GRACIOUS GOODNESS

THE TASTE OF MEMPHIS

Go, little book, and wish to all

Flowers in the garden, meat in the hall,

A bin of wine, a spice of wit,

A house with lawns enclosing it,

A living river by the door,

A nightingale in the sycamore!

—Robert Louis Stevenson, *Underwoods*

GRACIOUS GOODNESS

THE TASTE OF MEMPHIS

From Southern Homes and History
Photographs   Traditions   Choice Recipes

On January 17, 1959, an enthusiastic group
of civic-minded Memphis women signed the
charter which marked the beginning of the
Memphis Sinfonietta League. Their purpose
was to support a young and ambitious thirty-two
member orchestra, conducted by Vincent de Frank.
The Sinfonietta grew into the Memphis Symphony
Orchestra, one of the country's finest regional
orchestras. The Sinfonietta League became the
Memphis Symphony League, an organization of
some one thousand members dedicated to the
support of the Memphis Symphony Orchestra
through raising funds, increasing concert
subscriptions, and sponsoring educational
programs in the field of music.

All proceeds from the sale of this book
will benefit the Memphis Symphony Orchestra
through the support of the Memphis Symphony League.

First Edition First Printing
November 1989

Second Printing
May 1990

Third Printing
November 1991

Printing by Lithograph Printing Company, Inc.

Color Separations by Hanson Graphics of Memphis

Typography by Central Imaging

© 1989 by the Memphis Symphony League

Library of Congress Catalog Card Number
87-62419

ISBN 0-9619131-0-X

Printed in the United States of America

ROSES ON THE RIVER
(frontispiece and jacket cover)
Fragrant roses from a private garden
preside over an eighteenth century
Pembroke table set for a sunset
rendezvous on the bluff. The Dresden
china and the heirloom silver, in the
Whiting Lily design, are from the
collection of a grandson of George T.
Brodnax, founder of the fine, old jewelry
firm where so many Memphis and Mid-
South brides once chose their wedding
patterns. Awaiting the sunset seekers
is HEAVENLY FRESH COCONUT CAKE,
a Deep South favorite.

Note: Recipes set in small capitals
may be found in the index

THE COMMITTEE

Nancy Crosby, *Editor*

Susan Robinson, *Art Director*

Flo Snowden, *Flower Arrangements*

Sissy Long, *Research and Drafting*
   Photograph Commentaries

Carol Lynn Yellin, *Writer, Consulting Editor*
   Photograph Commentaries

Larry Kuzniewski, *Photography*
   Kuzniewski-Tomas Studio

Barbara Robertson, *Editorial Assistant*

Carol Cherry, *Recipe Testing Chairman*

Betty Jennings, *Recipe Acknowledgments*

Ruth Cunningham, *Recipe Classification*

Perre Magness, *Recipe Classification*

Walter P. Armstrong, Jr., *Wines*

Richard J. Reynolds, *Sauces*

Ellen and Richard Dixon, *Barbecue*

Anne Threefoot, *Picnics Chairman*

Babbie Lovett, *Picnics*

Anne Miller, *Picnics*

Mary Alice Quinn, *Picnics*

Mary Weymouth, *Picnics*

Roseann Painter, *Restaurants Chairman*

Barbara Harrington, *Restaurants*

Sophia Guidi, *International Recipes*

Marilou Awiakta, *Advisor*

Nancy Beck, *Advisor*

Nell Hughes, *Advisor*

Megan Turner, *Advisor*

Linda-Marie Goetze, *Production*

Cathy Knight, *Production*

Greg Stablein, *Production*

WITH SPECIAL THANKS

HANSON GRAPHICS OF MEMPHIS

THE PEABODY, MEMPHIS

LITHOGRAPH PRINTING COMPANY

OPUS 2

CENTRAL IMAGING

Dutch Akers
Patricia Atkinson
Marilou Awiakta
Diana Bailey
Rob Barnett, Vertical
    Market Software
Meg Bartlett
Frank G. Barton III
Nancy Beck*
Ron Belz
The Big Cheese
Jack Blair, Smith and
    Nephew Richards
Jerry Bower
Emmett Buford
Patricia Campbell
Pam Castleman
Shirley Sigler Chamberlin
Mary Winslow Chapman
Pat and Carroll Cloar
Anne Connell
Reva and Fred Cook
Dr. Charles Crawford
Ruth Crenshaw
Robert Crump
Nell Dickerson
Grace and Gene Dinstuhl
Marcia Dunlap
Andy Eugenio
Mildred Fall

George Falls
Family Tree Greenhouse
    Corinth, Mississippi
Kay Ferree
Brannon Galyean
Molly Gary
Goldsmith's Civic Garden Center
Goodwin's Greenhouses
Paul Hanson
Dr. John E. Harkins
Jean House
Sheila Hudson
Betty Hughes
Nell Hughes*
Sharon Hundt
Ann Hunt
Betty Hunt*
Buzzy Hussey*
Peter Hyrka
Peggy Jemison
Mickey Kee
Gail Kimball
Netta Sue Caudill King
Larry Kuzniewski
Kroger Food Stores
Kathy Laizure
Carroll Leatherman
Lichterman Nature Study Center
Debbie Litch
Sissy Long*

Babbie Lovett
Ed Lupo, Graphic Arts
    Associates, Inc.
Rick Mackie
Perre Magness
Martha McGuire*
Memphis Chamber of
    Commerce
Memphis Development
    Foundation
Memphis in May
    International Festival, Inc.
Memphis Pink Palace
    Museum
Memphis/Shelby County
    Public Library
Memphis/Shelby County
    Room
Betty Milford*
Charlotte Neal
Gloria Nobles*
Helen Norfleet
Lucia and Pete Outlan
Roseann Painter*
Alan Parsons
Betty Pidgeon
Ralph Potter
Libby Pritchard*
José Rodriquez
Ellen Rolfes

Dr. James E. Roper
Tattie Samuelson*
Elaine Schuppe*
Seessel's Supermarkets
Josie Sides
Raymond Skinner
Marilyn Skwor
Jennie Smith
Pete Smith
Flo Snowden*
Mary Stagg
Gaye Stanley
Margaret Taylor
Nancy Thomas
C. Fred Thompson
    Athens, Georgia
Pat Kerr Tigrett
Tommy Tubbs
Megan Turner
Sherri Turner
Dorothy Vawter
Ceil Walker
Ann Weihsmann
Mary and Tom Wells
Marge and Charlie White
Dixie and Bill Wolbrecht
Lynette Wrenn
Douglas C. Wynn
Carol Lynn and David Yellin
Florence Young

and many thanks indeed for the serendipitous naming of this book by Tara Burkhart at a meeting of the Hein Park Garden Club

*Members, Memphis Symphony League Initial Steering Committee

CONTENTS
With Commentaries and Photographs

FINISHING TOUCHES

FESTIVE TRADITIONS AND UNFORGETTABLE FLAVORS

PREFACE

When the members of the Memphis Symphony League decided to write and publish a cook book, they recognized a considerable challenge, for Memphis is blessed with a bevy of books about cooking—all good. Should there be yet another? Reassured by current wisdom that another cook book never spoils the broth, but rather, makes it richer, the committee members charged with producing this book set about not only gathering recipes, but also seeking ways to capture something of the essence of Memphis within the book's pages.

With its essential Southernness implicit in its name, *Gracious Goodness* went behind the scenes to homes, places of business, barns, boats, selected events, and to the river, to provide a glimpse of this city's history and way of life. At every turn we were met by the graciousness of our hosts and hostesses, underscoring the name and theme of our book; and the willingness of the volunteers who did the work that put it all together, die-stamped the entire book with the hallmark of Memphis—the volunteer's heart, doing what needs doing for the joy of it and the belief in it.

As you look at these photographs, we believe you will gain, as we did, an enhanced appreciation of the treasures all around us, some public, some private, worth guarding and preserving. As you read these commentaries and vignettes, we expect you will discover, as we did, a fresh understanding of the character of Memphis life, of the richness and color of Memphis history: tempered in the crucible of the past—the hard times, the good times; embracing a hospitality born of living at the river's edge, greeting friend and stranger alike, never knowing who will be deposited at the door; reared with a conservative soul created by living close to the land, dependent upon the vagaries of weather to get the crops in the barn; putting a value on old things—old ways, old manners, old friends—yet reaching for tomorrow with a frontiersman's vision, an "all things are possible" Memphis mindset that has given the country and the world so many enduring "firsts"; and cherishing relationships, for here people know all their cousins, the quintessential Memphis invitation is still to the small dinner party at home, and wanderers tend to return. And as you try these recipes, we believe you will realize that the one criterion that governed our selections was: Is it the best we can offer? We were reminded anew that the best requires time and patience—often the most important ingredients. And interestingly, we found the Southern love of sweets reigned supreme, for more recipes for desserts were submitted than for any other category.

We have had great fun along the way—delving into Memphis history, searching out articles for photographs, sorting recipes, and tasting our way through a veritable feast—learning and rediscovering the strength and grace of this city and its regional culture. Welcome to *Gracious Goodness*. It brings you a taste of Memphis, our hometown, a good place to live, with some of the most gracious people to be found anywhere in the world.

Nancy Crosby
Editor

A Toast to "The Proprietors"

The American republic was a very young country in 1820, but already, its Atlantic seaboard settlers were pouring over the Appalachian mountain ridges, looking for greener pastures in the west. One widely printed newspaper advertisement attracting their attention that year read, in part:

MEMPHIS, a New Town on the Mississippi

A town of the above name has been laid off on the east bank of the Mississippi, at the Lower Chickasaw Bluff, in the county of Shelby, state of Tennessee....Streets are wide and spacious, and between the front lots and the river is ample space, reserved as a Promenade.... MEMPHIS occupies a position perfectly accessible to steam-boats and vessels of every size and description,...opportunity is offered, at every season of the year, of traveling from this place to every quarter of the globe....The present number of inhabitants amount to about fifty souls, most of whom have settled there for commercial purposes. Several families of the first respectability have lately become residents.... MEMPHIS appears to combine advantages eminently calculated to make it a populous and flourishing town. No situation on the banks of the Upper Mississippi is more auspicious to health, or better suited to the rapid acquisition of wealth.

With this glowing description, Judge John Overton of Nashville, together with his fellow Tennesseans, General (soon-to-be President) Andrew Jackson and retired General James Winchester, had launched promotions for development of a parcel of riverbluff property they jointly owned. Located at the juncture of the Wolf and Mississippi Rivers, near the sites of military fortifications and trading posts, it was in territory Spain, France, England, and the United States had variously claimed over the centuries—even while the Chickasaw Indian Nation continued to regard it as their rightful hunting grounds. Queen Elizabeth I had assigned it to the colony of Virginia; King Charles I had transferred it to the Carolina colonies. The state of North Carolina, therefore, had arbitrarily decided in 1783 to sell grants of Chickasaw land in western Tennessee territory to land speculators, to help pay off its Revolutionary War debts.

One early buyer was John Rice, who paid five cents an acre for a five-thousand-acre tract on the Fourth Chickasaw Bluff, described in his deed as "beginning about one mile below the mouth of Woolf [sic] river at a white oak tree marked J. R." (Other boundary markers were a cottonwood tree and a mulberry tree.) After John Rice's death a few years later, Overton, Jackson, and Winchester acquired title to the property from his heirs through a sequence of land transfers and ownership divisions. When all Indian claims were settled (in the Chickasaw Cession of Tennessee territory negotiated in 1818 by General Jackson), each of their five thousand well-situated acres was suddenly worth eight dollars.

In 1819, this triumvirate of "proprietors," as they were known, laid out plans for a "populous and flourishing" city to be built on their land. General Winchester, a scholar of the classics, named it "Memphis," after an ancient Egyptian city on the great river Nile. As it turned out, none of them ever lived in their city, but they were its true founders. Their vision of a Memphis-that-could-be set the course for all that would follow.

TREASURED RECIPES

APPETIZERS AND SANDWICHES

PAPRIKA CHEESE BALL

Sure to get rave reviews, and best when made twenty-four hours in advance of serving.

1 8-ounce package Velveeta cheese, softened	2 cloves garlic, minced
1 8-ounce package cream cheese, softened	1 cup chopped pecans
	1 tablespoon paprika

Blend cheeses and garlic in food processor. Fold in pecans and form into one large ball or into two smaller ones. Sprinkle well with paprika. Chill and serve.

Serves 20

Mary Louise Grubbs

SUMMER GARDEN APPETIZER

A good fresh taste.

2 large tomatoes, skinned, seeded, and chopped	1 envelope unflavored gelatin
1 cup minced celery	¼ cup cold water
1 small onion, minced	¼ cup boiling water
1 small cucumber, peeled, seeded, and chopped	1 tablespoon Worcestershire sauce
1 green bell pepper, seeded and chopped	½ teaspoon Tabasco sauce
1 carrot, shredded	1 teaspoon crushed dried dill weed
2 tablespoons minced parsley leaves	1 teaspoon salt
1 4-ounce can chopped green chilies, well-drained	1 teaspoon paprika
	½ teaspoon cayenne pepper, optional
	1 cup mayonnaise

Place vegetables on paper towels, drain at least 30 minutes, and pat dry. Place in large bowl and set aside.

Dissolve gelatin in cold water. Stir in boiling water and set aside to cool. Add Worcestershire sauce, Tabasco sauce, and all dry seasonings to mayonnaise, mix well, and let stand briefly to blend flavors. Combine gelatin mixture and seasoned mayonnaise. Gently fold in vegetables to avoid mashing tomatoes. Place in decorative 6-cup mold or in large quiche dish and refrigerate overnight.

Garnish with sprig of fresh dill or parsley and serve with unflavored crackers.

Serves 20 to 30

Eleanor D. Hughes

FROSTED LIVERWURST MOLD

A recipe that evolved from something good into something wonderful.

1 pound liverwurst, room temperature	¼ teaspoon chives
Mayonnaise	1 8-ounce package cream cheese, softened
4 teaspoons Worcestershire sauce	Sour cream
1 tablespoon grated onion or more to taste	Dill weed to taste
	Dash or two cayenne pepper
1 teaspoon salt	1 2-ounce jar caviar
1 teaspoon pepper	Fresh parsley

Mix liverwurst with just enough mayonnaise to make it spreadable. Mix in 3 teaspoons Worcestershire sauce, onion, salt, and pepper. Mold into desired shape on serving plate and set in freezer until firm enough to frost.

Combine chives with cream cheese and just enough sour cream to make mixture easily spreadable. Add remaining 1 teaspoon Worcestershire sauce, dill weed, and cayenne pepper. Frost chilled mold with cheese mixture. Refrigerate until ready to serve.

Cover with caviar, garnish with parsley, and serve with rounds of rye bread or with favorite party crackers.

Serves 12 to 15

Rowene Neidow

BACON-CHEESE ROLL-UPS

Great blend of flavors.

1 loaf sandwich bread, thinly sliced	1 5-ounce jar cheese spread
Mustard	1 16-ounce package bacon

Remove crusts from bread and flatten each slice with rolling pin. Spread each slice lightly, but uniformly, with mustard and then with cheese spread. Roll up each bread slice and spiral the bacon around it, covering all bread.

Place roll-ups on rack and place rack on baking sheet with raised edges. Bake at 375 degrees until bacon is browned thoroughly, about 20 to 25 minutes. Cut each roll-up in 3 pieces. Serve hot.

Yields 60 roll-ups

Mrs. Henry B. Turner

MINIATURE PIZZAS

We've always heard good things come in small packages.

1 4¼-ounce can chopped ripe olives, drained	1 cup Hellmann's mayonnaise
2 tablespoons minced green onion	1 loaf party rye bread
2 cups grated Cheddar cheese	1 16-ounce package bacon, fried crisp and crumbled

Combine olives, onions, cheese, and mayonnaise, mix well, and chill. Spread mixture on bread and sprinkle with bacon. Place on ungreased baking sheet and bake at 300 degrees for 10 minutes or until cheese is bubbly.

Serves 12 to 16

Mrs. Donald R. Skwor

CRAB MEAT SPREAD

Water chestnuts add a very nice texture.

1 pound fresh crab meat	2 tablespoons soy sauce
½ cup minced water chestnuts	2 tablespoons minced green onions
½ cup mayonnaise	

Clean crab meat and shred. Combine with remaining ingredients, mix well, and chill. Serve on favorite crackers.

Serves 12 to 16

Elaine Schuppe

WATERMELON PICKLE WRAP-UPS

Salty and sweet and good.

1 10-ounce jar pickled watermelon rind	1 16-ounce package sliced bacon

Cut pickled watermelon rind in small pieces. Cut each strip of bacon in 3 pieces. Wrap watermelon rind in bacon and secure with toothpick. Bake at 375 degrees for 20 minutes or until bacon is browned. Drain on paper towel. Serve immediately.

Yields 38 to 40 wrap-ups

Mrs. Kenneth Vandervoort

COUNTRY TERRINE

An especially good hors d'oeuvre. Or, with a green salad, a great summer luncheon dish.

2 large onions, chopped	1 teaspoon thyme
2 tablespoons butter	1 teaspoon mace
½ pound cooked ham, diced	1 teaspoon allspice
1 pound fresh pork, finely ground	1 teaspoon rosemary
1 pound veal, finely ground	⅛ teaspoon ground cloves
1 pound chicken livers, finely cut with scissors	3 eggs, lightly beaten
1 pound fresh pork fat, ground	½ cup brandy
3 cloves garlic, minced	1 cup heavy cream
4 teaspoons salt	3 dashes cayenne pepper
2 teaspoons black pepper	1 large bay leaf, cut in half
	Chopped parsley

Brown onions in butter and combine with all other ingredients except bay leaf and parsley. Mix by hand until well-blended. Fill an oval 16-cup terrine or two glass loaf pans with mixture. Insert half bay leaf at each end of terrine or at one end of each loaf pan. Cover with heavy aluminum foil and set in pan of water. Bake 2½ hours at 350 degrees. Remove cover and bake 20 minutes more.

Cool with weight lying atop terrine or loaf pans. Pour off accumulated juices. After cooling, refrigerate for several hours before serving.

Sprinkle with generous amount parsley. Serve with slices of French bread, homemade mayonnaise, cornichons, cocktail tomatoes, sliced ripe olives, and sliced hard-cooked egg.

Serves 15 to 20

Mrs. Norfleet R. Turner

LO-CAL VEGETABLE DIP

Enjoy with an easy conscience.

1 to 2 green onions	1 package favorite dry dip mix
1½ cups low-fat cottage cheese	2 tablespoons light mayonnaise

Place green onions in food processor and mince. Add cottage cheese and process briefly to retain somewhat coarse texture. Blend in dip mix and mayonnaise.

Serve with favorite crisp fresh vegetables.

Serves 12

Mary Jane Richens

A Reception at Memphis Brooks Museum of Art in Overton Park

From its very beginnings as a tiny village carved out of a vast green forest, Memphis has been a park-rich community. The city's founding fathers donated a riverfront promenade and four downtown squares as recreational land for use by citizens. Succeeding generations of Memphis leaders have indulged similar civic urges, but never more grandly than in the early 1900s when two big woodland tracts on the edge of the city were purchased and turned into parks. One, Riverside Park to the southwest, became a favorite spot for picnics and for dances in the wooden pavilion. (In later years it would be renamed in honor of Dr. Martin Luther King, Jr.) The other, named Overton Park for one of the city's founders, was a 342-acre tract of virgin forest lying in the path of the city's rapid growth to the northeast. A portion of these woods was left intact and is today one of the city's most valued treasures. As described by award-winning author and one-time Memphian Peter Taylor, in his celebrated short story, "The Old Forest," this was "the last surviving bit of the primeval forest that once grew right up to the bluffs above the Mississippi River. Here are giant oak and yellow poplar trees older than the memory of the earliest white settler. Some of them surely may have been mature trees when Hernando De Soto passed this way."

But Overton Park has always offered more than unspoiled nature and recreational opportunities—sports fields, footpaths, bicycle trails, a nine-hole golf course. As conceived by Memphis architect Carl Gutherz in 1906, the park was also to be the site of an artistic, scientific, and educational complex, with an art museum as its nucleus. One citizen, Samuel Hamilton Brooks, was so intrigued with the plan that, after his death in 1912, his wife, Bessie, donated funds in his memory to build the museum, a small but exquisite Renaissance Revival marble structure that became Tennessee's first public art gallery.

The Memphis Brooks Museum of Art has been several times enlarged since, and has acquired prized holdings over the years, most recently the purchase of the magnificent *Ecce Homo* of Manfredi, circa 1610, and most notably, in 1952, when the Samuel H. Kress Foundation gave the museum part of its priceless collection of Italian Renaissance and Baroque painting and sculpture. The notion that the city had brought luck to entrepreneur Kress some years earlier when the first of his nationwide chain of successful variety stores was opened in Memphis may have helped inspire this gift. (The Kress Building, in all its rococo splendor and complete with lunch counter, is still open for business on Mid-America Mall—once known as Main Street.)

Today, the museum is an indispensable part of the city's cultural life. It helps bring to Memphis such events as the notable Ramesses the Great Exhibition (1987). It exhibits and purchases works by local and regional artists, some of whose works are also in galleries in other cities as well as in private collections around the world—Carroll Cloar, Veda Reed, Edwin Cooper "Ted" Rust, Adele Lemm, Mary Sims, Burton Callicott, Marjorie Liebman, Edward Faiers, Steve Yee, Lawrence Anthony, Harris Sorrelle, Louise Leahman, Ronald W. Pekar, Dorothy Sturm, Nancy Cheairs, and others. It provides extensive educational programs, including an innovative art appreciation project for the visually handicapped, developed and led by volunteers. The Brooks Museum's enduring vitality stems in great part from seven volunteer support groups, chief among them the Brooks Museum League.

Meanwhile, Carl Gutherz's dream of Overton Park as a total arts, scientific, and educational complex continues to be fulfilled. His original plan set aside thirty-six acres as the site for a zoo. Today, with some nineteen hundred animals on display in natural

THE PICTURE: *The Memphis Brooks Museum of Art has long been a centerpiece of the arts-educational-scientific complex conceived for Overton Park in 1906 by visionary Memphis architect Carl Gutherz. It was brought to reality in 1912 as Tennessee's first public art gallery, through a gift honoring Memphis art-lover, Samuel H. Brooks. Today it houses the state's most comprehensive art collection. Here, in the marble foyer of the original museum, light hors d'oeuvres await Brooks Museum League members who are attending a preview of the latest exhibit. Seen through the doorway is a part of the Kress collection, including the large tempera on wood painting,* **The Annunciation,** *by Italian artist Andrea Previtali, circa 1502-1528. The eighteenth-century silver punch bowl, a Brooks Museum League gift to the museum, was designed by William Adams. A French country ceramic bird holds a bouquet of Gerbera daisies, rubrum lilies, zinnias, salvia, nicotiana, and pink mini-carnations.*

THE FOOD: *The appetizing fare includes mushrooms stuffed with herbed cheese and pecans, vinaigrette-marinated cucumber slices, red bell pepper with snow peas, ZESTY BEEF LOG, VICTORIA TEA SANDWICHES, and SPINACH SANDWICHES. The punch is RUST'S REVENGE, named for Ted Rust, Director Emeritus of the neighboring Memphis College of Art.*

settings, and a fine aquarium, the Memphis Zoo regularly tops the listings of the city's most visited attractions. (A more curious claim to fame: For many years, the zoo's most famous resident was a lion named Volney, whose roar, recorded in the 1930s, can still be heard introducing vintage Metro-Goldwyn-Mayer movies on late-night TV.) Rising in the park nearby is a contemporary glass structure, the home of the Memphis College of Art which offers accredited B.F.A. and M.F.A. degrees. Nor have the performing arts been slighted. In past years, several generations of Memphians gathered under the stars on warm summer nights at Memphis Open Air Theatre, familiarly called the MOAT, at Overton Park Shell—the Mid-South's first outdoor theatre—to see familiar light operas such as *Desert Song, Naughty Marietta, New Moon,* and *Rose Marie,* with favorite stars Marguerite Piazza, Frances Greer, Eddie Roecker, Dorothy Kirsten, Mack Harrell, and Frank Hornaday, and to hear, in concerts through the years, artists as varied in style and appeal as bandleader Benny Goodman, bluesman Furry Lewis, jazz pianist Marian McPartland, rock stars Seals and Croft, and in 1954, a zoot-suited young singer making his first professional appearance, Elvis Presley.

With the advent of air-conditioning and television, the Shell fell into disrepair. But in 1986, a determined group of "Save the Shell" volunteers collected money and also provided much of the labor needed to restore the familiar landmark. The grand reopening concert drew an enthusiastic and nostalgic audience of some four thousand. The Shell is back in business, presenting such free performances as summertime jazz sessions, Navy Band concerts, and sunrise services on Easter morning.

ZESTY BEEF LOG

This is a winner.

1 2½-ounce jar dried beef, finely chopped
1½ tablespoons butter
1 8-ounce package cream cheese, softened
1 teaspoon prepared horseradish
1 teaspoon hot prepared mustard

Sauté dried beef in butter until slightly crisp, about 3 minutes. Set aside.

Mix cream cheese with horseradish and mustard. Shape cheese mixture into two rolls on wax paper. Cover on 3 sides with dried beef. Wrap in wax paper and chill one hour or more. Serve with Melba rounds.

Serves 8 to 10

Mrs. Fox Miller

QUICK CRAB TREAT

Simple and delicious. Great for unexpected company.

1 8-ounce package cream cheese, softened
1 6½-ounce can crab meat
Seafood cocktail sauce of choice

Spread layer of cream cheese in bottom of quiche dish and cover evenly with layer of crab meat. Top crab meat with thin layer of cocktail sauce. Serve with crackers.

Serves 8

Dianne D'Gerolamo

HIGH COUNTRY DIP

Great as a dip but also tasty on eggs.

1 6-ounce can ripe olives, chopped, with juice
1 4-ounce can green chilies, chopped, with juice
2 large tomatoes, chopped
3 to 4 green onions, chopped
2 tablespoons vegetable oil
1 tablespoon vinegar
1 teaspoon garlic salt
Salt and pepper to taste

Combine all ingredients. Let stand 3 to 4 hours, and drain. Serve with corn chips.

Yields 2½ cups dip

Mary Jane Newens
Denver, Colorado

VANISHING MEATBALLS IN SAUCE

An exceptional taste. They will quickly disappear.

Sauce
3 8-ounce cans tomato sauce
1 cup water
2 tablespoons parsley flakes
2 tablespoons onion flakes
1 tablespoon Italian seasoning
Salt and pepper to taste

Combine all ingredients and simmer in 4-quart saucepan. While sauce is simmering, prepare meatballs.

Meatballs
2 pounds ground chuck
1 cup bread crumbs
½ cup crisp rice cereal
3 tablespoons onion flakes
½ teaspoon garlic flakes
¼ cup parsley flakes
2 eggs, lightly beaten
1 teaspoon Italian seasoning
¼ teaspoon chili powder
¼ teaspoon cumin powder or less to taste
⅛ teaspoon salt
Freshly ground pepper to taste
Water as needed

Combine all ingredients and mix well. Add water so mixture is not too dry, but will form ball that keeps its shape. Use 1 tablespoon meat mixture for each ball. Place meatballs ½-inch apart on baking sheet. Bake 10 minutes at 350 degrees. Remove from oven, shake baking sheet to move meatballs around, and bake another 10 minutes. Carefully stir baked meatballs into sauce and cook another 30 minutes. Serve hot.

Yields 36 meatballs

Geri Cuoghi

CHEESE CHUTNEY SPREAD

A smooth yet piquant taste.

1 8-ounce package cream cheese, softened
1 cup grated Cheddar cheese
1 teaspoon curry powder
4 teaspoons sherry
½ to 1 cup chutney to taste
3 to 4 teaspoons finely chopped green onion
1 hard-cooked egg, grated

Combine cheeses and blend with curry powder and sherry. Shape into flattened round on serving tray and spread with chutney. Top first with onion and then with egg. Serve with crackers.

Serves 20

Katherine Morgan
Forrest City, Arkansas

OLIVE'S PARTY CRACKERS

A perfectly wonderful little tidbit.

1 cup corn oil	½ teaspoon lemon pepper
1 package favorite dry salad dressing mix	1 16-ounce package oyster crackers
1 teaspoon dill weed	

In large salad bowl, mix oil and dry ingredients. Add crackers and lightly toss. Spread on large baking sheet and bake 10 minutes at 350 degrees.

Serves 10 to 12

Katherine Leftwich
Forrest City, Arkansas

Variation

¼ cup Parmesan cheese	¾ cup vegetable oil
1 package favorite dry salad dressing mix	1 11-ounce package oyster crackers

Combine cheese, dressing mix, and oil. Gently stir in oyster crackers. Let stand 2 hours, and serve or store in tins with tightly fitting lids.

Madeline Henders

MEMPHIS HOT WINGS

Delicious! Serve with an ample supply of paper napkins and a fire extinguisher.

20 chicken wings	Paprika
4 tablespoons butter, melted	Pepper
Greek seasoning	1 cup favorite hot sauce

Wash wings and pat dry with paper towel. Cut at large joint making 20 drummettes and 20 wing sections. Place chicken pieces in large shallow baking pan. Brush with melted butter. Sprinkle with Greek seasoning, paprika, and pepper.

Broil 8 to 10 minutes. Turn pieces, brush with buttery juices from baking pan, and sprinkle with Greek seasoning, paprika, and pepper. Broil 8 to 10 minutes more, watching carefully so that chicken does not burn. Remove from broiler. Pour hot sauce over pieces and toss. Return to oven and bake at 350 degrees until tender, about 10 minutes.

Yields 40 hot wings

Teresa Cuoghi Edens
Albuquerque, New Mexico

BOUREKAKIA

Probably impossible to eat just one.

Pastry

1 cup all-purpose flour	1 egg, beaten
¼ teaspoon salt	1 tablespoon water
⅓ cup butter, softened	Olive oil

Mix flour with salt. Add butter, egg, and water. Knead with fingers until well-blended. Chill.

Divide dough in fourths. Roll dough as thin as possible on lightly floured board. Dough must be much thinner than pie crust. Cut in 3-inch rounds. Place a teaspoonful of either meat or cheese filling on each round of pastry. (Double pastry recipe if necessary to use all filling.) Fold and press edges firmly together with fork (may be frozen at this point). Brush pastry generously with olive oil. Bake at 450 degrees for 15 minutes or until golden brown. Serve while warm.

Meat Filling

4 medium onions, chopped	1 tablespoon chopped parsley
2 bunches green onions, chopped	½ teaspoon chopped mint
Olive oil	Salt and pepper to taste
1 pound ground beef	1 tablespoon butter
½ teaspoon dill	½ cup water

Brown onions in small amount olive oil. Add beef and brown, adding more olive oil if needed. Add dill, parsley, mint, salt, pepper, butter, and water. Stir well and simmer until no water remains.

Cheese Filling

2 cups crumbled feta cheese	1 egg, beaten

Blend cheese and egg.

Yields 6 dozen pastries

Evelyn Palmer

SAUERKRAUT BALLS

Unbelievably tasty! Try with horseradish sauce.

½ pound pork sausage
¼ cup finely chopped onion
1 16-ounce can sauerkraut,
 drained and minced
2 tablespoons fine dry
 bread crumbs
1 3-ounce package cream
 cheese, softened
2 tablespoons parsley

1 teaspoon prepared mustard
¼ teaspoon garlic salt
⅛ teaspoon pepper
¼ cup all-purpose flour
2 eggs, well-beaten
¼ cup milk
1 cup fine dry bread crumbs
4 cups vegetable oil

In skillet, cook sausage and onions until meat is brown and crumbly. Drain. Add sauerkraut and 2 tablespoons bread crumbs. Combine cheese, parsley, mustard, garlic salt, and pepper. Stir into sauerkraut mixture and chill.

When chilled, shape sauerkraut mixture into small balls and coat with flour. Combine eggs and milk. Dip floured balls in egg mixture and then in bread crumbs. Place in sizzling hot oil and brown. Drain on paper towel.

Note: May be fried and frozen in bags. Reheat on baking sheet at 350 degrees.

Yields 50 sauerkraut balls

Carol M. Cherry

MINIATURE QUICHE CUPS

Easy to put together on short notice.

1 egg, lightly beaten
¾ cup all-purpose flour
1 cup milk
½ teaspoon salt
⅛ teaspoon pepper

1 cup shredded sharp Cheddar
 cheese
½ cup crumbled cooked bacon,
 ham, or pepperoni

Combine egg, flour, ½ cup milk, salt, and pepper. Beat until smooth. Add remaining milk, cheese, and choice of meat.

Grease miniature muffin pans and fill each cup almost to top. Bake 20 minutes at 425 degrees.

Yields 24 quiche cups

Mrs. Harry Stone
New Haven, Connecticut

ESCARGOTS IN PUFF PASTRY

A delicacy for the esoteric palate.

4 to 5 snails
2 mushrooms, cut in fourths
½ teaspoon minced garlic
Butter

3 tablespoons heavy cream
3 tablespoons BROWN SAUCE
1 tablespoon diced tomatoes

Sauté snails, mushrooms, and garlic in butter. Add cream and reduce mixture by half. Add brown sauce and tomatoes. Simmer 1 minute.

Serve in puff pastry shell or in ramekin with garlic bread.

Serves 1

Holiday Inn, Crowne Plaza
Robert Harrington, Executive Chef

BOURBON BITES

So good—and the flavor is even better if made the day before.

3 pounds smoked link sausage
1 cup brown sugar

1 cup bourbon whiskey
1 cup chili sauce

Slice smoked sausage into pieces. Combine remaining ingredients, blend well, pour over sausage, and stir. Place in baking dish and bake covered for 2½ hours at 325 degrees. Serve hot in chafing dish.

Serves 16 to 20

Nancy Ricards Primeaux
Dallas, Texas

CHEESE ROLL

Found in a recipe collection from the twenties. Very good.

1 8-ounce package Cheddar
 cheese
1 8-ounce package American
 cheese
1 2-ounce jar pimientos

1 8-ounce package cream
 cheese, softened
1 tablespoon mayonnaise
2 small cloves garlic
Paprika

Combine all ingredients except paprika in food processor and blend. Separate into four portions. Form portions into rolls and sprinkle with paprika. Wrap in aluminum foil and chill. Serve with favorite crackers.

Yields 4 cheese rolls

Mrs. W. A. Fairchild

A Rooftop Supper to View the Great River Carnival

Memphis loves celebrations and has long enjoyed a reputation for having grand parties. The Great River Carnival of the 1980s is only the latest in a long line of elaborate festivals that began with the *Maifesten* organized in the 1850s by the city's German immigrants, featuring parades, music, and festival royalty. In 1872, Memphis held its first annual Mardi Gras when twenty thousand costumed spectators gathered in the streets to view the official state visit of the Grand Duke Alexis of Russia. Mardi Gras was succeeded in the 1930s by a week-long Cotton Carnival held each May to promote the city's premier business enterprise, and ruled over by a King and Queen chosen from families prominent in the cotton business. Carnival events included grand parades, pet shows, garden parties, fashion shows, and festivities of sponsoring secret societies. The riverfront became an amusement park with rides, shows, and cotton candy. The black community staged a Cotton Makers' Jubilee with dancing on Beale Street. A carnival highlight came on the first night at dusk, when fireworks exploded in a darkening sky above the river, and crowds lined the cobblestone landings downtown to await the arrival of the brightly lighted royal barge bringing that year's King and Queen and their court, dressed in glittering attire, to lead the carnival's opening parade down Main Street.

The Cotton Carnival gave way to an updated version, the Great River Carnival, when Memphis resolved that the time had come to celebrate (and promote) its prime, all-time attraction for residents and visitors alike—the mighty Mississippi River flowing past the city's doorstep. The advent of the Great River Carnival dovetailed with a revival in the mid-1970s of public interest and private investment in downtown Memphis, after decades of flight from riverfront to suburbs by businesses and residents alike. It coincided, too, with allocation of federal, state, and local funding to innovative downtown projects—such as building a park on a large, undeveloped, offshore sandbar, with a prosaic but memorable name.

Mud Island was what Memphians called the big deposit of silt that collected on the upriver side of an ocean-going vessel, aground and docked in Memphis in the winter of 1913. Spring's rising waters released the boat, but the newborn, left-behind island stayed put and kept growing; squatters took up temporary residence; an impromptu airport for small planes later appeared there. But no one knew how best to use this unexpected gift of urban real estate—not until the 1970s, when the Downtown Association asked architect Roy Harrover to create plans to turn it into a unique park. Today, linked to the mainland by a monorail tramway, Mud Island lures thousands of visitors annually with its special events such as the Catfish Festival, its amphitheatre concerts, its Mississippi River Museum (the nation's only museum celebrating river lore), its pavilion housing the legendary World War II B-17 bomber, *Memphis Belle*. Especially popular is Mud Island's five-block-long Riverwalk, an ever-flowing, contour model of the Lower Mississippi, with electronically controlled water levels matching those of the actual river, and grid maps of all riverbank towns and cities from Cairo, Illinois, to New Orleans, on which tiny streets are accurately laid out in slate and brass.

By 1989, nearly one billion dollars had been invested in downtown Memphis, etching the skyline with new, high-rise office buildings, giving new life to older buildings, and creating thousands of new residential units. A new generation of Memphians began moving downtown to work, to live, and to enjoy always-changing views of the great river.

THE PICTURE: *Festivals and celebrations have always been an integral part of Memphis life, and the great Mississippi River has ever been the focus of the city's most festive events. Many Memphians nowadays don't have to go downtown to enjoy these occasions. They already live there. Since the mid-1970s, developers have been busy in downtown Memphis. They have converted old warehouses, lofts, and factories into inviting shops, offices, and residences; they have turned old brick Front Street buildings, with their cotton classing room skylights, into studios; they have remodeled languishing hotels into apartments, and built posh new riverfront townhouses and condominiums. On this warm June evening, a small crowd in holiday mood has gathered on the spacious terrace of a new riverfront apartment, atop an office building that was once an old meat-packing plant. From here they will watch the opening fireworks of the Great River Carnival and enjoy the never-ending parade of boats, barges, and pleasure craft on the river below. The candlelit table, graced with a lone grandiflora magnolia bud afloat in a crystal bowl, is set for a late supper.*

THE FOOD: *Presented for the enjoyment of the party-goers are RYE ROUNDS, SCAMPI AL FRESCO, crisp vegetables with CURRIED DIP, meringue miniatures, and CHAMPAGNE WITH FRAMBOISE.*

SCAMPI AL FRESCO

The great taste of this dish belies its simplicity.

2 tablespoons olive oil
2 tablespoons butter
1 pound raw shrimp, peeled
3 tablespoons chopped Italian
   parsley

2 cloves garlic, chopped
1 teaspoon chopped fresh mint
Salt and freshly ground pepper
   to taste
Juice of 1 lemon

Heat oil and butter in skillet. Add shrimp and cook over high heat, stirring constantly. When shrimp turns pink, add remaining ingredients except lemon juice. When garlic begins to brown, add lemon juice. Continue cooking for 3 to 4 minutes, stirring occasionally. Serve hot or cold.

Serves 4 to 6

Ed Giobbi
Katonah, New York

HIDDEN TREASURE SHRIMP

Delicious and full of surprises.

1 pound cooked, peeled shrimp
½ pint cherry tomatoes
1 6-ounce can pitted ripe
   olives
½ head cauliflower florets

1 8-ounce can water
   chestnuts, drained
½ pound whole small
   mushrooms

Combine all ingredients and toss lightly to mix. Toss with dressing and chill. Serve in large clam shell with cocktail picks nearby.

Dressing
2 cups mayonnaise
½ cup prepared horseradish,
   drained
½ teaspoon Accent

2 teaspoons dry mustard
2 teaspoons lemon juice
½ teaspoon salt

Combine all ingredients and blend well.

Serves 12

Pat Klinke

RYE ROUNDS

Little rounds of blended flavor. Nice to have on hand in the freezer.

1 pound lean ground chuck
1 pound sausage

1 16-ounce box Velveeta cheese
1½ loaves party rye bread

Brown meats and drain. Add cheese and stir until melted. Spread on rye bread slices. Bake at 400 degrees until hot and bubbly, or freeze and bake later.

Serves 20 to 24

Samye L. Slagle
Duncan, Oklahoma

SHRIMP DIP

A welcome accompaniment to any gathering of friends.

1 8-ounce package cream
   cheese, softened
1 cup cooked and minced
   fresh shrimp
2 tablespoons chopped
   stuffed olives

2 tablespoons chili sauce
2 tablespoons chopped green
   onions
1 teaspoon lemon juice
Sliced stuffed olives

Stir cream cheese until smooth. Blend in shrimp, chopped olives, chili sauce, onions, and lemon juice. Chill thoroughly. Garnish with sliced olives. Serve with wheat crackers.

Serves 8 to 10

Louise Campbell

MOCK PIZZA MUFFINS

A great little treat—so simple to prepare.

2 English muffins
Mayonnaise
Jalapeño pepper cheese

1 tomato
1 medium onion

Slice muffins. Spread lightly with mayonnaise. Top with several cheese slices and 2 thin slices each tomato and onion. Bake at 350 degrees until cheese melts.

Yields 4 pizza muffins

Robbie L. Crosby

14

CHEESE-STUFFED SOURDOUGH BREAD

Great to take on picnics. Will stay warm almost an hour when wrapped in foil.

1 round loaf sourdough bread
2 cups grated sharp Cheddar cheese
1 8-ounce package cream cheese, softened
1 cup sour cream
1 tablespoon Worcestershire sauce
1 medium bunch green onions, chopped
1 2½-ounce jar dried beef, chopped

Slice top from loaf and save. Remove bread in pieces from inside loaf and wrap in foil. Mix cheeses with remaining ingredients. Fill cavity of loaf with cheese mixture. Replace top of loaf and wrap in aluminum foil. Bake 1½ hours at 350 degrees. During final 30 minutes, place wrapped bread pieces in oven and bake with stuffed loaf.

Remove top, place loaf on serving tray, and surround with bread pieces.

Serves 12

Mrs. Bill Patrick

CHEESE CRISPS

The kind of nibble that's at home in any company.

1 cup margarine
2 cups grated sharp Cheddar cheese
2 cups all-purpose flour
1¼ teaspoons dry mustard
1 teaspoon salt
2 cups Rice Krispies
1 to 2 dashes Tabasco sauce
Cayenne pepper to taste
Additional flour as needed for consistency

Combine all ingredients and mix well with hands. Pinch off pieces of dough to equal approximately 1 teaspoonful, place on baking sheet, and flatten with tines of fork. Bake at 350 degrees for 15 minutes or until golden brown and slightly dry.

Note: Do not substitute butter for margarine as consistency will change too much.

Yields 5 to 6 dozen crisps

Mrs. Arthur Fulmer, Jr.

CHEESE SQUARES

A tasty snack that is quick and easy.

2 loaves salt-rising bread, unsliced
½ cup butter, softened
¾ pound Cheddar cheese, room temperature
Dash Worcestershire sauce

Trim crusts from bread and cut loaves in eight thick slices. Cut each slice in 4 squares.

Blend butter and cheese. Add Worcestershire sauce and mix well. Spread cheese mixture on top and sides of each square. Place on baking sheet and chill in freezer for 30 minutes.

Remove as many as desired and bake 15 minutes at 400 degrees. Store remainder in freezer in plastic bag.

Yields 64 squares

Mrs. Fred Lawrence

HOT CRAB CRESCENTS

Exceptionally good.

1 pound snow crab meat, fresh or frozen
½ cup mayonnaise
½ cup shredded sharp Cheddar cheese
1 tablespoon minced green onions
1 8-ounce can refrigerated crescent dinner rolls
1 tablespoon capers

Flake crab meat. (If frozen, thaw and drain thoroughly, then flake.) Mix well with mayonnaise, cheese, and onion.

Separate rolls and shape into triangles. Cut lengthwise down middle of each for a total of 16 triangles. Spread each triangle with equal portions of crab mixture and sprinkle with 4 to 5 capers. Roll up loosely like a jelly roll, bend into crescent shape, and place on lightly greased baking sheet. Bake at 375 degrees for 15 to 18 minutes or until golden brown. Serve hot.

Yields 16 crescents

Mrs. Vincent de Frank

A Wedding Reception at Annesdale

Although many splendid wedding receptions in today's Memphis are held in churches, country clubs, or hotels, some families prefer the treasured traditions of a home reception. There is a timeless quality about a wedding celebration that takes place in a home where the bride has spent her childhood, among trees that she has climbed, and in rooms where she has dreamed about her wedding day. Such a gathering took place at Annesdale, a fine old Italianate mansion of handmade brick, following the wedding of the daughter of the house, a member of the family's fourth generation to grow up there.

Like a gracious paradigm of the past, Annesdale today sits atop a hill amid towering trees, its broad lawns surrounded by a shrubbery-bordered fence. Its handsome brick gate is guarded by stone lions whose gaze forever rests on a busy intersection of Lamar Avenue, a main thoroughfare that was once, long ago, an Indian trail. Built as a country home for a wholesale druggist in the mid-1850s, it was used briefly, after the Battle of Shiloh, as a military hospital for the wounded. In 1869, Colonel Robert C. Brinkley bought the home and its two hundred surrounding acres as a wedding gift for his daughter, Annie Overton Brinkley, and her husband, Colonel Robert Bogardus Snowden, a Shiloh veteran. (That was the same year the bride's father, a leading Memphis financier and railroadman, built a grand new Memphis hotel called the Peabody.) The newlyweds named their home Annesdale (Annie's Dale) for its new mistress, a granddaughter of Memphis founder John Overton, and they lived there in style, raising eight children, and entertaining lavishly. Family members still tell stories of the magnificent storehouse of provisions found deep in the basement of Annesdale; of barrels of oysters brought on riverboats from the Gulf, and fifty-pound tubs of butter cooling in the darkness. They remember caves dug in the yard to hold the ice cut from winter lakes and then covered with sawdust to be stored for summer months. They also recall that shopping expeditions, in the days when they involved traveling from Annesdale to downtown Memphis in a horsedrawn carriage, were all-day excursions, and usually ended with an overnight stay at the Peabody.

At the turn of the century, this elegant house became the centerpiece of a prestigious residential district, Annesdale Park. The Snowdens' two sons became real estate partners and, on the acreage adjoining Annesdale, by then easily accessible by trolley car, they built a cluster of homes enjoying all the latest modern conveniences—gas streetlights, sewers, water mains. Annesdale Park, once called "the South's first subdivision," is now known as the Annesdale-Snowden neighborhood, and has been recognized as a historical district in the National Registry.

Meanwhile, Annesdale itself, with its lofty tower and parklike setting, its carved cornices, hand-painted ceilings, and marble fireplaces, has gone its decorous way. Each generation, through the years, has celebrated its happy occasions in this stately old home, observing anew the long-cherished family customs.

THE PICTURE: *Many links to the history of Memphis can be found at Annesdale, a stately antebellum mansion that has been home, over the years, to several leading Memphis citizens. The house was the centerpiece of Annesdale Park, a turn-of-the-century residential district hailed as "the South's first subdivision," and is now a central landmark of the Annesdale-Snowden neighborhood, recognized as an historical district in the National Register. On this day, a young woman who is a fourth-generation member of the Memphis family that has long called Annesdale its home will be celebrating a special occasion. The table, graced by an arrangement of white calla lilies, dogwood blossoms, birch branches, Dutch iris, and stock presented in an antique silver basket with French Border design, is set for her wedding reception, and awaits the arrival of the bridal couple. In a time-honored family tradition, the bride, wearing the wedding veil worn by her mother, will cut the five-tiered, flower-decorated wedding cake with the Civil War saber of her great-grandfather, who fought at Shiloh.*

THE FOOD: *Between dances in an adjoining flower-bedecked room, wedding guests will enjoy a buffet supper offering crudités, PECAN CHEESE STRAWS, BRANDIED AND HERBED CHICKEN LIVER PÂTÉ, cheeses and fruit, and slices of beef tenderloin with little homemade POCKETBOOK ROLLS.*

BRANDIED AND HERBED CHICKEN LIVER PÂTÉ

For company that you like a lot!

½ cup butter	½ teaspoon pepper
2 medium onions, chopped	1 bay leaf
1 clove garlic, minced	⅛ teaspoon thyme
1 pound chicken livers	⅛ teaspoon oregano
1 tablespoon all-purpose flour	⅛ teaspoon tarragon
1 teaspoon salt	3 tablespoons brandy

Melt butter in large skillet and sauté onions and garlic until tender. Remove from skillet with slotted spoon. In same skillet, sauté livers until almost tender. Sprinkle with flour. Add salt, pepper, bay leaf, thyme, oregano, and tarragon. Cover and simmer over low heat for 1 to 2 minutes, or until livers are done. Discard bay leaf.

In food processor, combine liver mixture with onion mixture. Add brandy and process until smooth. Serve with crackers or with Melba toast.

Note: Can be frozen if wrapped first in plastic and then in foil. Or can be packed into small crocks for gifts.

Serves 12

Selma S. Lewis

PECAN CHEESE STRAWS

Elegant little cheese straws, perennially pleasing.

½ cup butter, softened	Pinch of salt
½ pound sharp Cheddar cheese, grated	Dash cayenne pepper
	1 cup finely chopped pecans
2 cups all-purpose flour	4 to 5 tablespoons ice water

Cream together butter, cheese, flour, salt, and pepper. Stir in pecans. Gradually add ice water, mixing well. Shape dough into roll and chill for easier handling. Press through cookie press or roll on floured board and cut in strips. Place on ungreased baking sheet, flatten with tines of fork, and bake at 325 degrees for 20 minutes or until golden brown.

Yields 4 dozen cheese straws

Patricia LaPointe

LITTLE PARMESANOS

Make a big, hot batch and watch them disappear.

1 3-ounce package cream cheese, softened	1 tablespoon chopped chives
	¾ teaspoon grated onion
¼ cup Hellmann's mayonnaise	⅛ teaspoon red pepper
2 tablespoons grated Parmesan cheese	25 to 30 2-inch bread rounds

Mix together cream cheese, mayonnaise, Parmesan cheese, chives, onion, and red pepper. Spread on bread rounds and place on ungreased baking sheet. Bake 15 minutes at 350 degrees and serve hot.

Serves 8 to 10

Mary Lou Adams

BLUE CHEESE DIP

A really outstanding taste.

1 8-ounce package cream cheese, softened	⅓ cup milk
	2 tablespoons chopped green bell pepper
4 ounces blue cheese, softened	2 tablespoons chopped fresh mushrooms
⅓ cup chopped thinly sliced ham	

Combine all ingredients and mix well. Chill at least 6 hours or overnight. Serve on whole wheat Melba toast or dark rye toast.

Serves 6 to 8

Eleanor Trezevant McKinney

PIGGYBACKS

Little nothings that are hard to beat.

Dijon mustard	1 16-ounce package bacon slices, halved
Saltine or club crackers	

Spread thin layer of mustard on cracker. Wrap half slice bacon around cracker and place on rack in broiling pan. Begin baking at 500 degrees but reduce temperature to 350 degrees when bacon starts cooking. Turn and bake until browned. Serve warm.

Serves 10 to 15

Lynn Warren Taylor

STUFFED MUSHROOMS MADEIRA

Mushrooms with winning ways.

12 large mushrooms, stems removed and reserved	3 tablespoons dry bread crumbs
2 to 3 tablespoons butter, melted	¼ cup finely grated Swiss cheese
6 tablespoons minced green onion	4 tablespoons minced parsley
2 tablespoons butter	½ teaspoon tarragon
1 tablespoon vegetable oil	Salt and pepper to taste
¼ cup Madeira	2 to 3 tablespoons heavy cream

Place mushroom caps in buttered baking pan and brush with melted butter. Chop mushroom stems and sauté with onions in 2 tablespoons butter and oil. Add Madeira and boil rapidly until reduced slightly. Remove from heat, add remaining ingredients, and spoon into mushroom caps. Bake 15 to 20 minutes at 375 degrees.

Serves 6

Barbara M. Robertson

SNOW PEAS WITH CRAB

Colorful, flavorful do-ahead delights. For a nice effect, arrange peas in pinwheel design on serving plate.

35 to 40 fresh snow peas	2 tablespoons mayonnaise
4 to 5 ounces fresh white crab meat	1 teaspoon fresh lemon juice
	Salt to taste

Snap off stem and remove string from snow peas. Blanch in large pot of rapidly boiling water for 30 seconds. Plunge immediately into cool water to stop cooking and to preserve green color. With small sharp knife, slit open curved seam of each snow pea. Set aside.

Mix crab meat with mayonnaise, lemon juice, and salt. With small spatula, generously fill each snow pea with crab meat mixture. Refrigerate until serving time.

Yields 35 to 40 snow peas

Eleanor C. Ricards
Houston, Texas

SPINACH SANDWICHES

Always a hit and rarely does anyone realize it's spinach.

2 pounds fresh spinach	1 loaf sandwich bread, thinly sliced
1 16-ounce package bacon	
Durkee's dressing	½ cup butter, softened

Wash and dry spinach, removing any tough stems. In food processor, chop enough spinach to measure 1 cup tightly packed. Careful—do not purée. Empty into 1-quart mixing bowl.

Cook bacon until crisp and crumble into bits. Add to spinach and moisten with enough Durkee's dressing for spreading consistency.

Trim crusts from bread and spread each slice with thin layer of butter. Spread half the bread slices with spinach-bacon mixture. Cover with remaining bread and cut each sandwich in fourths.

Yields 40 tea sandwiches

Mrs. M. V. Highsmith

OPEN-FACED MUSHROOM SANDWICH

Very good for a quick Sunday night supper dish.

2½ cups sliced fresh mushrooms	½ cup grated Parmesan cheese
2 tablespoons butter	1 tablespoon chopped chives
1 cup mayonnaise	6 thick slices bread
1 teaspoon grated lemon peel	Softened butter
1 tablespoon lemon juice	12 tomato slices
	Freshly ground black pepper

Sauté mushrooms in butter and set aside. Combine mayonnaise, lemon peel, lemon juice, cheese, and chives, and mix well.

Toast bread slices on one side. Turn and spread with butter. Top with 2 slices of tomato, a portion of mushrooms, and a dollop of mayonnaise mixture. Sprinkle black pepper on top. Bake at 350 degrees until hot and bubbly, then broil until lightly browned. Serve immediately.

Note: Mayonnaise mixture is very good as sauce on cooked spinach.

Serves 6

Elouise Deaton

OLIVE-NUT SANDWICH SPREAD

This is especially good on thin slices of rye bread.

2 3-ounce packages cream cheese, softened	1 cup chopped ripe olives, with 2 tablespoons juice reserved
½ cup mayonnaise	Dash pepper
½ to ¾ cup chopped pecans	

Mash cheese with fork and blend in mayonnaise. Add pecans, olives, olive juice, and pepper. Mix well and refrigerate 2 to 3 hours, or until mixture reaches consistency for spreading.

Yields 2½ to 3 cups spread

Mrs. Charles H. Samuelson

HOBO SANDWICH

Try it once and you'll be sold.

2 slices rye bread	Several thin slices cucumber
Mayonnaise	Lawry's seasoned salt
3 ounces roast beef, thinly sliced	Curry powder

Spread bread with mayonnaise and layer with roast beef. Top with thin slices cucumber. Add seasonings to taste.

Serves 1

Mrs. Harold Wilkins

DOTTIE'S CHEESE PUFF SANDWICHES

A delightfully different cheese sandwich.

¼ pound Cheddar or colby cheese, grated	8 drops Tabasco sauce
1 tablespoon catsup	⅛ teaspoon salt
3 tablespoons mayonnaise	1 egg white
1 teaspoon minced onion	2 English muffins

Combine cheese, catsup, mayonnaise, onion, and seasonings, and blend. Whip egg white until stiff. Fold into cheese mixture. Spread lightly on English muffin halves and place under broiler until cheese puffs.

Serves 2 to 4

Mrs. Mike Isom

PONTCHARTRAIN SANDWICH

An open-faced crab meat sandwich that's perfect for a summer luncheon.

1 8-ounce package cream cheese, softened	¼ cup mayonnaise
1 tablespoon Worcestershire sauce	6 Holland rusks
	Shredded lettuce
Dash Tabasco sauce	Tomato slices
	1 pound fresh crab meat, flaked

Season cream cheese with Worcestershire sauce, Tabasco sauce, and mayonnaise. Spread on Holland rusks. Place on each rusk a portion of lettuce, tomato slices, and crab meat. Chill and serve with small amount of dressing poured over sandwich. Add more dressing to taste. Garnish with sliced hard-cooked eggs, artichoke hearts, and 2 or 3 cooked shrimp.

Dressing

¾ cup vegetable oil	¼ cup water
⅓ cup sugar	¼ cup garlic wine vinegar
1 onion, grated	1 teaspoon paprika
¾ cup chili sauce	

Combine all ingredients, mix well, and chill.

Serves 6

Mrs. Thomas L. Hunt

VICTORIA TEA SANDWICHES

A perfectly delicious little spring tea sandwich.

1 8-ounce package cream cheese, softened	¼ cup minced green bell pepper
¼ teaspoon salt	¼ cup chopped cucumber
2 tablespoons lemon juice	¼ cup chopped celery
1½ tablespoons mayonnaise	1 loaf sandwich bread, thinly sliced
¼ cup minced onion	Softened butter
⅔ cup grated carrots	

Whip cream cheese lightly. Blend in salt, lemon juice, and mayonnaise. Drain vegetables, add to cheese mixture, mix, and chill several hours.

Trim crusts from bread, butter each slice lightly, and spread with vegetable mixture. Cut each sandwich in fourths.

Yields 40 tea sandwiches

Bobbye Bryant
Chicago, Illinois

SOUPS

CURRIED CREAM OF RED PEPPER SOUP

A soup-lover's dream.

½ cup chopped onion	1 cup heavy cream
1 clove garlic, minced	Salt and freshly ground pepper
4 tablespoons butter	to taste
1½ cups sliced red bell pepper	1 roasted red bell pepper,
1½ teaspoons curry powder	sliced in ¼-inch rings, for
2½ cups chicken stock	garnish

Sauté onion and garlic in butter 2 to 3 minutes over medium heat. Reduce heat, add sliced pepper, and cook 2 to 3 minutes more. Add curry powder and cook another 3 to 4 minutes. Add chicken stock and simmer 10 minutes or until pepper and onion are very soft. Purée mixture in blender. Return to saucepan and add cream, salt, and pepper. Heat slowly and serve hot, garnished with slices of roasted pepper.

Note: Roast pepper by heating under broiler or over gas flame, turning often until roasted evenly. Rinse with cool water and peel.

Serves 4 to 6

Ann Reynolds

CHICKEN SOUP WITH LEMON-EGG SAUCE

Like the Greek avgholemono, this Armenian soup is marvelously good. The smooth broth with the tang of lemon is just right.

1 large chicken	⅓ cup rice
8 cups water	2 eggs
1 teaspoon salt	Juice of 1 lemon
¼ teaspoon black pepper	

Place chicken and water in soup pot, add salt and pepper, and boil until tender. Remove chicken and strain broth. Return 6 cups broth to soup pot, add rice, and cook according to package directions. Set aside. (Save chicken for other uses.)

Beat eggs and lemon juice together. Remove 1 cup broth from soup pot and gradually add to egg mixture, stirring continuously. Place soup pot over low heat and blend in egg-broth mixture. Do not overheat or eggs will curdle. Serve immediately.

Serves 4 to 6

Vikki Bedeian

GENE SHAFER'S SUPERB CLAM CHOWDER

When the day is chilly and wet and preparation time is limited, this may be just what is called for.

4 6½-ounce cans minced	2 10¾-ounce cans cream of
clams, drained and juice	mushroom soup
reserved	1 10¾-ounce can cream of
6 medium potatoes, peeled	celery soup
and diced	4 tablespoons butter
1 medium onion, chopped	Salt and pepper to taste
3 to 4 cups milk	Tabasco sauce to taste

Combine clam juice, potatoes, onions, and small amount of water in 8-quart saucepan. Bring to boil and cook until potatoes are soft. Stir in clams and remaining ingredients and simmer 30 to 45 minutes. Add more milk if thinner consistency is preferred.

Serves 12

C. E. Hyde, Jr.

SERIOUS FISH CHOWDER

Filling, nourishing, and wholly satisfying.

1 cup chopped onion	1 14½-ounce can whole
1 cup chopped celery	tomatoes, chopped
3 tablespoons vegetable oil	1½ cups fresh corn
1 teaspoon salt	1 10¾-ounce can cream of
¼ teaspoon pepper	potato soup
Dash garlic salt	2 to 3 cups milk
1 small bay leaf	1 pound cod or other white fish,
1 10-ounce package frozen	cut in small pieces (if frozen,
mixed vegetables, cooked	thaw before using)

In large heavy saucepan, sauté onion and celery in oil until soft but not browned. Add seasonings and vegetables, cover, and simmer 30 to 45 minutes. Add potato soup, milk, and fish, cover, and simmer 30 minutes. Discard bay leaf before serving.

Note: For spicier taste, add ¼ to ½ teaspoon Old Bay Seasoning.

Serves 6

Bob Taylor

SOUL-SATISFYING MUSHROOM SOUP

Rich and brimming with hearty flavor.

1 medium onion, chopped
4 tablespoons butter
1 pound fresh mushrooms,
   sliced
1 potato, peeled and diced
1 cup beef bouillon
¼ teaspoon dried thyme

1 teaspoon chopped parsley
½ teaspoon salt
Pepper to taste
1 cup skim milk
2 cups heavy cream
3 teaspoons soy sauce
2 tablespoons dry sherry

Sauté onion in butter until clear. Add mushrooms and sauté until tender. Add potato, bouillon, thyme, parsley, salt, and pepper, and simmer until potato is soft. Place in food processor and blend until smooth. Return mixture to saucepan. Add milk, cream, and soy sauce, and slowly heat until serving temperature is reached. Stir in sherry just before serving.

Serves 6 to 8

Martha C. Witherspoon

FRESH TOMATO SOUP

Especially meant for the times when those wonderful summer tomatoes are ripe.

6 medium tomatoes or 2 pounds
   Italian plum tomatoes,
   cut in wedges
1 medium onion, chopped
1 rib celery, chopped
2 cups chicken broth
1 tablespoon tomato paste
½ teaspoon dried basil

½ teaspoon salt
¼ teaspoon freshly ground
   pepper
1 jalapeño pepper, seeded
   and chopped
1 bay leaf
Plain yogurt for garnish

Combine all ingredients except yogurt in 1½-quart saucepan and simmer uncovered 30 minutes. Strain soup, adjust seasonings, and serve topped with 1 teaspoon yogurt.

Note: For thicker, richer soup, place contents of strainer in blender, liquefy and stir into soup.

Serves 4 to 6

Carol M. Cherry

DRIED LIMA BEAN SOUP

A smooth soup that's divine. Takes time, but it's worth it.

2 cups dried lima beans
2 cups baked ham pieces plus
   ham bone
4 tablespoons vegetable oil
2 tablespoons butter
4 onions, quartered
1 14½-ounce can whole
   tomatoes with juice

1 clove garlic, minced
1 cup finely chopped celery
8 cups boiling water
1 tablespoon Worcestershire
   sauce
1 teaspoon salt
Dash freshly ground black
   pepper

Cover beans with water in large pot and soak overnight.

Leaving beans in water in which they soaked and working with a handful at a time, rub gently to remove skins, keeping beans moist with water in the process. Discard water and skins. Combine beans, ham and ham bone, oil, butter, onions, tomatoes with juice, garlic, and celery in large soup pot. Add boiling water and seasonings. Bring soup to boil, cover, and cook 3 to 4 hours over low heat. Stir occasionally, adding water if necessary.

Serves 6 to 8

Mrs. James L. Wiygul

MAIN EVENT VEGETABLE SOUP

A sturdy and filling main-dish soup.

1 large soup bone
1 pound pot roast, cut in
   stewing pieces
Garlic to taste
1 onion, coarsely chopped
Parsley to taste
Salt and pepper to taste
2 quarts water
½ cup barley
1 cup dry lima beans, rinsed

3 to 4 carrots, sliced
2 ribs celery, sliced
1 14½-ounce can tomatoes
   with juice
1 10-ounce package frozen
   green peas
1 7-ounce package spaghetti,
   broken in short pieces,
   cooked and drained, optional

Combine soup bone, meat, garlic, onion, parsley, salt, pepper, and water in large soup pot or Dutch oven. Bring to boil, cover, and simmer 1 hour.

Add barley, lima beans, carrots, celery, and tomatoes with juice, and simmer 1 hour. Skim, remove soup bone, and add peas and spaghetti. Simmer another 20 to 30 minutes, adding more water if needed.

Serve 6 to 8

Reva Cook

Homecoming Dinner in Holly Springs

On the last weekend of April each spring, when the small Mississippi town of Holly Springs opens its stately antebellum homes to the public, hundreds of Memphians join the annual Pilgrimage. There, less than an hour's drive from downtown Memphis, they can step back many years in time, and survey the sweep of events that have shaped an entire region. This historical community sprang up early in the nineteenth century on the site of a crossroads for several ancient Indian trails, a quiet glade of holly trees surrounding cool springs where travelers could rest and bathe in fresh waters. When the Chickasaws, in 1834, ceded six million acres of land in north Mississippi to be offered for sale by the United States Government, the town grew rapidly. One year after its incorporation in 1837, Holly Springs had some fourteen law offices, six physicians, two banks, five churches, three hotels, and several private schools. It became the seat of one of the state's most prosperous cotton-producing counties.

In those years, Holly Springs residents built many splendid homes that reflected the town's good fortune—houses with romantic names like Montrose, Grey Gables, Hamilton Place, Cedarhurst, Greenwood, Dunvegan, and Wakefield; houses that escaped destruction over the years and have been carefully preserved or restored. During the Pilgrimage, on daytime or candlelit evening tours, visitors can relive the past in these beautiful old residences. They can feel the presence of history at houses like Airliewood where General Ulysses S. Grant had his headquarters, or Walter Place where Mrs. Grant was in residence during what is still sometimes called, in this tradition-steeped town, The War.

Years before the Holly Springs Pilgrimage became an annual event listed on tourist calendars, however, regular visits to this nearby Mississippi community were customary for the many Memphis citizens whose family roots are there. One habitual pilgrim during the first half of this century was Edward Hull Crump, the fabled, long-time Memphis political leader who became widely known as "Mister Crump," through the lyrics of an early campaign song written by a talented young Beale Street musician named W. C. Handy. Each Sunday for many years, Mister Crump faithfully made the trip with his own family from Memphis to Holly Springs to visit his mother in the home where he grew up.

In 1883, Mrs. Mollie Crump, widowed by a deadly yellow fever epidemic, moved her three young children into a simple, one-story, white clapboard house that she had inherited from her great-uncle. She lived there until her death in 1940 at the age of ninety-three. Still known as Crump Place, this small, attractive home, built in 1838, is the oldest continually occupied residence in Holly Springs today. Its wide, wooden, columned porch, stretching across the entire front of the house, brings to mind long summer twilights, the lulling drone of cicadas, the lemony fragrance of magnolias, and the generations of Southerners who sat here rocking and fanning and talking as the fireflies became visible against the oncoming night.

THE PICTURE: *One of the many native Mississippians who found fame and fortune in Memphis was Edward Hull Crump, the city's most influential politician for some four decades. Crump Place in Holly Springs was his boyhood home. This simple but attractive house is now owned and lived in by another family, but for today, the table is set with heirloom pieces belonging to Crump family descendants, just as it might have been for some special family occasion years ago. The monogrammed silver place and butter plates are Baltimore Rose pattern by Kirk, and, like the stemware, the silver candelabra, and the silver flower basket, originally belonged to the Memphis Crumps. The soup tureen, circa 1840, the Spode china, the ecru lace table cloth and napkins were used in Mollie Crump's home in Holly Springs. The red roses were a family favorite, always on the table at Christmas and for other special occasions.*

THE FOOD: *GRANDMOTHER CRUMP'S CLEAR TOMATO SOUP was traditionally served as a first course at the Crump family's holiday dinners.*

GRANDMOTHER CRUMP'S CLEAR TOMATO SOUP

A generations-spanning soup that's still a family favorite. Especially good with a slice of French bread toasted with butter and Parmesan cheese.

1 28-ounce can whole tomatoes	Dash cayenne pepper
2 ribs celery, chopped	1 tablespoon apple cider
1 tablespoon chopped onion	vinegar
4 whole cloves	Lemon slices and fresh parsley
Dash salt	sprigs for garnish

Combine tomatoes, celery, onion, and cloves in saucepan. Cover and cook over low heat until tomatoes are soft. Remove from heat and add salt, cayenne pepper, and vinegar. Pour through sieve into second saucepan, mashing tomatoes against sieve for juice. Serve hot with lemon slice afloat in center of each serving and garnished with sprig of fresh parsley.

Serves 4

Louise Crump Wade
Baltimore, Maryland

CANADIAN CHEESE SOUP

A cheese soup with vegetables. Delicious!

2 cups chicken broth	½ 18-ounce package frozen
1 large potato, peeled and diced	broccoli and cauliflower
1 medium onion, chopped	½ cup heavy cream
¼ cup chopped celery	1 cup grated Cheddar cheese
½ cup sliced carrots	Salt and pepper to taste

Combine chicken broth, potato, onion, celery, and carrots in 1½-quart saucepan and cook until soft. Add broccoli and cauliflower, and simmer 10 minutes. Stir in cream, cheese, salt, and pepper, and heat until cheese is thoroughly melted. Do not boil. Add more broth if needed.

Note: May substitute ½ cup light cream or evaporated milk for heavy cream.

Serves 4

Carolyn H. Gates

VICHYSQUASH

If the name makes you smile, the taste will make you glow.

1 medium onion, chopped	1 cup milk
1 tablespoon margarine	Summer savory to taste
6 medium yellow squash,	Salt and white pepper to taste
sliced	Yogurt and chopped green
½ cup chicken stock	onion tops for garnish

Sauté onion in margarine. Cook squash in chicken stock for 15 minutes. Combine onion and squash, divide in two portions, and blend each in food processor until smooth. Combine portions, add milk and seasonings, and chill. Serve hot or cold, topped with yogurt and a sprinkle of onion tops.

Serves 6

Mrs. Ted Bratton

SHE-CRAB SOUP

A superb version of that low country classic.

7 tablespoons butter	2 tablespoons sugar
4 tablespoons all-purpose flour	½ teaspoon mace
1 cup heavy cream	¼ teaspoon pepper
2 quarts milk	2 teaspoons salt
¾ cup finely chopped onion	2 teaspoons Worcestershire
3 tablespoons chopped celery	sauce
1 pound crab meat	Finely grated peel of 1 lemon
3 hard-cooked egg yolks,	4 tablespoons sherry
crumbled, or equivalent	Tabasco sauce to taste
amount crab eggs	1 teaspoon soy sauce
½ teaspoon Angostura Bitters	

Melt 4 tablespoons butter in double boiler. Blend in flour until smooth. Add cream and milk, and cook over low heat until thick, stirring often, to make a white sauce.

Sauté onion and celery in remaining butter until tender, and add to white sauce, along with all remaining ingredients. Cook 20 minutes in double boiler over low heat. Serve immediately.

Serves 6 to 8

Anita Sage

MY SON BILL'S CATFISH GUMBO

Variation on a great old theme.

¼ cup vegetable oil	2 cups sliced fresh okra
½ cup chopped onions	2 teaspoons salt
½ cup chopped celery	¼ teaspoon thyme
½ cup chopped green bell pepper	1 tablespoon lemon juice
2 cloves garlic, minced	1 bay leaf
1 teaspoon brown sugar	Tabasco sauce to taste
2 cups fish stock	1 pound catfish fillets, cut
4 to 5 firm ripe tomatoes, cut	in 1-inch pieces
in wedges (or 14½-ounce	2 teaspoons filé powder
can tomato wedges)	3 cups cooked rice

Heat oil in heavy pot, add onions, celery, bell pepper, and garlic, and sauté until tender. Sprinkle with brown sugar, and stir. Add fish stock, tomatoes, okra, salt, thyme, lemon juice, bay leaf, and Tabasco sauce. Simmer 30 minutes.

Add catfish fillets and simmer 15 minutes more. Remove bay leaf, add filé powder, and stir. Let stand briefly. Serve over hot rice.

Note: Chicken stock or bottled clam juice may be substituted for fish stock.

Serves 4 to 6

Orline B. Woodward

MAMA'S CHICKEN SOUP

It is said it will cure the common cold and almost any other ailment.

4 to 5-pound young hen,	3 carrots, scraped and chopped
cut in pieces	4 teaspoons dried chicken soup
4 quarts water	base
1 large onion, quartered	1 to 2 teaspoons salt
3 ribs celery with leaves,	Cooked rice, cooked noodles,
chopped	or prepared matzo balls

Place hen in water in large soup pot. Bring to boil and skim. Add onion, celery, carrots, soup base, and salt. Cover and simmer until chicken is tender, about 2 hours. Remove chicken and reserve for other dishes. Strain broth and return to pot. Return carrots to broth and adjust seasoning. To serve, warm slowly and add rice, noodles, or matzo balls.

Serves 8 to 10

Lyda G. Parker

MINESTRONE

An authentic Italian vegetable bean soup. Serve it with hot Italian bread and lots of freshly grated Parmesan cheese.

1½ cups dried white beans	1½ cups peeled and diced
¾ cup olive oil	potatoes
3 medium onions, thinly sliced	1½ cups peeled, seeded, and
3 cloves garlic, minced	chopped Italian plum
Fresh green beans cut in 1-inch	tomatoes
pieces to measure 3 cups	1 large sprig fresh rosemary
3 cups diced zucchini	or ½ teaspoon dried
3 cups coarsely chopped	3 sprigs chopped fresh basil
cabbage	or 2 tablespoons dried
1½ cups thinly sliced carrots	9 cups beef stock
1½ cups chopped celery	Salt and pepper to taste
with leaves	Grated Parmesan cheese to taste

Cover dried beans with water and soak overnight. Drain.

Heat olive oil in large heavy soup pot over medium heat. Reduce heat to low. Add onions and garlic, and sauté, stirring occasionally, until onions are soft but not brown, about 10 minutes. Increase heat to medium. Stir in green beans, zucchini, cabbage, carrots, and celery. Cook 10 minutes, stirring to coat with oil. Add potatoes, tomatoes, crushed rosemary, basil, beef stock, and white beans to soup pot. Bring to boil over medium heat. Reduce heat to low and simmer, partially covered, until vegetables are very well done. Stir in salt, pepper, and cheese. Remove fresh rosemary before serving.

Serves 6 to 8

Sophia Guidi
Marco Island, Florida

BEEF BROTH

One of the basics.

3 pounds beef short ribs	1 carrot, julienne
1 beef knuckle, cracked	Bouquet garni
1 onion, studded with several	4 to 6 peppercorns
cloves	Salt to taste
2 ribs celery with leaves	8 cups water

Combine all ingredients and bring to boil. Gently simmer uncovered 2 to 3 hours, skimming foam from time to time. Strain broth through cheesecloth-lined sieve.

Yields 4 to 6 cups broth

Doris P. Harrell

Meeting the Future in Old Court Square

Memphis surely shares the lingering Southern nostalgia for old ways. But a regional reverence for the past has never prevented Memphians from adopting (or, quite as likely, inventing) convenient and imaginative new ways of doing things in the present. Over the years, Memphis has originated and successfully exported so many durable hallmarks—and a few fleeting fads—of twentieth-century American culture that the city has often seemed almost aggressively contemporary.

Consider this listing of Memphis "firsts"—a chronology of Memphis innovations that rapidly found favor elsewhere: *First drive-in.* (In 1906, when the Fortune-Ward soda fountain on Main Street offered "curb service" to motorists who parked outside and honked twice.) *First published blues music.* (In 1912, when W. C. Handy's "Memphis Blues" became available in sheet music.) *First supermarket.* (In 1916, when Clarence Saunders opened his revolutionary self-service grocery market, Piggly-Wiggly.) *First automobile lift.* (In 1925, when garage-owner Peter J. Lunati patented a rotary lift device to raise cars into the air on racks, letting mechanics work easily underneath.) *First Welcome Wagon.* (In 1928, when Thomas W. Briggs sent out teams of friendly, gift-bearing callers to extend warm welcomes to new Memphis residents on behalf of some local merchants.) *First Zoot Suit.* (In the late 1930s, when Beale Street tailor Louis Lettes made a swanky suit with an oversized jacket for his student assistant, Anderson Tate, thereby creating a style that would spread from Booker T. Washington High School in Memphis to St. Louis, Chicago, Los Angeles and the world.) *First Holiday Inn.* (In 1952, when Kemmons Wilson, acting on an idea that took shape on a motor trip to Washington D.C. with his wife and five children, built a new kind of "motel" on Summer Avenue, where young children could stay in the room with their parents at no extra charge. Its name inspired by the movie *Holiday Inn,* this prototype of the family-oriented roadside inn was so widely replicated thereafter, that the Memphis-based Holiday Corporation, which evolved from and includes Holiday Inns, Inc., is now the world's largest hotel operation, with more than eighteen hundred hotels in fifty-two countries and territories.)

Clearly, Memphis is a place where people have repeatedly turned good ideas into profitable reality. S. H. Kress opened his first five-and-dime store in Memphis. Both Greyhound and Trailways bus lines started in Memphis. The world's first termite-control program was developed in Memphis by the E. L. Bruce Company to safeguard their hardwood lumber. (Memphis has long been the world's leading hardwood marketplace.) Even local government caught the innovating spirit—Memphis was the birthplace of the country's first Motor Vehicle Inspection Bureau, and the first City Beautiful Commission. And then there was the idea for a "hub-and-spokes" air express service, first presented in a now-legendary term paper at Yale University which earned an unimpressive grade of C for business school student Fred Smith of Memphis. Undeterred, he returned home and formed a new company, Federal Express, to test his idea. Since 1973 when Federal Express planes made the first flights from their Memphis airport hub, Fred Smith's notion for getting a package from anywhere to anywhere else in the United States, "absolutely, positively overnight," has become a Fortune 500 wonder company that dominates the new industry it created.

That a city so bent on innovation for the future should also be intent on veneration of the past may, at first, seem curious. But it was always thus. Memphis, by geography no less than by mindset, has been a meeting place of old and new, a crossroads of past, present, and future, from its first years as a westernmost outpost of the Old South. Gazing west across the broad Mississippi River, seeing a vast new land empty of settlers but full of opportunity, new Memphians of the early 1800s kept their eyes fixed on the future. But their ears remained tuned to voices of the past, their allegiance pledged to the customs, attitudes, and experiences of the land "back east" whence they came.

This meld of new and old still characterizes today's Memphis. To observe it in strikingly visible form, visit old Court Square, one of four squares atop the riverbluff reserved for public recreation by the city's founders in 1819—the only one to have survived more or less intact. With its great old oaks and ancient magnolia trees, its nineteenth-century bandstand, and its familiar Hebe Fountain featuring a statue of the goddess of youth (installed in 1876 to celebrate the nation's centennial), this little two-acre downtown park has been, for generations, the symbolic center of the city. Seat yourself on one of Court Square's handsome Memphis-made oak and ornamental cast iron benches and watch the busy lunchtime scene—strollers, joggers, sidewalk vendors, flocks of resident pigeons awaiting handouts, young couples holding hands, oldsters napping in the sun. Then look about and enjoy close-up views of four landmark Memphis buildings, one opposite each corner of the Square. On the northwest is the now-classic, twenty-story Lincoln American Tower, erected in the 1920s, an approximate replica of New York City's Woolworth Building; facing the southwest corner is the eleven-story Dr. D. T. Porter Building, the South's first skyscraper (another Memphis innovation) when it was built in 1894. The imposing Exchange Building, completed in 1909 and housing for a time the Cotton Exchange, faces Court Square's southeast corner; and on the northeast corner, most arresting of all, is the three-story, domed and turreted, Moorish-style structure built in 1890 by the famous old Tennessee Club, reputedly the South's oldest social club.

From Court Square walk west now, toward the river. You will find yourself in the inviting new River Center Plaza with its eye-catching centerpiece, the modern French sculptor Arman's glorification of Memphis music, *Ascent of the Blues*—saxophones, trumpets, trombones, bass fiddles, and upright pianos are wrapped and stacked in an upward spiral of bronze. Also rising skyward here, just one block from Court Square, on the Front Street site formerly occupied by the old King Cotton Hotel, is one of the city's newest downtown office buildings. It is the twenty-one-story Morgan-Keegan Tower, housing a leading investment firm that, in the best Memphis tradition, does not hesitate to explore venturesome new ideas, particularly those Southern-based. The creative Memphis mingling of memories from the past, opportunities in the present, and visions for the future, continues.

OYSTER STEW

A grand old dish—always the same, always good.

1 cup chopped celery	2 cups light cream
1 medium white onion, chopped	2 pints large oysters
¼ cup butter	Salt and pepper to taste
1½ cups milk	

Combine celery and onions in small amount water and cook until transparent and tender. Drain, reserve vegetables, and mix with butter, milk, and cream in heavy saucepan. Heat until butter melts. Add oysters and simmer until edges of oysters curl. Season with salt and pepper, and serve hot with crackers.

Serves 8

Rosa Ann Keller

NEW ENGLAND CLAM CHOWDER

A dependable favorite.

2 slices bacon, chopped	1 10-ounce can whole baby
3 tablespoons butter	clams with juice
1 cup chopped onion	1 teaspoon salt or more to taste
1 cup chopped celery	¼ teaspoon white pepper
1 cup chopped carrots	2 tablespoons butter
½ cup chopped green bell	2 tablespoons all-purpose flour
pepper	2 cups light cream
1 clove garlic, chopped	1 whole pimiento, chopped or
3 tablespoons all-purpose flour	1 4-ounce jar diced
3 cups hot chicken stock	pimientos, drained
2 cups peeled and cubed	3 tablespoons chopped parsley
potatoes	

Fry bacon. Add 3 tablespoons butter, onion, celery, carrots, bell pepper, and garlic, and sauté briefly. Add 3 tablespoons flour, stirring until mixture becomes very dry. Slowly add hot chicken stock, stirring constantly, and simmer 10 minutes. Add potatoes, clams with juice, salt, and pepper. Simmer 10 minutes more and set aside.

In saucepan, blend 2 tablespoons butter and 2 tablespoons flour until smooth. Stir in cream to make smooth, thick sauce. Add pimiento and parsley, bring almost to boil, reduce heat, and simmer briefly. Combine sauce with clam mixture and refrigerate overnight. Bring almost to boil before serving.

Serves 6

Linda Lacey Frankum

LADY CURZON SOUP

History may award Her Ladyship plaudits, but it's the soup that's made her famous.

2 15-ounce cans turtle soup	2 egg yolks
⅓ cup minced fresh mushrooms	3 tablespoons heavy cream
2 tablespoons sherry	1½ tablespoons brandy
½ teaspoon curry powder	Parmesan cheese
1 teaspoon heavy cream	

In medium saucepan, bring soup just to boiling point. Remove from heat and set aside. Transfer ¾ cup soup to smaller pan. Add mushrooms and simmer 5 minutes. Stir in sherry. Return mixture to soup in medium pan.

Dissolve curry powder in 1 teaspoon cream. Beat egg yolks lightly with 3 tablespoons cream and brandy. Combine cream mixtures, add 1 cup soup, return to pot, and stir. Cook over low heat until slightly thickened. Sprinkle with Parmesan cheese just before serving.

Note: If turtle soup is unavailable, two 10½-ounce cans beef bouillon plus one 10¾-ounce can chicken broth will substitute nicely.

Serves 4

Walter P. Armstrong, Jr.

CREAM OF SPINACH SOUP

Rich, smooth, and wonderful.

2 tablespoons butter	1 soup can milk
1 10-ounce package frozen	1 soup can light cream
spinach, thawed	½ teaspoon salt
½ cup chopped onion	¼ teaspoon white pepper
3 tablespoons minced parsley	⅛ teaspoon nutmeg
2 10¾-ounce cans cream of	Dash Tabasco sauce, optional
celery soup	

Melt butter in large saucepan. Add spinach, onion, and parsley, and cook 5 minutes over medium heat. Purée mixture in blender and return to saucepan. Stir in remaining ingredients and heat, but do not boil.

Serves 6 to 8

Sara Beth Causey, Founding Director
Memphis Symphony Chorus

SANTA FE CHICKEN SOUP

Good with GUACAMOLE SALAD for Sunday supper.

1 tablespoon butter
½ cup chopped onion
1 clove garlic, crushed
1 14½-ounce can whole
    tomatoes, drained and
    crushed
1 4-ounce can chopped green
    chilies, drained
⅛ teaspoon freshly ground
    black pepper
3 pounds chicken wings
2 quarts water
1 16-ounce can pinto beans,
    drained
2 teaspoons salt

In Dutch oven or 4-quart saucepan, melt butter over low heat, add onion and garlic, and sauté until clear. Add remaining ingredients except beans and salt. Bring to boil, reduce heat, and simmer uncovered 1½ to 2 hours until meat falls off bones. Skim surface foam and remove bones. Add beans and salt, and simmer 15 minutes. Serve hot.

Serves 6 to 8

Carol M. Cherry

COUNTRY VEGETABLE SOUP

A great Sunday supper when the wind is howling and the fire is blazing. Try with green salad and STELLA'S DINNER TOAST.

1 cup navy beans
3 to 4 medium potatoes,
    peeled and halved
2 to 3 carrots, scraped and
    sliced
1 white turnip, peeled and
    quartered
2 onions, chopped
1 clove garlic, crushed
Bouquet garni (thyme, bay
    leaf, and parsley)
2 quarts cold water
1 small head cabbage, cut in
    thin strips
1 meaty ham hock
Salt and pepper to taste
Polish sausage, cut in about
    12 pieces

Soak beans overnight. Drain.

Combine beans, potatoes, carrots, turnip, onions, water, bouquet garni, and garlic in soup kettle. Slowly bring to boil, skimming several times, cover, and simmer 2 hours. Add cabbage, ham hock, salt, and pepper, and simmer 1 hour longer. (Soup will be thick.)

In skillet, steam sausage until puffed. Add to soup, simmer briefly, and serve.

Serves 4

Mrs. Norfleet R. Turner

BLACK BEAN SOUP

A combination of recipes—Brazilian, Mid-Southern, and Puerto Rican—which resulted in a black bean soup that is particularly delicious and, with its garnishes, visually appealing as well.

1 16-ounce package black beans
1 large ham hock (or 3 small)
    preferably smoked or
    country ham
2 large onions, chopped
4 cloves garlic, chopped
2 bay leaves
1 to 1½ tablespoons salt
1 to 1½ tablespoons black pepper
1 teaspoon curry powder
1 to 1½ cups dry sherry
4 quarts water
Thick slices avocado
Chopped green onions with tops

Rinse beans well and put in heavy 5 to 6-quart kettle. Add ham hock(s), onions, garlic, bay leaves, salt, black pepper, curry powder, 1 cup sherry, and water. Cover and cook over low heat for a minimum of 6 hours. (Beans can cook up to 10 hours or may be cooked a day ahead and reheated.)

Before serving, remove ham hock(s). Purée half of bean mixture in food processor, return to kettle, add remaining ½ cup sherry, if desired, and reheat. Serve garnished with avocado slices and onions.

Variation: For a one dish meal, add 1 pound sliced Polish sausage to original recipe and cook as above until very thick, but do not purée. Add ham pieces and serve over rice, garnished as above with addition of chilled mandarin orange slices.

Serves 6 to 8

Alice Bingham

CLARIFIED BROTH

For making a lovely, clear soup.

2 egg whites
2 ounces finely chopped
    raw lean beef
¼ cup minced green onion
Bouquet garni
BEEF BROTH
2 egg shells, crushed

Beat egg whites until frothy and mix with beef, onion, and bouquet garni. Stir into broth and add egg shells. Bring to boil, stirring constantly, and remove from heat. Drain through cheesecloth-lined sieve.

Doris P. Harrell

FRESH GREEN ASPARAGUS SOUP

Tastes like springtime. Typical of the "fresh is best" approach of this delightful East Memphis restaurant with a lunch-only format.

2½ pounds fresh asparagus
3 quarts water
1 teaspoon salt
½ to 1 teaspoon white pepper
6 tablespoons butter

Snap asparagus at tender point. Cut off tips and save. Slice remainder of asparagus into 2-inch pieces. Bring water and salt to boil. Add asparagus pieces and cook until tender. Remove with slotted spoon, reserving cooking water. Purée in food processor, gradually adding 2 cups cooking water to make very smooth soup. Add white pepper to taste and more salt if preferred.

Cook asparagus tips in remaining reserved water until tender. Remove with slotted spoon and set aside. Bring soup to boil. Stir in asparagus tips and butter. When butter is melted, serve immediately.

Serves 6

Just For Lunch, Etc.
Ann Barnes, Martha Fogelman,
and Wendy Fogelman, Proprietors

SPINACH SCHAV

Schav is a soup of Polish and Russian ancestry. Its main ingredient is sorrel, an herb with a tart, acidic taste. In this recipe, spinach and citric acid substitute for fresh sorrel which is not always available.

2 10-ounce packages frozen
   chopped spinach
2 teaspoons citric acid
   (found in canning section
   of store)
Dash sugar
Salt to taste
4 hard-boiled eggs, chopped
   and chilled
4 potatoes, peeled, boiled,
   chopped, and chilled
1 cup sour cream

Cover spinach with water and bring to boil. Stir in citric acid, sugar, and salt, cover, and simmer 30 to 45 minutes. (Spinach will turn a dull green.) Chill. Gently stir in eggs, potatoes, and sour cream, and adjust seasonings. Serve cold.

Serves 4 to 6

Reva Cook
Racelle Mednikow

MELON SOUP

Smooth and sweet with the taste of honey.

3 cups chopped cantaloupe
3 cups chopped honeydew
   melon
2 cups fresh orange juice
½ cup fresh lime juice
2 cups white wine or
   champagne
3 tablespoons honey
Fresh mint sprigs

Place 2 cups cantaloupe in blender and process until smooth. Repeat procedure with 3 cups honeydew. Combine processed melons with all other ingredients and mix. Serve garnished with remaining cup cantaloupe, finely chopped. Add 1 sprig mint per serving.

Serves 8

Mrs. Thomas G. Carpenter

SUSAN'S GAZPACHO

You may already have a gazpacho recipe, but you just might abandon it for this one.

6 tomatoes, peeled and chopped
2 28-ounce cans whole
   tomatoes, chopped
1 cup olive oil
2 cups beef stock
½ cup tarragon vinegar
Several dashes Worcestershire
   sauce
2 dashes Tabasco sauce
4 to 6 cucumbers, peeled,
   seeded, and chopped
2 green bell peppers, chopped
2 onions, chopped
4 cloves garlic, minced
2 to 3 tablespoons minced fresh
   parsley and chives
1 teaspoon basil
1 teaspoon tarragon
1 teaspoon marjoram
1 teaspoon thyme
1 teaspoon oregano
Sour cream
Curry powder

Combine tomatoes in food processor and purée. Mix together tomato purée, olive oil, beef stock, vinegar, Worcestershire sauce, and Tabasco sauce. Stir in cucumbers, bell peppers, onions, garlic, and all herbs, and chill. Serve with dollop of sour cream seasoned with curry powder.

Serves 20

Mrs. William H. Houston III
Washington, D.C.

Lunch with a View of the Dixon Gardens

Dressed informally, carrying their lawn chairs, quilts, blankets, and picnic baskets, the crowds gather early at the Dixon Gallery and Gardens on certain Sunday afternoons in the fall and the spring. They come to this large, beautifully landscaped East Memphis house, set among the ancient, towering oaks of some seventeen prime wooded acres, to enjoy one of the most pleasing diversions Memphis has to offer. Here, on broad green lawns framed with banks of azaleas and dogwood, they join their friends, spread their feasts, and settle back to listen to an outdoor concert by the Memphis Symphony Chamber Orchestra. Those who arrive early may stroll through the handsomely furnished rooms of this house which welcomes visitors with the same warmth it once did as a private residence, enjoying the experience of being at home, quite literally, among priceless works of art.

In the living room and throughout the gallery hang some of the British portraits and landscapes of the eighteenth and nineteenth centuries which, along with the many French and American Impressionist paintings, and French and British sculpture, were collected by the home's original owners. Bouquets of fresh flowers that repeat the artists' subtleties of colors are placed near these and other paintings throughout the house, a tradition established by those owners. The dining room, with its full-length windows opening onto the brick terrace, is still graced by the original wallpaper, hand-painted in a Chinese design, which the owners selected. Leaving this place, visitors sometimes express the feeling that they have been enjoying the gracious hospitality of good and generous friends—which is exactly how the former owners and residents, Hugo and Margaret Dixon, intended they should feel.

The story of the Dixon Gallery and Gardens began when Hugo Dixon, an Englishman in the cotton business, and Margaret Oates, a Memphian whose family was also in the cotton business, met on a transatlantic voyage. They were married in 1926, eventually made their home in Memphis, and for the next many years they devoted their time, resources, and imagination to the support of music and the arts. In 1940, the Dixons moved into the Georgian home they had built on Park Avenue, and there created a lovely park with open vistas, secluded walks, and formal gardens where statues from English castles stood among the tall Tennessee trees. At the same time, they filled their home with eighteenth-century English antiques and began collecting, with care and selectivity, works by such renowned artists as Renoir, Degas, Gauguin, Matisse, Cassatt, Bonnard, Vuillard, Pissarro, and Reynolds.

Having no heirs, the Dixons arranged before their deaths, a few months apart in 1974, to establish and endow the future Dixon Gallery and Gardens, which would make their home and their art collection available on a permanent basis to their chosen beneficiaries, the people of Memphis. In the years since, visitors to the Dixon Gallery and Gardens have enjoyed regularly scheduled art exhibits, flower shows, film series, and concerts in the gardens. A wide variety of educational activities is available also—lectures, garden workshops, wildflower seminars, and internships for college students in art history, horticulture and museum management. To provide galleries for the ever-growing permanent collections, a new wing was added in 1977—an elegant continuation of the home's classic architecture. New emphasis was focused on the decorative arts collections which include Sheffield silver pieces, Chelsea and Sèvres porcelain, Waterford crystal, Chinese porcelain and—one of the Gallery's significant acquisitions—the Warda Stout collection of eighteenth-century German porcelain, among the world's finest. In 1986, another large wing was opened, featuring a handsome foyer, an

THE PICTURE: The people of Memphis, in 1974, inherited a fortune from long-time cultural leaders, Hugo and Margaret Dixon—the carefully assembled art treasures collected by the Dixons over their lifetimes, and the splendid home in which these treasures were housed. In the years since, the Dixon Gallery and Gardens has become one of the city's cultural landmarks. In keeping with their desire to share with others their pleasures, a luncheon prepared for guests is pictured here, just as it might have been served by the Dixons in their dining room, looking out over the gardens on this rainy spring day. The table is set with Mrs. Dixon's vividly colored patent Mason ironstone. Her favorite round crocheted doilies and monogrammed napkins complement the simple Creighton monogrammed silver. In the arrangement of white hybrid lilies and deutzia in a Dixon family vase, the flowers are all of one color, as preferred by Mrs. Dixon, and are from the cutting garden, for no cuttings of blossoms or greenery from the formal gardens were permitted.

THE FOOD: The meal begins with a cold soup, SARAH STEVENSON'S SOUP, to be followed by MAGGIE DIXON'S TARRAGON CHICKEN ASPIC with HOMEMADE MAYONNAISE, English peas with water chestnuts, and braised celery with caviar. The dessert is homemade strawberry ice cream with sugar cookies.

auditorium, conference rooms, and an inviting gift shop filled with unique garden accessories, books, and unusual gifts.

Spacious new exhibit rooms were also provided to accommodate the Gallery's increasingly important special exhibits, such as the 1988 Auguste Rodin Exhibition, bringing to Memphis more than fifty of the French sculptor's familiar and lesser-known works, including *The Thinker* and *The Kiss.* Equally significant was the Dixon Gallery's presentation in November, 1987 of ''Masterpieces from the Armand Hammer Collection,'' which brought this exhibit of selected works from the renowned collection full circle. It was the final stop on a fifty-five-city, eighteen-country tour that had begun in Memphis eighteen years earlier. For many years, Dr. Hammer, the legendary international businessman, art collector, and philanthropist had maintained close ties with long-time Memphis art collectors such as businessman Morrie A. Moss and the Dixons. Because of them, in 1969, Dr. Hammer had chosen the Memphis Brooks Museum of Art as the starting point for the exhibition's tour; in 1987, he chose Dixon Gallery as the most suitable site for its final display. Not only that, to mark their role in the tour, Armand Hammer presented each of these Memphis galleries with a gift of one hundred prints by French artist Honoré Daumier. In announcing the gift to the Dixon Gallery at the opening of the 1987 exhibition, he said, ''Now Brooks and Dixon can have an exhibition together.''

SARAH STEVENSON'S SOUP

Unusual? Yes! But good? Very!

1 chicken bouillon cube
4 cups hot chicken broth
1 large potato
1 large onion
1 ripe banana
1 large crisp apple
1 cup heavy cream
½ teaspoon curry powder
Salt and white pepper to taste

Dissolve bouillon cube in broth. Peel potato, onion, banana, and apple, and cut in pieces. Cook in broth until very soft. Pour into blender and process until smooth. Stir in cream and seasonings. Serve cold or hot.

Serves 8

Mrs. W. L. Oates

CHILLED CREAM OF CUCUMBER SOUP WITH HERBS

Simply superb!

2 cucumbers, peeled, seeded, and sliced
1 cup water
2 slices onion
½ teaspoon salt
⅛ teaspoon white pepper
¼ cup all-purpose flour
2 cups chicken stock
1 bay leaf
2 whole cloves
¾ cup chilled sour cream
1 tablespoon finely chopped fresh dill
1 tablespoon finely chopped fresh chives
1 tablespoon grated lemon rind
Lemon slices, fresh dill, or more chopped chives for garnish

Combine cucumbers, water, onion, salt, and pepper in saucepan, and simmer covered over low heat until cucumbers are very soft. Cool mixture, purée in food processor, and set aside. Blend flour and ½ cup chicken stock in saucepan until smooth. Stir in remaining stock. Add cucumber purée, bay leaf, and cloves, and stir over low heat to blend. Simmer 2 to 3 minutes. Strain soup and chill in covered container.

Just before serving, stir in sour cream, dill, chives, and lemon rind. Serve very cold, and garnish with lemon slice, fresh dill, or chives.

Serves 6

Mrs. A. Arthur Halle, Jr.

TOMATO DILL SOUP

One of the best tomato soup recipes to be found.

½ cup vegetable oil
½ cup butter
3 medium onions, finely chopped
1 clove garlic, pierced with toothpick
7 to 8 unpeeled large ripe tomatoes or 2 28-ounce cans whole tomatoes, chopped
1 6-ounce can tomato paste
¼ cup all-purpose flour
3 14½-ounce cans chicken broth, heated
3 cups heavy cream
Salt and white pepper to taste
¼ to ½ cup chopped fresh dill or 2 to 4 tablespoons dried dill weed
8 drops Tabasco sauce

Heat oil and butter in large saucepan and add onion and garlic. Cook over low heat until onions are transparent but not browned. Increase heat, add tomatoes, and cook 5 to 6 minutes, stirring constantly. Remove garlic and add tomato paste. Mix flour with small amount broth and add to mixture, stirring until smooth. Very gradually add remainder of broth, stirring until thickened and smooth. Simmer 5 to 10 minutes over low heat. Purée mixture in food processor in batches and strain. Stir in cream, salt, pepper, dill, and Tabasco sauce. Serve hot or cold.

Serves 10 to 12

Mrs. Ron Hubbard

ICED CARROT AND ORANGE SOUP

Delightfully different combination.

2 tablespoons butter
1 pound new carrots, scraped and thinly sliced
1 onion, thinly sliced
3⅓ cups chicken stock
¼ teaspoon salt
1 teaspoon sugar
1 cup fresh orange juice, strained
⅔ cup heavy cream
1 teaspoon finely chopped chives

Melt butter in medium saucepan. Add carrots and onion, and sauté briefly until soft but not browned. Stir in chicken stock, salt, and sugar. Bring to boil, cover, and simmer 1 hour.

Remove from heat and purée in blender or food processor. Add orange juice and cream, blend briefly, and cool. Chill several hours and serve sprinkled with chives.

Serves 4 to 6

Palmeia Cooper

STRAWBERRY PATCH SOUP

Where the strawberries bloom, can paradise be far behind?

4 cups water	3 quarts strawberries, hulled
2 cups light red wine	and puréed
1½ cups sugar	1½ cups heavy cream
6 tablespoons lemon juice	¾ cup sour cream
3 cinnamon sticks	Whole strawberries

Combine water, wine, sugar, lemon juice, and cinnamon sticks in saucepan and bring to boil. Boil uncovered 15 minutes, stirring occasionally. Reduce heat, add strawberry purée, and cook 5 minutes. Remove cinnamon sticks and chill mixture.

Just before serving, whip cream and combine with sour cream. Fold into strawberry mixture. Serve in chilled cups, garnished with whole strawberries.

Serves 20 to 24

The Tennessee Club Restaurant
First Tennessee Bank

COLD PEACH SOUP

When summer's peach trees are laden and roadside stands are burgeoning with their fruit, serve your favorite guests this luscious soup.

5 large ripe peaches, peeled	2 tablespoons frozen orange
and sliced	juice concentrate, softened
¼ cup sugar	¼ cup sweet sherry
1 cup sour cream	Fresh peach slices and mint
¼ cup fresh lemon juice	leaves for garnish

Purée peaches with sugar in food processor. Add sour cream, lemon juice, orange juice concentrate, and sherry. Blend well, cover, and chill. Serve garnished with peach slices and mint leaves.

Serves 6

Mrs. W. Thomas Cunningham, Jr.
Richmond, Virginia

CAVIAR BORSCHT IN ICE BOWLS

A beautiful soup—rich in color, taste and appearance.

2 teaspoons minced onion	10 ounces plain yogurt
2 teaspoons minced celery	8 ounces Russian caviar
¼ cup chicken broth	Sour cream
1 8-ounce jar sliced beets,	
drained and juice reserved	

Simmer onion and celery in broth until onions are clear. Drain and place in blender with beets, and liquefy. Add yogurt and blend. Add reserved juice from beets as needed for consistency and chill.

To serve, ladle soup into ice bowls nestled in greenery on serving plates or place ice bowls within rim soup bowls. Gently stir in 1 tablespoon caviar per bowl. Be careful not to crush eggs in order to reserve the taste sensation as they are eaten. Add dollop of sour cream to center of soup and top with teaspoon of caviar. Serve with toast points.

Ice Bowls
Use two bowls, one smaller than the other. The size difference will determine the thickness of the ice bowl. Fill larger bowl half full of water and place smaller bowl inside it. Press smaller bowl inside larger until bowl rims are even. Add or reduce water as needed to bring water level near rims of bowls. When proper water level is reached, place masking tape across tops of bowls to hold them in place. Smaller bowl will form hollow for ice bowl as water freezes. Freeze at least 24 hours. Leaves, petals, or whole blossoms such as roses may be frozen inside ice bowl by placing in water between bowls before freezing.

To remove ice bowl from mold, dip bottom of larger bowl briefly in warm water. Briefly place warm water in top bowl.

Serves 4

Pat Kerr Tigrett

SALADS AND DRESSINGS

ORANGE AND ONION SALAD

An unlikely marriage, but destined to last.

4 tablespoons walnut oil
2 tablespoons orange juice
1½ tablespoons white wine
   vinegar
1 teaspoon salt
½ teaspoon freshly ground
   black pepper

½ teaspoon crushed dried
   rosemary
5 oranges, peeled and sectioned
1 medium red onion, thinly
   sliced into rings
1 large head romaine lettuce,
   torn in pieces

Combine oil, orange juice, vinegar, salt, pepper, and rosemary in jar. Shake well and pour into salad bowl. Add oranges, onion, and lettuce, toss gently to coat with dressing, and serve.

Variation: Grapefruit sections and juice may be substituted for orange sections and juice.

Serves 10

Claire B. Austin

HERBED TOMATOES

Great when those wonderful home-grown summer tomatoes are available.

6 medium tomatoes
⅔ cup corn oil
¼ cup cider vinegar
1 clove garlic, minced
¼ cup minced parsley
¼ cup thinly sliced green
   onions with tops

½ teaspoon thyme
1 teaspoon salt
¼ teaspoon cracked black
   pepper
Chopped green onions and
   parsley sprigs for garnish

Peel tomatoes and quarter. Mix together all other ingredients except garnishes, and pour over tomatoes. Marinate in refrigerator overnight.

Arrange tomatoes on serving platter, spoon portion of marinade over each tomato, and sprinkle with green onions and parsley.

Serves 6

Mrs. Hugh D. Brewer
Robinsonville, Mississippi

REBEL YELL SALAD

Definitely a salad with spirit.

1 3-ounce package black cherry
   gelatin
1 cup hot water
1 16-ounce can pitted dark,
   sweet cherries
¾ cup juice from cherries

¼ cup bourbon whiskey
Juice of 1 lemon
2½ cups miniature marsh-
   mallows
1 cup finely chopped pecans
Lettuce leaves

Stir gelatin in hot water until dissolved. Add cherries, cherry juice, bourbon, and lemon juice, and mix well. Pour into mold and refrigerate until partially set. Stir in marshmallows and pecans, and chill until firm. Serve on lettuce leaves.

Variation: Replace marshmallows with 3-ounce package cream cheese, shaped into small balls. Roll in pecans, carefully fold into partially set gelatin, and chill until firm. Serve on lettuce leaves.

Serves 8 to 10

Betty A. Jennings

PIQUANT FRUIT SALAD

The custard-like sauce is a delightful addition to this salad.

2 eggs, beaten
2 tablespoons white vinegar
2 tablespoons sugar
2 tablespoons butter
2 cups white seedless grapes
2 cups diced canned pineapple
2 medium bananas, sliced

2 oranges, peeled, sectioned,
   and cut in pieces
1 cup miniature marsh-
   mallows
1 cup heavy cream, whipped
Fresh cherries for garnish

Combine eggs, vinegar, and sugar in top of double boiler, and cook over medium heat until thick, stirring constantly. Remove from heat and stir in butter. Cool. Add fruit and marshmallows to cooled egg mixture and toss lightly to coat. Refrigerate 24 hours.

Just before serving, toss lightly with whipped cream and top with cherries.

Serves 6

Maxine Morse

SHRIMP SALAD WITH NOODLES

A wonderful salad. Avocado adds interest.

1 6-ounce package egg noodles	1 avocado, chopped
2 pounds small or medium shrimp, cooked and peeled	3 scallions, chopped
	Poppy seeds
1 cucumber, chopped	¾ cup mayonnaise
1 tomato, chopped	¼ cup Italian dressing

Cook noodles according to package directions and drain.

Combine all other ingredients, toss with noodles, and chill. (Best made well ahead to allow flavors to blend.)

Serves 8 to 10

Mrs. Jesse Anderson

DATE DELIGHT

The perfect date—good taste and good looks.

2 3-ounce packages cream cheese, softened	1 8-ounce can crushed pineapple, drained
1 cup heavy cream, whipped	1 cup chopped pecans
1 8-ounce package dates, chopped	½ teaspoon vanilla

Mix cream cheese with whipped cream. Stir in dates, pineapple, nuts, and vanilla. Place in champagne glasses and chill at least one hour before serving.

Serves 6

Mrs. J. W. McAllister

CHRISTMAS SALAD

Tangy and refreshing.

1 3-ounce package raspberry gelatin	1 8-ounce can crushed pineapple with juice
¾ cup boiling water	¼ cup cold orange juice
1 16-ounce can whole cranberry sauce	½ cup chopped pecans

Dissolve gelatin in boiling water. Add all other ingredients and mix well. Pour into 6-cup mold and chill until firm.

Serves 6 to 8

Mary Stagg

CHICKEN MOUSSE

A very nice luncheon dish.

3 envelopes unflavored gelatin	1½ cups minced celery
½ cup water	1 cup chopped or sliced ripe olives
4½ cups warm chicken broth	
1 cup mayonnaise	1½ cups chopped blanched almonds
5 to 6 cups diced cooked chicken	
1 teaspoon Worcestershire sauce	2 teaspoons salt
	½ teaspoon pepper
2 tablespoons lemon juice	1 cup heavy cream, whipped
1½ tablespoons grated onion	

Soften gelatin in water and add to warm broth, stirring to dissolve. Chill until syrupy.

Blend mayonnaise into partially jelled broth. Add chicken and all other ingredients except cream, and mix thoroughly. Fold in whipped cream. Place in 9 x 13-inch pan and chill until set. Cut in squares to serve.

Serves 12

Mrs. James K. Dobbs, Jr.

MOLDED AVOCADO SALAD

Deserves an Oscar for perfect casting.

1½ envelopes unflavored gelatin	½ cup sour cream
	1 teaspoon salt
¾ cup water	Dash Tabasco sauce
1 to 2 large avocados	Grapefruit sections and watercress for garnish
2 tablespoons lemon juice	
½ cup mayonnaise	

Soften gelatin in water in small saucepan. Stir over low heat until gelatin is dissolved. Chill until slightly thickened.

Peel and mash avocados to measure 1 to 1½ cups. Add lemon juice and mix well to retain freshness and color of avocados. Stir in mayonnaise and sour cream. Add salt and Tabasco sauce, mix well, and fold into gelatin. Pour into 4-cup ring mold (or 6 individual molds) and refrigerate at least 3 hours or overnight. Serve with grapefruit sections in center and watercress garnish around base.

Serves 6

Marion D. Kendall

A Special Tradition at Calvary Episcopal Church

Religion is and always has been an integral part of Memphis life, even in earliest days when the little settlement enjoyed a certain notoriety as a rough, rambunctious river town. Some of the city's present-day congregations, especially the venerable ones still located in downtown Memphis, actively ministering to inner city needs, can trace their beginnings to those pioneer days. One such is the First Presbyterian Church at Poplar and Third, erected to house a congregation organized in 1828 by a missionary to the Chickasaw Indians. The First Methodist Church on North Second, built in 1832 as the Wesley Chapel, was the first church building in Memphis; its congregation was founded in 1826 by a circuit rider who came to town every sixth Sunday to preach. (Prior to that, the first resident clergyman in Memphis, a black Methodist named Harry Lawrence, had preached in outdoor meetings to both black and white parishioners.) The Calvary Episcopal Church on Adams at Second, dedicated in 1844, is the oldest public building in continuous use in Memphis. Its founding members first came together as a congregation in 1832, in church services held on a flatboat on the Mississippi River. Nearby, on Adams, is St. Peter's Catholic Church, founded in 1840 by Irish immigrants. A few blocks away, at Fourth and Beale, is the First Baptist Church Beale Street, built between 1865 and 1869 to house the oldest black congregation in Memphis, dating back to 1854. And the city's earliest Jewish congregation, B'nai Israel, organized in 1853 and a forerunner of present-day Temple Israel, in 1858 leased (and two years later purchased) the Merchants and Farmers Bank Building at Main and Exchange, to be converted into Memphis' first synagogue.

Each of these congregations and many others in Memphis have made memorable contributions to the city's religious life, and each cherishes special traditions. For some sixty years, a treasured tradition of the Calvary Episcopal Church has been their series of Lenten lunches, prepared and served by women of the church, and sold at reasonable prices following noontime services each weekday during the forty days preceding Easter. It began in 1928 as the Calvary Waffle Shop, a fund-raising project. In an old building just off Front Street (in an alley known, because of its colorful past, as "Whiskey Chute"), women volunteers, using old-fashioned waffle irons that had to be heated on the stove, prepared and served the food, and washed the dishes with water carried in buckets from outdoor hydrants. Profits of two thousand dollars that first year helped renovate the church organ. After two years, the project moved to 109 Court Square, a building blessed with electricity and running water.

In 1933 the Waffle Shop settled down in its present site in the basement of the church. Today, more than sixteen thousand meals—some seven hundred daily—are served each season, to downtown business people as well as to visitors from other parts of the city and the tri-state region. The proceeds benefit a number of charities. Waffles prepared according to the original recipe are still featured, but the menu has been expanded over the years, offering other dependable favorites such as chicken hash, fish pudding, the Calvary salad plate, and chocolate silk pies, which keep satisfied customers returning year after year to enjoy the Calvary Lenten luncheons.

THE PICTURE: *A question regularly asked of new Memphis residents is this: "Have you found your church home?" The phrasing indicates the important role religion plays in community life and in the Memphis psyche—a place of worship is another home. A number of Memphis congregations can date their beginnings to the city's earliest years, and have cherished traditions developed over time that make churches and synagogues continuing centers of spiritual life in the community. The Calvary Episcopal Church's annual series of Lenten lunches, which began in 1928, is one such tradition. Held in the basement of the church following noontime services, the lunches are prepared by women of the church using recipes that have become favorites over the years, and several charities benefit from the proceeds. This plate of salads is set by the leaded casement windows of the enclosed passageway connecting the church sanctuary with the parish house, a setting known to generations of parishioners as the Bride's Walk. The red tulips are a seasonal reminder of an early spring.*

THE FOOD: *Presented here is an appealing plate of salads which includes CALVARY CHURCH CIRCLE TOMATO ASPIC, a shrimp mousse, chicken salad, and pear halves topped with specially seasoned cottage cheese.*

CALVARY CHURCH CIRCLE TOMATO ASPIC

An old favorite.

3 tablespoons unflavored gelatin	Dash Tabasco sauce
1 46-ounce can tomato juice	2 tablespoons Worcestershire sauce
½ medium onion, minced	1 tablespoon sugar
½ cup chopped celery leaves	1 teaspoon celery salt
¼ cup chopped parsley sprigs	1 teaspoon salt
4 tablespoons lemon juice	Artichoke hearts, optional

Dissolve gelatin in 2 cups tomato juice and set aside. Pour remainder of juice into saucepan and bring to boil. Stir in remaining ingredients except artichoke hearts. Reduce heat, cover, simmer 10 minutes, and strain. Add artichoke hearts, if preferred, and gelatin mixture, stirring to mix well. Pour into 5-cup mold or individual molds and chill until set. Top with dollop of homemade mayonnaise.

Serves 10 to 12

Mrs. W. L. Oates

STREIBICH'S SHRIMP MOUSSE

Unfailingly good.

2 envelopes unflavored gelatin	½ cup chopped celery
1¼ cups cold water	1 chopped sweet pickle
1 10¾-ounce can tomato soup	1 cup mayonnaise
1 8-ounce package cream cheese, softened	Dash lemon juice
5 teaspoons grated onion or ½ cup finely chopped green onions with tops	Tabasco sauce to taste
	1 pound shrimp, boiled, peeled, and deveined (cut in half if large)
½ cup chopped green bell pepper	Watercress or parsley sprigs for garnish

Dissolve gelatin in water. Combine soup and cheese in top of double boiler and cook over medium heat, stirring until blended. Stir in gelatin mixture and cool. Add onion, bell pepper, celery, pickle, mayonnaise, lemon juice, and Tabasco sauce. Add shrimp, mix lightly, and pour into 5½-cup mold. Refrigerate at least 4 hours. Serve garnished with sprigs of watercress or parsley.

Serves 8 to 10

Harold C. Streibich

A CLASSIC SPINACH SALAD

Especially good.

1½ pounds fresh spinach	6 slices bacon, fried crisp and crumbled
3 hard-cooked eggs, chopped	
1 8-ounce can water chestnuts, sliced	½ red onion, sliced in thin rings

Combine ingredients and toss lightly with dressing.

Dressing

½ cup vegetable oil	1 teaspoon salt
⅓ cup sugar	1 teaspoon paprika
⅓ cup catsup	1 teaspoon A-1 sauce
¼ cup vinegar	1 tablespoon minced onion
2 tablespoons sherry	

Combine all ingredients and mix thoroughly.

Serves 6 to 8

Sara Beth Causey, Founding Director
Memphis Symphony Chorus

LAYERED POTATO SALAD

This may become your favorite potato salad.

1 8-ounce carton sour cream	¾ cup finely chopped celery
1½ cups Hellmann's mayonnaise	1 cup finely chopped fresh parsley
1½ teaspoons prepared horseradish	8 to 9 medium red potatoes, boiled, peeled, and cubed
6 to 8 green onions with tops, finely chopped	3 to 5 slices bacon, fried crisp and crumbled

Blend sour cream, mayonnaise, and horseradish to make dressing. Mix onions, celery, and parsley. In serving dish, layer in order half of potatoes, dressing, and celery mixture. Repeat layers once. Sprinkle with bacon bits.

Serves 8 to 10

Mrs. Fletcher Johnson

VEGETABLE ANTIPASTO SALAD

A splendid little salad.

½ cup thinly sliced cucumber
½ cup thinly sliced onion
2 6½-ounce jars marinated
   artichoke hearts, drained
   and halved
1 14½-ounce can stewed
   tomatoes, drained

1 2-ounce can ripe olives,
   drained and sliced
½ cup thinly sliced green
   bell pepper
½ cup Italian salad dressing

In 1-quart dish, layer vegetables in order listed above, add dressing, cover, and chill several hours.

Serves 4 to 6

Anne Threefoot

CONGEALED FRESH GRAPEFRUIT SALAD

Tart, crunchy, and refreshing. An excellent salad.

3 envelopes unflavored gelatin
1 cup cold water
3 cups grapefruit juice
½ cup sugar
4 tablespoons lemon juice

4 grapefruit (or 4 16-ounce
   cans grapefruit, drained)
1 cup finely chopped celery
1 cup pecan or almond pieces

Soften gelatin in cold water. Bring 1 cup grapefruit juice to boil and mix with gelatin mixture. Stir in remaining grapefruit juice, sugar, and lemon juice. Chill until partially set.

Peel and section grapefruit, removing as much white membrane as possible. Stir into gelatin with celery and nuts. Place in individual molds or in large ring mold. Chill until firm.

Serves 10

Lois Sandusky

FRUIT SALAD ICE

Just one word will do—scrumptious!

1 8-ounce carton small curd
   cottage cheese
1 14-ounce can sweetened
   condensed milk
1 tablespoon fresh lemon juice
1 tablespoon Cointreau,
   optional

Dash salt
1 cup sliced fresh peaches
1 cup sliced fresh strawberries
1 ripe banana, chopped
Sour cream
Lettuce leaves

In food processor, combine cheese, milk, lemon juice, Cointreau, and salt, and blend until smooth. Add fruit and process very briefly, keeping texture of fruit. Pour into 5 x 9-inch loaf pan and freeze until partially set. Scoop into large mixing bowl and beat until light. Return to loaf pan and freeze until firm.

Cut in squares. Top with dollop of sour cream, garnish with whole strawberry or peach slice, and serve on crisp lettuce leaves.

Serves 6

Mrs. Henry W. Williamson

FROZEN TOMATO SALAD

Simply a wonderful salad.

1 14½-ounce can whole
   tomatoes
½ cup cottage cheese
1 8-ounce can crushed
   pineapple, drained
1 3-ounce package cream cheese

½ teaspoon Tabasco sauce
Pinch ground ginger
¼ cup mayonnaise
Onion juice to taste
Salt and pepper to taste

Place all ingredients in blender and mix thoroughly. Freeze in individual molds or in 5-cup mold.

Note: Can be used as soup. Simply chill until icy, but do not freeze.

Serves 8 to 10

Mrs. Allen Hughes, Jr.

MRS. B'S FIRST COURSE

Great summertime first course. Try serving in small glass cups within ice-filled compotes.

1 large avocado, coarsely chopped
1 14-ounce can artichoke hearts, drained and quartered
2 hard-cooked eggs, coarsely chopped
¼ cup finely chopped onion
¼ cup finely chopped celery
Russian dressing to taste
6 slices bacon, fried crisp and crumbled

Combine avocado, artichoke hearts, eggs, onion, and celery. Mix with Russian dressing. Top with bacon and serve.

Variation: Add crab meat or tiny shrimp and serve on leaf lettuce for a great luncheon salad.

Serves 4 to 6

Mrs. Crit Currie

GREEK SALAD

Hearty enough to serve as a luncheon dish all on its own.

1 head iceberg lettuce
1 small head endive
10 to 12 radishes, sliced
2 carrots, grated
4 to 5 green onions, sliced
1 4-ounce package feta cheese, crumbled
1 2-ounce can anchovies
1 cup pitted ripe olives

Tear lettuce and toss with endive, radishes, carrots, and green onions. Just before serving, add dressing and top with feta cheese, anchovies, and olives.

Dressing
2 tablespoons olive oil
2 tablespoons vegetable oil
2 tablespoons red wine vinegar
1 clove garlic, minced
¼ teaspoon oregano

Combine all ingredients, mix well, and chill.

Serves 4 to 6

Helen Vergos

SUPREME SALAD OF TORTELLINI

A fine recipe saved from a long-gone cooking class.

12 large spinach leaves
3 whole chicken breasts, cooked, boned, and diced
2 cups green seedless grapes
1 cup snow peas
1 large celery rib, chopped
1 small cucumber, sliced
1 6½-ounce jar artichoke hearts, drained
½ cup raisins
1 green onion with top, chopped
1 8-ounce can sliced water chestnuts, drained
1 8-ounce package tortellini, cooked, drained, and chilled
Spinach leaves for serving
1 11-ounce can mandarin orange sections, drained

Wash 12 spinach leaves thoroughly, pat dry, and tear in pieces. Combine with chicken, grapes, snow peas, celery, cucumber, artichoke hearts, raisins, green onion, and water chestnuts, and toss. Add tortellini and gently toss again. Add dressing to taste, toss, and serve on bed of spinach leaves garnished with orange sections.

Dressing
⅔ cup mayonnaise
½ cup freshly grated Parmesan cheese
⅓ cup fresh lemon juice
Salt and pepper to taste
Vinegar to taste
Garlic powder to taste
Onion powder to taste

Combine all ingredients and mix well.

Serves 6 to 8

Tina Edge

PORT WINE SALAD

Nice with a dollop of sweetened sour cream.

1 11-ounce can mandarin oranges, drained and juice reserved
1 3-ounce package black cherry gelatin
1 tablespoon lemon juice
1½ tart medium apples, diced
½ cup port wine
½ to 1 cup pecans

Combine reserved juice with enough water to measure 1½ cups and bring to boil. Add gelatin and stir until dissolved and mixture becomes clear. Set aside to cool.

Add oranges and all remaining ingredients, pour into 6-cup mold, and chill until firm.

Serves 8

Sally McAdoo

JOE'S FAVORITE SALAD

A do-ahead salad that never seems to wear out its welcome.

1 14-ounce can artichoke
    hearts, cut in small pieces
Italian dressing
1 head lettuce
1 cup grated Cheddar cheese

7 to 10 slices bacon, fried crisp
    and crumbled
Salt and freshly ground pepper
    to taste

Marinate artichokes in small amount dressing. Wash lettuce leaves and pat dry. Chill lettuce, cheese, and bacon.

In large salad bowl, tear lettuce in pieces and combine with artichokes, cheese, and bacon. Add dressing to taste, salt and pepper, toss and serve. Must be served cold.

Serves 10 to 12

Mrs. Joseph S. Hardison, Jr.

CHICKEN CRANBERRY MOLD

A pretty two-layer salad. Makes a special holiday luncheon dish.

2 tablespoons unflavored
    gelatin
¾ cup cold water
1 tablespoon soy sauce
1 cup mayonnaise
1½ cups diced cooked chicken
½ cup diced celery

¼ cup chopped pecans
1 8-ounce can crushed
    pineapple
1 16-ounce can jellied cranberry
    sauce
2 tablespoons lemon juice

In saucepan, soften 1 tablespoon gelatin in cold water. Place over low heat and stir constantly until dissolved. Remove from heat, stir in soy sauce, and set aside to cool. Blend in mayonnaise. Add chicken, celery, and pecans, mix well, and pour into 6-cup mold. Chill until top is sticky and slightly firm.

While chicken layer is chilling, drain pineapple and reserve juice. Add water to juice to measure ½ cup, and soften remaining tablespoon of gelatin in this liquid. Cook over low heat, stirring until gelatin is dissolved, and set aside. Break up cranberry sauce with fork. Stir in crushed pineapple and lemon juice, and add warm gelatin mixture. Chill until syrupy and spoon over chicken layer. Chill until set.

Serves 8 to 10

Mrs. A. Van Court Pritchartt

INDIAN SUMMER SALAD

For those long, lovely days that usher in the fall of the year. The apples and cider are so good.

1 3-ounce package lemon
    gelatin
2 cups hot apple cider
1 tablespoon lemon juice
1 cup chopped unpeeled apples

½ cup pecan pieces
½ cup sliced dates
½ cup sour cream
½ cup mayonnaise
Grated orange rind

Dissolve gelatin in hot cider, add lemon juice, and chill until syrupy. Fold in apples, pecans, and dates. Spoon into 1-quart mold and chill until set.

Cut in squares to serve. Combine sour cream and mayonnaise, mix well, and place spoonful atop each serving. Sprinkle with orange rind.

Serves 6 to 8

Mrs. Wilson Northcross, Jr.

ARTICHOKE OLIVE SALAD

There's a lovely delicate flavor in the dressing that is just perfect for this salad.

2 6-ounce cans ripe olives,
    halved
2 14-ounce cans artichoke
    hearts, drained and
    quartered

1 quart cherry tomatoes or
    medium tomatoes, cut in
    pieces

Combine all ingredients and toss lightly. Pour dressing over salad when ready to serve.

Dressing
1 cup olive oil or vegetable oil
½ cup fresh lemon juice
1 teaspoon salt

1 teaspoon oregano
2 cloves garlic

Combine all ingredients in jar and shake well. Refrigerate overnight.

Serves 6

June Merrell
Forrest City, Arkansas

Dinner at the Symphony Ball in Germantown

The people of Memphis, by tradition and by choice, are quick to volunteer their services for worthy causes. Ever since the state exceeded by more than tenfold its Mexican War enlistment quota in 1848, Tennessee has been known as the Volunteer State. And it was fearless volunteers, refusing to flee the city in the 1870s, who organized efforts that helped Memphis survive that decade's devastating yellow fever epidemics.

Today's Memphis, too, owes much of its vitality and livability to the dedication and fund-raising prowess of volunteer groups. They support two major art museums, two ballet companies, a year-round children's theatre, and a natural history museum; they organize book sales for the benefit of the Memphis and Shelby County Library and Information Service. They established and support Le Bonheur Children's Hospital, now a part of Le Bonheur Children's Medical Center, one of the country's finest, and they founded and raise funds to support Les Passees Rehabilitation Center, providing treatment for children with neuro-muscular developmental problems. They help finance and staff MIFA, the Metropolitan Inter-Faith Association, with its host of services including a food bank for the hungry, shelter for the homeless, emergency services, and Meals on Wheels. Volunteers plant and maintain gardens to beautify Memphis. They raise money for the unique artistic and archival programs of the nationally acclaimed Center for Southern Folklore. They operate a successful tearoom, the Women's Exchange, which also provides a sales outlet for products made by homebound artisans. Volunteers sweep stages, make costumes, sell tickets, play minor roles or star as leading players for Theatre Memphis. And the welcoming glow added to the nighttime Memphis skyline in 1986 with the lighting of the Hernando De Soto Bridge that spans the Mississippi River came largely from the ideas and fund-raising efforts of volunteers.

Hard work, good luck, and ingenuity are all required to sustain these many volunteer-supported projects, and a crucial decision for each group is how best to expend its fund-raising energies. In Memphis, a time-tested favorite choice is the ball. A number of these elaborate galas are held each year to benefit various causes—the Cancer Society, Opera Memphis, the Heart Fund, and others—but in size, elegance, and glamour, none surpasses the annual Memphis Symphony Ball. The city's first and still foremost charity ball had its beginnings in 1959 when the first Symphony Ball was held at the Memphis Country Club with Metropolitan Opera star Marguerite Piazza as featured entertainer. It has been going strong ever since, leaving Memphis a series of dazzling nights to remember.

Each Symphony Ball is more spectacular than the last, and volunteers from the Memphis Symphony League work through the year planning every detail of entertainment, menu, music, auction, and setting for these grand affairs. A tent in the country becomes an elegant ballroom of white silk and glowing candlelight; a cool, flowing stream is created as part of a Japanese garden motif; a warehouse on the river is transformed with thousands of fresh-cut roses covering its walls. Guests are entertained by singers like Andy Williams, Natalie Cole, Tony Bennett, or pianists such as Phineas Newborn or Memphis Slim, and they dance to the music of Peter Duchin or Lester Lanin or Marshall Grant—or Memphis' own Jim Johnson.

The Twenty-Seventh Annual Symphony Ball was held in the pavilion of the new Agricenter International, a sparkling, sixty-five-foot steel and glass pyramid on Germantown Road. This dramatic exhibition site for innovative agribusiness products and technology is part of a complex that contains hydroponic greenhouses, aqua gardens, an indoor riding arena, and is surrounded by one thousand acres of fertile

THE PICTURE: *High on any list of Memphis civic assets would be the good works done by volunteers. The institutions, activities, and events sponsored and funded by volunteers in the city are just that—good works. They are very good for Memphis, and involve lots of hard work for the volunteers whose tireless energy, boundless ingenuity, and limitless optimism assure support for a great variety of projects. But all work and no play is not the way of the most successful volunteer efforts in Memphis. Many volunteer groups rely on parties, balls, and other galas as fund-raisers. Of these, none has been more popular in recent decades than the annual Symphony Ball, planned, organized, promoted (and enjoyed) by volunteers from the Memphis Symphony League. Here, just outside the Agricenter International pavilion, a round, white-draped table has been set with the dinner's salad course for six guests at the Twenty-Seventh Annual Symphony Ball. The centerpiece is a mirrored pedestal supporting a bouquet of white bridal roses, stock, fuji mums, tuberoses, and azalea foliage. The vastness of the Agricenter's well-lit arena where dancing will go on until early morning hours is seen in the background.*

THE FOOD: *MARINATED BRIE AND TOMATO SALAD is presented on crisp lettuce leaves.*

demonstration farm fields. For this evening's festivities, guests explored the pavilion's acres of corridors, or browsed in small shops set up for the evening. They assembled in the amphitheatre for a performance by Sammy Davis, Jr., then moved on to the twenty-thousand-square-foot arena to enjoy dinner and dancing under a lofty dome that had been draped with shimmering white fabric, and festooned with streamers of silver lame and white flowers cascading from the center apex. By the time the evening was over, celebrants at the Memphis Symphony Ball had once again demonstrated how volunteers can raise a significant portion of the funds required to maintain an excellent regional symphony orchestra, and have fun doing it.

MARINATED BRIE AND TOMATO SALAD

A beautiful salad idea.

1 pound Brie cheese with rind removed, cubed	3 cloves garlic, minced
4 large tomatoes, peeled, seeded, and cut in pieces	2/3 cup extra virgin olive oil
1 cup snipped fresh basil leaves	1 teaspoon salt
	1/2 teaspoon freshly ground black pepper
	Green and red leaf lettuce

Combine cheese and tomatoes. Mix basil, garlic, olive oil, salt, and pepper for marinade. Pour over cheese and tomatoes, cover, and let stand at room temperature at least 2 hours. Chill and serve on bed of green and red leaf lettuce.

Serves 6 to 8

Betty K. Whitehead

YUM YUM SALAD

Tastes just like its name.

1 6-ounce package orange-pineapple gelatin	3/4 cup sugar
1 cup cold water	1 cup mayonnaise
1 20-ounce can crushed pineapple with juice	1 cup grated Cheddar cheese
	1 16-ounce carton non-dairy whipped topping

Mix gelatin with cold water and set aside. Combine pineapple and juice with sugar and cook at least 5 minutes. Stir into gelatin mixture while hot and set aside to cool. Chill until partially set. Fold in mayonnaise, cheese, and non-dairy topping. Place in 9 x 13-inch glass dish and refrigerate at least 24 hours.

Serves 6 to 8

Mrs. William E. Sheffield, Sr.

AMARETTO CHICKEN SALAD

A most unusual and delicious chicken salad.

1/2 cup slivered almonds	1 cup chopped celery
1/4 cup butter	1/2 cup mayonnaise
4 cups cooked and cubed chicken breasts	1 teaspoon salt
1 15 1/4-ounce can crushed pineapple, drained	Fresh pineapple slices
	Lettuce leaves

Sauté almonds in butter until golden brown, stirring to prevent scorching. Drain well. Combine half of almonds with chicken, crushed pineapple, celery, mayonnaise, and salt. Mix well, cover, and chill several hours or overnight.

Place pineapple slices on lettuce leaves and top with chicken salad. Spoon dressing over salad and sprinkle with remaining almonds.

Amaretto Dressing

1 cup mayonnaise	1/4 cup Amaretto liqueur

Combine ingredients, mix until smooth, and chill thoroughly.

Serves 6 to 8

Teresa Cuoghi Edens
Albuquerque, New Mexico

CRAB MEAT ASPIC

Passed down from mother to daughter, a favorite ladies' luncheon recipe that is especially good.

1 10 3/4-ounce can tomato soup	1/4 cup vinegar
1/2 cup water	3/4 cup diced green bell pepper
1 3-ounce package lemon gelatin	3/4 cup diced celery
	1 6 1/2-ounce can crab meat

Mix soup and water, and bring to boil. Remove from heat and add gelatin, stirring to dissolve. Add vinegar, bell pepper, celery, and half of crab meat. Mix and pour into individual molds. Chill until firm and serve with dressing.

Dressing

Remaining half crab meat	1/4 cup chopped green bell pepper
1 cup mayonnaise	
2 to 3 green onions, chopped	3 to 4 tablespoons sherry
1/4 cup chopped celery	

Combine all ingredients and mix well.

Variation: Double recipe. Pour into ring mold and chill until firm. Fill center with artichoke hearts or avocado slices, and serve with dressing.

Serves 6

Sissy M. Long

TUNA VEGETABLE SALAD

A dieter's dream.

1 12½-ounce can water-packed
  tuna, drained
1 to 2 small zucchini, thinly
  sliced
⅔ cup chopped celery
2 tablespoons minced green
  onion and tops
½ cup mayonnaise

2 tablespoons lemon juice
1½ tablespoons minced
  parsley
½ teaspoon dried dill weed
½ teaspoon salt
Dash pepper
Lettuce leaves
2 to 3 tomatoes, cut in wedges

Combine all ingredients except lettuce and tomatoes, stirring well. (Add more mayonnaise and lemon juice if mixture is too dry.) Chill and serve on lettuce leaves with tomatoes as garnish on the side.

Serves 4 to 6

Ann Kendall Ray

BROCCOLI SALAD

A special way to present broccoli.

2 10-ounce packages frozen
  chopped broccoli
1 10½-ounce can beef
  consommé
2 envelopes unflavored gelatin
¾ cup mayonnaise
1 3-ounce package cream
  cheese, softened
¼ cup fresh lemon juice

2 tablespoons Worcestershire
  sauce
1½ teaspoons Tabasco sauce
½ teaspoon salt
1 teaspoon pepper
4 hard-cooked eggs, chopped
1 4-ounce jar diced pimientos,
  drained

Cook broccoli according to package directions, omitting salt. Drain and chill.

Heat consommé in small saucepan. Sprinkle gelatin over consommé, stir until dissolved, and chill until thickened. Add broccoli and all other ingredients, mix well, and spoon into 6-cup mold. Chill until set.

Serves 10 to 12

Mrs. W. T. Whitley

FROZEN FRUIT SALAD

A good salad to make ahead and have on hand when needed. Cherries add nice flecks of color.

1½ cups sour cream
¾ cup sugar
⅛ teaspoon salt
2 tablespoons lemon juice
½ cup chopped pecans
2 cups crushed pineapple,
  drained

¼ cup chopped maraschino
  cherries or pitted dark
  Bing cherries, drained
2 large bananas, cut in small
  pieces
Mayonnaise

Blend sour cream, sugar, salt, and lemon juice. Combine pecans, pineapple, cherries, and bananas, and stir in sour cream mixture. Pour into 9 x 13-inch pan and freeze, preferably overnight.

Cut in squares and serve topped with dollop of mayonnaise and maraschino or Bing cherry.

Variation: Spoon into paper-lined muffin tins, cover with plastic wrap, and freeze. Great after-school treat for children.

Serves 10 to 12

Mrs. J. F. Lynch

PLEASANT HILL
CABBAGE AND ONION SALAD

A memorable salad.

1½ quarts shredded cabbage
  (about 1 large head)
1 large red onion, thinly sliced
  and separated into rings
1 cup sugar
1 cup vinegar

1 teaspoon celery seed
1 teaspoon dry mustard
1 teaspoon chopped parsley
1 teaspoon salt
¼ teaspoon pepper
1 cup vegetable oil

Alternately layer cabbage and onion in bowl, ending with layer of onion. Combine remaining ingredients except vegetable oil in saucepan and bring to boil. Stir in oil and drizzle hot mixture over cabbage and onions. Do not stir salad. Cover and refrigerate 24 hours.

Serves 12

Mrs. John Shea Buchignani

CHICKEN-FLAVORED POTATO SALAD

Everyone will ask the secret of the delicious taste.

4 pounds potatoes, peeled, cooked, and cubed to equal 9 cups
8 hard-cooked eggs, chopped
1½ cups chopped celery
½ cup minced onion
1 cup sweet pickle relish
2½ cups mayonnaise
4 tablespoons chopped pimiento, optional
2½ tablespoons chicken bouillon granules
¼ cup chopped parsley, optional
Lettuce leaves

Combine all ingredients except lettuce leaves in large bowl and toss. Cover and chill. When chilled, carefully toss salad again and serve on bed of lettuce leaves.

Serves 16

Mrs. J. T. Mahoney, Jr.

ANN'S HOT POTATO SALAD

Potato salad, oven-baked. Yummy.

6 medium potatoes
3 cups shredded American cheese
¼ cup butter
⅓ cup chopped scallions
¾ cup sour cream, room temperature
1 teaspoon salt
¼ teaspoon pepper
2 tablespoons butter

Cook potatoes in skins, cool, peel, and finely chop.

Combine cheese and ¼ cup butter in saucepan and cook over low heat until almost melted, stirring occasionally. Remove from heat and blend in scallions, sour cream, salt, and pepper. Fold in potatoes, place in greased 2-quart baking dish, and dot with remaining 2 tablespoons butter. Bake 30 minutes at 350 degrees.

Serves 8 to 10

Jacqueline Beane
Forrest City, Arkansas

AUNT BENA'S SALAD DRESSING

A delicious dressing.

1 cup Hellmann's mayonnaise
¼ cup catsup
2 tablespoons chili sauce
⅛ teaspoon garlic powder
10 stuffed olives, chopped

Mix together all ingredients and serve over lettuce wedge or salad greens.

Yields 1½ cups dressing

Mrs. J. W. McAllister

SISSY'S BUTTERMILK SALAD DRESSING

Keeps well and tastes great.

1 32-ounce jar Hellmann's mayonnaise
1 cup buttermilk
1 teaspoon onion powder
1 teaspoon garlic powder
1 teaspoon parsley flakes

Remove 1 cup of mayonnaise and save for other uses. Empty remaining mayonnaise into bowl, stir in all other ingredients until well-blended, and return to jar.

Yields 4 cups dressing

Mrs. Solon G. Freeman, Jr.

O'BRIEN'S FRENCH DRESSING

Many times tried and always true. It is especially good on fruit salads, particularly with avocado and grapefruit.

1 cup sugar
1 cup vegetable oil
½ cup catsup
1 teaspoon salt
Dash garlic salt
1 tablespoon Worcestershire sauce
½ cup vinegar
1 tablespoon grated onion

Combine all ingredients in food processor and blend for 1 minute.

Yields 2½ cups dressing

Lou Carson
Sikeston, Missouri

FRENCH DRESSING

Too good to miss. Make dressing several hours ahead, or even the day before, to allow flavors to blend fully.

½ cup corn oil
½ cup olive oil
2½ tablespoons white vinegar
2½ tablespoons red wine vinegar
4 tablespoons cold water
1 tablespoon Worcestershire sauce
½ teaspoon sugar
Dash hot sauce
4 tablespoons lemon juice

1 teaspoon instant minced onion
½ teaspoon parsley flakes
½ teaspoon paprika
¼ teaspoon chili powder
½ teaspoon Lawry's seasoned salt
½ teaspoon freshly ground black pepper
1 clove fresh garlic, minced

Combine all ingredients in pint jar and shake well.

Yields 2 cups dressing

Mrs. Philip Kaminsky

THE EMBERS RESTAURANT HONEY FRENCH DRESSING

For many years, The Embers, managed by Jack St. Clair, was a favorite Memphis restaurant, known, among other things, for its "bottomless salad bowl." This dressing, easy to make and infallible, was a favorite there.

½ cup catsup
½ cup honey
¼ cup cider vinegar
⅛ cup grated onion
¼ teaspoon ground cloves

1 teaspoon Worcestershire sauce
Freshly ground black pepper to taste
1 cup vegetable oil

Combine all ingredients except oil and mix well. Add oil gradually to mixture, stirring continuously. Store in refrigerator.

Yields 2½ cups dressing

Jack St. Clair, Former Manager
The Embers Restaurant

REMOULADE DRESSING

A perfection of flavors. Good with seafood as well as salads.

2 cloves garlic
1 egg
2 tablespoons red wine vinegar
1 cup vegetable oil
4 green onions with tops

2 ribs celery, cut in pieces
1½ tablespoons horseradish
1½ tablespoons Dijon mustard
½ teaspoon salt
¼ teaspoon Tabasco sauce

Chop garlic in food processor. With processor in operation, add egg and vinegar. Gradually add oil until well blended. Add remaining ingredients and blend until smooth.

Yields 1½ cups dressing

Frances Keenan Averitt

POPPY SEED DRESSING

Delicious on fruit salads of any kind. Try on salad of finely shredded red cabbage, thinly sliced avocado, and halved fresh grapes.

1½ cups sugar
2 teaspoons dry mustard
2 teaspoons salt
⅔ cup vinegar

3 tablespoons fresh onion juice
2 cups vegetable oil (never olive oil)
3 tablespoons poppy seeds

Mix sugar, mustard, salt, and vinegar. Add onion juice and stir thoroughly. Add oil slowly, beating constantly, and continue to beat until thick. Add poppy seeds and beat a few minutes more. Store in cool place or in refrigerator. Dressing will separate if it becomes too cold or too hot.

Note: To obtain onion juice, grate large onion on fine side of grater, or process in blender and then strain. (In either case, prepare to weep.)

Yields 3½ to 4 cups dressing

Mildred Blaine

EGGS, CHEESE, PASTA AND RICE

HONEY ALMOND BRIE

Brie unadorned is delicious enough, but these additions make it better yet.

1 miniature wheel of Brie (4½-ounce size)	4 apple slices
6 tablespoons honey	1 whole strawberry
Half of lemon	1 sprig fresh mint
1 ounce sliced, roasted almonds	4 sliced croûtons

Place Brie in individual baking dish. Cover with honey mixed with squeeze of lemon juice. Add almonds. Bake at 375 degrees for 10 minutes or until center begins to be soft. Remove from oven and garnish with apple slices, strawberry, mint, and croûtons.

Note: Sliced croûtons may be made by toasting very thin small slices of bread, or by frying slices in butter or oil until golden brown and very crisp.

Serves 1

Dux Restaurant
The Peabody

Variation: Use large wheel of Brie. Sprinkle generously with brown sugar, add almonds, and drizzle with honey and lemon juice. Bake at 375 degrees until sugar melts and center of cheese is soft. Serve surrounded with small slices of French bread.

VINEYARD EGGS

The ever-accommodating egg in a dish that was created on the spot for unexpected guests.

6 tablespoons butter	1½ cups heavy cream
2 tablespoons chopped shallots	Salt to taste
8 ounces fresh mushrooms, coarsely chopped	Paprika
	12 hard-cooked eggs, sliced
1 cup white wine	Triangles of buttered toast

Melt butter in shallow pan, add shallots and mushrooms, and cook 4 to 5 minutes over low heat. Add wine and simmer until mixture is reduced to ¼ cup. Add cream, salt, and enough paprika to color sauce well and cook just until thoroughly heated. Serve eggs on toast points and cover with sauce.

Serves 8

Catherine Vineyard

SCOTCH EGGS

Only the skirl of bagpipes could improve this bonny treat.

4 hard-cooked eggs	Fine bread crumbs or cracker meal
1 egg, beaten	
1 16-ounce package sausage, mild or hot	Vegetable oil

Dip hard-cooked eggs in beaten egg, and cover with thick layer of sausage. Dip again in beaten egg, then in bread crumbs or cracker meal. Fry 10 minutes in hot oil almost deep enough to cover eggs. Drain well on paper towel. Serve hot or cold.

Serves 4

Mrs. Henry B. Turner

SCALLOPS AND ZUCCHINI FETTUCCINE

The Grisanti name is synonymous with excellence in Italian cuisine. Here is something special from personal recipe files.

2 small zucchini	Freshly ground black pepper
1 pound bay scallops	2 tablespoons chopped fresh basil or Italian parsley
¾ cup butter	
2 cloves garlic, minced	1 pound fettuccine
All-purpose flour	½ pound green noodles
½ teaspoon salt	

Slice zucchini lengthwise into quarters and then into small pieces. Cut scallops into small pieces. Set both aside.

Melt butter over medium heat in large skillet. When foam subsides, add zucchini and toss over medium heat for 2 to 3 minutes. Add garlic, stir, and set skillet aside. Dredge scallops in flour, shaking off excess. Return skillet to heat and move zucchini to one side. Add scallops and fry quickly, tossing 1 to 2 minutes until lightly browned. Add salt, a few grains black pepper, and basil. Stir and remove from heat.

While preparing zucchini and scallops, cook pasta to al dente stage in boiling water according to package directions. Drain and toss immediately with scallops and zucchini. Serve piping hot.

Serves 6

Frank Grisanti's Italian Restaurant
Frank A. Grisanti, C.E.C.

GREEN CHILI SOUFFLÉ

A wake-up dish of spicy eggs.

1 12-ounce package grated
   Cheddar cheese
2 4-ounce cans green chilies,
   chopped
1 8-ounce block Monterey
   Jack cheese, grated
9 eggs, beaten

2 teaspoons ground cumin
2 teaspoons salt
2 teaspoons pepper
1 12-ounce can evaporated
   milk
2 5-ounce packages smoked
   baby link sausages

Lightly grease 9 x 13-inch baking dish with vegetable oil. Layer in order Cheddar cheese, green chilies, and Monterey Jack cheese. Mix eggs, seasonings, and milk, and pour over layers. Press sausages into mixture. Bake uncovered for 1 hour at 350 degrees.

Serves 10

Mrs. Robert Brommer

CHICKEN ROTEL WITH PASTA

A delicious main dish that has enduring appeal. Nice to divide and freeze half for another day.

8 whole chicken breasts
1 12-ounce package vermicelli
2 large green bell peppers,
   chopped
2 large onions, chopped
1 cup sliced fresh mushrooms
4 ribs celery, chopped

¾ cup butter
1 10-ounce can Rotel tomatoes
   with chilies
1 32-ounce package Velveeta
   cheese
2 tablespoons Worcestershire
   sauce

Simmer chicken in lightly salted water until tender, about 45 to 60 minutes. Remove chicken and skim fat. Cook vermicelli in broth, drain, and set aside. Reserve broth.

Sauté peppers, onions, mushrooms, and celery in butter until tender. Combine Rotel tomatoes with chilies and cheese in top of double boiler. Heat and stir until cheese is melted.

Skin and bone chicken, and cut in pieces. Combine chicken, sautéed mixture, cheese mixture, Worcestershire sauce, and vermicelli. Mix well, add 2 to 3 cups reserved broth, just enough to moisten well, and pour into buttered baking dish. Bake at 350 degrees for 30 minutes or until heated thoroughly.

Serves 12 to 14

Mrs. Maurice Stanley

CHEESE BLINTZES

A rich and creamy treat often served at traditional Thursday night Milchech Suppers. Or serve them at breakfast and give the day a special boost.

6 eggs, well-beaten
4 cups milk
3 cups all-purpose flour

1 teaspoon salt
Margarine

In large mixing bowl, blend eggs, milk, flour, and salt until smooth. Drop 2 tablespoons batter into heated, lightly greased small skillet. Tilt pan to spread batter thinly over entire bottom, like pancakes. Quickly brown bottom side lightly and when top looks dry, invert onto paper towel. When all pancakes have been made, put 1 tablespoon cheese filling in each center and fold opposite sides over each other to form a rectangle. Let stand 10 to 15 minutes, then pan-fry in margarine until browned on both sides. Serve with jelly and sour cream or applesauce.

Cheese Filling
3 8-ounce cartons ricotta cheese
3 eggs
1 tablespoon sugar

1 teaspoon grated lemon rind
1 tablespoon butter, softened

Blend all ingredients.

Yields 36 blintzes

Reva Cook
Racelle Mednikow

SQUASH BLOSSOM OMELET

Dining on blossoms can brighten one's day.

2 green onions, finely chopped
2 tablespoons butter
4 to 6 squash blossoms,
   sliced lengthwise twice

2 eggs, beaten
1 tablespoon milk
Salt and freshly ground
   pepper to taste

In small skillet or omelet pan, sauté onions in butter until transparent. Add squash blossoms and sauté lightly until barely wilted. Stir in eggs, milk, salt, and pepper. With spatula, pull omelet away from sides of pan as it cooks. Fold and serve immediately.

Serves 1

Virginia Caratenuto
Garfield, New Jersey

Remembering Piggly Wiggly at the Pink Palace Museum

On the day he opened his oddly named Piggly Wiggly grocery store in Memphis in 1916, Clarence Saunders, one of the most inventive entrepreneurs this nation has ever known, changed for all time the way America goes shopping. Customers were asked to take one of the wicker baskets stacked by the entrance, carry it around the store making their own food selections, then bring the basket to the counter and pay for their purchases at low prices made possible by savings in labor costs. Thus was born the self-service store, now universally known as the supermarket.

The idea was an instant success that rapidly spread nationwide and made Clarence Saunders an instant millionaire. Within just seven years more than twenty-six hundred Piggly Wigglys were flourishing throughout the United States. (The name was inspired by the zigzag route the first store's customers had to follow through aisles of well-stocked shelves—an ingenious marketing ploy.) To celebrate his good fortune, Saunders bought 155 acres of undeveloped land on Central Avenue in East Memphis and, in 1922, began building a palatial home—a huge mansion of pink Georgian marble with green tile roof, featuring an indoor swimming pool, billiard room, bowling alley, and large ballroom. Local newspapers labeled it the "Pink Palace." But in 1923, while construction and landscaping were still underway, Wall Street traders raided Piggly Wiggly, forcing the share price down until the New York Stock Exchange briefly suspended trading. Wiped out, Saunders declared bankruptcy. Developers bought his estate, complete with nine-hole-golf course and private lake, and there created the enduringly attractive Chickasaw Gardens residential district. Saunders, undaunted, went on to make and lose several other fortunes, including one, based on an ingenious key-based marketing device called a Keedoozle (Key-Does-All), which allowed customers to select items displayed behind glass, Automat-style, by turning a key in a slot, and then collect their keyed purchases at the check-out counter. But in those pre-World War II, pre-computer-age days, alas, that idea was ahead of its time.

Meanwhile, the Pink Palace itself and four surrounding acres had been donated to the city of Memphis to be used as a cultural center, art gallery, or museum. In 1930, after careful planning but with no major structural changes, the unfinished home Clarence Saunders and his family had never occupied opened its doors as the Memphis Museum of Natural Science and Industrial Arts. Popularly, and later officially, it was called the Pink Palace Museum, and it became an integral part of Memphis life. Even the empty indoor swimming pool was renovated and served, for a number of years, as the home of the fondly remembered Little Theatre, now Theatre Memphis. But the museum's main appeal was always to children, who loved the nature and science exhibits, the doll collection, the live beehive, the authentically designed hand-carved miniature tent circus with thousands of moving parts, the bird and animal collections, and the million-dollar planetarium where space science became reality for young visitors. (Interestingly, another favorite attraction for today's Memphis youngsters, the sixty-five acre Lichterman Nature Center on Quince Road, is located on a second estate once owned by Clarence Saunders, and is headquartered in the large, rugged, log-cabin-style home he built there.)

Since 1977, the Pink Palace's major exhibits have been housed in a new sixty-seven-thousand-square-foot addition built with funds generated by a volunteer group, the Friends of the Pink Palace. Here, permanent displays depict the natural environment and history of the region, and everyday lifestyles of the past—an 1830 log cabin, a Civil War battle scene, a full-sized replica of an early drug store. One impressive exhibit,

THE PICTURE: *For the Memphis Pink Palace Museum (originally known as the Memphis Museum of Natural Science and Industrial Arts), which began in the home built by Clarence Saunders, "father of the supermarket," there could be no more fitting exhibit than this replica of his first Piggly Wiggly store which opened in Memphis in 1916. A solid oak turnstile gives admittance to the store where shelves are lined with canned goods bearing labels of brand names, many of which have long since disappeared, and household items found in kitchens in the early years of the twentieth century. A snuff advertisement adorns the wall, flour is for sale in cotton bags, navy beans are available in gunny sacks for purchase in the amount needed. Old-fashioned scales and a cash register are visible in the background, and an old-fashioned glass milk bottle holds a bouquet of feverfew, resembling a daisy and reputed to be a cure for fever.*

THE FOOD: *Brown and white eggs are displayed in a replica of the original Piggly Wiggly customer's basket. Hams in sacks hang on the walls, candy jars are on the counters, and a selection of cheeses and pastas is displayed in the foreground.*

"From Saddlebags to Science," created by the Memphis-Shelby County Medical Auxiliary, documents Memphis medical history and includes over a thousand artifacts collected from Memphis physicians and their families. Every October, from 1972 through 1988, the Pink Palace lawn became the scene of the Mid-South Crafts Fair, and was dotted with tents and pavilions where weavers, potters, dollmakers, broommakers, and other artisans set up shop, and food-vendors offered their wares—perhaps none more popular than the hot, sugary, made-on-the spot doughnuts available each year. Visitors could see blacksmiths or glassblowers at work, or observe a sorghum mill in operation, or settle on the grass before outdoor stages and watch musicians, story-tellers, or cloggers entertain. Outgrowing its space, the fair moved its tents, tradesmen, and troubadours to a new site in October of 1989. Audubon Park is now its home. Proceeds from this festival help perpetuate the Pink Palace's educational programs.

PASTA PRIMAVERA FOR HUNDREDS

This can be easily multiplied to feed large numbers of people.

3 pounds assorted pasta (spinach, egg, farfel, shells)	½ pound snow peas, blanched
3 to 4 tablespoons raspberry vinegar	10 to 12 ripe olives, finely chopped
1 cup olive oil	6 to 8 green onions, cut in ¼-inch pieces
1 cup freshly grated Parmesan cheese	1 small red onion, finely chopped
1 bunch broccoli	2 tomatoes, diced
1 medium zucchini, sliced in thin rounds	Salt and freshly ground pepper to taste
1 10-ounce package frozen green peas, thawed	Sour cream

Cook pasta according to package directions. Rinse well in cold water to separate, and drain. Toss with vinegar, olive oil, and Parmesan cheese.

Cut broccoli in individual florets. Steam broccoli and zucchini about 3 minutes, keeping vegetables crisp. Toss green peas, snow peas, olives, green and red onions, tomatoes, broccoli, and zucchini with pasta mixture. Season with salt and pepper. Add just enough sour cream to coat pasta lightly. Serve at room temperature.

Serves 12 to 16

Louise Lancaster Keim
Hong Kong

RICE SALAD

An enticing make-ahead salad that improves with age.

3 cups cooked rice	American cheese cut in ¼-inch cubes to measure 1 cup
1½ cups diced celery	1 cup mayonnaise
1 10-ounce package frozen green peas, cooked and drained	1 teaspoon lemon juice
½ cup chopped pimiento, drained	Salt and pepper to taste
¼ cup minced onion	Sliced hard-cooked eggs
	Tomato wedges

Combine all ingredients except eggs and tomatoes and toss lightly. Adjust seasonings and chill. (Can be made 2 to 3 days ahead.) Garnish with sliced eggs and tomato wedges.

Serves 8

Dr. Frances Riley

TRIPLE CHEESE SOUFFLÉ

A creamy cheese treat.

1 pound Monterey Jack cheese, cubed	6 eggs, beaten
1 3-ounce package cream cheese, cubed	1 cup milk
1 8-ounce carton cottage cheese	2 teaspoons sugar
6 tablespoons butter, softened	1 teaspoon salt
	1 teaspoon baking powder
	½ cup all-purpose flour

Combine cheeses and butter, and mix well. Add eggs, milk, sugar, and salt, and stir well. Combine baking powder and flour, and add to cheese mixture, stirring to mix well. Bake in greased 11 x 14-inch baking dish for 45 minutes at 350 degrees.

Serves 8

Martha Milford Boyd
Fayetteville, North Carolina

EGGS AURORA

A creation made to match a dish discovered on a trip to Italy. Eggs with a tomato-flavored hollandaise and very good.

Aurora sauce	12 hard-cooked eggs, chilled
½ cup heavy cream, whipped	Fresh dill or fennel
¼ cup tomato purée	

Fold sauce, whipped cream, and tomato purée together. Halve eggs and cover with sauce. Garnish with sprig of fresh dill or fennel and serve immediately.

Aurora Sauce	
⅔ cup water	4 tablespoons lemon juice
1 teaspoon chopped shallots	¾ teaspoon salt
5 peppercorns	7 large egg yolks
Dash vinegar	Dash pepper
1 cup butter, softened	

Combine water, shallots, peppercorns, and vinegar in 1-quart saucepan. Cover and simmer 10 minutes. Strain and reserve seasoned water. Mix all other ingredients in blender. Add seasoned water gradually. Place mixture in double boiler and cook over boiling water for 10 minutes or until mixture coats wooden spoon, stirring occasionally. Sauce will be rather thick.

Serves 12

Claire B. Austin

CLASSIC MEXICAN RICE

Direct to Memphis from Brownsville, Texas, a town that likes its Texas-brand Mexican food.

1 cup uncooked rice
2 tablespoons vegetable oil
1 teaspoon mild chili powder
½ to ¾ teaspoon salt
1 small tomato, chopped

1 bunch green onions with tops, finely chopped
½ green bell pepper, finely chopped
2 cups water

Add rice to oil in large heavy iron skillet. Cook and stir over medium-low heat until rice is deep brown in color. Add chili powder and salt, and stir briefly. Stir in tomato, onions with tops, and bell pepper. Add water, stir again, cover, and cook over very low heat until all water is absorbed, about 25 minutes.

Remove cover and stir while steam escapes. Set aside briefly. Stir again and set aside once more. Stir again until all steam is gone and rice is dry.

Serves 6

Charlotte Neal

PASTA WITH FRESH TOMATO SAUCE

A superb sauce—a superb dish.

5 ripe tomatoes, peeled and coarsely chopped
1 cup coarsely chopped fresh basil
1 large clove garlic, minced
7 to 8 quarts water
2 tablespoons salt

1 tablespoon vegetable oil
1 16-ounce package thin spaghetti or linguini
1 10-ounce block mozzarella cheese, cubed
Salt and freshly ground pepper to taste

Combine tomatoes, basil, and garlic, and set aside.

Bring water to rolling boil and add salt and oil. Add pasta and cook to al dente stage. Working quickly, drain pasta and return at once to still-warm pot. Immediately stir in mozzarella. Heat of pasta will melt mozzarella cubes slightly. Stir in tomato mixture and season with salt and pepper. Transfer to hot serving bowl and serve at room temperature.

Note: If fresh basil is unavailable, use fresh watercress. Do not use dried basil.

Serves 6

Marguerite Piazza Bergtholdt

POPOVER SOUFFLÉ

One of those versatile dishes that every cook loves. Good for breakfast, lunch, or dinner. Try with roast beef gravy or with sweet butter and honey.

¾ cup all-purpose flour
¾ cup milk
2 eggs

Pinch salt
¼ cup butter

Combine flour, milk, eggs, and salt. Beat well, but do not overbeat.

Heat butter in 10 to 12-inch metal baking pan until frothy, add egg batter, and place in cold oven. Bake 15 minutes at 450 degrees. Reduce heat to 350 degrees and bake 20 minutes more or until brown and puffy.

Serves 4

Mrs. Norfleet R. Turner

BAKED MACARONI

A recipe from childhood days on Long Island, New York, when thirty-five cents bought the cheese, the macaroni, and the tomatoes from the neighborhood grocer.

2 28-ounce cans whole tomatoes
1 tablespoon Italian seasoning
2 cloves garlic, minced
1¼ teaspoons sugar
Salt to taste
Pepper to taste

⅔ to ¾ pound pepperoni, sliced
3 8-ounce packages elbow macaroni
1½ pounds grated American cheese

Mash tomatoes and heat until bubbly. Add Italian seasoning, garlic, sugar, salt, and pepper, and simmer 1½ hours. Add pepperoni and simmer for another 30 minutes. Cook macaroni according to package directions during last 30 minutes that sauce is simmering.

Place 1 cup sauce in bottom of large, deep, baking dish, and then begin layering in order macaroni, sauce, and cheese. Repeat layering procedure 2 more times. Bake at 350 degrees for 45 minutes or until top is deep golden brown.

Serves 8 to 12

Vincent de Frank, Conductor Emeritus
The Memphis Symphony

CANNELLONI BELLISSIMO

The stuff dreams are made of. Just the best thing imaginable.

Procedure
Prepare spaghetti gravy, filling, crêpes, and white sauce. Spread layer of spaghetti gravy in 9 x 13-inch baking pan. Place portion of filling on each crêpe and roll in jelly roll fashion. Layer crêpes on top of gravy and spread a thin layer of gravy over crêpes. Cover with white sauce. Top with bits of butter and Parmesan cheese. Bake 30 to 40 minutes at 350 degrees.

Spaghetti Gravy
3 cups minced onions	3 pounds ground beef, cooked and drained
3 cups minced celery with leaves	1 pound hot sausage, cooked and drained
2 teaspoons minced garlic	4 10¾-ounce cans chicken broth
1 cup olive oil	½ cup grated Parmesan cheese
8 tablespoons margarine	1 teaspoon Italian Seasoning
1 pound fresh mushrooms, finely chopped	½ teaspoon oregano
3 28-ounce cans tomatoes with juice, finely chopped	½ teaspoon crushed bay leaves
2 to 3 6-ounce cans tomato paste	Salt and pepper to taste
	Accent to taste

Sauté onions, celery, and garlic in olive oil and 4 tablespoons margarine. Set aside. Sauté mushrooms in remaining margarine. In large saucepan, combine sautéed ingredients with remaining ingredients. Simmer 1½ to 2 hours or until rather thick. (Recipe yields 2½ gallons gravy. Freeze unused gravy for later use.)

Filling
2 cups finely chopped onions	2 10-ounce packages chopped spinach, cooked and well-drained
2 teaspoons finely chopped garlic, optional	¾ cup light cream
½ cup olive oil	5 eggs
½ cup margarine	Salt and pepper to taste
3 pounds ground beef	Oregano to taste
2 pounds ground sausage, 1 hot, 1 mild	Accent to taste
2 cups chopped cooked chicken	

Sauté onions and garlic in olive oil and margarine, but do not brown. Cook beef and sausage until browned, then drain. Combine sautéed mixture and browned meats with chicken, spinach, and cream, and mix well. Add eggs one at a time, beating well after each addition. Mix in seasonings. (Recipe yields filling for 4 dozen crêpes. Freeze unused filling.)

Crêpes
1 cup milk	1 cup all-purpose flour
½ cup water	⅛ teaspoon salt
3 eggs, well-beaten	Margarine

Combine milk and water, and beat in eggs. Sift in flour and salt, and beat well until smooth. Lightly grease crêpe pan or small skillet with margarine. When margarine is very hot, pour in enough batter to cover bottom lightly, tipping pan from side to side to spread batter evenly. Cook until lightly browned. Turn and cook other side. Stack crêpes flat until ready to fill. (Recipe yields 10 to 12 crêpes; repeat as needed.)

White Sauce
½ cup butter	½ teaspoon white pepper
½ cup all-purpose flour	3 to 4 cups light cream
1 to 2 teaspoons salt	

Melt butter in saucepan. Stir in flour and seasonings, blending until smooth. Add cream. Stir constantly over low heat until desired consistency is reached. (Recipe yields 3 to 4 cups sauce; repeat as needed.)

Topping
Butter	1 cup grated Parmesan cheese

Yields 48 filled crêpes

Mrs. John Montesi

CUMIN RICE

An original from Stuttgart, Arkansas—the rice and duck capital of the world—where creative rice dishes perfectly accompany game.

⅓ cup chopped onion	1 tablespoon Worcestershire sauce
¼ cup diced green bell pepper	Dash salt
1 cup uncooked rice	¾ teaspoon cumin seed
2 tablespoons bacon drippings	
2 10½-ounce cans beef consommé	

In large skillet, sauté onion, pepper, and rice in bacon drippings. Add remaining ingredients and bring to boil. Stir, cover, and reduce heat to simmer. Cook 20 minutes or until rice is tender.

Serves 4

Audrey Weathers

The Longreen Hunt Breakfast

"Turn right at the sign of the fox." That is the direction given hunters and hilltoppers on the first day of fox-hunting season, to guide them to Longreen, the Bart Mueller farm near Rossville, Tennessee, in Fayette County, a short drive east of Memphis. A wooden fox stands as marker at the intersection of Highway 57 and the county road which leads south toward Longreen. At this farm, on the second Saturday in November each year, riders and spectators gather early in the morning. It is opening day of the Longreen Hunt, and they await the sound of the Master's horn announcing the start of the day's ride. Afterwards, they will return here for the traditional hunt breakfast.

With excitement sparkling like the crisp morning sunlight, hunters wearing the black hard hats and black hunting coats with green collars that signify membership in the Longreen Hunt, sit astride handsome hunter-jumpers that seem as eager to be away as do their riders. Among the group is the hunt's staff—the Master of the Fox Hounds (MFH) in his pink coat, the Whippers-in, who will be responsible for the hounds, the Outriders, who will keep watch on all concerned. As the horses move about, a pack of some fifteen Penn-Mary-Del (for Pennsylvania-Maryland-Delaware) hounds are brought out. The expectancy heightens, becomes almost palpable. At last, the traditional stirrup cup is poured, a bracing fortification against chill and spill; the clergyman intones his traditional prayer, seeking the Lord's blessing upon riders, hounds, and horses, asking that they come to the end of the day unhurt. Only then does the Master of the Longreen Hunt—Bart Mueller has held the post for more than thirty years—ride forward and sound his horn, the horn which "talks to the hunt," says "come on" to the hounds. Throughout the hunt, the Master's voice and horn will signal and control the hounds.

Now the hounds move ahead to seek the scent of the fox, and the whole assemblage follows. For the next several hours, they will range over fields and through woods of the adjacent Twin Hills Ranch, some six thousand acres, open to hunting, all fences paneled—the hounds after the fox, and the riders after the hounds. At the same time, the spectators have moved out for their sport of "hilltopping." In cars, trucks, and four-wheel-drive vehicles, they try to follow the field. Parking wherever the view is good, along dirt roads, atop hills, beside clearings in the wooded areas, they wait to hear the horn, and to watch the hounds and hunters emerge from the woods and fly across field and fence.

A good fox is highly esteemed and, after several exciting hunts, may become known by sight, even named. The hounds are after him, trying to guess his tricks, outsmart him, but the fox is smart—foxy. He may run for hours, sometimes in circles, sometimes for miles straight ahead; being a sporting fellow, he will sometimes run directly past his lair, ignoring it. When the fox finally ends the contest by going to ground or to tree, there is a special baying of the hounds, and all know that this hunt is over. But then the hounds pick up another scent, and the chase begins anew.

Mary Winslow Chapman, a member of the Longreen Hunt since its beginnings in the late 1950s, has captured in words the breathtaking essence of this sport: "There is nothing like the thrill of riding a perfectly marvelous horse, of going straight over everything you come to, every ditch, every fence, every stump, every stream. The horse is fearless—he takes his fences straight. The fox is noble—he runs with boldness. The hound has integrity—he never announces a false trail. The rider is courageous—he takes his jumps as he finds them. It's a fine, ancient feeling of doing what one should be doing."

THE PICTURE: *It's the opening day of the Longreen Hunt. On this clear fall morning, the hunt board is laid in the home of Mary and Bart Mueller at Longreen Farm. A ceramic fox presides over the table, which is also graced by hunting horns holding a rose, a single hybrid lily, and two chrysanthemums. Having risen early, having ridden hard and far and long, the hunters are beginning to arrive—dusty, perhaps a bit bruised, happily tired and hungry. They will soon be enjoying both the food and the tales to be told of the day. In the words of long-time Longreen Hunt member Mary Winslow Chapman, "A hunt breakfast is more, much more than a casual occasion. It has in fact a meaning all of its own, a relic from the past which, like everything connected with hunting, stems from deep, deep roots ... from a distant era. But if memory is lost, the emotion still lingers: A profound sense of belonging, a fundamental feeling of loyalty which along with other 'oldies', patriotism and religion, seem to call for recognition and celebration."*

THE FOOD: *Baked ham, sliced turkey, cheese, potato salad, and hot biscuits provide hearty accompaniment to the hunt breakfast's welcome GARLIC GRITS, HOT FIGGY FRUIT and the traditional APPLE DAPPLE CAKE.*

Ancient, indeed, for fox-hunting, with its intricate traditions strictly observed through the ages, had been popular in Europe and England for seven hundred years before it was introduced to Colonial America in 1650 by the first MFH in North America, Robert Brook. Brook arrived in Maryland from England in his own private ship with his family, servants, and a pack of hounds, the first of the well-known "Brook Hound" breed. It was some three hundred years later that a Marylander and avid hunter named Bart Mueller, with his friends, Walter Foster and Wib Magli, introduced traditional fox-hunting to the west Tennessee area. Returning home from military service after World War II, they settled in Tennessee, converted local riders to their enthusiasm for the sport, converted local saddle and trail horses to hunter-jumper style, and developed a pack of hounds from Tennessee and Maryland breeding. They founded the Oak Grove Hunt, and from that, in 1956, the Longreen Hunt.

A charming little book, *Longreen*, published in 1982 by members of the Longreen Hunt, offers an intriguing history of horsemanship and hunting in Shelby County and its neighboring areas. It includes stories of the local pony clubs for children, and depicts the magnificent training which has produced two members of U.S. Olympic equestrian teams—Melanie Smith Taylor, one of the top women riders in the world, and Mac Cone, now of Ontario, who has also been a member of the Canadian equestrian team. The book also tells of the rider who was perhaps the Longreen Hunt's most renowned member, novelist William Faulkner of Oxford, Mississippi. Faulkner once sent a blank check for his dues, requesting the proper amount be filled in by the secretary. The club was in a dilemma, not knowing whether to cash it or to frame it.

GARLIC GRITS

The versatility of grits makes them a great complement to many menus. Here the addition of garlic gives the definitive flavor.

1 cup grits	½ cup butter, melted
½ teaspoon salt	½ cup milk
4 cups boiling water	2 eggs, well-beaten
1½ cups grated extra sharp	1 small clove garlic, minced
Cheddar cheese	2 tablespoons butter

Add grits and salt to boiling water and cook 2½ to 5 minutes, stirring constantly. Remove from heat and add cheese, melted butter, milk, eggs, and garlic. Stir to mix well.

Melt remaining 2 tablespoons butter in large baking dish and spread evenly. Pour grits mixture into buttered baking dish and bake 1 hour at 350 degrees.

Serves 8 to 10

Mrs. Erich W. Merrill

HOLIDAY BREAKFAST STRATA

A perennial favorite with extra touches of flavor.

8 slices stale white bread	1 green onion, minced
Softened butter	¼ teaspoon paprika
1½ pounds sharp Cheddar cheese, grated	½ teaspoon dry mustard
2 pounds hot sausage, cooked, drained, and crumbled	½ teaspoon Worcestershire sauce
6 eggs	½ teaspoon salt
2½ to 3 cups light cream	⅛ teaspoon white pepper
1¼ teaspoons brown sugar	⅛ teaspoon cayenne pepper

Trim crust from bread. Butter and slice each piece in fourths.

Butter shallow 3-quart baking dish. Layer in order half of bread, cheese, and sausage. Repeat layers one time. Blend eggs, cream, brown sugar, onion, and seasonings, adding more cream if needed. Pour over layers, cover with foil, and refrigerate 24 hours.

Remove and let stand 2 hours to bring to room temperature. Place baking dish in shallow pan with ½-inch of water added. Bake uncovered 1 hour at 300 degrees. Let stand 20 minutes before serving.

Serves 8 to 10

Ann S. Adamson

MISS ALICE'S CHEESE SOUFFLÉ

An amazingly sturdy yet delicate soufflé that simply never disappoints.

6 tablespoons margarine	2 cups grated sharp Cheddar
6 tablespoons all-purpose flour	cheese
1½ cups milk	6 eggs, separated

Melt margarine in heavy saucepan over low heat. Remove from heat and gradually stir in flour. Return to low heat. Gradually add milk and cook, stirring constantly, until mixture thickens to consistency of heavy cream and is very smooth. Add cheese and remove from heat. Continue stirring until cheese melts. Cool until barely warm.

Beat egg yolks and stir into cheese sauce. Beat egg whites until soft peaks form and fold gently into sauce. With rubber spatula, scoop soufflé mixture into buttered 8-cup baking dish or soufflé dish. Bake 45 minutes at 300 degrees.

Serves 4 to 6

Mrs. William H. Houston III
Washington, D.C.

ANGEL HAIR PASTA

A heavenly way to serve pasta.

2 teaspoons salt	1 cup light cream or milk
1 tablespoon vegetable oil or olive oil	6 tablespoons grated Parmesan cheese
1 16-ounce package angel hair pasta	Pinch of nutmeg
½ cup butter, melted	Pinch of white pepper

Add salt and oil to large pot of water and bring to boil. Place pasta in boiling water, stirring occasionally to prevent sticking. Cook to al dente stage. Drain, quickly rinse with cool water, and drain again.

Return pasta to pot over low heat and add butter, lifting gently with two forks to coat. Gradually add cream, gently stirring and lifting pasta. Add Parmesan cheese 2 tablespoons at a time, mixing gently after each addition. Season with nutmeg and pepper and serve immediately.

Serves 6 to 8

Geri Cuoghi

Blessings from Afar at the Greek Bazaar

In 1860, Memphis was known as the fastest growing city in the United States. Much of that growth came from a steady influx of foreign-born. Almost seven thousand of the city's more than twenty-two thousand population had come to our shores as immigrants—all seeking the opportunities offered "only in America" and especially in Memphis during the thriving young city's preceding two decades of booming prosperity. Memphis readily welcomed these newcomers and made good use of their toil and talents, establishing a tradition that continues to the present day.

The largest group of early immigrants were the Irish, arriving in Memphis after the devastating potato famine in their home country during the 1840s. These hardworking laborers settled near downtown in an area where Jackson Avenue now merges with North Parkway. The yards around their small homes were decorated with clotheslines, and usually there was a resident goat, because the family could not afford a cow. The neighborhood became known alternately as Goat Hill or Irish Town. The Germans came next, by the hundreds, to escape political persecutions after the 1848 revolutions in Europe. Their influence in the cultural, financial, educational, and social life of the city was great. At one time, for example, nearly every member of the Memphis Philharmonic Orchestra was German. They built churches, began their own newspapers, established a German Mardi Gras or *Fasching,* an *Oktoberfest,* and a *Maifest* which many regard as a forerunner of today's Memphis in May celebrations. But their presence in Memphis faded when many Germans, fleeing the yellow fever outbreaks of the 1870s, moved to St. Louis or Cincinnati.

An old area of North Memphis known somewhat inelegantly as Pinch, or Pinchgut, was home to many of these immigrant newcomers over the years. Old-time Mississippi River flatboatmen, floating downstream, found the waters of Catfish Bay, at the mouth of Gayoso Bayou, a good landing place in the earliest days of Memphis. A natural eddy in the river, if it could be caught, allowed the boats to change course and turn easily in to the river's bank. If they disposed of all their goods, the flatboatmen abandoned their boats which could not return upstream. Poor settlers and backwoods drifters collected pieces of the abandoned wood and built crude dwellings. These shanty dwellers lived with an ever-present hunger that would label them as "pinch-gut." The name caught on, and through the years its use spread to include nearby districts, and the label united residents of the designated areas in a strange bond of pride. To have overcome the challenge of Pinch was a noteworthy achievement—an American success story in Memphis, begun by the Irish, and repeated by succeeding waves of Italian, Russian, Greek, and Jewish immigrants in the last decades of the nineteenth century and the first years of the twentieth.

Families opened shops there, and made their homes above the stores. Many of the names are familiar today. There was Rosen's Delicatessen, Dubrovner's and Makowsky's Butcher Shops, Ridblatt's Bakery, and Barzizza Brothers Import Foods. Anshei Mishne Synagogue stood near the city's first *Mikvah* (public bath house); other landmarks of the area were the Suzore Theatre, and Neighborhood House where immigrants learned English and were sworn in as U.S. citizens. Among those who once attended the district's Market Street School was a youngster named Abe Plough, who would become the founder of the pharmaceutical company Plough, Incorporated, now a major division of Schering-Plough Corporation. For many years, Abe Plough was one of the city's most generous and self-effacing philanthropists—though the true identity of the ubiquitous donor listing himself as Mr. Anonymous was one of the best-known "secrets" in

Memphis history. Nowadays, Pinch and its legends are achieving literary fame through the well-received fiction of Steve Stern, prize-winning young Memphis author of books such as *Lazar Malkin Enters Heaven* which have "The Pinch" as their setting.

The city's artistic, political, economic, and religious life has been immeasurably enriched by immigrants who have made Memphis their home—the Europeans, Chinese, and others who came early, and the Koreans, Japanese, Southeast Asians, East Indians, Middle Easterners, Latin Americans, and Russian Jews who are today's newcomers. As these new Americans weave the patterns of their own lives into the intricate tapestry of Memphis culture, they give this Southern city a rare and surprising blend of excitement and spirit.

DOLMATHES YIALANDJI

These meatless stuffed grapevine leaves are a very popular and traditional Greek dish. They are available by special order only at this long-established Greek-American restaurant, now in East Memphis, which had its beginnings in the early 1920s in downtown Memphis.

1 12-ounce jar of grapevine leaves
3 medium onions, finely chopped
¾ cup olive oil
¾ cup rice
1 teaspoon salt
½ teaspoon freshly ground pepper
1 tablespoon chopped fresh dill, or ½ teaspoon dried
½ cup fresh parsley, chopped, stems reserved
1 tablespoon chopped fresh mint
1 bunch green onions, finely chopped
¼ cup pine nuts, optional
Juice of 1 lemon
¼ cup water
Thinly sliced lemon rounds
Fresh dill

Remove grapevine leaves from jar, scald in hot water, and drain.

Sauté onions until transparent in ¼ cup oil. Add rice, salt, pepper, dill, parsley, mint, green onions, and pine nuts, and mix well. Add lemon juice and water, cover, and steam 10 minutes. Cool.

Separate grape leaves carefully. Snip off thick stems. Cut large leaves in half. Turn dull side of leaf up. Place 1 rounded teaspoonful of rice mixture at base of each grapevine leaf. Fold left side of leaf to center, then right side to center, and roll upward.

Spread parsley stems over bottom of deep 3 to 4-quart saucepan. Arrange stuffed leaves in layers over stems. Add more salt and pepper to taste and drizzle remaining ½ cup oil over dolmathes. Invert heavy ovenproof plate on top of dolmathes to keep them from falling apart during cooking, and cover with boiling water. Bring to quick boil, reduce heat, and cook 45 to 60 minutes until rice is done. Cool in saucepan.

To serve, arrange dolmathes on serving plate and sprinkle generously with more lemon juice. Garnish with lemon rounds and fresh dill.

Yields 3 dozen dolmathes

Jim's Place East Restaurant
Costa Taras, Dimitri Taras,
and Angelo Liollio, Proprietors

MACARONI-CHEESE DELUXE

Sour cream makes this saucy casserole extra-good and company-elegant.

1 7-ounce package elbow macaroni
2 cups small curd, cream-style cottage cheese
1 cup sour cream
1 egg, lightly beaten
¾ teaspoon salt
Dash pepper
1 8-ounce package sharp Cheddar cheese, grated
Paprika

Cook macaroni according to package directions and drain well. Combine cottage cheese, sour cream, egg, salt, and pepper. Add Cheddar cheese and mix well. Stir in macaroni. Place in greased 9-inch square baking dish. Sprinkle with paprika and bake 45 minutes at 350 degrees.

Variation: Slice fresh tomato, arrange slices atop casserole, and bake as directed.

Serves 6 to 8

Jacqueline Beane
Forrest City, Arkansas

WILD RICE MEDLEY

An all-in-one-dish dinner and a very good way to present wild rice.

1 cup wild rice
1½ pounds combined veal and pork, diced
2 tablespoons vegetable oil
1 large onion, diced
1 cup diced celery
1 6-ounce can mushrooms, chopped
6 ounces cashews, chopped
¼ cup chopped pimiento
2 10¾-ounce cans cream of mushroom soup
2 10¾-ounce cans cream of chicken soup
1⅓ cups water
⅔ cup milk
½ green bell pepper, chopped
¼ teaspoon Tabasco sauce
Salt to taste

Rinse rice and soak in water overnight.

Drain rice. Brown meat in oil. Add onion and celery, and sauté briefly. Combine rice, meat mixture, and all remaining ingredients, and stir to mix well. Place in baking dish and bake 2 hours at 350 degrees. Sprinkle a few extra cashews over top about 10 minutes before removing from oven.

Serves 8 to 10

Niki Balter

QUESADILLAS

An all-time favorite from a Mexican restaurant which has garnered a large and loyal Memphis following since it first opened its doors in 1974.

1½ cups grated Monterey Jack cheese	½ cup butter, melted
1½ cups grated Cheddar cheese	8 8-inch flour tortillas
	1 8-ounce jar Mexican salsa

Mix cheeses together and set aside. Pour 1 to 2 tablespoons melted butter upon each of two dinner plates and spread to cover. Place one tortilla on each plate and swirl in butter to coat one side. Spread one tortilla with ¾ cup mixed cheeses. Top with 2 tablespoons salsa. Place other buttered tortilla on top of filled tortilla, buttered side up, thus making the quesadilla. Set aside. Repeat process until 4 quesadillas are made, using more butter, if needed.

Heat non-stick skillet or griddle over low heat. Carefully slip one prepared quesadilla into skillet. Cook on one side 2 to 3 minutes or until golden brown. Using spatula and fingers, carefully flip quesadilla. Cook until golden brown. Remove to cutting board and slice in 4 to 6 pieces. Repeat for each quesadilla.

Serve with guacamole, more salsa, or sour cream.

Serves 6 to 8

Molly Gonzales' La Casita Restaurant

DUCKY RICE

Cook your ducks and save the broth to make this tasty rice. Good with duck, chicken, or beef.

½ teaspoon Greek seasoning	4 cups duck broth
½ teaspoon garlic powder	1 bag Success Rice
Salt to taste	

Stir seasonings into broth. Add bag of rice and cook as directed on package.

Serves 4

Dixie Wolbrecht

BEV'S VEGGIE LASAGNA

A grand collection of veggies in a fresh approach to lasagna. Be sure to try the variation using spaghetti squash.

1 medium eggplant, peeled, drained, and cubed, to measure 4 cups	¼ teaspoon black pepper
	9 drops Tabasco sauce
8 ounces fresh mushrooms, sliced	1 16-ounce carton 2% cottage cheese
⅓ cup olive oil	¾ cup grated Parmesan cheese
1 32-ounce jar Prego spaghetti sauce with mushrooms	2 eggs or 4 egg whites
	1 tablespoon parsley flakes
1 medium red bell pepper, sliced	1 8-ounce package lasagna noodles, cooked
1 cup chopped carrots	2 cups thinly sliced zucchini squash
3 cloves garlic, pressed	1 8-ounce package shredded mozzarella cheese
1 tablespoon minced onion	
1 teaspoon oregano	1 6-ounce package shredded Monterey Jack cheese
¼ teaspoon salt	

Sauté eggplant and mushrooms in olive oil. Add spaghetti sauce, bell pepper, carrots, garlic, onion, oregano, salt, pepper, and Tabasco sauce. Simmer 20 minutes. Mix cottage cheese with ½ cup Parmesan cheese, eggs, and parsley flakes.

In 9 x 13-inch baking dish, layer in order as follows, reserving enough sauce for top layer: noodles, spaghetti sauce, 1 cup zucchini, and half of mozzarella and Monterey Jack; noodles, cottage cheese mixture, and sauce; noodles, 1 cup zucchini, remaining mozzarella and Monterey Jack, and sauce. Bake uncovered on center rack 15 minutes at 400 degrees. Cover with foil, reduce heat to 350 degrees, and bake 45 minutes. Remove foil, sprinkle with remaining Parmesan cheese, and bake 10 minutes more or until Parmesan becomes crusty.

Variation: Substitute a 2 to 3-pound spaghetti squash for noodles. Pierce squash several times with sharp knife, place whole in shallow container, and cook in microwave oven on high, about 20 minutes. When knife can be inserted easily, squash is done. Slice in half lengthwise, remove seeds, and scoop out pulp to measure about 3 to 4 cupfuls. Toss with a little salt and margarine. Use all squash in one layer in bottom of baking dish, and then continue layering all other ingredients as above. (Squash pulp resembles spaghetti and adds a nice, crunchy texture.)

Serves 8 to 10

Beverly Elliotte Vance

VEGETABLES AND FRUITS

SUMMER SQUASH CASSEROLE

So good it almost tastes like dessert.

2 pounds yellow squash, sliced
1 large onion, chopped
½ cup margarine, melted
1 cup sour cream
½ cup grated Cheddar cheese

1 10¾-ounce can cream of
    chicken soup
Salt and pepper to taste
1 cup herb-flavored
    stuffing mix

Cook squash and onion until tender in small amount water, and drain. Combine all other ingredients except dressing mix, stir into squash-onion mixture, and place in 2½-quart baking dish. Sprinkle dressing mix on top and bake at 350 degrees for 30 minutes or until bubbly throughout.

Serves 12

Mrs. William N. Morris, Jr.

Variation: Substitute ½ cup chopped peanuts for grated cheese. Combine peanuts, dressing mix, and melted margarine and mix well. Place layer of peanut mixture in baking dish. Cover with layer of squash mixture and follow with layer of peanut mixture. Bake as above.

Mrs. Fred Betzel

MARINATED LIMA BEANS

Baby limas in a fresh bib and tucker.

2 10-ounce packages frozen
    baby lima beans, cooked
    until tender but firm

1 large red onion, thinly sliced
    and separated into rings
1 cup chopped fresh parsley

Combine all ingredients, toss, cover with marinade, and toss again. Chill at least 12 hours, stirring occasionally. Drain. Serve on lettuce leaves and garnish with extra sprigs of parsley.

Marinade
1 cup vegetable oil
1 cup tarragon vinegar
2 teaspoons sugar

1 teaspoon salt
1 teaspoon pepper
1 teaspoon celery seed

Blend all ingredients with electric mixer.

Serves 8 to 10

Nancy McConnico Beck

ZUCCHINI FRITTERS

No one ever seems to get enough of these marvelous things.

3 cups coarsely grated zucchini
1 egg, lightly beaten
Salt and pepper to taste
1 teaspoon baking powder

½ cup all-purpose flour
Melted butter
Freshly grated Parmesan
    cheese

Combine zucchini, egg, salt, and pepper, and mix well. Combine baking powder and flour, sift into zucchini mixture, and mix thoroughly. Drop by ¼ cupfuls onto lightly greased hot griddle and cook until lightly browned on both sides. Serve with melted butter and Parmesan cheese.

Yields 8 to 12 fritters

Ernestine Cunningham

CAN-DO BEAN CASSEROLE

Just try it!

4 15½-ounce cans kidney
    beans
4 12-ounce cans white niblet
    corn
4 16-ounce cans pork and beans

4 15-ounce cans beanless chili
1 cup Worcestershire sauce
1 28-ounce bottle tomato catsup
Bacon strips

Mix all ingredients and pour into large shallow baking dish. Top with bacon strips and bake 35 minutes at 350 degrees.

Serves 40

Mrs. N.S. Shobe

CARROT PUDDING

A smooth, sweet taste. Perhaps a substitute for sweet potatoes for Thanksgiving dinner?

2 cups cooked, mashed carrots
1 cup sugar
½ cup butter
2 tablespoons all-purpose flour
3 eggs

1 teaspoon baking powder
1 cup milk
½ teaspoon salt
1 teaspoon cinnamon
½ cup chopped pecans, optional

Mix all ingredients and pour into deep 2-quart baking dish. Bake at 350 degrees for 40 to 45 minutes or until firm and lightly browned.

Serves 8

Mrs. E. J. Adams

CRISP BUTTERED GREEN BEANS

Attractive and very good. A dish that is the antithesis of the traditional Southern way of simmering pole beans for hours with a piece of salt pork. One is well-advised to sample both.

2 pounds fresh pole beans, snapped and washed	2 teaspoons salt
	½ cup clarified butter

Drop beans into a pot of rapidly boiling unsalted water. Bring back to boil and add salt. Simmer uncovered until crisp and tender. Drain and plunge into ice water for 3 to 4 minutes. Spin dry, removing all water possible. Just before serving, toss gently for 1 to 2 minutes in heavy skillet over low heat, then add clarified butter, salt and pepper to taste, and serve at once.

Note: To clarify butter, melt slowly, skim foam, and pour off clarified liquid, leaving residue on bottom of saucepan.

Serves 8

Frances Keenan Averitt

ROT KRAUT MIT APFELN

Sit down to red kraut and apples—and conjure up Oktoberfest and castles on the Rhine.

2 tablespoons chicken fat	¼ teaspoon pepper
1 medium onion, sliced	2 whole cloves
2 tart apples, peeled and chopped	1 bay leaf
4 cups water	Juice of ½ lemon
½ cup red wine vinegar	1 medium head red cabbage, shredded
½ cup sugar	2 to 3 tablespoons all-purpose flour
½ teaspoon salt	

Heat fat in large saucepan. Add onion and apples, and sauté 3 to 4 minutes. Add all other ingredients except cabbage and flour. Bring to a boil and stir in cabbage. Cover and simmer 30 minutes or until tender. Just before serving, remove bay leaf and sprinkle flour over top of mixture to absorb liquid.

Serves 8 to 10

Elaine Schuppe

ARTICHOKE HEART CASSEROLE

Oh, so good. Every crumb will be consumed.

1 14-ounce can artichoke hearts, drained and liquid reserved	1 to 2 tablespoons lemon juice
	Dash Tabasco sauce or red pepper
Light cream	Dash Accent
2 tablespoons butter	1 to 2 cups grated sharp Cheddar cheese
2 tablespoons all-purpose flour	
1 egg yolk, well beaten	1 to 2 cups Ritz cracker crumbs

Combine reserved artichoke liquid with enough cream to equal 1 cup. Melt butter in top of double boiler. Add flour and stir until smooth. Gradually add cream mixture to flour mixture, stirring constantly over hot, but not boiling, water to make thick white sauce.

Remove 1 cup sauce and gradually add to egg yolk, beating constantly until mixture is thinned and well-blended. Stir thinned egg mixture back into sauce in double boiler. Add lemon juice and seasonings, and stir to blend.

Cut artichokes into halves or quarters. Butter 5-cup baking dish and alternately layer artichoke hearts and white sauce, ending with layer of sauce. Bake at 350 degrees for 20 to 30 minutes or until hot and bubbly. Remove from oven, cover with cheese, and continue baking until cheese melts. Cover with cracker crumbs and bake again until browned.

Serves 4

Mrs. Jere Crook, Jr.

SWEET POTATO TRIO

Just minutes to make. A good and different dish for a brunch.

1 29-ounce can sweet potatoes, mashed	4 large bananas, sliced
	½ cup orange juice
1 20-ounce can pineapple chunks, drained and ½ cup juice reserved	Juice of ½ lemon
	½ teaspoon cinnamon, optional
	Dash salt

Combine all ingredients including reserved juice and bake in buttered baking dish for 30 to 45 minutes at 350 degrees.

Serves 8

Mrs. Al Miller
Phoenix, Arizona

Summer Fruit and Vegetable Market at Collierville

For knowledgeable Southern gourmets, good Southern cooking can be defined most succinctly as "fresh fruits and vegetables." As lyrical as any of their odes to fried chicken, hot biscuits, or country ham, are their rhapsodies about such simple regional delicacies as green beans cooked with new potatoes, fried okra, sliced tomatoes and cucumbers with homemade mayonnaise, buttered beets, homemade applesauce, black-eyed peas, or peach cobbler—all fresh from the garden and hot off the stove.

That Memphis has always interpreted "fresh" produce to mean "freshest possible," is evidenced by a local cookbook, published in 1890, instructing cooks to use only vegetables that are gathered early in the morning, "as they are so much better with dew on them." In fact, daily shopping for the freshest possible produce to serve family and guests was a Memphis imperative as far back as the late 1850s when farmers brought their fruits and vegetables into town each day to be sold in two downtown markets— huge slate-roofed, brick-floored, three-hundred-foot-long sheds supported by steel girders. It was usually the head of the family, in those days, who took a market basket on his arm each morning and, accompanied by a servant more often than not, headed for the nearest farmers' market—on Poplar Avenue to the north, or on Beale Street to the south, where Handy Park is today. His goal was to finish his shopping early enough to get back home for breakfast.

Today's equivalent shopper might be a young suburban housewife in tennis attire, who has just finished carpooling the children to a soccer game, and is rushing to the local summer produce market on the town square of Collierville, some twenty minutes east of Memphis city limits on the old Indian trace known as Poplar Pike. Tradition claims that Collierville got its name from a stagecoach driver's habit of always shouting "Hello, Mr. Collier," to a local store owner, Jessie R. Collier, as the coach passed by. The arrival of a railroad in 1857 firmly established the town's importance as an agricultural trade center. Nearby dairy farms produced rich dairy products. In summer, farmers brought their vegetables in to market by the wagonload, and in the fall, gin platforms were crowded with bales of cotton waiting to be shipped.

The unspoiled beauty of the surrounding countryside has attracted many new residents who, like the old-time families, are determined that Collierville, as it grows, must keep its charm of yesterday. The town square, named Confederate Park in honor of the eighty-member town troop that marched off to the Civil War (the town was the scene of a battle which was the beginning of Sherman's March to the Sea), is regularly the scene of concerts, cheese carnivals, Christmas parades, watermelon festivals, and an annual fair. Church congregations hold old-fashioned bazaars. The Chamber of Commerce is housed in the old, restored train station, and in 1977, a log cabin of 1850s vintage that once served as a stage coach station on the old Holly Springs road to Memphis, was dismantled, moved to Collierville's town square, and reassembled.

The "freshest possible" produce can still be found in Memphis where farmers sometimes sell homegrown berries, melons, or tomatoes from their parked trucks, or at small neighborhood stalls. A growers' produce market at the new Agricenter International is also thriving. But nowhere does the farmers' market tradition continue more strongly than on the Collierville town square each summer, daily during the garden season.

THE PICTURE: *Local farmers line up their trucks on the Collierville town square each summer weekday, beginning in July, and offer a wide selection of freshly harvested, homegrown fruits and vegetables. Here, a bountiful supply of this produce is displayed on the weathered porch of an old log cabin, once a stage coach stop on the Memphis-Holly Springs road, that was removed to the square in 1977 as a monument to the past. A hundred-year-old ironstone buttermilk pitcher holds a bouquet of flowers gathered from private gardens and from roadsides in the area—brilliant yellow black-eyed Susans and bur marigold, blue salvia, globe amaranths, goldenrod, thoroughwort, and zinnias.*

THE FOOD: *Pumpkins, watermelon, Indian corn, and baskets of potatoes, eggplant, cucumbers, bell peppers, tomatoes, apples, gourds, squash, and hot peppers await the attention of shoppers.*

HERBED GREEN PEA SOUFFLÉ SALAD

Light and lovely. Perfect for a summer luncheon.

2 3-ounce packages lemon gelatin	¼ teaspoon celery salt
2 cups hot water	Dash Tabasco sauce
½ cup cold water	2 teaspoons minced onion
2 tablespoons vinegar	1 cup very thinly sliced unpeeled cucumber
1½ cups mayonnaise	1 cup finely chopped celery
1 teaspoon salt	2 cups shredded Cheddar cheese

Dissolve gelatin in hot water. Add all other ingredients except cucumber, celery, and cheese, and beat until well blended. Chill until partially set. Beat again until light and fluffy, and fold in cucumber, celery, and cheese. Pour into well-oiled 6-cup ring mold. Refrigerate until firm and serve with chilled herbed peas in center of ring.

Herbed Green Peas

2 10-ounce packages frozen green peas, cooked and chilled	⅓ cup favorite oil and vinegar dressing
⅔ cup thinly sliced pickled onions	½ teaspoon marjoram

Combine in order listed. Toss lightly.

Serves 8

Barbara B. Harrington

BUNDLE OF BEANS

Very simple to prepare. Especially good when time is in short supply.

2 16-ounce cans cut green beans, drained	½ cup vinegar
1 onion, sliced	1 teaspoon dry mustard
½ to 1 cup brown sugar	½ teaspoon seasoned salt
	4 slices bacon, cut in half

Wash beans thoroughly in cold water and drain well. Place in 9 x 13-inch baking dish and top with onion slices. Mix brown sugar, vinegar, mustard, and seasoned salt, and pour over beans. Top with bacon slices. Bake uncovered for 30 minutes at 350 degrees. Cover and bake 30 minutes more.

Serves 6 to 8

Peggy Worley

SPECIAL CARROTS

A dish that goes especially well with pork. Walnuts and carrots are a good combination.

2 pounds fresh carrots, sliced ½-inch thick	½ cup butter
2 small bunches green onions with tops, thinly sliced	1 3-ounce package broken English walnuts

Cook carrots in boiling water until barely tender, about 20 minutes. Drain thoroughly.

In large skillet, sauté onions briefly in butter. Stir in carrots and walnuts, and cook 5 minutes over low heat.

Serves 8

Mrs. James T. Dailey

SPANAKOPETA

A favorite at the annual Greek Bazaar where bouzouki music is in the background and the entire neighborhood is swathed in the tantalizing aromas of Greek cooking.

3 pounds fresh spinach	2 4-ounce packages crumbled feta cheese
1 bunch green onions, coarsely chopped	½ cup shredded Romano cheese
1 teaspoon dill weed	¼ cup olive oil
¼ cup chopped parsley	Salt to taste
5 eggs, lightly beaten	20 sheets phyllo
1 tablespoon farina or cream of wheat	1½ cups butter, melted

Wash spinach, drain, sprinkle with salt, and chop. Squeeze spinach well to remove excess moisture. Combine all remaining ingredients except phyllo and butter, and mix in spinach. Arrange 10 phyllo sheets in 11 x 15-inch baking pan, brushing each with butter. Pour in spinach mixture. Cover with remaining phyllo sheets, brushing each side with butter. Seal edges and pierce top with fork. Bake at 350 degrees for 45 minutes or until golden brown. Turn heat off and leave in oven 10 minutes. Remove and let stand 5 minutes before cutting.

Note: May substitute four 10-ounce packages frozen unchopped leaf spinach for fresh spinach. Do not sprinkle with salt.

Serves 20 to 24

Helen Vergos

ZEITOV FASSOLIA

An Armenian recipe for green beans in olive oil. Worth a try as soon as possible.

½ cup olive oil
1 medium onion, chopped
5 to 8 cloves garlic, chopped
1 pound fresh tomatoes, cut in small pieces

1 pound green beans, snapped
1 small red bell pepper, chopped, optional
2 to 3 carrots, chopped, optional
Salt and pepper to taste

Pour olive oil into iron skillet, add onion and garlic, and cook over medium-low heat for 10 minutes. Add remaining ingredients, cover, and cook over medium heat for 30 minutes or until vegetables are tender. Good hot or cold.

Serves 4 to 6

Hoorie Kissoyan

SCALLOPED POTATOES

The crisp crumb crust is an added plus to a very flavorful dish.

5 to 6 medium red potatoes
2 teaspoons grated onion
½ cup margarine, melted
3 tablespoons all-purpose flour
1 teaspoon Accent
1 teaspoon salt
¼ teaspoon pepper
¼ teaspoon paprika

½ teaspoon dry mustard
2½ cups milk
1½ cups grated American cheese
4 drops Worcestershire sauce
1½ cups crushed corn flakes
Paprika

Boil potatoes with jackets on. When done, peel and slice.

In medium saucepan over low heat, sauté onion in margarine until soft. Add flour, Accent, salt, pepper, ¼ teaspoon paprika, and mustard, blending until smooth. Gradually add milk, 1 cup cheese, and Worcestershire sauce, stirring until cheese is melted. Sauce may look too thin, but will thicken as it bakes.

In greased 3-quart baking dish, layer in order sliced potatoes, sauce, and 1 cup corn flake crumbs. Top with remaining cheese and corn flake crumbs, sprinkle with more paprika, and bake 30 minutes at 350 degrees.

Serves 6

Carolyn Todd

CHARLIE JEN'S SWEET-SOUR TOMATOES AND PEPPERS

Fond memories abide of Charlie Jen, talented Chinese architect and cook, who brought with him to Memphis wonderful recipes from his ancestral land. Here is one of the best.

4 ripe tomatoes
4 tablespoons vegetable oil
4 green bell peppers, cut in 1-inch squares

½ cup white vinegar
¼ cup sugar
1 teaspoon cornstarch

Cut each tomato into 8 equal wedges and place in serving bowl. Chill thoroughly.

Heat oil in heavy iron skillet until oil smokes. Add peppers and stir rapidly until covered with gray spots. Pour vinegar and sugar over peppers and continue cooking a few seconds until sugar dissolves and bubbles. Stir in cornstarch. As soon as liquid thickens, pour over cold tomatoes and serve immediately.

Serves 4 to 6

Mrs. Norfleet R. Turner

HEY HEY'S STUFFED BAKED POTATOES

An outstanding baked potato.

6 large potatoes, baked
¾ cup butter
¾ to 1 cup milk
2 eggs
1½ teaspoons salt
¼ teaspoon white pepper

¼ cup grated Cheddar cheese
4 slices bacon, fried crisp and crumbled
Cayenne pepper
Paprika

Slice potatoes in half lengthwise while hot and carefully scoop out centers without breaking skins. Set skins aside. Place potatoes in large bowl and beat 1 minute. Add butter and beat again. Add milk, eggs, salt, and pepper, and beat. Stuff shells with mixture and top with cheese and bacon. Sprinkle with cayenne pepper and paprika. Bake at 350 degrees until hot and bubbly.

Serves 8 to 10

Helen Turner

CAJUN STYLE CABBAGE

Even non-cabbage eaters have been heard to say, "When are we having that cabbage dish again?"

6 slices bacon	2 tablespoons vinegar
6 to 8 green onions with tops, chopped	1/8 teaspoon cayenne pepper or more to taste
2 14½-ounce cans whole tomatoes, drained	½ teaspoon salt
	1/8 teaspoon black pepper
1 medium head cabbage, coarsely chopped	

Fry bacon until crisp and remove from skillet, reserving drippings. Sauté onion in drippings until soft. Break up tomatoes and add with cabbage, vinegar, salt, and pepper to skillet. Cover and simmer 45 minutes. During last 10 minutes, add crumbled bacon.

Serves 6 to 8

Carol M. Cherry

BUXTON BAKED BEANS FOR A BUNCH

Just one of those grand recipes that perfectly serve church suppers, backyard picnics, or any other large convivial gathering.

5 28-ounce jars B&M beans	¼ cup malt vinegar
1 32-ounce bottle catsup	Dash Tabasco sauce
1 12-ounce bottle chili sauce	1½ cups dark brown sugar
1 teaspoon Worcestershire sauce	2 teaspoons salt
1 tablespoon garlic powder	½ teaspoon horseradish
1 tablespoon onion salt	8 to 10 pound canned ham, sliced and tied
1 teaspoon black pepper	1 cup sherry
½ teaspoon oregano	2 16-ounce cans whole cranberries
1 large onion, minced	
1 teaspoon celery salt	

Combine all ingredients except ham, sherry, and cranberries in very large baking dish, and bake 8 hours at 200 degrees. After 6 hours, place ham in center of beans. Mix sherry with cranberries, cover ham, and continue baking remaining 2 hours.

Serves 24

Mrs. Bertram H. Buxton

PEPPERONI ALLA BAGNA CAUDA

Sweet peppers with garlic cream. A selection from the always appealing Northern Italian cuisine of this fashionable Overton Square restaurant.

2 tablespoons olive oil	Freshly ground black pepper to taste
4 anchovy fillets	
1¾ teaspoons minced garlic	4 large pimiento peppers
3 cups heavy cream	4 leaves romaine lettuce
Salt to taste	2 tablespoons dry white wine

Preheat saucepan over medium heat. Add olive oil, anchovies, and garlic. Sauté until anchovies begin to dissolve. Add cream and simmer until reduced by half. Add salt and pepper. Remove from heat.

Warm peppers (halved or sliced) and then wilt romaine in wine over very low heat. Place peppers on romaine leaves on serving plates. Serve topped with warm sauce.

Serves 4

The Palm Court Restaurant
M. L. Cahhal, Executive Chef

FLORENTINE TOMATOES

Two favorites, tomatoes and spinach, with lots of added pizzazz.

4 tomatoes, halved	Salt and pepper to taste
1 10-ounce package frozen chopped spinach	Pinch of nutmeg
	1 tablespoon butter
1 tablespoon chopped onion	Grated Parmesan cheese
1 clove garlic, minced	Bread crumbs

Bake tomatoes 10 minutes at 325 degrees in buttered baking dish. Combine spinach and onion, cook according to directions, and drain well. Briefly blend spinach with garlic, salt, pepper, nutmeg, and butter in food processor. Place in saucepan, heat thoroughly, and heap mixture on tomato halves. Sprinkle with Parmesan cheese and bread crumbs, bake 10 minutes at 325 degrees, and serve immediately.

Serves 8

Mrs. Jerry W. Grise

MRS. STILL'S EGGPLANT CASSEROLE

A favorite from a legendary Mississippi Delta cook whose reputation still continued as she entered her nineties.

1 large eggplant, peeled and cut in cubes	1 cup sautéed fresh mushrooms
1 tablespoon sugar	1 16-ounce package sharp Cheddar cheese, shredded
1 green bell pepper, chopped	1 cup cracker crumbs
1 medium onion, chopped	Worcestershire sauce
2 tablespoons butter	Tabasco sauce
1 pound raw shrimp, peeled and deveined	Garlic salt
	Red pepper
1 10¾-ounce can cream of mushroom soup	Black pepper
	Paprika

Combine eggplant and sugar in small amount lightly salted water, boil until tender, and drain well. Sauté bell pepper and onion in butter until soft. Combine eggplant, sautéed peppers and onions, shrimp, soup, mushrooms, half of cheese and cracker crumbs, and add all seasonings, except paprika, to taste. Mix lightly and place in 2-quart baking dish. Top with remaining cheese and cracker crumbs, sprinkle with paprika, and bake 1 hour at 325 degrees.

Serves 8 to 10

Betty Jo Dulaney
Tunica, Mississippi

AMES PLANTATION GLAZED CARROTS

A sweet and tangy way to present carrots.

1 pound carrots, scraped and sliced	2 teaspoons lemon juice
½ cup butter, melted	Juice of 1 orange
2 tablespoons brown sugar	Grated rind of 1 orange
	1 tablespoon honey

Cook carrots in small amount water until tender. Drain and place in 1½-quart baking dish. Blend butter, sugar, juices, orange rind, and honey. Pour over carrots and bake 30 minutes at 325 degrees, turning carrots frequently to baste well.

Serves 4

Ames Plantation
Grand Junction, Tennessee

ZINGY BAKED TOMATOES

Draws raves every time. Even people who think they don't like baked tomatoes will like these.

1 medium onion, chopped	3 dashes Tabasco sauce
1 green bell pepper, chopped	¼ teaspoon Cajun vegetable seasoning
3 tablespoons butter	
4 14½-ounce cans tomato wedges with juice	Salt and freshly ground black pepper to taste
3 teaspoons light brown sugar	1 cup Pepperidge Farm stuffing mix
2 teaspoons Worcestershire sauce	1 cup grated Cheddar cheese

In large skillet, sauté onion and bell pepper in butter until onion is clear. Add tomatoes with juice, sugar, Worcestershire sauce, Tabasco sauce, seasoning, salt, and pepper, and mix well. Stir in stuffing mix and pour into buttered 3-quart baking dish. Sprinkle with cheese and bake 30 minutes at 350 degrees.

Serves 6 to 8

Ann Clark Harris

POTATO LATKES

A traditional holiday Chanukah dish, usually served with applesauce or sour cream.

5 large red potatoes, peeled	3 tablespoons matzo meal or all-purpose flour
3 eggs, beaten	
1 medium onion, finely grated	½ cup chicken schmaltz (fat) or margarine
½ teaspoon baking powder	
Salt and pepper to taste	

Grate potatoes very fine in food processor. Empty into colander and rinse with cold water. Drain well by mashing water from potato pulp. Combine potatoes with eggs, onion, baking powder, salt, pepper, and matzo meal, blending into smooth batter. Melt chicken schmaltz (or margarine) in skillet. Drop batter by tablespoonfuls into hot fat. Flatten each mound slightly and fry on both sides until brown and crisp. Drain on paper towels and serve warm.

Serves 6

Reva Cook

A Native American Feast on the Riverbluff

Most modern Memphians are vaguely aware that their city is located on the Fourth Chickasaw Bluff, one of several above-flood-level vantage points on the east bank of the lower Mississippi River. And, because "Chickasaw" has been locally used in the names of everything from a residential subdivision to a baseball team, they realize that the Chickasaw Indian tribe once inhabited the area. But few of today's Memphians reflect on how large a contribution Native Americans have made to their everyday lives. It is a rich heritage with a long history.

The well-situated land that the city now occupies welcomed its earliest human settlers eight to ten thousand years ago. And when the first European arrival, Spanish explorer Hernando De Soto, "discovered" the Mississippi River in 1541, somewhere near modern Memphis, he encountered Native Americans of still undetermined tribal affinity with a well-developed, centuries-old culture. Their thriving agricultural society was organized into a regional system of city-states stretching along the Mississippi to the south for forty miles, and connected by an efficient network of footpaths. Built along ridges which could be traveled "dry-shod" any season of the year, these Indian traces would become major arteries for today's traffic in Memphis—Lamar, Poplar, and Jackson Avenues—and were part of a foot-trail system covering most of the eastern United States. When the French explorers Marquette and Joliet visited the bluff in the late 1600s, the Chickasaw Indians, who by then had come to dominate the area, were traveling as far as the Gulf of Mexico to the south, the Atlantic Ocean to the east, and the Great Lakes to the north.

But the Native Americans were not just accomplished trailblazers who foreshadowed our modern mobility. They were, by custom and by choice, our earliest environmentalists, with an abiding love and respect for the land they inhabited. And what a bountiful land it was! Early travelers to the lower Mississippi valley described the wild strawberries, blackberries, plums, persimmons, grapes, and many varieties of nuts available there for the picking, not to mention the cultivated abundance of corn, peppers, tomatoes, beans, and squash. Wild turkeys could be captured with ease, it was said, not only because they were so plentiful, but also because the birds were so fat from eating acorns they were unable to fly. And a Chickasaw Indian swimming underwater with a hand net could catch, in just minutes, a day's supply of freshwater fish.

The great harmony with nature that characterized the culture and religion of our Native American predecessors has left indelible imprints on our lives today. Science, medicine, and industry have benefited from their time-tested use of wild and cultivated plants—herbs and cotton, for instance. Artists and designers are inspired by the timeless beauty of Native American artifacts, clothing, and household implements—their baskets and pottery made from patterns passed like recipes from generation to generation. Our modern diet is influenced by foods they ate (they liked barbecued meats, even bear ribs, it is said), and their methods of food preparation—simple, by custom, to enhance natural flavors.

It could, in fact, be argued that the justly celebrated "Southern hospitality" is simply a regional reflection of one of the most honored of all Native American traditions: The feast is open to all for as long as the food lasts.

THE PICTURE: *A vista from the Fourth Chickasaw Bluff, looking out over the wide Mississippi with nothing in view but water, trees, sky, and sandbars—much as the Chickasaw Indians must have seen the eternal river centuries ago. A feast has been spread on an heirloom blanket, offering modern versions of generations-old Native American recipes, served in vessels made by a contemporary Choctaw artisan in residence at Memphis State University's Chucalissa Indian Village and Museum on the outskirts of the city. Handwoven Choctaw and Cherokee baskets hold wild persimmons and Japanese persimmons, pomegranates, Osage oranges, ornamental gourds, shelf fungi, pine boughs, and branches of dogwood. Here, at De Soto Park, site of vanished Indian settlements long predating the arrival of Europeans, one feels the breezes, sees the sunlight and shadows, and senses in the great quiet, the forever presence of those who were here first.*

THE FOOD: *The feast includes ONE KETTLE STEW which was simmered for hours, CORN WITH BLACK WALNUTS, and warm BLACKBERRIES WITH CORN MEAL COBBLES, a cobbler with dumplings of corn meal, pecans and honey. When the meal is over, the feasters will depart, leaving all exactly as they found it.*

CORN WITH BLACK WALNUTS

A Native American dish that combines two readily available local foods in a highly complementary way.

6 to 8 ears fresh corn   ¾ cup black walnut pieces
Salt to taste

Slice corn from cob and bring to boil in lightly salted water. Reduce heat, cover, and simmer until done, about 7 to 10 minutes. Drain corn and toss with walnuts. Serve immediately.

Serves 4 to 6

Marilou Awiakta

BULGUR WHEAT WITH VEGETABLES

A delicious side dish.

2 tablespoons chopped onion   1 cup bulgur wheat (#2)
2 tablespoons chopped celery   2 cups chicken or beef broth
2 tablespoons diced carrots   Salt to taste
3 to 4 tablespoons butter

In 1½-quart saucepan, sauté onion, celery, and carrots in butter for 5 minutes. Add bulgur wheat, stirring and browning 5 minutes. Stir in broth and bring to slow boil, stirring well. Add salt, reduce heat, cover, and simmer 20 minutes until bulgur is soft and all moisture is absorbed.

Serves 6

Ann Kendall Ray

SIZZLING SAUTÉED MUSHROOMS

The hallmark of this popular East Memphis restaurant is its large platter of sizzling hot steak with sautéed mushrooms on the side.

2 pounds fresh whole   ½ cup butter
   mushrooms   8 ounces cream sherry

Combine mushrooms and butter in saucepan and sauté until mushrooms are tender. Bring mixture to boil. Add sherry, stir, and serve immediately.

Serves 8 to 10

Folk's Folly Prime Steakhouse
Humphrey E. Folk, Jr., Proprietor

MUSHROOMS À LA GRÉCQUE

Mushroom fanciers, front and center, please!

1 onion, finely chopped   1 pound fresh button
4 tablespoons olive oil   mushrooms
5 ounces dry white wine   ½ pound tomatoes, peeled,
Bouquet garni   quartered, and seeded
1 clove garlic   Chopped parsley
Salt and black pepper to taste

Sauté onion in 2 tablespoons oil until soft. Stir in wine, bouquet garni, garlic, salt, and pepper. Add mushrooms and tomatoes, and cook uncovered over low heat about 10 minutes, adding remaining oil if needed. Remove from heat and cool. Remove bouquet garni and garlic. Chill. Serve sprinkled with parsley.

Serves 6 to 8

Palmeia Cooper

ONIONS IN CREAM CASSEROLE

A delicious dish from a delightful downtown restaurant, open not only to bankers but to all who like dining they can bank on.

6 large yellow onions,   1 cup shredded Cheddar cheese
   sliced ¼-inch thick   Dash cayenne pepper
3 cups medium CREAM SAUCE   Salt and pepper to taste

Place onions in salted water, bring to boil, and cook 20 minutes or until tender. Drain and pat thoroughly dry with paper towels. Combine cream sauce, cheese, and seasonings in saucepan, and heat until blended. In buttered baking dish, layer portion of onions and cover completely with sauce. Repeat layers, ending with sauce. Top with croutons and sprinkle with paprika. Bake at 350 degrees until hot and bubbly.

Croutons
10 to 14 slices white bread   Butter (no substitute)

Trim bread and cut in ½ to ¾-inch squares. Melt butter and brush bread pieces. Place on baking sheet and bake at 250 degrees until very lightly browned.

Serves 10 to 12

Bankers Hours Restaurant
Union Planters Bank

EGGPLANT PARMESAN
WITH FRESH VEGETABLE SAUCE

The view of the river from Diane's Restaurant in its thirty-sixth floor location downtown almost makes lunch redundant, but this is one offering from a tempting menu that must not be overlooked.

½ cup all-purpose flour
½ teaspoon salt
Pepper to taste
1 eggplant, about 1¼ pounds, peeled and cut in 6 slices lengthwise

½ cup milk
¼ cup olive oil
Freshly grated Parmesan cheese

Combine flour with salt and pepper. Dip eggplant slices in milk and generously sprinkle with seasoned flour. Sauté in olive oil, turning from time to time until lightly browned.

Place slices in single layer in baking dish. Spread fresh vegetable sauce over top. Top with Parmesan cheese and bake at 350 degrees for 20 to 25 minutes or until heated through and bubbly.

Fresh Vegetable Sauce
1 cup chopped onion
Olive oil
½ pound ground round or chuck
1 cup peeled, seeded, and chopped fresh tomatoes

1 cup chopped celery
½ cup chopped green bell pepper
Salt and pepper to taste

Sauté onions in olive oil until clear and soft. Remove from skillet. In same skillet, sauté meat until partially cooked and crumbly. Add onions, cook briefly, and add tomatoes. Cook 5 minutes. Add celery and green pepper, and cook 10 minutes more. Season with salt and pepper.

Serves 4 to 6

Diane's Restaurant
Jane Genette, Rose Lou Heflin,
and Sue Sprunt, Proprietors

ARTICHOKE PIE

Definitely a recipe to file with the best.

2 6½-ounce jar marinated artichoke hearts, drained, chopped, and liquid reserved from 1 jar
1 small onion, finely chopped
1 clove garlic, pressed
4 eggs, beaten
¼ cup fine bread crumbs

¼ teaspoon salt
⅛ teaspoon pepper
⅛ teaspoon oregano
⅛ teaspoon Tabasco sauce
2 cups shredded sharp Cheddar cheese
2 tablespoons minced parsley

Heat reserved liquid in medium skillet, add onion and garlic, and sauté 6 to 8 minutes until onion is soft. Combine eggs, bread crumbs, salt, pepper, oregano, and Tabasco sauce. Mix in cheese and parsley. Add artichokes and mix well. Stir in sautéed onion and garlic. Pour mixture into deep pie pan and bake 30 minutes at 325 degrees. Cool briefly before cutting.

Serves 6

Mrs. Norfleet R. Turner

SPINACH O'PARMIGIANA

The name was devised to please an Irish relative, but the dish remains true to its Italian heritage.

2 10-ounce packages frozen chopped spinach
3 cloves garlic, minced
4 tablespoons olive oil

5 tablespoons butter
2 eggs, lightly beaten
⅓ cup grated Parmesan cheese
Salt to taste

Cook spinach according to package directions but decrease cooking time by half. Place spinach in sieve and press, draining all moisture.

In large skillet, sauté garlic in olive oil and butter until very lightly browned. Add spinach, mixing until thoroughly coated with oil and butter. Stir in eggs and cook until almost done, add Parmesan cheese and salt, and cook 2 minutes more.

Serves 6

Nicky Dwyer Ross
Forrest City, Arkansas

BROCCOLI STRATA

A perfect choice for lunch or brunch.

1 10-ounce package frozen broccoli	6 eggs, beaten
8 slices rye or wheat bread	1 cup milk
4 slices American cheese	1 cup light cream
1 2-ounce jar diced pimientos, drained	1 tablespoon chopped onion
	½ teaspoon prepared mustard
6 slices Swiss cheese	Salt and pepper to taste
	3 tablespoons butter, melted

Cook broccoli 3 minutes in boiling water and drain well. Toast 6 bread slices and arrange in ungreased 9 x 13-inch baking dish. On top of bread, layer in order American cheese, broccoli, and pimientos. Layer Swiss cheese over all. Combine eggs, milk, cream, onion, mustard, salt, and pepper, and pour over casserole. Cover and refrigerate at least 1 hour.

In food processor, make crumbs of remaining bread slices. Toss with melted butter, sprinkle over chilled casserole, and bake uncovered 1 hour at 325 degrees. Let stand 10 minutes before serving.

Serves 8

Mrs. Nicholas J. Nickl, Jr.

SAUCY OKRA AND TOMATOES

Those Southern favorites, okra and tomatoes, in a different presentation.

¼ cup sliced scallions	1½ cups sliced fresh okra
2 tablespoons butter	2 medium tomatoes, peeled and chopped
1 tablespoon all-purpose flour	
½ teaspoon salt	¾ cup soft bread crumbs
½ cup milk	2 tablespoons butter, melted
¼ cup grated sharp Cheddar cheese	

In medium saucepan, sauté scallions in butter until tender but not browned. Blend in flour and salt, and gradually add milk, stirring until thick and bubbly. Add cheese, stirring until blended. Fold in okra and tomatoes and pour into greased 1-quart baking dish. Combine bread crumbs and butter and sprinkle around edge of baking dish. Bake at 350 degrees for 30 minutes or until thoroughly heated.

Serves 6

Carolyn Todd

POTATO KUGELI

A great family dish, much like escalloped potatoes.

1 cup milk	6 large potatoes
6 tablespoons butter	¼ small onion, grated
1 to 2 teaspoons salt	¼ cup snipped parsley
3 eggs, well-beaten	

Combine milk, butter, and salt, and heat until butter is melted. Gradually add small amount of milk mixture to eggs, stirring constantly. Combine with remaining milk mixture in large bowl. Pare potatoes one at a time and grate immediately into milk mixture to prevent discoloration (grating is easily done in food processor). Add onion, mix well, and pour into well-greased 2½-quart baking dish. Bake uncovered 1¼ hours at 350 degrees. Sprinkle parsley on top before serving.

Serves 6

Mrs. Thomas E. Guenter

SPINACH TIMBALES

A delicious spinach custard. Try serving with a BUERRE BLANC sauce and julienne cucumbers.

6 ounces spinach leaves	Freshly ground black pepper to taste
2 eggs	
1 cup light cream	Dash nutmeg
½ teaspoon salt	1½ tablespoons butter

Wash spinach leaves, blanch in boiling water, drain, and squeeze dry. Chop coarsely and set aside.

Combine eggs, cream, salt, pepper, and nutmeg in bowl and mix well.

Melt butter in small skillet. When melted and bubbly, add spinach, and stir with fork over low to medium heat for 5 minutes. Combine with egg mixture. Generously butter bottom and sides of individual ramekins. Spoon spinach mixture into ramekins. Set in pan with water 1-inch deep and bake at 350 degrees for 30 minutes or until custards are set. To serve, slip knife blade around rim of each ramekin and invert custard onto serving plate.

Serves 4

Mrs. Winfred Sharp

STUFFED MIRLITONS

Mirlitons are infinitely adaptable to other flavors and foods because of their own delicate taste. A dish with a touch of New Orleans.

3 to 4 slices stale bread
3 large mirlitons
4 tablespoons butter
1 cup sliced green onions with tops
1 cup chopped onions
3 cloves garlic, minced
2 teaspoons thyme
2 whole bay leaves

1½ cups chopped ham or shrimp
3 eggs, lightly beaten
2 tablespoons minced fresh parsley
1 teaspoon salt
¼ teaspoon black pepper
Seasoned bread crumbs and grated Parmesan cheese

Cover bread with cold water. Squeeze to drain, and measure 2 cupfuls moistened bread. Set aside.

Wash mirlitons, cover with boiling water, and boil until tender but not soft, about 10 minutes. Drain at once and cool under running water. Cut in half lengthwise. Carefully scoop out each half, leaving shells at least ½-inch thick. Place shells on lightly greased baking sheet.

Coarsely chop mirliton pulp. Melt butter over low heat and stir in onions, garlic, thyme, and bay leaves. Sauté about 5 minutes. Remove from heat and mix in moistened bread, chopped mirliton, and ham or shrimp. Stir in eggs, parsley, salt, and pepper, remove bay leaves, and spoon mixture into shells. Sprinkle bread crumbs and cheese on top. Bake 20 to 25 minutes at 350 degrees.

Serves 6

Marguerite Piazza Bergtholdt

NOUVELLE BROCCOLI

A fresh approach to two favorite vegetables.

1 stalk broccoli with florets
1 medium potato, cooked and peeled

2 tablespoons butter
2 tablespoons sour cream
3 teaspoons dry dill weed

Cut broccoli in 2-inch pieces, boil 10 minutes in 1-quart saucepan, and drain. Combine broccoli, potato, butter, and sour cream in food processor and purée. Add dill weed and purée again. Heat in top of double boiler before serving.

Serves 4

Mrs. A. Arthur Halle, Jr.

KELLEY'S VEGETABLE PIE

Seconds will be in order for everyone.

2 bunches green onions, chopped
2 to 4 tablespoons butter
2 medium zucchini, sliced
3 medium yellow squash, sliced
8 ounces mushrooms, sliced thick

2 tomatoes, peeled, chopped, and drained
1 unbaked puff pastry crust
1 cup Hellmann's mayonnaise
1 cup grated mozzarella cheese

Sauté onions in butter until tender and remove from skillet. Briefly sauté zucchini and yellow squash in covered skillet. Combine onions, zucchini, yellow squash, mushrooms, and tomatoes, and pour into 10-inch pie plate lined with puff pastry. Mix mayonnaise and cheese and spread over top. Push mixture to edges to seal. Bake 1 hour at 350 degrees. Serve immediately.

Serves 6

Mrs. John Shea Buchignani

FRESH CORN SOUFFLÉ

Summertime, hot sun, tall cornfield, and corn just minutes off the stalk. What a wonderful thought and what a wonderful dish.

3 ears fresh yellow corn (do not substitute canned corn)
2 eggs
½ teaspoon salt

1 teaspoon sugar
1¼ tablespoons cornstarch
¼ cup milk
2 tablespoons butter, melted

Cut corn from cob and scrape cob for any remaining corn and juice. Place one egg in blender, add half the corn with juice, and mix well. Add remaining egg, corn, and juice. Blend 1 minute on highest speed, adding salt and sugar. Dissolve cornstarch in small portion of milk. Stir in remaining milk, add to blender with corn, and stir.

Brush melted butter over bottom and sides of 3-cup baking dish. Pour corn mixture into baking dish and stir slightly to mix butter with other ingredients. Bake 15 minutes at 350 degrees. Stir from the sides into center and bake 15 minutes more.

Serves 4

Martha E. Jayroe

A Polo Tournament Supper at Wildwood Farms

Fact: In 1986, the horse population of Shelby County, Tennessee, some sixteen thousand strong, was the second largest of any county in the United States. *Fact:* The current membership of the Memphis Polo Association, organized in 1954, is larger than the membership of the polo association of Newport, Rhode Island, where the first international polo match was held in 1886. *Fact:* The Germantown Charity Horse Show is the second largest all-breed show in the country.

Facts such as these, suitable for memorization by trivia fans, help explain why the Memphis area's reputation among informed sportsmen as "great horse country" is now international. The scene of much of this equine activity is Germantown, a fast-growing suburb east of Memphis, with an interesting past. In 1825, it became the setting for a bold social experiment. Frances Wright, a wealthy Scottish heiress, resolute idealist, non-conformist, and friend to Thomas Jefferson and Lafayette, purchased two thousand acres of wilderness in this area, as the site for her utopian Nashoba Plantation. Here, slaves whose freedom she had bought could live and work while awaiting transport to an independent life in the new Republic of Haiti. Doomed from the start by fevers, frontier hardships, rigors of climate, and rumors of scandals, the plan lasted only five years, but it made Frances Wright one of the most famous women of the nineteenth century, and prepared the way for other settlers who had already begun to arrive. The community that sprang up nearby was incorporated in 1841 as Germantown, but whether the name honored early-day citizens of German descent or the surveyor of town lots, N. R. German, is still unclear.

What is clear is that the village which developed here became one of the area's most appealing places in which to live. It is country on the edge of city and still has meandering greenery-laced lanes, and lovely antebellum cottages and plantation homes. But in recent years, in the face of accelerating growth—from a population of five thousand in 1972 to more than thirty-three thousand by 1989—Germantown has resorted to strict building codes and zoning laws as it struggles to preserve its wooded beauty, and the vintage village charm of its gingerbread-trimmed houses and fine old churches, However, the town has had no problem maintaining its ongoing fame among horse-fanciers. The well-established Germantown Charity Horse Show, where Tennessee walkers share star billing with appealing ponies and magnificent hunter-jumpers, grows more popular each year. And Germantown's renowned Wildwood Farms, with its four hundred acres of undisturbed pastureland and its miles of board fences reminiscent of Kentucky's rolling blue grass country, continues to be, as it has been for half a century, the site of fox hunts, steeple chases, polo matches, and all attendant ceremonies.

The great barn of weathered white-washed brick, when built in 1934 by Mr. and Mrs. W. L. Taylor, the owners of Wildwood Farms, was rated the second largest horse barn in America. With its vast indoor arena and exercise room, its slate roof, oak stalls, and graceful arched windows, it was also one of the most magnificent. Here the Taylors' fine harness and gaited horses—horses with fabled names like Seminole, Betsy Thompson, and Ocean Spray—practiced to win national honors throughout the country. At various times in Wildwood Farms' history, its fields have pastured polled Hereford cattle, and its kennels have nurtured prize fox hounds. The Memphis Polo Association has long had a practice field on Wildwood property, and a Taylor son is today a four-goal member of the Memphis team.

THE PICTURE: *Inside the Taylor's barn at Wildwood Farms in Germantown, with the entrance framing a view of grazing horses and fenced pastures beyond, a table has been set up for the traditional end-of-season picnic supper and cook-out. The table is covered with a handmade quilt and set with bright yellow, handpainted pottery in the Quimper pattern, from a French factory on the coast of Brittany. A silver trophy from the Memphis Invitational Polo Tournament holds an autumn bouquet of artemesia, hybrid lilies, and varieties of chrysanthemums.*

THE FOOD: *Supper menu for hungry riders is traditional—grilled pork chops with Cajun seasoning, OLD-FASHIONED SWEET POTATO PUDDING, sausage and cheese balls, PIGGYBACKS (broiled bacon-wrapped crackers), fresh tomatoes and kiwi vinaigrette, homegrown GREEN BEANS PROVINCIAL, and HOME BAKED BREAD. The finishing touch: famed transparent chess tarts from McLaurine's, a favorite family-owned Memphis bakery.*

Every fall, when tournament time arrives, the green polo field is ablaze with the bright colors of polo shirts, striped tents, and perhaps a hot air balloon landing in honor of the occasion. The mallet cracks hard against the ball, the thunder of galloping horses' hooves rises and falls, as ponies and players pass up and down the three-hundred-yard field. It is polo at its Tennessee best, a daredevil game of dash, nerve, skill, joyful insanity—and horse power.

GREEN BEANS PROVINCIAL

The tomato adds nice color and appealing taste with green beans.

1 16-ounce package frozen French-style green beans	½ cup chopped onion
	½ cup chopped celery
6 to 7 slices bacon	1 large tomato, diced

Cook beans according to package directions. Fry bacon and drain, reserving 2 tablespoons drippings. Sauté onion and celery in reserved drippings, and add to beans. Add tomato and simmer 8 to 10 minutes. Just before serving, top with crumbled bacon.

Serves 4

Mrs. Don A. Ramier, Jr.

TENNESSEE RED BEANS AND RICE

From old New Orleans and the bayou country, where red beans and rice were traditionally served on Mondays while the wash was drying in the South Louisiana sun. This Cajun recipe has a Tennessee touch and is not so spicy-hot as might be expected.

2 pounds dried red beans	1 tablespoon snipped parsley
1 pound hot country sausage	1 tablespoon Worcestershire sauce
1 pound smoked sausage, cut in 1-inch slices	1 tablespoon salt
1 pound baked ham, cut in 1-inch cubes	½ teaspoon coarsely ground black pepper
1 large hambone, sawn in pieces	⅛ teaspoon cayenne pepper
2 cups chopped onion	⅛ teaspoon crushed dried red pepper pods
2 cups chopped celery	
½ cup thinly sliced shallots (tops only)	2 whole bay leaves, broken in several pieces
½ cup chopped green bell pepper	8 cups cold water
	8 cups cooked rice

Soak beans overnight.

Drain beans. Cook and drain sausage. Place all ingredients except rice in heavy 8 to 10-quart soup pot (add more water if needed to cover ingredients). Bring to boil, reduce heat, and simmer 2½ to 3 hours until beans are tender and thick sauce has formed. Stir frequently, adding water if necessary to keep mixture moist. Serve over rice.

Serves 8 to 10

W. Kerby Bowling II

OLD-FASHIONED SWEET POTATO PUDDING

Just the way our grandmothers made it. The difference is in the grating.

4 eggs, beaten	5 tablespoons butter, melted
2 cups sugar	2 cups milk
½ teaspoon cinnamon	2 tablespoons vanilla
1 teaspoon allspice	3 tightly-packed cups grated raw sweet potatoes
¼ teaspoon ground cloves	
¼ teaspoon salt	

Mix together all ingredients except sweet potatoes. Stir in sweet potatoes, blend well, and pour into 2-quart baking dish. Bake 1½ hours at 350 degrees.

Serves 8 to 10

Lois Sandusky

Variation: Some Southern grandmothers added a splash of bourbon whiskey to their sweet potato pudding. The whiskey was kept for only three purposes: sweet potato puddings, hot toddies, and eggnog.

Rosa Ann Keller

HARDY APPLES

Now a favorite at the Longreen Hunt, this is a creation from vacation times at family cabins in Hardy, Arkansas, where children are always about in abundance. And having an affinity for red hots, they probably gave the true colors to this sweet side dish.

5 to 6 crisp apples, peeled and sliced	1 large lemon, squeezed and rind grated
1 cup sugar	1 small box Red Hots (about ⅘-ounce size)
Salt	
4 tablespoons butter	

Layer apple slices in buttered baking dish. Sprinkle each layer with sugar and a pinch of salt, and dot with butter. Pour lemon juice over layers and sprinkle with grated lemon rind. Stir red hots in small amount of water over medium heat until melted, smooth, and syrupy. Pour over apple layers and bake at 300 degrees until liquid is absorbed.

Serves 6 to 8

Mary Mueller
Rossville, Tennessee

GLAZED VEGETABLES AND APPLES

For parsnip lovers. A fresh taste for a winter's night vegetable dish.

1 pound carrots, peeled and
   sliced
1 pound parsnips, peeled and
   sliced
3 medium apples, cored and
   sliced

⅓ cup orange juice
⅓ cup light corn syrup
2 to 3 teaspoons salt
1 tablespoon grated orange rind
4 tablespoons butter

Cook carrots and parsnips in lightly salted boiling water until almost tender, and drain. Place carrots, parsnips, and apples in 2-quart baking dish.

In small saucepan, combine all remaining ingredients except butter and blend well over low heat. Pour over vegetables, dot with butter, and bake at 375 degrees for 25 to 30 minutes or until tender.

Serves 4 to 6

Mrs. Nicholas J. Nickl, Jr.

INEBRIATED PEACHES

Very good, and especially nice with a sugar cookie.

2 29-ounce cans peach halves,
   drained and juice reserved
½ cup brown sugar

4 tablespoons butter
½ cup bourbon whiskey
½ cup toasted pecans

Boil peach juice in small saucepan until reduced by half. Stir in brown sugar and butter, and blend well to make sauce. Add peach halves and keep warm until ready to serve. Before removing from pan, pour bourbon over peaches and blend with syrup. Place peaches in sherbet glasses, spoon sauce into cavity of each peach, and sprinkle with pecans. Add a sugar cookie on the side.

Serves 8 to 12

Frances Keenan Averitt

APRICOT CRUNCH

Such a versatile dish. Good for brunches, or as accompaniment for pork, or as dessert with ice cream or a dollop of whipped cream on top.

4 17-ounce cans peeled apricots
1 16-ounce box light brown
   sugar

1 16-ounce box Ritz crackers,
   crushed
1½ cups butter

In lightly greased 9 x 13-inch baking dish, layer in order half the apricots, half the brown sugar, and half the cracker crumbs. Dot with ¾ cup butter. Repeat layers. Cover and bake 45 minutes at 325 degrees. Uncover and bake additional 15 minutes or until juices bubble through and top is lightly browned and crusty.

Serves 16 to 18

Mrs. Greer Richardson

FANCIFUL FRUIT PIZZA

A pizza is a pizza is—well, is something wonderful.

1 18-ounce package refrigerated sugar cookies
1 8-ounce package cream
   cheese, softened
⅓ cup sugar

1 teaspoon vanilla
Fresh fruits of choice
½ cup orange marmalade
2 tablespoons water

Cut cookie dough in ⅛-inch slices. Line ungreased 14-inch pizza pan with overlapping dough slices. Bake 12 minutes at 375 degrees and cool.

Combine cheese, sugar, and vanilla, mix well, and spread over cookie crust. Arrange fruits (strawberries, green grapes, kiwi slices, banana slices, apricot halves) on top. Mix marmalade and water in small saucepan, heat, and stir briefly to make glaze. Spread over fruit and serve pizza sliced in wedges.

Serves 10

Susan Chamberlin Hall
Virginia Beach, Virginia

MEATS

NISHIKIMAKI

A very appealing vegetable-beef roll, authentically Japanese, from private recipe files. Exceptionally good.

½ to 1 carrot, cut in 2-inch strips	1 green bell pepper, cut in strips ¼-inch wide
7 ounces well-chilled lean beef, sliced paper thin	2 tablespoons all-purpose flour
2 ribs celery, cut in 2-inch strips	2 tablespoons vegetable oil

Boil carrot strips briefly. Lay out beef slices and fill each with portion of each vegetable. Roll in jelly roll fashion and fasten with toothpick. Flour beef rolls on all sides. Heat oil in skillet, add rolls, and brown, turning so that all sides brown evenly. Add sauce, increase heat, and stir to coat rolls. Remove toothpicks, cut rolls in bite-size pieces, and serve arranged on flat side to reveal design.

Sauce

2 tablespoons sugar	3 tablespoons Mirin
3 tablespoons soy sauce	(sweet sake)

Combine all ingredients and stir to blend.

Note: If Mirin cannot be found, substitute equal parts sake and sugar.

Serves 4

Mrs. Machiko Okamoto

PORK CHOPS IN WHITE WINE

An uptown treatment for the reliable pork chop.

2 medium onions, sliced	All-purpose flour
4 tablespoons butter	Salt and pepper to taste
4 pork chops, cut ½ to ¾-inch thick	½ to ¾ cup white wine
	1 teaspoon soy sauce

In large skillet, sauté onions in butter until slightly browned, and remove from skillet. Brown chops well on both sides. Place in 9 x 13-inch baking dish and sprinkle with flour, salt, and pepper. Top with sautéed onions. Mix white wine with soy sauce and pour over chops. Cover and bake 1½ hours at 350 degrees. If needed, add a little more wine as the pork chops cook. Serve with rice or noodles.

Serves 4

Mrs. William H. Morse

ITALIAN BEEF AU JUS

The aroma is marvelous and the taste, with the seasoned juices, is outstanding. And it's so simple to do.

5 to 6-pound Pike's Peak roast	2 teaspoons basil
1 package onion soup mix	½ teaspoon cayenne pepper
2 teaspoons dried oregano	or less to taste

Combine dry ingredients and sprinkle over roast. Place roast in heavy roasting pan or baking dish and pour 3½ cups water around it. Cover and bake 4 hours at 325 degrees. Slice and serve with individual bowls of seasoned juices and hot French bread for dipping.

Note: It is sometimes difficult with prepackaged cuts of meat to find a Pike's Peak roast, part of the end of the round. Perhaps your butcher can get one for you. If not, a sirloin tip will do.

Serves 6

Mrs. Erich W. Merrill

SISSY'S POOR BOY SPAGHETTI

A family favorite, resulting from experimentation, that became a hot hit.

1 16-ounce package bacon	Dash red pepper flakes
1 28-ounce can tomatoes	1 tablespoon salt
1 15-ounce can herbed tomato sauce	6 ribs celery, chopped
1 12-ounce can Hot Spicy V-8 juice	1 medium onion, chopped
½ teaspoon cayenne pepper	¼ green bell pepper, chopped
	2 12-ounce packages vermicelli

Reserve 4 slices bacon. Fry remainder until very crisp, and then crumble. In large saucepan, combine crumbled bacon, desired amount of bacon drippings, and all other ingredients except vermicelli. Cook over medium heat, stirring occasionally, until celery becomes soft.

Cook vermicelli approximately 7 minutes and drain. Place in two 2-quart baking dishes, pour tomato mixture over top, and mix thoroughly. Lay 2 slices reserved bacon on top of each baking dish and broil until bacon curls. Watch carefully to prevent scorching.

Serves 10 to 12

Didi Dwyer Montgomery

LAMB ROMA

A definitive flavor for an elegant lamb entrée.

1 4-pound leg of lamb, boned and netted	Salt and pepper to taste
3 to 4 cloves garlic, minced	Olive oil
½ cup finely chopped parsley	½ cup Rhine wine
1 teaspoon dried marjoram	Rosemary, fresh or dried
½ teaspoon dried rosemary	Cling peach halves, drained
¼ pound boiled ham or prosciutto	Capers, drained

Make about 12 deep cuts over entire surface of lamb without cutting netting. Combine garlic, parsley, marjoram, and rosemary. Cut ham in julienne strips, add to herb mixture, and stuff 2 teaspoons mixture into each slit in meat. Rub stuffed leg of lamb with salt, pepper, and any remaining herb-ham mixture.

Brown meat in small amount olive oil in skillet or deep roasting pan. Add ¼ cup wine, cover, and bake 70 to 80 minutes at 325 degrees, basting occasionally with remaining wine, until meat thermometer registers 125 to 130 degrees. It is essential that lamb not be overcooked (should be brown on outside and pink on inside). Let stand 15 minutes before carving. Serve sprinkled with fresh rosemary and garnished with peach halves filled with capers.

Serves 12

Mrs. Nicholas J. Nickl, Jr.

AUNT RUTH'S SAUSAGE STROGANOFF

An old family recipe with roots on both sides of the Mississippi. It has become a Memphis favorite, appearing in slightly different form in another Memphis cookbook, but good enough to print anew.

1 clove garlic	2 teaspoons soy sauce
2 pounds country sausage	2 tablespoons Worcestershire sauce
3 tablespoons all-purpose flour	
2 cups milk	Salt and pepper to taste
1 8-ounce can mushrooms	Paprika to taste
2 large onions, chopped	2 cups sour cream
2 tablespoons butter	Cooked rice

Rub large skillet with garlic. Add sausage and brown well over medium heat, pouring off grease as it accumulates. Dredge sausage in flour. Add milk and simmer until slightly thickened. Set aside.

Drain mushrooms, sauté with onions in butter, and add to sausage mixture. Add soy sauce, Worcestershire sauce, and seasonings, stirring gently. (Can be made ahead to this point.) When mixture bubbles, add sour cream. Serve over rice.

Note: Makes an excellent hot appetizer served from chafing dish with pastry shells, or with Melba toast for dipping. (Serves 25)

Serves 10 to 12

Gloria Polk Nobles

SAUTÉED VEAL TENDERLOIN WITH RED PEPPER SAUCE

A dining experience par excellence.

8 medallions veal loin	½ teaspoon grated horseradish
Vegetable oil	
2 shallots, chopped	Salt and pepper to taste
2 teaspoons dry white wine	10 red lettuce leaves
1 teaspoon brandy	Butter
1 cup heavy cream	Chopped fresh parsley
3 teaspoons puréed red bell pepper	Chopped shallots

Sauté veal medallions in hot oil to desired degree of doneness. Remove from pan and set aside. Pour off excess oil from pan. Add 2 chopped shallots and sauté lightly, taking care that shallots do not burn. Deglaze pan with wine and brandy, add cream, and reduce by two-thirds. Add red pepper purée and horseradish, cook a few minutes longer, remove from heat, and strain. Season with salt and pepper.

In separate pan, cook lettuce leaves with touch of butter and very small amount water until slightly wilted. Remove from pan and press water from lettuce with cloth. Arrange warm lettuce on plate, place veal on lettuce, and cover with warm sauce. Garnish with parsley and shallots.

Serves 2

Chez Philippe Restaurant
The Peabody Hotel
José Gutierrez, Chef de Cuisine

A Dinner Set for the King at Graceland

It has become clear, in the years since his death in 1977, that singer Elvis Presley was a singular phenomenon, a transforming influence in musical history. His records have outsold those of any other artist or group ever—a total of *one billion plus* and still climbing. His admirers say that only two names are recognized worldwide—Coca-Cola and Elvis.

To many throughout the world, the name Elvis is synonymous with the name Memphis. Certainly the legend of this Mississippi-born, Memphis-raised "poor boy" who grew up to be the uncontested King of Rock 'n' Roll is an indispensable part of Memphis mythology. It has also become a significant factor in the Memphis economy. Elvis devotees come by the thousands each day to Graceland, to see the twenty-three-room home where he lived the last twenty years of his life. They come as to a shrine, lining up to make the ninety-minute Graceland tour, lingering to drop a rose on his flower-strewn grave in the Meditation Garden next to the site of Graceland's one-time swimming pool, pausing to inscribe vows of eternal adulation on the graffiti-covered stone walls surrounding the estate. Each August, they come by the tens of thousands, to celebrate Elvis International Tribute Week and take part in the all-night candlelight vigil marking the anniversary of his death. All told, more than half a million pilgrims make their way to Memphis each year to pay homage to their idol, and to spend untold sums of money in his name, in souvenir shops, restaurants, lodging places, and at other Memphis tourist attractions all over town. All of which confounds critics, astounds philosophers, and delights the Memphis Chamber of Commerce.

The unstinting devotion of the ever-faithful Elvis fans who visit Graceland in such numbers is matched only by their insatiable curiosity about a place that was, for so many years, off-limits to them. When Elvis bought this thirteen-and-a-half-acre estate in 1957—a hilltop mansion built in the late 1930s on land that had once been part of a five-hundred-acre plantation named Graceland—he made it his guarded sanctuary. Returning home after Hollywood movie productions or concert tours where he was always besieged by adoring mobs, he would gather his family and close friends around him, and Graceland would become a secluded private club and amusement park. There, protected by stone walls, wooden fences, electronically controlled iron gates, watchmen, and karate-trained bodyguards, he and his old Memphis buddies from Humes High School would play pool or touch football, ride horses or motorcycles around the grounds, watch television on one of the home's fourteen sets. Occasionally they might emerge from Graceland's gates in a middle-of-the-night caravan of vehicles, en route to a Memphis movie theatre where Elvis had arranged impromptu private showings of a new movie or two, maybe more.

Not until Graceland was at last opened to the public in June of 1982, almost five years after Elvis died, were his fans permitted to enter this guarded kingdom and see its wonders: stairways with mirrored walls that once reflected the face of the King himself; rhinestone-studded sofa pillows reminiscent of the white rhinestone jacket in which Elvis often performed; the music room with his gold leaf grand piano; the TV room with his private soda fountain; the poolroom with pleated fabric walls and ceilings and twin Tiffany lamps hanging above the pool table; the "jungle room," where he recorded his last album, "Moody Blue"—a twenty-foot den with a waterfall (no longer functional) at one end, and "African animal furniture" upholstered in fake-fur fabric, including a circular throne-like chair large enough for two where the King liked to have his mid-afternoon breakfast.

THE PICTURE: *It was usually around midnight when the King and his entourage would arrive in the white-carpeted, mirror-paneled dining room at Graceland, and crowd around the glass-topped table under the crystal chandelier, ready for dinner. Pictured here is Elvis Presley's favorite dinner, just as it was often served. The oval pedestal table is set with mats of black linen overcovered with cotton lace. Simple Towle flatware, a plain Noritake dinner china, and oversized iced-tea glasses etched with the letters "E P" complete the setting. The high-backed gold chairs are upholstered in black velvet, and the eye-catching bouquet features bird-of-paradise, chrysanthemums, cyperus, and laurel.*

THE FOOD: *The meal is simple, but Elvis' favorite, according to his Aunt Delta Biggs—a grilled T-bone steak (which Elvis' devoted cook always cut in bite-size pieces after removing the bone), baked potato, canned spinach, green salad with Thousand Island dressing, and iced tea. Elvis wanted each food served on a separate dish, and seldom ate desserts.*

Last stop on the Graceland tour is the forty-foot-long trophy room, formerly a slot car racing track before it was expanded to become the depository for literally thousands of pieces of Elvis memorabilia—the countless awards he won, his one hundred and twenty gold records, the scripts of his thirty-one feature films, his jump suits, his U.S. Army uniform, his guitars, his photo albums, the messages he received from Presidents (Carter, Nixon, Johnson, Hoover). Here, as elsewhere at Graceland, some personal tributes from his admirers are on exhibit—an amateur artist's chalk rendering of Elvis and Priscilla Presley's wedding photo, a devoted fan's birthday poem to their daughter Lisa Marie. The fans loved Elvis, and the feeling was mutual. He never discarded gifts received from his faithful followers, it is said, and these mementoes reportedly fill two Memphis warehouses.

ONE KETTLE STEW

A Native American recipe updated for today's convenience.

1 pound beef stew meat, cut in 1-inch cubes	1 bay leaf
All-purpose flour	½ teaspoon summer savory
Vegetable oil	1 teaspoon sugar
2½ cups boiling water	½ tablespoon lemon juice
2 tablespoons chopped onion	½ teaspoon Worcestershire sauce
½ clove garlic	¼ cup tomato juice
1½ teaspoons salt	½ cup sliced carrots
¼ teaspoon pepper	½ cup diced celery
¼ teaspoon paprika	1 cup pearl onions
Dash allspice	1 cup peeled and cubed potatoes

Dredge beef cubes in flour and brown in hot vegetable oil in large heavy kettle, preferably cast iron. Add boiling water, onion, garlic, salt, pepper, spices, herbs, sugar, lemon juice, Worcestershire sauce, and tomato juice. Cover tightly and simmer 2 hours. Add more water if needed.

Add vegetables and cook 30 minutes more. Remove bay leaf before serving.

Serves 4 to 6

Marilou Awiakta

RAZORBACK CASSEROLE

When it's first and ten once again, call time out, and score some points of your own.

2 cups Rice Krispies	1 10¾-ounce can cream of celery soup
2 cups cooked rice	1 5-ounce can evaporated milk
1 pound medium-hot sausage, browned and drained	Rice Krispies and grated Cheddar cheese for topping
2 cups grated sharp Cheddar cheese	

In buttered baking dish, layer half of Rice Krispies, rice, sausage, and cheese. Repeat layers one time. Combine soup and milk, blend well, and pour over layers. Top with final layer of Rice Krispies and grated cheese. Cook at 350 degrees for 45 minutes or until bubbly and brown.

Serves 6

Katherine Leftwich
Forrest City, Arkansas

DR. WARRICK'S SICILIAN SPAGHETTI

A recipe brought back from Sicily after World War II and flavored with memories.

1 pound ground chuck	2 pinches crushed rosemary
1 medium onion, diced	½ teaspoon pepper or lemon pepper
1 medium green bell pepper, diced	½ teaspoon celery salt
1 6-ounce can tomato paste	Salt to taste
1 14½-ounce can whole tomatoes	Garlic salt to taste
1 clove garlic, minced	1 tablespoon Worcestershire sauce
½ teaspoon summer savory (if unavailable, use thyme)	1 7-ounce package spaghetti
	Parmesan cheese, freshly grated

Brown meat over low heat. Add onion and bell pepper, sauté, and drain well. Place in heavy saucepan and add tomato paste, tomatoes, and seasonings. Simmer at least 1½ hours, stirring occasionally. Add all salt during last ½ hour.

Cook spaghetti according to package directions. Top with sauce and sprinkle with Parmesan cheese.

Note: This recipe may be doubled or tripled. If tripled, increase cooking time to 2½ hours or more.

Serves 4

Mrs. Bill Herrington

SOUTHERN BELL SURPRISE CHOPS

Pork chops in disguise. A refreshingly different way to serve a standard favorite.

8 pork chops, thin breakfast-cut	2 eggs, beaten
3 tablespoons vegetable shortening	1½ cups plain white corn meal
Salt and pepper to taste	Lemon wedges

Remove bone and excess fat from pork chops. Pound chops between two sheets of wax paper to ⅛-inch thickness. In 12-inch skillet, melt shortening until water pops when dropped into skillet. Lightly salt and pepper chops. Dip into eggs and dredge in corn meal. Lay gently in hot shortening. Cook 1 minute on one side and ½ minute on other side, or until golden brown. Serve with lemon wedges.

Serves 4

Elizabeth Haney Bell

FILLET PAULETTE

An outstanding entrée from one of Memphis' most popular restaurants whose Old World ambience is always inviting, whether for lunch or dinner, Sunday brunch, or late night after-the-concert sweets.

2 4-ounce fillets of beef tenderloin	¼ tomato, julienne
Cracked pepper	½ cup heavy cream
2 tablespoons butter	Dash lemon juice
¼ onion, julienne	1 ounce white wine
¼ green bell pepper, julienne	2 tablespoons Worcestershire sauce

Encrust fillets with cracked pepper and sauté in hot butter in skillet. Remove and set aside. In same skillet, sauté onion, bell pepper, and tomato, adding tomato last. (Add more butter if necessary for consistency of sauce.) Add cream, lemon juice, wine, and Worcestershire sauce, and stir to blend. Place fillets in cream sauce and cook on high heat until sauce, boils. Remove fillets from pan, arrange vegetables on top, and pour cream sauce over all.

Serves 1

Paulette's Restaurant
George Falls, Proprietor

IRMA'S BRISKET

As Irma Ginsberg of Savannah, Georgia, was fond of saying to her many busy friends, "This dish can be prepared while you sleep."

1 package onion soup mix	1 6-pound beef brisket
3 tablespoons Heinz 57 sauce	

Sprinkle soup mix and sauce over entire brisket and wrap securely, fat side up, in heavy foil. Place in roasting pan, cover, and bake 1 hour at 500 degrees. Turn off heat but do not open oven. Let brisket stand in oven at least 8 hours.

Remove brisket from oven, reserve pan gravy, and chill. (If meat is done but not tender, rewrap and cook 45 to 60 minutes longer at 300 degrees.) Chill pan gravy and skim fat. Slice brisket thinly, place in gravy, and warm before serving.

Serves 10 to 12

Lyda G. Parker

KIBBIE

A spiced Lebanese dish with many variations. This one features beef with bulgur wheat.

1 cup bulgur wheat (#1)	2 teaspoons salt
2 pounds round steak	½ teaspoon pepper
1 large onion	½ cup butter, melted

Cover wheat with water and set aside to soak. Cut steak and onions into cubes and grind in small batches in food processor until somewhat like sausage in consistency. Drain wheat. In large bowl mix meat mixture with wheat, salt, and pepper. Knead with hands until well-mixed. Cover bottom of buttered 9 x 13-inch baking pan with portion of wheat mixture. Spread filling evenly over wheat layer. Make flat patties (tortilla-like) of remaining wheat mixture, lay them side by side on top of filling, and smooth edges together. Cut through kibbie layers with sharp knife to make diamond-shaped pieces. Drizzle with butter, making sure butter is drizzled into cuts. Bake at 350 degrees for 30 minutes or until browned.

Filling

2 tablespoons butter	1 teaspoon cinnamon
½ pound coarsely ground chuck or round	1 tablespoon lemon juice
1 small onion, chopped	3 tablespoons pine nuts
	Salt and pepper to taste

Melt butter in large skillet and brown meat. Add onions and cook until clear. Stir in cinnamon, lemon juice, pine nuts, salt, and pepper. Cover and simmer 20 minutes to blend seasonings.

Serves 10 to 12

Mrs. J. T. Jabbour

BACKSTAGE SPECIAL

A star attraction for hungry actors at cast dinners between Sunday matinées and evening performances at Theatre Memphis.

1 pound ground round steak	1 tablespoon chili powder
1 medium onion, chopped	or more to taste
1 clove garlic, chopped	1 15½-ounce can kidney
1 8-ounce can tomato sauce	or chili beans with juice
⅓ to ½ cup tomato juice	1 8-ounce bag corn chips
(or water or consommé)	Shredded lettuce
¼ teaspoon oregano	Chopped onion

Brown meat, onion, and garlic in skillet. Stir in tomato sauce, tomato juice, oregano, and chili powder. In greased 2-quart baking dish, alternately layer meat mixture, beans, and corn chips, ending with corn chips. Cover and bake 45 minutes at 350 degrees. Uncover and bake another 10 minutes.

Just before serving, top with shredded lettuce and onion.

Serves 4 to 6

Betty A. Jennings

CHAFING DISH BEEF BARBECUE

Great for buffet suppers or parties after the game. Makes its own sauce as it cooks.

1 3-pound chuck roast,	3 tablespoons sugar
well-trimmed	¼ cup Worcestershire sauce
1 yellow onion, chopped	1 teaspoon salt
1 28-ounce can whole	½ teaspoon pepper
tomatoes with juice	Dash Tabasco sauce, optional
½ cup water (or more	
tomatoes, if preferred)	

Place roast in large heavy pot. Mix all remaining ingredients, add to roast, cover, and simmer at least 3 hours. After 2 hours, break meat apart from time to time with wooden spoon, stirring occasionally. When meat is fully shredded, uncover and continue simmering to reduce liquid to desired consistency for barbecue. Serve from chafing dish on small party-sized buns.

Serves 18 to 20

Mrs. James Lowe
Iowa City, Iowa

ZUCCHINI PIZZA PIE

A great one-dish meal.

1½ pounds zucchini	1 large onion, chopped
1 cup shredded mozzarella	1 8-ounce can tomato sauce
cheese	2 teaspoons dried oregano
1 cup shredded Cheddar cheese	1 green bell pepper, cut in
2 eggs, lightly beaten	strips
¼ teaspoon salt	½ pound fresh mushrooms,
¼ teaspoon garlic salt	sliced
1 pound ground beef	⅓ cup grated Parmesan cheese

Shred and thoroughly drain enough zucchini to measure 4 cups. Mix zucchini with ½ cup mozzarella and ½ cup Cheddar cheese. Add eggs, mix well, and press mixture into greased 5 x 10-inch baking pan. Bake 10 minutes at 400 degrees.

Sprinkle salt and garlic salt in skillet over medium heat. Add beef and cook until crumbly. Add onion, cook until soft, and drain. Stir in tomato sauce and oregano, and spoon beef mixture over zucchini mixture. Arrange pepper strips and mushrooms on top and sprinkle with all remaining cheeses. Bake at 400 degrees for 30 minutes or until cheeses are bubbly.

Serves 6

Jane Chavis

STUFFED PORK SHOULDER

A great winter's night dish.

6 to 8 pound boned pork	Spiced peaches
shoulder (removing bone	
creates pocket for stuffing)	

Fill shoulder with stuffing and tie firmly with string. Roast 40 minutes per pound at 350 degrees. Garnish with spiced peaches.

Stuffing

4 cups soft bread crumbs	1 14-ounce can whole kernel
2 teaspoons salt	corn
4 tablespoons minced green	4 tablespoons butter, melted
bell pepper	2 eggs, beaten
2 tablespoons minced onion	

Combine all ingredients and mix well.

Serves 8 to 10

Evelyn Palmer

CHOUCROUTE

A heavenly dish.

5 cups sauerkraut	6 peppercorns
½ pound bacon	10 juniper berries
½ cup sliced carrots	2 to 3 cups beef bouillon
1 cup sliced onion	Salt to taste
4 sprigs parsley	3 smoked Polish sausages
1 bay leaf	Grey Poupon mustard

Drain and soak sauerkraut in cold water for 15 minutes, changing water every 5 minutes. Squeeze out as much water as possible and place in 3½ to 5-quart baking dish.

Fry bacon until soft but not browned. Add carrots and onion, sauté until onions are soft, and mix with sauerkraut. Tie small bundle parsley, bay leaf, peppercorns, and juniper berries in cheesecloth, and place in baking dish. Add beef bouillon, and salt lightly.

Lay circle of buttered parchment paper over contents, cover, and set on middle rack of oven. Bake 2½ hours at 300 degrees. Add Polish sausages cut in 2-inch lengths and continue baking 1½ to 2 hours longer or until all liquid is absorbed. Serve with mustard.

Note: If juniper berries are unavailable, substitute 1 cup dry white wine and ¼ cup gin.

Serves 6

Roma Marmon

ELEGANT BEEF TIPS

A splendid, in-a-hurry company dish.

4 sirloin strip steaks	2 tablespoons butter
Salt and pepper to taste	12 to 16 fresh asparagus
1 cup wild rice	spears (or broccoli), cooked
16 large mushrooms, sliced	

Season steaks with salt and pepper, and cook on grill. Slice in strips when done. While steaks are grilling, cook rice according to package directions. Sauté mushrooms in butter. To assemble for serving, layer in order wild rice, beef strips, and mushrooms. Spoon sauce over all and serve with asparagus topped with spoonful of sauce.

Sauce

1 cup butter	2 to 3 tablespoons dried parsley
6 egg yolks, lightly beaten	2 to 3 tablespoons tarragon
Juice of 2 to 3 lemons	flakes
2 to 3 tablespoons minced	Salt to taste
onion	Cayenne pepper to taste

Melt butter in top of double boiler over hot but not boiling water. As butter begins to liquefy, add egg yolks. Gradually add lemon juice, cooking and stirring until desired consistency is reached (too much will make mixture too thin). Stir in onion, parsley, tarragon, salt, and cayenne pepper, and serve immediately.

Serves 4 to 6

Mrs. Philip Kaminsky

SNOW-CAPPED LAMB CHOPS

Impressive in appearance and flavor.

6 sirloin lamb chops, cut ½-inch thick	½ cup sliced green onions (reserve tops)
2 tablespoons vegetable oil	1 3-ounce can chopped
Salt and pepper to taste	mushrooms, drained and
1 10½-ounce can beef	liquid reserved
consommé	3 tablespoons all-purpose flour
½ teaspoon thyme	1 tablespoon parsley flakes
½ cup chopped celery	1 cup sour cream

In heavy saucepan or Dutch oven, slowly brown chops in small amount hot oil, and sprinkle with salt and pepper. Drain. Add consommé, thyme, celery, and onions. Cover and simmer 30 to 45 minutes or until meat is done. Set chops aside.

In small bowl, blend reserved mushroom liquid slowly into flour and gradually stir into consommé mixture in saucepan. Cook over medium heat, stirring constantly until thickened. Add mushrooms and parsley. Place chops evenly in sauce and top with dollop of sour cream. Cover and heat 2 to 3 minutes. Sprinkle with reserved green onion tops.

Note: May be prepared ahead by cooking until done and setting chops aside, saving all pan juices. When ready to serve, prepare sauce as directed and proceed with remainder of recipe.

Serves 6

Margaret D. Wilson

CASSOULET TOULOUSAINE

The cassoulet is a classic dish whose ancestry lies in the southwest of France, said region having enriched the world with this grand mélange of tastes.

2 wild ducks, breasted and meat cubed
½ pound lean pork loin, cubed
½ pound lean loin of lamb, cubed
2 to 4 tablespoons vegetable oil
3 teaspoons chopped garlic
1 teaspoon thyme
2 bay leaves
½ to 1 cup dry white wine

2 cups chopped onion
4 cups chopped and crushed imported canned tomatoes
Salt and pepper to taste
6 cups canned white kidney beans (cannelini)
1 pound Polish sausage, sliced and sautéed
3 tablespoons fine fresh bread crumbs
2 tablespoons butter, melted

Lightly brown duck, pork, and lamb in portion of oil. Cover, reduce heat to medium-low, and cook 12 minutes. Add 1 teaspoon garlic, ½ teaspoon thyme, and 1 bay leaf, and stir. Add wine and mix well. Cover and cook 20 minutes.

Separately sauté onion and 2 teaspoons garlic in remaining oil for 5 minutes. Add tomatoes, salt, pepper, and remaining thyme and bay leaf. Cook 10 minutes. Add beans, sausage, and meat mixture. Pour into baking dish, sprinkle with bread crumbs, and drizzle with butter. Bake at 400 degrees for 10 minutes or until crumbs are lightly browned.

Note: Canned Italian tomatoes may be substituted for imported tomatoes, and great white northern beans for canned white kidney beans.

Serves 8 to 10

L. Jackson Powell

CHAR SU

Delicious thin slices of seasoned roast pork, Cantonese-style.

2 pounds pork tenderloin
½ tablespoon hoisin sauce
½ tablespoon heavy soy sauce
1 tablespoon light soy sauce

3 tablespoons sugar
½ teaspoon salt
Several drops red food coloring

Cut tenderloin across grain lengthwise into pieces 6 to 7-inches wide. Mix remaining ingredients, pour over meat, and marinate overnight, turning to coat evenly.

Line small roasting pan with aluminum foil and add 1 to 2 inches of water. Arrange meat on rack above water. (This prevents meat from drying out. Add more water during cooking time if necessary.) Roast 1¼ hours at 375 degrees, turning meat after 45 minutes. Slice very thin and serve hot or cold as hors d'oeuvre. Can also be served over rice as entrée, or added to stir-fry vegetables or to soup.

Serves 8 to 10 as hors d'oeuvre
    or 4 to 5 as entrée

Jeanine and Francis Mah

CONFUSED BEEF TENDERLOIN ON THE GRILL

Makes an elegant picnic sandwich. Frequent turning on the grill, so we are told, confuses the juices and creates a fine basting mixture.

1 8-pound tenderloin of beef, well-trimmed

Sandwich rolls
Durkee's Dressing

Place tenderloin in marinade and let stand for 2 to 5 hours, turning often.

Prepare charcoal grill. When coals are ready, grill tenderloin 10 to 15 minutes on each side, turning often to blend juices. Slice thin and serve on thick roll with Durkee's dressing.

Marinade
1 8-ounce bottle Italian dressing
1 5-ounce bottle soy sauce

Juice of 2 to 3 lemons
Freshly ground black pepper
Dash garlic powder

Combine all ingredients and mix well.

Serves 14 to 16

E. W. Atkinson

Sunday Afternoon Snack at the Ball Game

Professional sports first came to Memphis in 1902, along with a baseball team known during its brief lifetime as the Memphis Turtles. (The name was in honor of the team's playing field, located on a section of partially filled-in lowland called the Red Elms Bottoms, where poor drainage caused the infield to slope away from the pitcher's mound so steeply it resembled the back of a turtle.) But while baseball may be the oldest game in town, it's certainly not the only one. Sports-enthusiastic Memphis has something for everybody.

The Liberty Bowl Football Classic, a nationally televised post-season collegiate game, which moved from Philadelphia to Memphis in 1965, is presented annually during the Christmas holidays with a spectacular, patriotic half-time show. And beginning in 1989, one of the three U.S. military academy teams, the winner of the Commander-in-Chief's Trophy, will participate annually. Each year in February, the Volvo Tennis Indoor Championships are held at the Racquet Club of Memphis, where such internationally famed players as Borg, Connors, McEnroe, Edberg, Agassi, and Gilbert have accepted the winner's title. Summer brings the Professional Golf Association Tour's annual stop in the city, the Federal Express St. Jude Classic. All proceeds from the event (more than two and a half million dollars, to date) benefit St. Jude Children's Research Hospital in Memphis, founded in 1962 by entertainer Danny Thomas, and dedicated to the treatment of children's catastrophic diseases. In the fall, the Memorial Stadium parking lots are filled with tailgate parties when old football rivals like Memphis State University and Ole Miss (the University of Mississippi) meet. The Memphis State basketball team has twice made the NCAA Final Four, rising once to the finals, and MSU fans jealously guard their season tickets. The spring of 1987 brought yet another brand of spectator sports to the city, with the opening of the Memphis International Motorsports Park.

Baseball, however, because of a once and always team called the Memphis Chicks (in honor of the Chickasaw Indians), will eternally claim the number-one place in the affections of innumerable Memphis sports-lovers. Chicks enthusiasts love to swap stories about the glory days of the 1930s: When the mayor would give city employees a half-day holiday to assure a big opening day crowd for the Chicks. When the Chicks triumphed over teams like the Atlanta Crackers, the New Orleans Pelicans, the Chattanooga Lookouts, and the Arkansas Travelers to win the Southern League pennant. When players like Pete Gray, the one-armed ''King of the Southern League'' with a .333 batting average, packed the stadium, and was the hero of hundreds of young Chickasaw Buddies.

The Buddies were Chicks fans, aged five to fifteen, who attended every game in their blue Buddy caps, and followed the strict rules encoded on their Buddy Cards: (l) Root for the Chickasaws, and be respectful and polite to counselors, teachers, and parents. (2) Stay in the Buddy Section. (3) Be clean in body, talk, and play. (4) Do not throw things at the game. (5) Do not use tobacco.

After the team's old wooden stadium at Russwood Park burned in 1960, baseball all but disappeared from Memphis for a few years, along with the familiar Chicks. It made a comeback some years later as the Memphis Blues. Then, in 1976, local business-man and baseball fan Avron Fogelman became owner of a new Southern League team in Memphis. A contest was held to select a team name, and the overwhelming choice was ''The Chicks.'' Baseball was back in town.

THE PICTURE: *The Chicks are back in town, and on this late Sunday afternoon, the steel structure of the Chicks Stadium forms a wind tunnel of sorts, funneling a cool breeze across the crowd of spectators. Vendors roam the stands selling beverages and foods with inviting, nostalgia-enhanced aromas and flavors—popcorn, fresh-roasted peanuts, and that most appropriate of all baseball game treats, hot dogs. A pre-game warmup, in progress in the background with the home team at bat, is seen from the press box through the protective screen that guards fans in the stands from stray fly balls.*

THE FOOD: *A tray of all-American hot dogs is presented, each with a different topping or accompaniment. The glasses hold beer and a soft drink.*

CROWN ROAST OF PORK
WITH APPLE-WALNUT DRESSING

For those times when you want to present something especially wonderful.

Crown roast of pork, prepared   Salt and pepper to taste
  by butcher to allow   All-purpose flour
  1 to 2 ribs per person

Season meat with salt and pepper, and roast 20 to 30 minutes per pound at 350 degrees. One hour before completion of roasting time, remove from oven and lightly fill cavity with stuffing (do not pack). Return to oven for completion of cooking time.

When roast is done, pour drippings into small saucepan. Gradually blend in enough flour to make gravy.

Apple-Walnut Stuffing
2 tablespoons chopped onion   ½ cup chopped walnuts
2 tablespoons butter   Beef stock
1 package herb-flavored   Greek seasoning to taste
  stuffing mix   Paprika to taste
2 cups finely chopped
  unpeeled apples

Sauté onion in butter, add stuffing mix, and toss lightly. Mix in apples and walnuts. Add enough stock to hold stuffing together and season to taste with Greek seasoning and paprika.

Serves 6 to 8

Frances Keenan Averitt

SAVORY BAVARIAN GOULASH

Best made the day before for full flavor.

3 tablespoons vegetable oil   2 tablespoons vinegar
1 large onion, diced   1 tablespoon tomato paste
5 tablespoons Hungarian   2 tablespoons caraway seeds
  sweet paprika (no substitute)   ½ teaspoon marjoram
1 pound chuck roast, cut in   1 clove garlic, chopped
  1-inch cubes   8 cups water
All-purpose flour   4 large potatoes, peeled and
1 teaspoon salt   diced
½ teaspoon pepper

Heat oil in 3-quart saucepan and sauté onions until golden. Sprinkle with paprika and sauté 5 minutes, stirring constantly over very low heat. Coat beef heavily with flour. Add to onion and paprika mixture and stir well. Sear meat until dark brown in color and thick paste has formed. Sprinkle with salt and pepper, add vinegar, stir in tomato paste, and simmer 5 minutes. Add caraway seeds, marjoram, garlic, and water. Bring to boil, cover, and simmer gently 3 hours.

Add diced potatoes and cook slowly 30 minutes or until meat and potatoes are thoroughly cooked. Adjust seasonings and serve in deep bowls with a spoonful of sour cream on top.

Note: The secret of this goulash is in the thorough browning of the meat, creating the thick, dark paste, and the Hungarian sweet paprika.

Serves 6

Glenda Parsons
Cape Girardeau, Missouri

ENCHILADAS

For lovers of Mexican food, here's the real thing.

1 pound ground beef   2 10-ounce cans hot enchilada
½ cup chopped onion   sauce
2 tablespoons jalapeño relish   1 8-ounce package Monterey
1 16-ounce can refried beans   Jack cheese, grated
Salt to taste   1 6-ounce can sliced ripe olives
Corn oil   1 4 ounce can whole green
12 corn tortillas   chilies, chopped

Brown ground beef in skillet and drain. Add onion and sauté briefly. Add jalapeño relish, beans, and salt. Mix well, cover, and set aside.

Soften tortillas in hot oil in large skillet. Using 1 can enchilada sauce, dip each tortilla in sauce to coat. Spread half of remaining can enchilada sauce in bottom of 9 x 13-inch baking dish. Place generous tablespoonful of beef mixture onto tortilla shell. Roll up tortillas and place in dish, seam-side down. Top with remaining enchilada sauce, cheese, olives, and chilies. Bake 30 minutes at 350 degrees.

Serves 6

Nicky Dwyer Ross
Forrest City, Arkansas

TENNESSEE SPICED ROUND

A traditional recipe from Traveller's Rest, historic home of Judge John Overton, near Nashville, Tennessee. It requires a seventeen day preparation period prior to serving date. Incredibly good!

Step 1
17 to 20 pound round of beef	2 cups salt
2 cups brown sugar	1 teaspoon black pepper

Trim fat from round of beef. Do not remove bone. Mix brown sugar with seasonings and rub into meat, coating thoroughly. Cover and refrigerate overnight in large glass, porcelain, or enamel container.

Step 2
1½ tablespoons nutmeg	1½ tablespoons allspice
1½ tablespoons cinnamon	1½ tablespoons black pepper
1½ tablespoons ginger	1 tablespoon cayenne pepper

Remove round from refrigerator and allow juices to drain from it back into container. Mix spices and rub firmly into round. Return meat to container and refrigerate. Turn round in spiced marinade once a day for 2 weeks. Keep refrigerated.

Step 3
2 pounds beef suet	½ teaspoon ginger
1 teaspoon salt	½ teaspoon allspice
½ teaspoon nutmeg	½ teaspoon black pepper
½ teaspoon cinnamon	½ teaspoon cayenne pepper

Remove round from marinade. Discard marinade. Grind beef suet with salt and spices. Make deep holes with sharp paring knife in both sides of round and stuff seasoned suet into holes. Tie spiced round in heavy pudding bag or cheesecloth. (Tradition would require an old pillowcase, linen or cotton—no synthetics.) Cover round with water and boil in large covered pot 15 minutes per pound. Cool and refrigerate another day before serving.

Thinly slice spiced round horizontally. (Keep bone in round as it helps in carving.) Serve on nut bread with horseradish sauce and catsup.

Note: Keeps in refrigerator for 1 week. Freezes well.

Serves 40

Ellen Dixon

BROCCOLI-HAM ROLL-UPS

A perfect little luncheon dish.

4 tablespoons butter	2 cups grated Cheddar cheese
4 tablespoons all-purpose flour	½ pound Virginia country
½ teaspoon salt	ham, thinly sliced
1 teaspoon dry mustard	2 10-ounce packages frozen
2 to 2½ cups milk	broccoli spears, cooked

Melt butter in large skillet and blend in flour, salt, and mustard. Gradually stir in milk and cook until slightly thickened, stirring constantly. Add cheese and continue stirring until melted. Do not overcook.

Cut each ham slice in half and roll around broccoli spear. Place in greased baking dish and cover with cheese mixture. Bake at 350 degrees about 20 minutes or until bubbly.

Serves 6

Mary M. Sutton

BEEF ROULADEN

A good German recipe for spicy stuffed beef rolls.

4 large pieces boneless round steak, cut ¼-inch thick	All-purpose flour
	Butter or vegetable shortening
Salt and freshly ground black pepper to taste	4 cups water
	1 teaspoon Kitchen Bouquet
4 tablespoons prepared mustard	½ teaspoon oregano
4 slices uncooked bacon	1 small bay leaf
4 round slices onion	2 beef bouillon cubes
4 dill pickles, quartered lengthwise	

Season beef slices with salt and pepper, and cover each with 1 tablespoon mustard. Top each with slice of bacon and onion and 4 slices pickle. Roll beef tightly and tie securely with string. Lightly sprinkle rolls with flour and sauté in butter in heavy saucepan until browned. Add water, Kitchen Bouquet, oregano, bay leaf, and bouillon, bring to boil, and simmer 1½ to 2 hours.

Place beef rolls on serving platter and remove string. Remove bay leaf, thicken remaining liquid with flour to make gravy, and pour over rouladen (reserve some for gravy boat). Garnish platter with parsley.

Serves 4 to 6

Mrs. Helmut W. Grebe

GLAZED HAM LOAF

Rarely served that someone doesn't ask for the recipe. Good hot or cold. Try shaping into individual loaves for baking.

2 pounds cured ham, ground	1 cup milk
1½ pounds fresh pork, ground	1 onion, chopped
3 eggs	¼ cup finely chopped celery
1 cup bread crumbs	Salt and pepper to taste

Mix all ingredients, shape into loaf, and place in baking pan. Set pan in larger pan containing 1 to 2 inches water and bake ½ hour at 350 degrees. Pour off accumulated drippings and pour glaze over loaf. Continue baking 1½ hours, basting frequently. Serve with MUSTARD SAUCE SUPREME.

Glaze

1½ cups brown sugar	½ cup water
1 tablespoon prepared mustard	⅛ teaspoon ground cloves,
½ cup cider vinegar	optional

Combine ingredients, mix well, and boil 5 minutes.

Serves 10 to 12

Jean A. Morris
Little Rock, Arkansas

BEEF SALAMI

Makes a special homemade gift.

5 rounded teaspoons Morton's Tender Quick	2 teaspoons coarsely ground black pepper
1 teaspoon garlic powder	2 tablespoons peppercorns
2 teaspoons crushed red pepper	2 teaspoons mustard seed
2 teaspoons hickory-smoked salt	5 pounds ground beef

Combine seasonings, divide in five portions, and mix with beef, working with one pound beef and one part seasonings at a time. When all beef portions are seasoned, knead all 5 pounds together, cover, and refrigerate overnight.

On the second day, knead again and refrigerate.

On the third day, knead and roll in 1-pound logs. Place on rack on broiler pan and bake 4 hours at 225 degrees. Cool and wrap in foil. May be frozen.

Note: Morton's Tender Quick may be found either in canning section or in spice section of grocery store.

Yields five 1-pound logs

Mary Louise Grubbs

BARBECUE BRISKET

Put it in the oven and forget it. It will be ready when you are. So easy—so good.

1 4 pound beef brisket	1 5-ounce bottle Worcestershire sauce
1 4-ounce bottle liquid smoke	
Salt and pepper to taste	

Place meat lean side down on piece of heavy-duty foil, large enough to wrap around meat, in large shallow pan or roaster. Pour liquid smoke over brisket, seal in foil, and marinate overnight in refrigerator.

Pour off most of liquid. Season meat with salt and pepper, and cover with Worcestershire sauce. Place lean side up on foil, wrap, and bake 4½ hours at 300 degrees. Remove from oven, unwrap, and pour barbecue sauce over meat. Cover again with foil and bake another 1½ hours.

Chop and serve on buns, or slice thin and serve with remainder of sauce.

Barbecue Sauce

1½ cups catsup	½ cup brown sugar
¼ cup Worcestershire sauce	1 teaspoon celery salt
½ teaspoon sage	½ teaspoon Tabasco sauce

Combine all ingredients over low heat, stirring until well-blended.

Note: Barbecue sauce can be poured on brisket at beginning of cooking period. Beef may then be baked 6 hours without unwrapping.

Serves 12 to 14

Mrs. Don D. Varner

YAKITORI

Savory bits of Far East flavor.

2 pounds chicken thighs, boned

Cut each chicken thigh in 6 to 9 pieces and marinate in sauce for 1 hour. Thread pieces onto bamboo skewers. Broil at 350 degrees for 20 to 25 minutes or until well-done and tender, turning if necessary.

Sauce
5 tablespoons soy sauce
2 tablespoons sugar
1 tablespoon Mirin
  (sweet sake)
1 teaspoon Miso (bean paste),
  hot or sweet

½ teaspoon ginger extract
1 teaspoon sesame seeds,
  roasted
1 teaspoon sesame oil
1 green onion, chopped
⅓ teaspoon garlic powder

Combine all ingredients and blend well.

Note: Miso is available in specialty food shops or Oriental markets. Ginger extract may be made by peeling and grating fresh ginger, and squeezing through cheesecloth (powdered ginger is an acceptable substitute).

Serves 2 to 4

Mrs. Machiko Okamoto

SOUTHERN BAKED COUNTRY HAM IN A BLANKET

There's nothing better than country ham and this one gets special treatment.

10 to 12 pound country ham
1 cup brown sugar
2 tablespoons dry mustard
2 tablespoons ground cloves

1 teaspoon black pepper
4 cups all-purpose flour
1 liter ginger ale

Cover ham with water and simmer 15 minutes per pound on top of stove in covered pan. Remove skin and trim excess fat.

Combine sugar, mustard, cloves, pepper, and flour in mixing bowl. Gradually add ginger ale to flour until dough is of right consistency to roll out into pastry blanket. Cover ham with blanket and bake 20 minutes per pound at 325 degrees.

Remove blanket, slice ham, and serve hot or cold.

Serves 15 to 20

Mrs. Donald Thomas

FLANK STEAK SALAD

A great main dish salad that's good hot or cold.

1 2½-pound flank steak,
  trimmed and cut against
  grain in 4-inch wide strips
½ cup olive oil
½ cup red wine vinegar
¼ cup soybean oil
¼ cup teriyaki sauce

1 tablespoon lime juice
1 tablespoon Oriental chili
  sauce
1 tablespoon oregano
1 tablespoon thyme
¼ cup brown sugar

Place steak in shallow baking dish. Combine remaining ingredients and pour over meat. Cover and refrigerate overnight.

Remove meat from marinade and place in hot ungreased frying pan. Cook to medium-rare doneness. Slice diagonally across the grain into strips ¼-inch wide. Combine steak and salad vegetables, cover with dressing, and mix well. Serve at room temperature (or hot if preferred).

Salad Vegetables
1½ pounds onions, julienne
1½ pounds red bell peppers,
  julienne
1½ pounds green bell peppers,
  julienne

1½ pounds new potatoes,
  julienne
1 tablespoon rosemary
1 tablespoon salt
2¼ teaspoons pepper

Spread onions and peppers in oiled large shallow pan in one layer. Spread potatoes in another oiled shallow pan in one layer. Sprinkle rosemary, salt, and pepper over both. Place pans in oven and bake 15 minutes at 400 degrees. Remove onions and peppers, and cool. Bake potatoes 5 minutes more. Remove from oven and cool.

Dressing
½ cup soybean oil
6 tablespoons red wine vinegar
1½ teaspoons salt

2¼ teaspoons minced garlic
1½ teaspoons rosemary

Combine all ingredients and mix well.

Serves 12 to 14

Mary Gray Sasser

RÔTI DE VEAU NIVERNAISE

Divinely good.

4 tablespoons butter	Bouquet garni of 1 leek, 1
3 tablespoons vegetable oil	sprig parsley, 1 bay leaf,
3 to 4 pound eye of round	and few peppercorns
veal roast	1 tablespoon tomato paste
2 carrots, coarsely chopped	1 teaspoon salt
1 small onion, chopped	2 slices bacon
1½ cups chicken broth	

Combine 2 tablespoons butter and 2 tablespoons oil in 5-quart Dutch oven, heat, add roast, and sauté.

In skillet, lightly brown carrots and onion in remaining butter and oil. Add chicken broth, bouquet garni, tomato paste, and salt. Place bacon on top of roast. Bring broth mixture to boil, pour over roast in Dutch oven, cover, and bake at 300 degrees for 1½ hours or until done to taste.

Remove roast from Dutch oven. Skim fat from liquid. Strain liquid and reserve. Prepare gravy by stirring 2 tablespoons beurre manié into 1 cup reserved liquid and simmering several minutes. (If thicker gravy is desired, increase beurre manié and adjust liquid.) Serve with sliced veal.

Note: To make beurre manié, cream together equal parts butter and flour. Store in refrigerator and use to thicken soups and gravies. For thin gravy, use 2 tablespoons to 1 cup liquid. Simmer several minutes to remove floury taste.

Serves 6

Carol M. Cherry

SAUSAGE STRUDEL

A delicious treat. Great for brunch or special breakfasts.

2 medium cooking apples,	¾ cup dry bread crumbs
peeled and chopped	¼ teaspoon cinnamon
¼ cup raisins	⅛ teaspoon nutmeg
2 pounds fresh pork sausage,	2 eggs, beaten
cooked and well drained	2 tablespoons milk
2 tablespoons water	12 phyllo sheets
¾ cup chopped pecans	Melted butter

In skillet, cook apples and raisins in water until tender. Return sausage to skillet, and add nuts, 2 tablespoons crumbs, and spices. Mix eggs with milk, stir into mixture, and cool.

Place damp towel on work surface and cover with wax paper. Lay 2 phyllo sheets on top of each other on wax paper (do not get phyllo wet), brush with butter, and sprinkle with 1 tablespoon crumbs. Cover with 1 phyllo sheet, brush with butter, and sprinkle with 1 tablespoon crumbs. Repeat single sheet layering procedure three times (total 6 sheets per strudel). Spoon half of sausage mixture along long edge of phyllo, roll up lengthwise, using towel as aid, and place on greased baking sheet. Brush lightly with butter. Make second strudel with remaining sausage mixture and phyllo sheets. Make diagonal slits on top of each strudel. Bake at 350 degrees for 45 minutes or until golden brown. (May be frozen. Bring to room temperature before baking.)

Serves 12 to 14

Dorothye Moore

VEAL HAVARTI

Fresh herbs, fresh tomatoes, and Havarti—wonderful with veal.

1 2-pound veal round	1 medium onion, chopped
1 cup bread crumbs	1 to 2 cloves garlic, chopped
⅓ cup freshly grated Parmesan	3 large tomatoes, peeled
cheese	and mashed
1 teaspoon chopped fresh	1 tablespoon chopped fresh basil
oregano (½ teaspoon dried)	(1½ teaspoons dried)
2 eggs, beaten	1 to 2 dashes Tabasco sauce
Salt and black pepper to taste	¾ pound Havarti cheese, sliced
Olive oil	Freshly grated Parmesan cheese
2 tablespoons butter	for topping

Cut veal in several pieces and pound thin, about ⅛-inch. Mix crumbs with Parmesan cheese and oregano. Dip veal in egg and coat with crumbs. Season with salt and pepper. Pour olive oil into skillet to measure ⅛-inch deep and add butter. Sauté veal pieces until golden brown.

In separate pan, sauté onions and garlic in small amount of olive oil and butter. Stir in tomatoes, basil, and Tabasco sauce. Cover and simmer 15 minutes.

In baking dish, layer in order sauce, veal, and Havarti. Repeat layers once and top with layer of sauce. Sprinkle with additional Parmesan cheese. Bake uncovered 30 minutes at 350 degrees.

Serves 4 to 6

Mrs. Richard H. Mackie, Jr.

POULTRY

CHICKEN WITH FRUIT SAUCE

The sauce gives this chicken a delectable taste.

1 cup crushed corn flakes	1/4 teaspoon pepper
1/3 cup toasted sesame seeds	3 chicken breasts, halved
2 tablespoons chopped parsley	2 tablespoons butter, melted
1/4 cup grated Parmesan cheese	1 orange, thinly sliced

Combine corn flakes, sesame seeds, parsley, cheese, and pepper. Skin and bone chicken and pound each piece to 1/4-inch thickness. Dip chicken in butter and coat with seasoned crumb mixture. Place on lightly greased baking sheet and bake 20 minutes at 425 degrees.

Remove to serving dish, pour fruit sauce over chicken, and serve garnished with orange slices.

Fruit Sauce

3/4 cup fresh orange juice	1 teaspoon Dijon mustard
1/2 cup fresh lemon juice	1/4 teaspoon ground ginger
1/2 cup red currant jelly	2 tablespoons butter
1 tablespoon white wine	1 to 2 tablespoons cornstarch

Combine juices, jelly, wine, mustard, and ginger, and heat in saucepan until warm. In another saucepan, melt butter. Blend in 1 tablespoon cornstarch, and slowly add warm juice mixture. Cook over low heat until somewhat thickened, stirring constantly. Simmer 5 minutes and remove from heat.

Serves 4 to 6

Mark Robinson

CHICKEN RIGANATO

A chicken dish that couldn't be easier and couldn't be better.

2 medium fryers or broilers, cut in serving pieces	Juice of 2 lemons
Salt and pepper to taste	1 to 2 cloves garlic, minced
3/4 teaspoon oregano	1/4 cup butter
	1/2 cup water

Season chicken with salt, pepper, oregano, lemon juice, and garlic. Place in broiling pan, skin side up. Dot with butter and add water in bottom of pan. Bake uncovered at 350 degrees for 1 hour or until tender and golden brown, basting occasionally.

Serves 4 to 6

Helen Vergos

SWEET 'N' SASSY CHICKEN SALAD

Great summertime salad. A grand blend of flavors and texture.

3 cups cooked chicken, cut in bite-size pieces	1/2 cup chopped celery
1 cup cashews	1 cup fresh pineapple pieces
1/2 cup chopped scallions	1 apple, peeled and chopped
	1 cup raisins

Combine all ingredients and toss with dressing.

Dressing

3/4 cup mayonnaise	2 teaspoons lemon juice
3 tablespoons chutney	2 teaspoons curry powder
1/4 cup sour cream	

Combine all ingredients and mix well.

Note: For a nice taste, stir-fry chicken in peanut oil.

Serves 6

Brenda Wolf

ZUCCHINI CHICKEN BAKE

Full of flavor and all dressed-up for a special occasion.

2 boneless chicken breasts, halved	1 cup grated Parmesan cheese
5 tablespoons olive oil	1 pound small zucchini, sliced
1/4 cup lemon juice	1/2 cup chopped onion
Pepper to taste	1 6-ounce can tomato paste
1 bay leaf	1 teaspoon salt
4 tablespoons butter	2 eggs

Place chicken in shallow baking dish. Combine olive oil, lemon juice, pepper, and bay leaf, pour over chicken, and marinate 1 hour.

Melt butter in skillet. Remove chicken from marinade and sauté about 3 minutes on each side. Place in 2-quart baking dish and cover with half of cheese. In same skillet, sauté zucchini and onion about 5 minutes. Add tomato paste and salt, cook 5 minutes more, and pour over chicken. Beat eggs with remaining cheese and pour over chicken. Bake at 350 degrees for 20 to 30 minutes or until crust is golden brown and sauce is bubbly.

Serves 4

Mrs. Dale Riggins

POPPY SEED CHICKEN

A long-time favorite recipe-about-town. Good served over rice.

2 pounds boned chicken breasts
Celery leaves
1 small onion, chopped
1 clove garlic, chopped
1 cup sour cream
1 10 ¾ ounce can cream of chicken soup
2 tablespoons poppy seeds
6 tablespoons butter, melted
2 cups Ritz cracker crumbs

Combine chicken, celery leaves, onion, and garlic in large saucepan and cover with water. Cover and cook 30 minutes or until tender. Remove chicken and allow to cool.

Cut chicken in pieces and place in large baking dish. Combine sour cream, soup, and poppy seeds, and pour over chicken. Mix butter and cracker crumbs and spread on top of casserole. Sprinkle with more poppy seeds, cover with foil, and bake 30 minutes at 350 degrees.

Serves 6 to 8

John H. Sanguinetti III

LEMON CHICKEN SCALOPPINE

Light and luscious.

1 pound boneless chicken breasts
¼ cup all-purpose flour
½ teaspoon salt
¼ teaspoon pepper
2 teaspoons butter
2 teaspoons vegetable oil
3 tablespoons dry white wine
2 to 3 tablespoons fresh lemon juice
¼ cup chopped green onion

Pound chicken between sheets of wax paper. Combine flour, salt, and pepper in plastic bag. Add chicken and shake to coat. Heat 1 teaspoon butter and 1 teaspoon oil in skillet and sauté chicken 3 to 5 minutes on each side until browned. Transfer to warm platter. Combine remaining butter and oil with wine, lemon juice, and onion in skillet and boil until slightly reduced. Pour over chicken and serve.

Serves 2 to 3

Anne W. Brown

BARBECUED CHICKEN ON TOASTED BUNS

A traditional Southern dish, updated.

4 medium onions, chopped
2 cloves garlic, minced
4 green bell peppers, chopped
1 bunch celery, finely chopped
Bacon drippings
2 cups chicken broth
1 tablespoon prepared horseradish
Salt and pepper to taste
1 cup vinegar
2¼ cups chili sauce
1 14-ounce bottle catsup
½ cup Worcestershire sauce
Hot sauce to taste
1 tablespoon dry mustard
1 teaspoon curry powder
1 large hen, cooked, boned, and chopped

Sauté onions, garlic, bell peppers, and celery in bacon drippings. Add remaining ingredients except chicken, and simmer 1 hour.

Add chicken and simmer 2 to 3 hours more. Serve hot from chafing dish on toasted buns.

Serves 8 to 10

Mrs. William H. Houston III
Washington, D.C.

FIESTA CHILE CHICKEN

Combines the flavor of the Southwest with the versatile chicken and proves a cause for celebration.

4 whole chicken breasts
2 teaspoons salt
1 teaspoon pepper
1 bay leaf
1 10¾-ounce can cream of chicken soup
1 10¾-ounce can cream of mushroom soup
1 10-ounce can Rotel tomatoes with green chilies
12 corn tortillas, torn in small pieces
2 onions, finely chopped
3 cups grated sharp Cheddar cheese

Cook chicken in water with salt, pepper, and bay leaf. Remove chicken and reserve ½ cup stock. Cut chicken into large bite-size pieces and set aside.

Combine reserved stock, soups, and tomatoes with chilies, adjust seasonings, and mix well. In 3-quart baking dish, layer in order tortillas, chicken, soup mixture, onions, and cheese. Bake 30 to 40 minutes at 350 degrees.

Serves 6 to 8

Andrea Ricards Lapsley
Houston, Texas

Mother's Day at the Fourway Grill

For more than forty years, Mrs. Irene Cleaves, the Mississippi-born daughter of a Methodist minister, has been serving delicious food with caring kindness at the Fourway Grill, 998 Mississippi Boulevard. To open the restaurant, she and her husband Clint Cleaves raised fifteen hundred dollars soon after their marriage by mortgaging their home. Ask Mrs. Cleaves how the Fourway Grill got its name, and she explains: "From here you can go anywhere—north, south, east, and west." You can easily find your way back to the Fourway Grill, too, from any corner of the earth. Among the customers who have kept returning here over the years to enjoy mouth-watering, down-home treats are not only neighborhood residents, local politicians, downtown lawyers and businessmen, but also national celebrities, many of whose pictures adorn the restaurant walls: Nat "King" Cole, Dr. Martin Luther King, Jr., Lionel Hampton, Jesse Jackson, Alex Haley, Gladys Knight and the Pips, and Sugar Ray Robinson.

The Fourway Grill has, in fact, become a landmark in a neighborhood of landmarks. Mississippi Boulevard is lined with old houses and churches; a historic marker notes that Confederate troops once marched this way in pursuit of Union soldiers who had retreated behind the walls of a nearby state female college. Bethel Presbyterian church has provided a day nursery on this street for over fifty years. LeMoyne-Owen College, alma mater to scores of today's achieving black leaders of Memphis and the Mid-South, is nearby, and next door to the Fourway Grill is the notable old Mississippi Boulevard Church. Its long-time pastor, Reverend Blair T. Hunt, also served as principal of the neighborhood's Booker T. Washington High School, offering encouragement and guidance to young people for over thirty years, with "an iron hand in a velvet glove and a brass bell as his talisman." The bell, always carried with him, invariably got students' attention; legend has it that whenever the Warriors needed a touchdown at Booker T. Washington games, Reverend Hunt "just rang the bell and presto, they made it."

Elmwood Cemetery is a part of this venerable South Memphis neighborhood. To enter through its wrought-iron gates and walk down its narrow, carriage-size roads, beneath towering oaks, ancient magnolias and holly trees, hackberry and wild cherry, is to stroll through Memphis history. There is the stately Monument to the Confederate Dead keeping watch over rows and rows of small, stone markers bearing only a number. Famous local citizens whose names are engraved on the interesting old stone and marble monuments range all the way from one of the earliest civic leaders, John McLemore (who bought out the Memphis real estate interests of founding father General Andrew Jackson in 1823, and then, as a railroad builder, made—and lost—one of the city's first fortunes), to a man who was the dominant political power in Memphis and Shelby County throughout the first half of the twentieth century, the sometime mayor and congressman E. H. Crump. Here, too, is the final resting place of pioneer banker and real estate man Robert Church, known as "the South's first black millionaire," and remembered for creating Church Park on Beale Street, building the city's first public auditorium for blacks, and leading a depopulated, bankrupt Memphis back to recovery after the disastrous yellow fever epidemics of the 1870s, when he was the first businessman to buy bonds issued to fund repayment of the city's crippling debt. Most intriguing of all, perhaps, is the monument to a heroine of those dread epidemics. When yellow fever invaded Memphis in August 1878, Madame Annie Cook, proprietor of the Mansion House bordello on Gayoso Street, famous as "the wickedest spot between St. Louis and New Orleans," immediately closed down her establishment and turned its gilded and mirrored rooms into a hospital for fever victims. Nursing them, Annie Cook

THE PICTURE: *It is Mother's Day, and the Fourway Grill is expecting a large after-church crowd this Sunday. Two roses, one red and one white, mixed with a wisp of Baby's-breath, are placed on each table, carrying on the old Southern tradition of displaying roses on Mother's Day—white to remember a mother who is no longer living, red to pay tribute to one who is. The square white tables are covered with starched green cloths, the paneled walls are lined with plaques honoring the restaurant's owner, Mrs. Irene Cleaves, for her years of service to the community, and her contributions to the preservation of black heritage. Also on display are photographs of friends, neighbors, and celebrities who have gathered here through the years to enjoy big platters of such time-tested favorites as country-fried steak, neck bones, liver and onions, chitterlings, barbecued short ribs, vegetables that are delivered fresh each day by an old-time "market man," and fresh-from-the-stove desserts like Karo pecan pie, egg custard pie, and fresh peach cobbler.*

THE FOOD: *Pictured here are favorite Fourway Grill chicken dishes prepared— you guessed it—four ways: FOURWAY FRIED CHICKEN (served on a handsome ironstone platter that belonged to Mrs. Cleaves' mother), barbecued chicken, FOURWAY SMOTHERED CHICKEN with rich gravy, and FOURWAY BAKED CHICKEN AND DRESSING (corn bread dressing, of course).*

was herself struck down by the disease and died on September 11, 1878. A monument erected some years later over her unmarked grave in Elmwood Cemetery reads simply: "Annie Cook. A Nineteenth Century Mary Magdalene who gave her life to save the lives of others."

FOURWAY BAKED CHICKEN AND DRESSING

At the Fourway Grill, there is always a stock pot simmering on the back of the stove, rich with broth from chicken, turkey, and duck. Undoubtedly, the stock makes a crucial difference in this sumptuous dressing.

1 chicken, cut in 4 pieces	4 tablespoons margarine
Salt and white pepper to taste	1½ cups water
All-purpose flour	Paprika

Place chicken in lightly greased roasting pan and sprinkle with salt and pepper. Dust each piece with flour and place 1 tablespoon margarine on top. Add water to pan, cover, and bake covered 45 to 60 minutes at 350 degrees, occasionally basting with juices. Remove cover during last 15 minutes of baking time to allow chicken to brown. Sprinkle with paprika and serve with dressing.

Dressing

1 cup hot rich chicken broth, or more if needed	½ green bell pepper
5 to 6 corn muffins	2 eggs, beaten
1 cup cold water	4 tablespoons margarine, melted
6 biscuits or bread slices	2 teaspoons sage
1 small onion	Salt and black pepper to taste
4 ribs celery	

Pour broth over corn muffins and let stand for 15 minutes. Pour cold water over biscuits and let stand until biscuits are softened but not sticky. Mix together corn muffins and biscuits. Grind onion, celery, and bell pepper in food processor and add to bread mixture. Stir in remaining ingredients. (Mixture should be like very thick batter.) Add more broth if needed. Bake at 350 degrees for 45 to 60 minutes or until well set and lightly browned on top.

Serves 4

The Fourway Grill
Mrs. Irene Cleaves, Proprietor

FOURWAY SMOTHERED CHICKEN

One of those good, down-home dishes.

1 chicken	2 tablespoons all-purpose flour
Salt	Salt and pepper to taste
All-purpose flour	Water
Vegetable shortening	Cooked rice

Cut chicken in frying pieces, salt to taste, and dredge in flour. Melt enough shortening to measure 1 inch deep in skillet and heat to 350 degrees. Add chicken and fry, turning often until browned.

Remove crusty pieces and pour off all drippings except 2 tablespoons. Add 2 tablespoons flour to drippings and stir over low heat until smooth, adding water to make gravy. Season with salt and pepper. Place chicken in baking pan, cover with gravy, and bake at 350 degrees until heated thoroughly. Serve over rice.

Serves 4

The Fourway Grill
Mrs. Irene Cleaves, Proprietor

FOURWAY FRIED CHICKEN

The Fourway has its own way with fried chicken. It is served seven days a week to very happy customers.

1 chicken	1 egg
1 cup all-purpose flour	1 cup milk
Salt and pepper to taste	Vegetable oil

Cut chicken in frying pieces (2 breasts, 2 thighs, 2 legs, and 2 wings). Combine flour and seasonings in small paper bag and shake to mix. Blend egg with milk. Dip each piece of chicken in egg wash, toss in bag of seasoned flour to coat well, and shake off excess. Cook in hot oil in deep fryer for 20 minutes (oil must cover chicken). Chicken will rise to top when done. At that point, cook 5 minutes longer, drain briefly, and serve immediately.

Serves 4

The Fourway Grill
Mrs. Irene Cleaves, Proprietor

CHICKEN GOODY BAGS

A great little do-ahead treat for quick suppers for one or for several. Keep some on hand in the freezer.

6 chicken thighs, legs, or breast quarters	Salt
Lemon pepper	Vegetable oil

Season chicken pieces with lemon pepper and salt. Place each piece in square of foil, sprinkle each with 1 teaspoon oil, and wrap so that oil will not spill. Place on baking sheet and bake 35 to 40 minutes at 350 degrees. To brown, partially open foil package and broil 3 to 4 minutes.

Yields 6 goody bags

Marion D. Kendall

CHICKEN-WILD RICE CASSEROLE

Beware—there'll not be any left.

6 ribs celery, chopped	½ pound sharp Cheddar cheese, grated
1 onion, chopped	
3 tablespoons butter	1 6¾-ounce box mixed long grain and wild rice, cooked
2 cups chicken stock	
1 tablespoon Worcestershire sauce	1 hen or 4 whole chicken breasts, cooked, boned, and stock reserved
¼ teaspoon salt	
½ teaspoon pepper	1 3-ounce bottle stuffed green olives, chopped
1 10¾-ounce can cream of mushroom soup	
	1 cup chopped pecans

Sauté celery and onion in butter until tender. Add chicken stock, Worcestershire sauce, salt, and pepper, and simmer 15 minutes. Slowly stir in soup, cheese, and rice. Remove from heat and let stand for 1 hour.

Add chicken and olives. Place in greased 3-quart baking dish and sprinkle with chopped pecans. Bake at 350 degrees 30 to 45 minutes or until heated thoroughly.

Serves 10

Betty McMahon

CHICKEN ADEBO AND ITS COMPANION SOUP

A doubly-good, double-duty recipe.

Chicken Adebo

1 whole fryer plus extra chicken breast	½ cup white vinegar
	1 large onion, sliced
1 cup soy sauce	1 clove garlic, minced
½ cup water	2 cups cooked rice

Combine all ingredients except rice in heavy soup pot, cover, and cook 45 minutes over medium heat. When done, reserve wings, back, extra breast, and stock for Chicken Vegetable Soup Adebo. Serve remaining chicken pieces over rice.

Chicken Vegetable Soup Adebo

Reserved chicken pieces and stock from Chicken Adebo	1 15-ounce can herbed tomato sauce
2 cups mixed fresh vegetables, thinly sliced	½ cup barley
	1 teaspoon chili powder
1½ cups water	1 to 1½ cups V-8 juice

Bone and chop chicken and add with all other ingredients except V-8 juice to stock. Cook 45 minutes over medium heat or until vegetables are tender. Soup will be thick, but V-8 juice may be added if thinner soup is preferred.

Serves 4

Mrs. William H. Morse

CHICKEN MARSALA

Very simply prepared from an old Italian recipe.

2 chicken breasts, halved and skinned	1 medium onion, sliced
	¼ cup water
Salt and pepper to taste	½ cup Marsala
½ cup butter	

Season chicken with salt and pepper. Melt butter in large skillet. When very hot, add chicken, and brown on both sides for 5 minutes. Add onion and brown 2 minutes more. Reduce heat. Add water, cover, and simmer 20 minutes or until tender. Add Marsala and simmer another 10 minutes. If necessary, add more water. Serve over rice or noodles.

Serves 4

Mrs. Vincent de Frank

CHICKEN PINEAPPLE CURRY

Even non-curry fans will like this. Be creative with condiments.

2 medium onions, chopped
1 rib celery, chopped
2 apples, peeled, cored, and
  finely chopped
6 tablespoons butter
¼ cup all-purpose flour
1 tablespoon curry powder
1½ to 2 teaspoons salt
½ teaspoon pepper
½ teaspoon dry mustard
1 bay leaf
3 cups chicken broth
2 cups fresh pineapple
  chunks
1 cup light cream
4 cups chopped cooked chicken

In large skillet, sauté onions, celery, and apples in butter until tender but not browned. Sprinkle with flour and curry powder, stir, and cook 3 minutes. Add 1½ teaspoons salt, pepper, mustard, and bay leaf. Gradually stir in chicken broth and bring to boil. Add more salt if needed. Simmer 15 minutes over low heat, stirring occasionally. Remove bay leaf. Add pineapple and cream and cook 2 minutes. Add chicken to mixture and cook until heated through. Serve over rice.

Note: Substitute 1 cup coconut milk for 1 cup light cream. Extravagantly good!

Serves 4 to 5

Frances P. Elfstrom

FRIED CHICKEN STRIPS AND GRAVY

A different approach to the customary fried chicken. Makes a good appetizer when cut in small pieces.

8 to 10 boneless chicken breasts
Lawry's seasoned salt to taste
½ teaspoon paprika
¼ teaspoon garlic powder
Salt and pepper to taste
1 cup milk
½ cup all-purpose flour
Vegetable shortening

Season chicken well with seasoned salt, paprika, garlic powder, salt, and pepper. Dip chicken in milk, then in flour, and repeat process to coat chicken thoroughly.

Melt enough shortening to measure ½-inch deep in electric skillet. When shortening is hot, add chicken pieces and brown on one side. Turn chicken and cook until tender and browned on both sides, about 20 to 25 minutes. (Cooking time will vary according to size of chicken pieces.) Drain well on paper towels. Reserve pan drippings and crusty pieces for gravy.

Gravy

4 tablespoons pan drippings
2 tablespoons all-purpose flour
1 cup milk
1 cup hot water
Salt and pepper to taste

In smaller skillet, heat drippings, including crusty pieces. Blend in flour and stir until smooth. Gradually add milk and hot water, stirring constantly until mixture thickens. Add salt and pepper. (More liquid may be added if mixture becomes too thick.)

Serves 6 to 8

Edna Stiman

MAGGIE DIXON'S TARRAGON CHICKEN ASPIC

From carefully-kept Dixon family recipes through the courtesy of their former cook, Earl Louise Goosby.

1 3½-pound chicken
2 tablespoons chopped fresh
  tarragon (or 1 tablespoon
  dried)
¼ cup tarragon vinegar
½ cup dry white wine
1 onion, quartered
1½ teaspoons salt
8 cups water
1 envelope unflavored gelatin
2 tablespoons cold water
1 chicken bouillon cube
10 stuffed green olives,
  sliced in rings
4 ounces slivered almonds
HOMEMADE MAYONNAISE

Combine chicken, tarragon, tarragon vinegar, wine, onion, salt, and 8 cups water. Bring to boil, reduce heat, and simmer 45 minutes or until chicken is tender. Remove chicken and set stock aside to cool. Bone and dice chicken. Strain cooled stock and reserve.

Soften gelatin in cold water. Combine with 2 cups reserved stock (use bouillon cube to make more stock, if necessary) and pour ½ to ¾ cup mixture into bottom of chilled mold. Chill until partially set and then press olive rings onto top in desired pattern. Combine chicken, almonds, and remaining stock mixture and pour into partially set mold. Chill until set and serve with dollop of homemade mayonnaise.

Note: May also be made in individual molds, adjusting portions accordingly.

Serves 6

Mrs. Eric Catmur

A Cotton Man's Lunch from The Little Tea Shop

THE PICTURE: *The Weathersby Cotton Company is still doing business at the old stand, and mostly in the old way, on Front Street. Inside the cavernous old building, rough wooden bins cradle the soft cotton. Loose bits of fiber on the floors are swept up by porters in white cotton coats, and collected in long jute bags called "snakes" for return to the cotton gin to be reprocessed. Ancient dollies, dented and chipped by years of service at the railway station, stand by waiting to carry their heavy loads to the dock. The computers that hum in the Weathersby company's inner office are a concession to modernity, but the office walls are hung with old Shelby County maps and drawings of historic downtown buildings. This particular historic building also houses the unpretentious quarters of several other cotton merchants and an artist who paints in the natural daylight of a cotton classing room on the top floor. Each day the cotton men meet in the hallway and talk about crops, and they often lunch together at The Little Tea Shop just around the corner on Monroe, a favorite restaurant of Memphis cotton men since 1918. On this busy day, lunch was ordered in by one of the merchants, and the restaurant sent, as accompaniment, their decorative arrangement of cotton bolls, dried strawflowers, Baby's-breath, and yarrow.*

THE FOOD: *This is The Little Tea Shop's popular LACY'S SPECIAL, consisting of cornsticks split into halves, topped with baked chicken, covered with rich pan gravy, and served over rice. Along with this delectable dish (named for a well-known cotton broker who was one of the restaurant's frequent customers) comes SOUTHERN TURNIP GREENS and potlikker (the liquid from the pot where the greens were cooked), cole slaw, more cornsticks, the indispensable HOT PEPPER SAUCE to add extra flavor to the turnip greens, apple cobbler for dessert, and sweetened iced tea.*

Always, from the very beginning, cotton has played a leading role in the Memphis economy. It probably always will. But for several well-remembered decades, during the city's determined resurgence from war and pestilence, its twin societal traumas of the mid-eighteenth century, cotton played the hero, and it was a solo role. Memphis, with its easy accessibility—first by river, then by rail, highway, and air—is a natural trading and distribution center. In those days of crisis, however, there was little to trade other than the region's only large-scale export, its cotton crop. But the once-prosperous cotton planters were in trouble, forced to live and plant on credit, yet shunned by most investors. Finally, when Memphis cotton factors, the commission merchants who marketed the crop, began risking their own capital in loans to hard-up cotton planters, times got better—for cotton and for Memphis. The cotton factors then moved into all cotton-related industries—ginning, baling, compressing, binding, transporting, warehousing. By the 1880s, they dominated the now-thriving cotton trade, and the cotton trade dominated Memphis. A wisp of cotton classing room lint was the greatest badge of honor a Memphis businessmen could wear. Cotton was King.

Front Street, running along the top of the riverfront bluff from Jefferson to Beale, became known as Cotton Row, the home of the largest inland cotton market in the world. It was lined with the offices of cotton merchants—two- and three-story brick buildings that looked down on the steamboat landing below. From their windows the cotton men could watch bales of cotton that had been picked in the fields of Mississippi, Arkansas, or Tennessee, and transported to Memphis by riverboat and railroad, being unloaded on the cobblestone-paved levee and hauled by oxcart or mule-drawn dray up the steep incline to Front Street. There, bales piled on the sidewalk waiting to be moved into the warehouses, formed steep-walled corridors where buyers and factors stood making deals.

The Memphis Cotton Exchange, formed in 1874 as a kind of trade association to regulate cotton marketing, opened its first building in 1885. After several moves to larger quarters, it settled on the corner of Front and Union in 1922. Through the years, the Exchange issued crop reports, standardized the size of cotton bales, improved telegraph facilities and railroad handling, and inaugurated the direct shipment of Memphis cotton to European markets with "through bills of lading." Buyers from all over the world gathered on the Exchange floor. Automatic telegraph machines clattered away, cotton quotations from world-wide markets appeared on the big board, traders rushed to oak telephone booths lining the walls to relay prices to their home offices, and millions of dollars worth of cotton were bought and sold with a handshake as the contract.

Today, Memphis retains its primacy as the world's largest spot cotton market; Memphis merchants bring to market more than fifty percent of the nation's cotton. But individual office computers provide cotton traders with instant market information, making a central gathering point unnecessary. Many of the old Front Street personalities are gone, and many Memphis cotton firms, three of which are consistently among the world's largest, have left the Cotton Row Historic District for larger, more modern buildings. But a few cotton men hold fast to the old traditions, working in hundred-year-old Front Street buildings, meeting each day at lunch to talk about crop prospects and commodity prices.

LACY'S SPECIAL

The Little Tea Shop, established in 1918, is Memphis' oldest downtown restaurant still in operation. Now on the National Register of Historic Places, it is located just east of Front Street, Memphis' historic Cotton Row. It has always been a favorite of Memphians, but especially of cotton men who liked to simply walk around the corner for lunch. This particular dish was named for one of those men, C. A. Lacy.

2 chicken breasts, baked and sliced, with pan drippings reserved	2 tablespoons butter
	2 tablespoons all-purpose flour
	Hot chicken broth
2 cornsticks, split lengthwise	Salt and pepper to taste

Place chicken on top of cornsticks. Over low heat, blend butter and flour until smooth. Gradually stir in broth and reserved drippings to make gravy. Add salt and pepper. Pour gravy over chicken and cornsticks. Serve with rice covered with gravy and garnish with apple jelly on the side.

Serves 1

The Little Tea Shop
Suhair Lauck, Manager

POLLO ALFREDO

This is a family and company favorite. Easy to prepare and nice to take to a new neighbor or an ailing friend.

6 chicken breasts or 1 whole chicken cut in frying pieces	½ teaspoon basil
	¼ teaspoon rosemary
Paprika	1 10¾-ounce can cream of mushroom soup
Pepper	
Salt	1 4-ounce can sliced mushrooms, with juice
2 tablespoons butter	
½ cup chopped onion	Juice of ½ lemon
2 tablespoons chopped fresh parsley	½ cup slivered almonds
	¼ cup white wine or sherry

Wash chicken, drain, and pat dry. Sprinkle generously with paprika and pepper, season lightly with salt, and place in 9 x 13-inch baking dish. Melt butter, add onion and parsley, and sauté. Add remaining ingredients, mix well, and pour over chicken. Bake 1¼ hours at 350 degrees. Serve over rice or angel hair pasta.

Serves 4 to 6

Jo Anne Rossner

BARBECUED CHICKEN IN A SACK

The chicken is very tender and the sauce has a great taste.

3 pound fryer, cut in pieces	Salt and pepper to taste

Sprinkle chicken pieces with salt and pepper. Make roasting bag of heavy duty foil. Dip each piece in barbecue sauce and place in bag. Pour remaining sauce over chicken, seal bag, and place in roasting pan. Cover and bake 15 minutes at 500 degrees. Reduce oven temperature to 350 degrees and bake 1¼ hours more. Do not lift cover at any point before this time.

Open bag and continue baking 15 to 20 minutes to brown chicken, turning once or twice as needed. Serve in preheated baking dish.

Barbecue Sauce

3 tablespoons catsup	3 tablespoons brown sugar
2 tablespoons vinegar	1 teaspoon salt
1 tablespoon lemon juice	1 teaspoon mustard
2 tablespoons Worcestershire sauce	1 teaspoon chili powder
	1 teaspoon paprika
¼ cup water	½ teaspoon red pepper
2 tablespoons butter	

Combine all ingredients and mix well.

Serves 6 to 8

June Boyer Bleecker

MEMORABLE CHICKEN

Good friends, a rainy night, and a simple supper before a fire. Memories are made of moments like these.

3 cups chopped cooked chicken	1 medium onion, chopped and sautéed (or 1 tablespoon dried onion)
1 6¾-ounce box seasoned long grain and wild rice, cooked	
2 10¾-ounce cans cream of celery soup	1 cup mayonnaise
	1 8-ounce can sliced water chestnuts, drained
1 2-ounce jar sliced pimientos	
1 16-ounce can French-style green beans, drained	½ teaspoon salt
	¼ teaspoon pepper

Mix all ingredients and place in buttered 9 x 13-inch (or 3-quart) baking dish. Bake at 350 degrees for 30 minutes or until bubbly.

Serves 8 to 10

Elsie Keeton Burkhart

LEMON CHICKEN

A popular menu item at this long-favored restaurant featuring Mandarin cuisine.

2 whole chicken breasts, boned	1 cup self-rising flour
2 slices ham	Shredded lettuce
1 egg	Shredded fresh coconut
1 teaspoon vegetable oil	Fresh pineapple pieces

Slice chicken breasts lengthwise in butterfly fashion. Place slice of ham inside each breast. Combine egg, oil, and flour with just enough water to create rather thick paste and coat chicken. Deep-fry in medium-hot oil until lightly browned, and then deep-fry at maximum heat for 8 to 10 minutes. Remove chicken and drain thoroughly. Slice each breast in 5 to 6 pieces, coat with lemon sauce, and place on bed of shredded lettuce. Pour remaining sauce over chicken, top with coconut, and garnish with pineapple.

Lemon Sauce

Half of fresh lemon	1¼ cups pineapple juice
¼ cup lemon juice	3 tablespoons cornstarch
½ cup water	4 tablespoons water
¼ cup sugar	

Deeply score lemon half several times. Combine with lemon juice, ½ cup water, sugar, and pineapple juice in saucepan, mix well, and bring to boil. Dissolve cornstarch in 4 tablespoons water, stir into boiling lemon sauce, and cook until thickened.

Serves 4

Peking Restaurant

CHICKEN PUTTIN' ON THE RITZ

A tantalizing aroma from the oven adds to the enjoyment of this moist, tasty chicken with its light, crunchy crust.

3 whole chicken breasts, halved and skinned (or 3 breast halves and 3 drumsticks, skinned)	Vegetable oil
	20 Ritz crackers, crushed
	Paprika and/or Parmesan cheese to taste

Dip chicken in oil and drain excess. Roll in cracker crumbs. Sprinkle with paprika and Parmesan cheese. Do not salt. Bake in foil-lined baking pan at 350 degrees for 70 minutes or until tender.

Serves 6

Mrs. Jay W. McDonald

CHICKEN QUENELLES IN SHERRY SAUCE

Light, delicate, and divinely good. A superb first course.

½ cup butter	Paprika to taste
4 tablespoons all-purpose flour	1 teaspoon lemon juice
¾ cup water	½ pound chicken breasts, skinned and boned
¼ cup light cream	
½ teaspoon salt	6 cups chicken stock
Pepper to taste	5 large egg whites

Melt butter and blend in flour. Cook and stir 3 minutes over low heat, but do not brown. Add water, cream, salt, pepper, paprika, and lemon juice. Stir briskly but lightly with whisk until thickened. Set aside to cool thoroughly.

Bring chicken broth to simmer in large skillet. Cut chicken in pieces and purée in food processor. Add cooled butter mixture and blend. Add egg whites one at a time, blending well. Dip soup spoon into water and scoop portion of mixture. With second spoon, shape mixture into form of small egg. Slip into simmering chicken stock and poach approximately 5 minutes, turning once.

Serve quenelles in sherry sauce or serve sauce separately.

Sherry Sauce

3 tablespoons sweet butter	Tabasco sauce to taste
3½ tablespoons all-purpose flour	1 cup chicken stock
	½ cup light cream
Salt to taste	3 tablespoons dry sherry

Melt butter in heavy pan over low heat, and stir in flour. Add seasonings, stock, and cream, stirring until thick. Remove from heat and whisk in sherry.

Note: Quenelles may be cooked 1 to 2 days ahead and refrigerated, reserving stock to make sauce later.

Serves 8

Frances Keenan Averitt

FRIED CHICKEN SALAD

Good food and good jazz have brought a loyal clientele to this attractive New Orleans-style restaurant in Memphis' popular Overton Square.

Green Onion Dressing
1 egg and extra yolk	*1 tablespoon white vinegar*
½ cup finely chopped green onions	*¼ teaspoon salt*
1½ tablespoons Creole mustard	*1⅛ cups vegetable oil*

Blend egg and extra yolk 2 minutes in food processor. With processor running, add remaining ingredients except oil. Blend 1 minute and then slowly add oil. Chill thoroughly in refrigerator before starting salad.

Salad
2 eggs, beaten	*2 hard-cooked eggs, cut in wedges*
¼ cup milk	
½ to ¾ pound chicken breasts, skinned and boned	*Midget gherkin pickles*
Salad greens	*Ripe olives*
1 tomato, cut in wedges	*Alfalfa sprouts*
	Parsley sprigs

Combine beaten eggs and milk, and mix well. Dip chicken breast in egg mixture, roll in seasoned flour, and deep-fry at 350 degrees until golden brown. Chop and dip pieces in butter mix. Place chicken on bed of tossed greens and ladle dressing over top. Garnish with remaining ingredients.

Seasoned Flour
1 tablespoon salt	*½ teaspoon black pepper*
¾ teaspoon gumbo filé	*½ teaspoon garlic powder*
½ teaspoon onion powder	*3 cups all-purpose flour*
½ teaspoon paprika	

Sift together all ingredients.

Butter Mix
½ cup butter, melted	*¼ cup chopped parsley*
2 teaspoons garlic powder	

Blend all ingredients.

Serves 2

Café Toulouse
French Quarter Inn

OVEN-FRIED SESAME CHICKEN

Such an easy way to do chicken. Just pop it in the oven and forget it.

¼ cup soy sauce	*6 to 8 chicken legs, skinned (or 4 thighs or breast halves, skinned)*
4 tablespoons all-purpose flour (or flour and bread crumbs mixed)	
2 tablespoons sesame seeds	*2 tablespoons butter, melted*

Pour soy sauce in shallow dish. In another dish, mix flour and sesame seeds. Roll chicken in soy sauce and coat with flour mixture. Arrange chicken on foil-lined baking pan and drizzle with butter. Bake at 400 degrees for 40 minutes or until tender.

Serves 4

Mary Jane Richens

CHICKEN BURRITOS

A dish that will become a five-star favorite right away.

1 3-pound chicken	*1 8-ounce carton sour cream*
1 bay leaf	*½ small onion, chopped*
1 10¾-ounce can cream of chicken soup	*10 6-inch flour tortillas*
1½ cups shredded Cheddar cheese	*½ to 1 cup milk*
	Sliced ripe olives

Cook chicken with bay leaf. Bone and chop.

Mix together soup, ¾ cup cheese, sour cream, and onion. Combine a little more than half of mixture with chicken. Spoon portion of mixture onto each tortilla, roll up, and lay side by side in greased baking dish. Add enough milk to remaining soup mixture to make thin sauce, and pour over tortillas. Sprinkle with remaining cheese, top with olives, and bake at 350 degrees for 20 minutes or until cheese melts and casserole is thoroughly heated.

Note: For spicier dish, serve with salsa or sliced jalapeño peppers.

Serves 4 to 6

Linda Stablein

FISH AND SEAFOOD

FRICASSEE SHRIMP

A family favorite that will take many bows.

4 slices bacon, diced
2 large onions, finely chopped
1 green bell pepper, finely
    chopped
2 cloves garlic, chopped
1 cup butter
3 pounds fresh shrimp, peeled
    and deveined

3 tablespoons all-purpose flour
1 cup boiling water
Salt and pepper to taste
Tabasco sauce to taste
Worcestershire sauce to taste
Lemon juice to taste
Cooked rice

Sauté bacon, onions, pepper, and garlic until onions are transparent. Melt butter in separate large saucepan. Dredge shrimp in flour and fry in butter until just pink, about 3 minutes. Add bacon mixture, boiling water, seasonings, and lemon juice. Simmer 5 to 8 minutes, adding extra water if too thick, and adjust seasoning. Do not overcook. Serve hot over rice.

Serves 12

Jane Chase Holmgrain

CRANBERRY CRAB MEAT MOUSSE

Expect many compliments and requests for the recipe.

1 10¾-ounce can cream of
    mushroom soup
2 3-ounce packages cream
    cheese, softened
1 cup Hellmann's mayonnaise
1 cup finely chopped celery
1 cup fresh crab meat
Grated onion to taste

1½ teaspoons Worcestershire
    sauce
Salt and red pepper to taste
2 envelopes unflavored gelatin
½ cup boiling water
1 16-ounce can jellied cranberry
    sauce, chilled

Mix soup and cream cheese, cooking over low heat until well-blended. Remove from heat and stir in all ingredients except gelatin, water, and cranberry sauce. Dissolve gelatin in water and mix with crab meat mixture. Place in oiled mold and chill until firm. Serve on ¼-inch thick slices of jellied cranberry sauce.

Serves 6 to 8

Elise Wheeler

COQUILLES SAINT JACQUES

A delicious fish course. Easy to make ahead and brown in broiler just before serving.

1 cup water
Juice of 1 large lemon
1 teaspoon salt
2 pounds sea scallops, washed
    and drained
¼ cup finely chopped onion
¼ pound mushrooms, sliced
4 tablespoons butter
⅓ cup all-purpose flour

Dash white pepper
1 cup light cream
½ cup milk
1 cup Gruyère or Swiss cheese
½ cup dry white wine
1 tablespoon lemon juice
1 tablespoon chopped parsley
½ cup French bread crumbs
2 tablespoons butter, melted

In medium saucepan, combine water, lemon juice, and salt, and bring to boil. Add scallops, cover, and simmer 6 minutes. Remove scallops and drain on paper towels.

Sauté onion and mushrooms in butter for 5 minutes. Remove from heat, stir in flour and pepper, and blend well. Gradually stir in cream and milk, and bring to boil, stirring constantly. Reduce heat and simmer, stirring until very thick, about 4 to 5 minutes. Add cheese and stir until melted. Remove from heat and stir in wine, lemon juice, parsley, and scallops. Place mixture on 8 scallop shells or in 1½-quart baking dish. Mix bread crumbs with melted butter and sprinkle over scallops. Place shells on baking sheet. Broil 4 to 6 inches from heat for 2 to 3 minutes or until golden brown and bubbly.

Serves 8

Mrs. William B. Leffler

FISH GREEN GODDESS

An especially good way to serve fish.

4 fillets mild white fish
¾ cup Green Goddess salad
    dressing

Red pepper to taste
Crushed potato chips

Marinate fish in salad dressing for 1½ to 2 hours, turning once.

Arrange fish in ungreased 9 x 13-inch baking dish. Sprinkle lightly with red pepper and potato chips. Bake 35 minutes at 350 degrees.

Serves 4

Mrs. David Morse
Jackson, Mississippi

CREVETTES EN FROMAGE

An absolutely bound-to-please first course.

4 ounces shrimp, boiled and
  peeled
Salt and pepper to taste
1 4-ounce package Boursin
  cheese with herbs and garlic
½ 8-ounce package cream
  cheese
⅔ cup beef consommé, with
  4 tablespoons reserved
  for topping

Place several shrimp in each of four ramekins or other small serving dishes. Combine remaining shrimp, salt, pepper, cheeses, and consommé in food processor, and blend. Fill ramekins and top each with 1 tablespoon consommé. Chill 12 hours.

Serve with homemade Melba toast.

Serves 4

Patricia A. Cooper

SHRIMP MEMPHIS

Created by a newcomer to Memphis in celebration of his new city.

½ cup butter
¼ cup vegetable oil
¼ clove garlic, chopped
8 jumbo shrimp, peeled,
  deveined, and butterflied
1 cup all-purpose flour
1½ lemons
1½ cups beer, preferably dark
2 tablespoons bourbon whiskey
3 large fresh mushrooms, sliced
¼ cup chopped fresh parsley
1 cup brown rice, cooked

In large skillet, melt butter in oil over medium-high heat. Add garlic and brown. Coat shrimp with flour, place in skillet, and cook until pink, turning once. Squeeze lemons over shrimp. Add beer and bourbon. Top with mushrooms and parsley. Cover and cook 3½ to 5 minutes over medium heat. Serve over brown rice.

Serves 2 to 3

Arnold Wexler

SECOND-TIME-AROUND FISH

Many a fish fry yields some delicious leftovers. Here's a perfect way to serve the fish again.

2 tablespoons margarine
2 tablespoons all-purpose flour
1 cup hot milk
½ teaspoon dill weed
½ teaspoon Worcestershire
  sauce
1 teaspoon white pepper
1 teaspoon lemon juice
Salt to taste
¼ cup grated Parmesan cheese
1 tablespoon snipped parsley
1 cup flaked cooked fish, such
  as bream, bass, or crappie

In small saucepan over very low heat, melt margarine and gradually blend in flour. Slowly add milk, stirring constantly to keep sauce smooth. Add dill weed, Worcestershire sauce, pepper, lemon juice, salt, cheese, and parsley, stirring gently. Add fish to sauce, heat thoroughly, and serve on toast points.

Note: To serve as casserole, place fish in baking dish, cover with sauce, and sprinkle with cracker crumbs. Bake at 350 degrees until crumbs are browned.

Serves 4

Mrs. Hugh D. Brewer
Robinsonville, Mississippi

TUNA DELIGHT MOLD

A tuna dish that deserves star billing.

1 envelope unflavored gelatin
3 tablespoons water
1 6-ounce package lemon
  gelatin
1½ cups boiling water
3 tablespoons apple cider
  vinegar
2 10¾-ounce cans cream of
  chicken soup
1½ cups mayonnaise
1 cup finely chopped celery
2 tablespoons finely chopped
  onion
1 cup finely chopped green or
  ripe olives
1 cup finely chopped pecans
  or almonds
2 6½-ounce cans tuna,
  drained
1 teaspoon curry powder
Dash paprika
Dash dill weed

Soften unflavored gelatin with 3 tablespoons water in small container. Dissolve lemon gelatin in boiling water and add vinegar. Combine gelatin mixtures and chill until partially set.

In 3-quart bowl, mix remaining ingredients and combine with gelatin mixture. Pour into 9 x 13-inch baking dish or two 5-cup molds. Chill at least 3 hours or overnight.

Serves 10 to 12

Mrs. G. Vernon Drane

An Afternoon Fish Fry at Horseshoe Lake

Like birds migrating with the changing seasons, Memphians on holiday flock together each year to certain favorite retreats. Several particular places not too far from the city are uniquely Memphis hideaways where the same families may have lived as vacation neighbors for several generations. To the east, not far from the Civil War battlefield at Shiloh, there are lakeside cottages at Pickwick Dam on the Tennessee River where Memphis families go for fishing, houseboating, water-skiing, and sailing. There are beachside condominiums near the Florida fishing village of Destin, which is only a day's drive, or a brief flight, from Memphis and boasts the bluest water and whitest sand on the Gulf Coast. There are the comfortable rambling cottages at the old Chatauqua campground at Monteagle, Tennessee. And in the Great Smokies there are mountain lodges near Gatlinburg in East Tennessee, or Linville and Highlands in western North Carolina, where city heat can be forgotten on long walks beside cool streams and through deep woods filled with rhododendron in bloom.

Nearer at hand, to the west, Arkansas offers choice sites for vacation homes where Memphians love to gather for old-time houseparties, all-time family reunions, and weekends of boating, fishing, hunting, sailing, golf, tennis, and canoeing. One such favorite spot is Hardy on the Spring River. Eden Isle and Fairfield Bay on Greer's Ferry Lake in the Ozark foothills, and Bear Creek Lake with its rustic fishing cabins nestled in the woods of St. Francis National Forest, are other cherished places that, for years, have attracted many Memphians. Closest of all is Horseshoe Lake, less than an hour's drive from downtown Memphis, across the Mississippi River bridge in the fertile farmland of east Arkansas.

To reach Horseshoe Lake, you turn south off the interstate, onto a well-traveled two-lane highway that passes through fields of soybeans, corn, and rice. Soon, rising on the left, you will see a grass-covered levee built around 1929 by the U.S. Army Corps of Engineers to hold back the flooding waters of the Mississippi River. This earthen barricade changed one of the river's meanderings into a horseshoe-shaped lake. All the land around Horseshoe Lake was originally owned by three Memphis families, some of whose members still remember when it was remote territory accessible only by riverboat. They recall how electricity was generated by Delco battery, water came from artesian wells, and supplies arrived once a week by riverboat and had to be hauled overland by mule-drawn wagons. They also have some lighthearted memories of early-day diversions, such as treasure hunts when open-air biplanes landed in alfalfa fields to search for clues on surrounding farms. As transportation improved, these families entertained more and more guests, mostly from nearby Memphis; the guests enjoyed their outings, wanted to return often, and the area became a much-desired weekend retreat.

Today new construction fills almost every remaining lakeside lot, and Horseshoe Lake continues to be the home-away-from-home of scores of Memphis families who enjoy motorboating, sailing, water-skiing, hunting, and—above all—fishing.

THE PICTURE: *Under the lacy branches of a large cypress tree, on a pier that leads to a private boathouse, a mouth-watering feast awaits weekend guests at Horseshoe Lake in eastern Arkansas. The day's catch of local bream, bass, and crappie has been prepared by the "master chef," a Memphian displaying to an audience of hungry friends his skills at boning, skinning, breading (with a light tempura batter), and frying the fish. An ironstone crock of iced tea, and a bouquet of zinnias, Gloriosa daisies, Queen Anne's lace, sometimes called wild carrot, and a few yellow statice add fittingly rustic touches for this special occasion.*

THE FOOD: *Crisp, golden-brown HORSESHOE LAKE FRIED FISH, (fillets of local bass, bream, and crappie), deep-fried on the spot in the sizzling hot oil of a big metal fish fryer, platters of PASTA PRIMAVERA FOR HUNDREDS, HERBED TOMATOES with sliced red onions and cucumbers, sliced sweet Vidalias, HUSH PUPPIES (no fish fry can be without them), barbecued chicken, and grilled fresh Gulf shrimp—all calculated to satisfy the appetites of the convivial crowd that will gather on the rough wooden dock for this afternoon's fish fry. (The fish fryer was made to order for one of the Horseshoe fishermen by a local volunteer fireman.)*

129

HORSESHOE LAKE FRIED FISH

One of the beauties of Horseshoe Lake is that it is less than one hour's drive from Memphis—close enough to enjoy often, even on the spur of the moment. Its easy-going days and nights are perfect for friendly entertaining, and perhaps nothing suits those occasions more than a fish fry, particularly if it's the day's catch. However, no place better fulfills the old adage that, "There's only two kinds of fishin'—good and excellent. Excellent is when you catch somethin'."

Fresh large-mouth bass
Hot sauce
1 box Tempura batter mix

1 to 2 eggs, beaten
Black pepper to taste
Beer

Clean bass well, fillet, and rinse in cool water two or three times. Place fillets in solution of strong salt water and soak 20 to 30 minutes. Rinse thoroughly, place in pan, and add generous amount hot sauce. Marinate 30 to 45 minutes.

Meanwhile, prepare batter by combining Tempura mix with eggs, black pepper, and enough beer to make a thin batter. Heat cooking oil in fish fryer (or any large deep fryer). Drop a wooden match in the grease. When it flames, the temperature is right. Remove match. Coat fillets in batter and drop in hot oil. They will sink, but when done, will float to the top.

Note: This procedure works equally well with bream, but if using bream, omit hot sauce.

K. William Chandler

TRUITES À LA CRÈME

Spectacularly good.

1 trout, filleted
2 tablespoons butter
Salt and pepper to taste
1½ ounces brandy

½ cup heavy cream
2 tablespoons chopped almonds,
    browned in butter

Sauté trout fillets in butter 5 to 8 minutes on each side. Sprinkle with salt and pepper. Pour brandy over fish and flame. Place on hot serving platter. Bring cream to boil, sprinkle lightly with salt and pepper, and pour over fish. Sprinkle with almonds.

Serves 1

Nicole Lewis

BARBECUED SHRIMP BOYLEN

Created while on a visit to Hilton Head, South Carolina, and good enough to find its way there to the menu of a local country club, where it was given the French spelling of the name of its originator.

1 3¾-ounce can smoked
    oysters
1 3-ounce package cream
    cheese, softened

2 pounds large shrimp, peeled,
    deveined, and butterflied
1 16-ounce package bacon
1 cup barbecue sauce

Blend equal amounts oysters and cream cheese, and stuff shrimp. Wrap each shrimp with bacon slice. Thread onto skewer, cover with barbecue sauce, and grill over charcoal until bacon is done.

Serves 4 to 6

W. Kerby Bowling II

THE ADMIRAL'S STUFFED SHRIMP

An absolutely wonderful way to prepare shrimp.

1 egg, beaten
¼ cup milk
1¼ cups bread crumbs
½ teaspoon paprika
3 pounds large shrimp, peeled,
    deveined, and butterflied,
    with tails left on
1 pound crab meat, flaked
2 tablespoons mayonnaise
1 teaspoon dry mustard

1 teaspoon Worcestershire
    sauce
1 teaspoon Tabasco sauce
Salt and pepper to taste
1 medium onion, finely
    chopped
½ green bell pepper, finely
    chopped
⅓ cup margarine, melted

Combine egg and milk. Mix ¾ cup bread crumbs with paprika. Coat each shrimp well with egg mixture, then with crumbs.

Combine crab meat, mayonnaise, mustard, Worcestershire sauce, Tabasco sauce, salt, pepper, and remaining bread crumbs. Sauté onion and bell pepper in margarine, and add to crab meat mixture. Stuff shrimp with crab meat mixture and place in greased shallow baking dish. Bake at 400 degrees for 12 minutes or until browned.

Serves 6 to 8

Shirley Sigler Chamberlin
Millington, Tennessee

CRAB CAKES WITH CHILI CORN RELISH

The Mississippi is a long way from the Chesapeake, but never mind. This very special restaurant has departed, but this outstanding recipe will remain with us.

1 pound lump crab, special white or claw meat, flaked
1 cup finely diced red bell pepper
1 cup finely diced green bell pepper
¾ cup dry bread crumbs
⅔ cup Hellmann's mayonnaise
2 teaspoons Worcestershire sauce

1 teaspoon Tabasco sauce
1 teaspoon curry powder
½ teaspoon paprika
½ teaspoon dry mustard
2 large eggs, beaten
Dash or two fresh lemon juice
Salt and white pepper to taste
Dry bread crumbs for coating
Peanut or vegetable oil

Combine all ingredients except crumbs for coating and oil, and mix well. Divide into ¼ cup portions. On flat surface lightly sprinkled with remaining bread crumbs, form each portion into cake, turning once to coat on each side. Chill in freezer 10 minutes. Sauté cakes in enough hot oil to brown quickly, but do not deep-fry. Drain on paper towels and keep warm. Garnish with lemon wedges and serve with 1 tablespoon chili corn relish per cake.

Chili Corn Relish
1 46-ounce can V-8 juice
5 tablespoons chili powder
¼ cup butter
2 cups fresh sweet yellow corn
1 medium yellow onion, finely diced

1 extra large red bell pepper, finely diced
1 extra large green bell pepper, finely diced
Salt and pepper to taste

In 3-quart pot, mix V-8 juice with chili powder, bring to boil, and reduce by half. In large skillet, melt butter and brown corn over medium heat until golden, about 15 minutes. Add onion and bell peppers, cover, and cook 10 minutes over low heat. Add vegetables to reduced juice and bring to slow boil over medium-low heat. Add salt and pepper and cook 20 to 30 minutes until consistency is like slightly thinned honey, stirring occasionally (mixture should not separate when placed on plate). Store in airtight container. Keeps 1 week in refrigerator. (Yields 1 quart relish.)

Yields 16 cakes

The Market Place Restaurant

FLOUNDER STUFFED WITH MOUSSE

Takes time and tender loving care, but well worth it.

8 flounder fillets
Salt and pepper to taste
Cognac to taste
¼ cup chopped shallots
1 cup very dry white wine

¼ cup dry vermouth
½ cup fish stock
1 cup heavy cream
6 to 8 tablespoons butter, softened

Sprinkle fillets with salt, pepper, and cognac. Spread with mousse. Put two fillets together like a sandwich or roll into paupiettes. Place in buttered baking dish and sprinkle with shallots. Combine wine, vermouth, and fish stock, and pour over fish. Cover with buttered parchment paper. Bake at 350 degrees for 10 to 15 minutes or until fish flakes. To make sauce, pour juices into saucepan and reduce by half. Add cream and reduce by half again. Whisk in butter. Serve warm over fish.

Mousse
1 pound flounder
3 eggs
1 cup heavy cream

Salt and pepper to taste
¼ cup chopped parsley

Coarsely grind flounder in food processor and add eggs one at a time. Add cream, salt, pepper, and parsley and blend.

Variation: Substitute trout or salmon for flounder.

Note: If fish stock is not available, use bottled clam juice or chicken stock.

Serves 4 to 6

B. Mott Jones

SHRIMP PICKWICK

A jewel of a recipe.

1 8-ounce package cream cheese, softened
3 4-ounce jars frozen shrimp cocktails, thawed
½ cup chopped green onion

½ cup chopped bell pepper
½ cup chopped tomato
1 2-ounce can ripe olives, drained and chopped
1 cup grated mozzarella cheese

Layer ingredients in serving dish in order listed, and chill. Serve with Melba toast.

Serves 8 to 12

Terry Brown

SUNDAY-BEST TUNA MOUSSE

A definite departure from the usual tuna salad. Very tasty. Can also be used as a spread with crackers.

2 teaspoons unflavored gelatin	1 teaspoon vinegar
½ cup cold water	1 6-ounce can tuna, drained
¾ cup mayonnaise	1 cup finely chopped celery
Salt to taste	½ cup chopped stuffed olives
Paprika to taste	3 tablespoons minced pimiento

Heat gelatin and water in top of double boiler, stirring until dissolved. Cool. Combine gelatin with mayonnaise, salt, paprika, and vinegar, and blend until smooth. Fold in remaining ingredients. Pour mixture into greased 3½-cup mold and chill until set.

Serves 6 to 8

Eloise Mays

DOUBLE BATCH SHRIMP FLORENTINE

An easy company dish that's easy to plan ahead, as this freezes beautifully, ready to bake and serve.

4 10-ounce packages frozen chopped spinach	1 cup dry white wine
3 pounds shrimp, boiled and peeled	½ cup chopped scallions
	Salt and pepper to taste
½ cup butter	Paprika to taste
½ cup all-purpose flour	2 cups shredded Cheddar cheese
3 cups milk	

Line two 9-inch pie pans with aluminum foil. Thaw spinach and drain thoroughly, using paper towels to remove as much moisture as possible. Spread half of spinach in each pie pan and top with shrimp.

In saucepan, melt butter and stir in flour. Gradually add milk, wine, and scallions. Cook over low heat, stirring constantly, until sauce bubbles and thickens. Add salt and pepper and enough paprika for rosy color. Pour sauce over shrimp and sprinkle with cheese. Bake uncovered at 350 degrees for 35 minutes or until bubbly.

Serves 8

Sara M. Holmes

SEAFOOD DE JONGHE

An old favorite that is always welcome.

¾ cup butter, melted	½ cup red wine or sherry
1 cup bread crumbs	1 pound fresh mushrooms, sliced
2 teaspoons minced parsley	
½ teaspoon garlic powder	2 tablespoons butter, melted
⅛ teaspoon paprika	2 to 2½ pounds shrimp, boiled, peeled, and deveined
Dash cayenne pepper	
1 teaspoon salt	½ pound fresh crab meat

Combine ¾ cup butter, bread crumbs, parsley, and seasonings, and mix well. Add wine and set aside. Sauté mushrooms in 2 tablespoons butter and drain. In buttered baking dish, layer half of shrimp, crab meat, mushrooms, and crumb mixture. Repeat layers once. Bake 25 minutes at 350 degrees.

Note: Can be served on individual scallop shells, arranging shrimp, crab meat, and mushrooms as one layer and topping with crumb mixture. Bake at 350 degrees until browned.

Serves 6 to 8

Mrs. Philip Kaminsky

TUNA-ARTICHOKE CASSEROLE

Great for last-minute cooking, since most ingredients are readily at hand.

1 6½-ounce jar artichoke hearts	1 3-ounce can sliced mushrooms, drained
1 6½-ounce can white tuna, drained	1 tablespoon Worcestershire sauce
1 10¾-ounce can cream of celery soup	¾ cup grated Parmesan cheese

Arrange artichokes in greased 1-quart baking dish. Break tuna in large chunks and spread over artichokes. Mix soup, mushrooms, and Worcestershire sauce, and pour over tuna. Sprinkle with cheese and bake 20 to 25 minutes at 375 degrees.

Serves 4

Jean Tuttle

FILLET OF DOVER SOLE

Perfectly matched flavors: Dover sole with mushroom purée and wine sauce.

2 carrots, sliced	Salt and freshly ground black
1 onion, sliced	pepper to taste
2 tablespoons lemon juice	8 cups water
1 clove garlic, minced	1½ pounds Dover sole fillets
Fresh parsley, chopped	½ cup dry white wine
¼ teaspoon thyme	1 teaspoon butter
¼ teaspoon chervil	1 egg yolk, well-beaten

Combine all ingredients except sole, wine, butter, and egg yolk in saucepan, and boil 15 minutes to make court bouillon.

Poach fillets in court bouillon for 5 minutes, carefully remove from liquid, and place in small baking dish. Spread mushroom sauce over each fillet. Heat wine in small saucepan and add butter. Gradually blend with egg yolk and pour over fillets. Place under broiler, brown quickly, and serve.

Mushroom Sauce

1 pound mushrooms, finely chopped	2 teaspoons all-purpose flour
	½ cup heavy cream
2 tablespoons butter	Salt and pepper
2 shallots, chopped	

Sauté mushrooms in butter. Add shallots, cook until soft, and gradually stir in flour and cream. Season to taste.

Serves 4

Nicole Lewis

CURRIED EGGS AND SHRIMP CASSEROLE

Use the best curry powder available as it is the key to this dish.

1 pound medium shrimp, fresh or frozen	½ cup Hellmann's mayonnaise
12 hard-cooked eggs	1 10¾-ounce can cream of shrimp soup
¼ teaspoon salt	1 cup dry white wine
¼ teaspoon pepper	½ cup crushed seasoned
¼ teaspoon dry mustard	croutons
¼ to ½ teaspoon curry powder	½ cup grated Parmesan cheese

Cook shrimp in boiling salted water until pink. Drain and cool.

Cut eggs lengthwise. Remove yolks, mix with seasonings and enough mayonnaise to moisten, and stuff whites. Place in 9 x 11-inch baking dish. Arrange shrimp among eggs.

Blend wine into soup and heat to make sauce. Pour over shrimp and eggs and top with mixture of croutons and cheese. Bake at 350 degrees for 30 minutes or until bubbly and brown. Serve with hot, crusty bread.

Serves 8 to 10

Katherine Leftwich
Forrest City, Arkansas

SHRIMP AND ARTICHOKES FOR A CROWD

Great for a neighborhood supper, with tables set outdoors on a warm spring evening. A little moonlight wouldn't hurt.

3 pounds fresh mushrooms, sliced	12 14-ounce cans artichoke hearts, drained and chopped
½ cup butter	3 cups grated Parmesan cheese
2 cups dry sherry	Fresh parsley, chopped
12 pounds shrimp, boiled and peeled	

Sauté mushrooms in butter until tender. Add sherry and cook 5 minutes over medium heat. Gently combine mushroom mixture with shrimp and artichokes. Stir in white sauce, pour into buttered baking dishes, and top with Parmesan cheese. Bake 30 minutes at 375 degrees. Sprinkle with parsley and serve.

Note: May substitute chicken for shrimp or use combination of the two.

White Sauce

2 cups butter	1 to 2 teaspoons white pepper
2 cups all-purpose flour	Worcestershire sauce to taste
1 gallon milk	Paprika to taste
3 to 4 teaspoons salt	

Melt butter over low heat. Gradually blend in flour, stirring until smooth. Slowly add milk, stirring constantly until sauce is smooth and of medium-thick consistency. Blend in remaining ingredients. (Recipe yields 4½ quarts sauce.)

Serves 50

Nancy Hughes Coe

Dining Out in Style at Justine's

From its unlikely beginnings in 1948, in a fifty-dollar-a-month rented warehouse near the old bus barns on Walnut Street, to its present settled elegance in a beautifully restored antebellum home on Coward Place, Justine's has epitomized fine dining. This award-winning Memphis establishment, which former Metropolitan Opera director Rudolph Bing described without qualification as "the best restaurant in the United States," is the creation of Justine Smith, a petite, enterprising, Tennessee woman, and her Chicagoan husband, Dayton Smith. From the start, when she magically transformed the huge old abandoned warehouse—hanging globed lights on ten-foot cords from the tall ceiling, covering the twenty-foot windows with draperies she herself made from discount fabric, bringing in fine Baccarat crystal and Francis I silver from her own home to reflect the soft glow of hurricane lanterns on each table—she has spared no effort or expense to make every meal at Justine's a memorable experience. From the start, she has offered her customers a 103-item menu of classic French cuisine and has unfailingly served the freshest seafood in town—in the early days it was extravagantly flown in from Maine and Florida and delivered to the restaurant by taxi. From the start, most important of all, she has enjoyed doing so: "Every night was like having an elaborate dinner party in my own home," Justine once explained. Not since the long-gone days of sumptuous banquets at the famous old Gayoso Hotel, and lavish meals at Gaston House, the Court Square restaurant of French-born, Delmonico-trained chef John Gaston in the late 1800s, have Memphians been able to dine out in such elegant fashion.

Justine's move, in 1956, to its present location on Coward Place offered even more formidable challenges than refurbishing the Walnut Street warehouse had presented. The interesting old French Colonial house, built originally in 1843 and enlarged in the mid-1850s by a new owner inspired by the architecture he had seen on a steamboat trip to New Orleans, had subsequently been painted, remodeled, "modernized," and finally neglected, into a tragic state of disrepair. Justine and Dayton Smith stripped off fourteen layers of paint to reveal and restore the original pale pink stucco-like exterior; they repaired cornices and reclaimed the original marble entrance steps found buried in the yard. Inside, in the entry hall, they installed a splendid stairway balustrade from the old Gayoso Hotel, and, in the restrooms, they used the hotel's marble lavatories; they reworked all the carved moldings, and hung fine gold leaf mirrors above the original marble mantels in each room. Finally, they bought antiques from all over the world to furnish the historic building (which, with the self-assurance that befits a four-star restaurant, does not have so much as an identifying nameplate on the door).

What the Smiths did not remodel was the menu. It continues to feature all the justly celebrated Justine's specialties which, for some forty years, have pleased the discriminating palates of visiting opera stars, traveling business executives, and knowledgeable gourmets from around the world. And Justine's remains, as it has been for decades, the only place innumerable Memphis diners would dream of going to celebrate birthdays, engagements, anniversaries, and other assorted occasions of note.

THE PICTURE: *The table at Justine's, a favorite Memphis restaurant for four decades, is set with the owner's Georgian silver. As always at Justine's, a hurricane lantern is the centerpiece, and in the background is one of the restaurant's ever-present bouquets of fresh, fragrant roses intermingled with tuberoses. Arrangements of roses are found in every room at Justine's, and, in season, may have been cut from rosebushes at the owner's home, or may have come from the rose gardens that ornament the gazebo and brick-paved courtyard of the fine old nineteenth-century French Colonial mansion where Justine's has been located since 1956.*

THE FOOD: *Justine's has always specialized in seafood. Presented here are some of the restaurant's most popular offerings: OYSTERS JUSTINE (artichokes stuffed with seasoned oysters), fresh Gulf oysters on the half-shell; CRAB MEAT JUSTINE, and succulent Maine lobster. Vegetables that accompany a meal at Justine's may, in season, come from the one-acre vegetable garden at the owner's home, and may even have been harvested that morning by Justine Smith herself.*

OYSTERS JUSTINE

One of those dishes that insures return visits to this distinguished Memphis restaurant.

Oyster Sauce

½ cup butter	1 teaspoon Worcestershire
2 tablespoons all-purpose flour	sauce
½ cup chopped green onions	1 cup concentrated beef stock
½ cup chopped mushrooms	¼ cup chopped parsley
4 cups chicken broth	½ cup chopped artichoke
2 tablespoons sherry	hearts
½ teaspoon Tabasco sauce	Salt and pepper to taste

Melt butter in skillet and stir in flour. Add onions and mushrooms, and cook several minutes, continually stirring. Add remaining ingredients, mix well, and simmer 1 hour. Meanwhile, prepare fresh artichokes.

Artichokes

6 fresh artichokes	1 tablespoon salt

Cut off sharp points and slice a little off bottom so artichokes sit flat in saucepan. Add water to artichokes until almost covered and add salt. Cover and cook over medium heat for 45 minutes or until leaves can be easily removed. Cool and remove chokes from artichokes without removing leaves. Set aside. Prepare oysters.

Oysters

36 oysters in shell	4 tablespoons paprika
1½ cups vegetable oil	Salt and pepper to taste
2 cups all-purpose flour	

Remove oysters from shells and drain. Heat oil in skillet to frying temperature. Mix flour, paprika, salt, and pepper, and coat oysters. Fry until browned and crisp.

Reheat artichokes in a little water. Remove to serving dish, place oysters in each artichoke cup, and fill cup with hot oyster sauce. Serve immediately.

Serves 6

Justine's
Justine Smith

CRAB MEAT JUSTINE

A must when dining at Justine's.

½ cup butter	Dash Tabasco sauce
1 cup dry sherry	Dash or two lemon juice
½ pound fresh lump crab meat	French bread
Dash Worcestershire sauce	HOLLANDAISE SAUCE

Melt butter over medium heat. Add sherry, crab meat, seasonings, and lemon juice, stirring until thoroughly heated.

Place 2 tablespoons of mixture on thin slice of toasted French bread in individual ramekins. Top with Hollandaise sauce and bake at 425 degrees until sauce is lightly browned.

Serves 4 to 6

Justine's
Justine Smith

SMOKED SALMON CHEESE CAKE

This wonder of cold northern waters provides a delectable first course.

½ cup dry bread crumbs	1 tablespoon lemon juice
1 large onion, chopped	1 tablespoon minced fresh dill
3 tablespoons butter	or ¾ teaspoon dried
3 8-ounce packages cream	4 drops Tabasco sauce
cheese, softened	8 ounces smoked salmon,
4 eggs	chopped

Grease sides and bottom of 8-inch springform pan with vegetable shortening, coat with bread crumbs, and chill.

Sauté onion in butter until soft. With mixer or food processor, beat cream cheese until smooth. Add onion and remaining ingredients, and process until smooth. Pour mixture into chilled springform pan and place in large baking pan with enough hot water added to reach halfway up springform pan. Bake 1 hour at 325 degrees. Turn oven off and cool 1 hour in oven with door open. Remove from pan of water, cool on rack, and chill. Slice and serve garnished with sprig of fresh dill.

Serves 8 to 12

Ann Clark Harris

RAINBOW TROUT ALMONDINE

Stream-fresh and simply prepared. What could be better?

2 1-pound rainbow trout, cleaned and heads removed	½ cup slivered almonds, toasted
Salt and pepper to taste	Butter, melted

Sprinkle trout with salt and pepper. Wrap fish individually in foil and place in lightly buttered shallow pan. Bake at 350 degrees for 45 minutes or until tender to touch.

Open fish lengthwise and remove all bones and skin. Place halves center-up on buttered pan. Add toasted almonds and generously cover with butter. Briefly heat, being careful not to dry out meat. Carefully transfer to serving dish.

Serves 4

Josephine Conger

CATFISH VERA CRUZANA

The King Cotton Café, from its second floor aerie on Front Street where the old King Cotton Hotel once stood, affords a bird's-eye view of Confederate Park with its canopy of trees and glimpses of the river beyond. On a warm evening, diners may be treated to the sight of a horse-drawn carriage winding its way through the park. A nice ambience for presenting a menu that's billed as Delta dinin'.

4 5 to 7-ounce catfish fillets	4 small cloves garlic, chopped
2 cups white wine	4 tablespoons peanut oil or olive oil
4 tablespoons lemon juice	
2 tomatoes, diced	2 tablespoons red wine vinegar
1 medium white onion, diced	1 tablespoon cumin
¼ cup chopped cilantro	Grated Monterey Jack cheese

Lay fillets in baking pan and pour wine and lemon juice over tops. Bake at 475 degrees for 6 to 8 minutes or until fish flakes. (Reserve wine sauce to spoon over fish.) Combine remaining ingredients except cheese and spoon onto each fillet. Top with cheese and bake at 500 degrees until cheese melts and begins to brown.

Serves 4

King Cotton Café
Morgan Keegan Tower

OYSTERS ON THE SALT-RISE

The definitive taste of salt-rising bread gives nice individuality to this savory oyster dish.

1 loaf salt-rising bread	2 cups CREAM SAUCE or
1 12-ounce jar oysters, drained and juice reserved	1 10¾-ounce can cream of celery soup
½ cup chopped onion	Dash Worcestershire sauce
½ cup chopped celery	1 8-ounce can sliced water chestnuts, drained
2 tablespoons butter	

Trim bread, tear into small, coarse pieces, and toast at 200 degrees for 1 hour.

Line buttered shallow baking dish with toasted bread and cover with oysters. Sauté onion and celery in butter until soft and mix with sauce along with portion of oyster liquid. Add Worcestershire sauce. Pour sauce mixture over oysters. Layer water chestnuts on top and sprinkle with paprika. Bake at 350 degrees for 20 minutes or until bubbly.

Serves 4 to 6

Mrs. Percy Magness

LOBSTER THERMIDOR

One of the classics.

2½ pounds boiled lobster meat, cubed	¼ teaspoon paprika
3 tablespoons butter	2 tablespoons all-purpose flour
1 8-ounce can mushrooms, drained	2 cups light cream
½ cup sherry	2 egg yolks, beaten
¼ teaspoon salt	1 10¾-ounce can cream of potato soup
	Grated cheese

In 4-quart saucepan, briefly sauté lobster in butter. Stir in mushrooms, sherry, salt, and paprika. Sprinkle with flour and stir. Gradually add cream, egg yolks, and soup, and simmer until thick, about 2 minutes. Place in chafing dish and sprinkle with cheese. Serve in patty shells or over rice.

Note: May substitute shrimp for lobster or use a combination of both.

Serves 6 to 8

Mrs. Thomas G. Carpenter

SHRIMP MOSCA

Extra good blend of flavors.

2 pounds medium shrimp, unpeeled, heads removed	Freshly ground black pepper to taste
2 bay leaves	5 to 6 cloves garlic, crushed
½ teaspoon oregano	⅓ cup olive oil
½ teaspoon rosemary	3 tablespoons butter, melted
1 teaspoon salt	2 tablespoons dry white wine

Combine shrimp, seasonings, garlic, and olive oil. Pour butter over mixture. Marinate in refrigerator all day or overnight.

Remove from refrigerator and cook 10 to 15 minutes over medium heat. More butter may be added for extra sauce. Cool 25 minutes, add wine, and cook 5 minutes more. Remove from heat and let stand 10 minutes. Serve each person a portion of sauce with shrimp, and French bread for dipping.

Serves 4

Cecile Skaggs

WHITEHALL CRAB MEAT CASSEROLE

From the chef at the old Whitehall Hotel in Chicago, by way of a friend, to a personal recipe file.

½ pound fresh lump crab meat	3 tablespoons butter, melted
2 tablespoons chopped chives	3 eggs, well-beaten
2 tablespoons lemon juice	1¾ cups milk
3 cups cubed French bread, crust trimmed	1 tablespoon hot pepper sauce
3 ounces grated mild Cheddar cheese	½ teaspoon salt
	½ teaspoon dry mustard

Drain and flake crab meat. Toss with chives and lemon juice. In buttered 2-quart baking dish, arrange alternate layers of bread cubes, cheese, and crab meat. Drizzle butter over top. Combine remaining ingredients and pour over casserole. Cover with foil and chill overnight.

Bake uncovered at 350 degrees for 50 to 60 minutes or until puffed and golden.

Serves 6

Mrs. Robert E. Love, Jr.

GEFILTE FISH

This recipe was brought by a young wife from Warsaw, Poland when she came with three small children to join her husband in Memphis. From her home above a dry goods store on Beale at the turn of the century, this recipe has been passed down through generations to be traditionally served at Passover.

Stock

Bones from buffalo fish	Celery leaves, chopped
1 onion, chopped	5 quarts water
3 carrots, chopped	

Combine all ingredients in large soup pot and bring to rolling boil.

Fish Balls

2 to 3 medium onions, chopped	5 pounds buffalo fish, ground
4 carrots, chopped	3 to 4 teaspoons salt
6 ribs celery, chopped	1 teaspoon white pepper
5 eggs	½ cup matzo meal

Grate onions, carrots, and celery in food processor. Add eggs and purée. Place ground fish in large mixing bowl and add salt and pepper. Blend in puréed mixture. Add matzo meal and mix well, adding water as needed until fish mixture holds together well. Adjust seasonings. Moisten hands and make balls of fish mixture, about 2½ to 3 inches in diameter. Place one at a time in boiling stock. Reduce heat, partially cover, and simmer 2 hours, shaking pot occasionally.

Remove fish balls from stock with slotted spoon, cool, and refrigerate overnight. Strain stock and refrigerate to allow to jell. Serve fish balls with spoonful of jellied stock and horseradish on the side.

Yields 30 fish balls

Marilyn Iskiwitz Califf

LOW COUNTRY SHRIMP

A Carolina heritage that is very much at home beside the Mississippi.

1 to 1½ pounds Polish sausage, sliced in 1-inch diagonal pieces	3 to 4 ears of corn, broken in half
	3 pounds shrimp, unpeeled

Fill large pot one-third full of water. Add sausage, bring to boil, and simmer 5 minutes. Add corn, bring to boil, and simmer 5 minutes. Add shrimp, bring to boil, and simmer until shrimp are pink, about 10 minutes. Serve hot with small bowls of sauce for shrimp.

Sauce

½ cup butter	1 cup catsup
2 tablespoons lemon juice	Prepared horseradish to taste

Melt butter and mix in all other ingredients. Serve hot.

Serves 6 to 8

Nina F. Martin

SOPPIN' SHRIMP

Deliciously simple—just peel 'em and eat 'em. French bread for soppin' is a must.

5 pounds shrimp, rinsed and unpeeled	1 package dry Italian salad dressing mix
1 cup butter, melted	Onion powder, optional
1 10-ounce bottle Worcester-shire sauce	Celery seed, optional

Place shrimp in broiler pan. Blend butter, Worcestershire sauce, and salad dressing mix, and pour over shrimp. Sprinkle with onion powder and celery seed. Bake 45 minutes at 350 degrees, stirring occasionally. Serve hot or at room temperature but not chilled.

Variation: Mix 2 cups melted butter with one 16-ounce bottle Italian dressing, juice of 2 lemons, and 1 tablespoon coarsely ground black pepper. Pour over shrimp and bake as above.

Serves 8 to 10

Peggy Worley

SMOKED CATFISH

Everyone will come back for more.

2½ to 3 pound dressed catfish	Lemon wedges
Lemon juice	Chopped fresh parsley
Salt and pepper to taste	

Using fresh hickory chips, prepare water-type smoker. Sprinkle catfish with lemon juice, salt, and pepper. Smoke 3½ hours or until fish begins to flake. Garnish with lemon wedges and parsley. Serves as appetizer with crackers.

Serves 14 to 16

John S. Evans

MOUSSELINE OF SCALLOP

A standard from the menu at the lovely old Bradford House restaurant. Though the doors have closed, the memories linger. Recipe is adapted from cookbook of Jacques Pépin.

¾ pound scallops	½ cup heavy cream
½ teaspoon salt	1 cup heavy cream, lightly whipped
¼ teaspoon white pepper	
Pinch of curry powder	

Purée scallops in food processor. Add seasonings and ½ cup heavy cream, and purée again. Whisk scallop purée into 1 cup whipped cream. Spoon into buttered individual molds. Strike bottom of molds against top of counter to remove air pockets from mixture. Cover with buttered parchment paper and place in baking pan with water added to 1-inch depth. Bake at 350 degrees for 50 to 60 minutes or until set. Remove mousseline from molds and serve covered with sauce.

Sauce

1 cup dry white wine	½ teaspoon white pepper
½ cup water	2 tablespoons heavy cream
1 tablespoon vinegar	1 cup unsalted butter, cut in pieces
¼ cup chopped shallots	
½ teaspoon salt	Fresh parsley, chopped

Combine wine, water, vinegar, shallots, salt, and pepper. Mix well and cook over medium heat until mixture is reduced to ⅓ cup. Add cream and stir. Whisk in butter, a few pieces at a time, until melted and blended. Add parsley.

Serves 6 to 8

The Bradford House Restaurant
Wayne Reynolds, Former Proprietor

CIOPPINO

Variations on a family variation on a Portuguese theme. Distinctively good. Serve hot with crusty French bread and a chilled, crisp green salad.

2 quarts milk
2 pounds medium shrimp, peeled and deveined
1 3-ounce package crab and shrimp boil mix
1/4 teaspoon salt
3/4 pound sliced bacon, cut crosswise in 1/4-inch strips
5 medium yellow onions, chopped
2 to 3 green bell peppers, peeled and chopped
6 to 8 ribs celery, sliced in 1/4-inch pieces
2 medium Irish potatoes, peeled and diced in 1/2-inch pieces
1 pound fresh lumb crab meat
1/2 cup finely chopped parsley
1/2 cup dry sherry
Seasoned salt to taste
Freshly ground black pepper to taste
1 tablespoon paprika
2 teaspoons Worcesteshire sauce

Heat milk over low heat in 6-quart pot. In another pot, combine shrimp, shrimp boil mix, salt, and cold water. Bring to boil and boil 1 minute. Drain, rinse, and add to milk.

Cook bacon in skillet until well-done but not crisp. Drain and add to shrimp mixture. In same skillet, cover and cook onions and peppers over low heat about 30 minutes, stirring frequently. Add to mixture.

Boil celery and potatoes in salted water until tender but still firm, no longer than 10 minutes, and add to shrimp mixture. Stir in crab meat, parsley, sherry, and seasonings, and cook 2 or more hours over low heat to blend all ingredients. More milk may be added if mixture becomes too thick.

Note: Never boil cioppino as it will curdle.

Serves 12

Ted Rust, Director Emeritus
Memphis College of Art

VALENCIAN PAELLA

From the countryside in Spain, basically a rice dish with the added blessing of shellfish and chicken. Brought home to Memphis from a summer spent in Madrid.

8 pieces chicken
1 teaspoon oregano
1 clove garlic, minced
1/2 cup vinegar
1/4 cup olive oil
8 mussels in shells, thoroughly scrubbed
1 green bell pepper, chopped
1 onion, chopped
1 large tomato, quartered
8 clams in shells, thoroughly cleaned
1 teaspoon paprika
5 cups chicken broth
1 clove garlic
1/2 cup fresh parsley sprigs
1/4 teaspoon powdered saffron
1/2 teaspoon salt
6 cups cooked rice
12 shrimp, unpeeled

Marinate chicken overnight in mixture of oregano, minced garlic, and vinegar.

Fry chicken in olive oil in heavy skillet until nicely browned. Remove and place in deep heavy pot along with mussels. (Discard any mussels which have opened.) Combine pepper, onion, and tomato, and sauté in same skillet, adding more oil if needed. Mash tomato during cooking. Add clams and cook 10 minutes until shells open. Stir in paprika. Remove mixture from skillet and add to chicken and mussels. Stir in broth.

Thoroughly press and blend garlic clove, parsley, and saffron, adding small amount of broth to aid mixing. Add to pot along with salt. Add rice and stir all ingredients briefly. Cook 5 minutes more, add shrimp, and reduce heat. Cover and simmer 10 to 15 minutes or until liquid is reduced. (Discard any mussels which have not opened.) Garnish with lemon wedges.

Serves 6

Robbie L. Crosby

GAME

BARBECUED VENISON

Great addition to a holiday buffet.

Venison ham, well-trimmed
Pork roast, about half the
    size of venison ham
Salt and pepper to taste
Sesame oil

Soy sauce or Chinese oyster
    sauce
Garlic cloves
Favorite barbecue sauce

Season venison and pork generously with salt, pepper, sesame oil, and soy sauce. Refrigerate several hours, basting occasionally with additional sesame oil and soy sauce. Pierce meat on all sides and insert garlic cloves.

Place venison and pork in roasting pan, add 1 to 2 inches water, and cover with foil tent. Roast at 250 degrees for 4 to 6 hours or until meat falls off bone.

Chop meats. Mix together in baking dish with barbecue sauce, cover, and heat thoroughly to blend flavors.

Serves 16 to 20

Marguerite Piazza Bergtholdt

CHORIZOS-VENISON SAUSAGE

That special traditional Spanish sausage—with the added attraction of venison. Wonderful with BLACK BEAN SOUP, sautéed apples, red cabbage, and CORNSTICKS.

2 pounds venison
2 pounds pork shoulder
1 pound rindless pork fat
¼ cup wine vinegar
8 large cloves garlic, minced
1 to 2 4-ounce cans jalapeño
    peppers, chopped

¼ cup chili powder
1 tablespoon oregano
1 teaspoon ground cumin
2½ teaspoons coarsely ground
    black pepper
1½ tablespoons salt

In several small batches, place meats and pork fat in food processor and grind coarsely. In large mixing bowl, combine coarsely ground meat with remaining ingredients and mix thoroughly. Make patties of sausage and fry over medium heat until browned.

Note: Any unused portion of uncooked sausage may be frozen and fried later.

Yields 5 pounds sausage

Flo Snowden

VENISON BOURGUIGNONNE

At a dinner in his honor following a symphony performance, the visiting piano soloist, having recently dieted and lost forty pounds, advised apologetically that he must dine lightly. However, three servings of venison bourguignonne later, it was apparent his light diet was being played *rubato*.

4 pounds top round roast of
    venison
1 cup all-purpose flour
1 teaspoon salt
½ teaspoon pepper
½ teaspoon paprika
½ teaspoon garlic powder
¼ cup bacon drippings

¼ cup water
4 tablespoons butter
1 tablespoon sugar
2 pounds small white onions
1 pound mushrooms
3 cups Burgundy wine
1 small bay leaf

Remove all fat, bone, and silver skin from venison. Cut in large cubes. Combine flour, salt, pepper, paprika, and garlic in plastic bag, and shake to mix. Place meat cubes in bag and shake to coat with flour mixture. Place bacon drippings in heavy skillet, add meat, and brown over medium high heat. Transfer meat to 9 x 13-inch baking dish. Add ¼ cup water to skillet, stir to loosen browned bits, and pour over meat.

Wipe skillet with paper towel. Add 2 tablespoons butter and onions. Sprinkle sugar over onions, shaking skillet to thoroughly coat onions, and cook over medium heat until onions are browned. Scatter onions over venison in baking dish.

Melt remaining butter in skillet, sauté mushrooms until lightly browned, and add to baking dish. Pour wine over meat and vegetables, add bay leaf, cover, and bake 1 hour at 350 degrees. Remove cover, adjust seasonings, return to oven, and bake 15 minutes more. Remove bay leaf and serve.

Serves 8

Mrs. M. V. Highsmith

BAKED ORANGES FOR WILD DUCK

A wonderful complement for almost any wild duck dish.

4 large navel oranges, unpeeled
2 cups sugar
1½ cups water
Pinch of salt

Combine oranges, sugar, water, and salt in medium sauce-pan. Cover and cook 30 minutes over low heat. Add small amount of water, if necessary. Remove oranges with slotted spoon. Cut oranges in quarters and place in baking dish. Boil remaining liquid slowly for 5 minutes to make syrup and pour over oranges. Bake covered 30 minutes at 350 degrees. Serve as side dish with ducks.

Serves 4

Elizabeth J. Gilliland

WILD DUCK SUPERLATIVE

A duck blind can be one of the world's most beautiful places—no matter the cold. The dark woods becoming out-lined against the lightening sky at sunup, deep blues becom-ing a soft glow of pink and gold, and the sudden sound and sight of wild ducks have to rank among life's grandest mo-ments. It's all part of what makes duck taste so good.

4 wild ducks
3 eggs, beaten
1 cup bread crumbs
1 teaspoon salt
1 teaspoon pepper
1 to 2 tablespoons butter
Bacon drippings
¼ teaspoon paprika
2 whole bay leaves
4 whole cloves
2 cloves garlic, chopped
¼ cup wine vinegar
2 tablespoons Worcestershire
   sauce
1 teaspoon Kitchen Bouquet
1 tablespoon A-1 sauce
1 10-ounce jar red currant jelly
½ cup red wine

Fillet breasts and slice meat from legs. If large, cut in 3 to 4 pieces. Dip in beaten eggs and then in bread crumbs that have been mixed with salt and pepper. Place butter and bacon drippings in heavy saucepan. Add duck pieces and brown on all sides. Add all other ingredients except jelly and wine, and stir. Combine jelly and wine with small amount water, mix well, and pour over meat in pan. Simmer at least 1 hour or until tender. Remove bay leaves before serving.

Serves 8

Janis M. C. Iskra

DUCK SALAD

One of the best ways ever for serving duck.

6 ducks, preferably mallards
3 chicken bouillon cubes
1 large onion, quartered
7 ribs celery
Parsley flakes to taste
Salt and pepper to taste
1 green bell pepper, finely
   chopped
3 green onions, finely chopped
Tabasco sauce to taste
Dill to taste
Seasoned pepper to taste
1 tablespoon lemon or lime juice
Hellmann's mayonnaise
Sprig of dill or parsley

Place ducks in pot and cover with water. Add bouillon cubes, onion, 2 ribs celery, parsley flakes, salt, and pepper. Bring water to boil, reduce heat, and simmer covered until done, approximately 1 hour.

Remove skin and all bones from ducks, and chop meat by hand until very fine. Add bell pepper, green onions, and re-maining 5 ribs celery, finely chopped. Mix well. Add gener-ous amount Tabasco sauce, dill, and seasoned pepper. Mix in lemon or lime juice and enough mayonnaise to hold mixture together and mold. Garnish with sprig of dill or parsley and serve as spread for crackers.

Serves 8 to 10

Richard T. Ashman

BURGUNDY DUCK

Incredibly easy. In a word, a recipe that is just ducky.

2 wild ducks
Salt
¼ cup brown sugar
2 tablespoons catsup
2 tablespoons vinegar
2 tablespoons Worcestershire
   sauce
1 teaspoon paprika
⅔ cup Burgundy wine

Line heavy skillet with heavy foil. Wash and dry ducks, sprinkle with salt, and place on foil in skillet. Combine re-maining ingredients, mix well, and pour over ducks. Seal foil tightly and bake 3 hours at 300 degrees. Open foil and check for doneness by moving a leg on each duck. If leg moves eas-ily, duck is done. If necessary, cook another 30 minutes or more.

Serves 4

Mrs. Ted Lewis

The Sporting Life at Hatchie Coon Hunting Lodge

THE PICTURE: *The end of a dock, the river flowing by, a glimpse of an old duck blind—these are familiar scenes, for hunting and fishing were, are, and—if wildlife conservationists prevail— always will be among the prime diversions enjoyed by Memphis sportsmen. Few other American cities can claim so close a proximity to large and varied populations of fish, fowl, and game animals, or so rich a heritage of hunting history. In widely acclaimed books and articles, a Memphis writer named Nash Buckingham (1880-1971), left a record of his more than eighty hunting years, from early-day memories to latter-day wisdom. No one has more artfully communicated the age-old attraction, the exhilaration, of a sport that evolved from mankind's basic need for food. No one has more amiably described the countless pleasures—including pleasures having to do with the enjoyment of food—offered by the hunting and fishing clubs, many established a century or more ago, which have played a large role in preserving the traditions of the sport. This is Nash Buckingham's recollection of the seasonal cuisine of yesteryear, as prepared by clubhouse keepers at the Hatchie Coon Hunting Lodge near Marked Tree, Arkansas, the site of this picture: "Pre-breakfast coffee was slashed with choice brandy and a lump of butter; quite an eye-opening beverage if you've a mind to try it. Country hams, bacon, sausage, melons, berries, and scuppernongs—a cultivated muscadine grape—were 'home folks.' Maybe you'd sup on the haunch of a great turtle or a venison roast. Among fish offerings, 'fiddler' cats were the choice of many. Vegetables were in profusion, for the earth of those gardens would grow gold dollars." For present-day members, the tradition of good food, as pictured here, continues.*

THE FOOD: *Here, at the end of Hatchie Coon's dock on the unspoiled St. Francis River winding through the wilderness, a bowl of RED RIVER DUCKLINGS DUCK GUMBO awaits the attention of a hungry sportsman. It will be enjoyed with a thick wedge of corn bread and a cup of strong hot coffee. Someone has placed a wildflower bouquet of knotweed and cardinal flowers nearby.*

When the Chickasaw Indians ceded land in western Tennessee and northern Mississippi to the United States government in the early 1800s, they were relinquishing one of the North American continent's prized hunting grounds. Bears, deer, raccoons, rabbits, squirrels, and other small game ranged the uncut hardwood and cypress forests in infinite profusion. Wild turkeys, prairie chickens, partridge, and quail nested in the vast, unfenced fields. An abundance of fish—bream, largemouth bass, channel cat—filled the pristine waters of lakes, streams, and rivers. The sky was thick with waterfowl—geese, blue herons, great white cranes—that migrated between Canada and the Gulf of Mexico along the Mississippi Valley flyway. And across the broad river, in the marshes and bayous of Arkansas, there were great turtles, swans, and ducks—pintails, mallards, teals, wood ducks—in untold numbers.

Memphis was in the heart of this bountiful, newly opened territory, a veritable promised land to the bold frontiersmen of those early years. Seemingly inexhaustible supplies of game and fish were there for the taking by anyone with gun or pole—to feed their families, to share with friends and neighbors, to trade in local barter, or, after the coming of the railroads, to ship to game-hungry eastern markets. Several generations of young boys grew up in a world where hunting and fishing were as natural (and as necessary) a part of life as eating and sleeping. Then, with the passing of the years, the provider-hunter became, more and more, the sportsman-hunter. Shooting and fishing clubs that honored the rituals and fostered the camaraderie of the hunt appeared throughout the region—clubs with fine old names like Menasha, Beaver Dam, Five Points, Kingdom Come, Wapanoca Outing, and Hatchie Coon.

Nash Buckingham was a celebrated Memphis writer and storyteller, a shooting-man's writing-man whose works both spanned and epitomized the changes in the sporting life he reported first-hand. Born in 1880, "he started gunning in an era of unlimited bags" and won renown as "one of the finest wing shots of his generation." But by the time of his death in 1971, at the age of ninety-one, he had become one of the modern conservation movement's most eloquent advocates. The force of his later arguments, no less than the charm of his early writings, derived from vivid personal memories of an earlier time, a time he once called "the prodigal years." Memories of making Indian war bonnets as a child from the feathers of swans, geese, and ducks his father brought home to share with neighbors. Of his own first hunting trip at the age of twelve in the "primeval forest of alluvial Arkansas" where he lowered his first bobwhite, got his first glimpse of a prairie chicken, and marveled at the sight of thousands of white herons in flight, drifting overhead in the dawn's pink and silver light. Of shooting geese as a young man, "mostly Canadas but a few blues and snows too, from practically every worthwhile sand bar between Cairo, Illinois, and the Texas coastals." And memories of an outdoorsman's paradise at hunting and fishing clubs such as Hatchie Coon on the beautiful St. Francis River in Arkansas, which, in those days, could be reached only by handcar on a narrow-gauge tramway connecting to the Frisco Railroad. (As late as 1988, the quaint little tram was the only way in to the clubhouse when the water was up.)

Life at Hatchie Coon was "tranquillity itself," Buckingham wrote. "The great bottomlands of the St. Francis and Little River basins lay all but inviolate ... The clubhouse, built high on stilts above the crest line of the inevitable floods, provided a huge living room, cavernous fireplace, dining room, and kitchen. Sleeping quarters and baths accommodated goodly parties." Nash's description of the old club exemplified the true sporting life of those bygone days: "No automobiles, no outboard motors, no deep-freezers.... We would pole upstream to the saw-grassed spreads, shoot a limit of fifty woodies, then catch a limit of [fifty] bass en route to the clubhouse. After lunch there would be time for a snooze before the afternoon train back to Memphis, unless a two-day jaunt was planned.... Now, remember, these scenes were being enacted all over the South in the period 1889-1909."

Yet during those same years, almost unnoticed at first, paradise was being lost. Land drainage and droughts were beginning to take their toll on the breeding grounds of migratory waterfowl; commercial lumbering was getting started and would affect the natural habitat of wildlife; but unchecked market hunting, and unlimited bags by those hunters who used repeating rifles, pump guns, and autoloaders to take every piece of game that presented itself, were decimating the region's wildlife population. The swans were gone from Arkansas by 1890, the prairie chickens vanished soon after. By the turn of the century, chilling reports of dwindling wildfowl populations and the disappearance of upland game brought urgent calls for federal and state intervention to protect wildlife.

Some of those calls came from hunters and fishermen who not only supported passage of migratory bird laws and backed legislation to protect breeding grounds, but urged self-regulation by sportsmen as well. With the pressure of shooting making visible gaps in the migrations, the Boone and Crockett Club, as early as 1906, passed resolutions for action against autoloaders. Some hunting clubs had already adopted self-imposed daily bag limits of fifty ducks. (A generous restriction when, as Nash Buckingham later recalled in a magazine article called "The Prodigal Years," a party of twenty-two gunners on a Christmas week hunt at Wapanoca in 1898 could, and indeed did, bag eleven hundred ducks in a single day.) The clubs now lowered the limit to forty, and eventually supported much lower state and federal limits. Their members backed establishment of government wildlife refuges and helped organize the wildlife preservation efforts of private groups like Ducks Unlimited. Paradise could never be regained—not the heedless paradise of bygone days. But efforts to reclaim a semblance of that paradise by invoking the love of nature it represented began to pay off. By the second half of the twentieth century, conservation had become both the creed and the cause of true sportsmen.

Today, ducks still thrive in the marshy rice lands of Arkansas, quail and dove still populate the open fields of Mississippi, deer continue to roam in the Tennessee woods. And hunting and fishing clubs like Hatchie Coon still offer outdoorsmen a chance to enjoy good times, good friends, good food, and all the ancient traditions that accompany the sporting life.

RED RIVER DUCKLINGS DUCK GUMBO

A gumbo is a Cajun dish which is perfectly suited to all-day cooking, with its special aroma filling the house. Cajun dishes have made their way from the bayou country of South Louisiana up through the Delta to become Southern favorites, with infinite variations on the basic combination of meat or fish, okra, and spices. Here is one of those favorites—the first-place winner in the Third Annual Duck Gumbo Cook-Off in Stuttgart, Arkansas.

5 wild ducks	2 yellow onions, chopped
1 pound ham hock	1 bunch celery, chopped
5 quarts water	1 small banana pepper,
1 white onion, quartered	chopped
1 rib celery with leaves	1 green bell pepper, chopped
1 tablespoon Accent	6 cloves garlic, minced
2 tablespoons Creole seasoning	4 cups sliced okra
1 tablespoon Kitchen Bouquet	4 cups chopped tomatoes
10 bay leaves	1 pound smoked sausage, cut
1 tablespoon Cayenne pepper	in pieces
2 tablespoons Tabasco sauce	4 tablespoons filé powder,
Salt and pepper to taste	optional
1 cup vegetable oil	Cooked rice
1 cup all-purpose flour	1 cup chopped green onions
1 white onion, chopped	with tops
2 red onions, chopped	1 cup chopped fresh parsley

Add ducks and ham hock to 5 quarts water in large soup pot. Add quartered white onion, rib of celery, Accent, Creole seasoning, Kitchen Bouquet, bay leaves, Cayenne pepper, Tabasco sauce, salt, and pepper. Cook at least 1½ hours until stock is rich and until meat is tender and falls easily from bones. Remove meat from ducks and reserve along with pieces of ham. Chill stock and skim grease. Strain stock and reserve.

Heat oil in large heavy soup pot. Add flour to make a roux, stirring continually with wooden spoon over medium to medium-high heat, until roux is dark like chocolate, smooth and glossy. (Heat may need to be adjusted higher or lower during cooking.) This takes time, the stirring is long, the pot must be watched, but the roux must be right. Add white, red, and yellow onions, celery, peppers, and garlic. Cook and stir over medium-high heat until onions are transparent. The vegetable mixture may seem too thick, but will become more liquid as it cooks. Add okra, tomatoes, and sausage. Cook and stir 15 to 20 minutes until okra is tender.

Combine reserved meat and stock, heat briefly, and stir into vegetable mixture. Cover and simmer at least 4 hours. Remove from heat. Just before serving, stir in filé powder, if desired. (Or serve in shaker to be added to individual servings to taste.) Ladle gumbo into bowls and serve with scoop of rice on top. Sprinkle with green onions and parsley. Offer additional Tabasco sauce to taste.

Serves 15 to 20

Mrs. Arthur J. Sutherland III

WILD DUCK COOKED WITH TURNIPS

A prerequisite is an affinity for the delicate sweet taste of turnips. The gravy is spectacular. Try some on homemade biscuits.

2½ tablespoons bacon	2 cups hot water
drippings	1 tablespoon minced parsley
3 wild ducks, cleaned, cut in	2 teaspoons finely minced garlic
pieces and blotted dry	½ teaspoon thyme
1½ tablespoons all-purpose	Cayenne pepper to taste
flour	1½ teaspoons salt
1 medium white onion, chopped	½ teaspoon freshly ground
20 young white turnips, peeled	black pepper
and halved	Cooked rice

Heat bacon drippings over medium heat in heavy 6 to 8-quart saucepan. Brown duck pieces in hot drippings, turning them frequently to brown evenly. Remove duck pieces and set aside. Reduce heat to very low and gradually stir flour into drippings to make a roux. Cook 2 minutes, stirring constantly, and add onion. Continue cooking and stirring until onion is browned and roux is dark brown in color, approximately 15 to 20 minutes more. Add turnips and cook in roux for 2 minutes, turning several times. Gradually add hot water, stirring constantly. Add parsley and seasonings, and mix well.

Bring mixture to boil. Add browned duck pieces. Reduce heat and simmer 1¼ hours or until duck is tender when pierced with fork. Serve with rice, about ½ cup of pan gravy, and several pieces of turnips ladled over each portion.

Serves 6

Mrs. Norfleet R. Turner

SAUCY DUCKS

A sauce that is wonderful for any game of dubious freezer age.

3 wild ducks
Salt and pepper to taste
1 14-ounce bottle catsup
2 tablespoons Worcestershire sauce
1 tablespoon vinegar
6 dashes hot sauce
¼ teaspoon ground red pepper
¾ cup butter
1½ cups hot water
2 cloves garlic, chopped

Place ducks breast down in iron pot or roaster. Combine remaining ingredients, mix, and pour over ducks. Cover and cook at 350 degrees for 3 to 3½ hours or until meat falls off bones. Add water if needed.

Chop meat and mix well with sauce. Serve on buns.

Serves 6 to 8

Dr. Sam L. Raines

MRS. WALLACE CLAYPOOL'S WILD DUCK

Claypool's—one of the great old duck clubs where timeless memories were made and carried home. Many a hunter will remember the camaraderie of the lodge table and Mrs. Claypool's kitchen magic.

4 ribs celery, chopped
2 onions, chopped
1 green bell pepper, chopped
½ pound pork sausage
2 wild ducks
4 strips bacon
3 cups liquid (half water and half sherry and/or consommé)
2 tablespoons all-purpose flour

Combine celery, onions, pepper, and sausage, and mix well. Stuff ducks with generous amount sausage mixture and place in heavy saucepan. Lay 2 strips bacon over breast of each duck. Add liquid and bring to boil. Cover tightly and simmer over very low heat for 3½ to 4 hours until tender.

When ducks are done, remove to platter. Blend flour into liquid in saucepan, stirring until thickened. Pour over ducks and serve.

Serves 4

Flo Snowden

SUNDAY SCHOOL DUCKS

Scene I: The Sunday School class is coming for dinner—some ninety in number. Scene II: A power outage occurs and a freezer yields a flock of thawed ducks. Scene III: Enter baked ducks for a crowd. Curtain: Happy dinner guests praise the ingenuity of the hostess and the largesse of the host.

4 whole duck breasts
Seasoned salt
All-purpose flour
Vegetable oil
1 package onion soup mix
1 10½-ounce can beef consommé
1 10¾-ounce can cream of celery soup

Slice duck breasts in thin strips. Sprinkle with seasoned salt, dredge in flour, and brown in oil. Layer in baking dish and sprinkle with soup mix. Cover with consommé and celery soup. Cover and bake 2 hours at 350 degrees. Uncover during last half hour. Serve over rice.

Note: Recipe may be increased and adjusted according to number of ducks available and to number of guests—even ninety in number.

Serves 4 to 6

Dr. William F. "Chubby" Andrews

DUCKS WITH ORANGE SAUCE

Really easy, really tender, really good. The sauce is almost superfluous.

2 wild ducks
1 teaspoon salt
1 10½-ounce can onion soup
1 cup red cooking wine

Cut ducks in half and soak overnight in cold water to which salt has been added. Remove from salt water and place in roasting pan. Completely cover with undiluted soup, cover pan, and bake 3 to 4 hours at 350 degrees. Halfway through baking, add wine. Test with fork for doneness. Serve with orange sauce and wild rice.

Orange Sauce
1 orange, juice and rind
2 lemons, juice and rind
1 cup confectioners' sugar
1 tablespoon grated horseradish
2 tablespoons melted currant jelly

Grind orange and lemons. Combine all ingredients and pour into medium saucepan. Heat and serve.

Serves 4

Mrs. John D. Hughes

148

WILD DUCK WITH NOODLES

An at-home dish that warms a hunter's heart.

2 wild ducks	1 6-ounce package wide egg
4 ribs celery, sliced	noodles
1 cup celery leaves	½ cup butter, melted
1 teaspoon salt	Freshly ground black pepper
1 teaspoon pepper	Fresh parsley, chopped

Wash ducks well. Stuff cavities with sliced celery. Place in Dutch oven and cover with water. Add celery leaves, salt, and pepper. Cook over low to medium heat 1½ to 2 hours or until meat falls off bones. Set aside to cool. Remove meat and refrigerate. Strain broth and refrigerate overnight.

Skim all fat from broth. Bring broth to boil, add noodles, and cook until done, adding water only if necessary. Drain noodles, add duck meat and butter, and heat thoroughly, stirring occasionally. Add pepper to taste. Arrange on platter and garnish with fresh parsley.

Serves 4

Dr. Fontaine Moore

DUCK HASH

A supper-by-the-fire kind of dish—tasty, easy, comforting.

2 wild ducks	2 tablespoons Worcestershire
1 medium onion, chopped	sauce
1 small green bell pepper,	Garlic powder to taste
chopped	Greek seasoning to taste
1 dozen fresh mushrooms sliced	Salt to taste
2 tablespoons butter	Red pepper top taste
2 tablespoons all-purpose flour	Fresh fruit for garnish (grapes,
1½ cups chicken stock or beer	apple, pineapple)

Simmer ducks in salted water until tender. Remove skin and discard. Remove meat from bones and cut in small pieces.

In 12-inch skillet, sauté onion, pepper, and mushrooms in butter. Gradually stir in flour and blend well. Slowly add chicken stock, Worcestershire sauce, garlic powder, Greek seasoning, salt, and red pepper. Stir until mixture thickens. Add more liquid if needed (preferably broth from cooked ducks, or milk), and stir in duck pieces. Serve over toast or wild rice. Garnish with small skewer of fresh fruit.

Serves 4

Lucy Wilkinson

WILD DUCK WITH CANTONESE SAUCE

Makes getting up at 3:30 a.m. and freezing for hours in a duck blind more than worth it all.

2 wild ducks, giblets reserved	1 apple, quartered
Salt and pepper to taste	1 14-ounce bottle barbecue
½ cup all-purpose flour	sauce
1 cup bacon drippings	1 carrot, sliced lengthwise
1 onion, quartered	2 ribs celery, sliced
1 orange, quartered	½ cup water

Soak cleaned ducks overnight in salted water.

Drain ducks and set giblets aside. Sprinkle ducks with salt and pepper, and dredge in flour. Heat bacon drippings in heavy black iron skillet. Add ducks, sear on all sides, remove from skillet, and reserve drippings. Stuff ducks with onion, orange, and apple to absorb wild flavor. Place breast side up in Dutch oven, baste with barbecue sauce, and surround with carrot and celery. Add ½ cup water, cover, and bake 2 to 2½ hours at 350 degrees. Baste occasionally with more barbecue sauce. When done, remove onion, orange, and apple. Serve with choice of gravy or Cantonese sauce.

Gravy

Reserved giblets, chopped	2 tablespoons all-purpose flour
Reserved drippings	1 hard-cooked egg, chopped

Place giblets in small saucepan, cover with water, and cook until tender. Heat drippings remaining in black iron skillet, gradually stirring in flour until mixture thickens. Add giblets with pan juices, egg, and small amount water, stirring constantly to make gravy.

Cantonese Sauce

½ cup beer	1 tablespoon lemon juice
¼ cup dry mustard	1 teaspoon grated orange peel
1½ cups apricot preserves	2 tablespoons soy sauce

Combine beer and dry mustard. Blend until smooth and combine with remaining ingredients, pour into top of double boiler, stir to blend, and heat. Keep sauce hot until ready to serve, or simply reheat when needed. Sauce can be made first and spread on top of duck while roasting to give it a glaze.

Serves 4

Peggy Jalenak

FRIED DUCK

Something this easy shouldn't taste this good.

2 wild ducks	1/8 teaspoon dry mustard
1 cup all-purpose flour	1/8 teaspoon salt
1/8 teaspoon Greek seasoning	1/8 teaspoon pepper
1/8 teaspoon garlic powder	1 cup milk
1/8 teaspoon oregano	

Bone ducks and cut in 1-inch strips. Combine flour with all seasonings and mix well. Dip each strip in milk and then dredge in seasoned flour. Cook in deep fryer for 5 minutes or until lightly browned.

Serve as hors d'oeuvre with a sweet-sour sauce, or with pan gravy and rice as entrée.

Serves 4

Lucy Wilkinson

BAKED WILD DUCK

A very good dish with an especially good sauce.

2 wild ducks	2 tablespoons salt
2 teaspoons baking soda	4 tablespoons pepper
3 tablespoons vinegar	Butter
1 onion, sliced	All-purpose flour
1 potato, sliced	1 apple, sliced

Split ducks down back. Soak overnight in large pot with cold water, soda, vinegar, onion, and potato.

Remove ducks from water and wipe with cloth. Rub inside of each duck with salt, pepper, and butter. Sprinkle with flour, stuff with apple slices, and place breast down in baking dish. Add water 1/2-inch deep to baking dish. Pour sauce over ducks and cook at 350 degrees for 2 hours or until tender, basting often and adding hot water as needed.

Sauce
1/2 cup butter	1 cup chopped celery
Juice of 2 lemons	1 tablespoon prepared mustard
2 tablespoons vinegar	1 14-ounce bottle catsup

Combine all ingredients and mix well.

Serves 4 to 6

Carmen Phillipy

POTTED DOVES

A dove shoot is a memorable experience. It is sitting all afternoon in a hot cornfield watching for birds. It is an occasional hail of buckshot peppering hat and head. It is eager, sweet-tempered Labradors plunging into thickets to retrieve feathered quarry. It is sometimes an astounding barrage of gunfire signalling the fact that the one and only bird in every hunter's bead has made it in and out of the field. And it is barbecue suppers set out beneath the trees when day is done with dusty hunters either happy with their limit or happily anticipating another day's shoot. Dove season yields many a tasty morsel and many a tasty way to prepare them. Here is one especially good way.

40 dove breasts or 30 whole doves	1 cup all-purpose flour
2 quarts water	Black pepper to taste
1 bay leaf	1 teaspoon paprika
1 teaspoon peppercorns	1 teaspoon ground sage
1 tablespoon parsley flakes	Dash red pepper
4 teaspoons salt	1/3 cup vegetable oil
1 medium onion, chopped	1 12-ounce bottle beer
1 green bell pepper, chopped	2 tablespoons Worcestershire sauce
2 ribs celery, chopped	Cooked wild rice
5 tablespoons butter	

Place dove breasts or doves in pot and cover with water. Add bay leaf, peppercorns, parsley flakes, and 1 teaspoon salt. Bring to boil, reduce heat, and simmer covered for 40 minutes. Remove doves and pat dry with paper towels.

In small saucepan, sauté onion, bell pepper, and celery in 1 tablespoon butter, and set aside. In paper sack, combine flour, remaining 3 teaspoons salt, black pepper, paprika, sage, and red pepper, and shake to mix. Place doves in sack, several at a time, and shake to coat. Combine remaining 4 tablespoons butter with oil in large heavy saucepan. Place over medium heat, add doves, and brown. Add sautéed mixture, beer, and Worcestershire sauce. Cover and simmer slowly for 3 hours. (Add more beer if doves seem too dry.) Serve over wild rice.

Serves 10 to 12

Dr. Eph Wilkinson

DOVE PARMESAN

A versatile recipe that works equally well using ducks or fish.

Breasts of 12 to 15 doves	*½ cup Italian bread crumbs*
Salt and pepper to taste	*1 cup butter, clarified*
1 egg, beaten	*Juice of 1 large lemon*
1 tablespoon water	*¼ cup chopped fresh parsley*
½ cup Parmesan cheese	

Sprinkle dove breasts with salt and pepper. Whisk together egg and water. Toss together cheese and bread crumbs. Dip doves in egg mixture and then roll in cheese-crumb mixture. Place on baking sheet and refrigerate 15 to 20 minutes.

Pour ½ cup clarified butter into heavy skillet and brown doves quickly on medium-high heat. Remove to heated platter. Reduce heat to low and add remainder of butter, lemon juice, and parsley to skillet, stirring to blend. Pour over doves and serve immediately.

Note: If doves are frozen, thaw by soaking in salted water mixed with 1 tablespoon baking soda and 1 tablespoon vinegar. Rinse well before proceeding with recipe. If using frozen fish fillets in recipe, thaw without soaking.

Serves 4 to 5

Mrs. Lester Graves, Jr.

DOVE CASSEROLE

A very tasty way to prepare dove. Nice and crusty.

6 doves	*1 teaspoon finely chopped*
1 cup beef bouillon or sauterne	* parsley*
1 cup sliced fresh mushrooms	*1 medium onion, finely*
2 tablespoons butter	* chopped*
⅛ teaspoon thyme	*1 teaspoon salt*
⅛ teaspoon rosemary	*Cornstarch*

Place doves in large heavy skillet, add bouillon or sauterne, cover, and cook until meat falls off bones.

Sauté mushrooms in butter. Add thyme, rosemary, parsley, onion, and salt, and stir to blend. Remove meat from doves and add to mushroom mixture with remaining liquid from skillet. Stir in cornstarch for thickening, if needed. Place all ingredients in buttered baking dish. Bake at 350 degrees for 30 minutes or until crusty and brown.

Serves 4

Mrs. B. Snowden Boyle

DOVES CHASSEUR

Chasseur—the French word for hunter. Here is a sumptuous way to prepare the hunter's bounty.

1 teaspoon salt	*4 tablespoons Worcestershire*
½ teaspoon pepper	* sauce*
½ cup all-purpose flour	*⅛ teaspoon Tabasco sauce*
16 doves	*¾ pound mushrooms, sliced*
8 slices bacon, fried crisp,	*2 tablespoons butter*
* drippings reserved*	*1 teaspoon lemon juice*
⅔ cup consommé or water	*Fresh parsley, chopped*

Mix salt and pepper with flour. Season doves inside and out with additional salt and pepper, and dust lightly with seasoned flour. Heat 2 to 3 tablespoons bacon drippings in large Dutch oven. Brown doves on all sides in hot bacon grease. Arrange doves breast down in single layer and reduce heat to low. Add consommé or water, Worcestershire sauce, and Tabasco sauce, cover, and cook 20 minutes. Stir, turn doves, and cook another 20 minutes, adding more liquid, if necessary, to keep well-moistened.

Just prior to last 15 minutes of cooking time, sauté mushrooms lightly in butter and lemon juice. Add to doves. To serve, crumble bacon over doves and sprinkle with parsley.

Serves 8

Mrs. Norfleet R. Turner

DOVE BREAST PACKAGES

So easy to do. No muss, no fuss. Just does its own thing while you do yours.

3 dove breasts	*Soy sauce to taste*
¼ teaspoon beef bouillon	*Chopped parsley, oregano, or*
* granules*	* combination of herbs to*
Pepper to taste	* taste, optional*
1 strip bacon, cut in thirds	*1 to 2 tablespoons water*

Place 3 dove breasts on two layers of foil. Sprinkle with bouillon granules and pepper. Place bacon atop breasts and sprinkle with soy sauce and herbs. Add water, seal foil, and bake at 350 degrees for 1 hour. Check for doneness and if necessary, rewrap and bake 15 to 30 minutes more.

Serves 1

Mrs. Frank M. Norfleet

DOVE PIE

Four and twenty black birds baked in a pie? Not quite. But very likely just as good and just as fit for a king.

12 to 16 doves	Salt and pepper to taste
1 carrot, chopped	½ to 1 cup red wine
1 small bunch green onions, chopped	1 package dried brown gravy mix
1 rib celery with leaves, chopped	1 8-ounce can mushrooms
1 tablespoon chopped parsley	12 stuffed olives, sliced
1 tablespoon chicken bouillon granules	Pastry for 9-inch pie
	1 egg
	2 tablespoons milk

Soak doves in salted water overnight.

Drain doves and place in Dutch oven with carrot, onions, celery, parsley, bouillon, salt and pepper, and enough water to cover. Cook until doves are tender. Remove doves and set aside. Strain liquid, return to Dutch oven, and bring to simmer. Add wine and dried gravy mix. Add mushrooms, olives, and more water or wine, if needed, but gravy should be thick.

Bone doves, add meat to gravy, pour into baking dish, and cover with pastry. Mix egg and milk, and brush over top of pastry. Make slits in pastry and bake 30 to 35 minutes at 350 degrees.

Serves 6 to 8

Mrs. Arthur J. Sutherland III

A SIMPLE WAY TO ROAST A GOOSE

Perhaps Bob Cratchit never stood in a goose pit, searching the skies for the first sight of a flight of wild Canadas; nevertheless, the thought of roast goose does make us think of Christmas Past—of groaning boards and festive times. Here is a recipe that is simplicity itself.

1 young wild goose	Onions, quartered
Apples, quartered	Salt and pepper to taste
Oranges, quartered	Bacon slices

Firmly stuff goose with apples, oranges, and onions. Season with salt and pepper, prick skin several times with fork, and cover with bacon strips laid side by side. Secure legs and wings, and insert meat thermometer. Lay breast up on rack in roaster and bake 2 to 2½ hours at 325 degrees, basting often with drippings. Uncover during last 20 minutes of cooking.

Variation: Smoke a goose. Use brimming pan of charcoal mixed with 4 to 8 hickory brickettes soaked 15 minutes in water. Fill water pan with apple juice. Prepare goose as above, place in smoker on rack above apple juice, and cook according to manufacturer's instructions. (Check meat thermometer for doneness after 4 hours.)

Serves 6 to 8

Margaret Cobb Boyd

BAKED GOOSE

A grand way to cook one's goose.

2 wild geese	Seasoned salt
2 to 3 tablespoons salt	Garlic powder
1 tablespoon baking soda	Butter
1 tablespoon vinegar	1 to 2 tablespoons all-purpose flour
4 or 5 large potatoes	Dash Kitchen Bouquet
2 medium onions, chopped	
1 cup chopped celery	

Soak geese in water with salt, baking soda, and vinegar overnight. Change water and repeat at least once before cooking.

Peel, cube, and boil potatoes until tender and drain. In large bowl, combine potatoes, onions, celery, and seasoned salt, and gently mix to make dressing. Do not mash potatoes.

Rinse geese, pat dry, and sprinkle cavities with garlic powder. Stuff with potato dressing and rub with butter. Bake in covered roaster at 300 degrees for 3½ hours or until tender, basting with juices occasionally (or use meat thermometer as sizes of geese will vary). Remove cover for last half hour to brown geese. Remove geese from roaster and stir flour into pan juices, blending smoothly. Add water as needed to make gravy and dash of Kitchen Bouquet. (Dressing may be served as side dish.)

Serves 6

Mrs. Lester Graves, Jr.

WILD GOOSE MARTIN'S POINT WITH WILD RICE-SAUSAGE STUFFING

Martin's Point, on Maryland's beautiful Eastern Shore, is a favorite haunt of hunt-minded Memphians. It was also a favorite of James Michener, who chose it as part of the setting for his novel *Chesapeake*. Visits there sometimes yield geese—but always yield good times. "My heart knows where the wild goose goes …"

1 wild goose	1 large potato, peeled
Olive oil	and quartered
Salt	White onions, parboiled
1 large apple, peeled	¾ cup wild rice
and quartered	

Rub goose generously with olive oil. Rub salt inside. Stuff with apple and potato. Place in roaster, add 1 cup water, cover, and steam 1 hour at 300 degrees. Meanwhile, prepare wild rice for stuffing per package instructions. Remove goose from roaster, and discard apple and potato. Loosely fill cavity of goose with rice-sausage stuffing. Return to roaster and add 1½ cups water. Cover goose with butter-soaked tea towel or several thicknesses cheesecloth, and bake for 2 hours at 275 degrees. Remove cloth and bake uncovered 1 hour at 250 degrees. Meanwhile, place any remaining stuffing inside hollowed-out parboiled onions. Bake 40 minutes at 250 degrees. When done, reserve pan drippings for sauce.

Garnish goose with baked stuffed onions and orange slices. Serve with sauce and MUSCADINE PRESERVES.

Wild-Rice Stuffing

2 cups cooked wild rice,	1 medium onion, chopped and
well drained	sautéed in butter
½ pound mild sausage,	2 ribs celery, sliced
browned and drained	¼ cup chopped pecans
8 ounces fresh mushrooms,	Salt and pepper to taste
sliced and sautéed in butter	

Combine all ingredients and mix well.

Sauce

Reserved pan drippings	3 tablespoons all-purpose flour
3 tablespoons butter	Salt and pepper to taste

Skim grease from drippings. Melt butter in skillet and add flour, stirring until browned to make a roux. Blend in reserved drippings. Simmer and stir until sauce is of desired consistency. Adjust seasoning.

Serves 6

Mimi and Alex Dann

GAME CONSOMMÉ

When the judges for the Metropolitan Opera Mid-South Regional Auditions come to Memphis each year, this consommé is traditionally on the luncheon menu. Singularly good, it may be the reason that Memphis has sent so many singers to the Met.

2 pounds uncooked bones of	1½ pounds very lean, coarsely
venison, duck, dove, or quail	chopped venison or doves
1 pound lean venison	3 egg whites
½ pound meat from game birds	3 eggshells
2 medium onions	1 cup dry sherry
3 ribs celery with leaves	Chopped chives, sour cream, or
4 sprigs parsley	slices of lemon peel for
2 teaspoons salt	garnish
4 peppercorns	

Preheat oven to 450 degrees. Place bones from game in uncovered roasting pan and bake 30 to 40 minutes or until dark golden brown but not scorched. Add 1 to 2 tablespoons water to pan after first 15 minutes of browning, if needed.

Place bones in large stock pot. Add small amount water to roasting pan, scrape any brown bits adhering to pan, and add to stock pot. Add 1 pound venison and ½ pound game bird meat, onions, celery, parsley, salt, and peppercorns. Add 3 quarts cold water and bring slowly to a boil. Simmer gently for 1 hour. Correct seasonings, and simmer 1 hour longer or until meat is done. Skim surface occasionally.

Strain broth from pot through cheesecloth-lined colander. Cool and remove any accumulated fat on surface. To clarify stock, return broth to pot and add chopped venison. Beat egg whites until foamy, combine with broken-up shells of eggs and 1 cup of stock, stir, and return to pot. Bring slowly to boil, stirring constantly. Reduce heat and simmer 45 minutes. Solids will settle to bottom of pot. Remove broth with ladle and strain again through cheesecloth-lined colander to obtain clear consommé. Stir sherry into consommé just before serving. Garnish with chopped chives, dollop of sour cream, or lemon peel.

Note: Game bones may be all one variety, or mixture, or may be supplemented with chicken or beef bones, if necessary.

Serves 8 to 12

Mrs. M. V. Highsmith

Dinner for National Field Trial Judges at Ames Plantation

On the third Monday in February each year, dog-fanciers and hunting enthusiasts from near and far gather at the eighteen-thousand-acre Ames Plantation in Fayette and Hardeman Counties, just an hour's drive east of Memphis, for the start of the National Field Trial Championship. It is an an event of World Series-Superbowl-Kentucky Derby significance to the owners and handlers of bird dogs, with participants and spectators enjoying brisk days of hard riding and country cooking, and warm evenings of gracious dining in some of the beautifully restored (and still lived in) antebellum houses of nearby Grand Junction and La Grange, Tennessee.

Selected annually to compete in the National Field Trial are some twenty-four to thirty-eight prize-winning pointers and setters, chosen from some one thousand dogs from the United States, Canada, and other parts of the world. To qualify, the dogs must have won during that year at least two firsts in previous competitions elsewhere, and placed second or third in at least one other. Hunting in braces (pairs) for quail, and trailed by crowds of onlookers on horseback, the dogs' talents and endurance are tested for three hours over a fifteen mile course, running in sleet, snow, ice, drizzle—or sunshine—as the case may be. Only downpour or fog can halt the Field Trial, and even then the interruption is temporary.

Field trials were "born" in this country in 1874 at the old Greenlaw Plantation, now in the suburbs of Memphis. The first National Field Trial Championship was held in West Point, Mississippi, in 1896, but for almost a century now, the championship has been held at the Ames Plantation. In 1900, a wealthy Boston industrialist named Hobart Ames bought the fine old 1847 manor house, then called Jones Manor, on Cedar Plantation with its five hundred acres of surrounding land, as a winter home for himself and his wife. (He later increased his land to twenty-five thousand acres.) Then, as president of the Field Trial Association, a post he held for many years, he made it the scene thereafter of the association's National Championship. In succeeding years, under Ames' leadership, assisted by plantation manager Reuben Scott, the event became an increasingly significant affair, and the tradition was maintained by Mrs. Ames after her husband's death in 1945. When she died a few years later, her will, setting up the Julia Colony Ames Trust with the Bank of Boston to operate the plantation as a scientific research and wildlife preservation resource, for benefit of the University of Tennessee Institute of Agriculture, stipulated that the National Field Trial Championship would continue to be held there annually as a memorial to her husband. And so it has been, without interruption.

The activities get underway on the previous Saturday morning when owners and handlers gather for the drawing for bracemates and position. But the real crowds arrive for the competition itself, which begins the following Monday and continues for a week or ten days or more, as two braces of dogs are run each day, one in the morning and one in the afternoon, until all dogs have competed. The Field Trial is a spectator sport, open and free to all comers, and spectators as well as participants come from all over. There are Boston bankers, Texas cowboys, Japanese businessmen, Canadian ranchers, Mississippi planters. They wear all modes of dress—old khakis, blue jeans, reliable L. L. Bean outdoorswear, or very likely, sportswear from Dunn's, Inc. of Grand Junction. They ride all shapes and sizes of horses—even an occasional mule. Some in the gallery follow the action from cars or jeeps, driving along convenient roads.

Just before the running of each brace, when the two competing dogs are led by their handlers to the break away area, the drama is always the same. A hush falls over the crowd, sitting astride their mounts or shivering in the cold as they stand about awaiting the starting signal. The handlers kneel beside their dogs, holding their collars, stretching their tails to a point, smoothing their coats—as though their hands were molding from clay a perfect canine stance. At a signal from the judge, the handlers let go. The dogs are off. The handlers and judges follow on horseback, along with the mounted gallery which may number anywhere from five hundred to a thousand people. To the casual eye, the two small dogs look oddly insignificant, running across the wide winter fields, trailed by this huge gallery of riders on horseback. But the dogs are the stars, and everyone knows it.

The dogs make a cast around the edge of the field, sniffing, looking, while the handlers keep them on course by hand or voice signals. If a dog finds something, a single bird or a covey of quail, it will move in, tail up, trying to get as close as possible as quickly as possible without causing the bird to flush (or fly off); if necessary, the dog will instantly come from dead run to motionless statue. Meanwhile, the handler has raised his hat high to signal, "My dog on point." And until the handler gets there, dismounts, and attempts to flush the birds, the dog must remain on point—standing completely still, staunch, its entire body from nose to tail pointing toward the scent. When the handler fires one shell from his shotgun straight up into the air, the shot not only proves to the judges that the dog is gun-steady, staunch to flush and shot, it also says to the dog that a bird has been flushed and shot at, and the dog, having done its job well, remains staunch until it is released by the handler to resume the hunt. During the running of the braces, each dog is judged on the number of finds and on its ground race, for the competition is not decided on the number of finds alone, but also on a particular set of characteristics in evidence. Does the dog run fast or poke along? Does it completely cast around a field? Does it go to likely "birdy" places or just follow its handler's signals? Does it have bird sense and, as one owner put it, *savoir faire*? And does it meet the requirements of the Amesian Standard, among them " . . . speed, range, style, character, courage, and stamina—and good manners, always." At the end of each day the judges discuss that day's running and compare copious notes.

One of the great daily pleasures during the Field Trial is the noontime break when everyone—judges, owners, handlers, the gallery—gathers in the spacious Bryan Assembly Hall, named for former manager Jimmy Bryan, on the plantation grounds for a mid-day feast served cafeteria-style that features country treats such as barbecue, catfish, caramel meringue or pecan pie, prepared by local women from Grand Junction. Up the road, meanwhile, the staff at Ames Manor prepares the nightly dinner for their annual house guests—the trial judges and members of the Ames Foundation Board of Trustees and the Colony Trust—served according to the gracious traditions the Ameses established long ago.

On the final day, after the last brace is run, the judges will announce their decision from the steps of the manor house. There is only one top dog, no runner-up, and judges, dog, owner, and handler are photographed on the steps. The winning dog's name will be added to the roster of national champions. And the dog's owner will receive three rotating trophies to keep until the following year when, without fail, the crowds will again gather at Ames Plantation to enjoy one of the country's foremost sporting spectaculars.

SOUTHERN QUAIL

A favorite of the judges and other dinner guests at the National Field Trial at Ames Plantation. But let it be here recorded that although quail is a dinner specialty, it is always donated by friendly sportsmen from other hunts. The quail population at Ames is only for agricultural study and for Field Trial competition—never for the dinner table.

8 quail
Salt and pepper to taste
Butter, melted
1 6-ounce package brown
    and wild rice, cooked

½ cup chopped walnuts
½ cup chopped apples
4 strips bacon

Sprinkle quail with salt and pepper, and brush with butter. Mix rice with walnuts and apples, and stuff quail. Wrap each stuffed quail with strip of bacon and bake covered 1 hour at 350 degrees. Remove cover and bake 15 to 20 minutes more or until browned. Serve on top of rice mixture.

Serves 4

Ames Plantation
Grand Junction, Tennessee

QUAIL VÉRONIQUE

Hunting for quail is a delightful experience in itself—walking or riding through the fields, a well-loved dog on point, the flurry and thrill of a covey rise—and then there's the added delight of the delicate and wonderful taste of this lovely game bird.

4 quail
8 thin slices ham
4 tablespoons butter
Salt and pepper to taste
⅓ cup white wine

1½ ounces cognac
¾ cup white seedless grapes
4 thick slices bread
Butter

Stuff each quail with 2 slices ham. Sauté quail in butter until browned on all sides. Add salt, pepper, and wine. Cover pan and simmer 10 minutes. Remove cover, add cognac, and flame. Add grapes and cook 5 to 10 minutes more. Fry bread slices in butter until golden brown. Place 1 quail on each bread slice, spoon juices and grapes over quail, and serve.

Serves 4

Flo Snowden

PHOEBE COOK'S QUAIL

Something special. Perfect for a festive family holiday gathering.

8 quail
Salt and pepper

⅔ cup butter
1 cup light cream

Rub quail thoroughly with salt and pepper. Melt butter in iron skillet, add quail, and brown, basting and turning often, for 18 to 20 minutes. (Test one quail breast with point of sharp knife. If one is done, all will be.) Remove quail to hot platter.

Let skillet cool 2 minutes. Add cream, stir thoroughly, heat until warm, and pour over quail. Serve on toast.

Serves 4

Mrs. John W. Apperson, Jr.

QUAIL MADEIRA

Heritage Farms, a neighbor of Ames Plantation, has been in the same family since 1824, and quail hunts are very much a part of its long history. One of the great pleasures and traditions at Heritage is still the old custom of a group of friends gathering for a weekend with dogs and horses to hunt quail, and spinning stories in front of the fire when evening comes. Hunt suppers often include barbecue, Brunswick stew, and Quail Madeira.

8 breasts of quail
Salt and pepper to taste
½ cup butter
¼ cup chopped scallions
¼ cup Madeira

1 cup heavy cream
1 cup sliced fresh mushrooms
1 teaspoon paprika
Pinch of thyme

Wash and dry quail breasts and season with salt and pepper. Melt butter in heavy skillet, add scallions, and sauté. Add quail breasts and cook until lightly browned on all sides. Add wine and all remaining ingredients, cover, and cook over medium heat until quail is done, about 20 minutes. Serve over rice with pan gravy.

Serves 4

Peggy McKinnie Weaver
Heritage Farms
Hickory Valley, Tennessee

WILD TURKEY GUMBO

First, one must bag a wild turkey—no easy thing. But assuming this miracle has taken place, here is a great way to enjoy it. It takes place in three steps. If this seems long, just remember the hours spent in the woods tracking the birds, the camouflage and the mosquitoes, the pre-dawn arrival at the spot where hours of motionless sitting, calling, and watching lie ahead, and remind yourself that this is the easy part.

Step I—The Bird

1 large wild turkey, dressed	Black pepper
Creole seasoning	1 onion, quartered
Ground sage	2 ribs celery, cut in pieces
Garlic salt	1 lemon, halved
Lemon pepper	

Season turkey generously with all dry seasonings and stuff with onion, celery, and lemon halves. Place in smoker and cook according to manufacturer's instructions. When done, slice meat from turkey and serve (leave stuffing in bird). After sliced turkey has been eaten and enjoyed, prepare the stock.

Step II—The Stock

Turkey carcass, with remaining meat	Italian seasoning
	Garlic salt
2 bay leaves	Ground sage
Creole seasoning	

Place turkey carcass in large soup pot and cover with water. Add bay leaves and generous amount seasonings. Bring to boil, cover, and cook over high heat for 4 hours or until meat falls off bones. Remove all meat. Cool and strain stock. Reserve meat and stock for gumbo. Best made the day before making the gumbo.

Step III—The Gumbo

6 tablespoons vegetable oil	2 cloves garlic, minced
6 tablespoons all-purpose flour	½ cup fresh lemon juice
1 15-ounce can tomato sauce	½ cup Worcestershire sauce
2 10-ounce packages frozen sliced okra	2 to 3 tablespoons Tabasco sauce, (depending on one's tolerance for heat)
3 large onions, chopped	
1 green bell pepper, finely chopped	Creole seasoning to taste
	Salt and pepper to taste
1 bunch celery, finely chopped	

Heat oil in large soup pot. Gradually stir in flour to make a roux and cook, stirring continuously, until dark brown in color. Watch carefully, for if roux should become scorched at all, it cannot be used. Add tomato sauce and stir until well-blended. Reduce heat and cook until thickened. Add okra, onions, bell pepper, celery, garlic, lemon juice, Worcestershire sauce, Tabasco sauce, Creole seasoning, and salt and pepper, and cook over medium heat for 30 minutes. Add reserved stock and meat, and simmer 30 minutes more. Serve over rice. (Best served the next day, allowing the flavors to blend.)

Note: 2 to 3 pounds crab, shrimp, or oysters, or combination, may be added during last 15 minutes of cooking.

Serves 8 to 10

Mrs. John S. Evans

PHEASANT PÉRIGOURDINE

Of course, the best part of the recipe is in bringing home the pheasant. The rest is lagniappe.

2 pheasants	2 tablespoons pâté de foie gras
1½ cups port	¼ cup cognac
Salt to taste	¼ cup dry sherry
2 tablespoons butter, melted	2 teaspoons salt
2 tablespoons olive oil	Pepper to taste
1 tablespoon butter	4 chicken livers, finely chopped
3 green onions, chopped	2 truffles, finely chopped

Marinate pheasants overnight in port.

Drain pheasants and reserve wine marinade. Sprinkle pheasants with salt, brush with melted butter and olive oil, and roast 15 minutes at 400 degrees. Remove breast meat and cut in strips ½-inch wide.

Melt 1 tablespoon butter in skillet, add green onions, and sauté for 1 minute. Add pâté, cognac, and sherry, and flame briefly. Add reserved wine marinade, 2 teaspoons salt, pepper, and pheasant meat. Remove to platter. Stir chicken livers and truffles into skillet, cook until livers are done, and pour mixture over pheasant.

Serves 4

Flo Snowden

BREADS AND PASTRIES

LEMON BRAN BREAD

Unusually good flavor with a touch of zest.

2 cups sugar	1 cup milk
1 cup butter or margarine	1½ cups bran flakes
3 eggs, beaten	1 cup chopped walnuts,
1¼ cups all-purpose flour	optional
2 teaspoons baking powder	Grated rind of 2 lemons
¾ teaspoon salt	

Cream sugar with butter. Add eggs and mix well. Combine flour, baking powder, and salt, and add alternately with milk to egg mixture. Fold in bran flakes, walnuts, and lemon rind. Pour batter into two greased 4 x 8-inch loaf pans. Bake 50 to 60 minutes at 350 degrees. Pour topping over hot loaves and cool before removing from pans. For a less sweet loaf, omit topping.

Topping
Juice of 2 lemons   ½ cup sugar

Combine lemon juice and sugar, and stir over medium heat until sugar dissolves.

Yields 2 loaves bread

Peggy Tomford

TERESA'S BANANA MUFFINS

Delicious. Just a matter of minutes and there they are.

1¾ cups all-purpose flour	2 to 3 bananas, mashed
¾ cup sugar	2 eggs, beaten
1¼ teaspoons cream of tartar	½ cup vegetable oil
¾ teaspoon baking soda	¾ cup pecans, chopped

Mix all ingredients and pour into greased or paper-lined miniature muffin pans. Bake at 400 degrees for 18 minutes.

Yields 4 dozen muffins

Teresa Cuoghi Edens
Albuquerque, New Mexico

BRAN MUFFIN KEEPERS

A quick treat for breakfast. Batter can be kept in refrigerator up to 2 weeks.

1 15-ounce box 100% bran	1 cup vegetable oil
3 cups sugar	4 cups buttermilk
5 cups self-rising flour	4 eggs, lightly beaten

Combine dry ingredients. Stir in oil, buttermilk, and eggs. Pour into greased muffin pan and bake 15 to 20 minutes at 400 degrees.

Note: Raisins and nuts are a nice addition. Add either in the initial preparation of batter, or if stored in refrigerator for later use, add just before baking.

Yields 4 to 5 dozen keepers

Mrs. Frank M. Norfleet

STAND-BY BRAN MUFFINS

With this batter tucked away in the refrigerator, it's no trouble to bake a batch of muffins and serve with coffee when friends drop by. And the batter can be refrigerated up to four weeks.

1 cup bran buds	2½ teaspoons baking soda
1 cup boiling water	1 teaspoon salt
¾ cup margarine	2 cups Raisin Bran
1½ cups sugar	Raisins to taste
2 eggs, lightly beaten	Chopped pecans to taste
2 cups buttermilk	1 cup applesauce, blueberries
2½ cups all-purpose flour	or chopped dates, optional

In large bowl, mix bran with water and set aside to cool. Cream margarine with sugar, and add to cooled bran mix. Add eggs and buttermilk. Sift together flour, baking soda, and salt, and add to bran mixture. Stir in Raisin Bran, raisins, pecans, and optional choice. Bake in greased muffin pans 15 to 20 minutes at 375 degrees.

Yields 2 quarts batter

Martha McGuire

PEABODY MUFFINS

From the days of the old Peabody tearoom, muffins that were everyone's favorite. They are still being served today in this wonderfully restored hotel, now on the National Register of Historic Places. For many, they bring back memories of downtown shopping excursions and lunches with mothers and grandmothers, of the Peabody as a favorite luncheon spot for Memphis businessmen and visitors from the Delta and other places, and of the unforgettable wartime years of the forties when uniformed officers and enlisted men frequently filled the room. Corrine Hughes, tearoom hostess during the war years, remembers that customers were always called guests and that, upon arrival, they were offered hors d'oeuvres from a silver tray and later, mints and French pastries; that the room's antique mantel would be banked with magnolias, their fragrance filling the room; that the wonderful old lobby was a favorite place for many for reading newspapers and nodding a bit; that the music of the big bands of the time drifted from the adjacent Venetian Dining room where the bands played at noon, playing in the Skyway at night; and that the most expensive lunch cost eighty-five cents.

4 cups all-purpose flour	2 cups milk
1 tablespoon baking powder	2 eggs
2 cups sugar	½ cup butter, melted
½ teaspoon salt	1 tablespoon vanilla

Sift together all dry ingredients and make a well in the center. In separate bowl beat remaining ingredients thoroughly with fork. Pour into well all at once and stir quickly with fork until dry ingredients are slightly moistened. Do not beat or batter will become lumpy. Quickly drop batter into greased muffin tins, filling each slightly over half full. Bake 20 to 25 minutes at 400 degrees. Serve hot.

Yields 3 dozen muffins

Mrs. T. P. Hughes, Jr.

APRICOT TEA MUFFINS

A distinguished little muffin with the divine taste of apricots.

½ cup chopped dried apricots	2 cups all-purpose flour
½ cup boiling water	1 tablespoon baking powder
¼ cup margarine	1 teaspoon salt
⅓ cup sugar	4 tablespoons brown sugar
2 eggs	2 tablespoons margarine,
⅔ cup milk	melted

Pour water over apricots, cover, and let stand overnight. Drain.

Cream margarine and sugar. Beat in eggs and milk. Sift together flour, baking powder, and salt, and add all at once to mixture. Blend brown sugar and melted margarine, mix with apricots, and stir into batter. Fill greased muffin tins half-full and bake 15 to 20 minutes at 400 degrees.

Yields 12 to 18 muffins

Bobbye Bryant
Chicago, Illinois

APPLE MUFFINS

As good a muffin as can be found. And just suppose the apples are right out of the orchard with the early morning dew still upon them. Can't we dream?

1 cup raw honey	1 teaspoon nutmeg
1 cup vegetable oil	1 teaspoon cinnamon
1 teaspoon vanilla	½ cup nonfat dry milk
4 eggs	1¾ cups grated unpeeled
2½ cups whole wheat flour	apples
2 teaspoons baking powder	1 cup raisins, optional
½ teaspoon salt	Chopped nuts, optional
1 teaspoon allspice	

Combine honey, oil, vanilla, and eggs, and beat well. Mix all dry ingredients and stir into honey mixture. Fold in apples, raisins, and nuts. Fill paper-lined muffin cups two-thirds full and bake 12 to 15 minutes at 400 degrees.

Yields 24 muffins

E. Tucker Dickerson

Old Homeland Delicacies in the Greenlaw Addition

The city's first suburb was the thirty-block Greenlaw Addition, laid out in 1856 on undeveloped land along the river north of downtown Memphis by two enterprising brothers from Virginia. Some quarter of a century earlier, the Greenlaw brothers, William Borden and John Oliver, who were equal partners in everything they undertook, had arrived as youths in the new town of Memphis, without schooling or cash—a condition that proved to be no handicap whatsoever. Their first venture, a brickyard, rapidly expanded into a highly successful street and general contracting business. By the time they developed the Greenlaw Addition, they had already built several early Memphis landmarks, including the famous old Gayoso House, and had also petitioned, farsightedly but unsuccessfully, to develop an artesian well water supply for the city. (Not until 1887 would the artesian wells that still give Memphis one of its prime assets, a boundless supply of pure, sweet-tasting water, finally be tapped.) In subsequent years the brothers not only dabbled profitably in steamships, insurance, and railroads, but also built the city's two big public market houses, on Poplar and on Beale, as well as one of the South's finest theatres of the post-Civil War era, the Greenlaw Opera House.

Greenlaw Addition lay just north of the now vanished and nearly forgotten Bayou Gayoso (which marked the city's northern boundary for half a century) on a portion of General James Winchester's share of the historic John Rice land grant on which Memphis was founded. Since this was the first enlargement of the original city plan, Front Street, Main, and other downtown thoroughfares were extended northward into Greenlaw as wide, cobblestone boulevards, curbed with granite and lined with leafy sycamores. Indeed, one new east-west cross street was called Sycamore; others were named for the addition's investors and wealthy new residents.

Greenlaw, officially annexed in 1870 by an expanding Memphis, took on a unique diversity and vitality soon after the Civil War. The post-war, pre-yellow-fever city, its trade intact and its economy booming after several years of Northern occupation, was absorbing thousands of new residents—Southern farm families, white working-class Americans from the North or Midwest, immigrants, and new U. S. citizens, predominantly Irish and German. Attracted by reasonably priced property and its convenient location, many of these new Memphians from afar built, bought, or rented in Greenlaw; modest Queen Anne cottages and small neighborhood businesses began to appear among the larger homes. By 1890, Greenlaw's original population had grown to include skilled laborers (painters, plasterers, roofers, masons), neighborhood merchants (meat markets, feed stores, boot and shoe makers, druggists, bakers—many living above their shops in two-story brick buildings). Also, a sizable black community lived and worked in the area. Among the black-owned businesses were grocers, carpentry and blacksmith shops, and two restaurants. Notably, W. C. Handy's Knights of Pythias Band was headquartered in Greenlaw on North Fourth.

For many decades, as the city's fortunes peaked and ebbed, Greenlaw went its own eclectic, ethnic way, lending an enriching variety to Memphis cultural life. More recently, though, the area seemed in decline—until, once again, the historic Memphis "survival spirit" began to surface. Today, several self-help programs are at work revitalizing this historic district, and far-sighted preservationists are eying its landmark-quality old homes.

BURKLE'S BAKERY STRUDEL

Can hold its own with the best strudels of the world. A sweet, creamy, delectable pastry from the family recipes that made Burkle's Bakery a Memphis treasure.

3 cups bread flour	1 teaspoon salt
2 tablespoons cream of tartar	1 ounce ice water
10 tablespoons unsalted butter	1¼ cups unsalted butter,
2 large eggs	cut in thin pieces

In bowl of electric mixer, combine all ingredients except the 1¼ cups butter. Mix 5 to 6 minutes at medium speed until dough leaves sides of bowl and holds together well. Place dough on well-floured pastry board and let stand briefly to relax.

Roll out dough as thin as possible. Cover two-thirds dough with remaining butter and sprinkle lightly with flour. Fold unbuttered third into center of buttered two-thirds. Fold remaining buttered third over first third. Let rest 5 minutes. Roll out again on floured board. (If dough becomes too sticky to handle, refrigerate until slightly chilled.) Fold left third to center, fold right third to center, and then fold dough down center like a book. Let rest 5 minutes. Roll out again and repeat previous folding procedure. Let stand 1 hour. Roll out and repeat book folding procedure. Refrigerate overnight.

Bring dough to room temperature. Roll out as thin as possible and cut dough in half to yield two pieces each approximately 11 x 16 inches in size. Brush edges of dough with egg wash (2 egg whites whisked with small amount water). Spread filling lengthwise down center of each pastry. Fold left third of pastry into center. Fold right third into center about 1 to 1½ inches over edge of left third. Pinch ends together. Place with fold down on shallow ungreased baking pan. Push down on pastry ends to seal firmly. Brush top with egg wash and sprinkle with sugar. Bake at 400 degrees for 15 to 20 minutes or until golden brown.

Filling

1 cup sugar	3 8-ounce packages cream
½ cup butter, softened	cheese, softened
¼ cup orange juice concentrate	

Cream sugar and butter 3 to 4 minutes at medium speed until light and fluffy. Add orange juice concentrate and cream cheese, and mix 4 to 5 minutes. Filling should always be at room temperature before spreading.

Yields 2 world-class strudels

Herman Burkle

ORANGE WHEAT GRIDDLE CAKES

A delicious way to greet the day, especially when topped with yogurt or honey and fresh berries.

2 eggs	¼ teaspoon salt
¼ cup corn oil	½ teaspoon baking soda
1 cup whole wheat flour	⅔ cup orange juice
¼ cup oat bran	

Beat eggs and oil together. Sift dry ingredients together and add to egg mixture. Add enough orange juice to make batter pourable. Pour on heated and lightly oiled griddle. Turn when tops are covered with bubbles and edges are slightly dry. Serve immediately.

Yields 1 dozen 4-inch pancakes

Carol Lynn Yellin

BABKA

Babka is the traditional bread of Poland. It is usually served with jam or butter.

1 cup milk, scalded	½ cup butter, melted
2 packages yeast	4 eggs
¼ cup lukewarm water	1 egg yolk
½ cup sugar	4½ cups all-purpose flour
1 teaspoon salt	½ cup raisins

Cool scalded milk. Dissolve yeast in water, and stir into milk with all remaining ingredients except flour and raisins. Beat in 3 cups flour until smooth. Stir in remaining flour and beat 2 minutes. Add raisins. Cover with towel and let rise until light, about 1 hour. Pour into greased and floured 9-inch springform pan, cover, and let rise 1 hour more. Cover with topping and bake 1 hour at 350 degrees. Cool 10 minutes in pan before serving.

Topping

1 egg white	2 tablespoons sugar
1 tablespoon water	1 teaspoon cinnamon
2 tablespoons all-purpose flour	1½ tablespoons butter, softened

Whisk together egg white and water, and brush over top of babka. Mix remaining ingredients and sprinkle over top.

Serves 10 to 12

Ruth Jurand

SOUR CREAM BLUEBERRY PANCAKES

Blueberries, with all they connote, are the perfect addition to these marvelous pancakes.

1 cup milk
1 egg
¼ cup sour cream
1 cup all-purpose flour
1 tablespoon baking powder
1 tablespoon sugar
¼ teaspoon salt
2 tablespoons butter, melted
½ cup fresh blueberries

Combine milk, egg, and sour cream, and beat well. Stir together flour, baking powder, sugar, and salt, and add to milk mixture. Beat just until large lumps disappear. Stir in butter and fold in blueberries. For each pancake, pour ¼ cup batter onto hot, lightly greased griddle. Turn when tops are covered with bubbles and edges are slightly dry.

Yields 12 pancakes

Cecile Skaggs

HOMEMADE BANANA PANCAKES

A grand choice for a leisurely weekend breakfast.

1¼ cups sifted all-purpose flour
2½ teaspoons baking powder
¾ teaspoon salt
2 tablespoons sugar
2 eggs
½ to ¾ cup milk
3 tablespoons butter, melted
2 ripe bananas
¼ teaspoon cinnamon
¼ to ½ cup chopped pecans, optional

Combine flour, baking powder, salt, and sugar in bowl, and mix well. In separate bowl, beat eggs with milk and add butter. Blend bananas with cinnamon in food processor until liquefied and add to egg mixture. Gradually stir into dry ingredients, mixing only until moistened. Add pecans. Pour ¼ cup batter onto hot griddle, turning only once when tops are covered with bubbles.

Serves 4 to 6

Mrs. W. W. Cherry
Parkin, Arkansas

GRAMMY'S SWEET BISCUITS

A sweet biscuit with a German ancestry that made its way south from Pennsylvania. Really good with freshly brewed coffee or as a snack with a glass of cold milk.

8 cups all-purpose flour
1 tablespoon baking soda
½ teaspoon salt
1½ cups sugar
1 cup vegetable shortening
2 eggs, beaten
2 cups buttermilk
1 teaspoon vanilla
1 beaten egg white (or a little milk)
Cinnamon sugar

Sift flour, baking soda, and salt into bowl. Add sugar and mix together. Cut in shortening. Blend eggs, buttermilk, and vanilla, and add to dry ingredients. Knead well on floured board. Roll out thin and cut with biscuit cutter. Brush with egg white and sprinkle with cinnamon sugar. Bake 15 to 20 minutes at 375 degrees. Cool and store in covered container.

Note: Makes an excellent base for shortcakes.

Yields 3½ to 4 dozen biscuits

Jane A. Himes

MRS. ALICE CARTWRIGHT MANN'S WAFFLES

Waiting for melted butter and amber maple syrup—or perhaps a touch of yogurt and fresh raspberries. The batter is thick, but the waffles are light and fluffy.

3 eggs, separated
1¼ cups all-purpose flour
½ teaspoon salt
1 teaspoon sugar
½ teaspoon baking soda
1 cup buttermilk
¼ cup butter, melted

Beat egg yolks lightly. Beat egg whites until dry and stiff. Sift together flour, salt, and sugar. Add baking soda to buttermilk, stir into flour mixture, and add yolks and butter. Fold in egg whites and pour onto heated waffle iron. Cook until golden brown.

Note: Freeze waffles in plastic bag. Nice to have on hand to reheat and serve at a moment's notice.

Yields 3 cups batter

Rebecca Smythe Mann

ORANGE NUT BREAD

A steaming cup of tea, a slice of homemade bread, and quiet conversation with a very good friend. Life's special moments.

2½ cups all-purpose flour
1 cup sugar
½ teaspoon salt
½ teaspoon baking soda
1 tablespoon baking powder
1 cup chopped nuts
½ cup orange juice
2 teaspoons grated orange rind
2 tablespoons orange marmalade, optional
¾ cup evaporated milk
2 tablespoons butter, melted
1 egg, well-beaten

Sift flour, sugar, salt, baking soda, and baking powder together into medium bowl. Stir in nuts. Mix orange juice, orange rind, marmalade, milk, and butter into beaten egg. Add liquid ingredients all at once to dry ingredients, and stir until dry ingredients are moistened. Spoon batter into well-buttered 5 x 9-inch loaf pan and bake 55 minutes at 350 degrees. Let stand 10 minutes in pan. Remove to wire rack to cool. When cooled, wrap in foil and allow to season overnight in refrigerator before slicing.

Yields 1 loaf

Mrs. C. William Lantz

MRS. WILHITE'S CRANBERRY BREAD

Oranges and cranberries, reminiscent of sunshine and ocean breezes. Altogether wonderful.

4 cups sifted all-purpose flour
2 cups sugar
1 tablespoon baking powder
1 teaspoon baking soda
2 teaspoons salt
½ cup margarine
2 eggs, well-beaten
1½ cups orange juice
2 tablespoons grated orange peel
1 cup chopped nuts
2 cups chopped cranberries

Sift together flour, sugar, baking powder, baking soda, and salt. Cut in margarine. Mix together eggs, orange juice, and orange peel, and pour over dry ingredients. Mix just enough to moisten dry ingredients. Fold in nuts and cranberries. Spoon into three greased and floured 4 x 8-inch loaf pans. Bake 1 hour at 325 degrees.

Yields 3 loaves

Mrs. William H. Morse

GONGIE'S TEA DONUTS

Delicious little puffs, golden brown and sugar coated. Put on the teapot!

½ cup milk
1 egg, beaten
1 teaspoon vanilla
1 tablespoon vegetable oil
⅓ cup sugar
1⅓ cups all-purpose flour
2 teaspoons baking powder
¼ teaspoon salt
Vegetable oil for frying

Combine all ingredients except oil for frying, and mix well to make smooth batter. Pour enough oil into skillet or saucepan to deep-fry and heat to 375 degrees. Drop batter by teaspoonfuls into oil and deep-fry until golden brown, turning once. Sprinkle (or shake in bag) with confectioners', granulated, or cinnamon sugar.

Yields 9 to 12 donuts

Susan Gwynne Keathley

LEMON SCONES

Get out the Earl Grey and the homemade preserves.

4 cups all-purpose flour
3 tablespoons baking powder
¼ cup sugar
½ teaspoon salt
3 tablespoons and 1 teaspoon grated lemon peel
½ cup unsalted butter, cut into ½-inch pieces
2 eggs, lightly beaten and at room temperature
⅔ cup buttermilk
Heavy cream

Sift together flour and baking powder 3 times into deep bowl, adding sugar and salt the third time. Stir in lemon peel. Cut in butter until mixture resembles coarse meal. Blend in eggs and enough buttermilk to form soft, but not sticky, dough. Turn out onto lightly floured board and gently roll ½-inch thick, lightly flouring as necessary to prevent sticking. Cut with floured biscuit cutter. Place ½-inch apart on two greased and floured baking sheets, and brush with cream. Bake at 450 degrees for 12 to 15 minutes or until golden brown.

Yields 15 to 20 scones

Pamela Mortimer

ALMOND PUFF PASTRY

Simply delicious.

½ cup butter, softened
 (no substitutes)
2 cups all-purpose flour
2 tablespoons water

½ cup margarine
1 cup water
1 teaspoon almond extract
3 eggs

Cut butter into 1 cup flour and sprinkle with 2 tablespoons water. Mix with fork until ball is formed and divide pastry in half. Press each half into one 3 x 12-inch strip on ungreased baking sheet, keepings strips at least 3 inches apart.

Add margarine to 1 cup water and bring to rolling boil. Remove from heat and stir in almond extract and remaining cup flour. Return to low heat and stir continually until mixture leaves sides of pan and forms ball. Remove from heat, add eggs, and beat until smooth. Spread mixture over both pieces of pastry, covering well. Bake 1 hour at 350 degrees. Cool and frost (or freeze and frost later). Cut crosswise in slices 1-inch wide for serving.

Frosting
1½ cups confectioners' sugar
2 tablespoons margarine,
 softened

1½ teaspoons almond extract
1 to 2 tablespoons warm water

Combine all ingredients and mix well.

Yields 24 slices

Susan Chamberlin Hall
Virginia Beach, Virginia

SAUCE FOR DATE NUT BREADS

A sweet-sour sauce that heightens the flavor of any bread made with fruit and nuts.

1 cup sugar
½ cup butter

1 egg yolk, lightly beaten
2 tablespoons vinegar

Combine all ingredients in small saucepan and cook over low heat, stirring often, until smooth and creamy. Do not boil. Mixture will be rather thin while hot.

Yields 1 cup sauce

Minnie Morris McGregor
McCrory, Arkansas

DATE PECAN LOAF

So good during fall and winter months, and keeps a long time. A nice alternative for those who are not fond of holiday fruit cake. Superb with cream cheese, bourbon-flavored whipped cream, or with OLD FASHIONED BOILED CUSTARD.

1 cup sugar
4 eggs, well-beaten
1 teaspoon vanilla
1 cup sifted all-purpose flour

1 teaspoon salt
2 teaspoons baking powder
1 pound pecans, chopped
1 pound chopped dates

Gradually blend sugar with eggs and vanilla. Combine flour, salt, and baking powder, sift 3 times, and add to egg mixture. Alternately add pecans and dates to batter.

Grease sides of 8½-inch tube pan (or 2 loaf pans) and cover bottom with parchment paper. Pour batter into pan and bake at 325 degrees for 1 hour or until done.

Serves 24

Mrs. Albert A. McLean

HAWAIIAN BANANA NUT BREAD

"Sing me a song of the islands..." Luscious pineapple adds its own sweet flavor to that forever favorite, banana nut bread.

3 cups sifted all-purpose flour
2 cups sugar
1 cup chopped pecans or
 walnuts
1 teaspoon cinnamon
1 teaspoon baking soda
1 teaspoon salt

2 cups mashed ripe bananas
1 8-ounce can crushed pineapple, drained
¾ cup vegetable oil
3 eggs, beaten
2 teaspoons vanilla

In large bowl, combine all dry ingredients and set aside. In another bowl, beat together bananas, pineapple, oil, eggs, and vanilla. Add to dry ingredients, stirring just until moistened. Spoon into two greased and floured 5 x 9-inch loaf pans and bake 50 minutes at 350 degrees. Remove from oven, cover tops of loaves with foil, and bake 20 minutes more. Cool 10 minutes in pan.

Yields 2 loaves

Margaret S. Spain

Tea and a Private Journal at Goodwinslow

In 1824, when Memphis was a young and growing Mississippi River town, one of its three founding proprietors, Judge John Overton, was busy lobbying to make it the county seat of newly formed Shelby County, and thus assure the success of his investment. ("Commerce follows the courts" was the conventional wisdom of the times.) But the state selection committee, required by Tennessee law in those days to locate county seats no more than three miles from a county's geographical center, chose instead a place known as Sanderlin's Bluff on the Wolf River ten miles east of Memphis. Although it was in a wilderness inhabited only by trappers and Indians, when a wood frame courthouse was erected on this isolated site, there instantly grew up around it a prosperous community. The new town was named Raleigh by the first Shelby County circuit court clerk, in honor of the capital city of his home state of North Carolina. And, for a time, Raleigh's growth threatened to eclipse that of Memphis. Taverns and inns were built to accommodate attorneys who traveled from Memphis and surrounding areas to try their cases. Raleigh's citizens enjoyed fine mail service; they established an excellent school, the Raleigh Academy, for their children. The new community was fast becoming a cultural center.

Meanwhile, cotton, steamboats, and trains were bringing boom times (and many more lawyers) to rival Memphis. Then, ominously, the new railroads bypassed Raleigh. It was a crushing blow. The long ride to the courthouse by buggy or horseback, through dust or mud, became too much for Memphis lawyers. This time the courts followed commerce. In 1866, the lawyers succeeded in getting the county seat moved to Memphis.

Yet Raleigh persevered, and in the later years of the nineteenth century, it found a new identity—as a health resort. The medicinal value of the mineral springs water that bubbled out of a ravine near the center of town was first discovered in pioneer times when, according to a widely circulated legend, a Texas-bound family camping by the springs to await the death of their hopelessly sick infant claimed the miracle-working spring water cured the baby completely. For many years thereafter, Memphis druggists sold Baby Spring Water, bottled in Raleigh, to mothers concerned about the health of their families. And when health-conscious Memphians fled the city's yellow fever epidemics in the 1870s, quite a few decided to settle in Raleigh. Then, in 1891, good fortune came to Raleigh, quite literally, in the person of the North Carolina tobacco millionaire B. I. Duke, who visited the springs and decided they could become the site of a celebrated spa. Duke built the one-hundred-thousand-dollar Raleigh Springs Inn, a luxurious, up-to-the-minute resort hotel with electric lights throughout—even the flower beds were illuminated. It soon became the most fashionable vacation spot in the Mid-South. A year later Duke invested in an electric trolley line that brought riders from downtown Memphis directly to the door of the inn.

Raleigh at last had its rail link to Memphis, and those who enjoyed country living but whose business was in the city now became Shelby County's earliest commuters, retracing, in reverse, the Raleigh-bound travels of early Memphis lawyers. One Raleigh resident who made the hour-long ride to Memphis each day was a widely traveled, well-read attorney named William W. Goodwin. His unusual home, which he began building in 1875 and continued adding on to for the next twenty-five years, reflected his taste, travels, and interests. The twenty-room house (still occupied by Goodwin's descendants) is an eclectic architectural wonder with Italianate balconies, Tudor chimneys, even a Gothic tower with book-lined walls rising to a round glass skylight.

THE PICTURE: *A sense of history and a love of fine writing pervade the unusual home called Goodwinslow, built in 1875 in the town of Raleigh by William W. Goodwin, an attorney who was one of Shelby Country's early commuters. Here, too, lived his daughter, Anne Goodwin Winslow, a gifted author of books and writings that regularly appeared in* **The New Yorker,** *who made Goodwinslow a literary salon for the likes of Vachel Lindsay, Robert Penn Warren, John Crowe Ransom, Ford Madox Ford, Allen Tate, and Richard Halliburton. Winslow's daughter, grandson, and great-grandson still live here. On this day, the dining room windows of Goodwinslow are open wide to a summer morning breeze. In one corner of the room is a wooden harp, and beside the grand piano are bound books of music scores inscribed with the names of young ladies who grew up here. On the table is a mahogany tray set for tea with rose-colored Staffordshire in the Tonquin pattern, and old silver inscribed with the family name. A silver basket holds delicate blossoms from the garden's seventy-five-year-old perennial sweet pea vines.*

THE FOOD: *A cup of tea is poured, and loaves of sweet QUICK SALLY LUNN bread and WHEAT BREAD, still warm from the oven, are set out for the mistress of the house. Open for its daily recordings is a leather-bound, hand-written journal— another family tradition—with its mother-of-pearl quill pen.*

The Raleigh Inn burned down long ago, Raleigh's springs have long since dried up with a general lowering of the water table, and today's Raleigh, with its shopping malls and subdivision homes, is a bustling part of an expanding Memphis. But one remnant of the bygone Raleigh remains unchanged. Out of sight of the busy road, at the end of a long, winding, tree-guarded drive, set amidst a wide expanse of lawn and shaded by ancient magnolias, is William Goodwin's unique old mansion. It is called Goodwinslow now, for five generations of the Goodwin-Winslow-Chapman family who have lived there. There is a feeling, a spirit, in this house—bookish, quixotic, the last of its kind, a *grande dame* keeping pace only with itself, reserving the right of the aged to be as they please.

QUICK SALLY LUNN

An old Southern recipe with its roots in Europe. Did a French bread-seller really name it for the sun and moon—*soleil lune*—because of its golden top and lighter underside? Who knows? What is known is that from Colonial days forward, Sally Lunn has had legions of admirers. This particular recipe yields a beautiful hot bread, but uses no yeast.

2 eggs, separated
½ cup sugar
2 cups all-purpose flour
1 tablespoon baking powder
½ teaspoon salt
1 cup milk
½ cup butter, melted

Beat egg yolks and combine with sugar, mixing well. Sift together flour, baking powder, and salt, and add alternately with milk to egg mixture, beating well. Stir in butter. Beat egg whites until stiff peaks form and fold into batter. Pour into greased loaf pan, and bake at 375 degrees for 50 to 60 minutes or until done and browned on top. Sprinkle lightly with sugar, slice, and serve while still warm.

Note: Substitute 2¼ cups cake flour for lighter and more finely textured bread.

Yields 1 loaf bread

A combination of Southern recipes

NEVER-FAIL BISCUITS

Some people have been heard to say, "I could make these in my sleep." They really are quick and never-fail.

1 cup self-rising flour
⅔ cup milk
3 tablespoons vegetable shortening

Mix all ingredients and place on floured board. (Mixture will be very soft.) Knead 5 minutes, working in additional flour, until dough will roll out easily. Roll and cut with 2-inch biscuit cutter. Bake at 400 degrees for 20 minutes or until lightly browned on top.

Yields 1½ dozen biscuits

Ames Plantation
Grand Junction, Tennessee

WHEAT BREAD

A delicate wheat bread—particularly nice for a party. The Bundt design on the loaf is very pretty. Add a sprig of holly during the holidays.

⅓ cup vegetable shortening
3 cups lukewarm water
2 packages yeast
5 cups whole wheat flour
⅔ cup granulated sugar
½ cup all-purpose flour
2 tablespoons brown sugar
2 teaspoons salt
¼ cup butter, melted

Melt shortening in 2½ cups water. Dissolve yeast in remaining ½ cup water and stir into melted shortening. Combine dry ingredients and add to yeast mixture. Knead dough in greased bowl, set in warm place, and let rise until doubled in size. Knead again and put into greased large Bundt pan. Let rise until doubled in size. Bake 45 minutes at 350 degrees.

Remove from oven and pour butter around edges. Cool 10 minutes in pan and turn out on rack.

Yields 3 to 4 loaves

Flo Snowden

DELTA ROLLS

Good hot rolls, fresh from the oven, fragrantly wonderful. No commercial brand can ever come close.

2½ cups all-purpose flour
1 teaspoon salt
3 teaspoons sugar
1½ tablespoons vegetable shortening
1 package yeast
1 cup warm water
1 egg, beaten
Butter, melted

Sift flour, salt, and sugar together into bowl. Add shortening and cut in thoroughly. Dissolve yeast in water, add egg, and pour into middle of flour. Start mixing from middle, adding more flour if necessary to make soft dough. Roll out dough on floured board and cut in rounds. Dip top of each in butter and fold over. Place in baking pan and let rise in warm place until doubled in size, about 2 hours. Bake at 350 degrees for 20 minutes or until lightly browned.

Yields 1½ dozen rolls

Mrs. Winston Mosby
Helena, Arkansas

CHEESE BREAD

Too quick to believe. A wonderful way to perk up a simple supper.

3¾ cups buttermilk biscuit mix	1 egg, beaten
1¼ cups shredded sharp Cheddar cheese	½ teaspoon dry mustard
1½ cups milk	Sesame, poppy, or caraway seeds

Generously grease large loaf pan (or 2 small loaf pans or 1½-quart baking dish). Combine all ingredients in large bowl and beat vigorously for 1 minute. Pour into loaf pan. Sprinkle top with sesame seeds and bake 55 to 60 minutes at 325 degrees. Cool slightly before slicing.

Yields 1 loaf

Mrs. Henry T. V. Miller

COUNTRY APPLE COFFEE CAKE

A yummy coffee cake.

2 tablespoons butter	½ teaspoon cinnamon
1½ cups peeled and chopped apples	⅓ cup light corn syrup
1 10-ounce can refrigerated butter biscuits	1½ teaspoons bourbon whiskey
	1 egg
⅓ cup packed brown sugar	½ cup pecan halves or pieces

Using 1 tablespoon butter, generously grease bottom and sides of 9-inch round or 8-inch square pan. Spread 1 cup of apples in pan. Separate dough into 10 biscuits. Cut each biscuit in 4 pieces and place point side up over apples. Top with remaining apples.

Combine remaining tablespoon butter, brown sugar, cinnamon, corn syrup, bourbon, and egg, and beat 2 to 3 minutes until sugar is partially dissolved. Stir in pecans and spoon over biscuit pieces. Bake at 350 degrees for 35 to 45 minutes or until deep golden brown. Cool 5 minutes and drizzle glaze over warm coffee cake.

Glaze

⅓ cup confectioners' sugar	1 to 2 tablespoons milk
¼ teaspoon vanilla	

Combine ingredients and blend until smooth.

Serves 6 to 8

Elaine Schuppe

CORN MEAL YEAST BREAD

The best of two worlds—corn bread and yeast bread—all in one.

2 packages yeast	2 eggs, beaten
½ cup warm water	1 cup yellow corn meal
1½ cups scalded milk	5½ cups all-purpose flour
¾ cup butter	¼ cup butter, melted
½ cup sugar	2 teaspoons sesame seeds
1½ teaspoons salt	

Sprinkle yeast over water and set aside. In large mixing bowl, combine milk, butter, sugar, and salt. Cool to lukewarm and stir in yeast and eggs. Combine corn meal and 2 cups flour. Add to yeast mixture and beat 2 minutes on mixer's medium speed. Gradually add enough remaining flour until dough is soft and leaves sides of bowl. On floured surface, knead dough until smooth and satiny, about 5 to 10 minutes. Place in buttered bowl and brush with melted butter. Cover and let rise in warm place until doubled in size, about 1 hour.

Punch dough down, let rest 10 minutes, and divide in half. On lightly floured surface, roll each half into 9 x 12-inch rectangle. Beginning with 9-inch edge, roll dough tightly and seal final seam firmly. Seal ends of loaf and fold under. Place seams down in two buttered 5 x 9-inch loaf pans. Brush with butter and sprinkle tops with sesame seed. Cover and allow to stand until doubled in size, about 45 minutes. Bake at 375 degrees for 40 minutes or until loaf sounds hollow when tapped. Turn out of pans onto rack to cool.

Yields 2 loaves

Margaret D. Wilson

STELLA'S DINNER TOAST

Crisp and delicious!

½ cup margarine, melted	1 tablespoon parsley flakes
2 tablespoons grated Parmesan cheese	⅛ teaspoon garlic powder
	8 hamburger or hotdog buns

Mix together margarine, Parmesan cheese, parsley, and garlic powder, and spread on bread halves. Cut in halves again and bake at 250 degrees for 1 hour or until crisp. Serve hot or store in airtight container.

Yields 32 pieces

Mrs. William H. Morse

CRACKED SOYBEAN BREAD

A fragrant, sturdy bread, well blessed with protein. Heavenly when toasted and spread with jam and butter, or simply plain, fresh from the oven.

3 cups soy milk
2 packages yeast
3 tablespoons honey
¼ cup vegetable oil, warmed
1 tablespoon salt

6½ to 7 cups flour, half
  unbleached all-purpose flour
  and half bread flour
2 cups soy flour
½ cup cracked soybeans

Scald soy milk and cool until lukewarm. Sprinkle yeast over milk. Add honey, oil, and salt, and mix gently. Cover and let stand 10 minutes or until mixture foams.

Beat in 3½ cups combined unbleached flour and bread flour. (The combination of unbleached all-purpose flour and bread flour seems to improve texture and to facilitate rising of bread.) Beat in soy flour and soybeans. Add remaining flour in portions as needed, continuing to knead on lightly floured surface for 10 minutes or until dough is smooth and elastic. (Dough hook on mixer may be used.) Set aside to rise until increased by half.

Punch down, knead briefly, and let rise again until increased by half. Punch down, shape into 2 loaves, and place in lightly greased 5 x 9-inch loaf pans. Cover and let rise in warm spot until loaves increase by half. Bake at 350 degrees for 40 to 50 minutes or until golden brown.

Note: Soybeans and soybean products may be found in health food stores. A good food processor may be used to crack soybeans.

Yields 2 loaves bread

Mrs. Joseph H. Brooks

SLOW COOKER CORN STUFFING BALLS

A never-fail dish that is different from the usual corn bread dressing.

½ cup chopped celery with
  leaves
1 17-ounce can cream-style
  corn
¼ cup water
⅛ teaspoon pepper

1 teaspoon poultry seasoning
1 8-ounce package herb
  seasoned stuffing mix
2 eggs, lightly beaten
¼ cup butter, melted

Mix all ingredients except butter and shape into 8 balls. Place in slow cooker and pour butter over top. Cover and cook on low heat for 3 to 4 hours.

Serves 8

Patsy Kinney
Forrest City, Arkansas

YORKSHIRE PUDDING

Simple to make and simply elegant. Serve with a choice roast of beef.

2 eggs
1 cup milk
1 cup sifted all-purpose flour

½ teaspoon salt
2 tablespoons beef drippings

Beat eggs with milk. Sift together flour and salt, and stir into egg mixture. Beat batter until well-blended, occasionally scraping down sides (or use food processor, if preferred).

Heat 7 x 11-inch baking pan, ring mold, or muffin tins with about ¼-inch drippings in bottom. Pour batter into pan and bake 10 minutes at 450 degrees. Reduce heat to 350 degrees and bake 10 to 15 minutes more or until puffed and golden. Serve immediately.

Serves 4

Daphne Boyle

An Alumni Brunch at Rhodes College

Time magazine once described Rhodes College as one of "nine nifty colleges … institutions that are challenging the nation's elite schools." Memphis was pleased but not surprised. This Presbyterian-affiliated, coeducational liberal arts college of some 1300 students holds the oldest charter of any of the city's institutions of higher learning. (It was originally chartered in 1848 as a small Masonic college in Clarksville, Tennessee; after several name changes, it moved to its present campus in 1925 and became Southwestern.) It is strongly endowed. (Rhodes' capital assets represent one of the largest investments per student among private colleges in the nation.) It is strikingly handsome. (Thirteen of its graceful Gothic buildings, built of fine Arkansas sandstone, with gray slate roofs, and leaded casement windows, are listed on the National Register of Historic Places.) And its students have always been academic achievers. (Scholars, that is, as news stories inevitably pointed out in 1984 when the school was renamed Rhodes College in honor of its president emeritus, Dr. Peyton N. Rhodes.)

Rhodes College is one of twenty diverse degree-granting institutions of higher education in Memphis, each building its reputation for excellence and permanence in its own way. Consider, for example, the venerable LeMoyne-Owen College, one of the nation's oldest historically black institutions, which began as an elementary school in 1862 when the American Missionary Association sent a Miss Lucinda Humphreys to educate "contraband Negroes and freedmen" at Camp Shiloh near Memphis. The school was moved into the city the next year, and in 1871 it became LeMoyne Normal School, in honor of a generous Pennsylvania benefactor, Dr. Francis Julius LeMoyne. Today, LeMoyne-Owen College is a four-year, coeducational, private college offering degrees in arts, sciences, and business administration, with a noteworthy Cooperative Education Program that allows its nine hundred students to integrate academic learning with on-the-job training in their chosen fields.

Then there is Christian Brothers College, founded in 1871. It is a coeducational (since 1970) Catholic college, with over eighteen hundred students, that has distinguished itself in engineering studies—an unusual accomplishment for a private college. (Recently granted university status, the college has chosen to keep its name the same.) The school offers bachelor's degrees in electrical, civil, mechanical, and chemical engineering as well as in liberal arts, sciences, and business, and master's degrees in educational leadership, business, engineering management, and telecommunications. Its newest venture into advanced technology is the Center for Telecommunications and Information Systems, featuring courses and research services for area business professionals.

Memphis is a major regional medical center, thanks in part to medical studies offered at the University of Tennessee Center for the Health Sciences with its Colleges of Medicine, Nursing, Pharmacy, and Dentistry, and its graduate degrees offered in the allied health sciences. (There were two medical colleges in the city in 1846, extraordinary when Memphis was a river town of only some seven thousand souls. With a history encompassing the Civil War and disastrous yellow fever sieges, Memphis medical schools were reorganized many times, the last merging with the University of Tennessee College of Medicine in 1911 when that school was moved from Nashville to Memphis.) There is also the Southern College of Optometry and programs for health professionals at Shelby State Community College. Other local colleges and universities specialize in the visual arts (Memphis College of Art); in religion (Memphis Theological Seminary,

THE PICTURE: *An alumni group visiting the campus of their alma mater, Rhodes College, known for its academic excellence and one of the best-loved institutions of higher education in Memphis, will soon finish a nostalgic tour of academic halls and gather outside for brunch. Here, in a quiet corner of the campus, giant black oak trees stand as sentinels, guarding the beauty of Fisher Garden's lush green grass and luxuriant azaleas, planted in 1941. The generously provisioned table is set with silver bequeathed to Rhodes and ornamented with a bouquet of harlequin lilies, Gloriosa daisies, foxglove, and pink Gerbera daisies. In the background, Halliburton Tower can be seen rising above the treetops. This campus landmark is named for Memphian Richard Halliburton, adventurer, world traveler, and author of such books as* **The Royal Road to Romance.** *In 1939, in an attempt to cross the Pacific in a traditional Chinese junk, he was lost at sea during a typhoon, at the age of thirty-nine. The tower with its huge bronze bell that sounds the hour was given in Halliburton's memory by his parents, long-time supporters of the college. Inscribed on the bell is a quotation from Shakespeare: "The day shall not be up so soon as I, to try the fair adventure of tomorrow."*

THE FOOD: *The brunch offers cold avocado soup, HOLIDAY BREAKFAST STRATA, IS THAT ALL THERE IS? SOUR CREAM MUFFINS, DIDI'S FRENCH BREAD STRIPS, and a tempting assortment of fresh fruit.*

Crichton College, Mid-America Baptist Theological Seminary, Harding Graduate School of Religion); in technical studies (State Technical Institute at Memphis); and more.

Of all the Memphis institutions of higher learning, however, the biggest in scope, largest in enrollment, and broadest in outreach is fast-developing Memphis State University. Memphis State began as a state normal school in 1912, attained university status in 1957, and has been growing in size and stature ever since. With its sprawling urban campus, its more than twenty thousand students, its more than 750 faculty members, its six undergraduate schools, its graduate schools offering master's and doctoral degrees in over sixty disciplines, its law school, its comprehensive continuing education program, and its five state-supported academic Centers of Excellence in fields ranging from Earthquake Research and Information to an Institute of Egyptian Art and Archaeology, Memphis State University is a center of influence in the larger community.

IS THAT ALL THERE IS? SOUR CREAM MUFFINS

So delicately good and so easy to prepare that when the recipe is shared, the question is always asked, "Is that all there is?"

1 cup sour cream
2 cups self-rising flour

1 cup butter, melted
   (no substitution)

Mix sour cream with flour and stir in butter. Fill muffin pans almost to top as muffins do not rise much. Bake at 375 degrees until lightly browned.

Yields 1 dozen muffins

Mrs. James H. Daughdrill, Jr.

HOME BAKED BREAD

Freshly baked bread, announcing its arrival by a fragrance that soothes our souls. Unforgettable.

1 quart milk
1 cup sugar
1 cup vegetable shortening
2 packages yeast
½ cup lukewarm water

9 cups all-purpose flour
2 teaspoons baking powder
1 teaspoon baking soda
1 teaspoon salt
Margarine, softened

Combine milk, sugar, and shortening, mix, and bring to boil. Remove from heat and cool to lukewarm.

Dissolve yeast in water and add to milk mixture. Sift together flour, baking powder, baking soda, and salt. Add to milk mixture, mix with hands, then beat by hand until all lumps are gone. Let rise 4 to 5 times, stirring down dough each time.

Turn dough onto floured board, using only enough flour to make handling easier. Knead briefly, stretch to long roll, and cut in fourths. Place dough in 4 greased loaf pans. Let rise until doubled. Place on middle rack of oven and bake at 350 degrees for 35 to 40 minutes or until browned. Remove from oven and brush tops of loaves with margarine while still in pans. Cover pans with foil and a towel, and set aside to cool.

Yields 4 loaves

Marian Warren
Franklin, Tennessee

DIDI'S FRENCH BREAD STRIPS

Very rich and a little bit fancy. Serve as bread or as an hors d'oeuvre.

1 loaf fresh French bread
½ cup butter, melted
Garlic powder

Dill weed
Grated Parmesan cheese

Slice bread and cut each piece into 3 strips 1 to 1½-inches wide. With pastry brush, generously coat each strip with butter. Sprinkle each strip with garlic powder and lightly dust with dill weed. Top with generous sprinkle Parmesan cheese. Place on baking sheet and broil until toasted. Serve hot or cold.

Yields 4 to 4½ dozen strips

Didi Dwyer Montgomery

CONFETTI CORN BREAD

A super-good corn bread.

2 eggs, lightly beaten
¾ cup milk
⅓ cup corn oil
1 16-ounce can cream style corn
1 onion, minced or grated
1 2-ounce can chopped
   pimientos, drained
1 cup yellow corn meal

1 teaspoon salt
½ teaspoon baking powder
5 teaspoons sugar
1 4-ounce can chopped green
   chilies, drained, optional
¾ cup grated sharp Cheddar
   cheese

Combine all ingredients except cheese in large bowl and mix well. Pour into greased 9 x 13-inch baking pan and bake 40 to 45 minutes at 350 degrees. Remove from oven, sprinkle with cheese, and bake another 5 minutes. Cool and cut into squares.

Serves 6

Mrs. Jack Bugbee

TOASTED PITA PIECES

So good that friends have been known to invade the kitchen in search of more. Try with soups, or just as a snack.

1 15-ounce package pita bread   Lemon pepper to taste
Margarine

Slice through fold of pita bread to make 2 flat halves. Cut each half in fourths to yield 8 pieces. Spread margarine over each piece, sprinkle with lemon pepper, and toast 10 to 15 minutes at 350 degrees.

Note: Be as creative as you choose with toppings. Let your spice rack be your guide.

Yields 8 pieces per pita bread

Mrs. Arthur Fulmer, Jr.

SCOTTISH BISCUITS

Scrumptious scones. Great with berries and cream or with sweet butter and homemade *BLACKBERRY PRESERVES*.

2 cups all-purpose flour	2 tablespoons sugar
2½ teaspoons baking powder	¼ cup butter or margarine
¼ teaspoon baking soda	1 egg
½ teaspoon salt	¾ cup buttermilk

Sift together dry ingredients and cut in butter until crumbly. Beat egg into buttermilk and mix quickly into dry ingredients. Divide dough in half and place on cookie sheet. Pat each into smooth circle about ½-inch thick. Cut each circle into 6 to 8 wedges with flour-dipped knife, and bake 10 to 12 minutes at 425 degrees. Serve hot with lots of butter and homemade preserves.

Yields 12 to 16 wedges

Mrs. Hector Howard

IN-A-HURRY BREAD

Preparation time is unbelievably quick. Dough is light and rises beautifully.

2 cups very warm water	3 tablespoons vegetable oil
2 packages yeast	5 to 5½ cups bread flour
3 tablespoons sugar	Margarine, melted
3 teaspoons salt	

Combine water, yeast, and sugar, and let stand 10 minutes. Add salt, oil, and 5 cups flour, and knead (add remaining ½ cup flour if needed). Place dough in greased bowl, cover, and let rise in slightly warm oven until doubled in size. Punch down and allow to rest 15 to 20 minutes. Divide in half and shape in two greased 4 x 8-inch loaf pans. Brush loaves with margarine and bake 30 to 35 minutes at 350 degrees. Remove from pans immediately.

Yields 2 loaves

Mrs. James G. Sousoulas

POCKETBOOK ROLLS

Magic rolls that disappear before your eyes—the kind our grandmothers made.

2 tablespoons sugar	1 cup boiling milk
1 teaspoon salt	1 package yeast
2 tablespoons vegetable	2½ to 3 cups all-purpose flour
shortening	Margarine, softened

Combine sugar, salt, and shortening, and mix well. Pour boiling milk over mixture, stir, and cool to lukewarm. Mix in yeast. With wooden spoon, stir in flour and beat well. Cover and let rise until doubled, about 1½ to 2 hours.

Place dough on floured board and turn 2 or 3 times until dough loses stickiness. Roll out and cut in rounds. Fold each round, place in greased pan, and top with a little margarine. Let rise about 45 minutes. Bake at 350 degrees for 10 to 15 minutes until browned. If not serving immediately, bake at 350 degrees for 8 minutes and refrigerate when cooled. When ready to serve, finish baking at 350 degrees until lightly browned.

Yields 1 dozen rolls

Maryanna Popper

SWEETS

AUNT KATE'S DATE BARS

Wins friends and influences people.

1 cup sugar	1 cup pecans, chopped
3 eggs, separated	1 cup all-purpose flour
1 8-ounce package dates, cut in pieces	1 teaspoon baking powder
	Pinch of salt

Beat sugar and egg yolks. Add dates and pecans. Sift flour, baking powder, and salt together and add to mixture. Beat egg whites until stiff and fold into batter. Flour a 10-inch square baking pan and line with wax paper. Pour batter into pan and bake 1 hour at 300 degrees. Cool several minutes before cutting into bars. Roll in confectioners' sugar.

Yields 2 dozen bars

Betty Graves

BOURBON CREAMS

Just knowing one has a personal recipe from this fourth generation Memphis candy-making family is enough to make a sweet tooth smile.

3 12-ounce packages semi-sweet chocolate chips (or dipping chocolate)	½ cup butter, softened
	2 cups finely chopped pecans
	9 ounces bourbon whiskey
3 16-ounce boxes confectioners' sugar	¾ teaspoon invertase, optional

Melt chocolate in top of double boiler and keep warm over simmering water. Cream confectioners' sugar and butter. Add pecans, bourbon, and invertase. Mix well, form into small balls, and immediately dip in chocolate. Place on baking sheet lined with wax paper and chill. Store in cool place or refrigerator.

Note: Dipping chocolate and invertase (one commercial name is Convert-It) may be bought at candy manufacturing suppliers. Invertase causes sugar to liquefy so that creams have syrupy centers. Candy may be made without invertase, but texture will be firmer with no syrup.

Yields 6½ pounds creams

Grace Dinstuhl

CHOCOLATE BITTERSWEETS

A family favorite, and like a family, needs a little extra time and tender loving care, but the results are most rewarding.

½ cup margarine, softened	1 teaspoon vanilla
½ cup confectioners' sugar	1 cup plus 2 tablespoons sifted all-purpose flour
¼ teaspoon salt	

Cream margarine and sugar. Beat in salt and vanilla, and gradually add flour. Shape by half-teaspoonfuls into balls and place on ungreased baking sheet. Press hole in center of each. Bake at 350 degrees for 12 to 15 minutes until very lightly browned. Spoon filling into centers while warm. Chill and frost.

Nut Filling

1 cup sifted confectioners' sugar	2 tablespoons all-purpose flour
	1 teaspoon vanilla
1 3-ounce package cream cheese, softened	½ cup chopped pecans
	½ cup flaked coconut

Cream together sugar, cream cheese, flour, and vanilla. Stir in pecans and coconut.

Frosting

½ cup semi-sweet chocolate bits	2 tablespoons water
2 tablespoons butter	½ cup confectioners' sugar

Melt chocolate and butter in water over low heat, stirring occasionally. Add confectioners' sugar and beat until smooth. Use ½ teaspoon frosting per cookie.

Yields 3 dozen cookies

Mary Ann Cox

SWEDISH JAM SHORTBREAD

A quick way to fix a superlative sweet.

1 box Pillsbury Plus Butter Recipe cake mix	1 egg
½ cup finely chopped nuts	1 10-ounce jar raspberry jam or preserves
¼ cup butter, softened	

Combine cake mix, nuts, butter, and egg, and beat at low speed until crumbly. Press into greased and floured 9 x 13-inch baking pan. Spread with preserves. Bake at 350 degrees for 20 to 25 minutes, or until edges are lightly browned. Drizzle with glaze while warm. Cool completely and cut into bars.

Glaze
½ cup confectioners' sugar	½ teaspoon almond extract
2½ teaspoons water	

Mix ingredients until smooth.

Yields 3 dozen shortbread bars

Mary Jane Richens

PEANUT BRITTLE

A classic recipe

1½ cups sugar	¼ teaspoon salt
½ cup white corn syrup	2 cups shelled raw peanuts
¼ cup water	1 teaspoon soda

Coat 10½ x 15½ x 1-inch pan with margarine and set aside. In 4-quart heavy saucepan, combine sugar, corn syrup, and water. Bring to a boil and add salt. Gradually stir in peanuts, so that syrup continues to boil. Keep at rolling boil, reducing heat, if necessary, until peanuts pop and turn brown. Remove from heat, add soda, and stir well. Pour into prepared pan, and allow candy to spread. Cool, break into pieces, and store in airtight container. Candy will keep for a month—if undiscovered.

Yields 2 pounds candy

Mrs. M. V. Highsmith

CRÈME DE MENTHE SQUARES

Beautiful, tempting, and too good to believe.

2 cups sugar	1 cup sifted all-purpose flour
1 cup margarine, softened	½ teaspoon salt
4 eggs	4 squares unsweetened chocolate, melted
1 teaspoon vanilla	

Cream sugar and margarine. Add eggs, vanilla, flour, and salt. Mix in chocolate and pour into 9 x 13-inch greased baking pan. Bake 25 minutes at 350 degrees. Cool, cover with filling, and chill. Spread icing over filling and chill again. Store in refrigerator.

Filling
1 16-ounce box confectioners' sugar	½ cup margarine, softened Crème de Menthe

Cream sugar and margarine. Add enough Crème de Menthe for easy spreading consistency.

Icing
½ cup margarine, softened	1 square unsweetened chocolate, melted and cooled
1 16-ounce box confectioners' sugar	
1 teaspoon vanilla	Milk

Cream margarine and sugar. Add vanilla, chocolate, and enough milk for easy spreading consistency.

Yields 6 dozen squares

Linda S. Woods

CINNAMON THUMBS

Delicious, buttery, bite-size cookies.

1 cup butter, softened	1 teaspoon vanilla
5 tablespoons sugar	½ cup sugar
2 cups all-purpose flour	½ teaspoon cinnamon

Cream butter, 5 tablespoons sugar, flour, and vanilla. Form dough into small balls and shape into crescents about 2 inches long. Place on ungreased baking sheet. Bake 15 to 20 minutes at 350 degrees. Coat warm cookies in mixture of ½ cup sugar and cinnamon.

Yields 6 dozen cinnamon thumbs

Lou Carson
Sikeston, Missouri

Holiday Sweets in the Cooper-Young Neighborhood

The inevitable expansion of Memphis eastward from its river bluff beginnings was foreseen as early as 1819 when one of the city's first settlers, Solomon Rozelle from North Carolina, bought sixteen hundred acres of wilderness bordering what is now the Mid-South Fairgrounds. To make the land easily accessible to other settlers looking for a new home, Rozelle granted the Memphis and Charleston Railway (that would later become the Southern Railroad) free right-of-way across his property. But it was still too early for development of the area. Rozelle realized little on his investment, and his son, in 1848, sold 577 acres of the original tract to an Alabama man, William Cooper. As the Memphis city limits began to move steadily eastward, Cooper watched and waited. He began laying out a subdivision with streets intersecting the Memphis and Charleston rail line. (He named one street for himself.) Few lots were sold, however, until the city's recurring bouts with yellow fever in the 1870s made downtown living seem hazardous. Suddenly, Cooper's remote but easily accessible "suburb" began filling up.

Prosperity, in unexpected form, came to the new neighborhood a few years later. A race track called Montgomery Park was built on nearby land that is now part of the fairgrounds, and in 1884 it became the home of the prestigious Tennessee Derby. For many years thereafter, Memphis was one of the nation's horse-racing centers. During racing season, fleets of public hacks waited at the railway tracks to meet the crowds of fans en route to Montgomery Park. The glory days didn't last; in 1905, the state legislature outlawed pari-mutuel betting, and Montgomery Park closed down.

The district continued to thrive, nonetheless, thanks again to a railway. This time it was the Memphis Street Railway Company, which had virtually encircled the neighborhood with its new circuit line—from downtown, east on Madison Avenue to the Parkway (then called Trezevant), then south to Young Avenue, west on Young to Cooper Street, and north on Cooper to Madison again. (The rounded corners at Cooper and Madison and at Cooper and Young are silent reminders for today's Memphians of that long-gone era when electric streetcars needed lots of turning room as they hummed, sang, and swayed their way about the city, then reversed their wooden-slatted seats at the end of the line and headed back again.) More residents flocked to the area, more attractive homes were built—mostly bungalows and Queen Anne cottages, having various Colonial Revival styles, with wrap-around porches, high-pitched gabled roof lines, and intricate gingerbread trim. The neighborhood also saw a succession of enterprising businesses—from George Fleece's "oldest marriage institution in the South" offering loans in the early days to couples wishing to marry; to Summer's Drug Store at the turn of the century, selling its own liver pills, cold tablets, and almond ice cream; to the Keathley family bakers who developed in their home kitchen on Young Avenue a bargain culinary treat, the "nickel pie,"—pecan, coconut, apple, peach, raisin, and pineapple, all with the freshest ingredients— which made them a successful national company.

The Cooper-Young neighborhood, like several older areas in Memphis, is emerging from a period of decline and experiencing new life today. Its interesting old houses are being restored, one by one, by young families with children and young professionals investing in their first home, and new, small businesses are hanging out shingles in the commercial area.

THE PICTURE: *It is Christmas morning in this hundred-year-old classic Queen Anne cottage in the historic Cooper-Young neighborhood of Memphis. This charming residence, known as the Cheatham-Barron House, was built by one of the district's first homeowners, was later owned by one of the first professional firefighters in Memphis, and has been lovingly restored by its present owner. With its soft pink clapboard exterior and its gray carved gingerbread trim, it has the appearance of a life-sized doll house. Its nostalgic appeal is heightened by the holiday decorations on the front porch—wreaths of sweet-scented evergreens, toys to delight young hearts, and a tray of delicious-smelling home-baked goodies.*

THE FOOD: *An ageless treat for children of all ages, GINGERBREAD MEN.*

GINGERBREAD MEN

Run, run as fast as you can—or there won't be anything left in the pan.

1 cup brown sugar	1 egg
1¾ to 2 teaspoons ginger	3 cups all purpose flour
1 teaspoon cinnamon	1 teaspoon baking soda
¼ teaspoon ground cloves	½ teaspoon baking powder
1 teaspoon salt	¾ cup molasses
⅔ cup vegetable shortening	

Cream brown sugar, spices, salt, and shortening. Add egg and mix. Sift together flour, baking soda, and baking powder. Add dry ingredients and molasses to egg mixture, stirring until blended. Chill.

Roll dough ⅛-inch thick or slightly thicker on lightly floured pastry cloth with floured rolling pin. Cut with gingerbread man cookie cutter and place at least 1 inch apart on lightly greased baking sheet. (Cookies expand and must not join hands.) Bake 8 to 10 minutes at 375 degrees. Cool on rack. Decorate with white icing, currants or raisins, and candied cherries.

Yields 15 large gingerbread men

Susan Patton Robinson

MUMSEY'S COOKIES

A lovely tea cake from a cherished old recipe. Not very sweet and just a touch of citrus.

3½ cups margarine, softened	1 teaspoon vanilla
5 cups sugar	3 eggs
Grated rind of 2 oranges	7 cups all-purpose flour
Grated rind of 2 lemons	

Cream margarine, sugar, grated rinds, and vanilla until fluffy. Beat in eggs one at a time. Add flour, 1 cup at a time, mixing well after each addition. Form into rolls, 1½ inches in diameter, and refrigerate at least 1 hour or overnight. Slice thin and place on ungreased baking sheet. Bake at 350 degrees for 6 to 8 minutes until edges are browned.

Note: Dough can be frozen several months and used as needed.

Yields 20 dozen cookies

Ruth Meierhoefer

CHOCOLATE NUT CLUSTERS

A super-simple recipe—for super-good taste.

¼ cup margarine, softened	½ cup sifted all-purpose flour
½ cup sugar	¼ teaspoon baking powder
1 egg	½ teaspoon salt
1½ teaspoons vanilla	2 cups pecan or walnut halves
1½ squares unsweetened chocolate, melted	

Cream margarine and sugar. Mix in egg and vanilla. Blend in chocolate. Sift together dry ingredients and add to mixture. Stir in nuts. Drop by teaspoonfuls 1 inch apart onto ungreased baking sheet. Bake 10 minutes at 350 degrees. Do not overcook.

Yields 2 dozen clusters

Patricia K. Cremer

ORANGE DATE PINWHEELS

If cookies can taste like Christmas, these do. Scrumptious!

½ cup vegetable shortening	1 tablespoon grated orange rind
1 cup sugar	1½ cups sifted all-purpose flour
1 egg	½ teaspoon baking soda
2 to 3 teaspoons orange juice	¾ teaspoon salt

Cream shortening, sugar, egg, juice, and rind. Sift together flour, baking soda, and salt. Gradually add to creamed mixture, stirring well. Divide dough in half and place on wax paper. Shape each half into roll, wrap in wax paper, and chill.

Roll out each portion like pie crust between wax paper. Spread each half of dough with half of filling and roll as jelly roll. Wrap again in wax paper and chill (may be frozen at this point and baked later). Slice dough ¼-inch thick and place on greased baking sheets. Bake 10 minutes at 350 degrees. Do not overbake.

Filling

1 8-ounce package chopped dates	½ cup chopped pecans or walnuts
¼ cup orange juice	¼ cup sugar

Combine all ingredients and simmer until thick. Cool slightly before spreading over dough.

Yields 4 to 5 dozen pinwheels

Mrs. Lee Milford

JULIA'S OATMEAL COOKIES

Grand old oatmeal cookies. Brings out the child in all of us.

1 cup margarine, melted	½ teaspoon salt
½ cup granulated sugar	1 teaspoon baking soda
½ cup brown sugar	1 teaspoon cinnamon
2 eggs, lightly beaten	2 cups rolled oats
4 tablespoons milk	½ cup raisins
1 teaspoon vanilla	½ cup chopped dates
1 teaspoon almond extract	1 cup chopped nuts
2 cups all-purpose flour	

Combine margarine, granulated sugar, brown sugar, eggs, milk, vanilla, and almond extract, and mix well. Mix dry ingredients and stir into first mixture. Mix in raisins, dates, and nuts. Drop by teaspoonfuls onto greased baking sheet. Bake at 300 degrees for 15 to 20 minutes or until lightly browned.

Yields 8 dozen cookies

Tommie Kidd

FROSTED CASHEW DROPS

Crisp cashews in a cream cookie.

½ cup butter, softened	2 cups all-purpose flour
1 cup brown sugar	¾ teaspoon baking powder
1 egg	¾ teaspoon baking soda
1½ teaspoons vanilla	¼ teaspoon salt
½ cup sour cream	1¾ cups cashews, chopped

Mix butter, brown sugar, egg, and vanilla until creamy. Add sour cream. Combine dry ingredients and mix with egg mixture. Add cashews. Drop by tablespoonfuls onto ungreased baking sheet. Bake 10 minutes at 375 degrees. Frost while warm.

Frosting

1½ tablespoons butter, melted and very slightly browned	1 teaspoon vanilla
3 tablespoons light cream or milk	1½ to 2 cups confectioners' sugar

Combine butter, vanilla, and cream and mix well. Gradually add confectioners' sugar, stirring constantly until smooth.

Yields 5 to 6 dozen cashew drops

Dorothye Moore

PECAN SQUARES

A rich delight. Could give one a Croesus complex.

1 cup butter, softened	¼ teaspoon salt
½ cup sugar	Grated rind of large lemon
1 egg	3 cups sifted all-purpose flour

Butter 10½ x 15½-inch jelly roll pan and chill.

Cream butter and sugar. Beat in egg, salt, and lemon rind. Gradually add flour, beating until dough is smooth and holds shape. Place in chilled pan. Press dough firmly and evenly over bottom and on sides of pan. Prick dough on bottom of pan at ½-inch intervals with fork. Chill 10 minutes.

Bake at 375 degrees for 20 minutes until partially baked and lightly browned around edges. If dough puffs up while baking, prick again with fork. Remove from oven and spoon topping over crust, taking care to distribute pecans evenly. Bake 25 minutes at 375 degrees. Cool completely before slicing.

Pecan Topping

1 cup butter	¼ cup granulated sugar
½ cup honey	½ cup heavy cream
1 cup and 2 tablespoons dark brown sugar	20 ounces pecan halves

Cook butter and honey over medium-high heat until butter melts. Add both sugars and stir to dissolve. Boil 2 minutes. Immediately remove from heat and stir in cream and pecans.

Yields 2 dozen 2½-inch squares

Lyda G. Parker

FROZEN CREAM WITH FRUIT

Just delicious! And such a pretty sweet to serve.

1 8-ounce package cream cheese, softened	½ teaspoon vanilla
1 cup confectioners' sugar	1 cup light cream, whipped
	Fresh or frozen fruit of choice

Beat cream cheese until smooth. Beat in sugar, vanilla, and cream. Pour into 2-inch fluted paper cupcake liners placed in muffin tins. Freeze.

Just before serving, remove paper and spoon fruit around cream muffins.

Yields 8 cream muffins

Mrs. W. Thomas Cunningham, Jr.
Richmond, Virginia

Coffee in the Garden at Walnut Grove

When homesick Memphis expatriates reminisce about what they miss most, the city's year-round natural beauty is high on the list—springtime lawns carpeted with wildflowers, a summer profusion of leafy trees and flowering shrubs, colorful all-season flower gardens, lovingly preserved native woodlands, landscaped boulevards, parks and public buildings. The name Memphis, according to a much-quoted translation from the ancient Egyptian, means "Place of Good Abode." And in Tennessee it also means, according to local intent and national recognition, "The City Beautiful"—Memphis even has a City Beautiful Commission to attend to such matters.

The tradition derives not only from nature's endowments—a long growing season, generous rainfall, a temperate climate—but also from the good works of bygone Memphians who planted flowers and cultivated gardens, at first for their own enjoyment, and eventually to make their city more attractive. Some say it all started in 1918, when Mrs. J. P. Norfleet was landscaping the grounds of Walnut Grove, a new home she and her husband had built amid a cluster of walnut trees several miles beyond the city limits, beside a dirt road leading to Germantown. (Today, lined with fine homes, Walnut Grove Road is one of Memphis' officially designated scenic drives.) In that wooded sanctuary, Elise Norfleet planted ten *elegans superba* azaleas she had ordered from a Georgia nursery, in defiance of predictions that azaleas would never survive in Memphis. That same year she spotted some native azaleas growing in the Wolf River bottoms, dug them up, and transplanted them to her garden. The Walnut Grove azaleas flourished, and soon azaleas were appearing throughout the city.

Then, in 1922, while talking of their love of flowers at a dinner party, Elise Norfleet and two like-minded friends, Mrs. Hugh Heiskell and Mrs. S. B. Anderson, decided to organize the Memphis Garden Club. Their motto:

> Grow roses, that perfume thou mayst have and give.
> Grow cabbages, that thou mayst eat and live.
> For life is complex and its needs demand
> That cabbages and roses go hand in hand.

The Memphis Garden Club became a member of The Garden Club of America in 1925. In the ensuing years, they kept the faith, organizing flower shows and publishing a *Mid-South Garden Guide* that gardeners still find essential. Their numbers increased, and Memphis garden clubs were responsible for plantings of rose bushes, azaleas, and crape myrtles all over the city—along Riverside Drive, at the Veterans Hospital on Lamar, at the Mid-South Fairgrounds, at Overton Park. They also lobbied and campaigned in support of *Memphis Press-Scimitar* editor Ed Meeman's successful campaign to create Shelby Forest State Park on the banks of the Mississippi River just north of Memphis, and then planned the park's nature trails. In 1954, the garden clubs' efforts to find a common meeting place resulted in the Goldsmith family's gift of a Civic Garden Center in Audubon Park's Botanic Garden in east Memphis. There, today, you find plantings of irises (the Tennessee state flower), roses, dahlias, day lilies, daffodils, magnolias, an azalea trail, a dogwood trail, wildflower trails, even an herb garden. And the Japanese garden with its arched bridge spanning a small landscaped pond has been the setting for a number of weddings, not to mention innumerable photographs now preserved in family albums.

COCONUT KISSES

Just a wisp of a crisp little sweet.

2 egg whites	1 cup corn flakes
2/3 cup sugar	1 cup grated coconut

Beat egg whites until stiff and dry. Fold in remaining ingredients. Drop by teaspoonfuls onto ungreased baking sheet. Bake 15 to 20 minutes at 325 degrees.

Yields 1 dozen kisses

From the handwritten journal
of Mary C. Vance, 1933
Courtesy of Mr. and Mrs. Peter Norfleet

CREAM CHEESE COOKIES

A good non-sweet cookie that is just right with a bit of marmalade and a mid-morning cup of coffee.

1 cup butter, softened	1 egg yolk
1 3-ounce package cream cheese, softened	2 1/3 cups cake flour

Cream butter and cheese. Add egg yolk and mix well. Gradually stir in flour to make dough. Roll dough thin and cut with round cookie cutter. Place on ungreased baking sheet. Bake 15 to 20 minutes at 350 degrees.

Yields 2 1/2 dozen cookies

From the handwritten journal
of Mary C. Vance, 1933
Courtesy of Mr. and Mrs. Peter Norfleet

MOTHER'S KISSES

How children love them!

Leftover pie pastry	1/2 cup raisins
2 tablespoons butter, softened	1/4 cup nuts
1/4 to 1/2 cup brown sugar	1 teaspoon cinnamon

Roll pastry into 12-inch circle. Spread with butter and sprinkle with remaining ingredients. Roll jelly-roll fashion, place seam side down, and slice in pieces 1/2-inch thick. Lay pieces flat on greased baking sheet and gently press each with palm of hand. Bake 20 to 30 minutes at 350 degrees.

Yields 2 dozen kisses

Patricia B. Atkinson

SOTHEBY'S CHOCO-SCOTCH TREASURES

After completing a lecture series along with art appraisals in Memphis, a team of experts from Sotheby's was pleased to take a little tin of these culinary *objets d'art* back with them to New York whence a request for the recipe soon arrived by post. Now it's yours—no bidding necessary.

1 6-ounce package semi-sweet chocolate morsels	1 cup cocktail peanuts
1 6-ounce package butterscotch morsels	1 cup chow mein noodles, broken into 1/2-inch pieces
2 tablespoons creamy peanut butter	

Melt chocolate and butterscotch morsels in top of double boiler. Add peanut butter and stir until blended. Add peanuts and chow mein noodles. Cool slightly in refrigerator. (Do not allow to cool too long as mixture will become stiff and will lose shiny texture.) Drop by teaspoonfuls onto ungreased baking sheet. Store in a cool place until firm.

Yields 3 to 4 dozen treasures

Pat Klinke

MISS OLA'S YUMMY COOKIES FOR THE MUSIC CLUB

An excellent little sweet—rather like a meringue bar.

1/2 cup butter, softened	1/2 teaspoon salt
1 cup sugar	1 teaspoon vanilla
2 eggs, separated	1 cup brown sugar
1 1/2 cups all-purpose flour	1/2 cup nuts
1 teaspoon baking powder	

Cream butter and sugar. Beat egg yolks and add to creamed mixture. Sift flour, baking powder, and salt together into mixture, and beat. Add vanilla. Pour batter into greased and floured 9-inch square baking pan. Beat egg whites until stiff, gradually adding brown sugar. Fold in nuts and spread over batter. Bake 25 to 35 minutes at 375 degrees. Cool and cut in squares.

Yields 16 squares

Mrs. Henry W. Williamson

SOUR CREAM COOKIES

A rolled cookie just full of good things.

1 cup butter
2 cups sifted all-purpose flour
1 egg yolk, beaten
½ cup sour cream

Apricot preserves or
  orange marmalade
Flaked coconut
Chopped walnuts

With pastry blender, cut butter into flour until mixture resembles fine crumbs. Combine egg yolk and sour cream, and blend into flour mixture. Chill dough several hours or overnight.

Divide dough into 4 equal parts. Roll each portion into 10-inch circle on lightly-floured surface. Spread with preserves and sprinkle with coconut and walnuts. Roll in jelly roll fashion and place on ungreased baking sheet. Bake at 350 degrees for 20 minutes until lightly browned. Cool on rack and dust with confectioners' sugar. Slice ½ to 1-inch thick.

Yields 3 to 4 dozen cookies

Virginia Caratenuto
Garfield, New Jersey

POTATO CHIP COOKIES

Pretty cookies and oh! so good. Fun to have people guess the surprise ingredient.

½ cup butter, softened
½ cup margarine
½ cup sugar
1½ cups all-purpose flour

1 teaspoon vanilla
Plain potato chips
Confectioners' sugar

Cream butter, margarine, and sugar until thick and light in color. Add flour and vanilla. Lightly crush by hand enough potato chips to measure ¾ cup and fold into mixture. Drop by teaspoonfuls onto ungreased baking sheet. Bake at 350 degrees for 12 to 15 minutes until slightly browned at edges. Cool and dust with confectioners' sugar.

Variation: Add 16-ounce package butterscotch morsels to batter.

Yields 4 dozen cookies

Mrs. William H. Morse

EASY MICROWAVE FUDGE

Lazy day chocolate lover's delight.

1 16-ounce box confectioners'
  sugar
⅓ cup cocoa
⅔ cup mini marshmallows
  or 4 large ones, cut in pieces

½ cup margarine, sliced (if
  in stick form, cut in pieces)
¼ cup milk
½ teaspoon vanilla
1 cup chopped nuts

Combine sugar and cocoa in 1½-quart microwave-safe dish. Add marshmallows and margarine, and cook uncovered 2 minutes on full power. Stir, then beat in milk, vanilla, and nuts. Cook 30 seconds on full power. Beat well and pour into greased 8-inch square baking pan. Chill until firm.

Yields 64 1-inch squares

Karen Kalifeh

DOUBLE FROSTED BROWNIES

If there were Olympic Games for brownies, these would take home the gold.

1 cup butter, softened
2 cups sugar
4 squares unsweetened
  chocolate, melted
1 teaspoon vanilla

1 cup all-purpose flour
½ teaspoon salt
1 to 2 cups chopped nuts
4 eggs

Cream butter and sugar. Add chocolate, vanilla, flour, salt, and nuts. Beat in eggs one at a time. Pour batter into greased 9 x 13-inch baking pan. Bake 25 minutes at 350 degrees. Cool and cover with first frosting. Drizzle with second frosting and refrigerate. Cut in squares.

First Frosting
¼ cup margarine, softened
3 cups confectioners' sugar

5 tablespoons heavy cream
1 teaspoon vanilla

Cream together all ingredients.

Second Frosting
2 squares unsweetened
  chocolate

2 teaspoons butter

Melt ingredients together. Cool before using.

Yields 4 to 5 dozen brownies

Shirley Sigler Chamberlin
Milllington, Tennessee

An Historic Christening at Magevney House

THE PICTURE: *The Magevney House, next door to St. Peter's Roman Catholic Church on Adams Avenue in downtown Memphis, is one of the oldest homes in the city. In this cottage, in 1839, the Catholic Mass was said for the first time in Memphis. Now restored and maintained as a museum by the city of Memphis, this little "cracker box" house was the home of one of the founders of St. Peter's, a young Irish immigrant schoolmaster named Eugene Magevney, who came to Memphis to establish one of the city's first schools in 1833. Later, as a successful businessman, he became one of the city's most generous philanthropists. In 1840, Magevney married his Irish sweetheart, Mary Smyth, in the parlor of this cottage. It was the first Catholic wedding in Memphis. When their first-born daughter, Mary, was christened here the following year, it was the first Catholic christening in Memphis. Little Mary's christening dress, tucked and lace-trimmed by her mother, is one of the family heirlooms that can be seen at Magevney House today. The scene of the joyous reception which followed that christening has been re-created here, in the room where it took place. The table is set for a small gathering. Displayed on the lamp table in the background is the silver service given by Eugene Magevney to his second daughter, Kate, as a wedding gift. The secretary in the corner was part of the home's original furnishings. It holds a soup tureen which, like the cake server on the table, belongs to Magevney family descendants. In an alabaster vase is a graceful arrangement of Queen Anne's lace and sweetheart roses.*

THE FOOD: *The punch bowl holds tea-based AUTUMN GLOW PUNCH, typical of old punch recipes, that will accompany the white five-layer christening cake. Other treats offered include COCOONS, a plate of brownie-like sweets, HOMEMADE VANILLA WAFERS, and old-fashioned FRIED CUSTARD, all made from heirloom recipes.*

Set somewhat apart from the grand, elaborately decorated mansions in Victorian Village on Adams Avenue, and tucked modestly away under an old magnolia tree, there is a tiny, neatly painted clapboard house with green shutters and a cypress shingled roof. This unpretentious dwelling, next door to St. Peter's Roman Catholic Church, seems strangely out of place in the modern urban surroundings of downtown Memphis. As one of the last architectural reminders of Memphis as a very young city, it houses a vast store of local history.

It was once the home of Eugene Magevney, a young Irish immigrant who had studied to be a priest before he sailed for America in 1831. In Pennsylvania, he became a schoolmaster, applied for citizenship, and two years later moved on to Memphis. Magevney was then thirty-five years old; the city was but fourteen. In a log cabin which had originally served as a courthouse, he established a private school where, as a local historian later wrote, he "introduced the sons of affluent families to the mysteries of English spelling, the love of reading, the way to write clearly, and the rigid laws of mathematics." Since cash was scarce and land was cheap, many families paid the schoolmaster by deeding large acreages to him. (Not until 1848, when Magevney, as a duly elected city alderman, took the lead in organizing the city's public school system, would any tax moneys be used to pay teachers in Memphis.)

For a time, Magevney boarded in a home on the outskirts of town, but by 1837 he had saved enough money to buy a newly-built cottage on Adams Avenue, a "plain cracker box, with two rooms separated by a hall downstairs, and repeated upstairs." After several more years of saving, Magevney was able to send to Ireland for his bride-to-be, Mary Smyth, who had been waiting faithfully for his summons for twelve long years. She arrived in 1840 with a trunk full of furnishings for the little house, some seeds for flowers, and a bag of Irish peat to grow them in. They were married in the parlor of the cottage—the first Catholic wedding to take place in Memphis. A year later, their first-born daughter, Mary, was christened in that parlor. It was the city's first Catholic christening.

Memphis was booming in the 1840s, and Magevney, now a family man, gave up teaching to devote full attention to his real estate holdings. His wise investments and good management soon made him one of the city's most prosperous businessmen; his generosity made him one of its outstanding philanthropists. But the Magevneys continued to live simply. The man who had doubted his worthiness to be a priest became a founder and principal supporter of St. Peter's Church, the first Roman Catholic church in Memphis. It was built next door to the simple frame house on Adams Avenue, where Eugene Magevney continued to live until his death in 1873, during an outbreak of yellow fever. In the years that followed, the Magevney family honored his example of generosity, providing significant, sometimes pivotal, support to such institutions as St. Joseph Hospital, St. Peter Home for Children, and Christian Brothers College.

In 1940, the heirs of Eugene Magevney donated the little house on Adams Avenue, where he had lived and died, to the city he had loved. Still in its original location, restored and maintained as a museum, it stands now as a silent but eloquent witness to the struggles, the tragedies, and the triumphs of a younger Memphis.

COCOONS

A sugary butter cookie that never fails to please.

½ cup butter, softened	2 cups sifted all-purpose flour
4 tablespoons confectioners' sugar	1 cup finely chopped nuts
	1 teaspoon vanilla

Cream together butter and sugar. Add flour and mix well. Stir in nuts and vanilla (add 1 to 2 tablespoons cold water if mixture is too dry). Shape into small ovals—as the original recipe said, "…about the size of a bird's egg." Place on ungreased baking sheet so that cocoons do not touch each other. Bake at 325 degrees for 20 to 25 minutes or until lightly browned. Roll cocoons while hot in additional confectioners' sugar. Place on rack to cool.

Yields 3 to 3½ dozen cocoons

From the handwritten recipe collection
of Miss Genevieve Condon
Courtesy of Mrs. Noah Kimball

HOMEMADE VANILLA WAFERS

You can buy vanilla wafers in a box. But oh! the homemade…

½ cup butter or margarine, softened	2 to 3 teaspoons vanilla
½ cup vegetable shortening	2 eggs
⅔ cup sugar	1 teaspoon salt
	2½ cups sifted all-purpose flour

Cream together butter, shortening, and sugar. Add vanilla and mix. Add eggs one at a time, beating well after each addition. Sift salt with flour and stir into batter.

Drop by teaspoonful onto greased baking sheet and flatten by pressing with flat-bottom tumbler (dip tumbler in flour before pressing). Bake at 375 degrees for 8 to 10 minutes or until edges are delicately browned. Remove immediately from baking sheet.

Yields 6 dozen wafers

Mrs. Noah Kimball

FRIED CUSTARD

The lovely old Shadow Hill Tea Room, sitting gracefully on a hill amid tall trees in Hernando, Mississippi, just a quick drive south from Memphis, was a favorite dining-out spot for Memphians for many years, as well as for visitors from across the country. The Tea Room was in the home of its owner, Mrs. George Holmes, and was mainly a summer place with its big screened porch set with tables keeping company with comfortable wicker furniture. Though the Tea Room has long vanished, the treasures that came from the kitchen's venerable wood stove are remembered with pleasure and spoken of with love. As southern as magnolias and cape jasmine, this well-loved recipe, one of those treasures, has been the starting point of family menus for many happy occasions. The combination of the crisp coating outside and the creamy custard inside is superb.

4 cups milk	1 tablespoon butter
3 sticks cinnamon	1 teaspoon vanilla
6 eggs, separated	⅛ teaspoon salt
1 cup sugar	2 cups crushed cracker crumbs
4 tablespoons cornstarch	or crushed corn flakes
2 tablespoons all-purpose flour	Vegetable oil

Heat milk with cinnamon sticks in double boiler almost to boil. Discard cinnamon sticks. Cool milk slightly.

Store egg whites in refrigerator. Combine egg yolks and sugar, mix with 1 cup warm milk, and beat thoroughly. Combine cornstarch and flour, add 1 cup warm milk, and beat until smooth. Pour both mixtures into remaining milk in double boiler. Cook over medium heat until thick and smooth, stirring constantly. Remove from heat, add butter, vanilla, and salt, and beat well. Spread custard in buttered square baking pan and set aside to cool. Chill overnight.

Bring egg whites to room temperature and beat lightly. Pour oil 1-inch deep in skillet and heat to 350 degrees. Slice chilled custard in squares. Handling gently to keep shape, dip each square in egg whites, then coat lightly but evenly with crumbs. Gently lower into oil and fry, turning carefully until squares are golden brown on each side. Drain on absorbent paper and serve hot. May be briefly reheated in oven before serving, if necessary.

Yields 16 custard squares

Shadow Hill Tea Room
Courtesy of Mrs. James S. Dickerson

CHOCOLATE PRALINE SQUARES

Careful! These are extremely habit-forming.

Graham crackers
1 cup butter
1 cup light brown sugar
1 cup chopped pecans
6 1½-ounce Hershey bars

Cover bottom of 9-inch square pan with single layer of graham crackers. Melt butter in saucepan, add sugar and pecans, and cook 3 minutes or until mixture is blended and bubbly. Pour over graham crackers and bake 8 to 9 minutes at 350 degrees. Remove from oven and immediately cover with chocolate bars, spreading chocolate as it melts. Chill in pan until firm enough to cut into squares.

Yields 24 squares

Mrs. Norfleet R. Turner

ROCKY ROAD FUDGE

Just the best. No one can resist it.

1 12-ounce package semi-sweet chocolate chips
1 14-ounce can sweetened condensed milk
2 tablespoons margarine
2 cups dry roasted peanuts or pecans
1 10½-ounce package miniature marshmallows

Combine chocolate, milk, and margarine in heavy saucepan and cook over medium-low heat. Stir until well-blended and very hot, but do not boil. In large bowl, mix nuts with marshmallows, add hot chocolate mixture, and stir well. Line 9 x 13-inch baking pan with wax paper. Spread fudge in pan (or drop by teaspoonfuls) and chill at least 2 hours. Cut in 1-inch squares.

Yields 9½ dozen squares

Juanita Smith

GRAMMER'S BUTTER COOKIES

A long-treasured, supremely good family recipe from the old Swedish tradition of baking.

1 cup butter, softened
¼ cup granulated sugar
½ cup brown sugar
1 egg yolk, lightly beaten
2 cups all-purpose flour
1 teaspoon vanilla
Pecan pieces, or colored sugar, optional

Cream butter and both sugars. Add egg yolk, flour, and vanilla, and mix until smooth. Refrigerate until well-chilled.

Pinch small pieces from dough and form into small balls. Place on ungreased baking sheets and chill until firm. Press with fork and sprinkle with pecans or colored sugar. Bake at 350 degrees for 10 to 15 minutes or until lightly browned.

Note: Replace butter with margarine and delete egg yolk. Result: A delicious cookie for special diets.

Yields 4 to 5 dozen cookies

Mrs. Fletcher Johnson

POLISH WALNUT HORNS

Pretty to look at and luscious to eat.

1 cup butter, softened
1 cup cottage cheese, beaten
2½ cups sifted all-purpose flour

Combine all ingredients and mix well. Refrigerate overnight.

Roll dough out thin and cut in 2-inch squares. Spread each square with filling and roll in shape of cornucopia. Seal edges tightly and place on ungreased baking sheet. Bake 10 to 15 minutes at 350 degrees until lightly browned. Do not overbake.

Filling
½ pound finely ground walnuts
¼ cup sugar
1 egg white

Combine all ingredients and mix well.

Yields 3 dozen walnut horns

Vicki Bedeian

GALATOBOUREKO

It's hard to choose among Greek pastries, but this custard-filled sweet is one of the best. It is a favorite on the menu at this charming Greek-American restaurant whose authentic Greek dishes have brought it a devoted and ever-growing clientele.

½ gallon milk	½ teaspoon vanilla
2 cups butter	10 eggs, separated
1½ cups Cream of Wheat	1½ teaspoons orange extract
(do not use instant)	1 pound phyllo
1½ cups sugar	

In very large saucepan, combine milk, ½ cup butter, Cream of Wheat, ¾ cup sugar, and vanilla. Cook over medium heat until thickened, stirring constantly, about 20 to 30 minutes. Set aside to cool.

Combine egg yolks, orange extract, and remaining sugar, and beat well. Stir into cooled milk mixture. Beat egg whites until stiff but not dry, and fold into mixture.

Melt remaining butter, and brush bottom and sides of 12 x 18-inch baking pan. Layer the bottom and sides with 8 phyllo sheets, each one lightly brushed with butter. Carefully pour mixture into pan. Top with remaining phyllo, brushing each sheet with butter. Slice top layers of phyllo lengthwise 5 to 6 times. Pour remaining butter over top and sprinkle lightly with cool water. Bake at 350 degrees for 45 to 60 minutes or until puffy and golden brown.

Remove from oven and let stand 10 minutes. Pour syrup over hot pastry. Cool 1 hour and cut in squares. Store in refrigerator.

Syrup
2½ cups water	½ lemon
2 cups sugar	1 cinnamon stick

Combine ingredients and bring to boil. Reduce heat, simmer 15 minutes, and set aside to cool. Remove lemon and cinnamon stick just before pouring over pastry.

Yields 2 dozen 3-inch squares

The Unicorn Restaurant
Doris Anagnos, Proprietor

LULA'S APRICOT BALLS

A lovely confection, sweet yet tart.

1 pound dried apricots	1 cup sugar
1 large orange with peel,	1½ cups chopped pecans
seeded	Confectioners' sugar

Grind apricots using small blade of food grinder and set aside. Grind whole orange next, reserving juice. Combine apricots, orange with juice, and sugar in heavy saucepan. Cook 30 minutes over very low heat, stirring often as mixture burns easily. Cool and add pecans. Form into small balls using 2 teaspoonfuls mixture, and lightly roll in confectioners' sugar. Keep hands well dusted with sugar. Store in airtight container. Before serving, lightly dust again with confectioners' sugar.

Yields 2½ to 3 dozen balls

Maxine Croswell

MADELEINES

Dainty little tea cakes—pretty as a picture.

1¼ cups sifted cake flour	2 teaspoons finely grated
½ teaspoon baking powder	lemon rind
¼ teaspoon salt	1¼ cups butter, melted and
3 eggs	cooled
1 teaspoon vanilla	Confectioners' sugar
⅔ cup sugar	

Sift together flour, baking powder, and salt, and set aside. Beat eggs until light, add vanilla, and gradually beat in sugar. Continue beating until volume has increased four times in size. Fold in lemon rind, then gradually fold in dry ingredients. Stir in ¾ cup butter. Brush madeleine pans with remaining melted butter, and dust with flour. Spoon 1 tablespoon batter into each shell, filling it three-fourths full. Bake at 350 degrees for 12 to 15 minutes or until golden brown. Remove cookies from pans, place on wire rack, and sift confectioners' sugar over tops. Store in airtight container.

Note: Best if made at least 24 hours before serving. Madeleine pans may be found in most gourmet specialty shops or large department stores.

Yields 3 dozen madeleines

Mrs. Kenneth D. Bartee

DESSERTS

WARM FUDGE PIE

Good, better, best—a chocolate dream. Makes its own crust.

1½ squares unsweetened chocolate	1 cup sugar
½ cup butter	¼ cup all-purpose flour
2 eggs, beaten	Dash salt
	½ teaspoon vanilla

Melt chocolate and butter, remove from heat, and let cool slightly. Combine eggs and sugar. Add chocolate mixture and mix well. Add flour, salt, and vanilla. Pour into greased 8-inch pie pan and bake 30 minutes at 350 degrees. Serve warm with whipped cream or ice cream.

Serves 6 to 8

Mrs. Tracy Plyler

HUNDRED DOLLAR CHOCOLATE CAKE

Tradition has it that the originator of this recipe was paid one hundred dollars just for the list of ingredients.

½ cup butter, softened	½ teaspoon salt
2 cups sugar	2 teaspoons baking powder
2 eggs, separated	1½ cups milk
4 squares semi-sweet chocolate, melted	1 teaspoon vanilla
2 cups cake flour	1 cup chopped nuts

Cream butter and sugar. Beat egg yolks and add with chocolate to creamed mixture. Sift dry ingredients together three times and alternately add with milk to chocolate mixture, mixing well after each addition. Stir in vanilla and nuts. Beat egg whites until peaks are firm but not stiff and fold into batter. Pour into three greased and floured 9-inch cake pans. Bake 30 minutes at 350 degrees. Cool on rack and frost.

Frosting

2 eggs	½ cup butter
1½ 16-ounce boxes confectioners' sugar	1 teaspoon lemon juice
2 squares semi-sweet chocolate	1 teaspoon vanilla
	1 cup chopped nuts

Beat eggs, gradually adding sugar. Melt chocolate and butter in top of double boiler and add to egg mixture. Stir in lemon juice, vanilla, and nuts. If heavy frosting is desired, double recipe.

Serves 12 to 16

Mrs. George G. Lipsey

MAMA'S JAPANESE FRUIT CAKE

An absolutely gorgeous cake.

4 eggs, separated	1½ teaspoons vanilla
1 cup butter, softened	1 cup seedless raisins
2 cups sugar	1 cup chopped pecans
3 cups all-purpose flour	1 teaspoon allspice
2 teaspoons baking powder	1 teaspoon cinnamon
½ teaspoon salt	½ to 1 teaspoon ground cloves
1 cup milk	1 teaspoon nutmeg

Beat egg whites until stiff peaks form and set aside. Cream together butter, sugar, and egg yolks. Sift flour, baking powder, and salt, and alternately add with milk to creamed mixture. Add vanilla and fold in egg whites.

Pour half of cake batter into two greased and floured 9-inch cake pans. Combine raisins, pecans, and spices, stir into remaining batter, and pour into two additional 9-inch cake pans. Bake all four layers for 30 minutes at 350 degrees. Leave in pan 5 minutes, turn out onto wire racks, and cool completely. Spread filling over top of one plain layer. Top with one spiced layer and spread with filling. Repeat procedure with remaining layers. Allow to stand before serving, preferably overnight.

Filling

2 20-ounce cans unsweetened crushed pineapple, drained and 1 cup juice reserved (Add water if needed for full measure.)	Grated rind of 1 lemon
	2 6-ounce packages frozen coconut
	2 cups sugar
Juice of 2 lemons	2 tablespoons all-purpose flour

Combine all ingredients and mix well. Cook over medium heat, stirring occasionally, until thick and of spreading consistency. Filling may be refrigerated and kept up to 1 week.

Note: For a frosted cake, double filling recipe. Use half for filling and half for frosting.

Serves 10 to 12

Mrs. James H. Daughdrill, Jr.

FAMOUS BUTTERMILK PIE

An old Middle Tennessee recipe, this is much like a chess pie—absolutely great-tasting.

½ cup butter	3 eggs
1¼ cups sugar	1 teaspoon vanilla
1 tablespoon cornstarch	½ cup buttermilk
½ teaspoon salt	1 unbaked 8-inch pie shell

Cream butter until fluffy. Add sugar, cornstarch, and salt. Add eggs one at a time, beating well after each addition. Add vanilla and buttermilk. Pour into pie shell. Place in preheated 425 degree oven. Immediately reduce heat to 350 degrees and bake 40 to 50 minutes or until set.

Serves 6 to 8

Dr. Frances Riley

LEMON CUSTARD CAKE

An old-fashioned favorite whose good reputation spans more than half a century.

½ cup butter, softened	¾ cup milk
1½ cups sugar	1 teaspoon lemon extract
2½ cups cake flour	1 teaspoon vanilla
2 teaspoons baking powder	5 egg whites, stiffly beaten

Cream butter and sugar. Sift flour and baking powder together 3 times. Alternately add with milk to creamed mixture, beginning and ending with flour. Add lemon extract and vanilla, and fold in egg whites. Pour into four cake pans, greased and floured, and lined with wax paper. Bake at 350 degrees for 18 to 20 minutes or until lightly browned, testing for doneness. Layers will be thin. Cool. Stack layers, spreading filling on each layer, and frost cake with remainder.

Filling

5 egg yolks	3 tablespoons butter
2 eggs	Juice and grated rind of 2 large
2 cups sugar	lemons
2 tablespoons all-purpose flour	

Combine all ingredients in top of double boiler over hot water and cook until thick, stirring often, about 20 minutes. Cool before adding to cake.

Serves 10 to 12

Minnie Morris McGregor
McCrory, Arkansas

APPLE DAPPLE CAKE

A traditional favorite for the opening day breakfast at the Longreen Hunt.

1½ cups vegetable oil	1½ teaspoons cinnamon, optional
2 cups sugar	½ teaspoon nutmeg, optional
3 eggs, beaten	3 cups finely chopped raw apples
1 teaspoon vanilla	
2½ cups all-purpose flour	1½ cups chopped pecans or ½ cup chopped black walnuts
1 teaspoon salt	
1 teaspoon baking soda	

Combine oil, sugar, eggs, and vanilla, and mix well. Sift together flour, salt, and baking soda, and add to egg mixture. Fold in apples and nuts. Pour batter into greased and floured tube pan. Bake 1 hour at 350 degrees. Pour hot topping over cake while cake is still hot. Cool before removing from pan.

Topping

1 cup brown sugar	¼ cup milk
½ cup butter	

Combine all ingredients in saucepan and mix well. Cook 3 minutes over medium heat.

Serves 12 to 15

Mary Mueller
Rossville, Tennessee

MRS. KELSEY'S CARAMEL ICING FOR FRESH APPLE CAKES

Caramel and apples. Sweethearts forever.

3 cups sugar	1½ cups light cream
6 tablespoons butter, softened	1 teaspoon vanilla

Cream 2½ cups sugar with butter. Stir in light cream and bring to boil in large saucepan, stirring so that sugar does not cling to sides. Reduce heat to low. Caramelize remaining ½ cup sugar by cooking and stirring in heavy skillet over medium-high heat until sugar melts and turns brown. Add to cream mixture and continue cooking to soft ball stage. Remove from heat, add vanilla, and cool. Beat until thick enough to spread on cake.

Yields 2½ to 3 cups icing

Mrs. Howard Carrington

After-Concert Desserts with the Guest Artist

Memphis has an abiding affinity for the performing arts. Ever since 1824 when a small, entertainment-hungry band of early settlers formed a so-called Thespian Society to present a performance by a traveling comedian in a makeshift theater (known appropriately, no doubt, as the Blue Ruin), Memphis has been conducting an unremitting (and seldom unrequited) love affair with performing arts and artists— actors, actresses, singers, musicians—both home-grown and imported.

The first home-talent acting company, City Theatre, opened in a converted stable in 1842, and Memphis, since then, has always had one or more local theater groups. With the advent of the large opera houses (Greenlaw and, later, the Grand), and the fine, new Lyceum Theatre in the closing decades of the nineteenth century, Memphis became a regular stop on the schedules of the leading touring companies, from minstrels to Shakespeare. Memphis audiences applauded such theatrical greats as Joseph Jefferson, Edwin Booth, and Sarah Bernhardt.

And no one could have known it at the time, but when a one-act play entitled *Cairo, Shanghai, Bombay* was presented in Memphis on the night of July 12, 1935, on a stage in the garden of a private home, it was an event of historic importance. A young man named Tom Williams had written the play while visiting his Memphis grandparents that spring. This was the first (and apparently the only) performance of the earliest known dramatic work by one of America's greatest playwrights. (Thanks to the persistence of Memphis film and drama critic Edwin Howard, who resurrected the facts surrounding this almost-forgotten production, the event has now been memorialized by two local historical markers.) Young Tom Williams, using a nickname earned by his frequent visits to Tennessee relatives, would go on to achieve international fame as Tennessee Williams.

A stream of talented performing artists has poured out into the world from Memphis over the years. Singer Marie Greenwood, in 1885 at the age of twenty, made an impressive opera debut in New York, and later toured coast to coast with her own opera company. In the early 1900s, a beautiful red-haired Memphis actress, Florence Kahn, became leading lady to famed American actor Richard Mansfield, and was soon the toast of New York and London, where she married England's distinguished drama critic, Max Beerbohm. The fabled Front Street Theatre, begun as Theatre 12 in the basement of the old King Cotton Hotel by actor/director George Touliatos, during its brief but spirited existence (1957 to 1968) gave a number of well-known actors their start and sent them on to success elsewhere—George Hearn and Carrie Nye on Broadway, Stella Stevens and Macon McCalman in Hollywood, Dixie Carter and Barbara Cason in television. Memphis actress Cybill Shepherd has become a film and television superstar; also winning Hollywood's plaudits in recent years are such Memphis Children's Theatre alumni as actor Willard Pugh, and dancer Eric Henderson. The city has been a wellspring of opera talent, sending a whole roster of singers to the Metropolitan Opera—Mignon Dunn, sisters Patricia Welting and Ruth Welting, Nancy Tatum, Gail Robinson, Richard Vernon, and Kallen Esperian.

"Memphis music" is a term linked nowadays with rhythm and blues or rock 'n' roll, but the city's musical taste has always been eclectic—classical, popular, instrumental, vocal—and its musical appetite well-nigh insatiable. Memphis formed its own Philharmonic Society in the 1850s; Jenny Lind sang in Memphis; John Phillip Sousa conducted here; Kreisler and Rachmaninoff played here. The Beethoven Club, founded by six local women in 1888, has sponsored concerts by renowned musical performers, from Caruso to Sutherland, and is still going strong a century later. For many decades,

Memphis was one of eight American cities on the Metropolitan Opera's annual tour. And the Memphis Symphony, for nearly four decades, has welcomed to its stage such world-renowned guest artists as Isaac Stern, Itzhak Perlman, Leontyne Price, Van Cliburn, Zino Francescatti, Gina Bachauer, Lorin Hollander, Jean-Pierre Rampal, Lili Kraus, Aaron Copeland, Arthur Fiedler, Pablo Casals—an endless list—and a host of young, gifted performers whose music will reverberate through the great concert halls of the world for years to come.

Music, both classical and popular, is the concern of more than twenty Memphis associations, foundations, and performing companies. There's Opera Memphis and its eagerly-awaited productions that bring nationally celebrated opera stars together with accomplished Memphis singers. There's Roscoe's Surprise Orchestra—the surprise is that the audience never knows what new music it will hear—which regularly offers local music-lovers first-rate concerts of contemporary not to say avant-garde music. And the Blues Foundation annually sponsors and presents in Memphis the National Blues Music Awards. Dance, too, is on the creative move in the city. Memphis Concert Ballet and Memphis Classical Ballet feature local dancers and sponsor performances by visiting dance companies, while the Nubian Theatre Company offers exciting interpretations of traditional African dances.

Today, the link between Memphis and the performing arts is stronger than ever. So many new theatre, dance, and music groups have sprung up locally in the past fifteen years that the *Wall Street Journal* declared a "mini-renaissance in the arts" is occurring in Memphis. Live theatre, professional and amateur, is now presented year-round on some twenty local stages—university theatres, suburban community theatres in Germantown and Collierville, and dinner theatres. Not to mention the acclaimed Theatre Memphis which began as Memphis Little Theatre seventy years ago. Housed in a stunning, contemporary facility, its main stage, alternative stage, and touring company, ShoWagon, offer theatre virtually year round. It now boasts the country's second largest subscription audience for a non-professional company, and has represented the United States at international theatre festivals. There are the popular professional and local companies at Playhouse on the Square and Circuit Theatre, which have spawned such innovative ventures as Show of Hands, a deaf theatre group, and Blues City Cultural Center, presenting original work by Southern writers and artists. And Theatreworks, a small store-front theatre in the newly-designated South Main Historic District downtown, provides affordable performing space for emerging dramatists, actors, choreographers, and experimental theatre groups.

In Memphis, the arts nourish as they flourish. Ten local groups, often the offshoots of older arts organizations, now perform for young audiences, present performances by young artists, or both. Prime examples: the Memphis Youth Symphony and the Young Playwrights Showcase of the Memphis Children's Theatre, premiering first works by budding local dramatists.

Somewhere in town the curtain is always going up. The love affair continues.

CHOCOLATE GÂTEAU

A gorgeous dessert that takes top honors.

2¼ cups sugar
¾ cup butter, softened
1½ teaspoons vanilla
3 eggs
3 squares unsweetened
   chocolate, melted

3 cups sifted all-purpose flour
1½ teaspoons baking soda
¾ teaspoon salt
1½ cups ice water
Chocolate leaves for garnish

Butter and flour bottoms of two 9-inch square cake pans.

Cream sugar, butter, and vanilla together. Add eggs, beating until light and fluffy. Stir in chocolate. Sift flour, baking soda, and salt together, and add alternately with ice water to egg mixture, beating after each addition until smooth. Pour batter into cake pans and bake 35 to 40 minutes at 350 degrees. Cool 10 minutes in pan. Remove to cake rack and cool completely.

Place one cake layer on serving plate, top side down, and cover with mocha butter cream. Place second layer over first, top side down, and thinly frost top and sides. Spoon half of remaining frosting into icing bag with No. 30 star tube affixed. Pipe rosettes around sides and top, refilling bag as needed. (Chill bag in freezer 1 to 2 minutes if frosting becomes too soft.) Stick largest chocolate leaves into top of cake to form outer petals of a flower. Continue adding leaves in graduated sizes to form flower, ending with smallest pieces in center. Chill until both frosting and leaves are firm.

Mocha Butter Cream

5 cups brewed coffee
1 cup butter, softened
6 cups sifted confectioners'
   sugar

3 egg yolks
2 squares semi-sweet
   chocolate, melted

In heavy saucepan, bring coffee to vigorous boil, then reduce heat slightly and slowly boil until reduced to ½ cup coffee syrup, about 20 to 25 minutes. Cool and store in covered jar.

Cream butter with mixer until light and fluffy. Add 3 cups confectioners' sugar, beating until smooth. Add egg yolks and blend. Mix in remaining sugar. Add chocolate and ¼ cup coffee syrup, beating until blended and fluffy. (Reserve remaining coffee syrup for other uses.)

Chocolate Leaves

1 12-ounce package semi-sweet
   chocolate chips

Rose leaves or camellia
   leaves, washed

Place chocolate chips in ovenproof bowl in warm oven, about 150 degrees, leaving oven door slightly open. When chocolate has begun to melt yet still retains shape somewhat, remove from oven and beat until smooth. Pull a single leaf upside down over surface of chocolate. Tap leaf against bowl to remove excess. Place chocolate side up on baking sheet. Chill in refrigerator. When chocolate is chilled and hardened, peel off rose leaf.

Serves 10 to 12

Carol M. Cherry

COLD LEMON SOUFFLÉ

Light and tart. Rich, but not heavy.

5 eggs, separated
1½ cups sugar
¾ cup lemon juice
2 envelopes unflavored gelatin
½ cup water
1 teaspoon sugar

1 pint heavy cream
Pinch of salt
⅛ teaspoon cream of tartar
1½ to 2 dozen ladyfingers
1 cup heavy cream, whipped
Twisted lemon slices, optional

Beat egg yolks and 1½ cups sugar, gradually adding lemon juice until mixture becomes thick. In saucepan over low heat, sprinkle gelatin over water, add 1 teaspoon sugar, and stir until dissolved. Cool and add to lemon mixture. Partially whip 1 pint cream until thickened but not stiff, and fold into mixture. Combine egg whites, salt, and cream of tartar, beat until stiff peaks form, and fold into mixture. Line sides and bottom of 2-quart glass bowl with ladyfingers and fill with lemon mixture. Chill and serve topped with whipped cream. Or pour mixture into parfait glasses, chill, and garnish with twist of lemon.

Serves 12

Mrs. Philip Kaminsky

GLAZED CREAM CHEESECAKE

Is there a dessert more elegant than a superb cheesecake?

¾ cup coarsely ground walnuts	4 eggs
¾ cup finely crushed graham crackers	2 teaspoons vanilla
	1¼ cups sugar
3 tablespoons unsalted butter, melted	1 tablespoon fresh lemon juice
	2 cups sour cream
4 8-ounce packages cream cheese, softened	¼ cup sugar
	1 teaspoon vanilla

Combine walnuts, graham cracker crumbs, and butter. Tightly press into bottom of lightly buttered 9 or 10-inch springform pan.

Beat cream cheese until smooth. Add eggs, 2 teaspoons vanilla, 1¼ cups sugar, and lemon juice. Beat thoroughly, and spread over crust. Set pan on baking sheet, place in center of oven, and bake at 350 degrees. For a 9-inch pan, bake 50 to 55 minutes; for a 10-inch pan, bake 40 to 45 minutes. (Cake may rise slightly and crack, but will settle and be covered by topping.) Cool 15 minutes.

Combine sour cream, ¼ cup sugar, and 1 teaspoon vanilla. Spoon over cake, beginning at center and ending ½-inch from edge. Bake 5 minutes at 350 degrees. Cool and chill at least 24 hours, but preferably 2 to 3 days.

Using knife edge, loosen cake from pan and remove springform. Arrange berries, pointed end up, over top of cake. Spoon glaze over berries, allowing some to drip down sides of cake. Chill until glaze is set.

Strawberry Glaze

1 quart medium strawberries	¼ cup Cointreau
12 ounces red raspberry jelly	¼ cup water
1 tablespoon cornstarch	

Several hours before serving, wash, hull, and thoroughly dry strawberries. In saucepan, combine several tablespoons jelly with cornstarch, mix well, and add remaining jelly, Cointreau, and water. Cook over medium heat, stirring frequently, until thickened and clear, about 5 minutes. Cool to lukewarm, stirring occasionally.

Serves 10 to 15

Pamela McFarland

GLAZES FOR CHEESECAKES

Take your choice—you can't go wrong!

Lemon Glaze

½ cup sugar	⅓ cup lemon juice
4½ teaspoons cornstarch	1 egg yolk
¼ teaspoon salt	1 tablespoon butter, softened
¾ cup water	1 teaspoon grated lemon rind

In saucepan, combine sugar, cornstarch, and salt. Mix water, lemon juice, and egg yolk and add to sugar mixture. Cook over low heat, stirring constantly, until mixture comes to slow boil and thickens. Add butter and lemon rind. Cool slightly, but spread before glaze sets. Garnish with lemon strips and mint, if desired.

Patricia B. Atkinson

Chocolate-Apricot Glaze with Grand Marnier

1 18-ounce jar apricot preserves	2 squares unsweetened chocolate
Grand Marnier to taste	
2 squares German sweet chocolate	½ cup sugar
	½ cup heavy cream

Mix preserves with Grand Marnier and spread over cooled cheesecake. Chill. Combine both chocolates, sugar, and ¼ cup cream in top of double boiler and cook until thick, gradually adding remaining cream. Spoon over apricot layer. Glazes may intermingle, creating a pretty swirl.

Mrs. Philip Kaminsky

FLAMING PEARS

Pears with panache.

1½ cups sugar	Several drops red food coloring
1½ cups water	6 fresh pears
4 or 5 whole cloves	¼ cup brandy
3 slices lemon	

Combine sugar, water, cloves, and lemon slices in deep saucepan and bring to boil. Stir in food coloring. Peel pears, leaving stems on, and trim bottoms to sit flat in saucepan. Place in sauce and simmer 30 to 40 minutes or until tender.

Heat brandy, flame, pour over pears, and serve immediately.

Serves 6

Daphne Boyle

ENGLISH SUMMER PUDDING

Whether the berries are wild from the countryside or fresh from the garden, nothing better holds the taste of summer.

¾ pound bread loaf with crust removed	1 teaspoon lemon juice
¾ cup fresh raspberries	¼ cup sugar
¾ cup sliced fresh strawberries	¼ cup water

Cut bread into thin slices and use most to line 4-cup mold. Combine berries, lemon juice, sugar, and water, and simmer until most of water is absorbed, about 20 to 25 minutes. Spoon fruit mixture into bread-lined mold and layer with remainder of bread. Cover with wax paper, put small flat plate on top, and place a light weight on top of plate. Leave overnight in cool place. Serve with whipped cream or CUSTARD SAUCE FOR BERRY COBBLER.

Serves 4 to 6

Pat Kerr Tigrett

CANDIED VIOLETS

Make these lovely and edible bits of color in the springtime when violets grow wild, and store enough to use for the entire winter. Beautiful on cakes, soufflés, or candy.

36 violets, plus a few extra	8 to 10 drops violet extract, optional
1 egg white	
Purple food coloring, optional	½ cup sugar

Remove stems from violets, leaving just the flower. Cleanse in soapy water, rinse, and dry very carefully and thoroughly with soft paper towels.

Combine egg white, coloring, and extract, and beat until foamy. Dip each flower into egg mixture and then into sugar. Place violets on baking sheet. Use a toothpick to shape violets, keeping petals open. (A few extra will be needed as some will not survive the shaping procedure.) Heat oven at lowest temperature for 5 minutes. Turn off heat and place violets in oven to dry overnight. Store in airtight container in cool place. Will keep forever.

Note: Be sure violets have not been sprayed with herbicides or other chemicals.

Yields 36 candied violets

Carol M. Cherry

PRESBYTERIAN PATIENCE CAKE

Well worth the patience required for waiting five days before eating. Predestined to be good.

Filling

2 cups fresh or frozen coconut	1½ cups confectioners' sugar
1 16-ounce carton sour cream	1 teaspoon vanilla

Combine all ingredients and mix well. Refrigerate 24 hours.

1 box yellow butter cake mix	2 cups coconut, fresh or frozen
8 ounces non-dairy whipped topping, more if preferred	

Prepare cake according to directions on box. Bake in two 9-inch round pans. Cool cakes and split each layer in half. Place one layer split side up and spread with filling. Repeat with remaining layers. Frost cake with whipped topping and cover with coconut. Cover cake and refrigerate for 5 days.

Serves 12 to 14

Mary Lawrence Allen

ORANGE-RAISIN PUDDING

A special and unusual winter dessert, reminiscent of being home for the holidays with this fresh and spicy fragrance filling the comfortable kitchen.

Juice of 2 oranges	1 cup raisins
Juice of 1 lemon	1 egg
2 cups sugar	1 cup buttermilk
⅓ cup butter	1 teaspoon baking soda
Rind of 1 orange	2 cups all-purpose flour
Rind of 1 lemon	1 cup heavy cream, whipped

Mix juices and 1 cup sugar, and set aside for topping.

Cream butter and remaining sugar. Grind together citrus rinds and raisins, and mix with creamed mixture. Add remaining ingredients except heavy cream. Pour into 9 x 11-inch baking pan lined with parchment paper. Bake at 350 degrees for 45 minutes or until set. Pour reserved juice mixture over top of cake while hot. Cut in squares and serve warm topped with whipped cream.

Yields 2 dozen pudding squares

Sissy M. Long

BOURBON PUDDING

Simple and sophisticated all at once. A three-layer delight with a dash of sugar on top, custard in the middle, and a crisp cookie crust.

6 jumbo eggs, separated	4 cups milk
2 cups sugar	2 tablespoons bourbon whiskey
1 cup crushed vanilla wafers or crisp macaroons	1 teaspoon vanilla

To make pudding mixture, beat egg yolks with 1 cup sugar. Mix in vanilla wafers, milk, bourbon, and vanilla. Beat egg whites until soft peaks form and fold into mixture. Set aside.

Place remaining 1 cup sugar in non-Teflon tube pan and heat in oven at 350 degrees until sugar melts and turns brown. Swirl caramelized sugar to coat all sides of pan. Pour pudding mixture into tube pan and set in shallow baking pan of hot water. Bake 45 to 60 minutes at 325 degrees until set. Refrigerate in pan several hours or overnight.

Turn onto cake stand, slice in wedges, and top with bourbon-flavored whipped cream and chopped pecans.

Serves 10 to 12

Mrs. John Montesi

APPLE BROWN BETTY

A dish that has a long history of welcoming home-coming collegians.

6 to 7 medium tart apples, peeled and thinly sliced	1 cup all-purpose flour
½ cup granulated sugar	½ cup butter, softened
¼ teaspoon lemon juice	½ cup brown sugar
Pinch of cinnamon	2 tablespoons granulated sugar
	¼ teaspoon cinnamon

Combine apples, ½ cup granulated sugar, lemon juice, and cinnamon, and mix well. Pack into buttered glass baking dish. Mix flour and butter. Stir in brown sugar, 2 tablespoons granulated sugar, and cinnamon. Crumble mixture over apples. Bake at 400 degrees for 30 minutes or until lightly browned.

Serve warm with ice cream, sour cream, or whipped cream.

Serves 8 to 10

Mrs. Edward S. Kaplan

ORANGE DATE NUT CAKE

A cake that once celebrated a first child's arrival and promptly became a special-occasion cake. Delicious with GRANDMOTHER'S AMBROSIA.

1 cup margarine	1 teaspoon baking soda
2 cups sugar	2 tablespoons grated orange rind
4 eggs	
4 cups all-purpose flour	1 8-ounce package chopped dates
1 teaspoon baking powder	
½ teaspoon salt	1 cup chopped pecans
1⅓ cups buttermilk	1 teaspoon vanilla

Cream margarine and sugar. Add eggs one at a time. Sift together flour, baking powder, and salt. Mix buttermilk and baking soda. Add to creamed mixture alternately with dry ingredients. Mix orange rind, dates, and pecans with enough flour to coat, stir into batter, and add vanilla. Batter will be very thick. Pour into greased and floured tube pan. Bake at 325 degrees for 60 minutes or until thoroughly done. (Test with straw or cake tester.) Remove from pan and glaze while cake is still hot.

Glaze

2 tablespoons grated orange rind	Juice of 1 lemon
2 cups sugar	1 cup fresh orange juice

Mix all ingredients in saucepan and cook until thickened.

Serves 12 to 14

Mrs. John A. Edrington
Osceola, Arkansas

FROZEN LEMON DELIGHT

A perfect summertime dessert.

4 eggs, separated	Rind of 1 lemon, grated
½ cup sugar	1 cup heavy cream, whipped
Juice of 1 lemon	1 cup graham cracker crumbs

Combine egg yolks, sugar, lemon juice, and lemon rind, and beat well. Beat egg whites until firm peaks form and fold with whipped cream into egg mixture. Line 7 x 11-inch baking pan with ¾ cup graham cracker crumbs, spoon in lemon mixture, and sprinkle with remaining crumbs. Freeze.

Serves 12

Mrs. Richard L. de Saussure, Jr.

JOHN GRISANTI'S CHOCOLATE CHEESECAKE

Memphians have been in love with Grisanti's great Italian cooking since John's father opened his first restaurant in 1909 across from Central Station on South Main. The location has changed, but the excellence remains, including this sensational cheesecake.

1 cup butter, melted
3 cups graham cracker crumbs
1 12-ounce package semi-sweet chocolate chips
4 8-ounce packages cream cheese, room temperature
2 cups sugar
1 tablespoon cocoa
4 eggs
2 teaspoons vanilla
2 cups sour cream
1 cup heavy cream
1 teaspoon sugar
Grated chocolate
Pecans or maraschino cherries

Mix butter and graham cracker crumbs until crumbs are moistened (add more butter if mixture is too crumbly). Line sides and bottom of 10-inch springform pan with mixture and chill.

Melt chocolate in top of double boiler over simmering water and remove from heat. At medium speed, beat cream cheese until smooth, gradually adding 2 cups sugar. Beat in cocoa until blended. Add eggs one at a time, beating well after each addition. Beat in melted chocolate and vanilla. Stir in sour cream. Pour into chilled crust and bake 1½ hours at 290 degrees. Cool at room temperature and chill at least 5 hours before serving (cheesecake will set when chilled).

Combine cream and 1 teaspoon sugar, and whip until very thick. Spoon into pastry bag and decorate cake. Garnish with grated chocolate and pecans or maraschino cherries. To serve, remove from pan and slice thin.

Serves 16 to 20

John Grisanti

BRANDIED GRAPES

A superb dessert. Refreshing and light. Perfect with sugar wafers.

¾ cup honey
6 tablespoons brandy
1 tablespoon lemon juice
1 cup sour cream
1 pound red or green seedless grapes

Mix together honey, brandy, and lemon juice. Add sour cream and grapes, gently stirring until grapes are coated. Chill several hours. Serve in sherbet glasses.

Serves 4

Mrs. Wilson Northcross, Jr.

STRAWBERRY SQUARES WITH FRESH FRUIT

An old favorite with a new twist. So appealing decorated with fresh fruit.

1 box white cake mix with pudding
4 tablespoons all-purpose flour
1 3-ounce package wild strawberry gelatin
4 eggs
1 cup vegetable oil
1 quart strawberries, crushed
Strawberries and kiwi slices

In large bowl, sift together cake mix, flour, and gelatin. Add eggs one at a time, beating after each addition. Add oil and beat well. Add 1 cup crushed strawberries with juice to batter. Reserve additional ½ cup for frosting and drain remainder, reserving juice. Pour into greased and floured 9 x 13-inch baking pan and bake 35 to 45 minutes at 350 degrees. Do not overbake. Punch holes in cooled cake with skewer, drizzle reserved juice over cake, and frost. Cut in squares and garnish with strawberries and kiwi slices.

Frosting
½ cup reserved crushed strawberries
2 cups confectioners' sugar
½ cup butter, softened
Dash salt
½ cup frozen coconut, optional

Combine all ingredients and mix well.

Variations: In place of strawberry gelatin and mashed strawberries, use peach gelatin with fresh peaches (use yellow butter cake mix); or raspberry gelatin with raspberries; or blackberry gelatin with blackberries and blackberry wine.

Serves 15 to 20

Mrs. Winfred Sharp

Supper in a Carriage House Gazebo

When flat boats and paddlewheel packets crowded Memphis' port in the early nineteenth century, Adams and Jefferson Avenues were busy thoroughfares leading to the public landing on the banks of the Mississippi River. In the second half of the nineteenth century, Adams and Jefferson became two of the city's most fashionable addresses as affluent citizens—cotton factors, lumber merchants, bankers, railroad men, a carriage manufacturer, a steamboat captain, a former Confederate Army general—built splendid Victorian mansions along this tree-shaded street. But time and urban decay took their toll. By the mid-twentieth century, some of the street's finest homes had been torn down; others stood vacant or had become dilapidated tenements. When city officials, in 1959, announced they would be razing the Fontaine and Lee houses, it seemed the final blow. These one-time showplaces, given to the city and the Memphis Arts Association thirty years earlier to be used as an art academy, had been recently vacated when the Academy (today's Memphis College of Art) moved to new quarters in Overton Park. But if these grand old houses were demolished, what would happen to the area's other few surviving mansions?

What *did* happen surprised almost everyone. A determined band of Memphis citizens were dismayed by what they saw as rampant destruction of their city's architectural heritage; they decided now was the time and this was the place to stop the bulldozers. Joining forces with a few devoted preservationists already at work in the neighborhood, members of the Association for the Preservation of Tennessee Antiquities raised fifty thousand dollars for the restoration of the Fontaine House. Moreover, because of their campaigning and cajoling, some twenty other deteriorating Adams Avenue and Jefferson Avenue mansions were eventually reclaimed, and the area, lying almost in the shadow of downtown Memphis skyscrapers, officially incorporated itself as Victorian Village. (In 1972, it became the city's first residential district to be listed in the National Register of Historic Places, and its preservation is celebrated each fall at the Victorian Village Festival, when all Memphis is invited to visit the neighborhood.) These efforts, in turn, sparked formation of other agencies and groups that are now active in historic preservation throughout the city—Memphis Heritage, Inc., the Memphis Landmark Commission, the Shelby County Historical Commission, and the Center City Commission.

One person, more than any other, inspired the creation of Victorian Village and all that followed. Eldridge Wright, a design consultant, was the neighborhood's first preservationist. Drawn to the area by family roots, he bought a dilapidated Adams Avenue mansion in 1955 and restored it to vintage magnificence. But the reclamation of a small carriage house around the corner on Orleans Street was his greatest labor of love. This simple brick structure was all that remained of the original home, destroyed by the widening of Jefferson, of his great-grandfather, Luke E. Wright, a one-time Confederate officer who was the first Governor-General of the Philippines, first U. S. Ambassador to Japan, and Secretary of War under President Theodore Roosevelt. In 1966, Eldridge Wright began the restoration of this charming old building, enclosing its green lawn with a wall made of bricks salvaged from the original mansion.

THE PICTURE: *Hidden behind ivy-covered brick walls, the Wright Carriage House on Orleans Street between Adams and Jefferson Avenues re-creates the aura of an earlier, quieter era. Gracing the landscaped grounds is a small, octagonal gazebo of French design where meals are often served. This evening, a cool breeze is blowing through its gray lattice frame, and the dessert course of a summer supper awaits. In the background is the restored carriage house that once stood behind the home of General Luke E. Wright, a distinguished soldier and diplomat. It was remodeled in the late 1960s, and is used as an office by Luke Wright's great-grandson, Eldridge Wright, a leader in the movement to preserve the Memphis architectural landmarks that are now part of the Victorian Village near downtown Memphis. The small French iron table, its painted surface softened by time, is set for two. A butterfly gardenia lends its blossoms and fragrance. Pictures of bright-hued birds perched on a thistle branch ornament the old English dessert plates. The Coligney silver flatware was Luke Wright's wedding present to Eldridge Wright's parents. The ornate silver goblets, also heirlooms, are those in which Eldridge Wright's mother once served frosted mint juleps.*

THE FOOD: *GREAT-GRANDMOTHER WRIGHT'S CHARLOTTE RUSSE, in a bed of homemade lady fingers with fresh ripe raspberries and whipped cream, is made from a family recipe passed down for four generations. It is rich with the taste of sherry and memories of long ago.*

GREAT-GRANDMOTHER WRIGHT'S CHARLOTTE RUSSE

Simply a wonderful dessert, light as can be. Time has proved it a classic.

1 tablespoon unflavored
   gelatin
⅓ cup water
2 dozen ladyfingers

3 cups heavy cream
7 tablespoons confectioners'
   sugar
½ cup sherry

Dissolve gelatin in water over low heat and allow to cool slightly. Line sides and bottom of crystal bowl with ladyfingers, placing them vertically around sides.

Beat cream, sugar, and sherry until thick but not stiff and dry. Gradually add gelatin mixture, beating until well-blended. Pour into bowl. Split remaining ladyfingers lengthwise and garnish top in a single flower design, placing a few strawberries in center of flower. Or garnish with whipped cream, fresh raspberries, and gardenia leaves. Chill until set.

Serves 6 to 8

Eldridge Wright

JOY'S ORANGE WHIP

Light and luscious.

2 envelopes unflavored gelatin
2½ cups fresh orange juice
2 cups sugar
Dash salt
4 egg yolks

1 tablespoon grated orange rind
2 teaspoons grated lemon rind
3 tablespoons fresh lemon juice
1 cup orange sections
2 cups heavy cream, whipped

Dissolve gelatin thoroughly in ½ cup orange juice. Stir in sugar and salt. Beat together egg yolks and ½ cup orange juice, and stir into gelatin mixture. Cook over medium heat, stirring constantly, just until mixture begins to boil. Remove from heat. Stir in remaining orange juice, orange rind, lemon rind, and lemon juice. Chill, stirring occasionally, until mixture is partially set and mounds when dropped from spoon.

Stir in orange sections and fold in whipped cream. Pour into 2-quart mold, or into sherbet glasses, and chill until set.

Serves 10 to 12

Peggy Boyce Jemison

MAPLE SUGAR MOUSSE

For lovers of the special taste of maple syrup—lest there be some notion that it's only meant for pancakes and waffles.

1 cup maple syrup
1 pint heavy cream

3 eggs, separated

Boil syrup 1 minute and set aside to cool slightly. Whip cream until stiff. Beat egg whites until stiff peaks form. Fold whipped cream and egg whites together. Beat egg yolks well and gradually blend in warm syrup. Fold cream mixture into syrup mixture and freeze.

Serves 6 to 8

Mrs. M. A. J. Knox

KAHLUA COFFEE PARFAIT PIE

A typical scene among diners at Paulette's: Someone at the next table is served a towering slice of out-of-this-world pie. One look and all will power at one's own table deserts the premises. Result: Another order and another victory for Kahlua Coffee Pie.

Crust
1 7-ounce package flaked
   coconut
2 tablespoons all-purpose flour

4 ounces finely chopped pecans
½ cup margarine, melted

Combine coconut, flour, and pecans in large bowl. Add melted margarine and mix until all ingredients are well-moistened. Press into 10-inch metal pie pan. With back of wooden spoon, pack crust into sides and bottom corners of pie pan. Crust must be level with rim of pie pan to prevent burning when cooked. Bake at 375 degrees for 10 minutes or until golden brown. Cool completely before filling.

Filling
Coffee ice cream with
   chocolate chips
Heavy cream, whipped

Semi-sweet chocolate, grated
Kahlua

Pack crust 2 to 3 inches deep with ice cream. Freeze. To serve, top with whipped cream and sprinkle with grated chocolate. Pour 1 ounce of Kahlua on each slice just before serving.

Serves 8

Paulette's Restaurant
George Falls, Proprietor

BROWNIE BAKED ALASKA

Invented to please a chocolate-loving family. Gives a new twist to an old favorite.

Brownie layer, uncut, made
   from favorite recipe
1 quart vanilla or favorite
   ice cream, softened

5 egg whites
Sugar to taste

Cut brownie layer to fit into bottom of pie pan. Spread ice cream evenly over layer and freeze.

Beat egg whites into soft peaks. Gradually add sugar, beating until stiff peaks form. Cover ice cream with meringue, spreading to sides of pan to seal. Dab meringue in and out with back of spoon to form many little peaks with one large peak in center. Place under broiler just long enough to brown peaks. Slice and serve immediately.

Serves 8

Mrs. Philip Kaminsky

GERMAN SWEET CHOCOLATE PIE

A variation on a grand old theme.

1 4-ounce package German
   sweet chocolate
¼ cup butter
1 12-ounce can evaporated
   milk
1½ cups sugar
3 tablespoons cornstarch

⅛ teaspoon salt
2 eggs
1 teaspoon vanilla
1 unbaked 10-inch pie shell
1⅓ cups grated coconut
½ cup chopped pecans
1 cup heavy cream, whipped

Melt chocolate and butter over low heat, stirring until blended. Remove from heat and gradually stir in milk. Thoroughly mix sugar, cornstarch, and salt, beat in eggs and vanilla, and gradually blend into chocolate mixture. Pour into pie shell. Combine coconut and pecans, and sprinkle over top. Bake at 375 degrees for 45 minutes or until puffed and browned, watching carefully to see that coconut does not get too dark. (Pie filling will be soft, but will set when cooled.) Cool at least 4 hours before cutting. Serve with whipped cream on top.

Serves 8 to 10

Pamela McFarland

PEPPERMINT CHIFFON PIE

Light, airy, and delicious.

20 to 30 chocolate wafers,
   crushed
4 tablespoons butter, melted
3 eggs, separated
½ cup crushed peppermint
   sticks

½ cup sugar
1 envelope unflavored gelatin
1¼ cups milk
¼ teaspoon salt
Red food coloring
½ cup heavy cream, whipped

Mix wafers with butter and press into 10-inch pie pan. Bake 15 minutes at 350 degrees and cool.

In saucepan, beat egg yolks and add candy, ¼ cup sugar, gelatin, milk, and salt. Cook over low heat until candy and gelatin dissolve. Stir in a drop or two of food coloring and chill until partially set.

Beat egg whites until stiff peaks form, gradually adding remaining sugar. Fold with whipped cream into peppermint mixture. Pour into pie shell and chill. Serve topped with whipped cream and crushed peppermint candy.

Serves 8

Nancy McConnico Beck

MILLIONAIRE PIES

A lovely raisin and pecan tart.

1 cup seedless raisins, washed
4 tablespoons water
3 eggs, beaten
1½ cups sugar
2 tablespoons butter
2 tablespoons vinegar

1 teaspoon cinnamon
1 teaspoon allspice
1 teaspoon nutmeg
1 cup chopped pecans
8 individual baked tart shells
1 cup heavy cream, whipped

Simmer raisins in water 5 minutes. Combine water, eggs, sugar, butter, vinegar, and spices, add to simmering raisins, and boil until thick. Cool. Stir in pecans and spoon into tart shells. Top with whipped cream.

Note: Filling can be kept in refrigerator a week or more before putting in tart shells. Wonderful to have on hand for unexpected guests.

Serves 8

Dorothy Lancaster Moore
Blytheville, Arkansas

LEMON-KISSED BLUEBERRY TARTS

Blueberries are such wonderful little things. This touch of lemon makes them even more special.

Pastry

2 cups vegetable shortening, softened	5¼ cups all-purpose flour
1 tablespoon salt	1 cup ice water
	Whipped cream, optional

Mix shortening, salt, and flour with hands until smoothly blended. Make well in center and add water, mixing to make dough and adding more flour if dough is too sticky. Press portions of dough into individual 3-inch tart pans. (To freeze, put enough dough for 1 pie crust into individual plastic bags and place in freezer.) Bake at 400 degrees until lightly browned. Cool and pour in filling. Top with whipped cream, if desired.

Filling

2 cups blueberries, fresh or frozen	1 tablespoon cornstarch
½ cup sugar	Grated rind of 1 lemon
	1 tablespoon lemon juice

Divide 1 cup blueberries among 6 tart shells. In saucepan, crush remaining cup blueberries and add sugar, cornstarch, lemon rind, and lemon juice. Cook over high heat until clear and thick, and pour over berries.

Serves 6

Bobbye Bryant
Chicago, Illinois

CHOCOLATE CREAM POUND CAKE

Too rich for words—too good to miss.

2 Sara Lee pound cakes, cut in half lengthwise	2 tablespoons cognac
8 ounces sweet chocolate	1 pint heavy cream
¼ cup strong coffee	Chocolate curls

Combine chocolate, coffee, and cognac in top of double boiler and cook until smooth, stirring constantly. Cool. Whip cream and fold into chocolate mixture. Spread generously between layers and frost entire cake. Chill several hours or overnight. Serve garnished with chocolate curls.

Serves 8

Patricia B. Atkinson

MIXED FRUIT SHERBET

A great-grandmother's recipe with its origins in Kentucky, proving that something other than thoroughbreds makes the winner's circle.

3 cups sugar	1 15¼-ounce can crushed pineapple
3 cups water	3 large ripe bananas, mashed
Juice of 6 lemons	Milk
Juice of 3 oranges	

Combine sugar and water, bring to boil, and cook until sugar dissolves. Chill in refrigerator, preferably overnight. Stir in juices and fruits, and pour into 5-quart ice cream freezer. Freeze 10 to 15 minutes. Add milk up to "fill" line (or to within 2 inches of top of container). Continue freezing until set.

Serves 16 to 20

Betty A. Jennings

PARADISE PIE

The Red Apple Inn at Greer's Ferry Lake does seem to be a little bit of paradise, and it is a favorite vacation spot for Memphians and Arkansans. This pie is a traditional favorite on the Inn's menu.

3 egg whites	1 cup chopped pecans
1 teaspoon vanilla	¾ cup flaked coconut
1¼ cups sugar	1 cup heavy cream, whipped
20 soda crackers, crushed	

Beat egg whites and vanilla, gradually adding 1 cup sugar, until stiff peaks form. Fold in cracker crumbs and pecans. Line 10-inch pie pan with mixture and bake 15 minutes at 325 degrees. Cool.

Fold ½ cup coconut and remaining sugar into whipped cream and pour into pie pan. Sprinkle with remaining ¼ cup coconut, or more if preferred, and freeze.

Serves 8

The Red Apple Inn
Eden Isle
Heber Springs, Arkansas

CRANBERRY-ORANGE SHERBET

Colorful, tangy, and delicious.

2 cups fresh cranberries
1 medium orange, peeled,
    sectioned, and seeded
Rind of ½ orange

5 tablespoons orange liqueur
1 cup sugar
4 egg whites

Combine cranberries, orange sections, orange rind, and liqueur in food processor or blender, and purée. Add ¾ cup sugar and blend. Beat egg whites until stiff, gradually adding remaining ¼ cup sugar. Fold puréed fruit into egg whites. Pour into 1½ or 2-quart serving dish or mold, and freeze.

Serves 6

Roma Marmon

BAKED LEMON PUDDING

A delicious dessert with a baked-in surprise. Beneath a soufflé-like top is a layer of lemon pudding—a delightful combination.

1 cup sugar
3 tablespoons cornstarch
⅛ teaspoon salt
2 eggs, separated
1 cup milk

3 tablespoons lemon juice
1 teaspoon grated lemon rind
2 tablespoons margarine,
    melted

Sift ¾ cup sugar, cornstarch, and salt into large bowl, and set aside. Beat egg yolks until light and foamy, add milk, and gradually stir into sugar mixture. Combine lemon juice, lemon rind, and margarine, and add to sugar mixture. Beat egg whites until soft peaks form and gradually add remaining ¼ cup sugar, beating constantly until stiff peaks form. Fold into lemon mixture. Pour into buttered 1½-quart baking dish and place in pan of warm water. Bake at 350 degrees for 50 minutes or until set and browned on top. Place on rack to cool. Garnish with twist of lemon and serve warm or cold.

Serves 6 to 8

Sara M. Holmes

BLACKBERRIES WITH CORN MEAL COBBLES

The basis for this recipe is Native American cooking which made sweet use of readily available ingredients abundant in the forests and fields of the Fourth Chickasaw Bluff.

2 quarts fresh or frozen
    blackberries
1¼ cups sugar
1 cup stone ground corn meal
1 teaspoon baking powder
4 tablespoons butter, melted

½ cup buttermilk
¼ cup honey
1 tablespoon lime juice
½ cup chopped walnuts
Heavy cream

Rinse blackberries, drain, and sprinkle with 1 cup sugar (½ cup for frozen berries). Place in greased 2-quart baking dish. Mix together corn meal, baking powder, and remaining ¼ cup sugar, and make a well in center. Add 3 tablespoons butter and buttermilk to the well to make batter, stirring quickly to moisten. To make cobbles, drop batter by teaspoonfuls onto berries. Combine remaining tablespoon butter, honey, lime juice, and walnuts, and pour over top. Bake at 375 degrees for 30 to 40 minutes or until corn meal cobbles are browned. Serve warm with thick cream.

Serves 10 to 12

Marilou Awiakta

CHOCOLATE MINT MOUSSE

The taste of mint is a nice addition to the chocolate.

1 envelope unflavored gelatin
½ cup water
4 squares semi-sweet chocolate
10 chocolate mint wafers,
    finely crushed

⅓ cup sugar
1 cup milk, scalded
1 teaspoon vanilla
2 cups heavy cream

Soften gelatin in ¼ cup water. Melt chocolate with remaining water in top of double boiler. Add crushed mint wafers and blend well. Add sugar, milk, and gelatin mixture, blending well after each addition. Cool thoroughly. Add vanilla. Whip 1½ cups cream and fold into mixture. Pour into lightly oiled mold and chill until set. Whip remaining cream and use for topping.

Serves 10

Mrs. Solon G. Freeman, Sr.

THE ELEGANT SCHAUM TORTE

An airy dessert.

9 jumbo egg whites, room temperature	Ice cream or frozen yogurt of choice
3 cups sugar	Strawberries, peaches, or chocolate sauce
2 teaspoons vanilla	
2 teaspoons vinegar	

Whip egg whites until foamy, adding 2½ cups sugar ¼ cup at a time. Near the end of this process, add vinegar and vanilla. Fold in remaining ½ cup sugar with spatula. Wrap an aluminum foil collar around 10-inch springform pan to make it taller. Pour in mixture and bake at 300 degrees for 1 hour or until delicately browned. Chill thoroughly. When ready to serve, fill with ice cream and cover with fresh fruit or, in a moment of madness, chocolate sauce.

Serves 10 to 12

Mrs. Lawrence L. Cohen

BURNT CREAM

Always welcome, always good.

2 cups heavy cream	1 tablespoon vanilla
4 egg yolks	Granulated sugar for topping
½ cup granulated sugar	

Cook cream over low heat until bubbles form around edge of pan. Beat yolks and ½ cup sugar with wire whisk until thick, about 3 minutes. Gradually beat cream into egg mixture. Stir in vanilla and pour into lightly buttered custard cups. Set cups in baking pan with ½-inch water in bottom. Bake at 350 degrees for 45 minutes or until set. Chill.

Sprinkle each custard with 2 teaspoons sugar. Broil on top rack of oven until sugar becomes medium brown in color. Chill before serving.

Serves 6

Patsy Kinney
Forrest City, Arkansas

PUMPKIN SQUARES

Never underestimate a pumpkin—some turn into chariots, some turn into squares.

1 16-ounce can pumpkin	½ teaspoon salt
1 12-ounce can evaporated milk	1 box yellow cake mix
4 teaspoons pumpkin pie spice	¾ cup butter, melted
1 cup sugar	1 cup finely chopped nuts
3 eggs	Whipped cream, optional

Combine pumpkin, milk, spice, sugar, eggs, and salt, and mix well. Pour into greased 9 x 13-inch baking pan and sprinkle with cake mix. Drizzle butter evenly over mix and top with nuts. Bake at 350 degrees for 50 to 60 minutes until set. Cut in squares and serve topped with whipped cream.

Serves 12 to 16

Opal Caples

CHOCOLATE PIE

No life is complete without a first-class basic chocolate pie recipe. We offer this one, very easy and very good.

3 eggs, separated	¼ teaspoon salt
1 cup milk	4 tablespoons all-purpose flour
1 teaspoon vanilla	¼ cup butter
1 cup sugar	1 baked 8-inch pie shell
5 tablespoons cocoa	

Beat egg yolks in saucepan. Reserve whites. Add milk and vanilla. Sift together sugar, cocoa, salt, and flour, and add to egg mixture, stirring well. Add butter and cook over medium-high heat until thickened, stirring constantly. Pour into pie shell and top with meringue. Bake at 400 degrees for 10 minutes or until meringue is lightly browned.

Meringue

3 egg whites	6 tablespoons sugar

Whip egg whites until stiff, adding sugar gradually.

Serves 6

Mrs. Dan Scott, Jr.

SPICE CAKE

A cake in a pie pan, which is reason enough to try it.

⅓ cup solid shortening
1 cup sugar
1 egg, separated
½ teaspoon baking soda
⅔ cup sour milk (or substitute
   ⅔ cup milk mixed with
   1 tablespoon lemon juice)
1¼ cups all-purpose flour

½ teaspoon baking powder
½ teaspoon ground cloves
½ teaspoon cinnamon
¼ teaspoon salt
½ teaspoon vanilla
¼ cup chopped nuts
½ cup brown sugar
½ cup chopped nuts

Cream shortening, sugar, and egg yolk. Mix baking soda with sour milk and set aside. Sift together flour, baking powder, spices, and salt, and add alternately with milk mixture to sugar mixture. Add vanilla and ¼ cup nuts to batter and pour into greased 9-inch pie pan. Beat egg white until stiff peaks form. Add brown sugar, beat until glossy, and fold in ½ cup nuts. Spread over batter and bake 30 minutes at 350 degrees.

Serves 8

Dr. Sara B. Sanders

MINETRY'S MIRACLE

A glorious creation that will take its place in the dessert Hall of Fame.

2 dozen almond macaroons
1 cup bourbon whiskey
2 cups unsalted butter, softened
2 cups sugar
12 eggs, separated
4 squares unsweetened
   chocolate, melted

1 teaspoon vanilla
1 cup coarsely chopped pecans
2 dozen ladyfingers, separated
1½ cups heavy cream,
   sweetened to taste and
   whipped

Soak macaroons in bourbon and set aside. Cream butter and sugar until light and fluffy. Lightly beat egg yolks and add to creamed mixture. Beat in melted chocolate. Add vanilla and pecans. Beat egg whites until stiff peaks form, and fold into chocolate mixture.

Cover bottom of 10-inch springform pan with ladyfingers, standing remainder around sides of pan. Alternately add layers of chocolate mixture and macaroons. Chill overnight or at least 6 hours. Remove from pan and serve topped with whipped cream.

Serves 16 to 20

Mrs. Norfleet R. Turner

TWO CRUST "SLICE OF LEMON" PIE

A two-crust lemon pie that is divine.

1¼ cups sugar
2 tablespoons all-purpose flour
⅛ teaspoon salt
¼ cup butter, softened
3 eggs, well-beaten, with 1
   teaspoon egg white reserved
1 teaspoon grated lemon rind

1 lemon, peeled and sliced
   paper-thin
½ cup water
2 unbaked 8-inch pie shells
Sugar
Cinnamon

Combine sugar, flour, and salt, and blend with butter. Add eggs and mix until smooth. Add lemon rind, lemon slices, and water. Blend well, pour into one pie shell, and cover with remaining shell. Slit top several times, seal, and flute edges. Brush top with reserved egg white and sprinkle with sugar and cinnamon. Bake 30 to 35 minutes at 400 degrees.

Serves 6 to 8

Barbara B. Harrington

PERFECT PASTRY

A beautifully short, very forgiving pie crust. It simply will not go wrong.

1 cup all-purpose flour
½ teaspoon salt
½ cup vegetable shortening

1 teaspoon light cream
3 tablespoons boiling water

Sift flour with salt. With fork, mix shortening, cream, and water together until of consistency of cottage cheese. Stir in flour mixture well. Form into ball and thoroughly chill. Roll dough out on lightly floured board.

Note: Can be successfully doubled and also frozen, either as ball of dough or rolled out.

Yields 1 pie crust

Barbara M. Robertson

Special Treats to Honor a Beale Street Legend

There are, in all the world, only a few such streets—Broadway in New York, the *Champs Élysées* in Paris, Beale Street in Memphis—streets with names universally recognized and identities all their own. Streets that are forever part of, yet have come to represent more than, the cities with which their names are linked. They tell stories and sing songs about such streets: "If Beale Street could talk . . ."

Stretching eastward from Beale Landing, built in the early 1840s to accommodate the big new steamboats that were replacing Mississippi River flatboats, Beale Street was originally the main thoroughfare of the town of South Memphis. A prosperous early rival of Memphis until the two municipalities voted to merge in 1859, South Memphis was sometimes called "Sodom" because of its lavish lifestyle. It was a fitting birthplace for so legendary a place as Beale Street. Not much more than a mile long, Beale Street, in its little more than a century and a half of existence, has seen all, heard all, known all manner of men and women. It has welcomed roustabouts and robber barons, preachers and prostitutes, grocers and gamblers, dentists and conjurers. It has known pool halls and dance halls, barber shops and pawn shops, ice cream parlors and undertaking parlors, opera houses, and farmers' markets; it has seen mule trains and trolley cars, parades and riots, minstrel shows and civil rights marches. During the Civil War occupation of Memphis, a Union Army general named Ulysses S. Grant made his headquarters in a Beale Street mansion which still stands today, looking out on the street like a ghost of the past. In the early 1900s, a young black musician named William Christopher Handy wrote his songs in a room above a Beale Street saloon. In the early 1950s, a young white musician named Elvis Presley bought his first guitar in a Beale Street pawnshop.

Here, for many years, were the stylish homes of the old families of Memphis whose fortunes were made in antebellum boom times. Here, briefly, were schools for freed slaves, and hospitals for yellow fever victims. Here, from 1880 to 1914, housed in a spacious three-story mansion once owned by Robertson Topp, builder of the elegant Gayoso Hotel, was Miss Higbee's School for Young Ladies, attended by the young daughters of Memphis white society. And here at the same time, in the 1890s, housed in the basement of the First Baptist Church Beale Street, was the *Free Speech and Headlight* office from which a young black newspaperwoman named Ida B. Wells launched her lonely and heroic anti-lynching crusade which put her life in danger, forced her to leave Memphis, and made her famous as far away as London.

To Beale Street in its heyday—the 1880s through the 1920s—came a rich social and ethnic mix: Italians with their saloons, restaurants, and vaudeville theaters, and Jews with their clothing and department stores. In rooms above a Beale Street laundry, there was a Chinese Masonic lodge. The Metropolitan Opera Company of New York would perform twice a year at the Grand Opera House, on the corner of Beale and Main. And in the Church Auditorium, just a few blocks to the east, two thousand black Memphians would gather to listen to Booker T. Washington or W. E. B. Du Bois, to meet President Theodore Roosevelt, or to hear the music of W. C. Handy, the music that made Beale Street a legend.

Although W. C. Handy's minister father had viewed professional musicians as sinners, and made his talented son trade in his first guitar for a dictionary, the boy, nevertheless, learned to read music before he was eleven, bought a cornet when he was thirteen, and taught himself to play piano and violin. Seeking advanced musical instruction, he walked from his home town of Florence, Alabama to Birmingham, and

THE PICTURE: *A Beale Street-based bandleader named W. C. Handy gave the world a new kind of music when, in the early 1900s, he put on paper for the first time the sound of the blues—music with notes that bend, music that was described as "feelin' good about feelin' bad." He once wrote of Beale Street: "I had rather be there than any place I know." A few years ago, the Memphis home of W. C. Handy was moved to Beale Street, near the park named for him, and opened as a museum and as a home for the Memphis Blues Foundation. That house is the setting for this picture and in that house were written three of his most famous songs. Hanging on a wall in the house is a copy of the first page of the score of* Rhapsody in Blue, *inscribed to W. C. Handy by composer George Gershwin, who once told Handy, "Your music is the grandfather of mine." Displayed on the piano are Handy's own worn horn and some of the music he wrote. On a table nearby, a snack is set out, as though awaiting his return from a late night gig with his Memphis band. A stage-door bouquet of long-stemmed red roses adds the proper touch of elegance for one of the great musicians of the world.*

THE FOOD: *W. C. Handy's favorite dessert when on the road— DEEP-DISH APPLE PIE.*

soon become versed in everything from familiar band music to operas and symphonies. After working as a band and voice teacher in Alabama, as a member of a minstrel band traveling from Chicago to St. Louis, and as the director of the Negro Knights of Pythias Band in Clarksdale, Mississippi, W. C. Handy, in 1905, found his way to Beale Street. There, in a rented room above P. Wee's Saloon, he wrote notes that captured the blues on paper for the first time—rhythms, words, and music improvised by Southern blacks who hoed cotton, built levees, knew hunger, survived hard times, conquered stubborn mules, and mourned faithless loves. As Handy himself later pointed out, he did not invent the blues: "I got it from the Negro, put it on a silver platter, and handed it back to him just a little more beautiful."

He also handed that music to the world, and the world loved it—that music described as "feelin' good about feelin' bad." Handy tried out a few of the new tunes whenever his band played parades, funerals, conventions, or riverboat excursions. The "Handy sound" music began to be requested when the band played dance dates at the Memphis Country Club or the fashionable Alaskan Roof Gardens in the Falls Building. And during a mayoral election in 1909, Handy's Band played from the back of a wagon to attract lunchtime crowds for speeches on behalf of a young reform candidate named E. H. Crump. W. C. Handy even wrote a campaign song called *Mister Crump*. With its toe-tapping rhythm and mixed-message lyrics ("Mister Crump don't 'low no easy riders here ... I don't care what Mister Crump don't 'low, I'm gonna bar'l-house anyhow."), the song pleased both reformers and reprobates. E. H. Crump won the election handily, so to speak.

Published with a new title, *Memphis Blues,* and new lyrics, the song (containing the first jazz break) soon became a big sheet music hit nationwide, and Handy was on his way to fame and fortune. But before he moved to New York in 1918, he wrote such other classics as *Beale Street Blues,* and the immortal *St. Louis Blues*. And he left behind in Memphis a musical legacy that has made him one of the city's legendary greats, still remembered and honored by all, even though the Beale Street he knew has long since disappeared.

On today's Beale Street, the Victorian storefronts that survive have been renovated, their aging structures fortified. New restaurants and bars with new names and modern menus offer every kind of "Memphis Sound" music from rockabilly to jazz. But a few familiar names remain, and a few echoes of the old days linger. At A. Schwab's dry goods store, (established 1876), the motto is still "If you can't find it at Schwab's, you're better off without it." The Old Daisy Theatre, wearing a bright new coat of paint, presents regular showings of a multimedia show that recreates Beale Street's fabled past. And across the way, in a small park that is the site of outdoor concerts and festivals, there is a bronze statue of a man with a horn—W. C. Handy, the man for whom the park is named, the man who changed the world of music forever.

DEEP-DISH APPLE PIE

Deep-dish apple pie was W. C. Handy's favorite dessert when on the road, perhaps because his home in Yonkers had apple trees growing on the grounds. Shortly before his eighty-fourth birthday, in a letter written to his wife Louise's mother and dated October 18, 1957, Mr. Handy spoke of those apple trees. The following is an excerpt from that letter: ''My dear Mrs. Logan, I have been trying to write you for quite some time but find my work grows heavier and heavier with the days. I wanted to tell you about the beautiful wire fence…surrounding our property which your daughter supervised.…Everybody told me how the trees were loaded with apples…she got Mike to pick the apples off the trees and is sending some to everybody.…They are delicious. I am getting along fine and last night before going to bed I asked Louise for an apple pie; well, she gave me an apple cobbler and it was good, and I woke up this morning feeling fine.''

6 tart apples, peeled and sliced thin	¼ teaspoon nutmeg
	⅛ teaspoon salt
Juice of 1 lemon	Pie pastry, preferably
¾ to 1 cup sugar	made with butter
¼ teaspoon cinnamon	2 tablespoons butter, softened

Layer apple slices in deep 1-quart baking dish. Sprinkle each layer with lemon juice. Combine sugar, spices, and salt, and sprinkle portion over each layer. Cover with pastry, fold edges under ½ inch, and crimp with floured fork. Slash top several times and push butter into slashes. Bake 40 minutes at 375 degrees.

Serves 6

Mrs. W. C. Handy
Yonkers, New York

BROWN SUGAR PECAN CRUST

Fill with your favorite ice cream and topping.

1 cup all-purpose flour	½ to 1 cup finely chopped
½ cup margarine, softened	pecans
¼ cup brown sugar	

Combine all ingredients, mix well, and press into pie pan or 9 x 11-inch baking pan. Bake 15 minutes at 375 degrees. Cool.

Yields 1 crust

Sissy M. Long

SILK 'N' SATIN PIE

Very rich, very good, very chocolate.

1 12-ounce package semi-sweet chocolate chips	4 large eggs, separated
	1 teaspoon vanilla
¼ cup milk	1 baked 9-inch pie shell
¼ cup sugar	Heavy cream, whipped
Pinch of salt	

Combine chocolate, milk, sugar, and salt in top of double boiler over hot water, and cook until blended and smooth. Remove from heat and cool slightly. Add egg yolks one at a time, beating well after each addition. Blend in vanilla. Beat egg whites until stiff peaks form, and fold into mixture. Pour into pie shell and let stand 2 to 3 hours at room temperature. Serve topped with whipped cream (if chilled, let pie stand at room temperature at least 1 hour before serving).

Serves 8

Mrs. Oscar H. Green

QUEEN MOTHER CAKE

A regal dessert.

6 eggs, separated	1 cup finely ground almonds
⅔ cup sugar	6 ounces semi-sweet chocolate
¾ cup unsalted butter, softened	

Beat egg yolks and sugar until they ripple. Blend in butter and add almonds. Melt chocolate in double boiler and fold into egg mixture. Beat egg whites until stiff peaks form and fold into mixture. Pour into buttered and floured 10-inch cake pan and bake 45 minutes at 325 degrees. Cool 10 minutes in pan before turning out. Ice when completely cooled.

Icing

3 ounces semi-sweet chocolate	½ cup heavy cream

Melt chocolate in double boiler. Blend cream into hot chocolate with wire whisk. Set aside to cool.

Serves 8 to 10

La Tourelle Restaurant
Glenn Hays, Proprietor

HYPOCRITE PIE

Family history records that one young twig off the family tree once served himself a piece of this dessert. Thinking it was custard pie, he discovered apples on the bottom, whereupon he announced, "It's a hypocrite—it looks like what it's not."

2 to 3 medium apples, peeled and sliced	4 eggs
1 unbaked 9-inch pie shell	1 cup sugar
1½ cups milk	½ teaspoon nutmeg
¼ cup butter	1 teaspoon vanilla
	Dash salt

Lay apple slices in bottom of pie shell. Heat milk and butter until butter melts, and remove from heat. Beat eggs and sugar at medium speed until thick and lemon-colored. Add hot milk mixture, beating at low speed. Add nutmeg, vanilla, and salt. Pour over apple slices and bake at 350 degrees for 35 to 40 minutes or until set. Serve warm.

Serves 6 to 8

Mrs. M. V. Highsmith

CHOCOLATE SOUFFLÉ

A premier dessert for very special occasions or for very special people on any occasion.

3 tablespoons butter	⅛ teaspoon salt
3 tablespoons all-purpose flour	4 eggs, separated, plus
1 cup milk	1 extra egg white
½ to ⅔ cup sugar	
3 squares unsweetened chocolate	

Melt butter in heavy saucepan and mix in flour. Cook until well-blended and add milk, stirring until smooth. Add sugar, stirring until dissolved, and then add chocolate, stirring with whisk until grainy look disappears and sauce is thick and smooth. Add salt and set aside to cool. When cooled, add yolks and mix well. Beat egg whites until stiff peaks form and fold several large spoonfuls into cooled chocolate mixture, and then fold carefully into remaining egg whites. Gently scoop into soufflé dish and bake at 350 degrees until puffed, about 30 minutes. Serve hot with spoonful of OLD FASHIONED BOILED CUSTARD on top.

Serves 6 to 8

Frances Keenan Averitt

BEAUTIFUL GRAPE ICE CREAM

A very special dessert from a grandmother's receipt book. And even more tempting served in crystal dessert bowls and accompanied by a butter cookie.

1 12-ounce can frozen grape juice concentrate, thawed	1 20-ounce can crushed pineapple, drained
2½ cups sugar	1 teaspoon grated lemon rind
Juice of 4 lemons	1 quart heavy cream

Combine all ingredients and stir until well mixed. Pour into chilled 1-gallon canister of ice cream freezer and freeze until firm.

Serves 16 to 20

Joanne C. Moore
Frenchman's Bayou, Arkansas

TOFFEE TREASURE CAKE

A marvelous sour cream coffee cake with little bits of crunchy toffee bars providing delicious surprises.

1¼ cups sugar	1 teaspoon baking soda
1 teaspoon cinnamon	¼ teaspoon salt
½ cup butter, softened	¼ cup chopped nuts
1 8-ounce carton sour cream	5 ounces chocolate toffee candy
2 eggs	bars, coarsely crushed
1 teaspoon vanilla	¼ cup butter, melted
2 cups all-purpose flour	Confectioners' sugar, optional
1½ teaspoons baking powder	

Combine ¼ cup sugar and cinnamon, and set aside. In large mixing bowl, combine butter, sour cream, eggs, vanilla, flour, baking powder, baking soda, and salt, and blend at low speed until moistened. Beat 3 minutes at medium speed, scraping bowl occasionally. Pour half of batter into greased and floured Bundt pan or 9 x 13-inch baking pan. Sprinkle with 2 tablespoons cinnamon sugar. Pour in remaining batter and cover with remaining cinnamon sugar, nuts, and candy. Drizzle melted butter over top and bake at 325 degrees for 45 minutes or until cake springs back when lightly touched in center. Let stand in pan 15 minutes before turning out and sprinkle with confectioners' sugar.

Serves 14

Mrs. W. W. Cherry
Parkin, Arkansas

LEMON SNOW

Cool and refreshing, like a light snowfall.

2 cups water	4 tablespoons cornstarch
2 teaspoons grated lemon rind	4 tablespoons lemon juice
2/3 cup sugar	2 egg whites, stiffly beaten
1/4 cup water	(reserve yolks for sauce)

Bring 2 cups water and lemon rind to boil. Combine sugar, 1/4 cup water, and cornstarch, stir into boiling water, and cook until thickened. Remove from heat and add lemon juice and egg whites. Pour into 3-cup mold or individual dishes and chill until set. Serve topped with sauce.

Sauce

1 1/2 cups milk	1 teaspoon vanilla
3 tablespoons sugar	Pinch of salt
2 egg yolks, beaten	

Combine milk and sugar in heavy saucepan and heat until sugar dissolves. Mix small amount hot milk mixture with egg yolks and gradually stir into remaining hot milk mixture. Add vanilla and salt, and cook until mixture coats spoon. Chill.

Serves 4 to 6

Evelyn Burrell
St. Thomas, Ontario, Canada

CHILLED STRAWBERRY SOUFFLÉ

So berry good. You will love it.

1 1/2 cups sugar	1 cup heavy cream, stiffly
1 cup water	whipped
5 egg whites	1 cup puréed raspberries
1 cup puréed strawberries	

Dissolve sugar in water, bring to boil, and cook to soft ball stage. Beat egg whites until very stiff and carefully fold in sugar syrup. Freeze until partially set. Remove from freezer and very carefully stir in strawberries and whipped cream. Tie band of paper around upper rim of straight-sided soufflé mold to stand 1 inch above rim. Pour mixture into mold up to rim. Freeze 2 hours. (Soufflé should rise 1-inch over rim.)

Remove paper band and serve with raspberry purée.

Serves 8

Mrs. A. Arthur Halle, Jr.

MOTHER'S DELICIOUS RICE PUDDING

"Whatever's the matter with Mary Jane? We're having lovely rice pudding again."

1 tablespoon butter, softened	2 to 3 generous tablespoons
1/2 cup sugar	cooked rice
2 large eggs, separated	1 teaspoon vanilla
3/4 cup milk	1/4 cup raisins, optional

Cream butter and sugar. Beat in egg yolks. Add milk, rice, vanilla, and raisins, stirring well. Beat egg whites until stiff peaks form and fold into mixture. Pour into shallow glass baking dish and set in pan of water 1-inch deep. Lay sheet of aluminum foil over top to prevent too much browning. Remove toward end of baking time. Bake at 350 degrees for 50 to 60 minutes or until set. Serve warm.

Serves 4

Elizabeth Baker Parr

AIDA'S CHOCOLATE MOUSSE

Beautiful served in a lovely cut-glass bowl and garnished with whipped cream.

1 12-ounce package semi-sweet	2 cups heavy cream, whipped
chocolate chips	1 small angel food cake,
1/4 cup water	cut in 1-inch cubes
Pinch of salt	Chopped pecans
1/2 cup confectioners' sugar	Whipped cream for topping,
4 eggs, separated	optional

Combine chocolate chips, water, and salt in top of double boiler, and cook until chocolate melts. Add confectioners' sugar and blend. Beat egg yolks and add to chocolate mixture. Cool.

Fold whipped cream into cooled chocolate mixture. Beat egg whites until stiff peaks form, and fold into mixture. Fold in angel food cake pieces. Pour into 9 x 13-inch baking pan and refrigerate overnight.

Sprinkle with pecans and serve. Or offer pecans and whipped cream as choices for toppings.

Variation: Substitute 1/2 cup chocolate mini-chips for angel food cake pieces.

Serves 12

Madeleine Moore

CRÈME BRÛLÉE

One of those divine dishes that defy description—smooth, pale, creamy, wonderfully good. Try it with fresh strawberries or raspberries.

1 quart heavy cream	2 teaspoons vanilla
8 egg yolks	Brown sugar
½ cup granulated sugar	

Scald cream in heavy saucepan, but do not boil. Beat egg yolks, add sugar, and beat until creamy. Add scalded cream and vanilla. Pour through strainer into 1½-quart baking dish. Set dish in pan of hot water and bake at 350 degrees for 1 hour or until knife inserted in middle comes out clean. Cool.

Cover with brown sugar, about ½ inch deep. Place under broiler to caramelize sugar, watching carefully that it does not burn. Chill and serve.

Serves 8 to 10

Lola Malone

SORBET DE CHAMPAGNE

A lovely intermezzo, or a perfect light dessert.

1¼ cups sugar	⅔ cup plus 1 tablespoon pink
1¼ cups water	champagne
½ cup fresh lemon juice	2 egg whites

In heavy medium saucepan, dissolve 1 cup sugar in water, bring to boil, and remove from heat. Stir in lemon juice and ⅔ cup champagne. Strain through fine sieve into medium bowl, cover, and chill.

Dissolve remaining sugar in 2 tablespoons water in small saucepan over medium heat. Bring to boil, cook 1 minute, and remove from heat. Beat egg whites until foamy and add hot sugar syrup in thin, steady stream. Continue beating 3 to 5 minutes or until mixture is stiff. Quickly stir in champagne syrup (mixtures will remain separated) and pour into ice cream freezer canister. Add remaining tablespoon champagne and freeze according to manufacturer's instructions (mixture will freeze soft). Empty sorbet into container, cover, and freeze until firm, about 4 hours or overnight.

Serves 6 to 8

Carol M. Cherry

APRICOT TORTE

An elegant dessert that tends to linger in the mind—worthy of reverie.

3 cups sifted all-purpose flour	1 cup butter, softened
¾ cup sugar	1 egg
Pinch of salt	

Combine dry ingredients and cut in butter. Add egg and mix well. Divide dough into seven equal portions. Roll one portion at a time between wax paper, adding flour as needed to make dough more manageable. Turn 9-inch round cake or pie pan upside down, and grease and flour top. Lay rolled dough over top and trim around edges. Bake 10 to 12 minutes at 350 degrees. Repeat for remaining 6 portions, cooling each layer on rack. (Make ahead, stack with wax paper between layers, and store in airtight container.) Spread first layer with preserve filling (about 6 tablespoonfuls) and top with second layer. Spread second layer with sour cream filling. Continue layering in this manner, ending with preserves on top. Sprinkle top generously with sifted confectioners' sugar. Garnish with chopped pecans or chocolate-dipped glazed apricots, if desired. Chill at least 4 hours or overnight, and cut in thin wedges. Torte keeps for several days.

Preserve Filling
1 18-ounce jar apricot preserves

For smoother spreading, blend very briefly in food processor or warm in top of double boiler and press through sieve. (Cool preserves slightly before spreading.)

Sour Cream Filling

2 cups sour cream	1 cup chopped pecans
1½ cups confectioners' sugar	1 teaspoon vanilla

Combine all ingredients and mix well. Filling may seem thin, but is not intended as frosting. Filling soaks into layers.

Serves 12 to 14

Mrs. B. Mott Jones

BEVERAGES

BANANA PUNCH

Perfect for graduation parties and bridal showers. Easy to make ahead of time.

6 cups water
3 cups sugar
1 46-ounce can pineapple juice
1 12-ounce can frozen orange juice concentrate
1 6-ounce can frozen lime juice concentrate
6 ripe bananas
2 liters ginger ale
1 liter lemon-lime soda

Combine water and sugar, and boil 3 minutes to make simple syrup. Set aside to cool. Chill.

Combine juices. Purée bananas in processor and blend with juices until smooth. Combine simple syrup with banana mixture and pour into gallon-size containers. Cover and freeze overnight.

Thaw 2 hours before serving. Mix with ginger ale and lemon-lime soda in large punch bowl. (Champagne or white rum may be added if desired.)

Serves 40 to 50

Charlotte Neal

DEBUTANTE PUNCH

A pretty punch with a festive look, especially with an ice ring of whole strawberries, stems attached, afloat in punch bowl.

2 pints fresh strawberries
2 tablespoons sugar
2 tablespoons water
2 cups sugar
2 cups water
1 46-ounce can pineapple juice
9 to 11 ounces fresh lemon juice
1 bottle champagne (750 milliliter size) or 1 liter ginger ale, chilled

Hull and slice strawberries. Add 2 tablespoons sugar and 2 tablespoons water. Let stand at least 2 hours.

Stir 2 cups sugar into 2 cups water and boil 5 minutes to make simple syrup. Add pineapple juice and 9 ounces lemon juice. Squeeze sugared strawberries through cheesecloth to obtain 2 cups juice, adding water if necessary for full measure. Pour into juice mixture. Taste for flavor, add remaining lemon juice if necessary, and chill. Add champagne or ginger ale just before serving.

Serves 20 to 24

Peggy Carroll

APRICOT SOUR

An original version of an old favorite.

3 ounces apricot brandy
¾ ounce Triple Sec
2 teaspoons lemon juice
6 ounces orange juice
1 teaspoon sugar
1 cup ice cubes

Combine all ingredients except ice cubes in processor and blend briefly. Serve over ice.

Serves 2

Dr. J. Garland Cherry, Jr.

RUST'S REVENGE

Always a favorite at the annual Holiday Bazaar, now in its third decade, of the Memphis College of Art. Bazaar sales have soared, due partially to this holiday-spirited punch.

1 46-ounce can grapefruit juice
1 46-ounce can pineapple juice
1 46-ounce can apricot nectar
2 liters ginger ale
Gin, rum, or vodka, if desired

Combine all ingredients. Add ice before serving. Particularly nice served from an Academy hand-made pottery punch bowl.

Serves 20 to 25

Ellen Cooper Klyce
Ted Rust, Director Emeritus
Memphis College of Art

OLD-FASHIONED HOT SPICED TEA

Perfect for fall open house.

6 cups water
1 teaspoon whole cloves
1 inch-long cinnamon stick
2½ tablespoons black tea
¾ cup orange juice
2 tablespoons lemon juice
½ cup sugar

Combine water and spices and bring to boil. Add tea and steep 5 to 10 minutes. Strain to remove spices. Combine fruit juices and sugar, heat just to boiling point, stirring to dissolve sugar, and add to hot tea.

Serves 8

Martha Whitington

MULLED WINE

Perfect on a cold winter's night—particularly if there's snow on the ground!

1 cup sugar
4 cups water
Peel of ½ lemon
18 whole cloves

2 bottles Burgundy wine or claret (750 milliliter size)
12 cinnamon sticks

Dissolve sugar in water in large heavy pot. Add lemon peel and cloves, and boil 15 minutes. Add wine and heat gently, but do not boil. Remove cloves and serve in preheated mugs or cups. Add cinnamon stick for stirrer.

Serves 12

Kate Hawkins
Cedar Rapids, Iowa

VENETIAN APERITIF

Tastes good even without a gondola.

1 ounce Campari
1 ounce gin
1 ounce sweet vermouth
2 ounces orange juice

2 ounces apricot nectar
6 to 8 ice cubes, crushed
2 twists orange peel

Mix liquids with ice. Strain and serve in chilled champagne glasses with twist of orange peel for garnish.

Serves 2

Dr. Richard A. Atkinson

COOL BY THE POOL FRUIT DRINK

An icy, refreshing concoction with the cool taste of fruit.

1 10-ounce package frozen strawberries
1 20-ounce can pineapple chunks

1 12-ounce can frozen orange juice concentrate
Rum to taste

Combine strawberries, pineapple, and orange juice, and process in blender. Remove half of mixture and save for refills. To remainder, add rum and 20 ice cubes, and process again in blender.

Serves 8 to 10

Linda Meade Shea

PINK PARTY PUNCH

The almond flavor is what sets this punch apart.

3 quarts water
12 cups sugar
3 6-ounce packages strawberry gelatin
3 tablespoons almond extract

3 46-ounce cans pineapple juice
1 quart lemon juice, fresh or bottled
4 liters ginger ale, chilled

Bring water to boil. Add sugar and gelatin, and stir to dissolve. Add almond extract and juices. Stir well, pour into 5 half-gallon containers (milk cartons are perfect), and freeze.

Thaw until slushy, pour into punch bowl, and add ginger ale.

Serves 80 to 100

Madeleine Moore

WASSAIL WITH APPLE JACK

Just the thing for a holiday party or perhaps a neighborhood get-together. Serve with assorted cheeses and with a sweet or two.

3 whole oranges
20 whole cloves
1½ gallons apple cider
4 cups orange juice
1 cup lemon juice

4 cinnamon sticks
1 teaspoon cinnamon
6 whole allspice
Apple jack brandy

Stud oranges with cloves and bake 2 hours at 300 degrees.

Combine cider, orange juice, lemon juice, cinnamon, and allspice, and simmer 1 hour. Pour into punch bowl and float clove-studded oranges on top. Serve hot. Add apple jack to each serving as desired.

Serves 20 to 24

Glenda Parsons
Cape Girardeau, Missouri

A Box Party at the Orpheum

THE PICTURE: *When longtime local citizens reminisce about the pleasures of growing up in Memphis in the '30s and '40s (and they do), someone usually mentions birthday parties in the balcony boxes at the movie palace known as the Orpheum Theatre. These "box parties" were very special occasions for young Memphians. At the appointed matinee hour, the invited guests, dressed in their best finery, were delivered by parents to the Orpheum's balcony foyer. There, while the birthday honoree opened the gifts they had brought, they enjoyed a time of balloons and laughter, and consumed quantities of pink lemonade and iced cakes. Then—the cue they were waiting for—the great organ began to play. Showtime! Time to storm the auditorium and rush to their reserved box seats behind the polished brass rails overlooking the stage. Awaiting them there on each seat, as expected, was a small box of candy. Joy! The lights dimmed, the stage curtain parted revealing the big silver screen, and the children, quiet at last, settled back in their seats: Let the movie begin! Today, the sixty-year-old Orpheum Theatre, restored to its original gilded splendor by the devoted efforts of the volunteer "Friends of the Orpheum," is bringing the excitement of music, theatre, dance, and film to a new generation of Memphis audiences. But the excitement re-created here is that of an unforgettable old-time Orpheum "box party."*

THE FOOD: *Treats for young movie-goers of the past included OLD-FASHIONED PINK LEMONADE, iced cakes, and candy from Dinstuhl's, a local family firm which has provided four generations of Memphians with delectable sweets. (It was the tradition of the founder of this firm to place a small box of chocolates on each seat in the Orpheum's early opera days.) On the silver beverage tray, beside gaily wrapped birthday gifts, a small, beribboned nosegay of sweetheart roses and Baby's-breath awaits the honoree.*

Memphians love to be entertained. From earliest days, they have turned out in happy throngs to applaud everything from traveling medicine shows, to Mississippi River showboats, to circuses and carnivals, to modern-day rock concerts. They have also built and patronized an impressive series of local pleasure domes where shows of every kind have been presented regularly and profitably. One of the first was the Greenlaw Opera House at the corner of Union and Second, completed in 1866 at a cost of some two hundred thousand "very old-fashioned dollars," in the words of one latter-day historian. It seated sixteen hundred people, and beholders were awed by its "classical porticos," "spectacular stage," and "cavernous auditorium." Opera and Shakespeare were both presented there, the Mozart Musical Society performed there, but the Greenlaw, like other opera houses of the time, most often featured vaudeville and minstrel shows. After it burned to the ground in 1883, the new Lyceum Theatre at Third and Union, with seating for thirteen hundred, and nightly performances by a resident stock company, became Memphis' leading theatre. But it was soon surpassed by the new Grand Opera House on the corner of Main at Beale.

Built in 1890, the Grand Opera House was said to be the finest theater west of New York. Some of the greatest performers of the era appeared on its stage—singer Lillian Russell, actress Sarah Bernhardt, pianist Paderewski, and twice a year, New York's Metropolitan Opera Company. Among its amenities were a restaurant and billiard rooms; on its upper floors were the elegant private club rooms of the prestigious and prize-winning military drill team, the Chickasaw Guards, where several generations of Memphis debutantes were entertained at parties and balls. Fire destroyed the Grand Opera House, too, in 1923. But another grand theatre opened on the same site in 1928.

The million-dollar Orpheum, a vaudeville and movie theatre on the RKO-Orpheum circuit, was financed and built by local businessmen. It was the embodiment of the plush "movie palace" of the period—damask walls, velvet draperies, gilded arches, two magnificent crystal chandeliers, a nine-piece orchestra, and a staff organist playing the "mighty Wurlitzer." Vaudeville was doomed to gradual extinction by the growing popularity of the new "talking pictures," but before it finally expired, many show business legends appeared on the Orpheum stage—Duke Ellington, George Burns and Gracie Allen, tap dancer Bill Robinson, magicians Blackstone and Houdini, Louis Armstrong, Mae West, Count Basie, Milton Berle, the Mills Brothers, fan-dancer Sally Rand. Then, for several decades, the Orpheum prospered as one of the South's finest movie houses, showing choice first-run films every night of the week, including Sundays—even though Memphis was one of the last bastions of the old blue laws which outlawed Sunday entertainment and sports events. The Orpheum got around the restrictions by setting up tables on the tiled floors of the foyer and serving "Sunday suppers." Until the blue laws were repealed in the mid-1930s, as many as five thousand customers would show up to pay fifty cents for sandwiches and soft drinks, and receive free tickets to the movie inside. Each Sunday night the Orpheum's manager was arrested, and each Monday morning he went to court and paid a twenty-five dollar fine.

By the 1970s, movie attendance downtown had fallen off drastically. The Orpheum's original opulence had begun to tarnish. But the familiar landmark was rescued from destruction when it was bought by the Memphis Development Foundation in 1978, and restored to its former glory with five million dollars raised in 1982 by "Friends of the Orpheum," a group of local volunteers which included, among others,

Memphis actress Cybill Shepherd. Today, the rejuvenated Orpheum, resplendent once more in her best velvets, damask, and gilt, is presenting symphony pop concerts, Memphis Opera Theatre productions, and summer film series of classic Hollywood movies (complete with Wurlitzer organ music at intermission time). And a new generation of Memphis theatre-lovers is giving ovations (standing, often as not—an affable Memphis tradition) to the traveling productions of Broadway dramas and musicals that are bringing live theatre back to the Orpheum.

OLD-FASHIONED PINK LEMONADE

Tart, refreshing, and recommended for all ages.

1 pint strawberries	2 cups water
1 cup sugar	⅓ cup fresh lemon juice

Hull and slice strawberries, sprinkle with a little sugar and very small amount water, and set aside. Combine 1 cup sugar and 2 cups water in small saucepan, and boil 5 minutes to make simple syrup. Stir in lemon juice and cool.

Dilute cooled lemon syrup with water to taste. Squeeze berries through cheesecloth to extract juice. Add juice to plain lemonade and pour into tall ice-filled glasses.

Yields 3 cups syrup

Basic lemonade recipe from
the Josephine Cook Book, 1936
Courtesy of Mrs. John D. Walt

PAPPY'S HOT TODDY

"When grownups in the Faulkner family were sick, Pappy had an instant cure—his ever-popular Hot Toddy. It was guaranteed to cure or ease anything from the aches and pains of a bad spill from a horse to a bad cold, from a broken leg to a broken heart. Pappy alone decided when a Hot Toddy was needed, and he administered it to his patient with the best bedside manner of a country doctor....Pappy always made a small ceremony out of serving his Hot Toddy, bringing it up-stairs on a silver tray and admonishing his patient to drink it quickly before it cooled off. It never failed." (William Faulkner)

Heaven Hill bourbon whiskey	1 tablespoon sugar
(the Jack Daniels was re-	½ lemon
served for Pappy's ailments)	Boiling water

Fill heavy glass tumbler approximately half-full with bour-bon. Add sugar. Squeeze juice from lemon into glass and add the lemon half. Stir until sugar dissolves and fill glass with boiling water. Serve with potholder to protect patient's hand from hot glass.

Serves 1

The Great American Writer's Cookbook
Courtesy of Dean Faulkner Wells
Yoknapatawpha Press
Oxford, Mississippi

MISS ALICE'S SOUTHERN EGGNOG

Stout and memorable. A Southern holiday ritual.

6 eggs, separated	½ cup rum
1 cup sugar	1 quart heavy cream, whipped
1 quart milk	Grated nutmeg
1 pint bourbon whiskey	

Beat egg whites and ½ cup sugar until soft peaks form, and set aside. Combine egg yolks and remaining ½ cup sugar, and beat well. Add milk and blend. Stir in bourbon and rum. Gently fold in beaten egg whites and whipped cream. Refrig-erate overnight and serve with sprinkle of nutmeg on top.

Serves 12

Mrs. William H. Houston III
Washington, D.C.

AUTUMN GLOW PUNCH

Good hot or cold. So refreshing with its hint of spice.

8 cups cold water	2 46-ounce cans unsweetened
8 cups sugar	pineapple juice
4 cinnamon sticks, broken	2 46-ounce cans unsweetened
4 teaspoons whole cloves	orange juice
8 family-size teabags	4 cups lemon juice
6 cups boiling water	

Combine cold water, sugar, and spices in saucepan, and boil 5 minutes to make syrup. Steep teabags in boiling water. Blend juices in large pot, add tea and spiced syrup, and heat but do not boil. Strain to remove spices.

Make a day ahead of time to allow flavors to blend. Keeps in refrigerator indefinitely.

Serves 96 to 100

Elly Beasley
Heth, Arkansas

Afternoon Tea at the Peabody

The Peabody. For true Memphians the very name of this famous old hotel conjures up memories, pride, even a certain reverence. In truth, there have been two Peabody Hotels in Memphis. The original, on Main at Monroe, was an oasis of sedate elegance in a hustling, young river town. Built in 1869 by a Memphis entrepreneur, Colonel Robert C. Brinkley, it was the city's first steel framework building. Brinkley named it for his friend George Peabody, the financier and philanthropist who gave millions to promote education in the South, and whose investments had earlier helped bring a railroad to Memphis. Peabody never visited the hotel named for him, but a great many other dignitaries did, including presidents (Andrew Jackson and William McKinley) and generals (Robert E. Lee and Nathan Bedford Forrest). Its prestige was such that, when it was torn down in 1923, its successor, a luxurious five-million-dollar hotel which opened in 1925 on Union Avenue between Second and Third, was (and still is) called simply the Peabody. As a regional historian later wrote, "The Peabody is the Paris Ritz, the Cairo Shepheard's, the London Savoy of this section."

The lobby has white Alabama marble floors, beamed ceilings, wrought iron chandeliers, and a fountain, carved from one block of Italian travertine marble, rising from an octagonal pool where the Peabody ducks, the hotel's famous trademark, spend their days paddling and preening. This tradition began as a joke, years ago, when live mallard decoys from an Arkansas hunting expedition were deployed in the Peabody's fountain. The joke has become serious business. Each morning at eleven, before crowds of enchanted onlookers, a red carpet is rolled out. The web-footed celebrities are delivered by elevator from their "palace" on the Peabody's roof and, to the strains of the *King Cotton March*, parade single file across the lobby to the fountain. The ceremony is repeated in reverse at five each evening.

Several generations of Memphians have tales to tell about the Peabody—memories of debutante teas, fund-raising galas, Rotary and Kiwanis meetings, bridal luncheons, ginners' conventions, and Maid of Cotton fashion shows that took place there. As children, their downtown shopping expeditions with favorite aunts always included lunch in the Venetian Dining Room. They attended their senior proms in the Continental Ballroom and danced with their dates in the Skyway to the big bands of Les Brown, Paul Whiteman, Chuck Foster, Jack Teagarden, Clyde McCoy, and Tommy Dorsey. It was a special thrill knowing the dance music was being broadcast live on national network radio "... from the beautiful Skyway, high atop Hotel Peabody, the South's finest, one of America's best hotels, overlooking Ol' Man River in downtown Memphis, Tennessee." In summertime, before air conditioning, the dancing moved to the breeze-swept, moonlit Plantation Roof.

Hard times visited downtown Memphis in the early 1970s. In 1975, the Peabody closed its doors, and for several years it stood empty. It was a painful experience for Memphians to drive by its degenerating facade. A part of their heritage was gone. Then, with courage, optimism, imagination, and the aid of federal and local grants, Belz Enterprises, a family-owned Memphis company, undertook a twenty-five-million-dollar renovation of this historic landmark. Downtown revitalization was truly happening. Giant billboard announcements of the grand re-opening in 1981 resounded like a battle cry: "The Peabody. Now, again and forever!"

THE PICTURE: *The Peabody, Memphis' famous old grand hotel, is its stylish, elegant self again, after several years in shabby limbo during the late 1970s. A twenty-five-million-dollar renovation restored its former grandeur, and in 1981 a glorious re-opening took place. Today the Peabody is not only the symbol of a legendary bygone Memphis, but also a hallmark of a vital, emerging Memphis. Young business people gather for lunch at its chic restaurants, out-of-town visitors are treated to cocktails in its handsome lobby, wedding receptions take place in its ballrooms, music and dancing have returned to the Skyway and the Plantation Roof. And a new Memphis ritual has been established—afternoon tea in the Peabody lobby, served promptly at three each day from a red-lacquered, flower-bedecked tea cart, to the accompaniment of soft music from the grand piano. The tea table is set for two, the vase holds a single long-stemmed rose. In the background, the latest generation of the famous Peabody ducks are swimming in the pool of the fountain, which is crowned with its customary large and colorful floral arrangement. (It should be noted that restaurants at the Peabody never serve duck.)*

THE FOOD: *The tempting fare provided by the Peabody chefs includes little tea sandwiches of chicken salad, watercress, and smoked salmon, scones with whipped cream, and a delectable selection of pastries, served with a choice of several blends of tea.*

SUMMER ICED TEA

Nothing better on a summer's day when the humidity seems touchable. Add a sprig of mint pinched fresh from the garden and serve from a pretty, pottery pitcher.

1 quart boiling water	1 6-ounce can frozen lemon
7 individual-size tea bags	juice concentrate
1 6-ounce can frozen orange	2 cups sugar
juice concentrate	

Add tea bags to boiling water and steep 15 minutes. Pour into 1-gallon pitcher or jar. Add juices and sugar. Stir to dissolve sugar. Add water to fill container to top, stir again, and store in refrigerator.

Serves 8 to 12

Mrs. W. Thomas Cunningham, Jr.
Richmond, Virginia

CLYDE'S ICED TEA

When West Tennessean Isaac Tigrett established the first Hard Rock Cafe in London, he included some typical Southern foods on the menu. Among them is this refreshing drink, recalled from boyhood memories of Tennessee picnics, and originally created by Mr. Clyde, venerable major-domo of a Nashville family.

7 gallons cold water	18 small tea bags
8 cups sugar	2 quarts orange juice
25 whole cloves	3 cups lemon juice

Combine 4 gallons water with sugar and cloves, and bring to boil, stirring to dissolve sugar. Add tea bags and simmer over very low heat for 30 minutes.

Remove from heat, discard tea bags, and add juices and remaining 3 gallons cold water. Stir well to blend flavors. Strain to remove cloves. Serve in tall, ice-filled glasses.

Serves 125

Hard Rock Cafe
London, England

CHAMPAGNE WITH FRAMBOISE

From a visit to the Champagne region of France, where this delightful drink was served at a charming chateau-housed restaurant.

1 to 2 tablespoons fresh	Extra-dry champagne
raspberry juice	

Pour raspberry juice into chilled champagne glass. Add champagne and serve immediately.

Note: Juice from frozen raspberries will substitute nicely for fresh. Or, as a variation, add raspberry liqueur instead of juice.

Serves 1

Dr. Richard A. Atkinson

SANGRIA BLANCA

Great to serve from an ice cold pitcher on a hot summer day—or any time with Mexican food.

½ cup sugar	1 lemon, sliced thin
½ cup freshly squeezed	Ice cubes
lemon juice	1 liter club soda
1 bottle dry white wine	Orange slices, strawberries,
(750 milliliter size)	fresh pineapple spears, and
½ cup freshly squeezed	seedless grapes
orange juice	Mint for garnish
¼ cup orange-flavored liqueur	

In large pitcher, dissolve sugar in lemon juice. Add wine, orange juice, liqueur, lemon slices, and ice cubes, and stir well. Add club soda just before serving to preserve fizz. Offer with fresh fruit as accompaniment, and garnish with mint, if desired.

Serves 6

Carol M. Cherry

FINISHING TOUCHES

SAUCES

An Infinite Variety of Sauces

by Dr. Richard J. Reynolds

Sauces are the heart and soul of fine cuisine. It has been said that the English have a dozen religions and only one sauce, while sauces serve the French in place of a state religion. A ridiculous exaggeration, of course. Nevertheless, any true artist of saucemaking undertakes the task with an almost religious devotion.

In the world's finest restaurants, great attention is paid to the quality, flavor, and texture of the sauces that accompany various dishes. The *chef saucier* or sauce chef ranks second only to the *chef de cuisine*, who himself, it may be assumed, was at one point in his career a *chef saucier*. After all, what head chef could possibly direct a great kitchen without having first mastered the art of saucemaking? To protect the reputation of his establishment, especially if it is one honored by the *Guide Michelin's* rating, he must critically analyze and constantly appraise the quality of all the various sauces prepared and served under his regime.

Our word ''sauce'' is the same as the French word *sauce* which derived from the Latin *salsus*, meaning salted. But by common usage it can denote any appetizing amalgamation of ingredients, liquid or semi-liquid, created to accompany and complement a solid food. This clearly allows for endless variations. The French repertory of sauces comprises more than two hundred recipes (with numerous permutations). It not only encompasses brown and white sauces, milk- and stock-based sauces, butter and egg yolk sauces, hot and cold sauces that are designed to enhance enjoyment of all manner of meats, poultry, and cooked vegetables, but also includes various salad dressings and dessert sauces as well.

Although the list of sauces is quite formidable and the possible blendings of ingredients seem almost limitless, sauce preparation usually involves only a few steps. Fortunately, since the same basic saucemaking methods are employed over and over again, certain fundamental suggestions for preparation of sauces can be set forth.

The ingredients used in a sauce must obviously be of high quality. Inferior materials will produce an inferior sauce. Also, proper utensils are essential. The saucepan must be made of a heavy metal that maintains and distributes the heat evenly, since sauces scorch readily in spite of constant stirring, especially if prepared in a light saucepan. (If a lightweight pan must be used, an asbestos pad placed between the heat source and the bottom of the pan can alleviate the problem.) The saucepan should have a rounded bottom rather than a sharp angle where the sides and bottom meet, for the whisk used for stirring must reach and keep in motion all of the sauce to help avoid scorching. White sauces should always be made in an enameled, stainless steel or tin-lined copper saucepan. Aluminum tends to discolor sauces containing wine or egg yolks.

Most sauces begin with a roux (or thickening mixture) of butter and flour. In general, for each cup of sauce, melt one to two tablespoons of butter in the saucepan and heat until hot, but not sizzling. Add an equal amount of flour and, for a white sauce, stir the mixture constantly while cooking it over low heat until it barely begins to color. Roux for a brown sauce is cooked and stirred longer, until it takes on a rich brown color.

It is very important to cook the roux slowly. Starch cells in the flour burst under the influence of heat, and then combine or bind with the melted butterfat to form a mass that will be able to absorb six times its own weight of liquid. But if too much heat is used, the starch will burn. This shrinks the cells and thus diminishes or destroys the binding process which is essential to all saucemaking. It also imparts a bitter flavor to the sauce.

Next, the liquid is added, and again, until the sauce thickens slightly, it must be constantly stirred. Many experienced sauce chefs follow the general rule that a cold liquid, milk or stock, should be added to a hot roux. Conversely, if a hot liquid is to be added, the roux should be cool. It can be cooled quickly, if necessary, by immersing the pan in cold water.

The thickness of the sauce is in direct proportion to the amount of flour or starch used per cup of liquid. As a general rule, one tablespoon of flour is used for each cup of liquid to make a thin sauce. A medium or general purpose sauce requires one and one-half tablespoons, and a thick sauce requires two tablespoons of flour for each cup of liquid. For a soufflé base, use three tablespoons of flour for one cup of liquid.

Sauces that start with what may seem to be an inordinate amount of liquid and are thickened by slow and patient reduction are superior to those prepared with either more flour or less liquid. To reduce a sauce, the heat should be lowered and the sauce simmered while the liquid evaporates, until the volume is reduced by as much as one-half or more. Fat and insoluble particles rise to the surface during the reduction and should be skimmed off from time to time. Meanwhile, the sauce should be stirred only occasionally to prevent scorching. If the sauce is stirred too much during this phase of cooking, it will lighten in color. Generally, more liquid is used in brown sauces to lengthen the reduction process and permit better blending and concentration of the flavor.

In sauces made without a roux, egg yolks and butter are often the thickening agents. Well-prepared sauces, whether thickened with flour or egg yolk, have a body and consistency, known as *du corps*, that can be noticed as the mixture is stirred. When a sauce coats the back of a spoon, it is described as being *à la nappe* which means having the viscosity to cling to food.

A little fresh butter swirled into any sauce will improve the flavor and thicken the sauce a little. But be cautious, for too much stirring at this stage can prevent thickening. The butter should be swirled by moving the pan in a circular motion, and the pan removed from the heat before the butter is completely melted.

Finally, our sauce is ready. Long, slow cooking has fully blended its ingredients, and perfected its consistency. It is light without being liquid. It has a smooth texture and a fine flavor. It is glossy in appearance, decided in taste. Like all good sauces, it will complement and enhance the flavor of the food that it accompanies, neither overpowering it, nor being overpowered by it. It will, in short, add subtle pleasure to the enjoyment of the occasion. Let the feasting begin. But first, the blessing: "We thank Thee, Father, for the love/Which feeds us here below,/And hope in fairer realms above,/Celestial feasts to know " (C. H. Spurgeon). And last, the toast: *Bon Cuisine! Bon Appétit!*

SAUCES MÈRES AND VARIATIONS

The basic sauces are referred to as *sauces mères* (mother sauces) and are so called because they are used in the preparation of many other sauces. Here are some of the classic *sauces mères* and their variations:

Béchamel Sauce: Milk-based white sauce made with a *blanc* (white) roux.

Velouté Sauce: Stock-based sauce made with a *blond* (honey-colored) roux.

Brown Sauce: Stock-based sauce made with a *brun* (brown) roux.

Sauces au Beurre: Sauces such as Hollandaise that are made from egg yolks and butter without a roux.

Tomato Sauces: Tomato-based sauces, late arrivals on the scene because of a lingering early misconception that the tomato was poisonous.

To illustrate how one *sauce mère* can evolve into a sequence of other sauces, let us start with the simple Béchamel Sauce made of butter, flour, and milk:

Cream Sauce: Add cream to the basic Béchamel Sauce.

Mornay Sauce: Add egg yolks and cheese (preferably a hard non-oily one such as Parmesan or Swiss) to a Béchamel Sauce.

Or start with a stock-based Velouté Sauce as the *sauce mère*, and develop variations on that theme:

Bercy Sauce: Add shallots, lemon juice, white wine, and butter to a Velouté Sauce.

Sauce Suprême: Add cream and mushroom liquor to a Velouté Sauce.

Allemande Sauce: Add egg yolks and more cream to Sauce Suprême and it becomes Allemande Sauce, the richest of all white sauces.

With Brown Sauce as the *sauce mère*, a whole series of other sauces can be created:

Madeira Sauce: Add Madeira wine to Brown Sauce.

Périgueux Sauce: Add truffles to Madeira Sauce.

Périgourdine Sauce: Add more truffles, diced, to Périgueux Sauce.

Robert Sauce: Add white wine and Dijon mustard to Brown Sauce.

Thus, we see how *sauces mères* can lend themselves to limitless embellishments, according to the chef's knowledge and ingenuity. And we can understand why the infinite variety of sauces to be enjoyed continues to grow.

RJR

The sauce recipes on the following pages, unless otherwise noted, are from the collection of Dr. Richard J. Reynolds.

SAUCE MÈRE—BÉCHAMEL SAUCE

Milk-based white sauce with white roux.

2 tablespoons butter	¼ teaspoon salt
1 onion, finely chopped	3 peppercorns
4 tablespoons all-purpose flour	1 parsley sprig
3 cups scalded milk	Pinch of grated nutmeg

Melt butter in heavy saucepan over low heat. Add onion and sauté until soft and lightly colored. Gradually stir in flour and cook slowly, stirring constantly, until roux becomes golden in color. Gradually add milk, stirring vigorously with wire whisk until mixture is smooth and thick. Season with salt, peppercorns, parsley, and nutmeg. Cook over low heat for 30 minutes or until reduced by one-third, stirring often. Strain through fine sieve.

Yields 2 cups sauce

VARIATION—CREAM SAUCE

For poultry, fish, eggs, or vegetables.

2 cups BÉCHAMEL SAUCE	Salt and white pepper to taste
½ cup heavy cream	

Reduce Béchamel Sauce to 1½ cups. Gradually add cream and correct seasoning. If serving with fish, add a few drops lemon juice.

Yields 2 cups sauce

VARIATION—MORNAY SAUCE

For veal, poultry, fish, eggs, or pastas.

2 cups CREAM SAUCE	¼ cup grated Parmesan cheese
(made without onions)	Salt and pepper to taste
4 egg yolks, lightly beaten	Nutmeg to taste
¼ cup grated Swiss cheese	

Heat Cream Sauce until hot but not boiling. Remove from heat and add egg yolks and cheeses, stirring until blended. Correct seasoning.

Yields 2¾ cups sauce

SAUCE MÈRE—VELOUTÉ SAUCE

Stock-based sauce with golden roux.

2 tablespoons butter	½ cup sliced mushrooms,
4 tablespoons all-purpose flour	with stems
3 cups boiling white stock	Parsley sprigs
(chicken, veal, or fish)	Salt to taste
3 white peppercorns	

Melt butter in heavy saucepan. Add flour to make a roux, stirring constantly until light gold in color. Add stock, stirring vigorously with wire whisk. Add peppercorns, mushrooms, parsley, and salt, and simmer about 1 hour over low heat, stirring frequently and skimming occasionally, until reduced by one-third and consistency is as heavy cream. Strain through fine sieve and adjust seasoning.

Yields 2 cups sauce

VARIATION—SAUCE BERCY

For fish.

1 tablespoon chopped shallots	1 teaspoon lemon juice
¾ cup white wine	2 tablespoons butter
1½ cups VELOUTÉ SAUCE	

Cook shallots in white wine until liquid is reduced to 2 tablespoons. Add Velouté Sauce made from fish stock and cook 5 minutes over low heat. Remove from heat, add lemon juice, and swirl in butter.

Yields 2 cups sauce

VARIATION—SAUCE SUPRÊME

For meat, vegetables, eggs, or poultry.

2 cups chicken stock	1 cup heavy cream
3 mushrooms, sliced	Salt and pepper to taste
1 cup VELOUTÉ SAUCE	

Cook chicken stock and mushrooms until liquid is reduced by two-thirds. Add Velouté Sauce, bring to boil, and simmer until reduced to 1 cup. Gradually stir in cream and correct seasoning. Strain through fine sieve before serving.

Yields 2 cups sauce

VARIATION—SAUCE ALLEMANDE

Richest of all sauces—for meat, vegetables, eggs, or poultry.

2 egg yolks, lightly beaten	2 cups SAUCE SUPRÊME,
2 tablespoons heavy cream	heated

Mix egg yolks with small portion each of cream and Sauce Suprême. Add mixture to remaining Sauce Suprême and heat, stirring constantly, until very hot but not boiling. Remove from heat and add remaining cream.

Yields 2 cups sauce

VARIATION—SAUCE NORMANDE

For fish or oysters.

1 8-ounce package mushrooms	¾ cup fish stock
3 tablespoons butter	2 egg yolks, slightly beaten
1 tablespoon all-purpose flour	½ cup heavy cream

Sauté mushrooms in 1 tablespoon butter, and set aside, reserving cup mushroom liquor. Melt 2 tablespoons butter in saucepan and add flour, stirring and cooking until slightly colored. Add fish stock and mushroom liquor. Cook and stir over low heat for 10 minutes. Remove from heat. Mix egg yolks with cream, stir into sauce, reheat, and strain.

Yields 1⅓ cups sauce

VARIATION—ANDALOUSE SAUCE

For fish, poultry, and eggs.

1 cup VELOUTÉ SAUCE	Minced garlic to taste
2 to 4 tablespoons tomato paste	Minced parsley to taste
2 tablespoons chopped pimiento	

Combine all ingredients in heavy saucepan and cook over low heat just until well-blended.

Yields 1¼ cups sauce

SAUCE MÈRE—BROWN SAUCE (ESPAGÑOL SAUCE)

Stock-based sauce with brown roux.

⅓ cup diced onion	6 cups beef stock or bouillon
⅓ cup diced carrots	2 tablespoons tomato paste
⅓ cup diced celery	Bouquet garni (parsley, thyme,
3 tablespoons diced boiled ham	and bay leaf tied in
6 tablespoons clarified butter	cheesecloth)
4 tablespoons all-purpose flour	Salt and pepper to taste

Cook vegetables and ham in butter for 10 minutes over low heat. Blend in flour, cooking and stirring constantly over low heat for 10 to 20 minutes or until roux turns nut brown in color. Remove from heat.

Bring beef stock to boil and add to roux all at once, blending with wire whisk. Stir in tomato paste. Add bouquet garni and simmer partially covered for 2 hours or longer, skimming as necessary, until sauce is thick enough to coat spoon. Add more stock if sauce thickens too much. Remove bouquet garni, correct seasoning, and strain, pressing juice from vegetables. Chill and skim to remove grease.

Yields 3½ to 4 cups sauce

VARIATION—SAUCE DIABLE

For broiled chicken or roast pork.

2 tablespoons minced shallots	Black pepper
or green onions	2 to 3 tablespoons minced
1 tablespoon butter	parsley
1 cup dry white wine or	1 to 3 tablespoons butter,
⅔ cup vermouth	softened
2 cups BROWN SAUCE	

Cook shallots in 1 tablespoon butter for 2 minutes over low heat until soft but not brown. Add wine and boil rapidly until only 3 to 4 tablespoons remain. Add Brown Sauce and simmer 2 minutes. Season with enough pepper to give a spicy taste. Remove from heat. Just before serving, add parsley and swirl remaining butter into sauce a little at a time to preferred consistency and taste.

Yields 2¼ cups sauce

VARIATION—MADEIRA SAUCE

For fillet of beef, veal, chicken, liver, ham, or egg dishes.

½ cup Madeira or port
2 cups BROWN SAUCE

2 to 3 tablespoons butter,
softened

Boil wine until reduced to about 3 tablespoons. Add Brown Sauce and simmer 2 minutes. Taste for flavor and add more wine if needed, a tablespoon at a time. Simmer briefly to evaporate the alcohol and remove from heat. Just before serving, swirl in butter.

Yields 2 cups sauce

VARIATION—SAUCE PÉRIGUEUX

For fish, eggs, or chicken.

1 1-ounce can truffles, sliced
and juice reserved

2 to 3 tablespoons butter

Prepare MADEIRA SAUCE, adding truffle juice at beginning of reducing wine. Stir in truffles and simmer 1 minute. Remove from heat and swirl in butter.

Yields 2⅓ cups sauce

VARIATION—SAUCE ROBERT

For beef, pork, or chicken.

¼ cup minced yellow onion
1 tablespoon butter
1 cup dry white wine or
    ⅔ cup vermouth
2 cups BROWN SAUCE
3 to 4 tablespoons Dijon
    mustard

2 to 3 tablespoons butter,
softened
Pinch of sugar
2 to 3 tablespoons minced
parsley

Cook onion in 1 tablespoon butter in heavy saucepan over low heat for 10 minutes or until tender and lightly colored. Add wine and reduce to 3 to 4 tablespoons over medium-high heat. Add Brown Sauce and simmer 10 minutes. Adjust seasoning and remove from heat. Just before serving, beat in mustard, butter, and sugar, and stir in parsley.

Yields 2½ cups sauce

MARCHAND DE VIN SAUCE

For eggs, steak, or hamburgers.

8 shallots, chopped
1½ cups dry red wine
2 teaspoons meat glaze
½ cup unsalted butter, softened
1 teaspoon all-purpose flour

2 tablespoons chopped parsley
1 teaspoon lemon juice
Salt
Freshly ground pepper

Combine shallots and wine in large skillet and cook over high heat until liquid is reduced to ¾ cup. Add meat glaze and simmer to blend flavors. Strain through fine sieve, pressing shallots firmly to extract all juices. Beat butter until creamy and then beat in flour and parsley. Add lemon juice a drop or two at a time. Just before serving, bring liquid to simmer, whisk in butter mixture, and continue simmering until slightly thickened, stirring continuously. Correct seasoning.

Note: Meat glaze can be made by boiling consommé until reduced by three-fourths.

Yields 1 cup sauce

TOMATO COULIS

Tomato-based sauce with garlic and herbs. For boiled chicken or beef, hamburger, pastas, pizza, and eggs.

⅓ cup minced onion
2 tablespoons olive oil
2 tablespoons all-purpose flour
3 pounds ripe tomatoes, peeled,
    seeded, and chopped
½ teaspoon sugar
2 cloves garlic, crushed

Bouquet garni
⅛ teaspoon fennel
Pinch of coriander
Small piece dried orange peel
½ teaspoon salt
Tomato juice

Sauté onion in olive oil for 10 minutes until soft but not browned. Add flour and cook 3 minutes without browning over very low heat. Add remaining ingredients, cover pan, and cook 15 to 20 minutes over low heat to render juice from tomatoes. Remove cover and simmer 30 to 40 minutes over medium-low heat, stirring occasionally, until thick enough to hold shape in spoon. Add tomato juice if needed to prevent scorching or over-thickening. Remove bouquet garni and orange peel. Adjust seasoning and serve.

Yields 3 cups sauce

SAUCE MÈRE—SAUCES AU BEURRE HOLLANDAISE SAUCE

Egg yolk and butter sauce with no roux.

4 egg yolks
2 tablespoons water
1 cup butter, softened

Juice of ½ lemon
Salt and white pepper to taste

Combine egg yolks and water in top of small double boiler or heavy saucepan and beat until frothy and thick. Cook over low heat, gradually adding butter, and whisk constantly until thick. Season to taste with lemon juice, salt, and pepper.

Note: Hollandaise sauce is not served hot. If it is kept too warm, it will separate or curdle. If necessary to keep it warm for any length of time, it should be placed over warm water. A teaspoon of cornstarch beaten into the egg yolks at the beginning will extend the holding time.

If the sauce is too thick, beat in 1 to 2 tablespoons of hot water, stock, or cream. If the sauce does not thicken, the butter was probably added too quickly. In this case, rinse a mixing bowl with hot water and put in a teaspoon of lemon juice and a tablespoon of the sauce. Beat with whisk until the mixture thickens. Beat in remaining sauce a tablespoon at a time until each addition has thickened.

If the sauce curdles or separates, a tablespoon of cold water beaten into it will usually reconstitute it. If it does not, rinse a mixing bowl with hot water, add a teaspoon of lemon juice, a tablespoon of the sauce, and beat in the rest of the sauce in small increments.

Yields 1½ cups sauce

VARIATION—SAUCE MALTAISE

For asparagus or other vegetables.

1 tablespoon grated orange rind
2 to 3 tablespoons orange juice

1½ cups HOLLANDAISE SAUCE

Combine rind and juice. Beat spoonful at a time into Hollandaise Sauce.

Yields 1½ cups sauce

BÉARNAISE SAUCE

For steaks, fish, chicken, or egg dishes.

¼ cup white wine vinegar
¼ cup white wine
2 shallots, chopped
2 peppercorns, crushed
2 tablespoons minced tarragon
  or 1 tablespoon dried

1 tablespoon minced chervil
  or ½ tablespoon dried
4 egg yolks
1 cup butter
Salt

Combine vinegar, wine, shallots, peppercorns, tarragon, and chervil in heavy saucepan, and cook over medium-high heat until liquid is reduced to 2 tablespoons. Remove from heat and allow to cool slightly. Add egg yolks and whisk well. Return to low heat and add butter a little at a time, stirring constantly until thick. Strain through fine sieve and correct seasoning.

Note: For Sauce Choron, add 2 to 4 tablespoons tomato paste. For Sauce Colbert, add 1 tablespoon meat glaze melted in 1 tablespoon white wine to 1 cup Béarnaise.

Yields 1½ cups sauce

BEURRE BLANC

For boiled, baked, or broiled fish, shellfish, and vegetables.

½ cup vinegar
½ cup white wine
4 shallots, chopped
Juice of ½ lemon

Salt and white pepper to taste
2 tablespoons heavy cream
1 cup butter

Combine vinegar, wine, and shallots in heavy saucepan and cook until reduced to consistency of thick purée. Remove from heat and add lemon juice, salt, and pepper. Stir in cream. Beat in butter in small pieces until well-blended and sauce is creamy in appearance. If not served immediately, keep warm over lukewarm water.

Note: Butter will become oily if sauce is reheated or kept over water that is too hot. If this occurs, put one spoonful in cold mixing bowl and beat. Gradually beat in remaining sauce in small spoonfuls.

Yields 1 cup sauce

BLENDER HOLLANDAISE SAUCE

Good on eggs, seafood, and vegetables.

3 egg yolks	Dash cayenne pepper
2 tablespoons lemon juice	½ cup butter or margarine,
¼ teaspoon salt	melted

In blender, combine egg yolks, lemon juice, salt, and pepper. Cover and process briefly, turning blender on and off. Remove center of lid, set blender on high speed, and gradually add hot, melted butter in steady stream. Serve immediately or keep warm by setting container in 2 inches of hot, not boiling, water. Can also be stored in refrigerator and reheated in same fashion.

Yields 1 cup sauce

Trudie Weil

ITALIAN SPAGHETTI SAUCE

Italian sausage is the primary seasoning for this sauce. The taste is superb and deliciously complements lasagna, cannelloni, spaghetti, or any other favorite pasta. Meatballs can always be added. The sauce freezes beautifully.

2 pounds Italian link	1¼ teaspoons sugar
sausage	2 tablespoons instant minced
½ cup water	onion
1 6-pound, 6-ounce can	1 to 2 tablespoons garlic powder
whole tomatoes in juice	2 tablespoons Italian herbs
⅓ cup dry red wine	1 tablespoon chopped parsley
1½ tablespoons freshly grated	1 bay leaf
Parmesan cheese	Salt and pepper to taste

Pierce sausage links with fork. Place in baking pan with ½ cup water and broil, turning once, until browned. Reserve pan drippings.

Mash tomatoes and add remaining ingredients. Mix with sausage links and pan drippings. Simmer 4 to 6 hours or until mixture reaches desired consistency. Remove bay leaf before serving.

Yields 1 gallon sauce

Vincent de Frank, Conductor Emeritus
Memphis Symphony Orchestra

LEMON-PARSLEY SAUCE

Particularly good brushed on salmon steaks, grilled trout, or chicken.

½ cup butter, melted	1 clove garlic, minced
¼ cup lemon juice	½ teaspoon Nature's Season
1½ teaspoons chopped parsley	¼ to ½ teaspoon Tabasco sauce
½ teaspoon Greek seasoning	Garlic powder to taste

Combine all ingredients and mix well.

Yields ¾ cup sauce

June Merrell
Forrest City, Arkansas

PESTO SAUCE

Wonderful over pasta!

3 packed cups fresh basil	⅓ cup pine nuts or almonds,
leaves	optional
1½ cups freshly grated	3 cloves garlic
Parmesan cheese	1½ cups olive oil

Chop basil leaves in food processor. Add cheese, nuts, and garlic, and blend in processor, adding oil slowly, until paste is formed. Store in refrigerator.

Yields 2 cups sauce

Danette Watkins
Lepanto, Arkansas

MUSTARD SAUCE SUPREME

Great with all kinds of ham dishes and GLAZED HAM LOAF.

1 cup water	¼ cup butter
½ cup cider vinegar	1 egg
½ cup prepared mustard	1 tablespoon all-purpose flour
½ cup sugar	

Combine all ingredients and cook over low heat until thick, stirring frequently.

Yields 1½ cups sauce

Minnie Morris McGregor
McCrory, Arkansas

PICANTE SAUCE

Serve as topping for Mexican dishes, or *CHICKEN BURRITOS*, or as dip with chips.

1 28-ounce can whole tomatoes with juice	½ cup white vinegar
1 medium onion	1 teaspoon salt
1 green bell pepper	1 teaspoon sugar
2 jalapeño peppers	Cayenne pepper to taste
1 to 2 cloves garlic	Oregano to taste
	Ground cumin to taste

Combine tomatoes, onion, all peppers, and garlic in food processor and chop. Place in 2-quart stainless steel or enamel pan and add vinegar, salt, and sugar. Simmer for 30 to 40 minutes. Stir in remaining seasonings.

Yields 4 cups sauce

Tommie Kidd

RED PEPPER BUTTER FOR FISH

Particularly good on swordfish, tuna, redfish, and bluefish.

2 red bell peppers	Dash Tabasco sauce
1 cup butter, softened	¼ teaspoon salt
2 teaspoons lemon juice	½ teaspoon white pepper
½ teaspoon paprika	

Roast pepper over gas flame or under broiler until skin chars and blisters. Place pepper in paper bag, seal, and set aside. When cool, remove skin and seeds. Place in food processor and process until smooth, adding butter 2 tablespoons at a time. Add remaining ingredients and blend briefly. Top each serving of fish with 2 tablespoons red pepper butter.

Yields 1¼ cups butter

Memphis Petroleum Club
National Bank of Commerce

BREAD SAUCE

Serve with duck or any other fowl, or with roast, and offer *SHARP CRAB APPLE JELLY SAUCE* as a complementary taste.

2 cups light cream	Dash Tabasco sauce, optional
1 medium onion studded with 4 to 6 whole cloves	¼ to ⅓ cup finely crushed white bread crumbs
1 bay leaf	3 tablespoons butter, softened
Salt and white pepper to taste	

Combine cream, onion, and seasonings, and bring to boil in medium heavy saucepan. Reduce heat, add bread crumbs, and simmer 3 minutes. Remove onion and bay leaf. Whisk in butter until mixture is shiny and smooth. Keep hot over simmering water in double boiler or reheat, adding extra butter, if needed.

Yields 2 to 2½ cups sauce

Mrs. Norfleet R. Turner

SHARP CRAB APPLE JELLY SAUCE

Especially good with duck.

3 to 4 tablespoons butter	1 tablespoon freshly ground horseradish
1 cup crab apple or tart currant jelly	

Melt butter in small, heavy saucepan over medium heat. Add jelly and simmer over low heat, stirring gently until well blended. Stir in horseradish.

Yields 1¼ cups sauce

Mrs. Norfleet R. Turner

PLUM SAUCE

Great with *FRIED CHICKEN STRIPS* or chicken drummies.

1½ cups red plum jam	1½ tablespoons prepared horseradish
1½ tablespoons prepared mustard	1½ teaspoons lemon juice

Combine all ingredients in small heavy saucepan and stir over low heat until blended and warm.

Yields 1¾ cups sauce

Margaret M. Price

MY GRANDMOTHER'S MINT SAUCE

From Cheshire in England, a lovely sauce traditionally served with lamb. But serendipity led to trying it with strawberries. Delicious!

2 tablespoons chopped fresh
   mint
3 tablespoons sugar

1 tablespoon white vinegar
1 tablespoon lemon juice
3 tablespoons whipped cream

Combine mint, sugar, vinegar, and lemon juice, and stir until blended. Gradually add cream.

Yields ⅓ cup sauce

Daphne Boyle

BUTTERSCOTCH SAUCE

For ice cream or cold desserts.

1 cup brown sugar
⅓ cup butter, melted

⅓ cup heavy cream

In heavy saucepan, blend all ingredients and boil 5 minutes over medium-high heat without stirring. Remove from heat and beat 30 seconds or until foamy. Serve warm.

Yields 1⅓ cups sauce

CUSTARD SAUCE
FOR BERRY COBBLER

Good with any baked fruit dish.

1 egg
¾ cup sugar
1⅛ tablespoons all-purpose
   flour
Pinch of salt

1 cup milk
¼ cup butter
1 teaspoon vanilla

Beat together egg, sugar, flour, and salt. Add milk gradually and cook in top of double boiler until mixture thickens and coats spoon. Remove from heat and add butter and vanilla. Serve cold over hot berry cobbler.

Serves 6 to 8

Shirley Sigler Chamberlin
Millington, Tennessee

GRAND MARNIER SAUCE

For cakes, desserts, or soufflés.

1 cup milk
1-inch piece vanilla bean
4 egg yolks
½ cup sugar

¾ cup heavy cream
⅓ teaspoon salt
3 tablespoons Grand Marnier

Scald milk with vanilla bean added. Beat egg yolks until light and gradually add sugar, beating constantly. Stir in cream. Gradually add milk mixture and salt, beating briskly with whisk. Cook in double boiler over hot water, stirring constantly, until mixture coats spoon. Remove from heat, remove vanilla bean, and beat in Grand Marnier.

Yields 2 cups sauce

LU'S CHOCOLATE SAUCE

Delicious over ice cream.

⅓ cup cocoa
1 cup sugar
2 tablespoons all-purpose flour
Pinch of salt

1 cup boiling water
2 tablespoons butter
1 teaspoon vanilla

Sift together dry ingredients. Slowly pour boiling water over dry mixture, stirring well. Cook until thick, stirring constantly. Stir in butter and vanilla.

Yields 1¼ cups sauce

Melissa Robinson

FRUIT SAUCES

Lovely sauces may be made from jams and preserves. Apricot, strawberry, and raspberry are particularly good. Simply dilute jam with a small amount of water or light syrup, and heat slightly. Strain through fine sieve. Add liqueur of choice, if preferred.

WINES

The Pleasures of Wine

by Walter P. Armstrong, Jr.

"Wine," according to novelist Alexandre Dumas, "is the intellectual part of a meal." Certainly this is correct, for just as some knowledge of musical structure can add greatly to the appreciation of a great symphony, so some knowledge of oenology can enhance greatly the pleasure of drinking a quality wine. The enjoyment of fine wine is, like the enjoyment of great music, a cultural experience, not merely a means of sustenance or a source of stimulation. There are far less expensive and more effective means of assuaging thirst or achieving inebriation.

The appreciation of a trained palate for a truly great wine is unique; but it is an ability which anyone can easily acquire. It knows neither age nor sex; in fact, a good case can be made that in this respect women are better qualified than men, and so when hereafter I use the pronoun "he" it is merely for convenience and without reference to gender. As Cyril Ray, a British authority on wines, writes: "Whence comes the notion that women are less capable than men of appreciating and understanding wine? . . . Women can choose or match a scent or a soap or a toilet-water more promptly and more surely than a man, just as they can taste a sauce in the course of preparing a dinner, or can say, more decisively than any man not professionally engaged, that this cushion clashes with those curtains, or that such a scarf would never do with such a frock. A sense of smell; a sense of taste; and an eye for colour—most women have all these, and all they lack, to be amateurs of wine, is experience, and this they will never get if they always leave the ordering of wine to their husbands."

There are three distinct phases in the enjoyment of wine. First, there is its selection and acquisition. This activity is like any other hobby, such as the collection of stamps or rare books. The true oenophile will scrutinize the shelves of the local wine shops for unusual and untried vintages; haunt those of the cities which he visits in search of those unattainable locally; and seize avidly those opportunities which present themselves through special imports or the marketing of the personal collections of others to expand his own holdings. He will be an avid reader of catalogues, auction records, and books upon the subject, and, above all, he will exchange information and, where the occasion presents itself, examples of his successful search, with his fellow enthusiasts. He will, if possible, visit the vineyards from which the great wines come so that he may from personal experience recognize their source. And he will exercise restraint and patience in laying down those wines which require maturity, to be drunk when their qualities are fully developed.

But, fascinating as the collection of wines can be, full enjoyment can never be achieved so long as the cork remains in the bottle; its drinking, of course, is the ultimate experience which wine can provide. Some wines are made to be sipped delicately; some should be held in the mouth while their virtues blossom to their fullest; and some very few should be taken in sizeable swallows robustly but with veneration. Whatever the wine and however it may be drunk, it should be shared; for wine was not made for solitary drinking. And to enhance its qualities so that it may be appreciated to the fullest, it should be accompanied by appropriate food, lovingly prepared and served with consideration and aplomb.

Finally, there is the recollection in tranquility of the happy occasions upon which certain wines have been drunk with good companions. As the years go by, each acquires a patina of memory which serves to enhance its enjoyment immeasurably, even though the nostalgia may be somewhat saddened by the impossibility of repetition. As the cup touches the lips visions of faces, some long gone, rise up in the mind, and join the present company for a brief moment of pleasant reincarnation. And like the coral, each tasting builds upon all of the others until there exists an edifice of memory inaccessible to others but awaiting only the next encounter with the same wine to unlock its portals.

Often I am asked the question, what is your favorite wine? There is no answer, except that it is the wine I find most appropriate to the occasion. You may prefer an entirely different one. If so, by all means follow your own taste, not mine or anyone else's. If you find a wine that you like, lay down a few bottles for future sharing with your friends. If they do not join you in your enthusiasm for it, it is not necessarily the qualities of the wine which should be reconsidered.

Another question that I am often asked is, what should I pay for a bottle of wine? Again, there is no universal answer. It depends upon the individual. Obviously, the biggest bargain is the least expensive wine which returns the maximum benefit to the purchaser. This is going to vary widely depending upon the circumstances, including taste and economic resources. The best wine is not always the most expensive, although it is seldom the cheapest; and he who orders invariably from the top of the price list is showing his ostentation while revealing his ignorance. On the other hand, many a fine dinner is spoiled by serving an inferior wine. As a rule of thumb, I suggest the bottle of wine which you serve your guests should cost approximately the same as the cost of the meal per person, whether in a restaurant or at home. Of course, if you want a bottle of 1865 Lafite, know where and how to get it, and can afford it, then by all means buy it, but treat it as a possession to be treasured for the proper occasion, not as a status symbol. Great wine drunk too freely can be as cloying as any other surfeit.

The storage of wine is another subject which has developed a body of tradition more colorful than practical. Wine in the bottle is a living, organic substance and should be treated as such; but it need not be coddled and cared for like an invalid, and actually it is amazing how much mistreatment it can take and still survive. The only purpose of storing it upon its side is so that the cork will remain damp (and with fortified wines such as port and sherry even this is unnecessary) and thus not allow too much air to enter the bottle; if this is accomplished, the exact angle of placement is immaterial. Optimum storage conditions require that proper ventilation and a reasonable amount of air circulation should be provided, and of course, extremes of heat and cold should be avoided. Storage temperature should be as close to fifty-five degrees Fahrenheit as possible, though a reasonable variation is permissible; it is sudden changes in temperature which are harmful. Unless the wine is very old or stored for a prolonged period of time, the periodic turning of the bottles seems to me to be an affectation rather than a necessity, as does recorking. Caps should never be sealed with sealing wax, or with paraffin only if the wine is intended for a later generation. Within these limits, storage, including the quantity to be stored, depends largely upon available facilities. But in determining your location do not forget accessibility; the wine is there to be drunk, and it would be wrong to allow the difficulty of retrieving it to detract from the pleasure of that ultimate objective.

The prolonged storage of wine always involves some risk, no matter how careful you may be. White wines age more quickly than do reds, and should therefore be drunk younger. Some red wines age more rapidly than others, as do wines of certain vintage years, depending upon their constitution. Normally wine matures more quickly in half bottles, less so in magnums or jeroboams. But an imperfect cork or previous mistreatment can change these rules drastically.

After the wine has rested adequately in the cellar and hopefully reached its peak of maturity (which is really a plateau at which it may remain for some time) then proper thought should be given to its manner of drinking. Here the food, the occasion and the company are the primary considerations. "Every glass of fine wine given to the wrong person is robbery of the right person," said Earle Welby, author of *The Cellar Key*. So let yourself not be guilty of such theft. If necessary, emulate Voltaire, who said that he drank Corton but gave Beaujolais to his friends. But with the worthy, share the best of wines.

The wine should be brought from its resting place a substantial period in advance of serving and the bottle placed upright. White wine should, of course, be cooled and red wine served at room temperature. Both of these terms are, however, subject to broad interpretation. Cooled does not mean ice cold, nor does room temperature refer to the reading on the weather bureau thermometer in mid-August. A fair estimate would be in the one case ten degrees below storage temperature, in the other ten degrees above. But, here again, tastes may vary.

White wines should be uncorked shortly if not immediately prior to serving. I suggest the avoidance of all patented cork removers (with the sole exception of Screwpull, which is quite expensive) and reliance upon the standard French lever type corkscrew, which gives you adequate pressure upon the cork while at the same time letting you both see what you are doing and react promptly to any feeling of insecurity in the cork which might indicate impending breakage. Red wines should be allowed a breathing period before serving to permit their latent qualities to develop fully. This may be accomplished either by removing the cork and allowing the wine to stand in the bottle or by decanting. I recommend the latter only in the case of very old wine, where it may be necessary in order to separate the clear wine from the dregs.

Finally, proper wine glasses can contribute much to the enjoyment of wine. In the case of red wines, these should be reasonably large (but not immense) stemmed glasses, filled about one-third, so as to allow maximum surface exposure to the atmosphere while retaining the fragrance of the wine largely within the confines of the glass. Smaller glasses of a more open shape will serve for white wines where these factors are less important. One bottle of average size is considered to provide eight servings; but I find that with generous refills five is closer to the mark. Obviously, some persons will not drink as much as others, and it is better to provide a relatively small amount at the first pouring and let those who wish have more later.

Michael Broadbent, one of England's Masters of Wine and expert advisor to Christie's in the field, has written an excellent little book, *Wine Tasting*, in which he divides the process of evaluating a wine into three phases, in each of which certain characteristics are sought and analyzed. First, there is the appearance, in which the decisive elements are color, clarity and tone. Here a proper glass of clear crystal to be held by the stem is essential, as well as adequate illumination. Then there is the nose or bouquet, to the full appreciation of which a proper glass can again contribute much. Here the things to look for are cleanliness, grape variety, maturity, fruitiness and fullness or depth. Finally there is the actual taste, which may vary slightly as the wine is taken on the tip of the tongue, the roof of the mouth, and the back of the throat. The qualities here revealed are dryness or sweetness, body, flavor, acidity, tannin content, finish and aftertaste. Once you have satisfied yourself that a wine meets all of these tests (and remember some wines improve in the glass), relax and enjoy it. It may not be the best you have ever had, but it probably will not be the worst; and think of the multitude of comparisons, invidious and otherwise, with other wines which you have previously drunk that these fifteen points invite.

I have been fortunate in encountering very few bad bottles of wine, perhaps no more than a dozen in my entire career. The memory of those few encounters, however, remains vivid. Often I have been asked how one tells when a bottle of wine is bad. In a case where it has outlasted its life span, the question is superfluous, for the answer is obvious. Mr. Broadbent described the resulting odor as reminiscent of old socks; however, it reminds me more of rotting wet leaves. In either event, the result is unmistakable and disastrous, and the only thing to do is to abandon the wine, no matter how expensive (if you are in a restaurant, by all means send it back) and go on to something better. Young wines which have been spoiled by mistreatment develop a bitter taste which is equally characteristic.

But let us assume that the wine tasted has proven successful and deserving of being remembered. The next problem is the selection of adequate terms in which to describe its qualities. There, as in all fields of expertise, certain words of art are in common usage. Michael Broadbent lists and defines more than fifty such terms commonly used to describe the bouquet of wine and as many more which apply to its taste. These are all good English words easily understood by anyone; and while he also appends shorter lists of French and German terms, their use seems to me to be seldom if ever necessary, and smacks more of pretension than precision. Few of us are blessed with the aptness of poet and essayist Hilaire Belloc who when called upon to speak to the Chambertin at a formal dinner, responded: "And when I depart from this earth to appear before my beloved Lord to account for my sins, which have been scarlet, I shall say to Him: 'I cannot remember the name of the village; I do not even recollect the name of the girl, but the wine, my God, was Chambertin!' "

Almost every country in the world produces some type of wine, but many are of mediocre quality. Outstanding are the classified growths of French wines, which constitute only five percent of the total production of that country; but many others produce a limited quantity of high quality wines. Chile produces excellent white wine, and Australia good red, if properly aged. More Italian wine is imported into the United States than from any other country, and some of it is outstanding. Other countries produce special wines, such as Hungarian Tokay and Portugal's glorious ports. Spain has many good wines, including some quite acceptable sparkling wines. Greece also produces wine, but I should warn you that retsina is an acquired taste. If you are seriously interested in wine I suggest that you acquire a copy of Alexis Lichine's *New Encyclopedia of Wines and Spirits*, which is the bible of oenophilia; or, more compact and therefore less expensive, Hugh Johnson's *Pocket Encyclopedia of Wine*.

Frequently I am asked my opinion of California wines. Frankly, I think that the average California wine is just as good as the average French wine, particularly the whites; and other states also produce some excellent wines. But the best California wine does not in my judgment begin to compare with the best French wine, although it is beginning to be comparable in price.

The drinking, enjoyment and appreciation of wine has for millennia been one of the great pleasures of men of taste and culture. Although the Moslems consider it a sin, it is a recognized article of faith among certain of their sects that when their spiritual leader, the Aga Khan, raises a glass, the liquid changes from wine to water as it passes his lips, thus leaving him spotless but satisfied. And the Persian Prince Kai Kans Ibn Iskandar faced with a similar dilemma wrote to his son that although wine drinking "is a transgression, if you wish to commit a transgression it should at least not be a flavorless one. If you drink wine, let it be the finest; if you listen to music, let it be the sweetest; and if you commit a forbidden act let it be with a beautiful partner, so that even though you may be convicted of a sin in the next world, you will at any rate not be branded a fool in this."

Fortunately, our Judeo-Christian religion has always recognized the drinking of wine as a part of its traditional ritual. There are many references to wine-drinking in the Bible. My favorite is in the Book of Ecclesiastes (Ch. 9, v. 7), the words of the Preacher of Ecclesiastes, who was not generally noted for his optimism:

"Go thy way, eat thy bread with joy, and drink thy wine with a merry heart."

SELECTING THE RIGHT WINE FOR THE FOOD

Good food is a necessary accompaniment to good wine. Without each other, neither is complete. Certain wines traditionally go well with certain foods, but do not be bound by shibboleths; suit your own taste. The following are merely suggestions and guidelines to be used as a matter of convenience:

Hors d'Oeuvres: Any aperitif wine. Champagne is always good, and can be served throughout the meal. My own favorite is Kir (named for Canon Felix Kir, leader of the French resistance in Lyon) which is made by adding a teaspoon of Cassis to any light white dry wine. I do not recommend providing cocktails or highballs before a meal at which wine is to be served, although some authorities insist that a very cold, very dry martini is permissible.

Soup: Usually no wine is served, although a dry sherry is traditional with turtle soup.

Fish: A dry white wine. Chablis is considered particularly appropriate to shellfish.

Chicken: This presents a problem. Some prefer light red wine or a Beaujolais; others a dry white. And, when the dish is cold, a rosé is appropriate.

Lamb: A red Bordeaux or equivalent such as an American Cabernet.

Veal and Pork: A light red wine, although some prefer a dry white or even a rosé. (There is no wine that will stand up to ham.)

Beef and Fowl: A full-bodied red wine or a Beaujolais, or a Rhone wine. A Spanish Rioja is also acceptable.

Pasta: Obviously, Italian red wine, although a dry white goes well if there is a fish sauce. Among the American wines, Zinfandel is a popular counterpart.

Salad: No wine should be served with the salad; and the use of vinegar should be avoided, with lemon juice substituted. I also find that tomatoes detract from the enjoyment of wine.

Sweetbreads, Sausages, Etc.: A light red wine, although sweetbreads with a cream sauce go well with a dry white wine.

Cheese: Any full-bodied red wine, or Port.

Desserts: Champagne, sauternes, sweet German wines (Auslese) or American sweet Semillon.

Coffee: Brandy or Port.

Remember, these are not immutable rules like the laws of the Medes and the Persians. Follow them if you will, ignore them if you wish.

WPA, Jr.

STARTING A WINE CELLAR

A wine cellar may vary in size from a few bottles to hundreds of cases; in quality from a few personal favorites to the great cellars of the three-star restaurants of France. It is largely a matter of personal taste, space availability and willingness to make a substantial long term non-revenue producing investment. Therefore, I lay down no rules, but merely make a few suggestions for a beginning cellar which may prove of help to the novice:

Aperitif: Two bottles of good (but not necessarily the best) French champagne, or a Spanish or American counterpart. Other sparkling wines, such as Italian Asti Spumante or sparkling Vouvray, can be substituted. Two bottles of light white wine, such as a German Rhine or Moselle or a French wine of the Loire Valley, an Alsatian wine such as a Gewurztraminer or Riesling, or a corresponding American wine. South African white wine may be substituted. One bottle of dry sherry, Spanish, American, South African or Australian. One bottle of proprietary aperitif wine such as Byrr, Lillet, Dubonnet, or Campari. Here there is wide room for experimentation, and personal taste must govern.

White Bordeaux: Two bottles of dry white wine such as Graves or Entre Deux Mers, or American Sauvignon Blanc or Semillon. An Italian Soave or Chilean white wine may be substituted. One bottle of sweet white wine, such as a Sauterne or a Barsac, or a corresponding American sweet Semillon or Chenin Blanc; or a Hungarian Tokay.

White Burgundy: Four bottles, two of finer quality. Meursault is very popular, as is Pouilly-Fuisse, but the latter has become quite expensive. Saint Veran, which is not far removed, is much more reasonable in cost. And of course, Chablis is always acceptable. Among the great white Burgundies are Corton Charlemagne, Puligny-Montrachet and Chassagne-Montrachet. Similar American wines are Pinot Blanc and Pinot Chardonnay.

Red Bordeaux (Claret): Four bottles, two regional growths, such as Margaux, Pauillac, Saint-Julien, Graves, Saint-Emilion or Pomerol; and two chateau bottlings, not necessarily the best, but at least among the classified Grands Crus, of which there are many.

Red Burgundy: Four bottles, including two Beaujolais or Macon, and two classified growths such as Aloxe-Corton, Beaune, Gevery-Chambertin, Nuits-Saint-Georges, or Pommard. Or an American Pinot Noir, or an Australian counterpart.

Rhone: One bottle of Chateauneuf-du-Pape, Cotie Rotie, or Hermitage.

Italian: One bottle of Chianti Classico (look for the black cockerel on the neck of the bottle); and one bottle of Barolo.

Port, Sherry: One bottle of each, very dry, preferably imported, but some American imitations are quite good.

Brandy: One bottle of cognac, of good quality. Real cognac, of course, comes only from Cognac in France; but the Americans, Italians, Spanish and others make fair substitutes. And there is also Armagnac and, if you are experimental, Calvados.

This makes a total of twenty-five bottles, a reasonable number with which to start. I have not discussed vintages as any good chart can be your guide in that respect, and many are easily available. As experience is gained, quantities can be increased, and varieties broadened. The difficulty may be to stay within reasonable limits and not become too enthusiastic.

WPA, Jr.

LOCAL AND REGIONAL WINERIES

For those who may have an interest in local and regional wineries, we offer a sampling of those in and closest to Memphis. They represent a revitalization of area grape growing and wine making, and their wines rather consistently bring home gold medals in national and international wine testing events.

Laurel Hill Vineyard
Memphis, Tennessee

Wines are European-style, from Old World grapes grown in Laurel Hill's own estate vineyards in Lawrence County, Tennessee. Wines include Chardonnay, Riesling, Vidal, and Central Gardens Red, a blend of red grapes named for the winery's proximity to Memphis' historic Central Gardens District.

Monteagle Wine Cellars
Monteagle, Tennessee

Located, as their label reads, "high atop the Cumberland Plateau on majestic Monteagle Mountain," this winery offers thirteen different labels, including Assembly Blush, Sewanee White, and Cumberland Red, as well as Sauvignon Blanc and White Riesling. Grapes are from growers in the Tennessee towns of Savannah, Portland, and Gallatin, as well as from local vineyards in Sewanee and Jasper, Tennessee.

Winery Rushing
Merigold, Mississippi

Specializes exclusively in muscadine wines from grapes grown in nearby vineyards on the banks of the Sunflower River. (Muscadines are Southern natives, and they do not take kindly to growing much further north than Memphis.)

Claiborne Vineyards
Indianola, Mississippi

Wines from French-American hybrid grapes as well as vinifera (classic Old World-style grapes). The grapes are grown in Indianola in vineyards located close to the junction of Highways 49 and 82. One of the most popular labels is Bayou Rouge, a blend of several varieties, similar to wines of the Côte du Rhône region of France.

Wiederkehr Wine Cellars, Inc.
Wiederkehr Village on St. Mary's Mountain
Near Altus, Arkansas

Family-owned since 1880, this winery offers about thirty different varieties of wines pressed from French-American hybrids and European vinifera. Wines include Pink Catawba, Sangria, Alpine Chablis, Edelweiss, and Johannisberg Riesling. A very popular label is Cynthiana, made from a local grape called Cynthiana, discovered growing wild in Arkansas many years ago. Grapes are from the nearby family-owned Swiss Family Vineyards, as well as from contract growers in Arkansas and elsewhere.

Post Winery
Altus, Arkansas

Owned and operated by a fifth generation family of winemakers, this winery dating from 1880 offers thirty varieties of wines, including a sherry and champagnes, as well as such varietals as Chardonnay, Cynthiana, Niagara, and Vidal Blanc. It also sells non-alcoholic grape juices, pure from the crushed grape with no sugar added. Grapes are grown atop St Mary's Mountain in the Post Familie Vineyard, located in the Altus viticultural area. (The area around Altus, Arkansas, was officially recognized in 1984 as a viticultural, or grape growing, region known as Altus.)

HERBS AND SPICES

The Enhancements of Herbs and Spices

by Joseph Carey, C.E.C.

The French gastronome Brillat-Savarin once said: "You are what you eat." I can think of lots worse things to be than an herb. And duller things to be than a spice. Whether or not we accept Brillat-Savarin's premise, however, we should note that many people throughout history have found that the use of herbs and spices enhanced the quality of their foods—and, sometimes, their lives.

Though the distinction between herbs and spices is somewhat hazy, they differ in two basic ways. First, herbs are usually grown in the more temperate climes, while spices grow in the tropics. Second, because herbs generally come from the leaves of plants, they are mostly green in color. Spices, on the other hand, may come from the bark, flowers, roots, seeds, or fruits of plants, so they may be red, brown, black, or yellow, and are much more varied in appearance. But herbs and spices are alike in one respect—they share a long and important role in human history.

Probably the best working definition of an herb (we pronounce it "erb," the English "herb") is provided by the Herb Society of America: "A plant or plant part valued for its medicinal, savory, or aromatic qualities." The oldest known uses of herbs are medicinal. The Chinese Emperor Shen-Nung, who lived around 3700 B. C., compiled the first known herbal pharmacopoeia. Egyptian histories list over eight hundred medicinal herbs. Just about every classic Roman villa included an herb garden. Galen, physician to Marcus Aurelius, wrote a book with one hundred and thirty herbal remedies. And after the fall of the Roman Empire, the Christian monasteries and Arabic physicians carried on the tradition of the *bouquet garni* for several hundred years.

Early English colonists, particularly in the southern United States, considered herbs as important vegetables. They grew hyssop, lavender, chamomile, lemon balm, comfrey, borage, chervil, mint, basil, and parsley. Thomas Jefferson grew twenty-six kinds of herbs in his kitchen garden at Monticello. His personal favorite was nasturtium, and he used every part of the plant.

Today, fresh herbs are enjoying an ever-increasing popularity. When I was executive chef at a well-known restaurant in San Ramon, California, we had a ten-acre organic garden which included about thirty-five different herbs. In that year-and-a-half period, I learned more about fresh herbs than I had previously known in my entire life—one of the first revelations being that there are no hard and fast rules for cooking with fresh herbs. In our Memphis restaurants, we commonly use about a dozen fresh herbs. They include basil, thyme, lemon balm, sage, chives, tarragon, dill, mint, anise, oregano, parsley, and rosemary. We use them in soups, salads, sauces, and with meat, fish, and poultry. We use them in appetizers, entrees, even in desserts.

One of my personal favorites is basil. It is a key ingredient in the Genoan herb paste, *pesto*, a fragrant puree of basil, pine nuts, olive oil, garlic and fresh Parmesan cheese. We incorporate the *pesto* in soups, marinate lamb in *pesto*, flavor a dish of baked Tennessee goat cheese with it, and use it, of course, with fresh pasta. Another favorite herb of mine is oregano. This herb's flavor, like that of basil, alters significantly when dried. You *must* try both of these herbs fresh—chopped, sliced, snipped—at the earliest opportunity.

Growing your own herbs is not difficult. In the Mid-South, most herbs can be planted from either seeds or transplants in the spring, and will attempt to bloom in July and August. Aromatic herbs tend to be disease- and pest-resistant, and most do well in a sunny plot with fairly fertile soil and ample water. Some herbs, including chervil, sweet woodruff, violet, and wintergreen actually prefer shade. But the ancient notion that herbs thrive in poor soil is erroneous. They will survive in poor soil, but they flourish in fertile soil.

For your first herb garden, try parsley, thyme, basil, sage, rosemary, chives, anise and nasturtiums. Most of the herbs have beautiful blossoms but try to use most of the leaves before the plants blossom.

Spices, like herbs, have been around since ancient times. Many centuries before the world began buying their oil, the Arabs of the Middle East were making great fortunes in the spice trade. Over the years, they sent countless caravans of thousands of camels traversing the so-called spice routes to the east, to bring back the precious aromatic spices so much prized in Europe in a time when preservation of foods by canning, refrigeration, or freezing was unknown. Europeans had only the vaguest idea where the "East" was because the Arabs closely guarded all information on the sources from which they obtained the spices.

Not until the end of the thirteenth century did such knowledge become available. That's when Marco Polo returned home safely after two decades of travels in the Orient, only to be taken prisoner in a war between his native Venice and Genoa. It was during his two years of imprisonment by the Genoese that he dictated *The Book of Marco Polo* which told of his long overland journey, detailed his amazing adventures in lands ruled by the emperor Kublai Khan, and disclosed the secret sources of the spices in the process. Two centuries later, a young Genoese sailor named Christopher Columbus read of Marco's travels and decided he could find an all-water route to reach the spice sources of the Orient—by sailing west instead of east. He never quite made it, of course, for he discovered something far more important than spices on the way.

One of the earliest known spices was pepper. (Both black and white pepper come from the same plant, the *Piper nigrum*. Black peppercorns come from green berries, not yet ripe, which have been allowed to dry and darken in the sun. White peppercorns are from the fully ripened red berries which have been peeled.) Pepper's existence has been documented for at least four thousand years, and it was long considered the most valuable of all spices. We get the expression that a man is "worth his salt" because Roman soldiers were often paid in salt. But a man who was "worth his pepper" would have been far more valuable. In medieval France, a serf could buy his freedom for a pound of pepper.

Among the other spices originally brought from the east were cinnamon, nutmeg, cloves, ginger, mace, poppy seed and turmeric. Our favorite herb, basil, also came to us from the east. All of these spices and many more are still used in the Middle Eastern dishes we call "curries"—some East Indian dishes may have thirty or forty different spices in them. In the west, nowadays, these once-eastern spices are used primarily in baking.

But no matter whether you cook with them, heal with them, bathe in them, or make tea with them, feel free to use herbs with ease and spices with imagination. The mistakes will be minor and the rewards great.

INDIAN GINGER CHICKEN

A delicious creation rich in spices.

1 cup clarified butter
2 medium onions, minced
3 tablespoons minced garlic
2 tablespoons minced fresh
    ginger
1 tablespoon turmeric
1 teaspoon coriander
1 teaspoon decorticated
    cardamom
1½ tablespoons whole cloves
8 cinnamon sticks, broken
    in half
1 teaspoon cayenne pepper
1 teaspoon cumin

4 peppers, minced (serrano,
    jalapeño, or cayenne)
2 2½-pound chickens, skinned
    and cut in serving pieces
3 cups chicken stock
Salt and pepper to taste
2 cups tomatoes, peeled,
    seeded, cooked, and puréed
1 cup cashew butter,
    available in health food
    section at supermarket
1 cup unsweetened flaked
    coconut
1 cup plain yogurt

Heat clarified butter in large heavy saucepan. Add onions, garlic, and ginger, cover, and let stand 5 minutes. Add all dry spices and minced peppers, and cook 2 to 3 minutes over medium heat. Remove cloves and cinnamon sticks. Add chicken, chicken stock, salt, pepper, tomatoes, cashew butter, and coconut. Mix well, cover, and simmer 45 to 50 minutes.

Blend in yogurt and correct seasoning. Serve with rice pilaf.

Serves 8 to 10

Memphis Culinary Academy
Joseph Carey, C.E.C., Director

HERBED VINEGAR

Herbs fresh from the garden mixed with vinegar can make any salad well-dressed. Experiment a little. Try garlic with basil or oregano with hot peppers.

Fresh herbs (tarragon, basil,
    thyme, rosemary, etc.)

White vinegar, 5% acidity

Pack quart jar two-thirds full with any herb or combination of herbs. Bruise herbs with handle of wooden spoon and add vinegar to finish filling jar. Cover tightly and store 3 weeks in dark, cool place. Strain liquid and pour into decorative bottle containing sprig of fresh herb. Cork or cap tightly. (Makes a nice gift.)

Yields 1 quart vinegar

June Owens

DILL BREAD

Makes a dilly of a loaf.

1 package yeast
¼ cup warm water
2 tablespoons sugar
1 cup creamed cottage cheese
2 tablespoons butter, melted
1 egg at room temperature
2 teaspoons dill seed

1 teaspoon dill weed
1 teaspoon salt
1 tablespoon instant minced
    onion
¼ teaspoon baking soda
2½ cups all-purpose flour

Dissolve yeast in water and add sugar. Heat cottage cheese until lukewarm. Stir in yeast mixture, butter, egg, dill seed, dill weed, salt, onion, and baking soda. Add flour, mixing well, to make stiff dough. Let rise in warm place until light and doubled in size. Stir down dough, place in greased round baking dish, and let rise until doubled in size. Bake 40 minutes at 350 degrees. Brush top with butter while hot.

Yields 1 loaf bread

Patricia LaPointe

PHEASANT IN GINGER CREAM SAUCE ON FETTUCCINE

Just a whisper of ginger, but it is simply perfect.

1 pheasant
Olive oil
2 cups heavy cream
1½-inch piece fresh ginger,
    sliced

½ pound fettuccine
2 tablespoons butter
1½ tablespoons brandy
Chives to taste
Freshly ground pepper to taste

With very sharp knife, remove breast from pheasant and cut in ⅜-inch cubes. Marinate in olive oil 4 hours.

Combine cream and ginger in small saucepan. Cook until reduced to 1½ cups and strain.

Cook fettuccine in boiling water 5 to 8 minutes and drain. While pasta is cooking, drain pheasant meat and sauté in butter for 1 minute, stirring constantly. Add brandy and cook 1 minute more. Toss pasta with ginger-cream mixture. Place sautéed pheasant on top of pasta and sprinkle with chives and pepper.

Serves 2

Flo Snowden

HERBED-EGG CASSEROLE

A good way to use leftover Easter eggs.

¼ cup butter, softened	1 teaspoon marjoram
¼ cup all-purpose flour	1½ dozen hard-cooked eggs,
1 cup heavy cream	sliced
1 cup milk	1 16-ounce package bacon,
1 16-ounce package sharp	cooked, drained, and
Cheddar cheese, grated	crumbled
1 teaspoon thyme	¼ cup minced parsley
1 teaspoon basil	Buttered bread crumbs

Melt butter in saucepan over low heat. Add flour, stirring until smooth. Gradually add cream and milk, cooking and stirring to make medium sauce. Add cheese, thyme, basil, and marjoram, and stir until cheese is blended.

In greased 9 x 13-inch baking dish, layer in order half of eggs, bacon, sauce, and parsley. Repeat layers one time. Sprinkle with bread crumbs and bake at 350 degrees for 20 to 30 minutes or until bubbly.

Note: Sauce is very good over vegetables, especially broccoli or spinach.

Serves 8 to 12

Martha Whitington

SPICED SHRIMP

A wonderful way to treat shrimp.

2½ pounds uncooked shrimp	1 tablespoon salt
½ cup celery leaves	2 cups thinly sliced onions
¼ cup mixed pickling spices	7 bay leaves

Add shrimp, celery leaves, pickling spices, and salt to boiling water, and cook 10 to 12 minutes. Rinse and peel shrimp. Alternate layers of shrimp and onions in glass container. Add bay leaves, cover with dressing, and refrigerate at least 24 hours. Remove bay leaves before serving.

Dressing

1¼ cups vegetable oil	2½ teaspoons celery seed
¾ cup white vinegar	1½ teaspoons salt
2½ tablespoons capers	Dash Tabasco sauce
Dash juice from capers	

Combine all ingredients and mix well. Pour over shrimp.

Serves 8 to 10

Barbara Keathley

LEG OF LAMB CASTILLE

A dish sampled while on vacation in the Castille region of Spain. Experimentation finally produced a likeness of the original.

1 8-pound leg of lamb	Olive oil
Several cloves garlic, sliced	

Heat coals 1 hour in grill. Before cooking, move coals to one side.

Make numerous slits in leg of lamb and insert garlic pieces. Rub entire surface with olive oil and place meat thermometer in mid-portion of leg. Place meat on side of grill away from coals and cook very slowly, about 20 minutes per pound or to preferred degree of doneness. Baste every 15 minutes to create thick crust. Slice and serve.

Basting Sauce

2 cups olive oil	Fresh oregano
Juice of 2 lemons	Fresh rosemary
4 tablespoons Worcestershire	Fresh thyme
sauce	Garlic salt to taste
1 to 2 teaspoons ground cumin	Lemon pepper to taste

Combine olive oil, lemon juice, Worcestershire sauce, and cumin. Add fresh herbs to taste, garlic salt, and lemon pepper.

Serves 10 to 12

Dr. Max Painter

KIMIONOV KIOFTA

An Armenian dish of sautéed meatballs made with lamb and flavored with cumin.

1 pound ground lamb	1 tablespoon salt
⅓ cup bread crumbs	½ tablespoon cumin
½ cup milk	3 tablespoons butter

Combine all ingredients except butter and mix thoroughly by hand. Knead mixture 2 to 3 minutes and form into small balls about 1¼ inches in diameter. Sauté meatballs in butter until well-browned. Serve hot (can be prepared in advance, frozen, and reheated before serving).

Yields 35 meatballs

Siran Voskeritchian Patzsch

BAKED CHICKEN ROSEMARY

Company fare!

1½ teaspoons salt
1 teaspoon pepper
½ teaspoon paprika
4 chicken breasts
6 tablespoons butter
1 14-ounce can artichoke
  hearts

½ pound fresh mushrooms,
  sliced
2 tablespoons all-purpose flour
⅔ to 1 cup chicken broth
3 tablespoons sherry
1¼ teaspoons rosemary

Mix salt, pepper, and paprika, and sprinkle over chicken. Melt 4 tablespoons butter in skillet, add chicken, and cook until browned. Place in ungreased 3-quart baking dish and arrange artichoke hearts among chicken.

Add remaining 2 tablespoons butter to drippings in skillet and sauté mushrooms. Sprinkle flour over mushrooms and stir in broth, sherry, and rosemary. Simmer 4 to 5 minutes and pour over chicken. Cover and bake at 375 degrees for 40 minutes or until tender.

Serves 4

Mrs. John D. Hughes

CRAB IN A CURRIED SOUR CREAM AND BRANDY SAUCE

Indescribably delicious. Try it as soon as possible.

2 bunches scallions, sliced
½ cup butter
4 tablespoons all-purpose flour
3 ounces vermouth
1½ ounces brandy
¼ ounce sherry
⅛ teaspoon curry powder

⅛ teaspoon nutmeg
½ teaspoon salt
1 cup sour cream
1 pound fresh crab meat
Fresh bread crumbs
2 tablespoons butter, melted
1 tablespoon lemon juice

Sauté scallions in butter. Add flour and stir well. Add vermouth, brandy, sherry, spices, and salt, and simmer 10 minutes. Remove from heat and stir in sour cream and crab meat. Place mixture in small baking shells or ramekins (may be refrigerated at this point and baked later). Sauté bread crumbs in butter and lemon juice, and sprinkle over crab meat mixture. Bake at 400 degrees for 20 minutes or until bubbly and brown on top.

Serves 6

Bobbye Bryant
Chicago, Illinois

MUSSEL SOUP WITH SAFFRON AND ORANGE

Preparing mussels is something of an adventure. Eating them is something of a pleasure.

24 mussels, thoroughly cleaned
1 shallot, chopped
1 cup white wine
2 tablespoons beef or chicken
  stock
3 cups heavy cream

Juice of 1 orange
Pinch of powdered saffron
Black pepper to taste
1 orange, thinly sliced
Chopped parsley

Poach mussels with shallot in wine and stock until mussels open. Remove mussels, discard any which have not opened, and let cool. Return liquid to heat and reduce to ¼ cup. Decrease heat and add cream, orange juice, saffron, and pepper. Simmer 5 minutes, slowly reducing liquid. One minute before serving, add mussels to hot soup and serve garnished with orange slices and parsley.

Note: To prepare mussels, scrub thoroughly and rinse several times. Discard any which have opened. Remove the "beards," the sea strands extending from shells.

Serves 4

La Tourelle Restaurant
Glenn Hays, Proprietor

GRILLED SALMON WITH FRESH HERBS

Superbly good. If you have not tried fresh herbs, what better time to bring a few home from your favorite garden center?

1 lemon
3 to 5 pound salmon, cleaned
¼ cup fresh lemon balm

¼ cup fresh tarragon
¼ cup fresh oregano
1 clove garlic, minced

Squeeze lemon over inner surface of salmon and sprinkle with herbs and garlic. Place in greased hinged fish-cooker and grill 10 to 15 minutes on each side. (Fish will flake when done.)

Serve with rye crackers, homemade mayonnaise, capers, and finely chopped green onions with tops.

Serves 12 to 14

Roseann Painter

BEEF SHISH KABOB

An original family recipe from West Bengal in India.

1 pound very lean beef,
    preferably tenderloin
1 ginger root
½ medium onion
2 to 3 cloves garlic
2 heaping tablespoons low-fat
    plain yogurt
1 teaspoon coriander seed
1 teaspoon cumin seed
6 whole cloves

4 whole cardamom
2 cinnamon sticks
Black peppercorns to taste
1 teaspoon meat tenderizer
    or more if needed
Dash ground allspice
Salt to taste
2 to 3 tablespoons vegetable oil
Ground red pepper, optional

Pat meat with paper towels to absorb moisture. Cut in pieces 2 inches long, 1 inch wide, and ½ inch thick. (Meat slices more easily if partially frozen.) Scrape skin from ginger root and grind in food processor to yield 2 teaspoons fresh ginger. Combine ginger with onion and garlic, and grind to make ginger paste. Do not add water. Combine with yogurt and mix with meat.

Place coriander, cumin, cloves, cardamom, cinnamon, and peppercorns in skillet. Heat and stir until spices sizzle. Put into coffee grinder and grind very well (processor should not be used for this). Combine with meat tenderizer, allspice, salt, and vegetable oil. Add red pepper if hot mixture is preferred. Stir into meat mixture, cover, and marinate overnight or longer.

Thread meat on skewers with no spaces between pieces. Skewers must be long enough to rest on sides of grill so that meat is directly over coals but not lying on grill as meat will stick to it. Cook until lightly browned. Arrange skewers (1 per person) on platter, and surround with lettuce, lemon wedges, and slices of tomato, onion, and cucumber. Serve with *naan* (Indian flat bread, available in health food stores or other specialty stores) or with rice.

Note: Works equally well with chicken or with fish that does not flake easily, such as tuna and snapper. (Do not add meat tenderizer.)

Serves 3 to 4

Sofia Khandakar

SURPRISE WILD RICE CASSEROLE

The surprise is that there are no pecans and no wild rice in this delicious casserole. The lovely nutty flavor is from a particular rice grown in the Evangeline country of South Louisiana, evocative of the taste of wild pecans that grow in that area. Great with quail!

1 7-ounce box Konriko Wild
    Pecan Rice
3 tablespoons butter
4 tablespoons minced onion
3 tablespoons chopped green
    bell pepper
1 cup sliced fresh mushrooms
1 8-ounce can water
    chestnuts, chopped
1 6-ounce can pitted ripe olives
1 10¾-ounce can cream of
    mushroom soup

¾ cup light cream
¼ teaspoon salt
¼ teaspoon pepper
¼ teaspoon marjoram
⅛ teaspoon dill
⅛ teaspoon tarragon
⅛ teaspoon basil
⅛ teaspoon thyme
½ teaspoon curry powder
8 fresh mushroom caps,
    sautéed until barely tender

Cook rice according to package directions.

While rice is cooking, melt butter in saucepan and sauté onion and pepper 5 minutes. Add sliced mushrooms, water chestnuts, and olives, and heat briefly. Stir in soup, cream, and seasonings. Cook 10 minutes over very low heat. Add soup mixture to cooked rice and pour into greased 2-quart baking dish. Top with sautéed mushroom caps. Bake 8 to 10 minutes at 350 degrees.

Serves 6 to 8

Diane Chamberlin
Houston, Texas

BAY LEAF BARBECUE SAUCE

Prepared in minutes. Exceptionally good.

1 10¾-ounce can tomato soup
1 5-ounce bottle Worcestershire
    sauce
½ cup vegetable oil
2 tablespoons dry mustard
2 tablespoons salt

1 teaspoon black pepper
1 teaspoon red pepper
2 to 3 bay leaves, broken
Grated onion to taste, optional
1 cup vinegar

Mix all ingredients except vinegar in saucepan and cook 5 minutes over low heat. Remove from heat and add vinegar.

Yields 2 cups sauce

Mrs. Blanchard Tual

BUTTER SPREADS

Butter is the perfect host for various herbs to make delicious spreads.

Chive Butter
Good on fish, vegetables, or sizzling steaks. Divine on hot biscuits.

½ cup butter, softened
   to spreading consistency

1 to 2 teaspoons chopped chives,
   fresh or frozen only

Blend butter and chives. Place in oiled butter molds and freeze. If serving with bread, remove from freezer 15 to 20 minutes ahead; for other foods, serve at room temperature.

Yields ½ cup

Lemon Butter
Serve over artichokes, asparagus, broccoli, or fish.

¼ cup butter, melted
1 tablespoon minced fresh
   parsley

1 tablespoon lemon juice
Black pepper to taste

Combine all ingredients and blend.

Yields ¼ cup

Parsley Butter
Delicious served on potatoes and meats.

½ cup butter, softened
1 tablespoon minced fresh
   parsley
1 teaspoon lemon juice

½ teaspoon minced fresh
   summer savory
Salt and pepper to taste

Combine all ingredients and blend.

Yields ½ cup

Tarragon Mustard Butter
Serve at room temperature on steaks.

½ cup butter, softened
1 tablespoon Dijon mustard

¼ cup chopped fresh tarragon
   or 1 tablespoon dried

Combine all ingredients and blend.

Yields ½ cup

Carol M. Cherry

BISCOTTI DI VINO

Little wine-flavored cookies, perfect to package for holiday giving.

8 cups all-purpose flour
2½ cups sugar
¼ cup walnut chips
1 teaspoon baking powder
½ teaspoon anise seed
1 cup vegetable oil

1 cup solid vegetable
   shortening, melted
1 teaspoon vanilla
1 tablespoon rum
2½ cups dry white wine

Combine flour, sugar, nuts, baking powder, and anise seed, and mix well. Add all remaining ingredients and mix until thoroughly blended. Add more flour as needed until consistency is like bread dough. Pinch off small portion and form a thin roll about 2 inches long. Dip in sugar and shape, sugar side up, into an "S" on greased and floured baking sheet. Place in middle of oven and bake at 350 degrees for 35 minutes or until light brown. Cool before removing from pan.

Yields 16 dozen cookies

Velia Marinelli
Rockford, Illinois

FRUIT PRESERVE CAKE

This recipe works well with fig, peach, or pear preserves. It produces a moist cake that is not too sweet.

2 cups all-purpose flour
1 teaspoon salt
1 teaspoon baking soda
1 teaspoon ground cloves
1 teaspoon cinnamon
1 teaspoon nutmeg
1¼ cups sugar

1 cup vegetable oil
3 eggs
1 cup buttermilk
1 cup fig preserves
1 tablespoon vanilla
1 cup chopped pecans

Sift together flour, salt, baking soda, spices, and sugar. Combine dry ingredients with oil and beat well with electric mixer. Add eggs and beat well at medium speed. Add buttermilk, fig preserves, and vanilla, beating at low speed until lightly blended. Add nuts and continue beating until evenly distributed. Pour into greased and floured 10-inch tube pan. Bake at 325 degrees for 45 minutes or until cake springs back when lightly touched.

Serves 18 to 20

Mrs. M.V. Highsmith

SUGAR PLUM CAKE

The perfect ending after attending a performance of *The Nutcracker*. Children will love it.

2 cups sugar	½ teaspoon salt
1 cup vegetable oil	1 teaspoon baking soda
3 eggs, lightly beaten	1 cup buttermilk
2 cups all-purpose flour	1 cup chopped cooked prunes
2 teaspoons allspice	1 cup chopped pecans or
2 teaspoons nutmeg	walnuts
2 teaspoons cinnamon	Assorted gum drops

Combine sugar, oil, and eggs, and beat well with mixer. Sift flour with spices and salt. Mix baking soda with buttermilk and add alternately with dry ingredients to sugar mixture, beating well after each addition. Beat 2 minutes more at medium speed, add prunes and nuts, and beat 1 minute. Pour into greased and floured 12-cup Bundt pan and bake 1 to 1¼ hours at 325 degrees. Remove from oven, leave in pan, and pierce top with toothpick or skewer. Pour half of warm glaze over hot cake, and cool slightly. Remove from pan and pour remaining glaze over top. Decorate with small gumdrops.

Glaze

1 cup sugar	½ cup buttermilk
½ cup butter, melted	½ teaspoon baking soda

Combine butter, sugar, and buttermilk, and stir until creamy. Cook 1 to 2 minutes over high heat. Remove from heat and mix in baking soda. Cool slightly.

Serves 16

Peggy Jones

SPICY BLUEBERRY CAKE

Buy a batch of berries when the season arrives, use some while fresh, and freeze the rest for a midwinter feast.

1 cup butter, softened	¾ teaspoon cinnamon
2 cups sugar	½ cup milk
3 eggs	2 cups blueberries (fresh or
3 cups all-purpose flour	frozen, not packaged in
1½ teaspoons baking powder	syrup)
⅛ teaspoon salt	2 teaspoons sugar
¼ teaspoon mace	2 teaspoons all-purpose flour

Cream butter with 2 cups sugar until light and fluffy. Add eggs, beating well. Sift together 3 cups flour, baking powder, salt, and spices. Add to creamed mixture alternately with milk, beating well after each addition. Coat berries with remaining sugar and flour, then fold into batter. Pour into greased and floured 10-inch tube pan. Bake 50 to 60 minutes at 350 degrees. Cool in pan 15 minutes and turn out on wire rack. Glaze while cake is still hot. (This cake freezes well.)

Glaze

1 cup confectioners' sugar	½ teaspoon vanilla
⅛ cup hot water	Pinch of cinnamon

Mix all ingredients together.

Serves 14

Mrs. John E. Marcom
Jonesboro, Arkansas

MOTHER'S SPECIAL PUMPKIN PIE

Fresh pumpkin pie—a grand seasonal treat.

1 pie pumpkin	⅜ teaspoon allspice
⅔ cup molasses	⅜ teaspoon cinnamon
½ cup sour cream	⅜ teaspoon ground cloves
½ cup evaporated milk	⅜ teaspoon ginger
3 eggs, well beaten	⅜ teaspoon nutmeg
½ scant teaspoon salt	1 unbaked 10-inch pie shell

Clean pumpkin and cut up in large pieces. Place on baking sheet and bake at 400 degrees until pulp is just barely soft. Cool and peel. Place pulp in food processor and purée. Combine 1½ cups puréed pumpkin with remaining ingredients and blend well. Pour into pie shell and bake at 350 degrees for 50 to 60 minutes or until set.

Note: Substitute honey for molasses for milder, sweeter taste. For spicier taste, increase spices to ½ teaspoon each.

Serves 8 to 10

Linda-Marie Goetze

CONSERVES, CONDIMENTS
AND CONFECTIONS

A Little Something Homemade

by Phyllis Tickle

At the bottom of our stairwell, just where the hall turns in front of one bedroom and heads toward the den, there is a trunk. It is admittedly a weary trunk, having come across the waters with our European ancestors almost two centuries ago. But burnished by the hands of many grandmothers and repaired from time to time by those of many grandfathers, it still holds an honored spot in our decor and it still contains the *crème de la crème* of the family treasures.

One such treasure is a postcard. Faded to a mocha brown and spotted like an old woman with her age marks, it is dated August, 1908 and is the only penny postcard our children have ever seen up close. Its message is ornate, if not clear: "Dear Miss Maggie, I am beholden for the squirrel, my health being much improved as a result. Your Servant, George Osbourne."

In her later years, Great Aunt Maggie was fond of having our children visit her, probably because they were genuinely fond of listening to her stories. Their favorite was the one of George Osbourne's postcard.

Maggie would take the card out of her Bible and, holding it in her rough-lined hands, she would begin to remember. To recall what a dandy Mr. George Osbourne had been in the summer of 1908 when the fever had struck him; how the fever had wasted him down to almost nothing; how only broth would stay with him; and how there was no more meat from which to make him broth as the summer wore on. Then, with a little duck of her head, half modest and half proud, she would say, "But I was the best shot in Sullivan County in those days. Even the men'd tell you that. And there was this squirrel . . . only squirrel left in Sullivan County that August, I'd wager . . . come playing on my back fence one morning, just tempting me. So I took down my gun and got me that squirrel. I dressed it out, and I wrapped it up good, and I put a stamp on it. Then I went out to the mail box and I waited. Soon as the carrier came, I give it him and told him to fetch it down to George Osbourne's house for making him some broth. And he did that and they made George the broth and it cured him."

"Of course," she always ended her story, "of course, I say it's the care in something like that that does it. The strength is in the caring. Yessir, it'll do it every time, all that caring packed into just a little something homemade." Which is why, when Great Aunt Maggie died, the children took Mr. Osbourne's postcard out of her Bible and put it in the hall trunk. As I said in the beginning, space in the trunk is limited to only the most authentic and wisest of our treasures.

MEMI'S SPICED NUTS

Just the best nibbles. And a little tin of them makes such a welcome gift.

2½ cups pecan halves   ½ teaspoon salt
1 cup sugar   ½ cup water
1 teaspoon cinnamon   1½ teaspoons vanilla

Spread pecans in baking pan and bake 10 to 15 minutes at 350 degrees, moving pecans around several times. Set aside to cool. Combine sugar, cinnamon, salt, and water, and cook to soft ball stage. Remove from heat and add vanilla and nuts, stirring constantly until mixture becomes creamy and lighter in color. Continue stirring until mixture loses its luster and begins to harden. At that point, turn nuts onto large platter, separate, and allow to cool.

Yields 2½ cups nuts

Anne Filer Crosby

SPICY MOCHA MIX

Gives a delicious cup of comfort when the frost is on the pumpkin, or ice is on the eaves.

½ cup sugar   ¼ teaspoon allspice
¼ cup cocoa   Dash ground cardamom
2 tablespoons nonfat dry milk Milk
1 to 3 tablespoons instant   Vanilla bean
    coffee to taste   Rum, optional
¼ teaspoon cinnamon

Mix all dry ingredients together and store in airtight container. Put small piece vanilla bean in container with mix for added flavor. For one serving, stir 2 tablespoons mix into 1 cup hot milk. (Add 2 tablespoons rum, if preferred.)

Yields 1 cup mix

Cathy A. Knight

BLACKBERRY PRESERVES AND JELLY

Double results for half the effort!

3 pounds blackberries   5 cups sugar

Rinse berries well. Cook over low heat in heavy enameled 5-quart pot until juice is extracted. Add sugar and boil rapidly for 20 minutes. Strain and reserve juice. Fill sterilized half-pint jars two-thirds full with berries.

Boil reserved juice rapidly until candy thermometer reads 221 degrees. (Test small amount in saucer to see if juice will jell. Boil longer, almost to softball stage, if thicker jelly is preferred.) Skim foam from juice and pour into jars of berries, filling ½-inch from top and stirring to mix thoroughly. Pour remaining juice into separate sterilized jars to make jelly. Wipe rims of jars and seal.

Yields 4 half-pint jars each
        preserves and jelly

Dr. J. Garland Cherry, Jr.

PEACH CONSERVE

Capture summer in a jar, seal it tight, and save it for another day.

3 medium oranges, unpeeled   2 quarts sliced peeled peaches
2 small lemons, unpeeled   6 cups sugar

Cut oranges and lemons in quarters, and remove seeds and center membranes. Put in food processor and process 1 minute. Pour into heavy 4-quart saucepan. Process peaches until well-chopped, about 10 to 20 seconds, and pour into saucepan. Add sugar and stir over low heat until dissolved. Bring to boil and cook 30 minutes at slow, rolling boil, stirring every few minutes to keep from sticking. Pour into sterilized jars and seal. Water bath 10 minutes.

Water Bath Procedure:

Place jars on rack in canner or deep kettle. Cover with water 1 inch above lids. Quickly bring water to boil and boil 10 minutes, counting water bath time as soon as bubbles begin to flow over jars.

Yields 4 pints conserve

Mary Lou Adams

SWEET GARLIC PICKLES

These pickles won't last long. Seems no one can leave them alone.

1 gallon jar whole sour pickles, drained and sliced ½-inch thick
½ cup whole peppercorns
2 cloves garlic, finely chopped
5 pounds sugar

Mix all ingredients in plastic or enameled pan. Cover and let stand in cool place for 2 days, stirring twice daily with wooden spoon. On third day, fill sterilized jars with pickles and juice, tighten lids, and turn upside down until sealed.

Yields 4 quarts pickles

Ellen Davies Rodgers
Brunswick, Tennessee

SCOTTISH SHORTBREAD

A recipe that came with a young wife traveling from Scotland to America in 1909 to join her husband. It was always served with her freshly-brewed tea of which she said, "Unless the kettle boilin' be, ye'll nae hae a proper cup o' tea."

1 cup plus 2 tablespoons sugar
2 cups butter, softened
3 cups sifted all-purpose flour
1⅔ cups rice flour (no substitute)

Mix sugar and butter together with fingers. Gradually add all-purpose flour and rice flour, blending until mixture leaves hands clean. Shape in small pieces or in long rolls, slice, and prick tops with tines of fork. Bake at 275 degrees for 35 to 40 minutes or until very lightly browned.

Note: Makes a perfect holiday gift packed in colorful tins and tied with ribbon, preferably tartan plaid.

Yields 4 to 5 dozen cookies

Elizabeth Hutchinson Redfearn
Everett, Washington

FRIENDSHIP TEA

Nothing is better spent between friends than time, and how much better when it's time over teacups.

1 17-ounce jar powdered orange drink
1 cup sugar
½ cup presweetened lemonade mix
1 3-ounce package apricot or peach gelatin
½ cup instant tea
2½ teaspoons cinnamon
1 teaspoon ground cloves
¼ teaspoon allspice, optional
⅛ teaspoon ground cardamom, optional

Mix all ingredients together and store in airtight container. For one serving, stir 1½ tablespoons mix into 1 cup hot water.

Note: Wonderful to package as gifts in tins or jars.

Yields 4½ cups mix

Cathy A. Knight

PEACH CHUTNEY

Peaches are so good, whatever their guise.

3½ pounds firm peaches, peeled and pitted
½ cup chopped white raisins
½ cup chopped dark raisins
½ cup chopped candied ginger
1 cup chopped onions
2 cloves garlic, minced
1 chili pepper, seeded and chopped, optional
3½ cups sugar
½ teaspoon ginger, optional
1½ cups cider vinegar
¾ cup lime juice
¼ cup Worcestershire sauce
Grated rind of 1 lime

Slice peaches ¼-inch thick. Cover with brine (2 tablespoons salt to 1 quart water) and let stand 24 to 36 hours. Drain.

Mix remaining ingredients in non-aluminum 4 to 5-quart saucepan, add peaches, and simmer 45 to 60 minutes. Pour into sterilized jars and seal.

Yields 4 to 5 pints chutney

Mrs. Frank M. Norfleet

NUTS AND BOLTS

There are times in our lives when we just need to get down to nuts and bolts.

2 cups butter, melted	1 10-ounce box Chex Snax Mix
2 teaspoons salt	1 10-ounce box Cheerios
2 teaspoons Worcestershire sauce	1 9-ounce package pretzels, broken
1½ teaspoons garlic salt or 3 cloves garlic, crushed	1 6-ounce package sesame chips (found in health food stores)
1 teaspoon onion salt	
½ teaspoon celery salt	1 pound almonds, cashews, and pecans, or mixed nuts
Tabasco sauce to taste	

Blend butter with all seasonings. Combine Chex, Cheerios, pretzels, sesame chips, and nuts in baking pan, sprinkle with seasoned butter, and mix. Bake 2 hours at 250 degrees, stirring well every 15 minutes. Store in tins or jars.

Yields 3 pounds mix

Shirley Marshall

EASY BREAD AND BUTTER PICKLES

Somehow, when pickles are homemade, they just taste better.

10 large cucumbers, unpeeled and sliced in thin rounds	4 cups cider vinegar
6 onions, sliced in thin rounds	5 tablespoons mustard seed
½ cup uniodized salt	5 tablespoons celery seed
1 bag ice	½ teaspoon ground cloves
4 cups sugar	1½ teaspoons turmeric
	6 green bell peppers, julienne

Combine cucumbers and onions in large bowl, cover with salt, and mix well. Add ice to cover completely and gently stir until well distributed. Let stand in brine 3 hours, and drain. (If salt intake is limited, omit brine and chill vegetables for 24 hours.)

Combine vegetables with remaining ingredients in non-aluminum 6 to 8-quart pot and mix gently. Bring just to boil, remove from heat, and stir. Pour into sterilized pint jars and seal.

Yields 12 pints pickles

Mrs. A. Arthur Halle, Jr.

CRANBERRY CHUTNEY

The splendid cranberry in a spicy mixture of good flavors.

1 pound fresh cranberries	½ cup chopped, mixed candied peel and fruits
1 large tart apple, peeled and diced	¼ teaspoon ginger
2 cups brown sugar	¼ teaspoon ground cloves
¾ cup apple cider vinegar	¼ teaspoon allspice
½ teaspoon salt	¼ teaspoon dry mustard

Combine all ingredients in 3-quart saucepan and bring to boil. Reduce heat and simmer uncovered 15 minutes, stirring constantly. Cool and refrigerate or freeze in airtight containers.

Yields 2 pints chutney

Edna Sitler

STREIBICH'S HOT MUSTARD

This has a nice sweet 'n' sour taste.

1 1⅜-ounce can dry mustard	½ teaspoon salt
¼ cup all-purpose flour	Tarragon vinegar
¼ cup sugar	Boiling water

Mix dry ingredients together. Add tarragon vinegar, stirring until thick paste forms with no lumps. Thin with boiling water to desired consistency. (Will keep indefinitely in refrigerator.)

Yields 1 to 1½ cups mustard

Harold C. Streibich

TENNESSEE HOTS

Not for the faint-hearted!

1 gallon jar dill pickles, drained and thinly sliced	6 cups sugar
	1 2-ounce bottle Tabasco sauce

Combine pickles, sugar, and Tabasco sauce in gallon jar. Store 3 days, periodically inverting jar.

Note: For a delicious pimiento cheese, mix cheese with chopped fresh pimiento peppers, chopped Tennessee Hots, and mayonnaise.

Yields 1 gallon pickles

Geri Cuoghi

MARY E'S JEZEBEL SAUCE

A fine sauce that's even better if the jelly and preserves are homemade. So good with country ham.

1 12-ounce jar apple jelly
1 12-ounce jar peach preserves
½ teaspoon dry mustard
2 tablespoons horseradish sauce or more to taste

Mix all ingredients together and chill 2 days to blend flavors.

Note: Fill decorative jars to use as gifts.

Yields 3 cups sauce

Mary Ellen White
Fairfield Bay, Arkansas

SWEET DILLS

Dill pickles in disguise. Crunchy and good.

1 gallon jar dill pickles drained
5 pounds sugar
2 cups red wine vinegar
1 9¾-ounce package Mrs. Wages Sweet Pickling Spice
¼ cup vegetable oil
1 whole black peppercorn

Leave pickles in jar, cover with water, and let stand at least 4 hours. Drain. In 6 to 8-quart non-aluminum pot, combine remaining ingredients and bring to boil. Add pickles and bring to hard boil. Pour into sterilized jars and seal.

Yields 4 quarts pickles

Mrs. Fred Lawrence

PINEAPPLE PICKLE

Pickling pineapple is like gilding the lily. But the result in this case is very desirable.

2 20-ounce cans chunk pineapple, drained
1½ cups sugar
⅔ cup cider vinegar
½ cup water
1½ teaspoons whole cloves

Fill sterilized pint jars with pineapple chunks. Combine remaining ingredients and boil until liquid begins to thicken, about 10 to 15 minutes. Pour syrup into jars to cover fruit and refrigerate 7 to 10 days before using. Do not seal. (More syrup may be made and added if necessary.)

Yields 2 pints pickles

Josephine Conger

CARAMEL POPCORN

Hard to improve on popcorn—unless you add caramel to it.

2 cups popcorn kernels
1 cup margarine
2 cups brown sugar, firmly packed
½ cup light corn syrup
1 teaspoon salt
½ teaspoon baking soda
1 teaspoon vanilla

Pop kernels and set aside in large baking pan.

In saucepan, boil margarine, brown sugar, and corn syrup for 5 minutes over medium heat, stirring constantly. Remove from heat and stir in salt, baking soda, and vanilla. Pour caramel over popcorn and toss to coat. Bake 1 hour at 250 degrees, stirring every 15 minutes. Cool and store in airtight container.

Serves 10 to 12

Mrs. W. Thomas Cunningham, Jr.
Richmond, Virginia

CANDIED ORANGE SLICES

Such good little confections. And they travel well.

8 or 9 oranges
2 cups granulated sugar
¾ cup water
2 cups confectioners' sugar

Carefully peel oranges and slice peel vertically in ¼-inch wide strips. Place in heavy saucepan, cover with water, and bring to boil. Drain well. Repeat boiling and draining three times. Add granulated sugar and ¾ cup water, and bring to boil. Reduce heat and cook 30 to 45 minutes to soften peel. Drain thoroughly.

Place cake rack on baking sheet. Pour confectioners' sugar in plastic bag, add 1 cup orange peel at a time, and shake well to coat. Remove orange slices one by one and lay on cake rack. Chill overnight and store in air-tight container. (May be necessary to add confectioners' sugar before serving.)

Yield varies with size of oranges

Pat Cook
Duncan, Oklahoma

GRANOLA

For snacks at home or on the back-pack trail.

¼ cup vegetable oil	⅓ cup wheat germ
⅓ cup honey	¼ cup slivered almonds
2 cups rolled oats	3 tablespoons sesame seeds
½ cup raisins	1 cup shredded coconut

Mix oil with honey and set aside. Combine all other ingredients in large mixing bowl and toss together. Add honey mixture and stir well. Place in baking pan and bake 10 to 12 minutes at 350 degrees. Remove from oven and stir. Cool and store in jars or tins.

Yields 5 cups granola

Mrs. W. Thomas Cunningham, Jr.
Richmond, Virginia

DOGGIE BISCUITS

Wonderful holiday presents for the puppies on your list. Keep for months in tins.

3½ cups all-purpose flour	4 teaspoons salt
2 cups whole wheat flour	1 package yeast
1 cup rye flour	¼ cup very warm water
2 cups bulgur wheat	2 to 3 cups chicken broth
1 cup corn meal	1 large egg
½ cup nonfat dry milk	1 tablespoon milk

In large bowl, combine all flour, bulgur wheat, corn meal, dry milk, and salt, and mix well. Dissolve yeast in water and add with 2 cups broth to dry ingredients. Mix well with hands, adding more broth if necessary. Dough will be very stiff.

On floured surface, roll out dough ¼-inch thick. Cut in shape of 3 x ¾-inch dog bones and place on ungreased baking sheet. Mix egg with milk, brush biscuits lightly, and bake 45 minutes at 300 degrees. Turn off oven, but leave biscuits inside with door closed for several hours or overnight to dry.

Note: It is best if flour, bulgur wheat, and corn meal are medium-grind.

Yields 11 dozen biscuits

Carol M. Cherry

RIPE TOMATO RELISH

When your tomato vines give you a bumper crop, put some of their treasure into this delicious relish.

4 quarts ripe tomatoes, chopped and drained	4 large onions, finely chopped
4 cups sugar	4 green bell peppers, finely chopped
2 cups white vinegar	3 medium hot peppers, finely chopped
2 tablespoons uniodized salt	

Mix all ingredients in large saucepan and cook covered over medium-low heat until thick, about 1½ to 2 hours. Pour into sterilized jars and seal.

Yields 2 to 2½ pints relish

Maxine Morse

AUNT HELEN'S
SPICED CRANBERRY JELLY

A delicious, sweet, and spicy condiment for holiday giving.

3 sticks cinnamon	4 cups fresh cranberries, washed and drained
2 tablespoons whole cloves	2 cups sugar
1 tablespoon whole allspice	
2 cups water	

Tie spices in cheesecloth, place in water, bring to full boil, and boil 3 to 4 minutes. Add cranberries and continue boiling until all berries burst. Remove from heat and remove spice bag.

Mash berries in fruit press (or colander), discard skins, and reserve pulp and juice. Add sugar to pulp mixture and bring slowly to full boil, stirring constantly until sugar dissolves. Continue boiling until mixture falls in sheets from spoon, about 5 to 10 minutes, or until teaspoonful placed on saucer will set. Remove from heat and pour into sterilized jars.

Yields 6 to 7 pints jelly

Margaret Cobb Boyd

> Note: Some home canners prefer to water bath all pickles, relishes, jams, and jellies. Some do not. Please consult general canning guide, if undecided.

FESTIVE TRADITIONS
AND
UNFORGETTABLE FLAVORS

THE QUINTESSENTIAL BARBECUE

Barbecue in the South can be defined generically as good eating and good times. The barbecue can refer to anything from a simple, back-yard, family gathering, to a special dinner for convivial guests, to the occasion for community-wide froth and frenzy. Barbecue, specifically, can mean barbecued spareribs, barbecued pork shoulder, or most often, if you are a Memphian, the barbecue sandwich. The first food a Memphian seeks when returning home from afar, the food that can bring tears to the eyes in recollection, is the barbecue sandwich for which Memphis is famous—a big, soft bun filled to overflowing with bite-sized shreds of perfectly cooked barbecued pork, white or dark, a dollop of crisp or creamy cole slaw, and a generous slathering of barbecue sauce, hot or mild. Served with a side order of well-seasoned baked beans, and with your choice of beverage (the purist may well prefer a glass of cold Bulgarian buttermilk), a Memphis barbecue sandwich is...Ah, heaven!

ABOUT MEMPHIS BARBECUE

When Memphians say barbecue, they mean pork, and they mean pork shoulder, chopped or pulled, and pork ribs. They mean pork cooked one way: slowly, in a close place, on a grid over hot coals, the grease from the meat falling onto the coals and sending up a redolent smoke that singularly flavors the meat. Originally the pork prepared this way was cooked outdoors in a covered pit, hence the name pit barbecue. Nowadays, the word barbecue is often loosely used to mean anything cooked over coals, but barbecue lovers understand that that's only grilled meat. Real barbecuing, on the other hand, takes time. Southerners have a propensity for taking their time.

Memphis has barbecue restaurants all over the city, close to a hundred of them, and each one has its fans who proclaim their choice the best: Payne's, Corky's, Gridley's, John Wills Bar-B-Que Pit, Willingham's, Tops, Charlie Vergos' Rendezvous (which ships its famous ribs nationwide by Federal Express), and many more, including Bozo's in nearby Mason, Tennessee. The old barbecue drive-ins—like the Cotton Boll, Berretta's, the Pig 'N' Whistle—have disappeared in the path of the drive-through fast food places. Only Leonard's remains, the granddaddy of them all. Named for owner Leonard Heuberger, this oldest of Memphis barbecue restaurants started in 1932 as a seven-stool sandwich stand in South Memphis, and moved in the forties to its present location on Bellevue. In the forties and fifties Leonard's was "the world's largest drive-in restaurant" with 20 carhops serving a daily and nightly parade of customers, their cars parked under metal canopies. Today, people go inside to eat at Leonard's, where they can indulge in both barbecue and nostalgia, with the constant sound of chopping knife on cutting board punctuating all conversation. The walls are covered with pictures from Memphis' past—the 1872 steamboat *Robert E. Lee*, Cotton Carnival parades, the 1912 flood, A. Schwab dry goods store on Beale, a 1917 Piggly Wiggly, W. C. Handy and his band, and Elvis. Customers are from all walks of life. There are young people, men in overalls and in business suits, medical students in white coats, old couples, and people from the neighborhood. They all have one thing in common: they like barbecue.

To watch the cooking process at Leonard's is to understand what pit barbecue is all about. Leonard's started using pork shoulders, the best for barbecue, because they were by-products of the whole hog, usually ground up for scraps, and therefore inexpensive cuts. They were cooked a long time to get the fat out and to make the meat tender, and in the process, a Southern institution was born. The shoulders—sometimes as many as seventy-five at a time—and ribs are cooked in huge pits over low coals on grills about three feet above the fire. Preparation of the fire is important. The hickory chips are ignited in front of the pits, and after they blaze, they are beaten and scattered on the floor of the pits to give the right combination of ashes and smoke, and of coals glowing right under the meat, which must be over direct heat all the time. (One bag of chips lasts about one hour.) Leonard's has six old pits and three new ones, brick with iron doors and steel plates in front on the floor. And the fires never go out. James Willis, pit man in charge of all barbecuing at Leonard's, has been there since July 4, 1938. He says, "You have to tend to barbecue—barbecue can't be left to cook on its own. Somebody is here twenty-four hours a day. You have to start the basting when the meat is three-fourths done; too much basting makes the meat too brown. Then you cook it another one or two hours. Ribs take about three hours. You know they're done when you can take 'em and break 'em. Shoulders take more time; you have to know when to add fire and when to take the shoulders out. You know they're done when you can take out the bone without tearing the meat." And how do you know when that time comes? Says Mr. Willis, "I can look at it and tell." And why is Leonard's so good? "I think it's because they cook it better than anywhere else. And the sauce is eighty-five percent of your business. If you get a good sauce, you've got your barbecue."

ABOUT BARBECUE COOKING

State-of-the-art charbroiling seems to change almost daily, rediscovered with each issue of a newspaper, magazine, or cookbook. However, a few basic techniques for outdoor barbecuing, grilling, or smoking remain, and need to be to be reviewed from time to time, as do the various types of equipment available.

The direct method of smoking or grilling: (Damp wood technique) The food to be smoked or grilled is placed over a bed of charcoal which has burned down to a uniform, dusty gray color. Several chunks of damp hickory, mesquite, or other aromatic wood are placed on the coals. The damp wood gives off copious amounts of smoke to impart a unique flavor to the food. A hint: The wetter the wood the better. You can soak it in water for days or weeks in advance. With this technique, a grill cover may be left open or closed, or a combination of both.

The indirect method of smoking or grilling: In a conventional oblong charcoal grill with a cover a mound of charcoal is placed at one end of the grill. Use a *small* amount of charcoal starter fluid to light a *small* area in the center of the charcoal mound. After the charcoal has burned down, place several large pieces of fat over the charcoal. Place the meat to be cooked at the other end of the grill, and then close and vent the grill lid. As the fat cooks, it drips over the fire, producing much smoke. In a few hours, beautifully cooked meat emerges with little or no attention required.

Grills which utilize gas, propane gas, or electricity: Consult the equipment manufacturer's suggested techniques. Most of this equipment uses heated lava rock. Dripping fat on this lava rock is the primary source of the charbroiled smoky flavor imparted to meats.

The indoor grill: An excellent, versatile cooking apparatus which will give that charbroiled flavor to your favorite meats, rain or shine or snow. However, smoking techniques are obviously a no-no!

Cast iron or steel charcoal grills: This type grill is available, with or without a covering lid, in natural gas, propane gas, electric, or plain charcoal models. When real smoking techniques are called for, a grill lid is a necessity.

The kettle smoker: This equipment, combining smoke and steam to add an extra dimension to charcoal cooking, is excellent for slow-cooking large portions—turkey, game, whole fish. Manufacturers are quite precise and accurate on amounts of charcoal, water quantities, and cooking times for various meats. But once you master the basics, let your imagination run free. Not only may aromatic woods be added directly to the charcoal fire, but various condiments, such as apples, lemons, oranges, etc. may be added to the water to give unique flavors to your cooking. A minimum of "grill-side" attention is required. Best results if you don't peep.

The oil drum: An excellent cooking and smoking instrument which demonstrates quite well that good equipment can have simple beginnings.

For starting a conventional charcoal fire:

Charcoal fluid: Very easy and popular. However, be sure that the charcoal has burned down to a dusty gray color before you begin cooking. This allows the petroleum smoke and aroma to burn out of the charcoal.

The "tin can" method: A large forty-six-ounce juice can with lids removed at both ends is perforated throughout with large holes. Place a piece of newspaper at the bottom of the can and then place ten to fifteen charcoal briquets in the can. When you light the newspaper the flame migrates upward, igniting the charcoal, and the coals are then placed in the grill. Purists feel this method is superior since there is no chance for residual petroleum aromas or flavors in the food. It should be noted that manufactured versions of the "can" are readily available.

So now you're ready. Put on your favorite apron, hum a few notes of *On Top of Old Smokey*, and let the barbecue cooking begin!

Ellen and Richard Dixon

BOURBON-MARINATED RIBS

6 to 8 pound rack country-cut
   pork ribs

Pour marinade over ribs and chill overnight in covered pan, turning once. Remove from refrigerator 4 hours before grilling.

Cook ribs on charcoal grill for 1 hour, turning and basting with marinade. Place ribs in roaster, add any remaining marinade, and cover. Bake at 250 degrees for 1½ to 2 hours until tender and succulent.

Bourbon Marinade
1 large onion, minced
⅓ cup bourbon whiskey
⅓ cup cider vinegar
¼ cup soy sauce
¼ cup light brown sugar

2 tablespoons Dijon mustard
1 tablespoon lemon juice
1 tablespoon Worcestershire
   sauce

Combine all ingredients and mix well.

Serves 12 to 15

SMOKED CROWN RIB ROAST OF LAMB

1 crown rib of roast, cut to
   allow 2 ribs per person

Prepare smoker according to manufacturer's instructions. Place unstuffed rib roast on top of grill, insert meat thermometer, and cover smoker. Cook until thermometer reads 165 degrees, or to preferred degree of doneness.

Note: A crown roast must be ordered ahead of time. A most festive cut of meat, it lends itself to a large gathering or special occasion. Dilled sour cream, carrots with rosemary, tomatoes with basil, or spinach with pine nuts are excellent choices as accompanying dishes.

CHARCOALED LEG OF LAMB

10 to 12-pound leg of lamb
3 cups white wine
2 lemons, thinly sliced

1 tablespoon rosemary
1 tablespoon thyme

Place lamb in glass or plastic container. Blend wine, lemon slices, and herbs, and pour over lamb. Refrigerate 2 days, periodically turning leg to marinate entire surface.

Reserve marinade. Insert meat thermometer in fleshiest part of lamb. Cook in covered grill, turning every 15 to 30 minutes, until thermometer reads 165 degrees (or to preferred degree of doneness). Outside should be crusty, and inside pink and tender.

Cook marinade until reduced by half and serve as sauce. Serve lamb with new potatoes or rice, or with any side dish that will not shade its marvelous flavor.

Serves 8 to 10

PORK ADOBADO

1 4-ounce brick Achiote
   (made from annato seed)
Juice of fresh limes

3 to 5 pound Boston butt of
   pork, trimmed and fat
   reserved

Dissolve Achiote in enough juice to make thin paste. (The brick-red paste keeps the juices in the meat and imparts an earthy flavor with a subtle hint of garlic.) Deeply slash meat in crisscross pattern and generously cover with paste. Place in covered container and refrigerate 8 to 24 hours. Insert meat thermometer and cook 4 to 6 hours over charcoal fire using indirect method of smoking. (In rural Mexico, the meat is sometimes wrapped in a banana leaf and cooked underground.)

Note: Achiote is not easily found, except in the Southwest or in Yucatan, Mexico, but it is sometimes found in the Mexican section of specialty food stores. The paste is also good on chicken or grilled breakfast steaks.

Serves 8

MUSTARD-GARLIC PORK CHOPS

6 large center-cut pork chops,
  cut 1-inch thick
4 tablespoons unsalted butter

2 cloves garlic, pressed
Dijon mustard
White wine

Cut deep pocket in pork chop, slicing through middle of one edge.

Melt butter in pan, add pressed garlic, and cook 2 to 3 minutes over low heat. Set aside to cool. Insert 1 teaspoon each mustard and garlic butter in pocket of each chop, sealing edges with toothpick, and place chops in large baking dish. Drizzle with wine, leaving enough to cover bottom. Cover and chill 6 to 8 hours, turning chops at least once.

Grill each side of pork chop over open, hot fire 10 to 15 minutes.

Serves 6

BARBECUED HAM

1 picnic ham, skinned and
  trimmed, with fat reserved

Lay fat over hot coals. Score ham deeply with crisscross slashes and place on grill. Cook 6 to 8 hours, using the indirect method of smoking.

DIJON-LACED BEEF TENDER

2 cloves garlic, crushed
½ cup butter, melted
1 4-pound beef tenderloin

2 tablespoons Dijon mustard
2 cups red wine
Sour cream

Saute garlic in butter for 1 to 2 minutes. Slit beef two-thirds through lengthwise. Coat pocket with Dijon mustard, then with garlic butter. Tie beef with twine at 2-inch intervals and place in glass dish. Pour red wine over beef. Cover and chill overnight, turning at least once.

Remove from refrigerator at least 3 hours before grilling. Reserve wine marinade. Grill on four sides 5 minutes each or more, depending upon preferred doneness. While grilling beef, pour marinade into saucepan, reduce by half, and cool somewhat. Add sour cream to desired thickness. Serve warm, not hot, so that sour cream does not curdle.

Serves 10 to 14

BARBECUED SHRIMP

1 cup white wine
1 cup dry vermouth
½ cup brown sugar
2 tablespoons salt
2 teaspoons ground bay leaves
2 tablespoons oregano
2 tablespoons thyme
2 tablespoons rosemary
1 tablespoon poultry seasoning
6 cloves garlic, chopped
1 pound carrots, thinly sliced

12 tomatoes, peeled and
  chopped
8 green bell peppers, thinly
  sliced
6 onions, thinly sliced
8 ribs celery, thinly sliced
1 pound tiny fresh okra
2 cups Krinos Greek peppers
5 pounds unpeeled large shrimp
1 cup olive oil

Prepare grill with wet hickory chips over coals. In heavy saucepan, combine wines, brown sugar, and all seasonings, and blend well. Add all vegetables except okra and Greek peppers, cover, and bring to boil. Reduce heat and simmer 30 minutes over medium heat. Add okra, cover, and simmer 15 minutes. Add Greek peppers, cover, and remove from heat.

Divide and lay shrimp in two shallow baking pans. Pour ½ cup oil over each pan and stir to coat shrimp. Place pans on grill, close lid, and cook until shrimp are bright pink. Peel and stir into vegetable sauce mixture. Cool and chill overnight.

Heat in covered pan until boiling and serve with French bread.

Serves 8 to 10

ROMANIAN MITITEI

2 pounds lean ground beef
¼ cup beef stock or bouillon
2 teaspoons minced garlic
1½ teaspoons salt
½ teaspoon allspice

½ teaspoon ground cloves
¼ teaspoon dried thyme
¼ teaspoon coarsely ground
  pepper

Combine all ingredients and mix well with wooden fork. Form into cylinder-shaped sausages or into patties. Grill until crispy and brown. Great with PEPPERS IN OIL, feta cheese, and dill pickles.

Serves 6 to 8

Memphis in May's International Barbecue Contest

Some years back, composer Hoagy Carmichael wrote a song celebrating the justly acclaimed joys of *Memphis in June*. What people are celebrating these days, even though no one has written a song about it yet, is Memphis in May. Every year since 1977, during the city's month-long Memphis in May International Festival, Mid-Southerners and visitors from a selected foreign country enjoy together the sunny days, balmy nights, flowering greenery, and river breezes that make May such a special time in Memphis. They share other pleasures, too. The country being saluted each year—Japan, Canada, West Germany, Venezuela, Egypt, the Netherlands, Israel, Mexico, Australia, China, Great Britain, and Kenya have been among the nations honored—sends performing artists, special exhibits, and good-will ambassadors to Memphis to provide samplings of its culture, customs, foods, art, language, and history. Memphis, in turn, offers a city-wide series of home-flavored events for all to enjoy—children's programs; art exhibits; a sunset symphony; film festivals; all-day musicfests with rock groups, country-western bands, blues, jazz, and gospel artists; relay races and triathlons; even a Mississippi River canoe and kayak race. Most popular of all, perhaps, is the contest celebrating what is, without question, the city's most famous and most favored food—barbecue.

Memphis in May's International Barbecue Contest began without much fanfare in 1978, the festival's second year. It was held in a parking lot at Beale and Main with twenty-four entrants, and attracted about three thousand spectators. Today, Memphis in May's barbecue contest is billed as the world's largest. It is held at Tom Lee Park on the riverbluff, and is now limited to 175 cooking teams, representing businesses, groups, and individuals from Memphis, the Mid-South, and as far away as Canada or Ireland. Some eighty thousand spectators come by to watch the teams compete. Contestants are judged for culinary ability in preparing entries in three categories: whole hog, pork shoulder, and ribs. Memphis barbecue is always pork. They may also win awards for design of cooking edifices, originality of skits presented during the two-day contest, choice of costumes, even hog-calling skill.

In the days before the big contest weekend, tents, platforms, and pavilions are set up to house the cooking equipment—stoves ranging in complexity from old oil drums to pig-shaped cookers to elaborate ovens costing thousands of dollars. By Friday, Tom Lee Park is a village of barbecue pits, colorful tents, carefully wrought pavilions, and replicas of everything from ships to Japanese tea houses, all with appropriately costumed participants. When all-night cooking chores begin on Friday night, friends arrive to help contestants pass the time. The air is filled with the happy sounds of intermingling cookout parties, and the heavenly aroma of slowly roasting barbecue. On Saturday, more good times prevail as judges (and teams) spend the day sampling the results. That evening winners in all categories are announced, prizes totaling ten thousand dollars are awarded, and another chapter in the never-ending quest for a better barbecue, a perfect sauce, is over—until May in Memphis, next year.

THE PICTURE: *Barbecue is, undeniably, the first food of Memphis. It is also the centerpiece of one of the most popular events in the city's annual month-long Memphis in May International Festival—the annual barbecue-cooking contest held in Tom Lee Park on the banks of the Mississippi River. The cooking oven which has twice won for its owner the coveted grand championship trophy in Memphis in May's International Barbecue Contest is pictured here. His name is proudly engraved on its brass plate. A glimpse of one of the river's sandbars is visible beyond the cooking tent. On display in the foreground are the prize products of hours of careful cooking, so delectable-looking that a barbecue fancier can almost smell the fabled aroma.*

THE FOOD: *A pork shoulder, seasoned and browned by hours of slow cooking, sits on an old tree stump which travels with its owner wherever his barbecue is being judged, even, on one occasion, to Ireland. A rack of pork ribs rests on a pig-shaped cutting board once used to serve Julia Child her first taste of Memphis' famed barbecue. Baked beans and cole slaw, traditional accompaniments for barbecue, Memphis-style, are also offered.*

SOUTH-OF-THE-BORDER MARINADE FOR CHICKEN

1 cup orange juice	4 teaspoons cumin
1 cup tomato juice	4 teaspoons oregano
½ cup lime juice	2 teaspoons crushed red pepper
½ cup olive oil	8 teaspoons minced garlic
4 teaspoons paprika	Chicken pieces

Blend juices, oil, seasonings, and garlic. Pour over chicken pieces, turn to coat thoroughly, and place chicken in covered container. Marinate at room temperature if grilling within 6 hours; if not, refrigerate. Grill in closed charbroiler or on open grill.

Note: Meat may marinate 1 hour to 2 days beforehand. The marinade itself can be refrigerated for 3 days or frozen without losing its flavor.

Yields 3½ cups marinade

SMOKED CATFISH PÂTÉ

3 whole pond-raised catfish, skinned

Soak fish overnight in brine (¼ cup salt per 1 quart water).

Prepare coals in grill which has thermostat and lid. Place soaked hickory chips on hot coals. Put catfish on opposite end of grill and close lid. Monitor closed grill carefully to maintain 200 degree heat for 8 hours. Take fish from grill and discard darkest parts. (If using smoker rather than grill, use full pan of water and full pan of charcoal with 4 pieces water-soaked hickory chips. Smoke 8 hours.)

Pâté

2 cups boned grilled catfish	2 teaspoons chopped parsley
1 tablespoon lemon juice	1 8-ounce package cream cheese
1 tablespoon horseradish	½ onion, grated
¼ to ½ teaspoon salt	½ cup chopped pecans, optional

Briefly blend all ingredients in food processor. Shape into form of fish and chill overnight.

Sprinkle with pecans and serve with plain crackers.

Serves 6 to 8

SEPHARDIC SHASLYK

½ cup olive oil	2 pounds beef steak, cut in 1-inch cubes
2 tablespoons lemon juice	12 mushrooms
1½ tablespoons chopped parsley	3 tomatoes, sliced
1 teaspoon salt	3 onions, quartered
½ teaspoon pepper	2 bell peppers, cut in squares
2 cloves garlic, minced	

Combine olive oil, lemon juice, seasonings, and garlic, and blend well to make marinade. Add steak cubes and marinate overnight.

Just before cooking, remove meat, add vegetables, and stir gently to coat. Thread on skewers and grill. Best results may be obtained by combining items with similar cooking times rather than placing all on same skewer: mushrooms with tomatoes, and beef with onions and peppers. Food can then be attractively presented without undercooked meat or overcooked tomatoes.

Note: Serve with a dessert of mixed honeydew balls, green grapes, honey, and chopped fresh mint.

Serves 6 to 8

HOT POTATO SALAD

2 pounds potatoes, boiled, peeled, and sliced	4 slices bacon, fried crisp and crumbled, reserved drippings

Gently mix potatoes, bacon, and dressing with wooden fork. Salad keeps 1 week in refrigerator or all day and overnight in cooler on an outing.

Dressing

6 tablespoons Dusseldorf mustard	1 teaspoon salt
6 tablespoons beef consommé	½ bunch parsley leaves, minced
½ cup white wine vinegar	1 small onion, minced
¼ cup vegetable oil	Pepper to taste
2 teaspoons sugar	Bacon drippings

Mix all ingredients together with reserved bacon drippings, using wooden fork.

Serves 8

BARBECUED POTATOES

8 large potatoes, peeled
  and thinly sliced
1½ cups milk
1 cup grated cheese
¼ cup chopped onion
4 teaspoons catsup
4 teaspoons chopped parsley
1 tablespoon butter
½ teaspoon Worcestershire
  sauce
½ teaspoon salt
Dash pepper
Dash Tabasco sauce

Combine all ingredients in greased Dutch oven and mix. Cover and cook 1 hour over very low heat, or on one side of grill while cooking meat. Stir every 10 minutes.

Serves 6 to 8

BOLDINGS BEANS

1 pound dry pinto or black
  beans
Large meaty ham bone
2 large onions, chopped
1 teaspoon cayenne pepper
1 teaspoon ground coriander
½ teaspoon sage
½ teaspoon thyme
Salt and pepper

Soak beans in water for at least 6 hours. Drain.

While beans are soaking, cover ham bone with water in 3 to 5-quart Dutch oven and simmer until meat falls off. Remove bone. Add beans and remaining ingredients except salt and pepper. Simmer 1 hour or until done. Salt and pepper to taste and serve immediately.

Serves 6 to 8

SPRING ONIONS

1 bunch green onions

After removing main dish from grill, place onions on hot grill. Cook only until brown as overcooking tends to toughen onions.

Serves 2 to 4

ONIONS FIRST

3 large red onions, sliced
  paper-thin
1 lemon, sliced paper-thin
¼ cup vinegar
2 tablespoons lemon juice
1 teaspoon summer savory
½ teaspoon salt

Layer onions and lemon slices in serving dish. Combine remaining ingredients and pour over layers. Chill 8 hours, basting occasionally.

Note: Lemon tempers the onion flavor in this tangy relish. Try with fish, hamburgers, pork chops, or chicken.

Yield 2 cups relish

PEPPERS IN OIL

8 green bell peppers
Feta cheese, cubed
Greek olives
Scallions, sliced

Roast peppers on long fork over open fire, or broil halved peppers in oven until skin blisters. Immediately place peppers in covered dish or paper bag until cool, then peel and slice in 1-inch sections. Cover with marinade and let stand 5 hours. Drain and garnish with cheese, olives, and scallions.

Marinade
¾ cup olive oil
¾ cup wine vinegar
½ cup water
1 tablespoon paprika
1½ teaspoons salt
Black pepper to taste

Blend all ingredients well.

Serves 8

APPETIZER PEPPERS

1 16-ounce package sharp
  Cheddar cheese
1 bunch fresh cilantro
  with stems
1 teaspoon garlic salt
3 banana peppers per person,
  split and seeded

Combine cheese, cilantro, and salt in food processor, and blend. Stuff each pepper half and place on teflon baking sheet. Bake at 400 degrees until browned. Cool slightly before serving. (Makes a nice light luncheon dish, too.)

Yields 2 cups filling

Mr. and Mrs. William Browder

An Old-Fashioned Barbecue at Seven Hills Farm

If you leave downtown Memphis, cross the Wolf River and drive north through Frayser (a community originally settled by immigrant truck farmers, but now a busy urban residential neighborhood) until you come to the Loosahatchie River, you will find yourself on the doorstep of North Shelby County. That's the unofficial but enduring designation given to a wide expanse of land stretching north from the Loosahatchie to Tipton County, and east from the Mississippi River to Fayette County. North Shelby County has been called one of the Memphis area's best-kept secrets—a place long of memory, rich in history, and restful in pace.

Here, along the Third Chickasaw Bluff, you will find the vast fourteen-thousand-acre unspoiled wilderness of Meeman-Shelby Forest State Park, with its hiking and riding trails, its inviting cabins and campgrounds, its views of the great river, and its supply of deer, squirrel, and wild turkey, hunted in season by permit. One of the county's earliest settlements, Big Creek, was in North Shelby County. Here, too, are (or were) other old towns, some thriving, some found only on historical maps—places with colorful names like Cuba, Big Spring, Egypt, Rosemark, Jeter, Lucy. And here, amid the smaller communities, is the old and bustling township of Millington, which was once the home of Park Field, an Army base for training pilots in World War I. During the Depression, President Franklin D. Roosevelt considered dividing the land into forty-acre plots where sharecroppers could relocate and become landowners, but World War II intervened. In the early 1940s, it became the site of a permanent air training station for the United States Navy where, today, some twenty-two thousand sailors are regularly stationed. It is the country's largest naval base not located on water.

In the heart of this area lies Seven Hills Plantation, the oldest farm in Shelby County, continuously lived on since 1821 by five generations of the same family. Seven Hills is located on the two-thousand-acre land grant given in recognition of his military service to Revolutionary War veteran Andrew Rembert in 1789, when west Tennessee was still North Carolina territory. A cotton plantation in antebellum days, it later became a beef cattle farm; hay and forage crops are grown on its present-day three hundred acres. Rembert Place, the homestead begun by Andrew, was completed in 1845 by his versatile son, Samuel S. Rembert, a lover of classical literature, who named the plantation for the Seven Hills of Rome. (He also chose, from the works of Sir Walter Scott, the name for the nearby town of Woodstock.) A sometime author and inventor, Samuel's patents included one granted in 1850 for the first mechanical cotton picker (which he demonstrated but never manufactured), and another for a grain reaper.

At Seven Hills, time seems to have slowed down, paused for reflection. "A short distance away is a busy life," says Rembert H. Williams, Jr., Andrew Rembert's great-great-grandson, who is the current resident of Rembert Place. "But here—where the family has been, where the people who first owned the land are buried—it's another world." The sense of continuity that pervades a place like Seven Hills is experienced daily by Rembert Williams. He sleeps in the same bed in the same room where his grandmother was born and died, and where his father was born and died. (He tells his sister, who lives across the road, "When you get ready to die, get up and run across the street, because you know you have to die in *this* bed in *this* room.")

The home is filled with period pieces—fine old furniture, family portraits, framed memorabilia, and books, books, books. Indeed, Rembert Williams, in and of himself, is a fund of period information—a living storehouse of inherited memories: Stories of how

285

his mother's family moved to Shelby County from Brunswick County, Virginia, bringing with them a treasured recipe for Brunswick Stew which became a centerpiece of the big Fourth of July celebration and barbecue held yearly on the front lawn of Rembert Place, and attended by friends, neighbors, and kinfolk from miles around. (Traditionally, families migrating to west Tennessee from the Carolinas and Virginia in the early days formed groups to buy land together so their homes could be clustered—establishing that fabled Southern sense of "place" early on.) Tales of how his grandfather boated to Memphis in his sixty-five foot steamboat, which was moored on the Loosahatchie and burned three cords of wood a day. (Because of the lack of roads and bridges, much area travel in the early days was by skiff—on the Wolf, the Loosahatchie, the Mississippi, and, at one time, on Big Creek, a portion of which ran deep and wide through Seven Hills Plantation, with white sand and gravel on the banks.)

Today, in an era when most of the world seems to be moving in the fast lane, Seven Hills goes its own leisurely way. It remains a place for remembering the past—and celebrating the present. A family wedding for Rembert Williams' niece, his sister's child, was held on the front lawn of Rembert Place. An Oriental rug was laid on the grass in front of ancient magnolia trees. Wicker baskets of homegrown roses were everywhere, and tables were set up on the lawn for a champagne luncheon. A sixth generation was making new memories at Seven Hills.

BRUNSWICK STEW

In old Southern cook books, there is usually a recipe for Brunswick Stew—that legendary country concoction whose reputation has become sacrosanct with the years. It always included game of some sort, but a more up-to-date recipe will simply substitute chicken or beef, or both. There probably could not be a better description of the old-time stew than the one that follows as told by Rembert Williams. Perhaps after reading it, you may be inspired to stir up your own version—with or without squirrel.

It was brought by my great-grandparents from Brunswick County, Virginia, to Shelby County, Tennessee, in 1840. This has been handed down to each generation up to the present time. It is necessary to have a large black iron pot or kettle (the kind that was used for boiling clothes and making lard). It is necessary to swing this pot with a chain so it is somewhat six to eight inches above the ground in order that the fire will not be too close under the bottom and cause the stew to stick. It must be cooked anywhere from six to eight hours very slow.

First thing you must do is put some water in the pot and then you put your meat in. It was always a custom to kill a big fat hen or rooster and then, if you had some frying chickens, you could put some of those in there, too, and then a nice piece of fat beef. And then we used to go to the smokehouse and get a little strip of bacon. We put all this in the pot and cooked it until the chicken came off the bones. Then we took the bones out and added the vegetables, fresh butter beans (small and green), a few carrots, potatoes (cut very small), onions, and, of course, corn, but the corn wasn't put in until the stew was almost done. The base of it was tomatoes and you put more tomatoes than anything else.

There were other people in the community that used to have community stew and some people would bring beans, peas or cabbage. But my grandfather was very particular. He would not let them put any of this in because this was not true Brunswick stew that he had been used to. But some people still put that in it. There was one old man that always brought cabbage and there was always a big argument whether to put that cabbage into the stew or not. My grandfather always won 'cause he was generally the main one that supposedly knew more about it.

Also, it was not considered Brunswick Stew unless it had a couple of young squirrels, that had just been killed, put in there. My mother didn't like the squirrels because they had such tiny bones and when they were cooked up they were hard to pick out. Also, sometimes if they thought it didn't have enough fat they would put a little country butter in it to add a little flavor. Then they seasoned it with salt and pepper, to the taste, of course. Some liked it hotter than others, but then again, my grandfather didn't let them make it hotter because of the little children that were going to eat it.

Now the trouble of making Brunswick Stew is that it has to be stirred constantly and you have a stirring pattern as it bubbles along. You have to keep bringing it up from the bottom and keeping it turned over so it will not stick and someone has to stand there and do this until it is cooked. If it begins to get too thick and you want to cook more, then you continually add more water to it.

It is done when all the vegetables have cooked up so the meat looks like splinters and the tomatoes are all cooked up. Sometimes the butter beans were still together but nothing else. It was all cooked to pieces. Then you put the corn in last. When we had Brunswick Stew we always had crackers to eat with it and for dessert we had watermelon.

COUNTRY BARBECUE SAUCE

From a home in southwest Shelby County where hogs are raised and still used in the old way—cured ham, sausage, ribs, souse, lard, cracklings (those crisp bits that are left over when the fat is rendered into lard, and then go into that Southern corn bread called "cracklin' bread") and barbecue with its special sauce.

1 cup butter	1 24-ounce bottle catsup
1 medium onion, chopped	1 24-ounce can tomato juice
1 green bell pepper, chopped	1 6-ounce can tomato paste
1 rib celery with leaves, chopped	1½ cups white vinegar
	¾ cup brown or white sugar
3 cloves garlic, chopped	Salt to taste
1 tablespoon pinched fresh sage	1 cup bourbon whiskey
	Juice and rind of 3 lemons

Melt butter in large heavy saucepan. Add onion, bell pepper, celery, garlic, and sage, and cook until vegetables are lightly browned. Add catsup, tomato juice, tomato paste, vinegar, sugar, and salt, and simmer 2 to 3 hours over medium-low heat until thickened. About 30 minutes before completion of cooking time add bourbon, lemon juice, and lemon rind.

Yields 2 quarts sauce

Mrs. Oneitha Roane

WILLOW LAKE FARM BARBECUE SAUCE

Barbecues were the favorite form of entertainment for the Jeter family when at their farm in North Shelby County. Many friends from the cotton business on Front Street fished at Willow Lake and feasted on barbecued pork—often a whole hog—which was marinated and then cooked on a grill over a pit dug beside one of the cabins at the farm. The meat was cooked from late afternoon all through the night. The sauce was made by Mrs. Jeter in quantities to last throughout the year—and in her words, made "by taste and smell and how it looks, and stored in a cool place." Here is a scaled-down version of her recipe.

2 tablespoons dry mustard	2 cups catsup
2 teaspoons allspice	1 5-ounce bottle Worcester-
2 teaspoons paprika	shire sauce
2 teaspoons cayenne pepper	7 tablespoons prepared
2 teaspoons black pepper	horseradish
½ cup vegetable oil	¼ cup dark brown sugar
1 cup vinegar	

Dissolve spices in oil. Combine vinegar, catsup, Worcestershire sauce, horseradish, and sugar, and mix well. Stir in spice mixture. Add more vinegar for sharper, thinner sauce.

Yields 4 cups sauce

Mrs. J. Stovall Jeter

NEWBERRY COUNTY BARBECUE SAUCE

Different from Memphis sauces, this old family recipe is an excellent example of mustard-based sauces from the South Carolina midlands. Excellent on chicken.

1 cup butter, melted	1 tablespoon Worcestershire
Juice of 1 lemon	sauce
5 tablespoons prepared	1 tablespoon sugar
yellow mustard	Salt and pepper to taste
1 tablespoon white vinegar	

Stir all ingredients in small saucepan over low heat until well-blended to make sauce. Baste chicken or pork while cooking on grill or use on smoked turkey. Provide bottle of warm sauce to pour over meat when served, if desired.

Yields 1⅔ cups sauce

Dr. Richard Crooks
Greenville, South Carolina

THE INCOMPARABLE PICNIC

Memphians love picnics. Whether it be a duet for lovers or a family celebration at the campground, a picnic is a traditional way of sharing good food and friendship. And Memphians seem to have a way of making any picnic an enchanted occasion. It may be a child's outing in the park with hot dogs, or peanut butter and jelly sandwiches served from a paper sack, fried chicken served in The Grove at Ole Miss on a football weekend, thinly sliced tenderloin of beef on a croissant enjoyed on the green lawn of the Dixon Gardens and Gallery at a Sunday afternoon concert, or baked ham and new potato salad for the neighbors, on the picnic table in your own back yard. Whatever the outdoor fare, wherever the location, a picnic means a vacation from the kitchen, a time away from everyday cares and concerns. It represents a return to a kind of freedom we all seem to yearn for, seem dimly to recollect—that uncomplicated childhood freedom of long ago.

A PICNIC IS A PLEASURE PARTY

by Craig Claiborne

Most people think the word picnic is as American as clam chowder or corn on the cob, but it is believed by many linguists to be as French as fresh croissants. It derives from the French words *pique*, which means to pick, and *nique*, a small thing or trifle.

My preferred interpretation of the word can be found in the Oxford English Dictionary. Here's how that venerable volume defines a picnic: Originally, a fashionable social entertainment in which each person present contributed a share of the provisions; now, a pleasure party including an excursion to some spot in the country where all partake of a repast out-of-doors; the participants may bring with them individually the viands and means of entertainment, or the whole may be provided by someone who "gives a picnic."

I dote on being that person—always have since my childhood. We would have Sunday afternoon picnics in those days at a small lake near my birthplace of Sunflower, Mississippi, where we would gather and munch on barbecued chicken or spareribs, plus fresh-caught catfish that would be cooked on the spot in the open air.

Now that I live in East Hampton, New York, on Long Island, I frequently give picnics for special friends on a remote beach, at picnic areas near the lighthouse at Montauk Point a few miles distant, or simply on my own lawn. Wherever the portable feast, I always provide, in addition to the food hampers full of one or more tablecloths, real china for the food and real crystal for whatever the beverage, be it wine or iced tea.

The food is served as sunset approaches, and may vary from fried chicken to assorted pâtés, barbecued spareribs to lobster salad. Almost invariably, however, my picnics include stuffed eggs, the flavorings depending on the mood of the moment, a well-chilled white wine, and plenty of napkins.

Then comes the moment at the end of dusk when dishes *et cetera* are carefully packaged and we depart, taking care that there is not one crust of bread left behind to betray our presence.

Here are two recipes culled at random from recent gatherings on the beach or wherever.

Anchovy Stuffed Eggs
Cucumbers Swedish-Style

Craig Claiborne

ANCHOVY-STUFFED EGGS

6 large eggs, room temperature	Freshly ground black pepper to taste
3 tablespoons butter, softened	1 to 2 tablespoons anchovy
1 tablespoon mayonnaise	paste or finely chopped
1 tablespoon minced chives	unstuffed anchovies
Salt to taste	Anchovy fillets, optional

Cover eggs with cold water, bring to boil, and simmer 15 minutes. Immediately cool under cold running water. Peel and halve eggs, separating yolks from whites. Press yolks through sieve, blend with all other ingredients except anchovy fillets, and stuff egg whites. Garnish with anchovy fillets.

Serves 4 to 6

CUCUMBERS SWEDISH-STYLE

1 pound cucumbers, peeled	2 tablespoons finely chopped
6 tablespoons water	parsley
3 tablespoons white vinegar	Freshly ground black pepper
3 tablespoons sugar	to taste
Salt to taste	

Cut cucumbers in half lengthwise and, if desired, scrape out seeds. Cut halves crosswise in very thin slices to make about 2½ cups. Place in mixing bowl. Bring water, vinegar, sugar, and salt to boil in saucepan, stirring until sugar dissolves. Pour over cucumbers, cool, and chill. Drain, and serve sprinkled with parsley and pepper.

Serves 4 to 6

PICNIC PARTICULARS

Half the fun of a picnic is in the planning. Here are some recommendations for preparing and packing your feast:

The picnic basket: Invest in a good one. Size should be a major consideration. Select one large enough to carry the majority of your gear, yet not so large or heavy that it becomes cumbersome. Wicker is particularly nice and sturdy, and many styles are available, some with fitted appointments and some plain, waiting for your own pretty things.

Food containers and serving dishes: Plastic covered containers are another good investment. Lightweight, they can serve as both food containers and serving dishes. Purchase insulated carryalls for your hot/cold foods and beverages. Good quality plastic utensils are a must. (What a pity to have a plastic fork break at the neck as it plunges into a tasty morsel of cold, marinated chicken!) Very colorful and attractive dishes and glasses are available also in paper and plastic. But remember how lovely your china and glassware will look with sunlight—or sunset—upon them.

Picnic checklist: Don't forget: Bottle opener, insect repellent, cork screw, trash bag, small paring knife, handi-wipes, salt and pepper, matches. And what about binoculars and a birder's field guide, a wildflower book, and a camera for capturing the day?

Food preparation: Remember some common-sense rules for health and safety. Keep foods such as custards, meat salads, egg or potato salads, and moist sandwiches chilled (or, if the food so dictates, piping hot) to prevent growth of bacteria that can cause food-poisoning. Do not allow these foods to remain at room temperature for more than four hours. Chill thoroughly such cooked foods as fried chicken, baked ham, meat loaf, and fried fish before putting them in the picnic hamper or, better yet, into a cooler, if the food will not be eaten for several hours. For hot service, heat over the grill at the picnic site.

Picnic decor: Let your imagination run with the wind. That favorite quilt covering the bed in the guest room will make a delightful spread cloth for your feast. (You may want to place it over a plastic drop cloth to prevent grass stains.) Color-coordinate bright cotton napkins or use heavy-duty paper ones. And don't forget the flowers. If the garden is void of posies, pick up a pot of geraniums at a garden center or supermarket on the way out of town.

If one rule governs your moveable feast, consider this: Make it rich and keep it simple!

The Picnic Committee

The following recipes, unless otherwise noted, are from the collection of each picnic menu contributor.

TAILGATE PICNIC FOR A CRISP FALL DAY

"If this is fall, it must be football." And when Memphis State has a home game or when Ole Miss or UT is in town, it's party-time down South. Just pack your picnic, gather your friends, and head for Liberty Bowl Memorial Stadium. Go early, get a good parking place, and start the "play" before the game. No referees needed. Everyone knows the rules.

Hot Buttered Tomato Juice
Cheese-Stuffed Sourdough Bread*
Bourbon Marinated Ribs*
Can-Do Beans*   *Kraut Salad*
Crunchy Dill Pickles
Home Baked Bread*
The Best Chocolate Cake

*See Index   Anne Threefoot

HOT BUTTERED TOMATO JUICE

1 46-ounce can tomato juice	2 tablespoons butter
2 10½-ounce cans beef stock	1 teaspoon prepared mustard
1¼ cups water	½ teaspoon Tabasco sauce
2 teaspoons Worcestershire sauce	Lemon wedges

Combine all ingredients except lemon wedges and bring to boil, stirring to blend. Pour into insulated container. Serve in mugs with lemon wedges for garnish.

Yields 2 quarts juice

THE BEST CHOCOLATE CAKE

2 cups all-purpose flour	½ cup buttermilk
2 cups sugar	2 eggs
1 cup hot water	1 teaspoon cinnamon
½ to ¾ cup cocoa	1 teaspoon baking soda
½ cup butter	1 teaspoon vanilla
½ cup margarine	½ teaspoon salt

Sift together flour and sugar. Combine water, cocoa, butter, and margarine in heavy saucepan, and bring to boil. Stir into flour mixture. Mix in buttermilk, eggs, cinnamon, baking soda, vanilla, and salt. Pour into ungreased 9 x 13-inch baking pan and smooth to sides. Bake 35 to 40 minutes at 375 degrees. Remove from oven and immediately pour warm frosting over top. Cool in pan.

Frosting

½ cup margarine	1 16-ounce box confectioners' sugar, sifted
6 tablespoons milk or coffee	1 cup chopped pecans
¼ cup cocoa	
1 teaspoon vanilla	

Combine margarine, milk, and cocoa, and bring to rolling boil. Remove from heat and stir in vanilla, confectioners' sugar, and nuts.

Note: Certified chocolate lovers may already have this recipe with minor variations. However, it is so good that we dare not risk letting someone miss it.

Serves 12 to 15

Mrs. A. Claude Holt

KRAUT SALAD

1 16-ounce can chopped sauerkraut, drained	1 cup sliced celery
1 cup sliced onion	½ cup diced green bell pepper
	1 2-ounce jar chopped pimiento

Mix all ingredients together. Stir in marinade and refrigerate overnight in covered container.

Marinade

¾ cup sugar	Dash red pepper
½ cup vegetable oil	Salt and black pepper to taste
¼ cup vinegar	

Combine all ingredients and mix well.

Serves 8

GOOD OL' POTATO SALAD

8 large potatoes, cooked,
  peeled, and diced
6 hard-cooked eggs, chopped
2 onions, chopped
1 green bell pepper, chopped
½ cup chopped celery

½ to ¾ cup sweet pickle relish,
  drained
½ cup chopped stuffed olives
1 tablespoon prepared mustard
Mayonnaise as needed

Combine potatoes, eggs, onions, bell pepper, celery, pickle relish, and olives. Mix mustard with mayonnaise and stir gently into salad.

Serves 10 to 12

BANANA NUT CAKE
WITH PRALINE FROSTING

⅔ cup butter, softened
2 cups sugar
3 eggs
2¼ cups sifted all-purpose
  flour
1 teaspoon baking soda

½ teaspoon baking powder
¼ teaspoon salt
⅓ cup buttermilk or cream
3 mashed ripe bananas
1 teaspoon vanilla
¾ cup chopped pecans

Cream butter with sugar, gradually adding sugar. Stir in eggs one at a time, beating well after each addition. Sift together flour, baking soda, baking powder, and salt. Alternately add flour mixture and buttermilk. Fold in bananas and vanilla. Stir in pecans. Pour into two 9-inch cake pans lined on bottom with wax paper. Bake 25 to 35 minutes at 375 degrees. Cool and frost.

Praline Frosting
1 cup light brown sugar
¼ cup milk
3 tablespoons vegetable
  shortening

2 tablespoons butter
1 cup sifted confectioners'
  sugar
1 cup finely chopped pecans

Combine brown sugar, milk, shortening, and butter. Bring to boil and cook 3 minutes. Remove from heat and stir in confectioners' sugar, beating until smooth. Add pecans and spread while warm. (Frosting can be thinned with a few drops of milk.)

Note: It is a fact that this cake is so good that it once brought forth a proposal of marriage. Matchmakers, take heed!

Serves 8 to 12

PICNIC AT PICKWICK LAKE

Pickwick Lake, at Pickwick Landing State Park, two pleasant hours east of Memphis on Highway 57, is a year-round getaway place for scores of Memphians whose vacation sites may be either lakeside in the form of cottages or waterborne in the form of houseboats or sailboats. The area was named for *Pickwick Papers* by the local postmaster in the early 1930s, Dickens being his favorite author. This lovely 600-acre state park, only 20 minutes away from the historic site of the Battle of Shiloh, offers good fishing, well-kept marinas for all kinds of water sports, and a delightful inn with great fried catfish. Entertaining at Pickwick is easy-going, and any reason is a good one for a no-trouble-at-all picnic, whether for a few city friends, for whom some neighbors may add their boats or pontoons for enjoying the water and sun, or just for family. And if it rains? No problem—just move the picnic to the porch for games, dancing, or just enjoying present company. The menu will be flexible, but will generally include tried and true favorites.

Barbecued Chicken
Fried Tennessee River Catfish Nuggets
with Tartar Sauce*
Baked Beans   *Everyone's Favorite Coleslaw*
Good Ol' Potato Salad   *Sliced Tomatoes*
Banana Nut Cake with Praline Frosting

*See Index

Mrs. Baxter Southern

EVERYONE'S FAVORITE COLESLAW

1 small head cabbage, shredded
1 bunch green onions with
  tops, chopped
2 carrots, grated
½ cup mayonnaise

¼ cup sour cream
2 tablespoons sugar
½ teaspoon salt
⅛ teaspoon pepper
Green bell pepper rings

Toss cabbage with onions, and carrots. Combine mayonnaise, sour cream, sugar, salt, and pepper. Add to vegetables and fold until well-coated. Refrigerate 2 to 3 hours, stirring occasionally to insure good mixing of vegetables and dressing. Serve garnished with bell pepper rings.

Serves 8 to 10

Jo Anne Rossner

PORCH PARTY AT MONTEAGLE, TENNESSEE

Monteagle, nestled in the mountain greenery of the Cumberlands near the University of the South at Sewanee, was begun in 1882 as the Monteagle Sunday School Assembly of the Methodist Church. It was patterned after the Chatauqua Institute in New York with its educational, cultural, entertainment, and religious programs. Memphians and Mid-Southerners have been meeting there for 107 years in family cottages with rambling rooms, inviting porches with swings and wicker rocking chairs, and wide-open windows which welcome the mountain air. It is in the best sense a summer place, where life slows down and actually appears to take a step back in time to some remembered place where everyone seemed to keep a simpler, different pace. There's activity enough for all—lectures, tennis, musicales, old fashioned games, and always twilight prayers. One of the most popular pastimes in Monteagle is the porch party, an informal get-together meant for visiting, exchanging news of the day, and, in general, sharing laughter and good times.

Cocktail Cake
Crab Meat Loaf
Finger Sandwiches
Curried Dip with Fresh Vegetables
Pecan Cheese Straws*
Olives and Potato Chips

*See Index

Mrs. John R. Pepper II

COCKTAIL CAKE

1 round loaf bread
1 cup ground ham
1 cup grated cheese of choice
1 cup grated hard-cooked eggs
1 cup grated carrots
½ cup minced onion
Mayonnaise
1 8-ounce package cream cheese, softened
Milk
Worcestershire sauce to taste
Pimiento strips
Sliced olives

Trim crust from bread and slice in 3 to 5 round layers. Mix ham, cheese, eggs, carrots, and onions with enough mayonnaise for spreading consistency. Spread layers with equal portions of mixture and stack like a cake. Blend cream cheese with small amount milk for spreading consistency. Add Worcestershire sauce and frost cake with mixture. Garnish with pimientos and olives arranged in pretty design. Add candles if there's a birthday!

Serves 12

CURRIED DIP

1 cup Hellmann's mayonnaise
2 teaspoons grated onion
1 teaspoon curry powder
1 teaspoon garlic salt
1 teaspoon prepared horseradish
1 teaspoon vinegar

Combine all ingredients, mix well, and chill at least 6 hours before serving.

Yields 1 cup dip

CRAB MEAT LOAF

1 10¾-ounce can cream of mushroom soup
1 tablespoon unflavored gelatin
3 tablespoons water
1 8-ounce package cream cheese, softened
1 cup mayonnaise
1 6½-ounce can crab meat
1 bunch green onions, finely chopped
1 cup chopped celery
1 tablespoon lemon juice

Heat soup. Dissolve gelatin in water, add to soup, and cool slightly. Blend cream cheese with mayonnaise and add to soup. Stir in crab meat, onions, celery, and lemon juice. Pour into oiled 5 to 6-cup mold and chill overnight or until firm. Serve with HOMEMADE MELBA TOAST.

Serves 8 to 10

ARTICHOKE HEARTS WITH CAVIAR

1 8-ounce package cream cheese, softened	1 8½-ounce jar artichoke hearts, drained and chopped
2 tablespoons sour cream	2 teaspoons grated onion
2 teaspoons mayonnaise	Dash garlic salt
1 teaspoon lemon juice	1 3-ounce jar caviar, drained

Blend cream cheese, sour cream, mayonnaise, and lemon juice. Add artichokes, onion, and garlic salt. Shape mixture into mound, flatten slightly, and spread caviar on top. Serve with favorite crackers.

Serves 8

ARMENIAN BEAN SALAD

2 cups dried navy beans	1 bunch parsley, chopped
¼ to ½ cup olive oil	Lemon juice to taste
2 to 3 large onions, chopped	Salt and pepper to taste

Cover beans with water and cook until tender but still firm. Drain and immediately rinse with cold water. Place in bowl, add olive oil, and toss very gently. Add onions, parsley, lemon juice, salt, and pepper, and gently toss again. Cover and chill several hours before serving.

Serves 8 to 10

Kallen Esperian Machen

PASTA SALAD WITH SALMON

1 8-ounce package shell macaroni, cooked	2 tablespoons chopped onion
1 16-ounce can red salmon, drained, boned, and skinned	2 tablespoons chopped pimiento
2 hard-cooked eggs, chopped	2 tablespoons sugar
½ cup chopped pickles	2 tablespoons vinegar
½ cup chopped celery	½ cup mayonnaise
	Salt and pepper to taste

Combine macaroni, salmon, eggs, pickles, celery, onion, and pimiento. Blend sugar, vinegar, and mayonnaise, and pour over salad. Season with salt and pepper, and toss gently but thoroughly. Chill before serving.

Serves 6

┌─────────────────────────────────────┐
│   │

POOLSIDE
ON A WARM EVENING

"Summertime, and the livin' is easy..." Hot summer nights are the perfect setting for a casual gathering beside the pool. Nothing is hurried, the company is always good, and the mood is right for lingering.

Artichoke Hearts with Caviar
Assorted Crackers
Pasta Salad with Salmon
Armenian Bean Salad
Almond Squares

The Picnic Committee

ALMOND SQUARES

½ cup butter, softened	½ teaspoon salt
½ cup sugar	Grated rind of 1 lemon
1 cup all-purpose flour	

Cream butter with sugar until light and fluffy. Add remaining ingredients and mix thoroughly. Spread in greased 7 x 11-inch baking pan and bake 10 minutes at 375 degrees. Cover with hot topping and bake 15 minutes more. Chill and cut in squares.

Topping

½ cup butter	½ cup sugar
1 cup almond chips	½ cup heavy cream

Melt butter in heavy saucepan. Add almonds and sugar, and cook 3 minutes over medium heat, stirring constantly. Add cream and bring to boil. Remove from heat.

Yields about 6 dozen squares

Mrs. Jimmy Haskins
Union City, Tennessee

A Gourmet Picnic at the Sunset Symphony

For more than a decade, Memphis has been restructuring its skyline with new buildings, revitalizing its downtown with new businesses, and repopulating its riverbluff with new residents. What is happening here, some say, may be nothing less than a well-timed resurgence of that most basic of Memphis urges—to gather at the river. There is one celebration that invites all of Memphis to do just that. It is the Memphis Symphony Orchestra's annual Sunset Symphony, held in Tom Lee Park down by the riverside on the last Saturday night in May. This outdoor concert, the grand finale of the month-long Memphis in May International Festival, is rapidly becoming a hardy Memphis tradition, surrounded by rituals that have developed spontaneously. For one thing, just about everybody who shows up brings along food and drink, making the Sunset Symphony one grand community picnic. For another, the audience demands that certain favorite musical numbers be included in the concert year after year.

The fact that the Sunset Symphony takes place in Tom Lee Park receives no particular notice during the evening's festivities, but the setting gives the concert special meaning for Mississippi River buffs. This park honors a black river worker who was on the scene in his small motorboat, around dusk on the afternoon of May 8, 1925, when an overloaded excursion steamer, returning to the city, capsized and sank some twenty miles below Memphis. With no other help at hand, Tom Lee single-handedly saved thirty-two lives. He pulled the struggling swimmers from the deep, swiftly moving currents one by one, and ferried them to the nearest sandbar, a feat made more remarkable because he himself could not swim. The last person Tom Lee was able to save on that fateful evening was a young Memphis woman named Margaret Oates, who had stayed afloat by clinging to her parasol—she had managed to pop it open, trapping a pocket of air beneath it. Some years later, when the city renamed Astor Park at the foot of Beale Street in Tom Lee's honor, a thirty-two foot granite obelisk was erected there as a memorial to him. The monument's inscription, after recounting Lee's heroism, concludes with heartfelt words: "His good deeds were scattered everywhere that day and into eternity." Listed as a donor, one of "the grateful people of Memphis" perpetuating the memory of Tom Lee is Hugo Dixon, who had met and married Margaret Oates the year after her dramatic rescue. Perhaps today's Dixon Gallery and Gardens, the home and art collection the Dixons together bequeathed to the city in 1974, should be counted as part of that ripple effect—one of the scattered and ongoing good deeds that seem somehow to have resulted from Tom Lee's bravery.

In recent years, the Sunset Symphony audience has numbered as many as two hundred thousand. Many arrive early to claim choice places, and Tom Lee Park soon fills with crowds sitting on blankets spread on the grass; other people perch on the river embankment above the park, lean from the windows of nearby office buildings, crowd the balconies and terraces of new riverfront condominiums. As they wait for the music, they spread their feasts—some simple, some elaborate. The scene becomes a delightful hodgepodge of silver candelabra and plastic ice chests, elegant linens and simple vinyl tablecloths, bottles of fine wines and cans of beer. To the west, the sky's brilliant hues change dramatically, moment by moment, as the sun sinks below the horizon, beyond the fields and trees of the river's floodplain in Arkansas—one of the grandest sights along the length of this mighty river. The musicians, dressed in white formal jackets and colorful pastel evening gowns, take their places on the platform at the bluff's edge. Cool breezes blow, and the last sparkling reflections of the setting sun dance across the river's

THE PICTURE: *Memphis is a picnic place. Memphians picnic wherever and whenever the mood strikes, the weather permits, and the occasion demands—in their own back yards, on the picnic grounds of the city's many parks, on tailgates in football stadium parking lots. Or, as in the case here, on the bluffs above the Mississippi River, listening to the Sunset Symphony held in Tom Lee Park each year to mark the end of the Memphis in May International Festival. The elegant picnic pictured here, one of hundreds being served on the bluff this day, is presented from a wicker basket and served on wicker plates. A silver wine cooler and fluted wine glasses furnish suitably festive touches. The embroidered linen cloth, a family treasure, is a reminder of picnics past. A small basketful of Queen Anne's lace bravely holds its own in the heat of the day.*

THE FOOD: *A wicker serving tray holds chilled fresh pineapple spears, green grapes, and luscious red strawberries, with accompaniments of sour cream and brown sugar. Other delights include BLENDED CHEESE MOLD, and a CURRIED PÂTÉ WITH COGNAC. Glass mugs of COLD ZUCCHINI SOUP are offered, along with CUCUMBER ROUNDS WITH CHICKEN SALAD, and delicate ham sandwiches on Dijon bread.*

flowing waters. Dusk comes in a rush; candles are lit; a baby's cry is heard in the distance, as the conductor raises his baton.

For the next two hours, the music echoes through all of downtown. On the riverbank, there is more laughter, more food, more conviviality. A familiar melody brings smiles; with another, voices sing along; couples hold hands as they sway to the rhythms. Then, at last, the essential moment arrives: The sound of *Ol' Man River* fills the air, sung just the right way, (by James Hyter, one of the city's favorite soloists), at exactly the right place, on the banks of the Mississippi. As the deep bass voice descends to the definitive low note of this popular classic ("... and you'll land in ja-a-a-il"), the crowd goes wild, applauding, cheering. Encores are demanded again and again, until, eventually, consensus is reached that the orchestra can proceed to its final selection of the evening—another all-time favorite, Tchaikovsky's *1812 Overture.* The familiar music swells to the awaited climax. The sounds of clashing cymbals and a booming cannon (from the U. S. Naval Air Station at nearby Millington, Tennessee) bring forth a brilliant explosion of fireworks in the night sky above the river, continuing for some minutes after the music ends. Then the last burst fades into darkness. The crowds gather their blankets and baskets, and turn toward home. The concert's enchantment, the festival's excitement, have ended for another year. But the river, Ol' Man River—he just keeps rollin' along.

COLD ZUCCHINI SOUP

You will simply love this soup.

1½ to 2 tablespoons finely
  chopped green onions
1 clove garlic, minced
3 tablespoons butter
1 pound zucchini, unpeeled
  and sliced in thin rounds

2 cups heavy cream
1 cup chicken stock
1 teaspoon salt or to taste
½ teaspoon curry powder
Green onion tops, finely
  chopped for garnish

Sauté onions and garlic in 1 tablespoon butter, and set aside. Simmer zucchini in 2 tablespoons butter for 10 minutes. Blend with onion mixture in food processor. Add cream and remaining ingredients, and blend well (may have to mix in two portions, depending on size of processor). Serve cold, garnished with sprinkle of onion tops.

Chicken Stock
1 chicken
2 leeks, chopped
1 onion, quartered

Minced fresh parsley to taste
Salt and pepper to taste

Cover chicken with water and add remaining ingredients. Bring to boil, reduce heat, and simmer 40 to 45 minutes. Remove and bone chicken, reserving meat for other uses. Strain stock and chill.

Serves 6 to 8

A Matter of Taste Restaurant
Nina Hammond Tayloe, Proprietor

BLENDED CHEESE MOLD

All excellent blend of tastes.

Stuffed olives, sliced
Pimiento strips
3 8-ounce cartons cottage
  cheese, drained well
1 pound sharp Cheddar
  cheese, grated

4 ounces blue cheese,
  crumbled
1 medium onion, grated
5½ tablespoons butter, melted
Salt and pepper to taste

Decoratively arrange olives and pimientos in bottom of buttered 5 to 6-cup mold. Combine remaining ingredients, mix well with hands, and press firmly into mold. Chill at least 12 hours or overnight. Serve with crackers or HOMEMADE MELBA TOAST.

Serves 20

Anne Threefoot

CURRIED PÂTÉ WITH COGNAC

Elegant and extra-good.

1 pound chicken livers
1 medium onion, chopped
4 tablespoons butter
¾ cup chicken broth,
  heated slightly
2 tablespoons cognac

1 tablespoon Worcestershire
  sauce
½ teaspoon paprika
½ teaspoon curry powder
½ teaspoon salt
⅛ teaspoon pepper

Sauté livers and onion in butter until lightly browned. Add ½ cup warm broth and simmer gently until livers are done. Place in blender with cognac, Worcestershire sauce, and seasonings, and blend 15 seconds at high speed. Add more broth if needed and blend until smooth. Pour into mold and chill until firm. Serve with Melba toast or crackers.

Serves 10 to 12

Mary Weymouth

CUCUMBER ROUNDS
WITH CHICKEN SALAD

Just the best little things.

2 cucumbers
1 large chicken breast, cooked,
  boned, and finely chopped
1 hard-cooked egg, finely
  chopped
Mayonnaise to moisten

2 tablespoons chopped fresh
  parsley
Salt and pepper to taste
Sandwich bread
Fresh parsley sprigs, optional

Slice ends from cucumbers, remove seeds with apple corer, and peel in strips for striated effect. Combine chicken, egg, mayonnaise, parsley, salt, and pepper, and fill hollowed cucumbers. Wrap in plastic wrap and chill 2 to 3 hours or overnight. Cut 26 rounds from bread slices with small cookie cutter and spread with mayonnaise. Cut stuffed cucumbers in ¼-inch slices and place on bread rounds. Garnish with parsley.

Yields 26 rounds

Mrs. Richard T. Ashman

PICNIC IN THE GROVE AT OXFORD

A short drive south from Memphis—just "down the road a piece"—will bring you to the University of Mississippi (Ole Miss) in the historic town of Oxford, the home of William Faulkner and a second home to many Memphians. Tailgating at Ole Miss is the great tradition identified with every home football game. It means parking in The Grove among the stately oaks—older than the institution itself—which stand sentinel over the center of the campus, offering a cathedral canopy of leafy shade. It means picnicking from the trunk of the car, a spirit of camaraderie, and that unique bond of loyalty so characteristic of the Ole Miss family.

Creamy Cucumber Soup
Southern Fried Chicken*
French Green Bean Salad
Deviled Eggs   Tomato Slices
Homemade Mayonnaise
Southern Style Loaf Bread
Pecan Tassies

Mr. and Mrs. Martin Michael
Coldwater, Mississippi

*See Index

SOUTHERN STYLE LOAF BREAD

1 cup boiling water	1 egg
1 cup vegetable shortening	1 package yeast
1 cup sugar	1 cup lukewarm water
1 teaspoon salt	6 cups self-rising flour

Stir together boiling water, shortening, sugar, salt, and egg, and set aside to cool slightly. Dissolve yeast in lukewarm water and add to egg mixture. Add flour 1 cup at a time, stirring well after each addition. Chill overnight in greased airtight container.

Put dough in two greased loaf pans and let rise several hours. Bake 40 minutes at 325 degrees.

Yields 2 loaves

CREAMY CUCUMBER SOUP

2 10¾-ounce cans cream of celery soup	2 small cucumbers, chopped
2 cups milk	½ cup sliced stuffed olives
2 small green bell peppers, chopped	2 cups sour cream
	2 tablespoons lemon juice
	Thin cucumber slices, optional

Combine soup, milk, bell peppers, cucumbers, and olives in blender, and process 2 minutes. Remove from blender, stir in sour cream and lemon juice, and chill at least 4 hours. Garnish with cucumber slices.

Serves 10 to 12

FRENCH GREEN BEAN SALAD

1 16-ounce can French-style green beans, drained	1 small onion, chopped
1 16-ounce can English peas, drained	2 ribs celery, chopped
	1 red bell pepper, chopped
	1 small pimiento, chopped

Combine all ingredients, mix, and cover with marinade. Chill 24 hours. Drain salad before serving.

Marinade

1 cup sugar	¼ cup water
1 cup cider vinegar	1 teaspoon salt
½ cup vegetable oil	¼ teaspoon paprika

Combine ingredients and blend well.

Serves 12

HOMEMADE MAYONNAISE

1 cup vegetable oil	½ teaspoon dry mustard
1 egg	⅛ teaspoon red pepper
1 tablespoon lemon juice	⅛ teaspoon paprika
½ to 1 teaspoon salt	

In blender, combine ¼ cup oil with remaining ingredients and mix well at high speed. Reduce to low speed and gradually add remaining oil, blending well. (Recipe cannot be doubled.)

Yields 1 cup mayonnaise

PECAN TASSIES

1 3-ounce package cream
   cheese, softened
½ cup butter, softened
1 cup all-purpose flour
¾ cup brown sugar, firmly
   packed

1 egg
1 tablespoon butter, softened
Dash salt
⅔ cup pecan pieces

Mix cream cheese and ½ cup butter in small bowl until smooth. Stir in flour and mix well. Chill 1 hour. Shape dough in 24 one-inch balls and press one ball into each cup of ungreased miniature muffin pans to form tiny pie shells.

Combine sugar, egg, butter, and salt in small bowl, and beat at medium speed with mixer until smooth. Layer ½ teaspoon pecans, 1 teaspoon mixture, and another ½ teaspoon pecans in each pastry shell. Bake at 325 degrees for 20 to 25 minutes or until filling is set.

Yields 24 pies

CHILDREN'S PICNIC

Children love picnics, whether at the park, at the lake, or in their own backyard. Just remember to keep things simple and serve food that you know little folks like. They will thank you with happy faces, squeals of laughter, and a few impulsive hugs—maybe even a quick kiss on the cheek complete with mustard.

Walking Salad
Hot Dogs Sans Grill
Potato Chips
Banana Crush Slush   *After School Cookies*
Cold Drinks

Anne Miller

WALKING SALAD

1 small to medium apple
   per child

Peanut butter
Raisins

Wash and core apple. Fill with peanut butter and top with raisins.

HOT DOGS SANS GRILL

Preheat wide-mouth insulated vacuum jug by filling with boiling water. Let stand a few minutes, and then empty. Refill with boiling water almost to top, secure lid, and transport to picnic site. Put hot dogs in jug, seal, and let stand 10 to 15 minutes. Remove from water with tongs and serve on buns with condiments.

AFTER SCHOOL COOKIES

2 cups sugar
½ cup milk
½ cup margarine
¼ cup cocoa

Dash salt
2½ cups rolled oats
½ cup peanut butter
1 teaspoon vanilla

Combine sugar, milk, margarine, cocoa, and salt in saucepan, and bring to boil over medium heat, stirring constantly. Boil 1 minute and remove from heat. Stir in oatmeal, peanut butter, and vanilla. Continue stirring until mixture is cool enough to drop by teaspoonfuls onto baking sheet. Let stand until hardened.

Yields 3 to 4 dozen cookies

Hollye Spiotta

BANANA CRUSH SLUSH

1 12-ounce can frozen orange
   juice concentrate
1 6-ounce can frozen lemonade
   concentrate
3 cups pineapple juice

3 bananas, mashed
2 cups sugar or to taste
2 to 3 cups water
Lemon-lime soda to taste

Combine all ingredients except lemon-lime soda and blend until sugar dissolves. Chill. Just before serving, add soda.

Yields 2 quarts juice

When the weather is nice and spring is nudging at one's senses, the lure of Memphis out-of-doors is irresistible. The fragrance of honeysuckle, jasmine, magnolias, and roses seems to be everywhere. Grab a blanket or a quilt, spread it under a tree, and have supper outside—instant picnic.

Baked Ham
Black-Eyed Pea Salad
Sliced Tomatoes and Vidalia Onions
New Potatoes in Mustard Vinaigrette
Corn Light Bread
Lemon Danish Squares

The Picnic Committee

BLACK-EYED PEA SALAD

2 15-ounce cans black-eyed peas, drained	1 cup vegetable oil
	¼ cup wine vinegar
1 onion, thinly sliced	1 teaspoon celery seed
1 4-ounce jar chopped pimiento	½ teaspoon salt
1 clove garlic	½ teaspoon black pepper

Combine all ingredients and mix thoroughly. Refrigerate 2 days in covered container. Remove garlic clove after 24 hours. (Keeps 2 weeks.)

Serves 6 to 8

CORN LIGHT BREAD

2 cups white corn meal	1 teaspoon salt
1 cup all-purpose flour	2 cups buttermilk
1 scant cup sugar	3 tablespoons vegetable oil
1 teaspoon baking soda	

Sift together all dry ingredients. Combine buttermilk and oil, and add to dry mixture. Stir well and pour into oiled loaf pan. Bake 45 to 60 minutes at 350 degrees.

Serves 12

Martha Ellen Maxwell

NEW POTATOES
IN MUSTARD VINAIGRETTE

1½ pounds new potatoes	2 tablespoons mayonnaise
Chopped green onions or chives to taste	1 teaspoon dry mustard
	1 teaspoon sugar
6 tablespoons vegetable oil	1 teaspoon lemon juice
2 tablespoons white wine vinegar	Salt and freshly ground black pepper to taste

Cook potatoes in salted water until tender, and then drain. (Do not overcook.) Slice thin while still warm, place in bowl, and add onions. Combine remaining ingredients in jar and shake until well-blended. Pour over potatoes and toss lightly. Cover and chill.

Serves 4

LEMON DANISH SQUARES

1 cup all-purpose flour	1 cup granulated sugar
½ cup confectioners' sugar	3 tablespoons lemon juice
½ cup butter, softened	½ teaspoon baking powder
2 eggs	2 tablespoons all-purpose flour

Cream together flour, confectioners' sugar, and butter. Press into 8-inch square baking pan. Bake 20 minutes at 350 degrees. Mix remaining ingredients and pour over crust. Bake 25 minutes at 350 degrees. Cut into bars while warm and sprinkle with granulated or confectioners' sugar.

Yields 16 squares

Maxine Morse

SALADE NIÇOISE WITH BASIL DRESSING

1 clove garlic, halved
1 head Boston lettuce
10 salad tomatoes, quartered
½ pound potatoes, boiled, peeled, and cut in large cubes
3 hard-cooked eggs, quartered
1 cucumber, peeled and thinly sliced
1 red bell pepper, sliced in rings
1 green bell pepper, sliced in rings
1 cup grated peeled carrots
1 cup cooked and cut fresh green beans
⅔ cup small ripe olives

Rub bottom and sides of large wooden salad bowl with garlic halves. Line with lettuce leaves. Arrange all other ingredients decoratively in bowl. Pour dressing over salad or serve separately.

Basil Dressing
½ cup olive oil
2 tablespoons red wine vinegar
Salt and pepper to taste
8 to 10 fresh basil leaves, minced

Blend oil, vinegar, salt, and pepper. Add basil and let stand a few minutes to blend flavors.

Serves 4 to 6

CLAFOUTI

3 eggs, beaten
⅔ cup sugar
Dash salt
1¼ cups all-purpose flour
1 cup milk
3 tablespoons butter, melted
1 teaspoon vanilla
2 pounds cherries, pitted
Confectioners' sugar

Blend eggs, sugar, and salt. Add flour, milk, butter, and vanilla, and mix well. Spread cherries on bottom of greased 9-inch cake pan and cover with batter. Bake 1 hour at 350 degrees. Serve sprinkled with confectioners' sugar.

Serves 6

PIQUE-NIQUE IN AN ARTIST'S STUDIO

Memphis is blessed with an appealing variety of styles of painting by the artists who make this city their home. A visit to an artist's studio is always a treat. In the converted barn which serves as a studio for Sam Bjorklund, guests may be entertained in the style of the *pique-nique* reminiscent of the years the Bjorklunds spent in France.

Melon with Prosciutto
Assorted Cold Cuts (pâté, salami, smoked ham)
Assorted Cheeses (Roquefort, brie, goat cheese)
Ratatouille
Salade Niçoise with Basil Dressing
Crusty French Bread
Fresh Strawberries
Clafouti

Mr. and Mrs. Sam Bjorklund

RATATOUILLE

3 large onions, chopped
1 pound zucchini, sliced
1 pound eggplant, peeled and sliced
½ cup olive oil
2 red bell peppers, seeded and sliced
1 green bell pepper, seeded and sliced
½ pound ripe tomatoes, peeled, seeded, and chopped
10 fresh basil leaves
1 teaspoon crushed thyme
2 cloves garlic, crushed
Salt and pepper to taste

In large heavy saucepan, sauté onions, zucchini, and eggplant in olive oil for 5 minutes over medium heat. Add bell peppers and tomatoes, and cook a few minutes more. Add garlic, basil, thyme, salt, and pepper. Cover and simmer 30 minutes or until tender. If there is too much liquid, remove lid and allow water to evaporate by cooking over high heat. Watch carefully, stirring occasionally, to avoid scorching. Serve hot or cold.

Serves 6

SYMPHONY IN THE GARDENS

The setting for these annual open-air performances of the Memphis Symphony's chamber orchestra is perfection. The beautiful greenery and grounds of the Dixon Gallery and Gardens with their graceful dogwoods, towering oaks, abundant azaleas, and carefully chosen statuary could not be more inviting to the hundreds of picnic-bound music fanciers who gather there on certain Sunday afternoons in the fall and spring. Casual picnickers may place their baskets or coolers side-by-side with someone whose picnic may be placed on a low table complete with candelabra and a hired-for-the-evening waiter in black tie. The feeling is friendly, the music fun, and the crowd in fine fettle.

Spiced Shrimp*
Caviar Pie with Melba Toast
Cherry Soup
Herb-Marinated Beef Tenderloin
Asparagus Vinaigrette   Layered Potato Salad*
Chocolate Almond Bars

Les Gourmands Supper Club
Kay and Gardner Brooksbank
Barbara and Roy Keathley
Kay and Vic Robilio
Carmine and Wynn Smith
Carol and Jim White

*See Index

CHERRY SOUP

1 16-ounce can pitted sour red cherries, drained and juice reserved	2 teaspoons cornstarch
	¼ teaspoon cinnamon
	¼ teaspoon salt
½ cup orange juice	½ cup claret
¼ cup sugar	Sour cream

Reserve several cherries for garnish. Chop remaining cherries and combine with reserved juice, orange juice, sugar, cornstarch, cinnamon, and salt in saucepan. Cook over medium heat, stirring constantly, until mixture reaches boiling point. Boil 30 seconds, remove from heat, and stir in claret. Served chilled with dollop of sour cream topped with whole cherry.

Serves 4

CAVIAR PIE

6 hard-cooked eggs	Dash Tabasco sauce
½ cup butter, softened	1 cup sour cream
Seasoned salt to taste	2 4-ounce jars caviar, drained
6 green onions, minced	

Press eggs through sieve and mix well with butter and seasoned salt. Pat into 9-inch quiche dish and chill 1 hour. Before serving, sprinkle onions over egg mixture. Blend Tabasco sauce with sour cream, spread over onions, and top with caviar. Serve with buttered Melba toast.

Serves 10 to 12

Nancy Gibson

HERB-MARINATED BEEF TENDERLOIN

7 to 8-pound beef tenderloin	2 tablespoons mixed herbs
2 cups dry red wine	(thyme, rosemary, chives,
3 shallots, minced	marjoram, and tarragon)
6 to 7 parsley sprigs	½ teaspoon Dijon mustard
3 tablespoons vegetable oil	Salt and pepper to taste

Place meat in glass container. Mix remaining ingredients for marinade and pour over meat. Cover and chill 6 to 8 hours or overnight, turning several times. Pat beef dry and grill 4 inches from coals to preferred doneness. Chill and slice thin. Serve with horseradish sauce.

Serves 12 to 16

CHOCOLATE ALMOND BARS

1 cup butter, softened	1 cup sifted all-purpose flour
½ cup brown sugar, firmly packed	1 cup quick oats
	2 8-ounce Hershey bars
½ cup granulated sugar	2 teaspoons butter
2 egg yolks	½ to 1 cup sliced almonds
1 teaspoon vanilla	

Cream butter with both sugars. Add egg yolks and vanilla, beating until light. Stir in flour and oats, mixing thoroughly. Spread mixture in greased 9 x 13-inch baking pan and bake 20 minutes at 350 degrees. Remove from oven and let stand 10 minutes. Melt Hershey bars with butter, stirring until smooth, and frost. Sprinkle with nuts. Allow chocolate to harden before cutting into bars.

Yields 3 to 4 dozen bars

WEST INDIES CRAB SALAD

1 pound fresh lump crab meat, flaked
1 medium onion, finely chopped
½ teaspoon salt
¼ to ½ teaspoon freshly ground black pepper
½ cup vegetable oil
6 tablespoons cider vinegar
½ cup ice water

Spread half of crab meat in bottom of glass bowl. Top with half of onion, salt, and pepper. Repeat layers. In order, pour oil, vinegar, and ice water over top layer. Cover and chill at least 2 hours. Before serving, toss lightly but do not stir.

Serves 4 to 6

GULF COAST GAZEBO LUNCHEON

For a great number of Memphians, going to the beach means a drive to the Florida Gulf Coast with its beaches of dazzling sugar-white sand. Scores of Memphians make this southward trek yearly to soak up the beauty of water and sand, sun and sky, and wind-blown clumps of sea oats. There is nothing lovelier than a picnic with family or friends in this tranquil setting—perhaps in a gazebo on a high dune overlooking the Gulf of Mexico.

West Indies Crab Salad
Homemade Melba Toast
Salmon Mousse with Cucumber-Dill Sauce
Fresh Sliced Tomatoes
Wonderful Frozen Fruit Dessert

Anne Miller

SALMON MOUSSE WITH CUCUMBER-DILL SAUCE

1 10½-ounce can beef consommé
1 tablespoon unflavored gelatin
1 16-ounce can red sockeye salmon, drained, boned, and skinned
1 cup mayonnaise
1 tablespoon Worcestershire sauce
1 tablespoon tarragon vinegar
1 small onion, grated
Juice of large lemon
Dash Tabasco sauce
Salt and pepper to taste

Heat consommé, add gelatin, and stir until dissolved. Add salmon and remaining ingredients, and process in blender until smooth. Pour into lightly oiled 1½-quart mold or 10 to 12 individual molds. Serve with cucumber-dill sauce.

Cucumber-Dill Sauce
½ cup shredded cucumber
½ cup mayonnaise
2 tablespoons minced fresh dill, or 2 teaspoons dried
2 tablespoons prepared mustard
2 tablespoons minced chives or onion
Coarsely ground black pepper or lemon pepper to taste

Squeeze moisture from cucumber and mix with remaining ingredients. Chill.

Serves 10 to 12

WONDERFUL FROZEN FRUIT DESSERT

3 oranges, juice and pulp
3 lemons, juice and pulp
1 20-ounce can crushed pineapple with juice
3 bananas, mashed
1 cup sugar
⅓ cup Cointreau or kirsch

Mix all ingredients together, pour into shallow pan, and freeze. For transporting to picnic site, spoon mixture into plastic container with lid. Wrap in newspaper, then in heavy duty foil, and place in cooler with ice.

Serves 8

HOMEMADE MELBA TOAST

1 loaf fine-grained sandwich bread, unsliced

Chill bread 2 to 3 days for easier slicing. Trim crusts, slice thin, and cut each slice in halves. Place on baking sheet (butter very lightly, if preferred). Bake at 275 degrees for 1 hour or until lightly browned. Cool and store in covered container.

Yields about 3½ dozen toast halves

Patricia A. Cooper

Feasting on a Mississippi River Sandbar

Speak of pleasure boating on the Mississippi, and what may come to mind are visions of the fine old steamboats, many with luxurious dining rooms and overnight accommodations for river travelers, which in former years crowded the Memphis port. The once-famous Lee Line, established in Memphis just after the Civil War by Captain James Lee, had thirty-six such paddlewheelers operating at various times, and had terminals in Cincinnati, Cairo, St. Louis, and Vicksburg. Nostalgia for the old romantic age of steamboat travel remains strong today. The local *Memphis Queen* and her four sister boats offer frequently scheduled sight-seeing excursions up and down the river, and dinner cruises in summer months, with passengers strolling the decks or dancing to the music of jazz and blues bands. Replicas of the classic sternwheelers, the beloved *Delta Queen* and the newer *Mississippi Queen,* make Memphis a port of call on their regular trips between New Orleans and Cincinnati. It is glorious to be on board as the boat leaves port, the sounds of its deep steam whistle mixing with the wheezy old tunes played on the steam calliope and calling up age-old memories. It is pure magic to be on the river as the water catches the glow of sunset, then gradually becomes pewter in color, and the lights of the city come on in the distance. One seems to hear a deckhand's timeless call, sounding the river's variable depths: "Mark twain—safe water."

But there is another kind of boating, riverboating for pleasure, that is a private way of life for many Memphians. These boaters regularly embark on river travel from the Memphis Yacht Club's new marina at the mouth of the Wolf River in Mud Island Harbor, just south of the Hernando De Soto bridge that carries motorists across the Mississippi River. Their crafts include everything from small speedboats or sailboats to big cabin cruisers and houseboats with full living quarters, and their cruises can keep them on the water anywhere from a few hours to a few months.

The Mississippi is a river to the world for these boating enthusiasts. They may go up the Mississippi to Cairo, Illinois, then up the Ohio River to Paducah, Kentucky, where they enter the Tennessee River and may travel on to Kentucky Lake, Pickwick Lake, or to Guntersville Lake in Alabama or other beautiful lakes along the way. Or they may travel down the Mississippi to New Orleans, on to Mobile, Alabama, through the Intracoastal Waterway, up the Tombigbee through the locks to the Tennessee River, thence again to the Ohio, the Mississippi, and home to Memphis—a mighty round-trip. If they go downriver past Helena, Arkansas, on the west bank of the Mississippi, they can enter the Arkansas River and follow it as far upriver as Tulsa, Oklahoma. Shorter cruises are more frequent, however, and for these outings, boaters like to go up the Mississippi— always go upriver, common wisdom suggests, so you can head home with the current, should something go wrong with an engine. Also, the water is often clearer upstream— so clean sometimes that swimming and water-skiing become delightful. Several boats may make the excursion together, and tie up at sandbars to spend the night. The boaters play games on the sandbar, horseshoes or baseball, perhaps; they build bonfires of driftwood and gather 'round to roast marshmallows and tell river stories. Sometimes they show movies under the stars, the projector powered by a boat's generator. There have been theme cruises with crews in appropriate costumes—pirates, say, or Gay Nineties; on Labor Day, there's a traditional cruise downriver to Helena for a fish-fry. For many years, a flotilla of several boats has gone about ten miles upriver and tied up at a sandbar to celebrate New Year's Day, even making the cruise in snow occasionally, with heaters on the boats and the campfire on the sandbar keeping them snug.

THE PICTURE: *This private houseboat, steel-hulled and of unusual design, was modeled after the early packet boats, with a pilot house and a shallow draft for shore (or sandbar) landing. Earlier in the day it left its slip at the Memphis Yacht Club marina next to Mud Island, one of the nation's most beautiful and unusual city parks. After an excursion upriver, where it was determined that the water was too low to allow a sandbar landing, the boat has made its way to a sandy bank on the Arkansas side where three generations of a family of boating enthusiasts, who first took to the river in the early 1930s, will gather for a chili supper. On a folding table set up on the sandbar is a small runner, woven by a family member from reeds and grasses that grow along the riverbank. A favorite piece of Mississippi River driftwood holds the arrangement of reeds, sumac, and trumpet vine, gathered near the river.*

THE FOOD: *The food was prepared at home and has been kept in the galley so that no part of this day of leisure on the water need be given to kitchen duty. The meal will feature FLOTILLA CHILI COOK-OFF WINNER, served with corn chips, GUACAMOLE SALAD, mugs of cold drinks, and MARTHA'S NEW YEAR'S DESSERT.*

Traveling the always-changing, often treacherous Mississippi River, whether on long cruises or short, requires real navigational skills. Hazards include the swiftness of the ever-flowing current, drifting debris, the wash from passing barges, and shifting channels—even the sandbars can become elusive between voyages, as they appear and disappear unnervingly. But members of the Memphis Yacht Club are well-versed in boat safety procedures. The club grew out of a U.S. Coast Guard Auxiliary formed during the Second World War to patrol the river when the active guards were called to duty. Later the auxiliary became a temporary Coast Guard Reserve unit that promoted boating safety with such events as dinghy races and "Man Overboard" drills. A fellowship developed among the participants; they went on to form the Memphis Yacht Club which continues the promotion of boat safety to the present time.

Meanwhile, the club's members, river travelers all, continue to re-create that most American of idylls. As they cruise, contemplating the varied wonders of this continent's great river, and gazing on its many wooded stretches of still primitive shoreline, Huck Finn lives once more—afloat again on the waters where time stands still.

MISSISSIPPI MUD

Ingredients easy to keep on boats, and preparation time in seconds—this is frequently served on sandbar picnics by the Memphis Yacht Club flotilla.

1 5-ounce bottle Pickapeppa   1 8-ounce package cream
   sauce (no substitute)   cheese, softened

Pour half of Pickapeppa sauce over block of cream cheese. Spread on crackers.

Serves 6 to 8

Katherine Hinds Smythe

FLOTILLA CHILI COOK-OFF WINNER

One of the many high-spirited events of the Memphis Yacht Club during its outings on the river was the great Chili Cook-Off. This winner is a winner indeed—a spicy, rich chili with Texas origins. Prepare to take your time. You'll be so pleased you did.

2 pounds stew meat, cubed,   1½ cups water
   fat trimmed and reserved   4 tablespoons chili powder
Salt and pepper to taste   3 tablespoons cumin powder
4 tablespoons olive oil   4 tablespoons Masa flour,
3 medium onions, chopped   available in specialty
3 to 4 cloves garlic, chopped   food stores
1 28-ounce can tomatoes   6 cups cooked rice
1 8-ounce can tomato sauce

Melt fat trimmings in heavy skillet. Add meat a little at a time, brown over very high heat, and season with salt and pepper. Remove meat and drippings from pan, and set aside. Add olive oil, onions, and garlic to skillet, and cook slowly until onions are soft and clear, about 5 to 10 minutes. Return meat and drippings to skillet. Add remaining ingredients except flour and rice, and mix well. Cover and simmer over very low heat for 8 to 10 hours. Check occasionally and add water if chili cooks down too much.

Just before serving, stir Masa flour into 1 cup water to create paste. Slowly stir portions of paste into chili until desired thickness is achieved. Serve over rice. And, if possible, on a Mississippi River sandbar.

Serves 6 to 8

Bob Jorgensen

MARTHA'S NEW YEAR'S DESSERT

A favorite dessert for the Memphis Yacht Club's flotilla when it goes up river on New Year's Day to a choice sandbar in the Mississippi. Whatever the weather, no matter how cold, the boats go out with one exception—when there's too much ice.

½ cup butter, softened   1 3-ounce package instant
2 cups chopped pecans   chocolate pudding
1 cup all-purpose flour   2½ cups milk
1 cup sifted confectioners'   1 3-ounce package instant
   sugar   vanilla pudding
1 8-ounce package cream   2 1½-ounce Hershey bars,
   cheese, softened   grated
2 8-ounce cartons Cool Whip

Mix butter, 1 cup pecans, and flour, and spread in bottom of 9 x 13-inch baking pan. Bake 25 minutes at 350 degrees. Cool thoroughly. For first layer, blend confectioners' sugar, cream cheese, and 1 carton Cool Whip, and spread over crust. For second layer, prepare chocolate pudding using 1¼ cups milk and spread over cream cheese layer. For third layer, prepare vanilla pudding using remaining 1¼ cups milk and spread over chocolate pudding. For fourth layer, cover vanilla pudding with half of second carton Cool Whip, reserving remainder for other uses. Sprinkle with chocolate and remaining pecans. Chill and cut into squares.

Serves 12

Martha Stanley

GUACAMOLE SALAD

A favorite among food lovers everywhere.

3 avocados, mashed   Salt to taste
2 tomatoes, peeled, chopped,   Red pepper to taste
   and strained   Cumin to taste
2 green onions, minced   Chili powder to taste
2 tablespoons olive oil   Mayonnaise
½ clove garlic, minced   Lemon juice

Combine all ingredients except lemon juice and mayonnaise and mix gently. Add enough mayonnaise mixed with lemon juice to adjust consistency.

Serves 6

Kathryn Jorgensen

STUFFED CHICKEN BREASTS

4 chicken breasts, boned, skinned, and halved	¼ teaspoon tarragon
	¼ teaspoon salt
1 cup dry bread crumbs	1 to 2 eggs, beaten
1 tablespoon paprika	6 tablespoons butter

Place chicken breasts between wax paper and pound to ¼-inch thickness. Place 2 tablespoons filling in center of each. Fold one side over and roll up. Secure with toothpick if necessary. Combine bread crumbs with seasonings. Dip roll into beaten egg and coat with seasoned bread crumbs. Chill 15 minutes in freezer. Melt butter in baking pan and add chicken, turning to coat. Bake 50 minutes at 375 degrees. Serve hot or cold.

Filling

1 cup chopped cooked ham	2 tablespoons chopped parsley
½ cup grated onion	½ teaspoon salt
¼ cup fresh bread crumbs	¼ teaspoon tarragon
2 tablespoons butter, melted	Freshly ground pepper to taste

Combine all ingredients and mix well.

Serves 8

BLACK CAVIAR MOUSSE

2 4-ounce jars black caviar	½ cup water
1½ tablespoons grated onion	2 cups sour cream
1 teaspoon grated lemon peel	1 cup heavy cream, lightly whipped
¼ cup chopped parsley	
2 envelopes unflavored gelatin	Pepper to taste

Combine caviar, onion, lemon peel, and parsley, and set aside. In medium saucepan, sprinkle gelatin over water and stir over low heat until dissolved. Remove from heat and stir in 1 cup sour cream. Fold gelatin mixture and remaining sour cream into caviar mixture. Fold in whipped cream and pepper. Pour into lightly oiled 6-cup mold and chill until set, about 4 to 6 hours. Garnish with parsley and serve with toast points or crackers.

Serves 16 to 20

ITALIAN SPINACH PIE

2 11-ounce packages pie crust mix	3 eggs, beaten
	1 16-ounce carton cottage cheese
1¼ cups grated Parmesan cheese	
	1 16-ounce carton ricotta cheese
Ice water	
2 10-ounce packages chopped spinach, thawed and drained	1½ teaspoons salt
	¼ teaspoon nutmeg
	⅛ teaspoon pepper

Combine pie crust mix, ½ cup Parmesan cheese, and enough ice water to form a ball. Roll out half the dough and line springform pan. Brush with egg wash (1 tablespoon water mixed with 1 beaten egg yolk). Mix remaining ingredients and pour into pan. Roll out remaining dough and cover spinach mixture, sealing edges. Slash top and brush with remaining egg wash. Bake 1½ hours at 375 degrees. Serve warm or cold.

Serves 8 to 10

BOURBON CHOCOLATE TORTE

¼ cup dark raisins
¼ cup bourbon whiskey
7 squares semi-sweet chocolate
8 tablespoons butter, softened
3 eggs, separated

⅔ cup sugar
⅔ cup ground blanched
  almonds
3 tablespoons all-purpose flour
Pinch of salt

Soak raisins in bourbon for 10 minutes. Melt chocolate in top of double boiler. Remove from heat and add butter 1 table-spoon at a time, stirring until smooth. Set aside to cool. Lightly grease sides and bottom of 9-inch round cake pan. Line bottom with parchment paper. Grease paper and dust with flour, tapping to remove excess.

In large mixing bowl, beat egg yolks well. Add sugar ⅓ cup at a time, beating until pale yellow and smooth. Reduce speed to low and beat in chocolate. Stir in almonds and flour. Add raisins and bourbon. Add salt to egg whites, beat until soft peaks form, and stir one-third of egg whites into batter. Fold in remaining egg whites. Pour batter into pan and bake 20 minutes at 375 degrees. Cool 20 minutes in pan on wire rack. Remove from pan and cool completely before removing paper. Glaze and let stand overnight before serving.

Glaze

3 squares semi-sweet chocolate   3 tablespoons butter, softened

Melt chocolate in top of double boiler. Add butter 1 table-spoon at a time, stirring until smooth. Remove from heat and cool 10 minutes.

Serves 10 to 12

BEEF BRISKET IN FOIL

6 to 7 pound beef brisket
1 10-ounce bottle barbecue
  sauce
¾ cup beer

1 package onion soup mix
3 to 4 tablespoons liquid smoke
Cracked black pepper

Place brisket on large sheet of heavy-duty foil. Pour barbecue sauce, beer, soup mix, and liquid smoke over meat. Sprinkle with generous amount of pepper. Seal in foil, place in baking pan, and bake 4 hours at 350 degrees. Cool and slice thin.

Serves 12 to 16

Anne Threefoot

SUMMER SUPPER IN THE TREETOPS

A picnic supper on a balcony—glassed-in or open air—in a handsome high-rise is a beautiful way to rise above it all while staying at home, taking in the view from above the trees.

Beef Brisket in Foil
Crab Meat Eggs
Vinaigrette-Marinated Sliced Tomatoes, Onions,
Asparagus, and Artichokes
French Bread with Sweet Butter
Berry Baskets

The Picnic Committee

CRAB MEAT EGGS

6 hard-cooked eggs, halved
1 6½-ounce can crab meat
½ cup chopped celery
½ cup mayonnaise

¼ cup chopped green onions
1 teaspoon minced parsley
Salt and white pepper to taste

Remove yolks, mash, and mix with remaining ingredients. Stuff egg halves and chill before serving.

Serves 6

BERRY BASKETS

3 large eggs, separated
½ teaspoon vinegar
¼ teaspoon vanilla

Dash salt
1¼ cups sugar
Glazed berries of choice

Combine egg whites, vinegar, vanilla, and salt, and beat until soft peaks form. (Save yolks for other dishes.) Gradually beat in sugar until mixture is very stiff. Spoon 14 to 16 small mounds onto baking sheet lined with parchment paper. Shape into shells with back of spoon. Bake 45 minutes at 275 degrees. Remove from paper immediately. Cool and fill with glazed fresh berries.

Yields 14 to 16 shells

Mary Gray Sasser

PICNICS BY THE NUMBERS

Countryside, lakeside, or wherever, picnics are favorite outings with family and friends. Here is a flexible formula for planning a variety of picnics. Menu selections are divided into four categories. Choose one selection from each category, put them together—any combination is a winner!—and let your imagination take charge. Have a hobo picnic and wrap it in large, brightly colored fabric squares or bandannas. Or use individual brown paper sacks tied with colorful cotton dish towels to be used as napkins. Or pack servings in children's plastic sand buckets.

Meats
Cornish Hens with Rice Salad Stuffing
Fried Drumsticks
Thin Strips of Melon Wrapped in Dried Beef
Turkey Rolls

Salads
Deauville Salad
Fresh Country Garden Salad
New Potato Salad
Sunflower Broccoli Salad

Sandwiches
Cream Cheese and Pecans on Raisin Bread or Pumpkin Bread
Curried Egg-Cheese Salad Sandwiches
Fruit Sandwiches
Shrimp Sandwiches

Desserts
Sugar and Cinnamon Sandwiches
Fresh Strawberries
Mixed Fruit in Cantaloupe Half
Buttermilk Tea Cakes
Fried Pies

Babbie Lovett

CORNISH HENS WITH RICE SALAD STUFFING

8 Cornish hens
8 tablespoons butter

Lemon pepper to taste
8 teaspoons water

Wash hens and pat dry. Rub each hen with 1 tablespoon butter and season with lemon pepper. Place 1 teaspoon water in cavity, wrap in foil, and bake at 375 degrees for 1 hour or until tender. Open foil during last 15 minutes of baking and baste with juices to brown hens. When done, pour off drippings and cool. Put ¼ cup rice salad stuffing in each hen, wrap again in foil, and chill. Serve in wrapping.

Rice Salad Stuffing
2 cups cooked rice
¾ cup chopped celery
¼ cup chopped apple
¼ cup chopped green bell pepper

¼ cup chopped fresh parsley
1 green onion, chopped
Salt and pepper to taste
Mayonnaise to taste

Combine ingredients and mix well.

Serves 8

TURKEY ROLLS

8 slices smoked turkey breast
Horseradish sauce or
    Durkee's salad dressing

Alfalfa sprouts

Spread turkey slice with dressing of choice. Sprinkle with sprouts, roll, and secure with toothpicks.

Serves 4 to 8

DEAUVILLE SALAD

1 head endive, sliced
1 York apple, cubed
1 cup chopped celery
¾ cup vegetable oil

¼ cup red wine vinegar
2 to 3 tablespoons Dijon mustard

Combine lettuce, apple, and celery. Blend oil, vinegar, and mustard, pour over salad, and toss.

Serves 8

FRESH COUNTRY GARDEN SALAD

2 large tomatoes, peeled and
  chopped
1 cucumber, peeled and
  chopped
1 small red onion or 4 to 5
  green onions, chopped
1 green bell pepper, chopped
2 ribs celery, chopped
Sugar
Wine vinegar to taste
Olive oil to taste
Salt and pepper to taste

Combine all vegetables and sprinkle with sugar. Add vinegar, olive oil, salt, and pepper. Toss lightly and chill.

Serves 4 to 6

NEW POTATO SALAD

12 small new potatoes,
  unpeeled
4 green onions with tops,
  chopped
3 parsley sprigs, chopped
Sour cream to taste
Dill to taste
Salt and pepper to taste

Boil new potatoes until tender. Cool and cut in fourths. Toss lightly with green onions, parsley, and sour cream. Season with dill, salt, and pepper.

Serves 4

SUNFLOWER BROCCOLI SALAD

4 cups chopped broccoli,
  washed and drained
½ pound bacon, fried and
  crumbled
1 cup raisins
1 medium red onion, chopped
1 4-ounce package salted
  sunflower seeds
1 2-ounce package almonds
1 cup mayonnaise
2 tablespoons red wine vinegar
2 tablespoons sugar

Combine broccoli with bacon, raisins, onion, sunflower seeds, and almonds, and chill. Mix together mayonnaise, vinegar, and sugar. Pour over broccoli mixture one hour before serving.

Serves 6 to 8

Carolyn H. Gates

PUMPKIN BREAD

1 16-ounce can pumpkin
1 cup vegetable oil
⅔ cup water
4 eggs, lightly beaten
3½ cups all-purpose flour
3 cups sugar
2½ teaspoons cinnamon
2 teaspoons nutmeg
2 teaspoons baking soda
1 teaspoon salt

Combine pumpkin, vegetable oil, water, and eggs. Sift together all dry ingredients and beat into pumpkin mixture. Pour into two greased 5 x 9-inch loaf pans or three 1-pound coffee cans filled half-full. Bake 30 minutes at 350 degrees, then reduce heat to 275 degrees and bake 1 hour more. Let stand 10 minutes before removing from pan.

Yields 2 or 3 loaves

Jeanne Burrow

CURRIED EGG-CHEESE SALAD SANDWICHES

6 hard-cooked eggs, chopped
1 cup shredded Cheddar cheese
½ cup chopped stuffed olives
½ cup mayonnaise
1 teaspoon curry powder
¼ teaspoon pepper
Sandwich bread
Crisp lettuce leaves

Combine eggs, cheese, and olives. Blend mayonnaise with curry powder and pepper, and add to egg mixture. Spread over bread and add lettuce leaves to sandwiches.

Serves 4

FRUIT SANDWICHES

1 15¼-ounce can crushed
  pineapple
1 15-ounce box raisins
1 cup pecans
Mayonnaise
Boston brown bread or
  WHEAT BREAD

Drain pineapple and reserve juice. Grind raisins and pecans, and mix with pineapple. Add just enough mayonnaise and reserved juice to make pineapple mixture spreadable. Spread on lightly buttered bread.

Yields 3½ to 4 cups spread

SHRIMP SANDWICHES

2 cups boiled and peeled medium shrimp	1 small onion
2 hard-cooked eggs	½ to 1 cup mayonnaise
1 medium dill pickle	1 teaspoon lemon juice
	Salt and pepper to taste

Combine shrimp, eggs, pickle, and onion in food processor, and chop. Add remaining ingredients and mix well. Spread on sandwich bread or French bread rounds.

Yields 3 cups sandwich spread

SUGAR AND CINNAMON SANDWICHES

Mix preferred amounts of sugar and cinnamon. Trim crusts from sandwich bread and spread bread with sweet butter. Sprinkle with sugar-cinnamon mixture, and cut in halves or squares. (Children love them....grown-up children, too.)

BUTTERMILK TEA CAKES

½ cup vegetable shortening	1 teaspoon baking powder
1 cup sugar	¼ teaspoon salt
1 egg, beaten	½ teaspoon baking soda
1 teaspoon vanilla	½ cup buttermilk
3 cups all-purpose flour	

Cream shortening with sugar. Add egg and vanilla. Sift together flour, baking powder, and salt. Stir baking soda into buttermilk, and add alternately with dry ingredients to sugar mixture. Place dough on lightly floured board and knead in just enough flour to handle easily. Roll out, cut with round cookie cutter, and place on ungreased baking sheet. Bake at 375 degrees for 12 to 15 minutes or until lightly browned. Sprinkle with extra sugar while warm.

Yields 3 to 4 dozen tea cakes

FRIED PIES

A marvel of Southern cooking, great for picnics or for box lunches on motoring trips. And old wood stoves might have had a few tucked into the warming oven for the lucky person who found them.

4 cups all-purpose flour	1 cup margarine, softened
¼ teaspoon salt	¾ cup ice water

Combine flour and salt. Cut in margarine until mixture resembles corn meal. Mix with enough ice water to make firm dough. Cover and chill until ready to use (will keep a week in refrigerator).

Roll small piece of dough on lightly floured surface into thin oval shape, about 5 x 8-inches. Put 2 heaping tablespoons of chilled filling on one end of oval, leaving 1-inch margin of dough for sealing pie. Dip finger in water and moisten dough around filling. Fold opposite end over filling and press edges together with fingers, then with tines of fork (do not cut through). Heat oil to 375 degrees and deep-fry until golden brown. Drain on several very thick paper towels at least 30 minutes. (Pies may be baked 25 minutes at 400 degrees on baking sheet rather than fried.)

Apple Filling

Package dried apples	Sugar
1 to 2 tablespoons butter	Ground cloves or apple pie spice

Cook dried apples as directed on package using only two-thirds of water recommended. When tender, mash and add remaining ingredients to taste. Chill before filling pies.

Peach or Apricot Filling

Prepare dried peaches or apricots as above (peaches and apricots may also be combined). Substitute cinnamon to taste for other spices.

Yields 8 pies

Mrs. John Berry Holder
McCrory, Arkansas

SIMPLY SOUTHERN

More than any other region, the South leaves its ineradicable mark upon its children. No matter how far they roam or how long they stay away, Southerners are likely to reveal their Southernness in subtle ways. They can be recognized by the pleasure they take in conversation with intimates and strangers alike, and the frequency with which they speak of distant relatives, usually with familial titles attached. They may well display a passion for lost causes, a tolerance for eccentrics, and an appetite for odd vegetables like okra and purple hull peas. Southerners, often as not, will have good manners, amiable dispositions, and a sweet tooth. Their spoken words will probably be marked by loving attention to vowels and benign neglect of consonants; their written words will sometimes indicate a penchant for story-telling. And always, Southerners will know each other by an unmistakable, accommodating warmth and a shared, instinctive understanding—generations deep.

1893: Notes on Southern Living
From Miss Lula Stovall's Journal

Like many another young lady of the period, Miss Lula Stovall faithfully recorded the events of her daily life in a personal diary. Portions of her journal for the year 1893, when she was living in her widowed mother's home on the Woodstock-Cuba Road in North Shelby County, were included in a book privately published almost a century later, in 1984 (A History of Cuba Tennessee, by author Shirley Sigler Chamberlin, lifelong resident of the area, and a descendant of one of its pioneer families). Presented below are some representative excerpts from Miss Lula's journal, simple jottings about everyday activities that marked the passing of the seasons. That her writings so often concerned food—the growing, gathering, preparing, eating, sharing of food—reminds us of the many ways that food shaped the lives of people in Tennessee and elsewhere in those times. In addition to Lula and her mother, the Stovall household in 1893 included Lula's two brothers, an uncle, and a young cousin. They and other relatives who lived nearby are frequently mentioned in the diary excerpts that follow.

Jan. 12. Cousin Asher brought us a nice treat, apples, raisins, and candy from Cuba. Berry went to the bottom hunting. *Jan. 27.* Sent Mrs. Matt Etheridge some potatoes, she is sick. Boys picked cotton. Hung our meat. Parched coffee and churned. Snow about gone.

Feb. 2. Started me a quilt "Sunshine & Shade." *Feb. 13.* At Maggie's most of the day helping cook for the log rolling tomorrow. Made the sacks to put our meat in this morn. *Feb. 17.* Sent two dozen eggs to Cuba. Got five papers, three dailys, *Commercial* and *Baptist.*

Mar. 4. (Sat.) Today is the inauguration of President Grover Cleveland. May he remember the Golden Rule and act accordingly. *Mar. 10.* Virgie and myself been cleaning off the front yard all day. The boys planted potatoes. Had the best jelly-roll for dinner. *Mar. 20.* Momma made a pot of soap. I fixed my gown. Made some hominy. The boys plowing. *Mar. 29.* Set out a row of bridal-wreath.

Apr. 8. Reset my box flowers. *Apr. 12.* Taken off some more little chicks. Washed my clothes ready to boil. *Apr. 16.* Went to preaching at Bethuel. Splendid sermon from Mr. Rinshaw. *Apr. 20.* Dr. Henning came to see Maggie. Said she has malarial fever. Mr. Rowe went to Memphis for ice. . . . Maggie ate ice constantly for three hours.

May 1. Bad day for the opening of the "World's Fair" [in St. Louis]. *May 13.* Eddie brought back some strawberries. Had us all over to eat supper with them. *May 22.* Resurrected the beds. Varnished some things. Green apple pies for dinner were splendid. *May 25.* Got the quilt out real nice. Charlie came for a setting of eggs. Played a piece on the organ for the first time in months. *May 30.* Got up a little after three. Got breakfast and Berry and myself went to Memphis.

June 3. Made caramel cake and lemon custards, blackberry jam. *June 4*. Got dinner before I went to church at Embury. Children's Day. . . . Raspberries and cake for dinner. *June 8*. A fruit agent here this evening. A poor old woman stopped at the gate for water. Walking to Memphis with two children. *June 29*. Canned my berries, made a little jam and nearly a quart of plum jelly. We were at Mr. Bud Trotter's awhile tonight. Like to be out such lovely moonlight nights.

July 3. Uncle Russel and the boys have gone to Grass Pond fishing. Will stay all night. *July 6*. All went to Memphis. Paid five dollars for my hat. . . . but couldn't help it.

Aug. 1. Cooked three cakes for the picnic, made light-bread. *Aug. 2*. Finished cooking for the picnic. Have a real nice basket fixed. *Aug. 24*. Made a gallon of peach sweet pickle. A crowd of us went to preaching at Big Creek tonight. 'Twas awful dusty. *Aug. 25*. We sent to Cuba and bought a nice watermelon. Fixed the rind for pickles.

Sept. 1. Played two or three pieces on the organ. Cooked two cakes and some custards. Uncle Lee went to the lodge. *Sept. 9*. Ernest Rowe ate dinner with us. Had Irish potato custards. Best I believe I ever made. Finished "The Scarlet Letter." *Sept. 11*. Made nearly a gallon of apple preserves. We all had a game of Lotto. *Sept. 23*. Cooked a caramel cake, four transparent custards, and three sweet potato custards.

Oct. 12. Mr. Rickman sent a nice basket of grapes. Mamma and myself worked on a couple of hickory shirts. The boys finished digging sweet potatoes. Made about thirty bushels. *Oct. 20*. We came to Memphis and then on out to Brunswick on the twelve o'clock train. . . . to Mamie's. Several here today. For dessert, cake and peaches and grated pudding. *Oct. 27*. Mamma and myself gathered in things to make some pickles.

Nov. 11. Miss Trent, the young lady that will teach the Independence School, came out in the buggy. She will board with us. Birds for supper. *Nov. 22*. The boys all went hickory nut hunting. Got about three bushels. *Nov. 23*. Had such a sweet serenade last night. So nice to be awakened by beautiful music. Fixed our squares for the crazy quilt today. *Nov. 30*. The men folks all went bird-hunting. Brought twenty home.

Dec. 16. Killed hogs today. Five weighed 855 lb. and about 14 gal. of lard. It's a good time but tiresome. *Dec. 18*. Stuffed some sausage. Some of Miss Mary's children came and spelled a while practicing for Friday eve. *Dec. 19*. Fixed the bed bolsters and pillows. Put new feathers in some. . . . Having such wonderful weather and beautiful nights. *Dec. 22*. All went down to the spelling match at Independence. Went to a party at Mr. Oscar Branch's. Five of us in a wagon. *Dec. 23*. Cooked four cakes and eight custards. Cleaned up and straightened around in general. *Dec. 25*. Well this is Christmas. The Lord has been very good to us and I am so thankful. Had a good dinner.

Breakfast at the Home Place

THE PICTURE: *Memphians who came to the city from the surrounding country-side remember with fond nostalgia the pleasures and fulfillments of a way of life centered on the farm, and ordered by the cycles of nature. It is a life still chosen by many in the region—a new generation of farmers who must cope with subsidies and complicated farm programs, but continue to plant their crops with hope, raise their children with love, welcome their guests with graciousness, and find time to enjoy what may properly be described as the finer things of life. This early-morning farm breakfast, set out on a favored, old iron table on the cool front porch pictured here, will be shared by a young farmer and his wife on his return from a sunrise visit to the fields. A simple bouquet of home-grown zinnias adds just the right welcoming touch. Known as the Home Place, this two-story, white-frame Victorian farmhouse is on the family-owned Bartlett plantation just outside Como, Mississippi, some forty miles and minutes from Memphis. It is home to members of the third generation of Bartletts to farm this land. The house, built in 1971 to replace the old family home that had burned, incorporates antique doors, window shutters, hardware, and fine woods collected from the surrounding area, and was erected with the help of friends and neighbors during an old-fashioned "wall-raising party."*

THE FOOD: *The morning fare includes crisp slab bacon, FLUFFY COTTAGE CHEESE PANCAKES soaking in butter, and fresh sorghum molasses that may have been made not far away, in a crude mill turned by a single mule. The fresh, sweet peaches were picked in an orchard nearby. The small lake seen in the background provides bream, crappie, bass—and a quiet place to think and dream.*

A warm welcome awaits newcomers to Memphis, and residents of the city go out of their way to make them feel at home. (After all, this is the place where Welcome Wagon originated.) Yet city folk who move to Memphis from many other metropolitan areas—especially from one of the great urban sprawls of continuously-adjoining cities and suburbs found mostly on the east or west coasts of America—will probably be disoriented at first, and then disarmed, but ultimately charmed by a large city whose roots are still so firmly set in the culture and kindnesses of rural and small-town life. Literally as well as figuratively, Memphis lives close to the land.

You notice it first in the landscape: how the approach to the city from nearly every direction is marked by a change of scene that moves almost directly from fields and farms to apartments, condominiums, and high-rise office buildings with no intervening expanse of suburbs; how downtown skyscrapers offer fine views, just across the Mississippi River, of the fertile Arkansas flood plain with its verdant fields of rice, cotton, and soybeans. Somehow, this physical closeness both symbolizes and emphasizes the importance of agriculture to the Memphis economy—not just the long-established primacy of cotton and the Cotton Exchange in the city, but the growing recognition of Memphis as a key distribution center for agricultural products, the expanding role that the new Agricenter International plays in exchange of agricultural information and dissemination of innovative agricultural technology, and the increasing corporate presence of agribusiness headquarters in the city.

More noticeable to newcomers on an everyday basis, however, is the easygoing ambience, the relaxed lifestyle—an unexpected persistence in big-city Memphis of some agreeable small-town American attitudes. Memphians typically describe themselves as friendly, they tend to attribute friendliness to others, and a pervasive amiability seems to characterize most exchanges with Memphis salespeople, bus drivers, waiters, waitresses, bank tellers, repairmen, even the casual passerby on the street. If one recently proposed test of urban reserve were applied to Memphis drivers, many would flunk: Big-city drivers, it is said, will stare straight ahead when stopped for a red light, to avoid any unwanted eye contact with strangers. Small-town drivers, on the other hand—like Memphis drivers—will spend the interval studying occupants of cars in the next lanes, hoping to spot a friend.

Many Memphis trend-setters remember growing up in the small towns and rural counties of eastern Arkansas, northern Mississippi, and western Tennessee, often on land that had been in their families for several generations. Thus, the city seems to have imported from those areas, in almost undiluted form, an ingrained neighbors-and-kinfolks mind-set. Many Memphis families still have friends and relatives living on farms and in small towns nearby. They still "go home" for weddings and funerals. On summer evenings, they still like to settle down in high-backed rockers and porch swings and "visit." In surprising numbers, prosperous Memphians will tell you they long to return someday (perhaps when they retire) to the land and life they remember so fondly. Meantime, they are very much at home in urban Memphis, preserving the best of their agrarian heritage, while helping make Memphis the friendly and outgoing city it is.

ABOUT SOUTHERN FOODS

After tasting black-eyed peas for the first time, a Mid-Westerner asked her Southern friend, "Do you eat normal foods, too?" Southerners enjoy all kinds of foods, but they do have a particular liking for certain things that are a part of their regional history—vegetables flavored with bacon drippings or salt pork, hot breads, fried chicken, catfish, and country ham, and always, a little something sweet. The following vignettes, menus, and recipes offer a glimpse of Southern living as Memphians and their nearby neighbors have experienced it. Included with recipes from menus are a selected collection of other Southern favorites.

PEAR HONEY

A really old-time treat, this is homemade at its best. Combined with sweet butter and hot biscuits, it is superb. Or try it over ice cream. It requires a special pear, the country kind—firm and apple-shaped with brownish-red skin and a hard, grainy texture. These are sometimes called preserving pears, sand pears, September pears, or Kieffer pears.

3 quarts peeled and coarsely ground fresh pears (use food grinder rather than food processor to extract more juice)	5 to 5½ cups sugar 3½ cups water 1 20-ounce can crushed pineapple with juice

Mix all ingredients and boil 1 to 1¼ hours in deep pan, stirring often, until mixture becomes amber-colored and syrupy. Pour into sterilized pint jars and seal while hot. Pear honey should be rather thin and syrupy, not thick like preserves or jelly.

Note: Preserving pears are generally home-grown and should be picked from the tree. Do not use pears that have brown spots, have fallen to the ground, or have been pecked by birds. If you do not have access to a friendly pear tree, pears may be purchased from produce store or farmers' market.

Yields 6 pints

Millard C. Harville
Pope, Mississippi

FLUFFY COTTAGE CHEESE PANCAKES

Great with hot, sautéed apple slices and thick country bacon.

1 cup large or small curd cottage cheese 4 eggs	¼ cup all-purpose flour ¼ teaspoon salt Fresh fruit of choice

In blender combine all ingredients except fruit and blend well on high speed. Mix in fruit. Cook pancakes in hot skillet or on griddle, turning when tops are covered with bubbles and edges are slightly dry.

Yields 1 dozen 5-inch pancakes

Barbara Walston Brunner

MUSCADINE PRESERVES

Gather ye muscadines while ye may—for finding them is the real challenge in making these preserves. These large, dark southern grapes grow mostly in the wild. In old wooded areas, the clusters of fruit bend from the branches, drop to the ground, or grow out of reach. But they are many times wonderful and worth the trouble to find. With a little luck, you may find them at farmers' markets.

Muscadines, however many you can find	1 cup sugar to every cup of muscadine pulp and seed

Wash muscadines and discard bad ones. Pop grapeskins to remove pulp (an easy way is to push muscadines against the bottom of a pan). Boil skins with a cup of water (or more if needed) in large pot, stirring until a soft, somewhat mushy mixture occurs. Cook pulp in another pot, stirring hard with wooden spoon, until seeds separate and pulp becomes soft and takes on creamy appearance. Push pulp through sieve to remove seeds, stirring hard with spoon and pressing against sides of sieve. Scrape bottom of sieve from time to time to remove pulp that clings there.

Combine cooked skins and pulp with sugar in large pot and bring to boil, stirring frequently. Simmer, continuing to stir, until a small portion dropped into cold water is somewhat jellied, rather like soft ball stage in candy-making (or test on small plate). Pour into sterilized jars, add jar tops, and seal when cooled.

Yield depends upon muscadine harvest

Mrs. Charles W. Olim

RED EYE GRAVY

The real thing. Great with grits and hot biscuits.

Fry slices of country ham. Pour off excess fat, leaving some drippings and crusty pieces in skillet. Stir in a little water, add 1 tablespoon sorghum, and pour in ½ to 1 cup coffee. Stir and heat and pour over ham. Serve remainder in gravy boat.

SOUTHERN BAKED COUNTRY HAM

Country ham is so good that it defies description.

12 to 15 pound country ham with bone (preferably Marten or Miller)	*2 cups chopped celery leaves*
	1 cup honey or sorghum molasses
2 apples, sliced crosswise	*1 46-ounce can pineapple juice*

Place ham on rack in roaster with skin side down and cut side up. Cover ham with apple slices (use toothpicks to hold in place), then celery leaves, honey, and juice. Close roaster vent and boil on stove top until strong steam develops. Bake at 300 degrees for 1½ to 2 hours or until bone moves. Remove from oven, take out rack, and turn cut side of ham over into juices. Open vent and marinate overnight.

Skin ham. Garnish with pineapple slices, cherries, and brown sugar. Place on baking sheet and bake 10 to 15 minutes at 250 degrees. Cool and refrigerate 24 hours before slicing.

Serves 15 to 20

Ellen Davies Rodgers
Brunswick, Tennessee

ABOUT GRITS

Grits are great just cooked as directed on the package, dressed with butter, and seasoned with salt and pepper. For a special taste, substitute chicken broth for water in cooking.

COUNTRY MORNING BREAKFAST

Any child who grew up in the country in the South, or who visited grandparents in the country, enjoyed many rich experiences, including one called breakfast. Morning came early in the country, before daybreak. Children who wanted to help had to rub sleepy eyes and scramble out of feather beds in a hurry. Activity in the kitchen could be heard throughout the house, as the giant stove—in the old days, a wood stove with its warming ovens, and reservoirs for hot water—started its collaboration with skillets and coffeepots and biscuit pans. Breakfasts were hearty—no liquid diets or cholesterol-consciousness here. With chores to be done, energy was needed. The result was a heavenly combination of aromas and flavors that was forever unforgettable: a large coffeepot with steam rising from it, fresh country butter and sweet cream, jams and jellies from the pantry, biscuits made from scratch out of the old flour bin, thick slabs of bacon and country ham from the smokehouse, red-eye gravy, eggs sunny-side up, homemade applesauce or stewed, homegrown apples, and maybe little skillet puffs—pie pastry triangles fried golden brown and dusted with powdered sugar. And after breakfast? There weren't enough hours in the day for all that awaited a child—wading in the creek and sliding down the bank, swinging on grapevines hanging from trees, chewing sugar cane, making maypop dolls, skipping down orchard paths for green apple treats, perching on cotton wagons waiting at the gin, climbing into hay lofts and telling ghost stories, and maybe, just maybe, an afternoon visit to the general store for strawberry pop and ice cream to be eaten with a flat wooden spoon.

Slab Bacon, Thick-Sliced
Country Ham with Red Eye Gravy
Fried Eggs   Buttered Grits
Stewed Apples
Hot Biscuits and Sweet Butter
Pear Honey and Muscadine Preserves

Nancy Lewis

HOT FIGGY FRUIT

Perhaps everyone has a favorite hot spiced fruit recipe. The addition of figs puts this one in a class of its own.

1 16-ounce can pear halves	½ cup butter, melted
1 20-ounce can pineapple spears	1 tablespoon brown sugar
1 16-ounce can peach slices	1 teaspoon curry powder
1 17-ounce can figs	1 teaspoon ground cinnamon
	½ teaspoon ground nutmeg

Drain fruit well and pat dry with absorbent towel. Arrange fruit in 7 x 11-inch baking dish. Mix together remaining ingredients and sprinkle over fruit. Bake 50 minutes at 325 degrees.

Serves 8

Mrs. Norfleet Sledge

ANGEL BISCUITS

A light, little dream of a biscuit with that heavenly taste of yeast bread. Serve piping hot with butter and PEAR HONEY.

½ teaspoon baking soda	3 tablespoons sugar
2 cups buttermilk	5 teaspoons baking powder
1 package yeast	1¼ teaspoons salt
5 tablespoons warm water	1 cup vegetable shortening
5 cups all-purpose flour	

Dissolve baking soda in buttermilk; dissolve yeast in water. Set both aside. Sift together dry ingredients. Add shortening and blend well. Add buttermilk and yeast mixtures, stirring until well-mixed. Divide dough in thirds and knead several times on floured surface. Roll out each third ½-inch thick and cut with small biscuit cutter. Place on greased baking sheet, brush tops with butter, and let rise 1½ hours. Bake at 425 degrees for 12 to 15 minutes or until lightly browned.

Note: Place unbaked biscuits on baking sheet, cover with foil, freeze, and then store in plastic bags in freezer until needed. Remove from freezer, let rise 3 hours, and bake as above.

Yields 4 to 5 dozen biscuits

Anne Filer Crosby

BREAKFAST COFFEE CAKE

Proof again that homemade is best.

2 cups sugar	1 teaspoon baking powder
1 cup margarine	¼ teaspoon salt
2 eggs	½ cup finely chopped pecans
1 cup sour cream	2 tablespoons brown sugar
½ teaspoon vanilla	½ teaspoon cinnamon
2 cups sifted cake flour	Confectioners' sugar

Cream sugar with margarine and eggs. Gently stir in sour cream and vanilla. Sift together flour, baking powder, and salt, and fold into sour cream mixture. Spoon half of batter into greased and floured 10-inch tube pan. Mix pecans with brown sugar and cinnamon, and sprinkle half over batter in pan. Cover with remaining batter and pecan topping. Bake 55 to 60 minutes at 350 degrees. Leave in pan until almost cool. Sprinkle with confectioners' sugar.

Serves 16 to 20

Mrs. John R. Adams

BESS' PECAN CINNAMON TOAST

One of those ageless favorites that take their place in family histories. From a much-beloved octogenarian cousin who invented this wonderful thing.

1 small loaf sandwich bread, trimmed and sliced thin	½ cup butter, softened Cinnamon to taste
1 cup sugar	½ to ⅔ cup pecan chips

Cut bread slices in halves. Mix sugar and butter, and add enough cinnamon to make mixture rather dark. Spread on bread and place on baking sheet with raised sides, arranging so that edges touch. Sprinkle evenly with pecans. Bake at 350 degrees for 15 minutes or until lightly toasted.

Note: To reheat, wrap in foil and warm 10 minutes at 300 degrees.

Yields 3½ dozen pieces

Mrs. Bland C. Cannon

BACON-WRAPPED QUAIL

Makes breakfast a memorable event.

1 quail	Salt and pepper to taste
Milk	Bacon slices
1 generous tablespoon butter	

Soak quail in milk several hours or overnight. Pat quail dry, place butter inside, and sprinkle with salt and pepper. Cover quail with strips of bacon (strip of lean is especially good) and bake until done. Brown under broiler and serve hot.

Serves 1

Carroll Leatherman

BAKED OYSTERS IN CREAM SAUCE

Oysters, brought in barrels upriver from the Gulf, were staples in Memphis and Delta homes. They always made an appearance at Christmas.

Butter baking dish, and layer first with cracker crumbs and then with uncooked oysters. Dot generously with butter and season with salt and pepper. Repeat layers once, cover with CREAM SAUCE, sprinkle with more crumbs, and bake at 350 degrees until browned and bubbly.

Sarah Meador

MARY'S STICKY BISCUITS

These "stickies" are great and a favorite Delta dish.

2 dozen day-old biscuits	1 pint heavy molasses,
Butter	preferably sorghum

Split biscuits, butter each half, and toast briefly in oven or under broiler. Line baking dish with layer of biscuits, toasted side up. Top with more butter and pour molasses over all. Continue layers until all biscuits are used. Cover with molasses, and bake until hot clear through and molasses is absorbed in biscuits.

Serves 8 to 12

Nancy Stovall
Stovall, Mississippi

CHRISTMAS MORNING PLANTATION BREAKFAST

Southerners are at home with traditions. Like initials carved in a special tree, they bring back time and place. Every family has its own traditions for the Christmas season. For some there may be a dinner before or after church services on Christmas Eve, a dinner whose menu never varies, lest complaints come loud and clear. And Christmas morning may find one family having coffee and sweet rolls in tandem with the delighted discoveries of Santa's surprises, while another will have a sumptuous breakfast after opening all their gifts. On Delta plantations, now as often as not called farms, these were breakfasts to remember. There would be much gathering in, with arrivals of family from the city and from the country, each falling into his or her accustomed place in the rhythm of the familiar and expected, and always at least one much-loved old dog—usually of the hunting variety—making everyone welcome before taking a long nap, stretched out in the middle of everything. It would be a rare home that would not be decorated with magnolia leaves and holly branches gathered on the place, with a very tall Christmas tree cut from the land, and there would always be a sprig of mistletoe, provided by a fearless child who had climbed the tree for it, or brought down by some handy hunter's gun. The fare would be festive, for it would be the only meal of the day until a grand dinner was served as dusk fell and embers were stirred again in huge, old fireplaces.

Little Splits of Champagne on Ice
or
My Mother's Mississippi Delta Egg Nog*
Fresh Orange Slices
Bacon-Wrapped Quail
Baked Oysters in Cream Sauce
Scrambled Eggs Surrounded by Sausage Patties
Skillet Tomatoes*
Grits with Butter
Mary's Sticky Biscuits
Angel Biscuits with Homemade Preserves

Carroll Leatherman
Commerce Landing Plantation
Robinsonville, Mississippi

*See Index

COMPANY'S COMIN' HOT ROLLS

A great basic recipe that yields wonderful hot rolls and leads to the best sweet rolls you'll ever taste.

1 package yeast	4 cups all-purpose flour
1 cup lukewarm water	1 egg
¼ cup sugar	1 teaspoon salt
½ cup butter, melted and cooled to lukewarm	½ cup butter, melted and kept warm

Dissolve yeast in lukewarm water in mixing bowl. Mix sugar with lukewarm butter and beat into yeast mixture. Sift in 2 cups flour and then add egg, beating well after each addition. Sift in remaining flour with salt, beating well. Cover bowl and refrigerate until 2½ to 3 hours before serving (can chill overnight).

Knead, roll out ⅓-inch thick, and cut with 2-inch cutter. Dip each roll in butter, fold in half, and place side-by-side in 11 x 17-inch baking pan. Let rise in warm place 2 hours or until doubled in bulk. Bake at 400 degrees for 10 minutes or until browned on top. Serve immediately.

Yields 4 dozen rolls

Sweet Rolls
Make basic roll recipe, but increase sugar to ⅓ cup.

½ cup raisins	2 tablespoons cinnamon
1 cup brown sugar	½ cup butter, melted
2 teaspoons nutmeg	

Cover raisins with warm water. Mix together sugar and spices. Place half of dough on floured board, knead, and roll out ⅛ to ¼-inch thick. Brush with half of butter and spread half of sugar mixture over dough. Drain and dry raisins, then sprinkle half over dough. Roll in jelly roll fashion and slice in 12 pieces. Place in 11 x 15-inch baking pan and brush tops with butter. Repeat procedure with other half of dough. Let rise 2 hours or until doubled in bulk. Bake at 400 degrees for 10 minutes or until browned on top.

Yields 2 dozen rolls

Mrs. William D. Galbreath

BAKED COUNTRY BACON SLICES

Make a lot of these. Everyone will love them.

2 eggs, beaten	Plain corn meal
1 scant teaspoon dry mustard	Thick slices of slab bacon,
1 scant teaspoon tarragon vinegar	or commercial brand sliced thick
Crushed saltine crackers	

Combine eggs, mustard, and vinegar, and heat to form a paste. Combine equal parts saltine crumbs and corn meal. Coat bacon in paste and dredge well in crumb mixture. Lay bacon on baking sheet and bake 15 minutes at 400 degrees.

Note: Adjust both coating mixtures to what is needed to coat bacon used.

Yield depends on amount of bacon used

Anne Connell

BREAKFAST SOUFFLÉ

A grand brunch dish. Especially good with its nip of hot peppers.

12 slices bread, trimmed	2 cups cubed ham, preferably
1 7-ounce can Ortega chili peppers, chopped and juice reserved	country ham
	3 cups milk
	6 eggs
1 pound grated Cheddar cheese	

Butter both sides of each bread slice and cut in fourths. Layer half of bread in greased 9 x 13-inch baking dish. In order, top with half of cheese, all of peppers, and half of ham. Repeat layers with remaining bread, cheese, and ham.

Combine milk with eggs and reserved juice, beating well, and pour over casserole. Bake at 350 degrees for 50 to 60 minutes or until browned on top. (This will not rise or puff up, but will be thick and bubbly when done.)

Serves 12

Anne Connell

THE BEST CHEESE GRITS

There may not be a better recipe for cheese grits. This one first appeared in a delightful book called *Delta Dining* from Marks, Mississippi. It bears repeating.

1 cup grits (not instant)
1 6-ounce package Kraft garlic cheese
½ cup margarine
2 eggs
1 cup milk
Grated Parmesan cheese

Cook grits according to package instructions. While grits are still hot, add cheese and margarine, stirring until cheese melts and ingredients are blended. Beat eggs with milk and stir into hot grits mixture. Pour into baking dish, sprinkle with Parmesan cheese, and bake 45 minutes at 350 degrees.

Note: Recipe doubles beautifully. Use 3-quart baking dish.

Serves 8

Mrs. Bob Carson
Marks, Mississippi

ERNEST HUGHES' BEULAH ISLAND APPLES

From the fabulous cook at Beulah Island Hunting Club near Rosedale, Mississippi.

3 cups sugar
1 cup water
Juice of 2 lemons
1 9-ounce package Red Hots
8 apples, peeled and cored
½ cup lemon juice

Combine 2½ cups sugar, water, juice from lemons, and red hots, and bring to boil. Reduce heat and simmer until light syrup forms, stirring constantly until red hots are melted. Add apples and cook until soft, but do not overcook. Place apples in baking dish and cover with half of syrup. Combine remaining syrup with ½ cup lemon juice and remaining ½ cup sugar, and cook until as thick as molasses. Serve garnished with sprig of mint or, if during the holiday season, sprig of holly.

Serves 8

Anne Connell

DELTA HOUSE PARTY BRUNCH

The Mississippi Delta—that legendary land that forms a rough triangle from Walls (just outside Memphis) to Greenwood to Vicksburg with the river to the west, is peopled with folk of a peculiar mind set. To them, distances mean nothing for they often live a long way from friends and neighbors in their towns and on their farms, and visiting means getting on the road. To drive a hundred miles from one town or farm to another for a tennis game, a round of bridge, a birthday luncheon, and to do it often, is not unusual at all because friends are friends, and good times are important. Memories are made here, the generational kind. Things change little, and then, only slowly. Times are sometimes easy, sometimes hard, depending on the weather and the crops, but times are always good when friends get together. This is a flat land, rich land for growing cotton and soybeans, land dotted with towns named for families whose plantations, often stretching from the levee across thousands of acres, put the towns on the map—names like Dockery, Bobo, Crenshaw, and Stovall; with colorful names like Alligator, Merigold, Money, and Minter City; Midnight, Friars Point, and Sunflower Landing; and not to be forgotten—Hushpuckena. One of the most pleasant happenings in the Delta is the house party, a week-end of parties often moving from house to house for brunches, lunches, and dinners, occasioned by a wedding, or a dove shoot, or the visit of a favorite friend or relative—or likely as not, for no reason at all except that it sounded like a good idea. House party days are spent in the pursuit of happiness and hallmarked by the telling of stories and the listening to them. A typical brunch might include:

Memphis Mornings*
Deep-Fried Stuffing Balls
Broiled Bacon-Wrapped Chicken Livers
Baked Country Bacon Slices
Breakfast Soufflé
The Best Cheese Grits
Ernest Hughes' Beulah Island Apples
Assorted Small Pastries

*See Index

Anne Connell

MISS BEA'S FRIED CORN

Miss Bea, a tall woman, was in the habit of walking into her garden early in the morning to pick a few ears of fresh corn. The story goes that her son, when very young, once became quite frightened watching his mother walk into the corn patch and seemingly disappear. Which tells us the corn grew tall in Clarksdale, Mississippi, where Miss Bea lived.

12 ears sweet corn	Salt and freshly ground black
2 tablespoons butter	pepper
¾ cup milk	

Cut corn from ears and scrape cob for juices. Melt butter in heavy skillet over medium heat and sauté corn 5 minutes, stirring frequently. Add milk, stirring constantly. Cover and cook 10 to 15 minutes over low heat until milk is absorbed, stirring occasionally. Season to taste.

Serves 6 to 8

Marilyn Iskiwitz Califf

CLICK'S BLACK-EYED NEW YEAR CASSEROLE

According to Southern tradition, New Year's Day must be greeted with black-eyed peas and hog's head for good luck. With just a little variation, here's a good dish for preserving that time-honored custom.

1 pound hot or mild pork sausage	Freshly ground black pepper to taste
1 large onion, chopped	½ teaspoon dry mustard
4 16-ounce cans black-eyed peas, drained	½ teaspoon oregano
	½ teaspoon marjoram
2 14½-ounce cans whole tomatoes with juice, chopped	½ teaspoon chervil
	½ teaspoon monosodium glutamate
1 tablespoon Worcestershire sauce	1 bay leaf

Brown sausage. Add onion and cook 5 minutes, stirring occasionally. Add remaining ingredients, draining some of grease if there seems to be too much. Place in 3-quart baking dish and bake 1 hour at 350 degrees. Remove bay leaf before serving.

Serves 10 to 12

Ann Clark Harris

SWEET POTATO CARAMEL

Sweet potatoes all dressed up.

6 large sweet potatoes	1 teaspoon vanilla
½ cup brown sugar	½ cup slivered almonds,
¼ cup butter	toasted

Wrap potatoes in foil and bake 3 hours at 300 degrees.

Peel and mash potatoes while hot. Whip potatoes with brown sugar, butter, and vanilla. Pour into buttered, deep 2½-quart baking dish. Make well in center of potato mixture and fill with caramel sauce. Top with almonds and bake at 350 degrees for 30 to 40 minutes or until bubbly.

Caramel Sauce

1 cup sugar	½ cup butter
1 cup light cream	

Combine ingredients in large skillet and cook over medium heat until honey-colored.

Serves 8

Roma Marmon

VEGETABLE JAMBALAYA

Delicious, bright, and colorful. Wonderful for a summer supper.

2 tablespoons chopped onion	3 ears sweet corn, corn cut from cob and cob scraped
2 to 3 slices bacon, cut in small pieces	1 teaspoon Worcestershire sauce
½ pound fresh okra, chopped (or 10-ounce package frozen)	½ to 1 teaspoon salt
1 14½-ounce can whole tomatoes	⅛ teaspoon pepper
	Cooked rice

In large skillet, sauté onion and bacon until bacon is rather crisp. Add okra, cover, and cook 20 minutes over medium-low heat. Add tomatoes, break up with spoon, and cook 5 minutes more. Stir in corn and scrapings from cob, Worcestershire sauce, salt, and pepper, and cook 10 minutes. Serve over rice.

Serves 6

Marion D. Kendall

SKILLET TOMATOES

Almost a stewed tomato. A marvelous combination of flavors.

Ripe tomatoes   Brown sugar
Butter

Cut tomatoes in thick slices. Melt butter in skillet, add tomatoes, and sauté thoroughly on both sides. Sprinkle with brown sugar and continue cooking until sugar is absorbed and tomatoes are darkened. Serve hot.

Servings depend upon
   number of tomatoes

Carroll Leatherman

TURNIP GREENS
WITH CORN MEAL DUMPLINGS

A different way to have your corn bread with your turnip greens. Very good, too.

9 cups water
2 cloves garlic
3 to 4 bunches fresh turnip
   greens, washed and trimmed
1 pound turnips, peeled and
   quartered

5 slices bacon, fried crisp and
   crumbled, drippings
   reserved
1 teaspoon sugar
1 teaspoon salt
½ teaspoon crushed red pepper

Bring water to boil in 6-quart saucepan. Add remaining ingredients and reserved drippings. Cover and simmer 1½ hours. Remove 1 cup pot liquor (juice from greens) for dumplings.

Dumplings
1½ cups white corn meal
½ cup all-purpose flour
1 teaspoon baking powder
1 teaspoon sugar
½ teaspoon salt

1 cup pot liquor
3 tablespoons margarine,
   melted
1 egg, beaten

Thoroughly mix dry ingredients. Quickly stir in remaining ingredients. Spoon rounded tablespoons of batter into saucepan holding greens. Cover and simmer 30 minutes.

Serves 6 to 8

Phyllis Brannon

SOUTHERN TURNIP GREENS

Old ways are sometimes the best ways when it comes to cooking. There is no improvement to be found in this method of cooking that queen of the southern vegetable patch, the turnip green.

2 quarts water   3 to 4 bunches turnip greens
⅛ pound lean salt meat   1 teaspoon baking soda

Bring water to boil in large stock pot. Add salt meat. Keep water and meat at slightly rolling boil for 2 to 3 hours.

Soak turnip greens in sink filled with cold water for 1 hour, swishing greens occasionally. Drain and run cold water over them while picking leaves from stems. Rinse 6 to 8 times under cold water until thoroughly clean. Fill sink with cold water and add greens and baking soda. Let stand a few seconds. Remove greens and squeeze out all water. Put greens in stock pot with meat and cook rapidly 20 to 25 minutes. The liquid in the pot becomes a marvelous pot liquor, to be served with corn bread. Taste greens for tenderness and cook longer if necessary.

Note: For an extra special, extra Southern touch, add 8 to 10 leaves of poke sallet (a "weed" found growing in yards and along roadsides that most locals can point out to you) that have been well washed and boiled separately in plain water. Stir into greens when tender.

Serves 3 to 4

Ernestine Cunningham

HOT PEPPER SAUCE

Pepper sauce sprinkled over turnip greens—or any other kind of greens—is a must! If peppers are from a home garden plot, they may carry a little extra warmth.

Whole hot peppers, red or   Cider vinegar
   green, or mixture of both   ½ teaspoon salt

Rinse peppers well and fill half of quart jar. Heat enough vinegar to fill jar, add salt, and pour into jar. Seal and let stand at least 7 days. Transfer vinegar and peppers to smaller jars for serving. Serve with greens. (Some like it on black-eyed peas, also.)

Yields 1 quart sauce

Prince Ella Hayes

A Summer Lawn Supper at Davies Manor

At the end of a long grove of oak trees which line a narrow, one-time carriage path stands Davies Manor, believed to be the oldest home in Shelby County. Construction of this two-story plantation home near Brunswick, Tennessee began in 1807. It was built beside an ancient Indian mound, and is one of the few structures in West Tennessee dating back to the years before the Chickasaw Cession of land to the United States government in 1818. Resting firmly on its original native sandstone boulders, it still reflects a touching mixture of pioneer practicality and quiet dignity achieved by the combined efforts of its several builders.

The earliest section of the home, a plaster-chinked log house consisting of a twenty-foot-square parlor with low-beamed ceilings, and a bedroom of similar dimensions above, was probably built by a Chickasaw Indian chief, although no official written records exist. The second owner, a planter from Virginia named Joel W. Royster, added another wing sometime after 1831, and connected it to the first by an open-air passageway, a so-called dogtrot. In 1851, the house and some two thousand surrounding acres were bought by the Davies family which has owned the property ever since. In succeeding years, the dogtrot was enclosed and a small columned porch was added, giving the simple farmhouse the lofty air of a Southern colonial mansion.

Today, this grand old place is open to visitors. The Davies descendant who is the current owner of the plantation, Mrs. Ellen Davies Rodgers, gave the home and surrounding grounds to the Davies Manor Association in 1976. The association maintains the property and conducts tours every Tuesday afternoon, May through October. Mrs. Davies, living nearby in her comfortable country home, The Oaks, continues to supervise the farm operation, producing soybeans, corn, hay, and cotton, and raising Angus cattle on the land.

A visit to Davies Manor is a trip back into another century. The home's unique charm invites visitors to stay a while, to linger by the old fireplace, to take pleasure in the look of the crisp white curtains against the hand-hewn logs of oak, to admire the antique fourposter bed, dressed in quilts and ruffles. Davies Manor is the regular meeting place of several patriotic organizations—the Zachariah Davies chapter of the Daughters of the American Revolution, and chapters of the Children of the American Revolution, and the Sons of the American Revolution. It was also the focal point of the town of Brunswick's year-long homecoming celebration in 1986 that included a watermelon festival, gospel singing, an ice cream supper, a tour of a cotton gin, and an antique quilt show where Brunswick Stew was served. The year of festivities ended with the fifty-third lighting of the Davies Plantation Christmas tree.

A monument to old days and old ways, Davies Manor is, and will remain, a solid fortress against change, a symbol of the proud persistence of historical awareness in modern Memphis.

THE PICTURE: *In the shade of a giant magnolia tree, a lawn supper has been set out for members of the historical society that is meeting on this summer evening at Davies Manor, believed to be the oldest home in Shelby County. This unique, old two-story plantation house, located near Brunswick, Tennessee, on the old stage coach route from Memphis to Nashville, is open to touring visitors one afternoon a week during the summer months, and is often the scene of such gatherings as this. The surrounding farm, still in operation, is lovingly supervised by a granddaughter of the Davies family, which has owned the land since 1851. The table here is covered with white linen, set with Davies family cut-glass and silver, and decorated with fresh-cut roses from the private garden near the manor.*

THE FOOD: *The menu—a typical, old-time, small-town, pot-luck supper—includes SOUTHERN BAKED COUNTRY HAM, a squash casserole, CRUNCHY POTATOES AU GRATIN, SPINACH SOUFFLÉ, fresh hot rolls, homemade plum preserves, SWEET GARLIC PICKLES, PLANTATION POUND CAKE, and syllabub custard with brandied cherries.*

SPINACH SOUFFLÉ

A quick and easy potluck dish, great for church suppers and dinners-on-the-ground.

2 15-ounce cans whole spinach, drained and chopped	Salt and white pepper to taste
1 10¾-ounce can cream of mushroom soup	2 eggs, separated
¼ teaspoon garlic salt	½ cup grated mild Cheddar cheese
	Browned bread crumbs

Combine spinach, soup, garlic salt, salt, and pepper. Beat egg yolks until fluffy, add cheese, and blend into spinach mixture. Beat egg whites until stiff and fold into spinach mixture. Pour into well-buttered baking dish lightly coated with bread crumbs. Top with additional bread crumbs and bake at 350 degrees for 25 to 30 minutes or until bubbly.

Serves 8 to 10

Ellen Davies Rodgers
Brunswick, Tennessee

CRUNCHY POTATOES AU GRATIN

A good old standard with a different approach. The water chestnuts add a nice texture.

5 large potatoes	3 hard-cooked eggs, sliced
1 8-ounce can water chestnuts, sliced	1 cup grated mild Cheddar cheese
1 10¾-ounce can cream of potato or celery soup	Salt and white pepper to taste

Boil potatoes in jackets until tender. Cool, peel, and slice. In well-buttered 2-quart baking dish, layer half of potatoes, water chestnuts, soup, eggs, and cheese. Repeat layers once. Add seasonings. Bake at 350 degrees until cheese is melted and bubbly.

Serves 10 to 12

Ellen Davies Rodgers
Brunswick, Tennessee

GRANDMOTHER'S AMBROSIA

The sweetest of sweets. Gorgeous in an antique cut-glass bowl.

Oranges	Fresh coconut
Sugar	

Peel oranges, and with sharp knife, remove sections from white membrane. Arrange orange sections in layers in pretty glass bowl, generously sprinkling each layer with sugar and coconut.

Nancy Y. Donovan

LUCILLE'S BANANA SALAD

A great-grandmother's traditional recipe that has been making its way to family picnics for nearly a century.

1 20-ounce can unsalted peanuts	½ cup water
1 egg, beaten	2 teaspoons all-purpose flour
½ cup sugar	1 tablespoon heavy cream
½ cup vinegar	4 bananas, firm and barely ripe

Spread peanuts on baking sheet and toast 10 minutes at 350 degrees. Grind peanuts in food processor (yields about 3¼ cups).

Combine egg, sugar, vinegar, water, and flour in top of double boiler, stirring and cooking until thick. Set aside to cool. Stir in cream.

Cut each banana in 3 equal pieces. Roll in sauce, lightly scraping off any excess, then roll quickly and lightly in ground peanuts. Place on wax paper and store in tightly sealed container. (Bananas may darken slightly, but will keep through the day.) Arrange on platter to serve.

Note: Use only small amount of ground peanuts at a time as sauce will drip from bananas, and fresh peanuts must be added from time to time.

Serves 6 to 8

Shirley Sigler Chamberlin
Millington, Tennessee

AUNT GERTRUDE MERRIN'S PICKLED OKRA

Try to eat just one.

Okra, whole and very small	1 quart vinegar
Garlic cloves, sliced	2 quarts water
Dill weed	1 cup salt
Hot peppers	1/8 teaspoon alum
Carrot pieces, optional	

Soak okra overnight in ice water. Wipe dry before filling jars.

Pack sterilized jars with okra (alternating ends), garlic, dill weed, and hot peppers. Add carrot and/or celery pieces if desired. Combine remaining ingredients to make brine and boil 3 minutes. Cover okra with brine. Do not cap tightly until all bubbling has stopped. Let stand at least 6 weeks. Serve chilled.

Yield depends upon amount of okra

Mrs. James A. Prewitt III

GRANNY'S CHOW-CHOW

Sweet memories of childhood, of being allowed to turn the old food grinder in preparing the relish. The aroma in Granny's kitchen was unforgettably wonderful. So was Granny.

1 quart green tomatoes	2 cups vinegar
2 quarts cabbage	1 tablespoon mixed pickling
6 onions	spice
6 red bell peppers	1 tablespoon dry mustard
6 green bell peppers	1 1/2 teaspoons celery seed
3/4 cup salt	1/2 teaspoon turmeric
2 1/2 cups sugar	

Grind all vegetables in food processor (or food grinder). Add salt and place in cheesecloth bag. Hang bag so that liquid drains into container beneath it, and let stand overnight to drain.

Squeeze remaining liquid from bag and empty bag into large pan. Add remaining ingredients and boil 20 minutes. Pour into hot sterilized jars and seal.

Yields 8 pints

Nancy R. Crosby

MARINATED VIDALIA ONIONS

Vidalia season! Brief and sweet, but ever prompting more delicious ways to serve these treasures, large yellow onions whose delicate flavor is dependent upon the particular soil of Vidalia, Georgia. Try Vidalias sliced in rings, dipped in buttermilk and flour, then salted and fried. Or tuck a little butter and brown sugar inside and bake them. And as soon as you can, try them marinated.

1/2 cup white vinegar	1/2 cup mayonnaise
1 cup sugar	Dill seed to taste
2 cups boiling water	Chopped parsley to taste
4 Vidalia onions, sliced and	Celery salt to taste
separated into rings	Sprinkle of paprika

Mix vinegar and sugar in water until sugar dissolves. Pour over onions and marinate several hours or overnight. Drain well.

Mix mayonnaise with remaining ingredients. Pour over onions and toss to mix well. Serve as a vegetable side dish, as relish, or coarsely chopped as spread for crackers.

Serves 8 to 10

Mrs. Percy Magness

COLD TOMATO COBB

A treasured classic.

6 large ripe tomatoes	1/4 teaspoon coarsely ground
1 small white onion, minced	black pepper
1 1/2 teaspoons salt	

Plunge tomatoes briefly into boiling water, rinse immediately with cold water, and remove skin. Chop tomatoes coarsely in food processor or blender, and mix with onion and seasonings. Place in freezer until chilled but not frozen. Stir when frosty and serve in chilled bouillon cups with dollop of topping.

Topping

5 tablespoons mayonnaise	1 teaspoon curry powder
1 tablespoon minced parsley	

Combine all ingredients and mix well.

Serves 8

Mrs. W. L. Oates

SUNDAY DINNER AT GRANDMOTHER'S HOUSE

Southerners are connectional. They love to touch fingers with the past. They know their aunts and uncles, and cousins three and four times removed. And they have a special relationship with their grandmothers, for it is they whom the family chooses to gather around, most often on Sundays after church. Although today we live in a fast-food era and we sometimes seem to live in a fast-forward frame of mind, for many Southerners, still, Sunday dinner at Grandmother's house is the centerpiece of the week. She it is who knows everyone's favorite food and sees that they get it, who keeps all secrets, who remembers when, who can name all the faces in the faded photographs. She it is who has time to answer letters, and to listen, and who has lived long enough to provide some sensible words of wisdom to young, impatient hearts. She is a haven, and although now she may play tennis and love to travel when once she quilted and made jam, she still somehow manages to be there when you need her. She's your mother's mother, or your father's mother—or if you're blessed indeed, you'll have both. Heading for her house is the sweetest of journeys.

Herbed Pork Roast
Rice and Gravy
Skillet Squash   Fresh Green Beans
Marinated Vidalia Onions*
Pocketbook Rolls*
Mother's Egg Custard Pie*
or
Plantation Pound Cake*
with
Old-Fashioned Boiled Custard*

*See Index

Netta Sue Caudill King

HERBED PORK ROAST

The aroma is heavenly, and so is the taste.

1 6-pound pork loin	Few celery leaves
3 teaspoons salt	Several parsley sprigs
1 teaspoon pepper	3 bay leaves
1 teaspoon thyme	4 whole cloves
1 teaspoon nutmeg	2 10½-ounce cans beef
2 carrots, sliced	consommé
2 onions, sliced	1¼ cups water
2 cloves garlic	

Rub meat with mixture of salt, pepper, thyme, and nutmeg. Bake uncovered 20 minutes at 450 degrees in large Dutch oven. Place vegetables and remaining seasonings around roast. Pour consommé and water over all. Cover and bake at 350 degrees until roast is well done, about 35 minutes per pound, or until meat thermometer reads 170 degrees. Remove roast to platter.

Remove garlic, cloves, and bay leaves. Using potato masher, thoroughly blend vegetables with juices in pan to make sauce. Thin with small amount water if necessary and serve with roast.

Serves 12

Nancy McConnico Beck

SKILLET SQUASH

Two recipes in one, because the sautéed squash straight from the skillet is as good as the baked version.

1 pound yellow summer squash or zucchini	¼ cup water
	Salt and pepper to taste
¾ cup diced onion	2 teaspoons sugar
3 to 4 slices bacon, fried crisp,	2 to 3 eggs
crumbled, 4 tablespoons	¼ cup milk
drippings reserved	½ cup buttered bread crumbs

Slice squash. Sauté in bacon drippings in large skillet with onion. Add water, seasonings, and sugar. Cook and stir until water evaporates. (Can be served at this point. Delicious!) Beat eggs with milk, stir into squash mixture, and pour into buttered baking dish. Sprinkle with bread crumbs and bacon, and bake at 350 degrees for 20 minutes or until bubbly.

Serves 6 to 8

Mrs. William H. Houston III
Washington, D.C.

CHICKEN AND DUMPLINGS MY WAY

A down-home favorite that cannot be improved on.

Dumplings

3 cups all-purpose flour	½ teaspoon paprika
1 teaspoon baking powder	½ cup vegetable shortening
1 teaspoon salt	¾ to 1 cup ice water

Sift together dry ingredients and cut in shortening. Add enough water to make somewhat stiff dough. Chill.

Broth

1 5 to 6-pound hen	Dash garlic salt
3 celery ribs, chopped	1 tablespoon butter
1 teaspoon salt	Pepper to taste

Combine all ingredients except butter and pepper, cover with water, and bring to boil. Reduce heat and simmer 1 to 1½ hours until meat easily pulls from bone. Remove chicken from broth, skin, bone, and chop. Set aside.

Roll out dough ¼-inch thick on floured surface and cut in 3 x 1-inch strips. Bring broth to rolling boil. Stretch each dumpling strip and drop into broth one at a time. Reduce heat to medium, cover, and cook 10 minutes. Remove lid and cook 10 minutes more. Add chicken, butter, and pepper to taste. Serve hot in bowls.

Serves 8 to 10

Barbara M. Robertson

CHICKEN IN THE JUG

Definitely different and very good.

3 whole boned chicken breasts, halved and each half cut in 3 strips lengthwise	Salt and pepper to taste
	1 onion, thinly sliced
1 cup blended whiskey	½ cup butter, cut in pieces
	Seedless grapes

Marinate chicken in whiskey for 2 to 2½ hours. Place chicken in shallow baking dish, season with salt and pepper, and add whiskey marinade. Cover with onion slices and dot with butter. Bake 30 minutes at 375 degrees. Baste with pan juices. Add clumps of grapes and place briefly under broiler to brown chicken. Serve over toast points.

Serves 4 to 6

Nancy McConnico Beck

ERNESTINE CUNNINGHAM'S FABULOUS CORN PONES

Corn pones, hoe cakes, johnny cakes, ash cakes—call them what you will. Whether baked, or fried in bacon grease or shortening, hot breads made from corn meal have been comforting accompaniments to the Southern table from time immemorial.

2 cups white unbleached corn meal	½ teaspoon salt
	½ teaspoon sugar
2 tablespoons vegetable oil or bacon drippings	Boiling water

Combine corn meal, oil, salt, and sugar, and stir well with wooden spoon. Add enough boiling water to make a thick, but not stiff, mush that can be easily handled. Keeping hands moist with cold water, form batter into pones (a shape somewhat like a flattened lemon) about ½-inch thick. Bake 25 to 30 minutes at 450 or 500 degrees. Pones should be crisp outside and like corn bread inside.

Yields 16 corn pones

Mrs. Norfleet R. Turner

CORNSTICKS

The self-rising meal provides a nice shortcut. Anything that puts the cornbread on the table a little faster is a little blessing.

1½ cups milk	1 egg
2 tablespoons bacon drippings or vegetable shortening, melted	2 cups self-rising corn meal
	1 tablespoon sugar

Combine all ingredients and mix until well-blended. Grease cornstick pan or black iron skillet and heat in oven until grease sizzles. Pour batter into hot pan and bake at 425 degrees for 20 to 25 minutes or until golden brown.

Yields 12 cornsticks

Ames Plantation
Grand Junction, Tennessee

Country Hams From an Old Whitehaven Smokehouse

Among pioneers arriving from the east to seek fortunes in the brand-new town of Memphis in the early 1800s, there were a few venturesome souls who moved across Nonconnah Creek to the south, and settled on land they had bought from the Indians for fifty cents an acre. This area, now known as Whitehaven, was called "the dark corner" in those days because low-lying swamps were hidden in the deep forest of oaks and poplars. But its land proved to be most fertile, and the newcomers stayed on and prospered. Eventually, comfortable new homes began to replace the original log cabins—houses such as the charming, white frame cottage built in 1869 by the son of one of the early settlers, a stock farmer named Ferdinand Farrow, who raised fine carriage, saddle, and race horses. Behind the house (called Faronia, a derivation from the family name), he built another small structure, a smokehouse, which was considered a necessity for early Memphis homes so that meats could be deliciously preserved by familiar methods long used in Virginia, North Carolina, and East Tennessee.

Both buildings survived for more than a hundred years, even as Whitehaven became one of the fastest-growing areas of an expanding Memphis. At last, however, progress being inevitable, Faronia was torn down to make way for a new suburban shopping center. But its little smokehouse was rescued. A great-granddaughter of Ferdinand Farrow, the home's original owner, had the hand-hewn logs, beams, and shingles carefully dismantled and moved by truck to the large, grassy back lawn of her Collierville home, where they were just as carefully reassembled. There, resting under an old walnut tree, the gray and weathered smokehouse stands today, a monument to the strength of family loyalty and the appeal of old-time flavors.

The preservation of this one old smokehouse symbolizes, somehow, the Mid-South's continuing devotion to real country ham, its ongoing appreciation of the skill and care that produces it—a painstaking process perfected in the days of the earliest settlers, when the first silver frost that covered the ground each autumn always brought the ritual of killing the hogs that would provide meat during the long winter months. Next came the careful steps of bleeding the meat, hand-rubbing the hams in salt and sugar, packing them in large wooden salt bins in the smokehouse for six weeks, and, finally, hanging them from iron hooks above smoking hickory chips until full flavor and proper preservation were assured.

In today's era of commercial meat-packing, there are few still practicing the art. But one family-owned Memphis business, Lipscomb Country Hams, just east of the city on Highway 70, is in its third generation of processing smoked meat by methods that capture all the old flavors, and conjure up memories of hot biscuits, red-eye gravy, and thick slabs of country ham for breakfast. The Lipscomb Company ships its ham and bacon to all fifty states and to points around the world. Mrs. Lipscomb also gives her customers cooking hints on how and when to fry, bake, or boil country hams or country-cured bacon. They include some surprises, such as: "Wrap country ham in aluminum foil to bake, and for extra moisture add Coca-Cola or Seven-Up before closing the foil." Or: "To make red-eye gravy, pour off most of the grease after frying the ham and turn up the heat until the skillet is smoking; then add one or two ounces of water—or better still, some say, strong coffee."

THE PICTURE: *An old farm lamp guards the door of this century-old smokehouse, snatched from the path of the bulldozers in modern Whitehaven, to be preserved intact near a country pasture in Collierville. At the smokehouse entrance stand earthen-colored pickling jars that once held young green cucumbers, and gave forth the strong, sweet aroma of cloves and other spices. Inside, hams and country bacon hang from the sturdy beams on iron hooks. On the floor of the smokehouse is an old iron pot that holds hickory logs, symbolic of the smoking process that slowly but surely cures and flavors the meat.*

THE FOOD: *Slab bacon and country hams—the genuine article.*

GRITS AND GRILLADES

Grits—agreeable, versatile, and altogether lovely. Although plain grits with salt, pepper, and a pat of butter can hardly be improved upon, grits combine wonderfully with many other foods and flavors. Grits with grillades is a Deep South favorite.

Grillades

3 pounds veal cutlets, cut in small strips	1 pound mushrooms, thinly sliced
½ cup all-purpose flour	5 tomatoes, peeled and chopped
2 teaspoons black pepper	2 tablespoons tomato paste
3 teaspoons salt	4 tablespoons minced parsley
1½ cups butter	1 teaspoon thyme
4 tablespoons vegetable oil	1 cup red wine
2 cups minced green onion	2 cups water
1 cup minced green bell pepper	3 teaspoons Cajun seasoning
2 cloves garlic, minced	

Dredge cutlets in mixture of flour, pepper, and 2 teaspoons salt. In large heavy skillet, heat 1 cup butter with oil, add veal, brown on both sides, and remove from skillet. Reduce heat, add onion and bell pepper, and sauté until tender. Add garlic and sauté briefly. Remove from heat.

In another skillet sauté mushrooms in remaining ½ cup butter. Mix with tomatoes, tomato paste, parsley, thyme, and remaining teaspoon salt. Mix veal, sautéed mixtures, wine, water, and Cajun seasoning in Dutch oven, and bake 1 hour at 350 degrees. Serve over grits.

Grits

6 cups water	1½ cups milk
1½ cups regular grits	4 eggs, separated
½ cup butter	1 cup grated extra sharp Cheddar cheese
1 teaspoon salt	

Bring water to boil. Add grits, butter, and salt, stirring constantly. Add milk. Reduce heat, cover, and cook until creamy and soft, about 5 minutes. Remove from heat. Beat egg yolks and add with cheese to grits. Beat egg whites until fluffy and stiff, and fold into grits. Pour mixture into baking dish and bake 25 to 30 minutes at 400 degrees.

Serves 8 to 10

Beneva Mayweather
Mayweather Catering

THE HOLLYWOOD FRIED DILL PICKLES

The Hollywood is a local restaurant ten miles north of Tunica, Mississippi, fifteen minutes from the Tennessee-Mississippi state line. Open only on weekends, it has a loyal clientele that loves to sample the specialties of the house: fried catfish, marinated catfish, frog legs, steaks, and fried dill pickles. The restaurant was housed until recently in a 130-year old building that was at various times a plantation, a commissary, a stage coach stop, and a railroad station. The building burned, but the Hollywood returned and is in business once again, to the delight of its customers. Here is one of the favorite menu items, created on the spot when the kitchen had no more catfish to fry, but lots of batter and lots of pickles.

Vegetable oil	¼ cup milk
1 cup all-purpose flour	1 can beer
1 tablespoon baking powder	1 quart dill pickles, sliced thick or thin
1 tablespoon paprika	
2¼ teaspoons red pepper	

Heat vegetable oil to 350 to 375 degrees. Mix dry ingredients with milk. Add enough beer to make medium-thick batter. Dredge pickles in batter to coat lightly and fry immediately in hot oil. Batter will puff and turn a deep red-brown color. Serve hot.

Yields 1 quart fried dill pickles

The Hollywood Restaurant
Robinsonville, Mississippi
Sterling Owen, Proprietor

GEORGIANNE'S OKRA AND TOMATOES

A down home dish that is wonderful.

2 pounds equal amounts sliced fresh okra and peeled fresh tomatoes cut in wedges	½ medium onion, finely chopped
2 tablespoons butter	Salt and pepper to taste

Combine all ingredients and cook 1 hour over low heat or until of stewed texture. Do not add water.

Serves 4 to 6

Mrs. William H. Houston III
Washington, D.C.

BIG BATCH FISH FRY

When you want something good and you want a lot of it.

15 pounds catfish fillets   Vegetable oil

Fill cooking vat with oil and heat to 360 degrees. Just before frying, dip fillets in batter, shake off excess, and roll in breading. Deep-fry fish until done, about 1 to 2 minutes after fillets float to surface.

Batter
7½ cups plain wheat flour   2 tablespoons baking powder
3 tablespoons salt   Beer or water

Combine dry ingredients with enough liquid to give consistency of thin pancake batter.

Breading
7¼ cups plain corn meal   1 tablespoon lemon pepper
4½ tablespoons seasoned salt   Cayenne pepper to taste,
3½ tablespoons salt   optional
1¼ tablespoons black pepper

Thoroughly blend all ingredients.

Serves 20 to 30

Ralph Potter
The Catfish Congregation Cooking Team
Tunica, Mississippi

GRILLED CATFISH

A prize-winning recipe.

Mesquite wood chips   Cajun seasoning
5 to 7-ounce catfish fillet   Brown sugar
Fresh lemons

Thoroughly soak mesquite wood chips. Build a charcoal fire, and spread it when ready.

Squeeze lemons over both sides of fillet. Sprinkle seasoning and brown sugar over both sides and gently rub in. Put fish in wire fish cooker sprayed with Pam. Lay mesquite chips over coals. Put basket on the grill, close lid, and cook 7½ minutes per side. The sugar will glaze over and seal in the moisture, while the outside edges get a little crisp.

Serves 1

Frank G. Barton III
Marion, Arkansas

FISH FRY!

A catfish is a fish with whiskers. It comes in all sizes. Catfish are found in most parts of the world, in fresh water and salt water; in their natural habitat, they find their food near the bottom of ponds and rivers and therefore are thought of as scavengers. But in the South the catfish has moved uptown—and when people speak of eating catfish today, they most often mean pond-raised and grain-fed fish, scientifically produced for the table, cleaner and better tasting than their country cousins. Catfish farming is spreading over Arkansas and Mississippi like the river at flood stage and has become a profitable business. Catfish restaurants abound. Catfish cooking contests are plentiful, with one of the larger ones being held annually on Memphis' Mud Island. Catfish can be grilled, marinated, blackened, barbecued, smoked, put into gumbo, or fried. The catfish fry is found at all kinds of southern events, particularly in small towns and rural communities—church festivals, men's club gatherings, Ducks Unlimited banquets, dove shoots, or as a way for businesses to say thank you to their customers. And it is a traditional campaign trail accompaniment, where people come to eat while listening to speeches from the stump. In fact, the catfish fry is perfect anytime a group wants to get together, wants something to eat, and plenty of it. A fish fry is the simplest of festivities. All that is required is a large pot, a sturdy fire, a tasty breading, and lots of hot cooking oil. Everyone has one perfect recipe for mixing up the breading—and therein lies the fame of many a cook. The time-honored go-alongs are hush puppies, coleslaw, french fries, and some sinfully sweet dessert.

Big Batch Fish Fry
Grilled Catfish
Thick-Cut French Fries   Creamy Coleslaw
Sweet Garlic Pickles*
Hush Puppies*
Judith's Fudge Cake Bars*

Frank G. Barton III
Marion, Arkansas

*See Index

TENNESSEE RIVER CATFISH WITH MUSTARD SAUCE

A great way to serve a great fish.

2 pounds catfish fillets
½ cup all-purpose flour
½ cup corn meal
Salt and black pepper to taste
Vegetable oil

Thoroughly dry fillets with paper towels and dredge in mixture of flour, corn meal, and seasonings. Let stand 10 minutes. Heat oil to 375 degrees in deep-fat fryer, and fry fish 4 to 5 minutes until golden brown. Drain and serve with warm mustard sauce.

Mustard Sauce
¾ cup minced onion
2 tablespoons unsalted butter
½ cup dry white wine
1 cup heavy cream
½ cup minced parsley
2 tablespoons Dijon mustard
Salt and black pepper to taste

Sauté onion in butter over low heat until softened but not browned. Add wine and cook uncovered over medium heat until liquid is absorbed, about 5 minutes. Add cream and reduce by one-fourth. Remove from heat and stir in remaining ingredients. Keep warm.

Serves 4

Dr. Richard J. Reynolds

CATFISH ON THE GRILL

Though not customarily considered among the elite of fish, the catfish is one of the world's best and most delicately-flavored white fish. This recipe may well help create a catfish fan club.

2 catfish fillets
1 clove garlic, minced
Soy sauce
Blackened fish seasoning
Freshly ground black pepper
Sesame oil
Lemon juice
Lemon slices

Sprinkle each fillet with all ingredients except lemon slices. Place in lightly oiled hinged fish-cooker and grill 5 minutes on each side. Serve with lemon slices.

Note: To cook in oven, season each fillet as above and bake 20 minutes at 350 degrees without turning.

Serves 2

Barbara Walker Hummel

FRIED CATFISH NUGGETS WITH TARTAR SAUCE

Some Memphians, we are told, have successfully used this dish as an initiation rite for Yankee visitors.

Self-rising corn meal
2 teaspoons black pepper
Peanut oil
2 pounds catfish fillets, cut in nuggets (some markets sell pre-cut nuggets)

Fill plastic baggie half-full with self-rising corn meal. Add black pepper and shake to mix. Heat peanut oil in deep-fryer or deep skillet. Put nuggets in baggie, a handful at a time, and shake to coat. Fry in hot oil until golden brown, drain on paper towels, and serve with tartar sauce.

Tartar Sauce
1 cup mayonnaise, homemade
½ cup chopped dill pickles
¼ cup chopped onion
2 tablespoons chopped parsley
Tabasco sauce to taste

Combine all ingredients and mix well.

Serves 6 to 8 as appetizer

Ellen and Richard Dixon

HUSH PUPPIES

Crisp, wonderful little morsels that perfectly accompany fish. And it may be true that they were once tossed under the table to a favorite hound with the admonition, ''Now hush, puppy!''

1 cup corn meal
1 cup all-purpose flour
1 teaspoon baking powder
1 teaspoon sugar
1 teaspoon salt
1 egg
¾ cup milk
Dash red pepper
½ cup chopped green onion tops
1 tablespoon grated onion
Vegetable oil

Mix corn meal, flour, baking powder, sugar, and salt together well. Combine egg, milk, pepper, onion tops, and onion, add to flour mixture, and stir well. Heat oil to 375 degrees. Drop batter by spoonfuls into deep-fryer and cook until golden brown. Drain on paper towels.

Yields 2 dozen hush puppies

Mrs. John J. Hughes
Whitefish, Montana

WILTED LETTUCE SALAD

As Southern as can be, and so good.

1 large head Boston or	2 teaspoons sugar
leaf lettuce	Several green onions with
6 to 8 bacon slices	tops, chopped
⅓ cup vinegar	Pepper

Tear lettuce in bite-size pieces and add onions. Fry bacon until crisp, drain, and crumble over lettuce and onions. Pour off all but ⅓ cup drippings from skillet. Add vinegar and sugar, and heat to boiling, stirring constantly. Pour over salad, toss until well-coated, and season to taste. Serve immediately.

Serves 6

Rose Redfearn

BAKED SALMON CASSEROLE

A recipe from a great-grandmother who lived at Twin Gables in historic LaGrange, Tennessee. As a young girl, this same great-grandmother, while living in a nearby community, attended the Young Ladies' Academy in LaGrange, studying embroidery and china painting. Originally in the APTA cookbook, currently out of print, this recipe, having won its laurels through several generations, called for reprinting.

Saltine cracker crumbs	7 hard-cooked eggs, sliced
1 15½-ounce can pink salmon,	Paprika
drained	Butter
Dry mustard	1½ to 2 cups milk
Freshly ground black pepper	

(Divide salmon and cracker crumbs so as to have at least 3 to 4 layers, as the crumbs act as a binder.) Cover bottom of greased 1½-quart baking dish with cracker crumbs. Add layer of salmon and sprinkle with mustard and pepper. Add layer of sliced eggs. Repeat layers until all salmon is used, but top with layer of crumbs and sprinkle with paprika. Place pats of butter over top. Slowly pour enough milk over top to moisten casserole throughout, taking care not to disturb crumb layers. Bake at 350 degrees until all milk is absorbed and casserole is lightly browned. Serve hot.

Serves 4 to 6

Eleanor D. Hughes

SUMMER SUPPER ON THE PORCH

Summer comes to the South with its bags packed to stay. When it moves in, present company moves over and adjusts itself for the duration. Summer warms you to the bone, sends you looking for fans, and sets you sipping iced drinks. Fragrances hang almost tangibly on the air—newly-cut grass, honeysuckle, magnolia, quick summer rain showers—and breathing becomes a new experience. A certain languor sets in that directs all activity. To move too fast is to court disaster—or at least, heat stroke. When this sizzling season arrives, Southerners opt for the out-of-doors when the sun has gone down and perhaps a transient breeze is stopping by. Many get no farther than the screened porch—a perfect place for a simple supper, some comfortable conversation, and a sense of slipping into the evening with the spark of lightning bugs decorating the trees and the night sounds of katydids, whippoorwills, bobwhites, the occasional bark of a far away dog, and best of all, the serenade of a mockingbird claiming the chimney for his bed and breakfast. There is the rhythmic sweep of the ceiling fan barely moving the air, and the squeak of the glider going nowhere in style. And if little ones are around, a lap will soon be invaded and a little head resting on a friendly shoulder will soon grow heavy as grownup talk gets boring. A favorite supper might include:

Tomato Dill Soup*
Baked Salmon Casserole
Wilted Lettuce Salad
Ernestine Cunningham's Fabulous Corn Pones*
Fresh Peach Cobbler*
Homemade Ice Cream

*See Index

Anne Lee Filer

FRIED GREEN TOMATOES

Many Southern vegetables are delicious fried.

Slice tomatoes, dredge in corn meal, and season with Season All (or salt and pepper). Fry on both sides in hot oil until golden brown. Drain and serve. (Try same procedure with zucchini or okra.)

Mary Hewitt

SUPPERTIME AT CAMP MEETING

For over one hundred and sixty years, the Taylors of Tabernacle United Methodist Church and Campground, descendants of the Richard Taylor family, have been holding camp meeting the first week of August just outside Brownsville, Tennessee. And the cousins come home from all over the world, as well as from Memphis, only an hour's drive away. Amid a grove of ancient oaks, they open their campground houses with their tin roofs and dogtrot hallways, houses made of rough-hewn planks of cypress and other native woods. They fire up their wood cook stoves, shake out their muslin curtains, and hang the porch swings. No one minds that the porch has a roof but no floor—only the clean-swept earth and sawdust. No one minds that the air-conditioning is by ceiling fans and open windows. The families have their minds on other things. Every day there is a morning prayer service, and every evening a rousing hymn-sing followed by preaching delivered by a visiting Methodist minister invited for the week. Morning and evening smoke rises over the campground as the mighty old stoves do their duty, and every evening mosquito lanterns and candles dot the landscape at each cabin, and the smell of popcorn floats on the air. The meals at Camp Meeting, often prepared by a fourth generation of cooks, are something to look forward to all year long. Breakfast alone is an event to dream about, and waking up to the smell of coffee on the fresh country air is heady stuff. Dinner generally includes at least two entrees, always hot breads, summer vegetables in profusion, homemade relishes, and sumptuous desserts—pies and cakes, with as often as not a serving of sliced fresh peaches from the famed Brownsville orchards.

Stuffed Peppers
Southern Fried Chicken
Black-Eyed Peas with Sweet Tomato Jelly
Fresh Butter Beans   Corn Pudding
Sliced Homegrown Tomatoes
Sorrelle's Easy Pickles
Corn Bread Muffins
Blackberry Jam Cake
with Fresh Peaches and Cream

Margaret Taylor

STUFFED PEPPERS

A great family dish for a great family place—Camp Meeting.

6 *large green bell peppers,*   1 *small onion, minced*
  cored   1 *cup cooked rice*
1 *pound ground beef*   ½ *teaspoon salt*
1 *tablespoon vegetable*   ⅛ *teaspoon pepper*
  shortening   3 *tablespoons grated Cheddar*
1 *cup chopped fresh or*   *cheese*
  canned tomatoes

Parboil peppers in salted water for 5 minutes and drain. Brown beef in shortening and drain. Simmer tomatoes and onion until onion is tender. Combine with meat. Add rice and seasonings, and blend well. Stuff mixture into peppers and cover each with 1½ teaspoons cheese. Place in baking dish and bake at 350 degrees for 20 minutes or until cheese melts.

Serves 6

Margaret Taylor

SORRELLE'S EASY PICKLES

Amazing how quickly a gallon of pickles disappears.

1 *gallon whole dill pickles*   4 *tablespoons mixed pickling*
3 *cups sugar*   *spice*
1 *teaspoon alum*

Drain pickles, reserving liquid, and cut into ¾-inch thick slices. Return pickles to jar, add sugar, and cover with reserved liquid. Wrap alum and pickling spice in cheesecloth and place in jar. Invert pickle jar every 24 hours for seven days. During the next four weeks, invert every other day.

Yields 1 gallon pickles

Sorrelle Woodson Maher
Brownsville, Tennessee

SOUTHERN FRIED CHICKEN

Southerners have an inherited taste for things fried. And nothing is more well-received in more Southern homes than fried chicken.

1 chicken, cut in pieces to
  include the wishbone
All-purpose flour

Salt
Vegetable shortening or lard

Dredge each piece of chicken in flour and sprinkle with salt (or mix flour and salt in paper bag, add chicken one piece at a time, and shake to coat). Melt enough shortening to measure 1 inch deep in heavy black skillet, and heat until oil is hot enough that a drop of water will sizzle but not hot enough to smoke. Add chicken and fry uncovered 25 to 30 minutes until golden brown, turning occasionally to cook evenly. Drain on absorbent paper. Serve with hot biscuits and pan gravy.

Pan Gravy

Pan drippings from chicken
2 to 3 tablespoons all-purpose
  flour

Water
Milk, optional
Salt and pepper to taste

Pour off grease after frying chicken, leaving 2 to 3 tablespoons pan drippings with some crusty brown pieces in skillet. Mix flour with a little water to make a paste. Over medium heat, gradually blend paste with hot pan drippings, stirring until smooth. Gradually add water (or a mixture of milk and water), stirring and cooking until gravy is of desired consistency. Season with salt and pepper.

Serves 4

*Generations of Southern cooks
whose names are legion*

SWEET TOMATO JELLY

Sweet tomato jelly and sweet memories, too, of this wonderful accompaniment to other wonders of Southern gardens.

8 cups canned whole tomatoes
  with juice

2 cups sugar
Butter to taste

Combine all ingredients in heavy saucepan and simmer until mixture jells somewhat, stirring frequently. Serve over hot field peas or black-eyed peas, lady peas or cream peas, purple-hull peas or crowder peas. (Need we say more?)

Yields 3 to 3½ pints jelly

Epps McConnico Turner

CORN PUDDING

Quick and easy.

1 16-ounce can whole kernel
  corn (or creamed corn)
1 egg, beaten
¼ cup sugar

2 tablespoons butter, melted
½ teaspoon salt
Pepper to taste

Combine all ingredients and mix well. Bake at 375 degrees for 30 minutes or until set and browned.

Serves 4

*Averil Taylor
Brownsville, Tennessee*

BLACKBERRY JAM CAKE

Just combining the words blackberry, jam, and cake tells you something good is on the way.

1 cup raisins
1 cup burgundy wine,
  or grape juice
1 cup chopped citron
1 cup chopped pecans
3½ cups all-purpose flour
2 teaspoons baking powder
1 teaspoon baking soda

1 teaspoon salt
1 cup butter, softened
1 cup sugar
5 eggs
1 cup seedless blackberry jam
¾ cup buttermilk
1 tablespoon confectioners'
  sugar

Soak raisins in wine overnight.

Drain raisins and reserve wine. Mix raisins, citron, and pecans in ½ cup flour. Sift together remaining flour, baking powder, baking soda, and salt. Cream butter until smooth and gradually add sugar, beating until fluffy. Add eggs one at a time, beating thoroughly after each addition. Add jam and beat until smooth. Alternately add dry ingredients and buttermilk, beating until smooth. Blend in reserved wine. Stir in floured fruits and nuts. Pour batter into greased 9-inch tube pan and bake 1¼ hours at 350 degrees. Cool and dust with confectioners' sugar.

Serves 10 to 12

*Ruby Johnson
Brownsville, Tennessee*

MINTED ICED TEA

Fresh, friendly mint, best picked right from the backyard.

2½ cups boiling water	½ cup fresh lemon juice
3 family-size tea bags	Rind of 1 lemon
6 cups water	6 mint sprigs, gently
1 cup sugar	crushed

Pour boiling water into pitcher (pottery is best), add tea bags, and steep 15 minutes. Remove tea bags, stir in remaining ingredients, and let stand briefly to blend flavors. Remove mint. Serve in tall ice-filled glasses garnished with additional mint sprigs.

Serves 10

Mrs. W. Thomas Cunningham, Jr.
Richmond, Virginia

MINT JULEP

According to the dictionary: "Julep (joo'lip), n. sweet drink, variously prepared and sometimes medicated." Perhaps, but in the South it is unvaryingly composed of crushed mint, crushed ice, simple syrup, and the medication, which is the best bourbon available, all of which is served in a frosted container, preferably silver, called a julep cup. The julep's origin in this country is debatable, being claimed on both sides of the Blue Ridge, but its taste and effects are undisputed and have inspired a certain poetry in the Southern psyche.

1 cup sugar	Bourbon whiskey
1 cup water	Crushed ice
Fresh mint sprigs	

Combine sugar and water, and boil 5 minutes to make simple syrup. Bruise several mint sprigs and combine with 2 teaspoons syrup. Add 2 jiggers (3 ounces) bourbon and stir carefully and well. Pour into julep cup packed with crushed ice and garnish with sprig of mint. (Use remaining syrup for additional servings.)

Serves 1

From the collective Southern consciousness
by way of several old hand-written journals.

MY MOTHER'S MISSISSIPPI DELTA EGGNOG

Rich, thick, utterly delicious. Almost has to be eaten with a spoon rather than drunk from a cup.

1 dozen eggs, separated	1 quart heavy cream, whipped
1½ cups bourbon whiskey	Grated nutmeg
¾ cup sugar	

Beat yolks until light and add whiskey drop by drop, alternating with ½ cup sugar. Gently fold in whipped cream. Beat whites until soft peaks form, gradually adding ¼ cup sugar. Fold into eggnog mixture and sprinkle with nutmeg.

Serves 24

Linda Nobles Allen

SHERRY COBBLER

A delightful, cool drink, light and refreshing. Second cousin to the julep.

2 lumps sugar	Shaved ice
Fresh mint	2 jiggers lemon juice
2 jiggers water	2 jiggers sherry

Crush sugar and several mint leaves in bottom of glass or julep cup. Stir in water. Fill two-thirds full with crushed ice and add lemon juice and sherry (one jigger equals 1½ ounces). Garnish with sprig of fresh mint.

Serves 1

From the hand-written journal
of Mrs. Mary C. Vance, 1933

MEMPHIS MORNINGS

A festive taste. Nothing simpler for a brunch punch.

Frozen orange juice concentrate   White wine or champagne

Substituting wine for water, dilute orange juice concentrate as directed on can.

Servings vary
   with amount of concentrate

Sophie Coors

S'MORES

One is never enough. You'll want s'more.

Roast a marshmallow over the fire, place it on a graham cracker, top with squares of Hershey bars, and cover with another graham cracker. Good!

MRS. STILL'S DELTA PECAN PIE

Life wouldn't be half so good without pecan pies.

4 eggs, well-beaten	*1 teaspoon vanilla*
½ cup butter, melted	*⅛ teaspoon salt*
1 cup dark or light corn syrup	*1½ cups chopped pecans*
½ cup sugar	*1 unbaked 8-inch pie shell*

Combine eggs, butter, corn syrup, sugar, vanilla, and salt, and mix well. Add pecans and stir briefly. Pour into pie shell and bake 45 minutes at 325 degrees.

Serves 6 to 8

Mrs. William H. Houston III
Washington, D.C.

MOTHER'S EGG CUSTARD PIE

The simplest of old-fashioned pies. Always delicious.

1 unbaked 9-inch pie shell	*5 egg yolks*
¾ cup butter, softened	*1½ cups light cream*
1⅓ cups sugar	*1½ teaspoons vanilla*
¼ cup all-purpose flour	*Nutmeg*

Prick bottom of pie shell with fork and bake 5 minutes at 325 degrees. Cool.

Cream butter and sugar, and blend with flour. Add egg yolks one at a time. Stir in cream and vanilla. Pour into pie shell and sprinkle top with nutmeg. Bake 50 to 60 minutes at 325 degrees. Top will be golden brown.

Serves 6 to 8

Netta Sue Caudill King

BONFIRE BY THE LEVEE

The Mississippi Delta was made of centuries of silt deposited by the river when it overflowed its banks. In the past, plantation owners in the delta built dikes around their farms to protect them from the flooding river, but in 1882 the U.S. Corps of Engineers began the building of a mighty levee. Today the protection comes from that levee—green slopes of relative safety, running down both sides of the river, following at a discreet distance from its banks the path of Ol' Man River. Cook-outs are sometimes held beside the levee after the first frost has killed the mosquitos. A flatbed truck or a four-wheel vehicle or a sturdy station wagon will wind its way across the fields of soybeans or cotton, follow narrow, dirt service roads, then climb the levee, cross it, and descend to the river side to deposit people and food and whatever equipment is needed. A roaring bonfire will be built and blankets will be spread for sitting. Guests will gather around for barbecue, or cook hamburgers or hot dogs over the fire, and finally, have something sweet, such as that childhood favorite, S'mores—so named because you always want some more. In the distance, boats and barges ply the river, sometimes the Delta Queen or the Mississippi Queen with their running lights and cabin lights trailing ribbons of gold in the water, recalling a time when the river was not just a highway but was a lifeline to the homes along the way, bringing supplies and news and the mail; when the blowing of a steamboat whistle enthralled everyone within earshot. As William Percy said, in his evocative book of essays, *Lanterns on the Levee,* "There is no sound in the world so filled with mystery and longing and unease as the sound at night of a riverboat blowing for the landing—one long, two shorts, one long, two shorts."

Barbecue or Hot Dogs
Buns and Condiments
Cold Drinks and Coffee
S'Mores

Jenny and Graham Smith
Waverly Plantation
Proctor, Arkansas

A Southern Feast at Cottondale

Southern cooking has come to mean so many things to so many people that it is difficult to describe, let alone define. The term seems to be variously synonymous with good, old, hot, and gravy. It is the antithesis of quick, easy, and dietetic. In the accustomed manner of the region, Southern cooking takes its time—the very words conjure up thoughts of long summer days, early morning trips to the garden, plenty of hours spent in the kitchen, and more spent at the table. It assumes, sometimes even requires, grains that are stone-ground, ingredients that are unprocessed, and foods that are fresh and homegrown as well as homemade. Like the South itself, it is full of surprises and contradictions. Good Southern cooking often evokes the simple, homey sentiments of comfort and joy—those fluffy white buttermilk biscuits ("Butter them while they're hot, now …") and that little pinch of sugar ("to bring out the flavor") in the fresh butter beans cooked with ham hock. It may also produce feelings of careless abandon (those ten eggs in the pound cake!) and a downright reckless sense of indulgence—the crisp layers of that strawberry shortcake, soaking in the thick sweet juice of ripe berries. Not to mention all that whipped cream!

This culinary style is eclectic, incorporating foods and cooking techniques from three continents, and adapting to the taste preferences of three races of humanity. The early settlers in North Carolina and Virginia who later moved west to Tennessee and Memphis, were Europeans, predominantly Anglo-Americans from the British Isles, who enjoyed hearty fare, simply prepared. As they learned to live on harvests from the land, they adopted with happy results many of the exotic new foods and unfamiliar food preparation methods of their new neighbors, the Native Americans. To this interesting mix was added the culinary skills of Afro-Americans, who helped shape the development of Southern cooking and enhanced the flavor of Southern food with the distinctive seasonings and rich spices of their African heritage.

Some purists claim that real Southern cooking tastes best when set out on a sturdy kitchen table and eaten from plain, pottery dishes. Others say paneled dining rooms, polished mahogany sideboards, white damask table linen, soft candlelight, and lovely old silver, crystal and china are proper accompaniments for fine Southern dinners. But all agree that the best Southern cooking is found in private homes where many of its secrets remain mysteries, and guardians of those secrets are aggravatingly imprecise in giving instructions. A cookbook compiled in 1905 by the ladies at Grace-St. Luke's Church in Memphis offers this comment on bread-making: "No description can be given to ascertain these points. It requires observation, reflection, and a quick nice judgment to decide when all is right."

The same can be said of Southern cooking in general. Seeing is learning, tasting is knowing, and experiencing is everything.

STRAWBERRY SHORTCAKE

Shortcake the old-fashioned way, just as presented in a charming, handwritten cook book, now out of print, of perfectly delightful recipes.

Pie crust   Whipped cream
Strawberries

Use any good pie crust pastry. Roll out and cut with tea cup. Bake until brown. Wash strawberries and add sugar. Let set for 15 minutes. Spread whipped cream on crust, and then a layer of strawberries. Top with pie crust, and add cream over crust. Add one whole strawberry on top for garnishing and 1 teaspoon of syrup from strawberries.

My Dining Generation
Margaret B. Wynn
Courtesy of Douglas C. Wynn
Greenville, Mississippi

FRESH PEACH COBBLER

A beautiful crust and peaches in their own syrup, sweet and cinnamony. Makes the peach season the best time of year.

Double recipe PERFECT PASTRY   1 tablespoon cinnamon
10 to 12 peaches   Butter
1 cup sugar

Peel peaches and slice. Combine sugar and cinnamon, add to peaches and gently stir together.

Roll out one layer of pastry and line baking dish. Spread peaches over pastry, spooning in all juices. Dot liberally with butter. Roll out second layer of pastry in rectangular shape and cut lengthwise in strips. Weave strips across top lattice-fashion and seal at edges. Spread small amount butter over top and sprinkle with sugar. Bake at 350 degrees for 40 to 50 minutes or until sugary syrup bubbles up and crust is crisp and light golden-brown.

Serves 8 to 10

Nancy R. Crosby

PROCESSOR BEATEN BISCUITS

Beaten biscuits are an epicurean wonder. And they are called beaten biscuits because years ago the dough was indeed beaten, at great length, with whatever was heavy and handy, be it an ax-handle, a heavy stick, an iron rod, or some like weapon. Beating and folding gave the dough its unique layered texture. The invention of a mechanized wringer, called a biscuit brake, made the procedure easier for the cook so fortunate as to own one. But today the food processor does the work and may bring about a revival of this completely wonderful morsel—small, flaky, smooth, pale, and destined for a happy life filled with paper-thin slices of country ham.

3 cups all-purpose flour   ¼ teaspoon baking powder
2 teaspoons salt   ⅓ cup vegetable shortening
½ teaspoon sugar   ½ cup milk

Combine flour, salt, sugar, baking powder, and shortening in food processor with steel blade and process 30 seconds. Add milk and process 30 seconds more. Dough will form ball. Separate into several pieces, return to processor, and process 15 to 30 seconds until ball forms again.

Roll dough out ⅛-inch thick on lightly floured board. Fold once and roll out again. Repeat folding and rolling twice, dusting top very, very lightly with flour each time to prevent sticking. Roll out to ¼-inch thickness and cut with small biscuit cutter, 1½ to 2 inches in diameter. Pierce through each biscuit several times with tines of fork. Place on ungreased baking sheet and bake at 400 degrees for 12 to 15 minutes or until lightly browned.

Note: These biscuits do not rise much. They will literally pop apart at the least pressure when done.

Yields 2 dozen biscuits

Mrs. William P. Halliday, Jr.

BANANA ICE CREAM

Smooth and delicious, a special blend of flavors.

2½ cups sugar	3 cups mashed bananas
5 tablespoons all-purpose flour	3 cups heavy cream
¼ teaspoon salt	2 tablespoons vanilla
6 eggs, lightly beaten	1½ tablespoons almond extract
5 cups scalded milk	

Mix sugar with flour and salt, and gradually add eggs. Gradually stir into hot milk, and cook over low heat until mixture thickens and coats spoon, stirring constantly. Cool. Add bananas, cream, vanilla, and almond extract. Freeze until set.

Yields 1 gallon ice cream

Clarene P. Russell

IDA'S HOMEMADE PEACH ICE CREAM CUSTARD STYLE

From an Arkansas plantation just across the river, a luscious ice cream with a boiled custard base. Must be reserved for the time when the peach crop comes in.

6 cups peeled and mashed ripe peaches	4 cups milk
2½ cups sugar	1 12-ounce can evaporated milk
2 tablespoons all-purpose flour	1 cup heavy cream, whipped
½ teaspoon salt	1 tablespoon vanilla
3 eggs, beaten	

Combine peaches and 1 cup sugar, and set aside. Combine flour, salt, and remaining sugar. Add eggs and blend well. Cook over low heat, gradually adding milk and evaporated milk, and stir constantly until mixture thickens and coats spoon. Allow mixture to cool. Fold in whipped cream and add sweetened peaches and vanilla. Pour into ice cream freezer—preferably the hand-cranked kind—and freeze. After cream is frozen, remove dasher and leave container in brine. Tightly pack container with towels to insulate entire freezer and allow ice cream to "set up."

Yields 1 gallon ice cream

Mrs. C. William Lantz

MISSISSIPPI TEA CAKES

From a great-grandmother who was the wife of a Civil War doctor in Atlanta, Mississippi. With readily available ingredients, these cookies were made by the washtubful for any big gathering in those days. Great with OLD-FASHIONED PINK LEMONADE.

2 cups sugar	1 teaspoon baking soda
1 cup butter, softened	⅓ cup buttermilk
6 egg yolks, separated	4 cups all-purpose flour
1 tablespoon vanilla	

Cream sugar with butter. Add egg yolks one at a time, and beat until light and fluffy. Add vanilla. Stir baking soda into buttermilk, and alternately add with flour to mixture, beating after each addition. Drop dough by spoonfuls onto very lightly greased baking sheet and bake at 350 degrees for 6 to 8 minutes or until edges are lightly browned.

Yields 5 to 6 dozen cookies

Mrs. Kenneth D. Bartee

CHAPLAIN CHARLIE'S PRALINES

In mid-November when the pecans start coming in, the pralines start going forth from the chaplain's kitchen. This recipe has made its way up the Mississippi Valley from New Orleans through several generations of one family.

4 cups pecans	½ cup water
1 cup granulated sugar	5 tablespoons butter
1 cup light brown sugar	¼ teaspoon salt
½ cup light corn syrup	1 tablespoon vanilla

Spread pecans on baking sheet and bake at 400 degrees until lightly toasted, stirring every 5 minutes. Set aside to cool.

Combine both sugars, syrup, and water in heavy 3-quart saucepan and cook to soft ball stage. Remove from heat, stir in pecans, butter, and salt, bring to rolling boil for 1 minute. Remove from heat and stir in vanilla. Set pan in sink filled with cold water and stir until mixture begins to thicken. Drop by spoonfuls onto buttered aluminum foil and allow to harden. If mixture hardens in pan, melt over low heat and continue spooning. Wrap individual pralines in plastic wrap when cooled.

Yields 4 dozen pralines

Chaplain Charles McKnight

AMES BANANA PUDDING

The proof of the pudding is in the eating. Prove away.

¾ cup sugar	3 egg yolks
2 tablespoons all-purpose flour	1 teaspoon vanilla
¼ teaspoon salt	1 12-ounce box vanilla wafers
2 cups milk	6 medium bananas, sliced

Combine sugar, flour, and salt in heavy saucepan, and stir in milk. Cook over medium heat until thickened, stirring constantly. Simmer uncovered 15 minutes, stirring occasionally. Beat egg yolks, add 2 tablespoons hot milk mixture, and blend. Return to remaining hot milk mixture and cook 5 minutes, stirring constantly. Remove from heat and add vanilla.

Line bottom of 1½-quart baking dish with vanilla wafers. Top with layer of bananas. Pour thin layer of pudding over bananas. Repeat layers of wafers, bananas, and pudding, ending with pudding. Bake at 425 degrees for 5 minutes or until very delicately browned. Top with meringue and bake at 350 degrees for 12 to 15 minutes or until meringue is delicately browned.

Meringue

3 egg whites	6 tablespoons sugar
1 teaspoon vanilla	

Beat egg whites with vanilla until soft peaks form. Gradually add sugar and beat until glossy.

Serves 6 to 8

Ames Plantation
Grand Junction, Tennessee

JUDITH'S FUDGE CAKE BARS

Occasionally life requires a large dose of chocolate.

1 cup butter	1 cup all-purpose flour
3 squares unsweetened chocolate	1 cup chopped nuts
2 cups sugar	2 eggs, well beaten
	2 teaspoons vanilla

Melt butter with chocolate in top of double boiler. Mix in remaining ingredients. Pour into greased 7 x 11-inch baking pan and bake 1 hour at 300 degrees. Cut into bars or squares while hot and store in covered container while warm.

Yields 20 bars

Mrs. Bruce Campbell

ANGEL BROWNIES

A very special brownie, divinely good.

1 cup butter	1 cup all-purpose flour
2 squares unsweetened chocolate	1 cup chopped nuts
4 eggs, well beaten	1 teaspoon vanilla
2 cups sugar	Confectioners' sugar

Grease 9 x 13-inch baking pan and line with foil. Melt butter with chocolate in heavy saucepan. Remove from heat and add remaining ingredients. Spread in pan and bake 40 minutes at 350 degrees. Take out of oven and refrigerate immediately. Let chill 3 to 4 hours or overnight.

Remove foil and cut in 1 x 3-inch bars. Gently shake in bag of confectioners' sugar. Place immediately in airtight container and let stand several hours before serving. (Brownies will be very hard when cut, but will become like chocolate clouds as they warm to room temperature in container.)

Yields 3¼ dozen bars

Mrs. George Mitchell III

A TRIFLE TIPSY

A great holiday dessert, festive and full of flavor.

Bourbon whiskey to taste	Whipped cream
Boiled custard	Slivered almonds
Sponge or yellow cake, sliced in strips	Maraschino cherries

Add bourbon to cold boiled custard. Layer half of cake in bottom of trifle bowl, and cover with half of custard. Repeat layers. Cover and refrigerate at least 24 hours to allow cake to season. Before serving, top with whipped cream, a sprinkle of almonds, and cherries.

Boiled Custard

1 cup sugar	3 eggs, well-beaten
1 tablespoon all-purpose flour	4 cups scalded milk

Sift sugar with flour and add eggs, beating well. Gradually add hot milk, beating with mixer until blended. Pour into double boiler and cook until mixture coats spoon, stirring constantly.

Serves 8 to 10

Kay Ferree
Jackson, Tennessee

COUSIN BETTY'S FRUITCAKE

This recipe was hand-delivered to Goodwinslow in 1890, having traveled all the way from Memphis to Raleigh, first by L&N Railway to the end of the line, and thence by buggy. It was sent by Cousin Betty with the following instruction written on the envelope: To Mrs. W.W. Goodwin/To be delivered by Her Handsome Husband/City.

2 pounds raisins	1 pound sugar
2 pounds currants	1 dozen eggs, separated
1 pound citron	½ cup cider vinegar
½ pound candied cherries, optional	1 teaspoon baking soda
	1 cup molasses
1 pound all-purpose flour	1 cup brandy
2 teaspoons nutmeg	½ pound walnuts, chopped
1 teaspoon cinnamon	½ pound pecans, chopped
1 teaspoon mace	1 pound almonds, chopped
1 pound butter	

Dredge fruit in portion of flour. Sift spices with remaining flour.

Cream butter and sugar. Beat egg yolks, add vinegar, and beat into creamed mixture. Sift baking soda into molasses, mix, and beat into batter with spiced flour. Mix brandy with floured fruit and stir into batter. Add nuts. Beat egg whites until stiff peaks form and fold into batter. Line four 5 x 9-inch loaf pans or two large tube pans (called chimney pans in those days) with baking parchment paper. Bake loaf cakes 3 hours at 275 degrees. Bake tube cakes 2¾ hours at 275 degrees. Cool and let stand 24 hours.

Wrap each cake in brandy-soaked linen and set aside to season. The longer the seasoning, the better the cake.

Serves 35 to 40

Mary Winslow Chapman

GRANDMOTHER LEATHERMAN'S BRANDY SAUCE CIRCA 1841

Fruit cakes and plum puddings alike take a great fancy to this vintage brandy sauce whose elegant blueprint has been passed down through generations.

½ cup butter	2 egg yolks
1 cup sugar	1 cup brandy, heated

Cream butter and sugar in top of double boiler. Stir in egg yolks. Add brandy very slowly, 1 tablespoon at a time. Bring to boil for 1 minute, stirring constantly with wooden spoon. Sauce is done when mixture forms thread when poured from spoon. Be extremely careful not to overcook, as sauce will curdle.

Yields 2 cups sauce

Mrs. M. A. J. Knox

ARKANSAS BLACKBERRY COBBLER

Best when you grow your own blackberries and have had the fun of picking them.

3 cups fresh blackberries	3 tablespoons all-purpose flour
1½ teaspoons vanilla	½ cup butter, sliced
1½ cups sugar	

Place fruit in unbaked 9-inch processor pastry shell and sprinkle with vanilla. Mix sugar with flour, pour over fruit, and top with butter. Cut remaining pastry into strips and arrange over fruit. Bake 10 minutes at 450 degrees, then at 350 degrees for 40 minutes or until slightly browned.

Processor Pastry

1½ cups all-purpose flour	2 to 3 tablespoons ice water
½ cup cold butter	

Briefly mix flour and butter in food processor. Add ice water and process until dough forms a ball. Chill several minutes before using. Recipe must be doubled for cobbler.

Note: Recipe works equally well with fresh peaches or apples.

Serves 6

Danette Watkins
Lepanto, Arkansas

OLD-FASHIONED BOILED CUSTARD

Great over PLANTATION POUND CAKE, or ladled over CHOCOLATE SOUFFLÉ, or served in punch cups. A heavenly mixture.

4 eggs
1 cup sugar
2 tablespoons all-purpose flour
Dash salt
4 cups scalded milk
1 teaspoon vanilla or more
   to taste
Whipped cream, optional

Beat eggs, sugar, flour, and salt together in very heavy 3-quart saucepan or top of 2-quart double boiler. Add milk gradually, stirring constantly, and stir over medium-low heat until mixture coats spoon. Remove from heat, add vanilla, and strain into large bowl or pitcher. Chill. Serve plain or topped with whipped cream.

Serves 6

Martha Whitington

CHRISTMAS PECAN CAKE

A perfect gift—whether for the family dinner table or that of a friend.

3 cups sugar
2 cups butter, softened
10 eggs, separated
4 cups sifted all-purpose flour
1 cup bourbon whiskey
2 pounds white raisins
2 pounds pecan pieces
1 tablespoon nutmeg

Cream sugar with butter, and beat in egg yolks one at a time. Alternately add, in small portions, 3 cups flour and bourbon. Combine remaining flour with raisins, pecans, and nutmeg, and add to batter. Beat egg whites until stiff peaks form and fold into batter. Pour into large tube pan or three small loaf pans well-greased and lined on bottom with two layers of wax paper. Fill two-thirds full and bake 4 hours at 250 degrees in tube pan or 3 hours at 250 degrees in loaf pans. Cool completely before removing from pan. Wrap in cloth soaked in bourbon, and then wrap in foil. After one week, resoak cloth. Soak again two weeks later.

Serves 24

Mrs. Henry T.V. Miller

PLANTATION POUND CAKE

Dear old pound cake—a pound of butter, a pound of sugar, a pound of flour, and always, ten eggs. Here is a supremely good version, with a little more sugar and a little less flour. A gorgeous cake.

3 cups sugar
2 cups butter, softened
10 eggs, room temperature
3 cups all-purpose flour
1 teaspoon salt
1 teaspoon vanilla

Cream sugar with butter. Add eggs one at a time, beating well after each addition. Sift flour with salt, add to egg mixture, and beat 2 minutes on medium to high speed. Add vanilla and beat again. Pour into greased and floured tube pan and bake 1½ to 2 hours at 300 degrees. (After cake rises, about 1 hour into baking time, lay piece of foil loosely over top of cake and continue baking.) Allow cake to stand briefly before removing from pan.

Note: This cake may be made with the addition of 1 teaspoon baking powder with splendid results. Some prefer it; some do not.

Serves 12 to 16

Ellen Davies Rodgers
Brunswick, Tennessee

ALABAMA SWEET POTATO PIE

A versatile, no-nonsense fellow, the sweet potato, with an interesting history. However, the only history needed is to know how good it is, whether baked and eaten with butter, or fried, or used in puddings and pies.

3 large sweet potatoes, baked
   or boiled, and peeled
1 cup milk
¾ cup butter
1½ teaspoons lemon extract
1½ cups sugar
½ teaspoon cinnamon
½ teaspoon allspice
½ teaspoon ground cloves
2 unbaked 9-inch pie shells

Mash sweet potatoes while hot. Mix with remaining ingredients and pour into pie shells. Bake at 300 degrees for 1 hour or until crust is brown and filling is set.

Serves 12 to 16

Mrs. James Stewart Cox

BREAD PUDDING WITH BRANDY SAUCE

Bread pudding—essentially Southern, born of thrifty cooks who threw nothing away—has become one of the most delectable desserts around. This winning recipe with New Orleans roots further proves the Deep South culinary gifts of a past winner of the Memphis in May Barbecue Festival.

10 slices day-old French bread (about 1-inch wide slices)	4 cups milk, scalded
1/3 cup butter, softened	4 eggs, beaten
1 cup sugar	1 teaspoon cinnamon
1 cup heavy cream	1 teaspoon vanilla
	1/2 teaspoon nutmeg

Break bread into pieces in large mixing bowl. Cream butter and sugar, and blend in cream. Gradually stir in hot milk and pour mixture over bread, gently turning with large wooden spoon to moisten. Let stand 15 minutes. (There must be enough bread to absorb the liquid. French bread slices about 1-inch wide are perfect. If using other sliced bread, or biscuits, use equivalent amounts.)

Add eggs, vanilla, and spices, turning bread mixture several times with spoon, and pour into lightly buttered large baking dish. (One-half cup raisins may be added, and spices may be omitted, if preferred.) Set dish in pan of hot water and bake at 350 degrees for 45 to 60 minutes, or until set, slightly puffed, and browned. (Test with knife inserted into middle of pudding to see if set.) Serve hot with brandy sauce.

Brandy Sauce

3 egg yolks, beaten	1 teaspoon vanilla
1 1/2 cups milk	1 tablespoon cornstarch
2 cups confectioners' sugar	1/4 cup water
1/2 cup butter, softened	1/4 cup brandy or dark rum

Combine egg, milk, sugar, butter, and vanilla in top of double boiler. Stirring constantly, cook over low heat until thoroughly heated but not boiling. Dissolve cornstarch in water and add to mixture, stirring until thick. Remove from heat and add brandy. Cool somewhat and serve.

Serves 8 to 10

John Wills Barbecue Pit
John Wills, Proprietor

LEMON SAUCE FOR BREAD PUDDING

From an Arkansas plantation kitchen. Delicious!

4 egg yolks	1 1/2 cups milk, scalded
1/2 cup sugar	4 tablespoons lemon juice
4 tablespoons all-purpose flour	

Beat egg yolks slightly, and stir in sugar and flour. Gradually add to hot milk and cook over low heat until thickened. Remove and add lemon juice.

Yields about 2 cups sauce

Mrs. C. William Lantz

BUNTYN CAFE COCONUT PIE

Memphis restaurants which feature Southern home-style cooking continue to draw the faithful home. Like a good tonic, they seem to be required at intervals, lest *haute cuisine* or fast food get the better of us. Premier among all, the Buntyn Cafe opened as a one-room diner in 1927, across from the old Buntyn Station railway depot. Passengers could buy a nickel sandwich, or for a dime, a tall piece of coconut cream pie. Owned by one family for the last forty years-plus, the Buntyn Restaurant, as it is known today, has been featured in various travel magazines as a 'must' in Memphis. It has made its reputation on its fried chicken, its vegetables, and its homemade rolls, pies, and cobblers.

1 baked and chilled 10-inch pie shell	5 teaspoons cornstarch
5 eggs, separated	1/4 cup butter, softened
2 1/2 cups sugar	1 cup flaked coconut
4 cups whole milk	1 teaspoon coconut flavoring
	Pinch baking powder

Combine egg yolks and 2 cups sugar in top of double boiler. Stir in milk and bring to a boil. Make a paste of cornstarch mixed with a little water and blend into hot mixture, cooking and stirring until thick. (Add more cornstarch, if needed.) Add butter, coconut and flavoring, stirring until thick. Pour into pie shell.

Beat egg whites until stiff, gradually adding remaining sugar and pinch of baking powder. Top pie with meringue, sprinkle with a little more coconut, and place in 325 degree oven to brown meringue. Chill before serving.

Yields 1 tall pie

The Buntyn Restaurant
Betty and Milton Wiggins, Proprietors

OLD-FASHIONED VANILLA ICE CREAM

Get out the freezer, pour in the salt, and line up the children to turn the crank. The turning and the waiting make it extra good.

2 quarts heavy cream	1½ cups sugar
2 cups milk	¼ teaspoon salt
4 eggs, lightly beaten	1 teaspoon vanilla
½ cup sweetened condensed milk	

Heat 2 cups cream with milk in top of double boiler. Mix eggs with condensed milk, sugar, and salt, and blend in small portion of hot cream mixture. Gradually add to remaining cream mixture. Cook, stirring constantly, until mixture reaches 176 degrees or just coats spoon, about 5 minutes. Cool. Stir in vanilla and remaining cream. Freeze in electric or hand-cranked ice cream freezer according to manufacturer's instructions.

Note: A master recipe, superb as is, but try adding chocolate, coffee, fresh peaches, strawberries, peanut brittle, peppermint—or whatever—to create your own favorite.

Yields 1 gallon ice cream

Carol M. Cherry

CHESS PIE

No one knows the origin of the name "chess" pie. So simple to make, with the ingredients always at hand, some say it was called "jus' pie," which over the years became "chess pie."

2 tablespoons all-purpose flour	½ cup milk
2 cups sugar	½ cup butter, melted
4 eggs, lightly beaten	1 unbaked 9-inch pie shell

Mix flour with sugar. Add eggs and milk, beating lightly until well-mixed. Add butter and stir to blend. Pour into pie shell and bake 15 minutes at 450 degrees, then reduce heat to 325 degrees and bake 45 minutes.

Note: Pinch of nutmeg may be used as flavoring, if desired.

Serves 8

Catharine Richey Hinton

Variation: For a lemon chess pie, replace ¼ cup milk with ¼ cup lemon juice and 3 tablespoons lemon rind.

Cathy Knight

HEAVENLY FRESH COCONUT CAKE

The ultimate dessert. Nothing is better than fresh coconut.

2 fresh coconuts	2 teaspoons salt
4 cups all-purpose flour	6 egg whites
2⅔ cups sugar	2 cups heavy cream
5½ teaspoons baking powder	3 teaspoons vanilla

Reserve coconut milk and grate coconuts. Sift flour, sugar, baking powder, and 1½ teaspoons salt. Repeat sifting. Beat egg whites with remaining salt until stiff peaks form. Whip cream until stiff and fold lightly into egg whites with wire whisk. Alternately add in thirds dry ingredients, coconut milk, and vanilla, folding gently into mixture. Pour into four greased and floured 9-inch cake pans. Bake 20 to 25 minutes at 350 degrees. Cool. Spread frosting over first cake layer and sprinkle with grated coconut. Repeat process until all layers are stacked. Spread remaining frosting over entire cake and cover with coconut.

Icing

4½ cups sugar	6 egg whites
1 cup water	⅓ cup confectioners' sugar
6 tablespoons white corn syrup	

Combine sugar, water, and corn syrup, and boil until soft ball stage is reached (234 to 240 degrees) or until soft ball forms when small portion of syrup is dropped into cold water. Beat egg whites until stiff peaks form. With mixer on, add hot syrup to egg whites in steady stream until all syrup is used. Continue mixing while adding confectioners' sugar.

Serves 20

Joyce Ferguson
West Memphis, Arkansas

HOT FUDGE SAUCE

The richest topping of all for ice cream.

1 cup sugar	2 tablespoons all-purpose flour
¾ cup milk	Dash salt
¼ cup cocoa	1 teaspoon vanilla

Combine all ingredients except vanilla in heavy saucepan and boil 2 minutes, stirring constantly. Remove from heat, add vanilla, and serve warm.

Yields 1½ cups sauce

Hollye Spiotta

LA VADA'S LEMON PIE

A very special cook at a very special grandmother's house caused a child to have a lifelong love for this pie. No egg yolks are used, resulting in a creamy, light color.

1¾ cups water	5 tablespoons cornstarch
¼ cup lemon juice	4 teaspoons all-purpose flour
1 tablespoon butter	2 teaspoons grated lemon rind
1 cup sugar	1 baked 9-inch pie shell

Mix all ingredients except pastry in top of double boiler over medium heat until thickened. Let mixture cool slightly before pouring into pie shell. Cover with meringue and place under broiler until peaks are lightly browned.

Meringue
4 egg whites, room temperature   ½ cup sugar

Whip egg whites until soft peaks form. Gradually add sugar, beating until stiff peaks form.

Serves 6

Mrs. Laine Friedman Agee

PATIENCE CARAMEL PIE

As old-fashioned as hoops and crinolines, and well-named. It takes patience to stir until this delicious mixture thickens.

2 cups sugar	Pinch of salt
2 cups scalded milk	3 eggs, separated
2 tablespoons cornstarch or	2 teaspoons vanilla
4 tablespoons all-purpose	1 baked 10-inch pie shell
flour	4 tablespoons sugar

Cook ½ cup sugar in skillet over medium heat until browned, stirring constantly. Remove from heat and add hot milk. Sift together 1½ cups sugar, cornstarch, and salt, and blend in small amount milk mixture. Add egg yolks and beat well. Stir into remaining milk mixture, add vanilla, and cook until thick, stirring constantly. Pour into pie shell and let cool.

Beat egg whites until stiff peaks form, adding remaining sugar 1 tablespoon at a time. Spread over pie and bake at 325 degrees for 15 minutes or until lightly browned.

Serves 8

Lucia Outlan

MEMORIAL DAY HOMECOMING DINNER ON THE GROUND

Southerners have long memories, and they like it that way. It's how they've been raised. And nowhere is this more evident than on Memorial Day at country churches. Kith and kin come from far and near to decorate graves, walk among old tombstones in family plots, and speak of departed relatives. All make their way indoors for the services in the church where, on the end of the pew, will always be a great-aunt or cousin who can answer everyone's whispered question about the identity of someone across the aisle. When the service ends, everyone leaves the church and gathers beneath trees on the grounds where long tables have been prepared. Families "spread" together—that is, combine their bounteous cooking. Certain foods always appear—baked ham, fried chicken, stuffed eggs. There will be casseroles of all kinds, and usually potato salad. But it's the desserts that steal the show, each person bringing her blue-ribbon best, and insisting that everyone try it. The result is that everyone has a taste of at least two, and sometimes three, desserts. That Southern sweet tooth has a field day! One conversation is sure to be repeated with only the names and a few details changed. It goes like this: "Well, of course, you're Doris's (or Jim's or Mary's) child. I went to grammar school with your mother (or father or aunt)." And suddenly, comfortingly, you're in your rightful place. You've been identified. You've come home.

Mrs. Still's Delta Pecan Pie*
La Vada's Lemon Pie
Patience Caramel Pie
Heavenly Fresh Coconut Cake
Old-Fashioned Vanilla Ice Cream
Double Chocolate Cake
Buttermilk Ice Cream
Sugar Wafers
Blue Ribbon Apple Pie
Chess Pie

Nannie P. Riley
Eudora, Mississippi

*See Index

BUTTERMILK ICE CREAM

Simple, old-fashioned, and luscious. More like a buttermilk ice. The zest of lemon is essential, and a MISSISSIPPI TEA CAKE on the side would be perfect.

1 quart whole buttermilk
¾ quart whole milk
1½ cups sugar

Grated rind and juice of
2 lemons

Mix all ingredients and freeze.

From the hand-written recipe journal
of Mrs. E. H. Crump
Courtesy of Mrs. Frank C. Pidgeon, Jr.

SUGAR WAFERS

An elegant, crisp little cookie.

1 cup butter, softened
1 cup sugar
1 egg
1½ cups cake flour
¼ teaspoon salt

½ teaspoon vanilla
Sugar, cinnamon sugar,
  coconut, or grated orange or
  lemon peel for topping

Cream butter with sugar and beat in egg. Sift flour with salt and gradually add to sugar mixture, beating well. Stir in vanilla. With measuring spoon, place batter by teaspoonfuls onto lightly greased baking sheet. Keep well separated. Sprinkle with topping of choice. Bake at 300 degrees for 12 to 15 minutes or until lightly browned around edges. Let stand several minutes until crisp before removing from baking sheet.

Note: The same amount of all-purpose flour can be used. Cake flour gives a finer texture and a somewhat thinner cookie. Bake on sunny days. These cookies do not like rain.

Yields 6 dozen cookies

Mrs. Frank M. Norfleet

BLUE RIBBON APPLE PIE

Supremely simple, supremely good. Adapted from a much-requested and closely-kept recipe from the old Camel Restaurant, now only a fond memory, but once a favorite gathering place for lunch and dinner in Memphis' medical center complex.

1 double recipe PERFECT PASTRY
1 17-ounce can apple pie filling
1 cup sugar

¼ cup butter, melted
2 tablespoons all purpose flour
½ teaspoon cinnamon

Prepare pastry ahead as it must chill thoroughly.

Combine all other ingredients, reserving about ⅓ to ½ cup juices from mixture. Roll out half of pie pastry and line a 9-inch pie pan. Pour apple pie mixture into crust. Use remaining pastry to top pie in latticework fashion. Bake at 350 degrees about 60 minutes, or until crust is a light golden brown. About 30 minutes into baking time, brush top of pie with reserved juice and continue baking.

Serves 8

Barbara M. Robertson

DOUBLE CHOCOLATE CAKE

Deeply chocolate, and doubly wonderful. Try it with ice cream and HOT FUDGE SAUCE.

8 1½-ounce Hershey bars
1 cup margarine
2 cups sugar
4 eggs
1 16-ounce can Hershey syrup
1 teaspoon baking soda

1 cup buttermilk
2½ cups all-purpose flour
½ teaspoon salt
1 cup chopped pecans
2 tablespoons vanilla

Melt Hershey bars in double boiler.

In mixing bowl, cream margarine with sugar. Add eggs, syrup, and melted candy bars. Stir baking soda into buttermilk. Sift flour with salt, and add to chocolate mixture alternately with buttermilk. Add nuts and vanilla, and pour into greased and floured tube pan. Bake at 350 degrees for 1¼ to 1½ hours, or until top springs back when touched.

Serves 12 to 16

Mrs. John Adams

ACKNOWLEDGMENTS
AND
SELECTED BIBLIOGRAPHY

PHOTOGRAPH AND COMMENTARY ACKNOWLEDGMENTS

The Memphis Symphony League is so very appreciative of the gracious hospitality and help afforded this cook book committee by all the persons listed below. They opened their homes and barns and boats and gardens and places of business to us—and they opened their hearts as well. They provided us priceless information and personalized assistance. Their interest helped carry the spark of this venture, and without them, we would never have succeeded in our endeavor.

Roses on the River (frontispiece)

Connie and Dunbar Abston
Margaret Boyle Falls
Lucy Barboro Fisher
Jean and Henry Williamson

The Proprietors

Ginger Austin
Vance Boyd
William Boyd
Virginia Overton McLean
Memphis Pink Palace Museum:
  Ronald C. Brister, Curator of
  Collections
Memphis/Shelby County Room,
  Memphis/Shelby County
  Public Library:
  Dr. James R. Johnson, Manager,
  History Department;
  Patricia M. LaPointe,
  Reference Librarian
Musette and Allen Morgan
Mary Elizabeth Overton
Lee Winchester

A Reception at Memphis Brooks Museum of Art in Overton Park

Leona Faiers
Louise Hays, President,
  Brooks Museum League
William Heidrich, Director
Mary Jane Miller

A Rooftop Supper to View the Great River Carnival

Alice Bingham
Clarence Day
Mary and Tom Wells

A Wedding Reception at Annesdale

Flo Snowden
May and Tom Todd

Homecoming Dinner in Holly Springs

Vadah Cochran
Carita and Robert Crump
Holly Springs, Mississippi,
  Chamber of Commerce
Marshall County Library,
  Holly Springs, Mississippi
Marie Moore
Louise Crump Wade
Jane and Roger Woods

Meeting the Future in Old Court Square

Burch, Porter, and Johnson:
  Frances Lawson, Manager
Jobe Taylor, former Maitre d',
  The Tennessee Club
Fred C. Smith

Lunch with a View of the Dixon Gardens

Margaret and Eric Catmur
Dixon Gallery and Gardens:
  Moussa Domit, former Director
Mrs. Charles P. Oates
Mrs. Thomas Day Oates
Megan Turner

A Special Tradition at Calvary Episcopal Church

The Reverend Douglass M. Bailey
Jane Barton
Peggy Hancock
Gloria Nobles
Flo Snowden
May Todd

Dinner at the Symphony Ball in Germantown

John W. Barringer
Peter Hyrka
Tom Wells
Betty Whitehead

Remembering Piggly Wiggly at the Pink Palace Museum

G. A. Crosby
Memphis Pink Palace Museum:
  Brad Evans, Public Relations
  and Marketing Coordinator

The Longreen Hunt Breakfast

Mary Winslow Chapman
Imogene Erb
Karen Erb
Mary and Bart Mueller

Blessings from Afar at the Greek Bazaar

Reva Cook
Sophia Guidi
Dr. John E. Harkins
Dr. James E. Roper
Sophia Sousoulas
Helen Vergos
The Reverend Nicholas L. Vieron

Summer Fruit and Vegetable Market at Collierville

Mr. and Mrs. H. W. Cox, Jr.
Catharine Richey Hinton
Percy McKinney
Lucia Outlan
Mrs. James Russell
Peggy Turnipseed

A Native American Feast on the Riverbluff

Marilou Awiakta
Frances Hill
Grady John, Choctaw potter,
  Chucalissa Indian Museum
Melissa Lehman
Mattie Panther
Jean Rosemary Smith
Jeffie Solomon
Carol Welch

A Polo Tournament Supper at Wildwood Farms

Audrey Taylor
Lynn Warren Taylor

A Dinner Set for The King at Graceland

Mrs. Delta Biggs
Mrs. Willie Pauline Nicholson
Jack Soden, Executive Director, Graceland

Sunday Afternoon Snack at the Ball Game

George Lapides

Mother's Day at the Fourway Grill

Mrs. Irene Cleaves

A Cotton Man's Lunch from The Little Tea Shop

Dean Ethridge
Sam Hollis
Suhair Lauck
Frank Weathersby

An Afternoon Fish Fry at Horseshoe Lake

Jeanne and Bill Arthur
Anne and Walter Broadfoot
Gee-Gee and Bill Chandler
Linda Grisham Smith

Dining Out in Style at Justine's

Janet Smith
Justine and Dayton Smith
Megan Turner

The Sporting Life at Hatchie Coon Lodge

Barbara and John Apperson
Patricia B. Atkinson
Ron Hickman
Lucy and Eph Wilkinson

Dinner for the National Field Trial Judges at Ames Plantation

Ames Plantation:
  Dr. James Anderson, Manager;
  Dr. Rick J. Carlisle, Assistant
  Manager; Joyce Burchfield,
  former hostess, Ames Manor
Dr. Frank A. McKnight,
Robert R. Milner,
Robert R. Milner, Jr.,
Dr. Marcus J. Stewart

Old Homeland Delicacies on the Greenlaw Addition

Mrs. A. C. Treadwell Beasley
Mr. and Mrs. Herman Burkle
CoDe North
Peggy Jemison
Perre Magness
Louise Greenlaw Mann
June Beasley Mann
Memphis/Shelby County Room,
  Memphis/Shelby County
  Public Library
National Ornamental Metal
  Museum, Inc.: James A. Wallace,
  Director

Tea and a Private Journal at Goodwinslow

Mary Winslow Chapman

An Alumni Brunch at Rhodes College

Mrs. James H. Daughdrill, Jr.
Fascinating Foods: Martha Brahm
Loyd Templeton, Jr.

Holiday Sweets in Cooper-Young Neighborhood

Nancy Coe
Cooper Street Antique Mall
Libba Gardner
Nell Hughes
The Idlewood House: Ginny Barron
Nicole Jans Midtown Antique Gallery
Beverly Taliaferro
Randle Witherington

Coffee in the Garden at Walnut Grove

Eleanor Currie
Leroy Montgomery
Helen Norfleet

A Historic Christening at Magevney House

Consignments
Brannon Galyean
Gail Kimball
Dianne and Dick Magevney
Magevney House:
  Marjorie Holmes, former Curator;
  Marie Brown, Assistant Curator
Memphis Pink Palace Museum:
  Dr. Douglas R. Noble, Director
  of Museums; Ronald C. Brister,
  Curator of Collections

After-Concert Desserts with the Guest Artist

Carol and Garland Cherry
Beverly and Harlan Gates
Meg Reid
Joy and Russel Wiener

Supper in a Carriage House Gazebo

Megan Turner
Eldridge Wright

Special Treats to Honor a Beale Street Legend

The Blues Foundation, Inc.: Joe Savarin,
  Founder and Executive Director
Memphis/Shelby County Room,
  Memphis/Shelby County Public
  Library: Dr. James R. Johnson, Manager,
  History Department; Patricia M. LaPointe,
  Reference Librarian
Mrs. Harry Godwin
Mrs. W. C. Handy, Yonkers, New York
Wyer Handy, New York, New York
Memphis Pink Palace Museum:
  Dr. Douglas R. Noble, Director of
  Museums; Roy R. Young, Conservator
Davis Tillman

A Box Party at the Orpheum

Dinstuhl's Candies
Mrs. Howell E. Long
Sissy M. Long
The Orpheum Theatre:
*   Pat Halloran, President;*
*   Vincent Astor, former House Manager*

Afternoon Tea at the Peabody

Ron Belz
Kay Ferree
The Peabody: John Voegler, General
*   Manager; Alan Parsons, Director*
*   of Catering*

Saucemaking in an East Memphis Kitchen

Megan and Norfleet Turner

A Wine Cellar
in the Central Gardens District

Alice and Walter Armstrong

Carter Seed Store on Front Street

Jeanne and Don Rodgers
Jack R. Tucker, Jr.

Gifts from the Hearth at Cedar Hall

Sally and John Greene
Jeannette and Jay Rainey

Memphis in May
International Barbecue Contest

Ellen and Richard Dixon
John Willingham

An Old-Fashioned Barbecue
at Seven Hills Farm

Patricia B. Atkinson
Patricia M. LaPointe
Martha Jane Pulliam Tibbs
Rembert Williams, Jr.

A Gourmet Picnic at the Sunset Symphony

Madge and Ross Clark
Babbie Lovett
Anne Threefoot
Mary Weymouth

Feasting on a Mississippi River Sandbar

Kathryn and Bob Jorgensen
Laura and Bob Schwartz
Marjorie Schwartz
Katherine and Ham Smythe

Country Ham from an
Old Whitehaven Smokehouse

Catharine Richey Hinton

A Summer Lawn Supper at Davies Manor

Ellen Davies Rodgers

Breakfast at the Home Place

Betty Jean Atkinson
Meg and Mike Bartlett

A Southern Feast at Cottondale

Jake Saunders
Megan Turner

Coffee and Laces with a View of the Bridge

Dinstuhl's Candies
Pat and John Tigrett

RECIPE TESTERS

Our testers have been wonderful beyond words. Gracious Goodness *is forever grateful for the gift of their time, talent, tenacity, and taste buds that have made this book a reality. Each recipe has been carefully tested, some as many as four times. We can recommend each one with confidence but with the understanding that some recipes require a little experience to achieve the best results. As a cook book compiled in 1905 by the ladies at Grace-St. Luke's Episcopal Church in Memphis commented on breadmaking: "No description can be given to ascertain these points. It requires observation, reflection, and a quick nice judgment to decide when all is right."*

Laine Agee
Sylvia Ashman
Patricia Atkinson
Claire Austin
Jacqueline and Colmore
  Beane
Nancy Beck
Marguerite Piazza
  Bergtholdt
Peggy Betzel
Tish and Don Blackard
Ann Blecken
Marion Bolks
Margaret Cobb Boyd
Helen Brandon
Phyllis Brannon
Donna Brommer
Anne Brown
Francie Brunt
Bobbie Buehl
Elsie Burkhart
Jeanne Burrow
Lois Buxton
June Caffey
Nell Caldwell
Judith Campbell
Kitty Cannon
Opal Caples
Stephanie Caratenuto
Oneida Carpenter
Ginger Chapman
Nancy Chase
Carol Cherry
J. Garland Cherry, Jr.
Karen Cherry
Kay Cohen
Janet Cox
Ruth Crenshaw
Ann Creson

Bissie Crosby
Nancy Crosby
Robbie Crosby
Geri Cuoghi
Mimi Cuoghi
Polly Daniels
Nancy Davis
Jane de Witt
Elouise Deaton
Lauran Dellinger
Jan Donelson
Marcia Dunlap
Teresa Edens
Marsha Evans
Joyce Ferguson
Jacqueline Freeman
Helen French
Alice Fulmer
Nancy Fulmer
Virginia Galyon
Margaret Giusti
Linda-Marie Goetze
Mary Ann Goetze
Rita Goetze
Barbara Graves
Pat Graves
Sarah Green
Sophia Guidi
Margaret A. Halle
Ann Clark Harris
Shirley Herrington
Tootsie Hickman
Joanna Higdon
Willena Highsmith
Sara Holmes
Jane Holmgrain
Josie Howser
Marily Hughes
Dorette Humphries

Sharon Hundt
Betty Hunt
Buzzy Hussey
Peggy Jalenak
Peggy Jemison
Betty Jennings
Susan Jenny
Joann Johnson
Nancy Lou Jones
Deanna Kaminsky
Phyllis Kaplan
Janet Kennon
Tommie Kidd
Pat Klinke
Cathy Knight
Mary Koch
Kathy Laizure
Patricia LaPointe
Bette Lathram
Susan Lawless-Glassman
Katherine Leftwich
Vivian Leiting
Gail Lewis
Debbie Litch
Sissy Long
Pat Love
Sherry Mahoney
Lisa Mallory
Amber Mathis
Carrie Mathis
Heather Mathis
Peggy Mathis
Charlene Mattingly
Emily McAllister
Sybil McAtee
Helen McClure
Anne and Randy McCord
Martha McGuire
Ruth Meierhoefer

Irma Merrill
Lou Moffatt
Londena Montesi
Didi Montgomery
Dorothye Moore
Irene Morse
Maxine Morse
Betty Moth
Jo Myhr
Charlotte Neal
Rowene Neidow
Carmella Nickl
Gloria Nobles
Jean Norfleet
June Owens
Roseann Painter
Kitty Palmer
Lyda Parker
Ann and Jim Pate
Ron Perel
Anne Plyler
Betty Pyeatt
Joan Ramier
Ann Ray
Betty Redfearn
Michael Redfearn
Billye Reed
Meg Reid
Anne Reynolds
Sandy Riggs
Frances Riley
Barbara Robertson
Mark Robinson
Judy Rogers
Peggy Rolfes
Martha Roper
Nicky Ross
JoAnne Rossner
Barbara Runyan

Sara Sanders
John Sanguinetti
Ann Schultz
Elaine Schuppe
Marjorie Schwartz
Sally Sharp
Tommy Shobe
Cecile Skaggs
Samye Slagle
Hollye Spiotta
Greg Stablein
Linda Stablein
Dorothy Steen
Freddie Stevenson
Jean Stringfellow
Lois Strock
Lisa Stubblefield
Theresa Sutherland
Sarah Symmes
Joanne Tabor
Anne Threefoot
Jo Threlkeld
Bette Tilly
Virginia Tobias
May Todd
Martha Towne
Meg Turner
Martha Vandervoort
Jodie Varner
Dorothy Vawter
Catherine Vineyard
Saralyn Weiss
Anna Leita Werkhoven
Lucy Wilkinson
Jean Williamson
Rose Wiseman
Martha Witherspoon
Dixie Wolbrecht
Peggy Worley

BOOKS

Adair, James. *The History of the American Indians.* London: Edward and Charles Dilly in the Poultry, 1775. Edited under the auspices of the National Society of Colonial Tennessee. Johnson City, Tennessee: The Watauga Press, 1930.

Bartram, William. *Travels Through North and South Carolina, Georgia, East and West Florida.* Philadelphia: James and Johnson, 1791. Edited by Mark Van Doren. New York: Dover Publications, 1928.

Bing, Rudolph. *5000 Nights at the Opera.* Garden City, New York: Doubleday, 1972.

Brown, William F. and Buckingham, Nash. *National Field Trial Champions.* Harrisburg, Pennsylvania: The Telegraph Press, 1955.

Buckingham, Nash. *De Shootin'est Gent'man.* New York: Charles Scribners Sons, 1941.

_____. *Mark Right!* New York: The Derrydale Press, 1936.

_____. *Tattered Coat.* New York: G. P. Putnams Sons, 1939.

Capers, Gerald M., Jr. *Biography of a River Town.* Chapel Hill: University of North Carolina Press, 1939.

Chamberlin, Shirley Sigler. *A History of Cuba, Tennessee.* Millington: Shirley S. Chamberlin, Publisher, 1984.

Chapman, Mary Winslow. *I Remember Raleigh.* Memphis: Riverside Press, 1977.

Coppock, Paul R. *Memphis Sketches.* Memphis: Friends of Memphis and Shelby County Libraries, 1976.

_____. *Memphis Memoirs.* Memphis: Memphis State University Press, 1980.

Crawford, Charles W. *Yesterday's Memphis.* Miami: E. A. Seeman Publishing, 1976.

Davies-Rodgers, Ellen. *The Great Book, Calvary Episcopal Church, 1832-1972.* Memphis: Plantation Press, 1974.

Dykeman, Wilma. *Tennessee, A Bicentennial History.* New York: W. W. Norton. Nashville: American Society for State and Local History, 1975.

Evans, George Bird. *The Best of Nash Buckingham.* New York: Winchester Press, 1973.

Greenlaw Generations. Cookbook sponsored by CoDe North and the Junior League of Memphis. Memphis: Hamilton Printing, 1985.

Harkins, John E. *Metropolis of the American Nile.* Sponsored by the West Tennessee Historical Society. Woodland Hills, California: Windsor Publications, 1982.

Historic Black Memphians. Compiled by Selma Lewis and Marjean Kremer for exhibit by Memphis Pink Palace Museum, in cooperation with Metropolitan Inter-Faith Association, 1979.

History of Medicine in Memphis. Edited by Marcus J. Stewart, M.D. and William T. Black, Jr., M.D. Co-edited by Mildred Hicks. Jackson, Tennessee: McCowat-Mercer Press, Inc., 1971.

Jemison, Peggy Boyce, *A History of The Cooper Young Neighborhood.* Memphis: Metropolitan Inter-Faith Association, 1977.

Jemison, Peggy Boyce, *Greenlaw Rediscovered.* Memphis: Metropolitan Inter-Faith Association, 1979.

Longreen, 25 Years of Horse Sport in West Tennessee. Compiled by members of the Longreen Hunt. Edited by Mary Winslow Chapman. Memphis: Towery Press, 1982.

Magness, Perre. *Good Abode.* Memphis: The Junior League of Memphis and Towery Press, 1983.

Malone, James H. *The Chickasaw Nation: A Short Sketch of a Noble People.* Louisville: J. P. Morgan, 1922.

McCorkle, Anna Leigh. *Tales of Old Whitehaven.* Jackson, Tennessee: Mercer Press, 1967.

Memphis Brooks Museum, Painting and Sculpture Collection. Compiled and researched by Sally Palmer Thomason. History by Douglas K. S. Hyland. Memphis: Mercury Printing, 1984.

Mid-South Garden Guide. Compiled by Memphis Garden Club. Memphis: 1954.

Miller, William D. *Mr. Crump of Memphis.* Baton Rouge: Louisiana State University Press, 1964.

Ornelas-Struve, Carole M. and Coulter, Frederick Lee. *Memphis, 1800-1900,* 3 Vols. A Pink Palace Museum Book. New York: Nancy Powers Publisher, 1982.

Percy, William Alexander. *Lanterns on the Levee: Recollections of a Planter's Son.* Baton Rouge and London: Louisiana State University Press, 1941.

Plunkett, Kitty. *Memphis: A Pictorial History.* Norfolk, Virginia: The Donning Company Publishers, 1976.

Roark, Eldon. *Memphis Bragabouts.* New York: McGraw-Hill, 1945.

Robinson, Francis. *Celebration, The Metropolitan Opera.* Garden City, New York: Doubleday, 1979.

Roper, James. *The Founding of Memphis, 1818-1820.* Memphis: The Memphis Sesquicentennial, Inc., 1970.

Sense of Place: Mississippi. Edited by Peggy W. Prenshaw and Jessi O. McKee. Jackson, Mississippi: University Press of Mississippi, 1979.

Taylor, Peter. *The Old Forest and Other Stories.* Garden City, New York: Doubleday, 1985.

Taylor, Peter. *A Summons to Memphis.* New York: Alfred A. Knopf, 1986.

Tennessee Women, Past and Present. Narrative by Wilma Dykeman, Selected additional material edited by Carol Lynn Yellin. Memphis: Tennessee Committee for the Humanities, and Tennessee Coordinating Committee for International Women's Decade, 1977.

Weeks, Linton. *Memphis: A Folk History.* Little Rock: Parkhurst Publishers, 1982.

OTHER SOURCES

"Ames Plantation." Brochure, no date.

"The Answerbook," *The Commercial Appeal* Special Section, 1987.

Awiakta, Marilou, "Native Americans." Paper prepared for *Gracious Goodness,* 1986.

"Brooks Art League Handbook." History, 1986.

Brooks, John, "A Corner in Piggly Wiggly." *The New Yorker,* June 6, 1959.

Brown, Mrs. Stephen Toof, "History of the Memphis Garden Club." Compiled, 1966.

"Brunswick, Tennessee Festival." Calendar of events, 1986.

Calvary Church Lenten Luncheon Menu, 1986.

"Center City Commission Annual Progress Report." 1985.

"Center City Commission Strategies Plan, 1985-2000." Report by Long-Range Planning Task Force of Memphis, Jim Ross, chairman. May 24, 1985.

"Chicks." Brochure compiled by Coca-Cola Bottling Company, 1986.

"Christian Brothers College." Brochure, no date.

The Commercial Appeal. Scattered issues, daily and Sunday, 1934-1987.

Cook, Reva, "History of the Pinch." Compiled for the Sheraton Hotel and the Memphis Symphony League Epicurean Committee, 1983.

Cortese, James, "The Memphis Sound: Pushed Through A Horn Until It Was." *Memphis 1819-1969, A Sesquicentennial Supplement to the Commercial Appeal,* May 25, 1969.

Darnell, J. Millon, "Germantown, Its History and Its Future." Brochure, 1986.

"Davies Manor." Brochure, May 1, 1982.

"Dixon Gallery and Gardens." Brochure, 1985.

Dawson, David, "Slouching Toward Elvis." *Southern Magazine,* August, 1987.

"Faith in the City." Calvary Church brochure, 1986.

Finger, Michael, "Tom Lee: A Hero's Tale." *Memphis Magazine,* June, 1987.

"Fox Hunting." *Encyclopedia Britannica,* Vol. XI, p. 892, 1968.

"From Egypt to Memphis: Two Old New Citizens." *Memphis State College of Communication and Fine Arts Publications,* June, 1986.

Graceland Press Packet, 1985.

"Holly Springs 48th Annual Pilgrimage." Brochure, 1986.

Hopkins, John L., "The Cheatham-Barron House, ca. 1883-1886." Article, August 3, 1986.

Howard, Edwin, "Memphis' Mark on Tennessee Williams Being Reciprocated." *Memphis Business Journal,* July 2-6, 1984.

Hunt, Blair Theodore Papers. Memphis-Shelby County Public Library and Information Center, 1979.

Insigner, Wendy, "The Best Quail Day in the World." *Town and Country,* February, 1986.

Institute of Egyptian Art and Archaeology Newsletter, Memphis State University, Summer, 1986.

Jalenak, Natalie, "Great Acts to Follow." *Memphis Magazine,* Vol. XI, No. 5, 1986.

King, Gail, "Top Dogs: the World Series of Pointerdom." *Wall Street Journal,* February 27, 1986.

Linx, Southwestern at Memphis College Annual, 1945, 1946, 1947, 1948.

"Little Tea Shop." Menu and history, no date.

"LeMoyne-Owen College History." Brochure, no date.

Lollar, Michael, "Justine's." *The Commercial Appeal Mid-South Magazine,* July 12, 1987.

Magness, Perre, "Jews Came to Memphis in the 1840s." *The Commercial Appeal,* Neighbors Section, April 7, 1988.

Memphis Garden Club Minutes, 1921.

Memphis Business Journal. Scattered issues, 1986-1987.

Memphis Magazine City Guide, Vol. X, No. 5, 1985-1986; Vol. XI, No. 5, 1986-1987; Vol. XII, No. 5, 1987-1988.

Memphis Press-Scimitar. Scattered issues, 1935-1983.

"Memphis State." Brochure, no date.

Matthews, Cynthia, "High-Goal Polo." *Town and Country,* January, 1986.

"The Orpheum Theatre." Marquee Program, Memphis, 1985.

The Peabody Press Packet, 1985.

"Pink Palace." Brochure, no date.

"Rhodes College Historical Summary." Brochure, 1985.

"River and City Just Keep Rolling Along Together." *Memphis, 1819-1969, A Sesquicentennial Supplement to the Commercial Appeal,* May 25, 1969.

Sorrels, William, "The First 150 Years." *Memphis, 1819-1969, A Sesquicentennial Supplement to the Commercial Appeal,* May 25, 1969.

Sousoulas, Mrs. James, "The Greek Bazaar in Memphis." Paper prepared for this book, 1986.

"State Tech." Brochure, no date.

Thomas, William, "Inside Graceland." *The Commercial Appeal,* Special supplement, May 2, 1982.

_____. "Beale Street's Heyday." *The Commercial Appeal Mid-South Magazine,* May 31, 1987.

"Today's Quimper," *Country Living,* July, 1986.

Tennessee Garden Club Minutes, 1932.

Victorian Village Arts and Pops Festival Newspaper, 1984.

"Welcome to the Lichterman Nature Center." Brochure, no date.

"Willingham's Restaurant." Menu and brochure, no date.

Weathers, Ed, "Memphis: An Introduction." *Memphis Magazine,* Vol. X, No. 5, 1985.

Weathersby, Frank, "The Memphis Cotton Exchange, 1873-1973." Address to the Memphis Cotton Exchange, 1973.

INTERVIEWS

In compiling research for the commentaries that accompany the photographs in this book, the following persons were interviewed:

Dr. James Anderson
Mr. Walter P. Armstrong, Jr.
Mr. Vincent Astor
Mrs. E. W. Atkinson
Marilou Awiakta
Mr. Don Bartlett
Mr. and Mrs. Mike Bartlett
Mrs. Frank G. Barton, Jr.
Mrs. James Barton
Mrs. Delta Biggs
Dr. Delano Black
Mrs. James Burchfield
Mr. and Mrs. Eric Catmur
Mr. and Mrs. William Chandler
Mary Winslow Chapman
Mrs. Irene Cleaves
Dr. Charles Crawford
Mr. Robert Crump, Jr.
Mrs. Crittenden Currie

Maestro and Mrs. Vincent de Frank
Mrs. Edward Falls
Mrs. Henry Hancock
Mrs. W. C. Handy
Dr. John E. Harkins
Dr. George Hays
Mrs. J. Karr Hinton
Mrs. Eleanor D. Hughes
Ms. Cary Jehl
Mrs. Frank Z. Jemison
Ms. Happy Jones
Mr. George Lapides
Ms. Suhair Lauck
Dr. William E. Long
Dr. Frank A. McKnight
Mr. James McKnight
Mr. Leroy Montgomery
Ms. Mary Montgomery

Mrs. Bart Mueller
Mrs. Willie Pauline Nicholson
Mr. and Mrs. Peter Norfleet
Ms. Helen Norman
Mrs. Charles P. Oates
Mrs. Thomas Day Oates
Mrs. Joseph Oliver
Mrs. William F. Outlan
Mrs. Van Pritchartt, Jr.
Mrs. Jay Rainey
Mr. and Mrs. Don Rodgers
Mrs. Ellen Davies Rodgers
Dr. James Roper
Mrs. James Russell
Mr. Joe Savarin
Mrs. Merrill Schwartz
Mr. and Mrs. Robert W. Schwartz
Mrs. Dayton Smith
Mr. and Mrs. Hamilton Smythe III

Mrs. Robert G. Snowden
Mrs. James Sousoulas
Dr. Marcus J. Stewart
Mrs. Arthur Sutherland III
Mr. Jobe Taylor
Lynn Warren Taylor
Mrs. W. L. Taylor
Mr. Loyd Templeton, Jr.
Mrs. Thomas H. Todd, Jr.
Mr. Jack Tucker
Mr. and Mrs. Norfleet R. Turner
Mrs. Pete Vergos
Mr. Frank Weathersby
Mr. Tom Wells
Mr. Rembert Williams, Jr.
Mr. John Willingham
Mr. James Willis
Mr. Randle Witherington
Mr. Eldridge Wright

INDEX OF RECIPES

OFFEE AND LACES
ITH A VIEW OF THE BRIDGE

*n a downtown balcony, overlooking
l'Man River and Riverside Drive,
e day has come to a close with
ndlelight, coffee and laces—coffee
which whipped cream, amber
gar, cinnamon sticks, and chocolate
rls can be added. Providing a touch
Old-World beauty to the setting is
antique lace place mat from the
ivate collection of Pat Kerr. A sprig
crape myrtle lends its summery
esence. The lights on the bridge,
uch like a brightly-etched initial
l' for Memphis, recall the evening
September 5, 1986, when many
ousands of Memphians on the
erbank and on Mud Island
tended the gala ceremony marking
e official lighting of the Hernando
Soto bridge, complete with
sic by the Memphis Symphony,
nicking, a parade of boats
stooned with lights, fireworks—
d exuberant cheers.*

Folks, I've just been down,

Down to Memphis town,

That's where the people smile,

Smile on you all the while,

Hospitality,

They were good to me,

I couldn't spend a dime

And had the grandest time…

—*The Memphis Blues*
Music by W. C. Handy
Lyrics by George A. Norton